The University of **Law**

incorporating The College of Law

The University of Law, 133 Great Hampton Street, Birmingham B18 6AQ
Telephone: 01483 216041   Email: library-birmingham@law.ac.uk

Birmingham I Bristol I Chester I Guildford I London I Manchester I York

Market Abuse and Insider Dealing

Market Abuse and Insider Dealing

3rd Edition

By

Professor Barry Rider OBE

Professorial Fellow, Centre of Development Studies,
University of Cambridge

Professor Kern Alexander

Chair for Banking and Financial Market Law, University of Zurich
Professorial Fellow in Financial Regulation, Centre for Risk Studies,
University of Cambridge

Stuart Bazley

Visiting Professor in Financial Regulation and Compliance Law,
BPP University Law School
Director, Medius Consulting

Jeffrey Bryant

Barrister and Specialist Prosecutor CPS Proceeds of Crime Service

Bloomsbury Professional

Bloomsbury Professional Ltd,
Maxwelton House,
41–43 Boltro Road,
Haywards Heath,
West Sussex,
RH16 1BJ

© Bloomsbury Professional Ltd 2016

Bloomsbury Professional, an imprint of Bloomsbury Publishing Plc

A CIP Catalogue record for this book is available from the British Library.

While every care has been taken to ensure the accuracy of this work, no responsibility for loss or damage occasioned to any person acting or refraining from action as a result of any statement in it can be accepted by the authors, editors or publishers.

Any views expressed in this book are those of the authors and not of the CPS.

ISBN: 978 1 78043 495 7

Typeset by Compuscript Ltd, Shannon

Printed and bound in Great Britain by CPI Group (UK) Ltd, Croydon, CR0 4YY

About the authors

Professor Barry Rider has taught financial and related areas of the law in the University of Cambridge since 1976. He is currently a Professorial Fellow in the Centre of Development Studies. He has held many senior academic appointments including Director of the Institute of Advanced Legal Studies, University of London. He currently holds a chair in comparative law at Renmin University, China, a chair in commercial law at the University of the Free State, South Africa and a chair in financial law at BPP University. He has held and continues to hold a number of visiting professorships and senior fellowships around the world. He holds doctorates from the University of Cambridge, University of London, University of the Free State and Penn State University (Dickinson Law School) in the USA. Professor Rider has also served as an international civil servant and was for many years head of a special intelligence and mutual legal assistance unit in an inter-governmental organisation. He has served on secondment and as a consultant with many international organisations including the IMF, World Bank, Asian Development Bank, Islamic Financial Services Board, Commonwealth, EU, various UN agencies and numerous national agencies. He has also served as Special Advisor to the Trade and Industry Select Committee of the House of Commons. He has practiced law in the City of London and is a Master of the Bench of the Honourable Society of the Inner Temple. He is the author of many books and other publications on financial law, corporate law and economic crime. He was made an Officer of the British Empire for his services to the prevention and control of economic crime by Her Majesty the Queen in 2014.

Professor Kern Alexander, Chair for Banking and Financial Market Law University of Zurich, and Professorial Fellow in Financial Regulation, Centre for Risk Studies, University of Cambridge. Formerly, the Specialist Adviser to the Parliamentary Joint Select Committee on the Financial Services Act 2012, and Member of the Expert Panel on Financial Services for the European Parliament (2009–14).

Stuart Bazley is a director at Medius Consulting in London and a Visiting Professor in Financial Regulation and Compliance Law at BPP University Law School. Stuart has over 30 years' experience working in the financial services industry, including senior roles as an in-house lawyer, General Counsel, Head of Compliance and Money Laundering Reporting Officer. He has also lectured on the law relating to financial regulation and compliance since 1998. Stuart now works as an expert regulatory consultant, advising on market and sales practice compliance, regulatory misconduct and enforcement matters, predominantly for firms operating in the securities, wealth management and corporate banking sectors.

About the authors

Jeffrey Bryant is an employed barrister in the Crown Prosecution Service, where he is a Specialist Prosecutor and Crown Advocate in the Proceeds of Crime Service. Jeffrey was the reviewing lawyer in the leading Supreme Court case of *R v Waya* [2013] 1 AC 294 on proportionality in the Proceeds of Crime Act 2002 and has had oversight of all proportionality arguments in the appeal courts since, including the Supreme Court cases of *R v Ahmad* [2015] 1 AC 299 and the forthcoming *R v Harvey*. Jeffrey also specialises in mutual legal assistance and has acted on behalf of numerous overseas governments freezing assets in England and Wales. Jeffrey is a visiting lecturer on LL.M. courses at BPP University and has been a contributing editor, since 2003, to the leading work *Mitchell, Taylor and Talbot on Confiscation and the Proceeds of Crime*.

Preface

Even if there is an ideal time for a new book or edition, which in the fast moving world of financial regulation there never can be, to bring together the many aspects of this work would render it impracticable. The pace of development in the law, its administration and interpretation, in both the criminal and civil dimensions, together with perhaps the even more significant inter-related realms of regulation and compliance, is today such that there never can be a final word on an issue, or for that matter an entirely topical analysis. Nonetheless, we have done our best and where the relevant law is particularly dynamic we have attempted to predict at least its trajectory.

Concern about the harm to confidence in the integrity of the markets caused by those who take advantage of privileged information in their own dealings is nothing new. Indeed, it is not only in our own time that the markets and financial system has been traumatised by a crisis of confidence. Some of the earliest laws relating to trade outlaw attempts to artificially interfere with the proper function of the markets and ensure their fairness. While having better information and being better able to use it are factors which in most societies are considered not only acceptable but commendable, others come into play when the information in question could not have been obtained by the most diligent competitor or counterparty and, indeed, the information was taken in a manner or from a source that others would consider to be unfair. Those who appropriate for their own, or for that matter another's benefit, information belonging to someone else, have an unfair advantage and no matter whether as a matter of logic, let alone traditional legal analysis, this can reasonably be expected to justify remedies, it brings the fairness of the market as a whole into disrepute. It is the concern to promote and preserve public confidence in the expectation of fair dealing in the markets that has, at least in Britain, justified our attempts to control the abuse of inside information. Of course, in recent years the influence of various initiatives within the European Union has resulted in a wider concern to address the taking advantage of asymmetric access to information even where such has not been appropriated or misused.

The law that has developed to address these issues in a prohibitive and remedial manner is both complex and multi-layered. While the criminal law is mostly found in statute, the law relating to market abuse operates in what is to English jurisprudence a relatively new world between criminal law and the civil law. The specific laws and regulatory provisions also function within the context of the general law and other structures of regulation ranging from the Code on Takeovers and Mergers to in-firm compliance systems. The range of potential legal and regulatory responses to even a simple case of insider dealing is both complex and often uncertain. The perception that insider abuse is still a major issue in most markets and the traditional approach of the criminal law has not served as a significant deterrent and has led to regulators such as the Financial Conduct Authority and the US Securities and Exchange Commission renewing their commitment to 'stamp out' insider dealing by whatever means are at their lawful disposal. Consequently it is important to consider the control of insider trading and related abuses in the rather wider context of financial crime and therefore in this third edition we have addressed in more depth issues such as the new fraud law and money laundering.

There is another important dimension that in this new edition we seek to further develop. Earlier discussions of insider dealing law have understandably tended to concentrate on the legal and regulatory liabilities of those who engage in the abuse of inside information. However, today as in the case of money laundering, the impact of the law and especially the regulatory system is in practice rather greater for those who find themselves, innocently or otherwise, as facilitators of objectionable transactions. A serious and very real responsibility has been cast on financial intermediaries and professional advisers to assist in the maintenance of integrity in the markets. Indeed, as we have seen post the financial crisis associated with the so-called sub-prime scandals, enforcement has bitten on the institutions that have failed to police their own staff and customers. In the real world, authorised persons, those who manage them and those who are engaged in compliance, are more likely to find themselves subject to legal and regulatory sanctions than those who actually engage in the abuse of inside information or for that matter who engage in other profitable crimes. The obligations that anti-money laundering laws, anti-insider dealing regulations and increasingly anti-corruption laws impose on those who handle other people's financial transactions to conduct due diligence and operate effective controls to discourage and expose such activity are onerous and well policed. Therefore, the control of insider dealing and related abuses is a very real and topical concern for all those who operate in the financial sector. In this new edition we expand our discussion of these issues and give particular emphasis to the role and responsibilities of compliance.

As we have seen only too well with the financial chaos stemming in part from the failure of banks to operate effective risk control systems, all financial markets are to a greater or lesser degree inter-dependent. Consequently, the laws and systems of one jurisdiction cannot be considered in isolation. Those engaged in objectionable or even merely facilitative activities may well be subject to the reach of other regulatory and legal systems. Most significantly in practical terms is the long arm reach of US securities law and, in particular, the concern of the US Securities and Exchange Commission to protect the integrity of its own national markets. Indeed, the criticism that has been made of the failure of the SEC to prevent and adequately control a series of recent scandals makes it almost inevitable that it will continue to adopt a robust enforcement stance. Therefore this edition, as did the second, attempts where relevant to address the legal and regulatory issues that may arise when other jurisdictions and in particular the USA seek to assert their authority.

With many developments in the substantive law – both in statute and case law, regulation and best practice – which frankly are too numerous to detail here, much of the text has been re-written and to some degree re-structured. There is also a great deal of new material in this edition, reflecting not only these developments, but also the emphasis that we have placed on institutional responsibility and accountability whether for failures in compliance or in terms of accessory liability.

The authors have attempted to draw upon their unique combination of expertise and practical experience in presenting in a clear and constructive manner an admittedly complex and dramatic body of law and regulation. Indeed, we are delighted that Jeffrey Bryant has joined us with his deep knowledge and experience as a prosecutor of financial crime. Given the topicality and fast moving nature of our subject matter we have sought the advice of many involved in the day-to-day administration of the relevant law and in particular compliance systems. It would be invidious to name particular individuals who have been of such assistance, but their advice and support has always been much appreciated and valued, albeit not always followed! We are particularly grateful for the support and advice that we have received from our publisher Mr Andy Hill and his colleagues, whose advice we have been scrupulous in following!

Professor Barry Rider OBE

Professor Kern Alexander

Professor Stuart Bazley

Mr Jeffrey Bryant

February 2016

Contents

Contents

Contents

Table of cases

Table of cases

Table of statutes

Table of statutes

Table of statutory instruments

Chapter 1

The nature of insider dealing and market abuse

INSIDER DEALING IN PERSPECTIVE

1.1   The commonly held view is that insider dealing is a problem of the twentieth century and, more specifically, the last quarter of the century. It is certainly the case that, over the last 40 years, there has been considerable interest in the topic in many countries. The media and, in particular, the press regularly carry stories of those in positions of trust taking advantage of price-sensitive information to further their own interests.[1] Most jurisdictions have in recent years enacted legislation specifically to deal with the problem of directors and officers of companies taking advantage of information that they receive by virtue of their privileged positions by dealing in their company's securities. Indeed, an increasing number of countries seek to discourage the 'misuse' of material information almost no matter in what circumstances it was obtained. In a work such as this it is not feasible or particularly useful to attempt to analyse in the depth required the laws and regulations of even the more significant financial markets around the world. On the other hand it may be helpful to identify the constituent elements in what is generally considered to be objectionable and worthy of legal and often criminal liability. Insider dealing is not, of course, confined to those holding office in a company and many regulatory systems impose prohibitions on anyone who acquires such information with knowledge that it is from a privileged source. On the other hand, despite the amount of law that has been created, there is considerable scepticism as to whether it does provide sufficient protection for investors and the markets.

1.2   In fact, the problem of insiders abusing information that they obtain by virtue of the special relationship that they have with their company is not a new one. It is possible to find references to insiders taking advantage of their privileged position to dump over-valued securities on the market in official reports as early as the seventeenth century.[2] Furthermore, the taking

---

1   See for example, Hector Saints, 'City must join insider trading fight' and Editorial, 'The FSA must stop insider trading' *Financial Times* 23 April 2007, V Harvey, 'The war against insider trading' *Financial Times* 21 October 2013 and H Wilson, 'Bank tells City to stamp out the scandals' *The Times*, 27 February 2015.
2   See, for example, B Rider, C Abrams and M Ashe, *Guide to Financial Services Regulation* (3rd ed, CCH 1997), at Ch 1; B Rider and H Ffrench, *The Regulation of Insider Trading* (Macmillan 1979), and G Gilligan, *Regulating the Financial Services Sector* (Kluwer 1999), Ch 4.

advantage of privileged information or, at least, information that the other party could not obtain, is as old as human nature. While history may not record examples of the abuse of such information on securities markets, there are countless examples from many countries of people profiting in one way or another from such information. Indeed, in many cultures, no opprobrium necessarily attached to such conduct and in some it would have been regarded inopportune, if not ungracious, not to have utilised the advantage in question. It is still the case that very few jurisdictions seek to impose constraints, let alone legal prohibitions, on the use of privileged knowledge in dealings other than in securities.

1.3   While most systems of law do, to some degree, protect the confidentiality of information in specific circumstances, they do not necessarily interfere in transactions with third parties who have been disadvantaged by the use of information obtained in breach of a duty of confidentiality. Few legal systems go anywhere near imposing an obligation on someone in possession of superior information to disclose this to another contracting party. Even when that other party could not have obtained the same information with the greatest diligence, in most jurisdictions there will be no duty to disclose or warn him. To require equality of information in such circumstances would undermine any incentive that a person would otherwise have to conduct research or acquire material information. Regarding decisions relating to the disposal of property and the conduct of commerce, it is necessary to have the best information that is available and therefore the acquisition of superior information should not be discouraged, let alone penalised.

1.4   Why should we, therefore, be concerned when such transactions occur in regard to intangible property and, in particular, in securities of public companies? Of course, the development of corporate enterprise has necessitated that we look at our ordinary laws and their application to new areas. While it is convenient for us to attribute a legal personality to the corporation for a variety of sensible and important reasons, this legal fiction inevitably gives rise to implications for those who deal with, or are involved in, the enterprise. For example, the corporation is interposed between the shareholders and the enterprise's property. In the vast majority of legal systems, shareholders do not own the company's property. It is only the company as a separate legal person that owns its assets. The shareholders' property is confined to their 'share' in the enterprise. The value of this 'share' will depend on many things, albeit most significantly, the value of the enterprise's assets and the productivity of their use. The important thing to note, however, is that we are not dealing with absolutes and value in this context will be determined by what another is willing to pay or exchange for the share in question. When we consider the value of other securities such as bonds and derivatives, the relationship with quantifiable and assessable property becomes even more remote. It is clear, therefore, that, in determining the value of securities, knowledge of events that are likely to affect the decision of others as to whether to acquire or dispose of ownership and upon what terms, plays a much greater role than in regard to many other forms of wealth. It is also clear that there will be persons who, by virtue of their position in or in relation to the enterprise, will be in a very privileged position in obtaining and assessing price-relevant information. Thus, quite early on in the development of the common law, obligations were cast upon those responsible for issuing new securities and, in particular, shares, to ensure fair and adequate disclosure of all material information relating to the enterprise and not to take advantage of their privileged position. In most jurisdictions today, such obligations have been placed on a statutory footing.[3]

1.5 Where insiders deal in the market in the securities of the issuer with which they enjoy this privileged access to its information, it is not difficult to see why many consider they should be held to similar responsibilities. While the situation is not quite the same as when the issuer itself offers securities of unknown value to the market, in the perception of those in the market, the dissimilarity is not fundamental. Those in a position of stewardship over the company's enterprise are taking advantage of their position to derive profit that is taken at the expense of those in the market. Given the conceptual and practical difficulties in fitting this sort of conduct within the scope of traditional civil or criminal causes of action, it is hardly surprising that most countries have enacted legislation specifically prohibiting those in possession of inside information from taking advantage of it. Indeed, in most systems, the prohibitions extend somewhat further than to those who would ordinarily be considered to occupy positions of trust within a company. While the unfairness of such misconduct more than justifies the intervention of the law to discourage abuse, it does not necessarily justify the development of remedies for those who happen to transact with an insider.[4] Obviously, in practical if not legal terms, there are considerable differences between the matching of parties to a particular transaction, on or off the market.

1.6 In the result, the regulation of insider dealing has and will no doubt continue to throw up a host of issues that would not ordinarily be encountered in the control of other anti-social conduct. The sophistication of the financial environment within which the law and regulatory mechanisms operate, compounds the practical and legal difficulties confronting those seeking to administer and apply the law. While the control of insider abuse has much in common with the prevention and interdiction of money laundering and even corruption, the crafting of legislation and the development of supporting regulatory mechanisms involve issues of peculiar complexity and sensitivity. Despite these problems, the efficacy of anti-insider dealing regulation has, in many countries, become almost a litmus test for the efficiency and competence of the wider regulatory structure overseeing the markets and the conduct of business in the financial sector.

1.7 Consequently, in practical and political terms, the control of insider abuse is a significant issue. While the various philosophical justifications for regulation may be argued about, it is the case that in many countries it is now recognised that the presence of such laws is required if investor confidence in the integrity of the markets is to be preserved and promoted. From perhaps a somewhat cynical perspective, it matters little if such empirical evidence as there is, is equivocal as to the extent of the problem of insider dealing and the harm it occasions. If enough people think it occurs and for whatever reason – including jealousy – consider this is unfair, confidence in the reputation and therefore the efficiency of the market will be eroded. Consequently,

3   See, for example, the Financial Services and Markets Act 2000, Pt VI and see Chapter 9 below.
4   For further discussion on this see B Rider 'Insider Trading – A Crime of our times?' *Current Legal Problems, Current Developments in Banking and Finance Laws* (D Kingsford Smith ed) 1989; B Rider 'The Control of Insider Trading – Smoke and Mirrors!' 1 *International and Comparative Corporate Law Journal* (1999) 271 and B Rider 'Civilising the Law – The use of Civil and Administrative Proceedings to enforce Financial Services Law' 3 *Journal of Financial Crime* (1995) 11.

those who are responsible for the protection of the markets have a responsibility to act. Whether this is through the medium of the criminal law or some other mechanism, it is in the public's interest that it be seen that insider dealing is not condoned.

WHAT IS INSIDER DEALING?

Who are insiders?

1.8   The classic example that is often given of insider dealing is where a director of a company learns in a board meeting that his company's profit forecasts are about to be revised to a significant extent and then goes onto the stock market and trades on the basis of this information before it is made publicly available. In such circumstances, he has clearly taken advantage of his position and the information that came to him by virtue of his seat on the board. He has manifestly misused the confidential information that was entrusted to him in the proper performance of his duties as a director or, in the words of US federal law, misappropriated it. It would also be generally regarded as falling within the notion of insider dealing if he persuaded another person to deal in the securities of his company or disclosed the information to a third person knowing that he would be likely so to deal or otherwise misuse the information.

1.9   It is accepted that this notion of insider dealing would extend to the misuse of confidential information to avoid a loss as well as to make a profit. It matters not whether the director takes advantage of the information to buy more securities in his company in the expectation that their price will rise on publication of the information or whether he sells securities in the fear that the market price will decline. It should, however, be noted that the law might not always offer a remedy or sanction in the latter case. It requires a degree of sophistication that is not always found in the law, to regard a loss avoided as a profit, which should be rendered accountable to the company.

1.10   It is not, of course, only company directors that will in the ordinary course of their duties acquire price-sensitive information. Indeed, it is probably more likely that in most companies there are many other insiders who will come into possession of such information rather more regularly than the directors. Having regard to the obvious relationship that a director has to his company, it remains to be seen whether such persons would be rash enough to risk exposure to public criticism by engaging in insider dealing. Furthermore, it cannot be taken for granted that most company directors would be willing to risk their position and the financial and other benefits that arise as a result of their office by engaging in abusive deals.

1.11   The notion of insider dealing is broad enough to encompass all those who, by virtue of their position in the company or who, by their business or professional relationship with the company, are likely to have access to privileged information. For the sake of convenience, it is perhaps useful to describe such persons as primary insiders. They are all subject to the common denominator of enjoying a special relationship with the company that gives them access to the price-sensitive information in question. Indeed, in US jurisprudence, they have often been referred to as 'access insiders'. Debate has taken place as to whether those who obtain such information in breach of their duties attaching to the relationship in question should be regarded as primary insiders. For example, is it appropriate to regard an office cleaner, who, while having access to a company's premises by virtue of her employment directly or indirectly with the company, obtains price-sensitive information by rummaging in the rubbish bins, as a primary insider? Although it is arguable that all those who abuse price-sensitive information should be sanctioned, for the sake of convenience in drafting rules and laws, most jurisdictions distinguish between those who obtain such information in the proper and lawful exercise of the duties attaching to the relationship that they have with the relevant company and those who do so essentially outside the scope of those responsibilities.

1.12   In practice, it is usual to throw the net rather wider and regard primary insiders as insiders, not only of the company with whom they are in this relationship, but also issuers that are closely related to it and to other issuers, such as a potential offeree company. Consequently, it will be considered to be insider dealing when a director of a company, having learnt that his company intends to make an attractive takeover offer for the shares of another company, acquires shares in that other company before the offer is announced.

Secondary insiders

1.13   It is also considered to be insider dealing when a person, while not in an access relationship to the issuer, acquires the relevant information in circumstances where he knows that it is unpublished price-sensitive information and comes from an insider source and then deals or encourages another to deal. Thus, although the office cleaner in the example referred to above might not be considered to be a primary insider, her abuse of the information obtained from what she appreciates is an 'inside source', would generally be considered to amount to insider trading. In some cases, it will even be considered objectionable for this tippee or secondary insider to pass the information on to yet another person in circumstances where they know or should appreciate that the information is likely to be misused.

Inside source

1.14   The law and, indeed, morality in most societies, therefore necessitates proof of a relationship between the source of the information and the person who is to be accused of insider dealing. The price-sensitive information must be obtained by virtue of this relationship. It is the relationship that taints it and renders improper its use for personal benefit. Of course, the notion of relationship is stretched far beyond what the law would normally consider to be relationships of a fiduciary quality or, for that matter, necessarily giving rise to a duty of confidentiality. The extent to which it is necessary to establish that the relevant information is obtained by virtue of the privileged access that the relationship gives to the person concerned is a matter for debate. Logically, if the information can be shown to have been obtained from some other and outside source, then its use by a person who is clearly in a special relationship with the company should not be considered to be insider dealing. However, in most systems of law, there will be a 'presumption' that if a primary insider is in possession of price-sensitive information in regard to the securities of the issuer with which he has an access relationship, then the 'inside information' was obtained pursuant to this relationship.

Inside information

1.15   Information is a very vague and ill-defined concept in many legal systems. However, in the context of insider dealing, it is generally not necessary to refine a definition that does more than indicate that it possesses a quality sufficient to influence the decision of the person who has access to it to deal in particular securities. In other words, the information that the person accused of insider dealing has in his possession must be such as would influence his decision to buy or sell. In the UK, as in most legal systems, it is enough if the information would influence the mind of a person who would be likely to deal in the relevant securities. Thus, materiality is objective and is determined by reference to the particular class or group of investors that would ordinarily be likely to deal in the securities in question. This gives the test of materiality sufficient flexibility to accommodate narrow and highly specialised markets. The more specific and precise the information is, the more likely it is that it will influence the mind of a reasonable person.

1.16   Some systems of regulation seek to define materiality not so much in terms of the impact on the investor, but on the market. Obviously, the more significant the impact that the information once disclosed is likely to have on the price of the securities the more influential it will be on the mind of an investor. On the other hand, tests that focus on whether the information is likely to affect the decision of an investor encompass not only the relevance of price, but also other market factors. Generally speaking, it is enough to establish materiality of information that it would be a factor in taking a decision; it need not be the determinant or an especially significant factor.

1.17   The information must be inside information. In other words, it must have a quality which ties it to the issuer in whose securities the dealing takes place. We have already discussed this issue in terms of the relationship that the person accused of insider dealing must have, directly or indirectly, with the source of the information. Obviously, relevance will be bound up with materiality in most conceivable cases. The information need not be generated within, by or for the benefit of the issuer in whose securities the dealing takes place. For example, it would be objectionable for a director of a company which intends to make an attractive takeover offer for the securities of another company to deal in the securities of that other company on the basis of this knowledge. The information in such a case may be regarded as being inside information obtained through his insider nexus with his company, but its relevance is to the market in that other issuer's securities.

1.18   While the information involved in most cases of insider abuse will be confidential or at least obtained in a relationship that might be expected to give rise to obligations of confidentiality, it is not always that the information will be such that could be protected as 'confidential' information. There will be cases where the information is too tentative to be protected as proprietary information, but which would still meet the test of materiality. It is also the case that there will be situations when the information is not confidential to a particular person or entity. In the result, it is clear that inside information is not always confidential information. Of course, in the United States, the courts have fashioned the so-called 'misappropriation theory' to justify liability for insider dealing. This approach sanctions the 'misappropriation' of information that belongs to another person. Dealing on the basis of such information will constitute a misappropriation, as will improperly disclosing it to another in circumstances where that other utilises it. The notion that information belongs to another person who will often obtain the same by the inside source is a difficult one for many legal systems. For example, while many legal systems are prepared to protect confidential information as if it were a form of property, not all by any means consider information capable of being a species of property.[5]

1.19   Inside information has sometimes been described as 'privileged' information. In the legal sense, privileged information is a concept even narrower than that of confidential information. Consequently, it is preferable to contemplate the notion of privilege, as referring to the circumstances in which it is acquired, rather than the information itself. Where a person in a special relationship or an access relationship acquires information by virtue of his position, then his access may be described as having been made possible in privileged circumstances. To describe, however, inside information as being privileged information in the traditionally accepted legal sense of the word is misleading.

1.20   The information to be inside information must not be in the public domain. Obviously, the value of the information to the person who deals upon it is that it is not publicly available. While it is not necessary for the information to be secret in the sense of being confidential, as we have seen, it must not be accessible to those who could ordinarily be expected to deal in the relevant securities. Many regulatory systems provide that the information should, at the time of its misuse, be unpublished. Much will therefore depend upon what publication means in this context. At one end of the spectrum, if information has been released into the public domain through a press announcement or a regulatory disclosure, then it ceases to be inside information. On the other hand, what if the company is prepared to make the information available only to analysts or other market professionals, possibly on a selective basis? The nature of the market and the sophistication of the financial environment within which the disclosure takes place will inevitably bear upon the question whether the information has been sufficiently published or not.

1.21   It is the case, however, that in most jurisdictions including the UK, provided that the information is freely available to those who would be likely to deal in the relevant securities, there is adequate public disclosure. It has been argued that the fact that the information is publicly available does not entitle those who had pre-publication knowledge to deal before there is an opportunity for the information to be adequately disseminated and even 'digested'.

The transaction

1.22   Insider dealing requires that the person in possession of the information does something partly, at least, in reliance on the information in question. It is not necessary that he does something that he would not have done had he not possessed the information. This would require a much too high standard of materiality and introduce difficult issues of causation. On the other hand, it is generally accepted that for insider dealing to occur the person concerned must enter into a transaction himself, procure or encourage another to enter into a transaction or disclose the information to another in circumstances where

---

5   See, for example, *Oxford v Moss* (1978) 68 Cr App R 183, in which it was held information was not property for the purpose of the law of theft, discussed at 2.27.

that other is likely to abuse the information. Merely desisting from trading would not, in most people's perception, amount to insider dealing. Of course, if a transaction has already been initiated, failing to complete it might well be sufficient.

1.23   The buying or selling need not necessarily relate to securities of the company with which the person concerned is in an access relationship. We have already referred to the fact that many systems of regulation would sanction the use of information pertaining to a transaction or arrangement between the insider's own company and another corporate issuer. It is also the case that dealing in the securities of related companies on the basis of relevant unpublished information would also be considered insider dealing. Dealings in securities other than equity securities that are price-affected by the information would be considered to be insider dealing in the UK and most other jurisdictions. Thus, acquiring options to acquire or dispose of underlying securities would be objectionable, as would dealing in other types of derivative securities. The question is simply whether the decision to deal in the relevant securities is influenced by the information that the person concerned has acquired and is using improperly.

1.24   The term 'insider dealing' is wide enough to encompass deals on or off an organised securities market. While a number of legal systems have effectively confined the operation of their legal rules to transactions that occur on an organised securities exchange or on or through an organised over-the-counter market, the elements of the abuse are the same whether the transaction is on a market or in a private direct transaction. One of the reasons why jurisdictions have confined the operation of their laws to public markets is the idea that the wrong indicated by insider dealing is one against the market as a whole. It saps confidence in the integrity and fairness of the market. Consequently, some have made available only their criminal justice system to sanction this essentially public wrong or, rather, crime. Off-market transactions are left to the ordinary law which governs the commercial dealings of private persons. The fallacy is to attribute the description of insider dealing to one type of transaction and not to the other. While there may be justifications for distinguishing market and off-market insider transactions in regard to the remedies that are made available and in relation to enforcement, the nature of the abuse and its elements are the same. Therefore, it is appropriate to regard insider dealing as taking place on organised markets as well as in private and even face-to-face transactions.

Unauthorised disclosures

1.25   It has already been pointed out that most systems of insider dealing regulation would regard disclosing inside information to another person, without the appropriate authority, in circumstances where that other person is likely to abuse the information, as a form of insider dealing. Merely disclosing information even if there is an expectation that the recipient will himself deal, is not 'dealing' in any real sense of the word. While it is possible and common place to attribute the transactions of an agent to the principal and therefore the deals of the agent to the deals of the 'insider', it is less easy to describe procuring or encouraging the dealing of another as insider dealing. Nonetheless, the term insider dealing is often employed in such an expansive manner, as it is in the UK.

1.26 Where a person, without authority, discloses unpublished and material information in the knowledge that the recipient might well utilise the information for dealing, then it is at least arguable that the person should be held responsible for what is indirectly the exploitation of the information in question. In the UK, as in most systems of law that regard such unauthorised disclosures as tantamount to insider dealing, it matters not whether the recipient actually engages in transactions which would themselves be considered insider dealing. For example, while the informant might be culpable, the recipient who deals on the basis of the information may not be aware that the information emanates from an inside source. A failure to appreciate the status of the information might well in any case bring into issue its materiality.

1.27 Such conduct will, however, only be considered objectionable when the primary insider discloses the relevant information without proper authority. It is not always easy to decide if a particular disclosure is legitimate or not. As a general rule, if the disclosure is made with the actual or implied authority of the person concerned to make or authorise disclosure, then it will not be objectionable. There may be cases where, while the relevant officer of the company has authority to disclose information, he does so not for a proper purpose, but perhaps to facilitate improper transactions on the part of another. In most systems of law, agents have authority only to engage in actions that are properly motivated. Therefore, a disclosure that is motivated by improper considerations, such as a desire to promote a false market, would not be legitimate and justifiable even when a primary insider has no authority to disclose information. It may well be on the facts appropriate and legitimate for him to do so, for example, 'blowing the whistle' on misconduct. Provided that such is done for a purpose that would be considered proper and is not dishonest, it is hard to see that such conduct could be described as fostering insider abuse. The line between what is acceptable and what is not is not always clear. Difficulties have arisen in the case of selective disclosures to analysts and private briefings, as we shall see.

The inside nexus

1.28 While over the last three decades most jurisdictions have enacted laws specifically prohibiting insider dealing and penalising infractions of the law, outside the US and one or two other jurisdictions, such as the UK, France and Australia prosecutions have been rare and have only occasionally resulted in convictions. The reasons why so few cases of insider abuse end in convictions are many and varied. However, it is not uncommon to find that the specific offences that have been created to address the problem of insider abuse require the prosecution to prove, to the high standard of the criminal law, a set of facts which in practice renders many cases incapable of successful prosecution. For example, the former offence of insider dealing in the UK required the prosecution to establish no fewer than 12 separate facts. Proof of the requisite state of mind, or *mens rea*, was particularly onerous. The record for successful prosecutions for fraud and economic crime involving complex factual situations and sophisticated business activity is not impressive in the vast majority of legal systems. On the other hand, there is the perception that insider dealing does occur at a sufficiently significant level in many markets to be a matter of concern to those who are charged with promoting and maintaining their integrity. It is also the case that in many jurisdictions, including the UK the efficacy or otherwise of the regulators' ability to deal efficiently and seemingly effectively with cases of insider abuse had become almost an acid test of their competence and ability to protect investors. Faced with this challenge it is perhaps not surprising that attempts have been made to simplify the essential elements for establishing the 'offence' of insider dealing.

1.29 A number of institutions, including the International Monetary Fund, have embarked on programmes to develop a more useable model of regulation, but it is the European Commission that has achieved most, at least in terms of statutory material. The European Commission initially attempted to do this through its company law harmonisation programme and then later as part of its initiative to ensure equivalence of protection and the creation of a level 'playing field' in the financial services industry. In doing so there has been – apart from in the United States – a tendency to move away from the need for an essentially fiduciary nexus and to base the prohibition on what might be described as 'fraud on the market' concepts. In doing so, the emphasis has been placed, at least as far as the law is concerned, on the misuse of privileged information from the standpoint of those in the market and not from the position of the company. Although the initial European directive[6] which seeks to co-ordinate anti-insider dealing laws within the EU is very much orientated to the market and ensuring the integrity of dealings in a market context, it still adheres in part to the more traditional notion that insider dealing signifies the involvement of persons who would be considered by virtue of their positions to be corporate insiders, namely directors, officers and substantial shareholders, albeit these primary insiders need not have this relationship with the issuer of the securities to which the abuse relates. Thus, in the context of this particular Directive we are still in the realm of company law and traditional issues of governance, although conceptually somewhat on the periphery. Of course, the Market Abuse Directive[7] is a rather different creature and reflects a much wider and more market-orientated approach in line with the development of the law in the UK after the Financial Services and Markets Act 2000.

1.30 Although, as we have indicated, there is a tendency, in at least some jurisdictions, to fasten upon the unfair use of all information that is not adequately disseminated, at this point in time, the notion of insider dealing involves three basic elements. First, the existence of information which is not publicly available, or at least is not available to those who would be likely to deal in the securities to which it relates, but, if it were, it would be likely to influence their decision to deal and upon what terms. In other words, there must be material, non-public information. Secondly, those in possession of the information must be aware that it emanates, directly or indirectly, from an inside source. Thirdly, they must then deal in the securities that would be affected by the information. It is also usually thought to be insider dealing when the possessor of the information encourages another to deal or improperly discloses the information to another in circumstances where it is likely that that other person will deal or encourage another to deal.

6   Directive 89/592/EC (1989) OJ L334/30.
7   Council Directive 2003/6/EC (2003) OJ L96/16; Directive 2003/124 (2003) OJ L339/70 and Directive 2004/72/EC (2004) L 162/70. See generally on the background to this R Alexander, *Insider Dealing and Money laundering in the EU: Law and Regulation* (Ashgate 2007), and generally Chapters 4 and 5 below.

How far should we cast the net?

1.31 We have looked at what might be described as the constituent elements of what is ordinarily conjured up by the term 'insider dealing'. Before proceeding with our discussion, it would be useful to explore the various arguments as to who should be regarded as an insider. We have already looked at the traditional categories and raised the distinction between primary or access insiders and those who obtain the relevant information through such a person and are thus more appropriately described as secondary insiders. However, even in relation to this simplistic distinction, there are issues which would be useful to discuss in the wider context of who may properly and appropriately be considered to be an insider and thereby subjected to additional obligations. It is also important to remember that, under the laws of most jurisdictions, the determination of who and who is not to be considered an insider has serious implications for those dealing with them and, in particular, receiving and utilising information from them. A person who deals with an insider is dealing with an inside source and, consequently, any communication from that insider will be from an inside source subjecting that person to the obligations of being an insider himself.

Access insiders

1.32 The classic notion of insider dealing, as we have already indicated, involves a person closely associated with an issuer, taking advantage of material unpublished information that has come into his possession by virtue of his relationship to the company. While there are no doubt instances of persons in an access relationship to an issuer engaging in such conduct, as we have already indicated, it must surely be unlikely that corporate insiders would be prepared to risk their position and employment by engaging in such egregious conduct. Consequently, most of the cases that have come to light involving primary insiders acting in such an unsophisticated and blatant manner have involved individuals whose conduct may fairly be described as an aberration, possibly motivated by exceptional pressures or financial needs. In fact, in a high proportion of cases, the amounts of money involved have also been relatively small. Most corporate insiders would not in the ordinary course of events be able to raise very significant amounts of money to risk on insider trading within the requisite time frame. Those insiders who are prepared to violate the trust reposed in them and engage in a more systematic abuse of their position would tend to utilise nominees, sell or even barter the information in question. Obviously, the more sophisticated the attempts are to evade detection, the less likely it is that the insider will be identified or rendered amenable to sanctions. In those jurisdictions that have developed regimes for the control of insider abuse, in the case of primary insiders, it is on the whole only the relatively 'innocent' and foolish – perhaps arrogant who get caught.

Those in the market

1.33 Professor Henry Manne suggested in 1966, in his controversial book *Insider Dealing and the Stock* Market,[8] that primary insiders would, because of the risks that they face, be far more likely to exchange items of inside information rather than trade on it themselves. While this was thought

---

8   The Free Press (US).

somewhat fanciful, there are examples of insiders indulging in this activity or selling information. Obviously, the more disassociated the eventual dealing is from the relationship through which the information was obtained, the more difficult it is for action to be taken against the insider who has betrayed his fiduciary obligations. Indeed, the relevant information is effectively laundered in the same manner as criminal property, often using very similar devices. In countries where anti-insider dealing regulation is developed, a significant proportion of cases involve dealing on unpublished price-sensitive information by financial intermediaries. Such persons are often in a much better position to evaluate the impact of information and exploit it, as compared with the ordinary corporate executive. They are also able to organise exploitation to maximum effect through the use of derivatives and other trading devices. The relevant information in many of these cases is either obtained from a primary insider or relates to the financial activity of the issuer in question.

1.34 There has been debate as to the extent to which 'market information', as opposed to information that is generated from within the company, can properly be regarded as inside information. For example, the decision of a substantial shareholder to liquidate his holding, while not inside information in the conventional sense of the word could well be highly price-sensitive. While it would generally be thought inappropriate to stigmatise the actual transaction by the substantial shareholder as objectionable, as he is possessed of nothing more than the knowledge of his own intentions, those who are privy to this might be thought to be in a rather different situation. It should be noted, however, that many systems impose disclosure obligations, primarily to the market, when a transaction would have implications for the control of a company. Of course, this is justified on much wider considerations than the abuse of what might be considered privileged information. The then Department of Trade stated 'a company, its members and the public at large should be entitled to be informed promptly of the acquisition of a significant holding in its voting shares ... in order that existing members and those dealing with the company may protect their interests and that the conduct of the affairs of the company is not prejudiced by uncertainty over those who may be in a position to influence or control the company'.[9] In the United Kingdom, as we shall see in our discussion of market abuse, such obligations are imposed primarily through the listing agreement and the rules promulgated initially by the Financial Services Authority. However, under the Companies Act 1948[10] a statutory obligation was placed on substantial shareholders to disclose and report their own holdings and those associated with them. This obligation has been transferred as a result of the intervention of EU legislation[11] from corporate law to the regulatory system established under the Financial Service and Markets Act 2000.[12] In addition to the disclosure of shareholdings above

---

9   See Disclosure of Interests in Shares (1980) and generally AJ Boyle et al, *Boyle and Birds' Company Law* (9th edn, Jordans 2014).
10   See the Companies Act 1985, Pt VI which extended and re-enacted these provisions. Note in particular the powers that companies have to investigate the beneficial ownership of their shares and that who are interested in them, see *Re Technology Investment Trust plc* [1988] BCLC 256 in Pt 22, Companies Act 2006 replacing the relevant provisions in the 1985 Act.
11   See Directive 88/627 EC (1988) OJ L348/62 and Directive 2001/34/EC (2001) OJ L184/1.
12   See s 1266 of the Companies Act 2006 introducing new Financial Services and Markets Act 2000 ss 89A–89G and Companies Act 2006 (Commencement No 1 Transitional Provisions and Savings) Order 2006, SI 2006/3428, Sch 3 and Implementation of the Transparency Directive and Investment Entities Listing Review, FSA CP06/4 March 2006, Ch 3 and Implementation of the Transparency Directive, FSA PS06/11, October 2006, Ch 3.

a certain level, most developed regulatory systems impose obligations on individuals and companies, once certain thresholds have been crossed, to announce their intentions and or make a public offer.[13] There are also provisions for the mandatory aggregation and disclosure of shareholdings in cases where persons act in concert to 'warehouse' securities if the aggregated holding exceeds the requisite 'disclosure threshold'.[14]

1.35   There are a number of important considerations, however, that need to be addressed if the regulatory net is thrown over market information that does not have some additional quality to it, other than being merely material and non-public. Mention has already been made of the important role that analysts and other intermediaries play in the financial services industry. It is important that what are widely considered to be quite proper and even beneficial operations in the market are not undermined. The position of market makers is particularly sensitive. In many markets, certain professionals will be charged with a responsibility to provide a market, either way, in a selection of securities. This facilitates liquidity and stability and assists in the maintenance of an orderly market. It is the case, however, that such dealers will, because of their specialised relationship with the issuers in whose securities they make a market, come into possession, or themselves generate, information of a price-sensitive nature. Having said this, however, it is also important to note that market makers, given their obligation to remain in the market, albeit within certain limits and be willing to trade, are particularly exposed to insider dealing and manipulative practices on the part of others. Consequently, market makers in many countries have often been at the forefront of those calling for stricter control of insider dealing. Generally speaking, the beneficial role performed by such market professionals is recognised in law by effectively exempting what they do in the ordinary and proper course of business as a market maker.

The corporate issuer

1.36   Discussion has also taken place in several jurisdictions as to whether the issuer can be sensibly regarded as an insider of itself. There is no objection, under the laws of most countries, to a company being considered an insider and to legal liability attaching to the corporation in the ordinary way. What has been said in regard to the intention of a person to act in a certain manner applies as much to a company as it would to an individual. However, where the issuer intends to act in a manner which would affect the price of its own securities or for that matter a related company's, there is an increasingly widely held view that it is properly cast in the role of an insider. Of course, the circumstances in which a company can deal in its own capital are regulated and in many countries it is illegal for a company to deal its own securities or give any third person financial assistance to do so.[15] However, in certain circumstances, companies may be able to repurchase and cancel stock or redeem preference shares. Where this is permitted, the issuer would be bound to ensure that the holders of these securities are in no way prejudiced by the existence of unpublished information which might affect the value of the securities to be acquired or redeemed. Consequently, the company would have to make a full

---

13   See General Principle 10 and Rule 2.2 of the Takeover Code.
14   See *supra* at 9.
15   See generally Part 18 of the Companies Act 2006 and 2.11 and generally Chapter 9.

and fair disclosure. In such circumstances, the directors of the company would also have a duty to ensure that whatever is done by the company is done in its best interests.

'Scalpers' and 'gun jumpers'

1.37   From a conceptual standpoint, a somewhat related issue is that of 'scalping'. In its simplest form, 'scalping' involves a journalist or analyst trading in securities that he has written up or, for that matter, expressed reservations about, in an article or report prior to its publication. Depending upon the circumstances, there is little doubt that comments of a favourable or negative character can have a profound and predictable impact on the price of securities. The problem is that the information upon which the journalist trades has no insider nexus with the relevant issuer. It may well amount to nothing more or less than the fruits of his or her work and reflections, based upon widely available and verifiable facts. On the other hand, using advance knowledge that the article is likely to have an impact on the market to make a profit or, for that matter, avoid a loss, is objectionable. It has the character of betting on a certainty which is compounded by an abuse of position. Where the dealing is by an individual other than the person who wrote it, then it is often relatively easy to construct an argument that would bring that person within the reach of the ordinary theories of insider liability. It is where the journalist or analyst himself trades that the real difficulty arises.

1.38   While most systems of regulation would consider this unethical, few actually attempt to impose specific legal sanctions. In the United States, the 'misappropriation theory' has been used with considerable effect to impose liability on anyone who uses, without proper authority, 'inside' information that belongs to another. Consequently, if the article has been prepared by the journalist in the course of his employment or under commission, then it is arguable that the information can only be used for his employer's purposes. If he seeks to take personal advantage of it by trading prior to publication, he would be guilty of insider dealing. Of course, in many jurisdictions and in particular common law legal systems, it is probable that the ordinary law would impose liability on an employee who sought to profit in such a manner.[16]

1.39   In the present context, the term 'gun jumping' is often applied to the same sort of conduct as 'scalping'. However, it is wider in the sense that it involves those, other than the person or persons responsible for the creation of the information or opportunity, seeking to take advantage of it before it is published. It is also applied to those who deal immediately on publication of the information before others have had an opportunity to assess it properly. Those who are privy to unpublished price-sensitive information and then, without authority, seek to exploit it, may well fall within the purview of anti-insider dealing laws. Under the European directive on insider trading, provided that the person seeking to exploit the information is aware that the source of the information is classified as a primary insider, even though they may have no relationship with the issuer of the securities in question, an offence would be committed. As we have already pointed out, the directive creates a class of primary insiders, members of which may or may not happen to be in an access relationship to the company in question. Where, however, the information is

---

16   See for example *Brandeaux Advisers (UK) Ltd v Chadwick* [2010] IRLR 244.

not obtained from a person who happens to be a director, officer or substantial shareholder of any company, the issue of liability is rather more problematical. Where the dealing takes place after the information has been disclosed, then, very few jurisdictions require those with advance knowledge to hold back for a period to allow dissemination, let alone digestion.

1.40 While 'jumping the gun' may be considered to be unfair, it must also be remembered that analysts do play an important role in refining information and thereby improving the quality of investment decisions. The costs of providing this service to the market needs to be met and it is important not to place those who develop such information at a competitive disadvantage in reaping the benefits of their own work. Perhaps the appropriate dividing line between what is acceptable use by the originators of such information and what is not, is the distinction between utilising the work product itself, as opposed to seeking to benefit from its market impact, once it becomes known.

Shareholders

1.41 Primary insiders are those who have a clear and defined relationship with the company to which the inside information 'belongs' or, in the case of those jurisdictions that have followed the European directives, any company. Although, as we have seen, it can be misleading to describe this relationship as always resembling a fiduciary or confidential relationship, in the majority of cases, those in an access relationship to the relevant information will be subject to legal obligations similar to those of a fiduciary or an agent. Many jurisdictions, however, include in the class of primary insiders substantial shareholders and, in some cases, all shareholders. In the vast majority of legal systems, the relationship between a shareholder and his company and with other investors is purely contractual and does not involve obligations of a fiduciary or confidential character.

1.42 In the laws of many countries shareholders have no right in law to special or privileged access to corporate information. Indeed, in many cases they have no right even to inspect the books of the company. Creditors, other than pursuant to special contractual arrangements that may be made, have both in law and practice even less access to the company. It is appreciated, however, that some shareholders, by virtue of the size or relevance of their holdings, may well have an influence on the management of the issuer and thereby, in some respects, be in the same position as an 'access insider'. In such cases, it may be appropriate simply to consider them to be potentially secondary insiders. Having said this, however, there is a tendency, which is not particularly logical to expand the category of 'presumed insider' to encompass those shareholders with a substantial interest in a class of equity or to, at least in Europe, all shareholders.

1.43 The extent to which professional criminals and, in particular, organised criminals have engaged in the abuse of price sensitive information as opposed to manipulative and fraudulent activity is an issue of some controversy. There are cases in the USA, Australia, Hong Kong and Japan where it is clear that organised crime has deliberately set about obtaining price sensitive information and then used it either by dealing itself or by selling it to others. Price-sensitive information has been obtained by illicit listening devices, bribery, extortion and penetration. While there has been relatively little discussion of such risks in the UK, there have been cases where criminals have attempted and occasionally succeeded in exploiting unpublished price sensitive information.[17] We will see when we discuss the substantive offences of insider dealing that in certain circumstances the receipt and misuse of inside information, in circumstances where it is appreciated that the information is from an inside source, would constitute a criminal offence. The market abuse provisions which are discussed in Chapters 4 and 5 are potentially more relevant. Such activity rarely, however, occurs in isolation and therefore it may well be that other offences, under the general law, will also be relevant.[18] While considerable steps have been taken in recent years in identifying the risks presented by organised crime and in responding to it,[19] to many criminals insider dealing appears as a potentially high reward and relatively low risk enterprise.

1.44   A related issue to that of organised criminals seeking to obtain and then exploit price sensitive information is the possibility that those who know that something very adverse to a company is about to occur deal in its securities or those of a related issuer in anticipation of the impact of this event on the price of the securities in question.[20] There have been cases where it is suspected that criminals have done this and the issue has arisen in regard to terrorist acts. For example, it was entirely predictable that the markets would be adversely impacted by the outrages on 9/11 and especially the price of insurance companies' securities would be adversely affected. The investigations that took place were broadly inconclusive, however, since then it is thought that certain terrorist organisations have become rather more sophisticated and there have been examples of such conduct. While this is abhorrent it is highly questionable whether in most cases anti-insider dealing laws are relevant. This takes us back to the question whether one's own intentions can be considered a form of inside information. While such pre-knowledge might be properly considered to constitute privileged information when used by another, there are real conceptual and other issues in the case of the perpetrator of the relevant event being cast in the role of an insider trader. Of course, this is not to say that there are not in almost every system of law adequate other offences which can be utilised without these difficulties. It is important to keep firmly in mind the nature of the abuse that anti-insider dealing laws are designed to address, which is after all relatively specific. While we might increasingly consider insider abuse to be fraud or at least analogous to fraud,[21] there are real problems in attempting to stretch the traditional offences related to misuse of privileged information too far, as the Americans have discovered under their law which is admittedly predicated, at least historically, on notions of fraud.

17   See generally K Hinterseer, *Criminal Finance* (2000) Kluwer; B Rider 'The enterprise of Crime' in *Money Laundering Control* (B Rider and TM Ashe eds) (Sweet and Maxwell 1996); B Rider, 'Policing the City – Combating Fraud and Other Abuses in the Corporate Securities Industry' (1988) 41 *Current Legal Problems* 47 and B Rider 'Organised Crime in the UK' Memorandum 15, *Organised Crime, Minutes of Evidence and Memoranda*, Home Affairs Committee, House of Commons (HMSO) 16 November 1994. The new offence of participating in the activities of an organised crime group might be relevant in this context; see s 45 of the Serious Crime Act 2015.

18   See Chapters 6 and 7.

19   See generally A Leong, *The Disruption of International Organised Crime* (Ashgate 2007) and D Masciandaro (ed), *Global Financial Crime* (Ashgate 2004) and B Rider (ed), International Financial Crime (Edward Elgar 2015), generally.

20   In *Ipourgos Ikonomikon v Georgakis* the European Court of Justice considered that a large shareholder and certain directors of a Greek company has taken advantage of inside information when they agreed to engage in a series of market transactions to boost the value of their company's securities. See European Court of Justice (3rd Chamber), 10 May 2007 and [2007] All ER (EC) 1106 and [2007] 3 CMLR 4.

21   See *R v McQuoid and Melbourne*, Unreported, Southwark Crown Court, 9–27 March 2009.

Chapter 2

Insider dealing: the civil law

A WRONG TO THE MARKET OR THE COMPANY?

2.1   In Chapter 1 we have discussed the reasons why insider dealing is considered wrongful and should therefore be discouraged. However, much of the discussion and analysis of the practice has focused on the relationship of the insider to the company with which he has an insider status. The very name of the concept – insider dealing – imports a relationship of proximity and privilege. Consequently, the early law in many jurisdictions fastened on those in a close relationship with or to companies. Thus, misuse by insiders of privileged information has been regarded by many commentators as involving primarily issues of company law. Indeed, in many countries it is discussed almost as part and parcel of the law relating to directors' duties. Of course, today we recognise that the problem of insider dealing is a much wider one than directors taking advantage of information that comes into their possession while discharging the duties of their office. In fact, such empirical research as has been undertaken clearly indicates other than in the most underdeveloped markets that abuse of inside information is not by such persons. They are too exposed and have rather too much to lose. Having said this, there are many examples of insiders manipulating corporate events to their own advantage. In those markets where there is a high incidence of owner control over the management of issuers, what takes places can often involve the misuse of unpublished price-sensitive information, albeit it often appears rather more as a matter of manipulation or self-dealing rather than insider dealing.

2.2   As our attempts to regulate the abuse of privileged information have become more sophisticated, we recognise more clearly that the abuse of inside information is not merely damaging to the relationship of stewardship that insiders will often be in. It has serious and wide implications for the market as a whole and in particular for the confidence and trust that other investors have in the fairness and proper operation of the relevant market. Consequently, regulatory regimes today tend to concentrate more on the damage that the abuse of unpublished price-sensitive information may have on the market. It is partly for this reason that in the United Kingdom resort has been made to the criminal law. While in Chapter 3 we will see that a comprehensive system of control has been developed within the criminal law to address insider dealing, this has been significantly expanded by the market abuse provisions administered by the Financial Conduct Authority. This we address in some detail in Chapter 4. It is important to appreciate that the law on market abuse emphasises the relationship of insider dealing to manipulation and moves away from the requirement that the relevant opportunity for abuse derives from a privileged relationship. The common law and in particular the civil law still, however, have a very important role to play. Apart from the indirect impact of the specific offences of insider dealing on the civil law, largely as a result of the doctrine of illegality, the law relating to insider abuse has no real impact on the underlying common law. Indeed, failure to appreciate this in regard to the impact of fiduciary duties has occasioned difficulties and uncertainties.[1] It should also be noted that in the context of the partial codification of directors duties in Chapter 2 of the Companies Act 2006, it is provided in section 170(4) 'the general duties shall be interpreted and applied in the same way as common law rules or equitable principles, and regard shall be had to the corresponding common law rules and equitable principles in interpreting and applying the general duties'. Thus, the traditional common law remains of considerable significance in our present discussion. It should also be remembered that the perimeters of fiduciary law are themselves not always certain[2] and as Frankfurter J in *SEC v Chenery Corporation*[3] observed: 'to say that a man is a fiduciary only begins the analysis; it gives direction to further inquiry. To whom is he a fiduciary? What obligations does he owe as a fiduciary? In what respect has he failed to discharge these obligations? And what are the consequences of his deviation from duty?'

CONFLICTS OF INTEREST

2.3   Directors and, in many countries, officers of corporations are properly regarded as 'stewards' of the corporate enterprise or at least the company. It is a matter for debate in each legal system as to the extent it might also be appropriate to encompass within such a concept others, such as controlling or even substantial shareholders, employees and other agents of the enterprise. Suffice it to say that most systems of law, given the onerous responsibilities of stewardship, sensibly confine the notion to those who really are in a proper relationship of trust and confidence to the company.

2.4   The notion of stewardship is ancient and has changed little over time. Lord Chancellor Herschell, in the leading English case of *Bray v Ford*[4]

---

1   See for example B Rider 'The Fiduciary and the Frying Pan' (1978) *Conveyancer* 114; B Rider (ed), *The Regulation of the British Securities Industry* (Oyez 1979), Chapter 5 and C Nakajima and E Sheffield, *Conflicts of Interest and Chinese Walls* (Butterworths 2002), and in particular the Law Commission, *Fiduciary Duties and Regulatory Rules: A Consultation Paper* (1992) No 124.

2   See P Birks, 'The Content of Fiduciary Obligation' (2002) 16 *TLI* 34 and see A Stafford and S Reading, *Fiduciary Duties, Directors and Employees* (2nd edn) (Jordan Publishing 2015) for a comprehensive discussion of the role of equity in this context and generally R Pearce, J Stevens and W Barr, *The Law of Trusts and Equitable Obligations* (5th edn) (Oxford University Press 2010).

3   (1943) 318 US 80 at 85.

4   [1896] AC 44. See also the classic statement of fiduciary responsibility predicated on loyalty of Millett LJ in *Bristol & West Building Society v. Mothew* [1998] Ch 1 at 1, 'The distinguishing obligation of a fiduciary is the obligation of loyalty. The principal is entitled to the single-minded loyalty of his fiduciary. This core liability has several facets. A fiduciary must act in good faith; he must not make a profit out of his trust; he must not place himself in a position where his duty and his interest may conflict; he may not act for his own benefit or the benefit of a third person without the informed consent of his principal. This is not intended to be an exhaustive list, but it is sufficient to indicate the nature of fiduciary obligations. They are the defining characteristics of the fiduciary. As Dr. Finn pointed out in his classic work *Fiduciary Obligations* (1977), p. 2, he is not subject to fiduciary obligations because he is a fiduciary; it is because he is subject to them that he is a fiduciary.'

emphasised that it is an inflexible rule that the courts will not permit a person in a fiduciary relationship to place himself in a position where his own interests conflict with those he is bound to serve. Nor is he to be permitted to derive an unauthorised benefit – a 'secret profit' – from his position of trust. He must be loyal to his principal. Of course, with all such simple rules, their application in practice is anything but simple. For example, there is still debate as to whether Lord Herschell intended to require those in a fiduciary position to eschew all conflicts of interest and duty no matter how insubstantial or theoretical. Nor is it certain whether the rule that a fiduciary should not benefit – without express authority – from his position is a separate rule or stems from the primary obligation to avoid all conflicts of interest. It is also uncertain as to how far it is appropriate to apply these rules to the situation where a fiduciary is in a conflict of duties to different principals, as opposed to merely his self-interest. A broad approach could create serious problems for those in several fiduciary relationships. Also, there is the real problem of financial intermediaries who engage in activities which might well produce conflicts between their different customers.[5] While Chinese Walls and similar devices may inhibit the flow of actual information from one function within the bank to another, they do not address the essential conflict of duty that the bank has placed itself in.

2.5   While it is certain that those in a position of stewardship or a fiduciary relationship must not subordinate without a clear mandate, the interests of the person for whom they act or serve to their own, it is unclear how conflicting duties might be resolved. For example, would a trustee be under a duty to use inside information that he learnt by virtue of some other relationship for the benefit of the trust? It might be less easy for him to excuse himself when the information in his possession indicates that the trust will suffer a serious loss unless he takes action. Indeed, it has been said that a stockbroker may be under a duty to ensure that privileged information that he possesses does not work to the disadvantage of his client.[6] To what extent it could be argued that a broker may come under a duty to search out such information or act upon information of a positive quality which results in profits rather than the avoidance of an otherwise certain loss is rather more debatable. These issues are addressed in rather more detail in Chapter 8.

2.6   While the trust is a creature of the common law, other systems of law impose obligations on individuals not too dissimilar to those under discussion. For example, in civil law jurisdictions, agents and those operating under mandate might well be held to duties of good faith and care which would give rise to issues not unrelated to those discussed above.[7] The misuse of privileged information and opportunity would also be condemned by Islamic law.[8] In most common law jurisdictions, it is generally thought that liability under the fiduciary law is, in large measure, strict. Thus, if a person in a fiduciary

---

5   See Chapter 8.
6   See G Cooper and B Cridlan, *The Law of Procedure of the Stock Exchange* (Butterworths 1971), at p 104. But see the comment of Lord Browne-Wilkinson in *Kelly v Cooper* [1993] AC 205, 'stockbrokers … cannot be contractually bound to disclose to their private clients inside information disclosed to the brokers in confidence by a company for which they also act'.
7   See C Nakajima, *Conflicts of Interest and Duty* (Kluwer 1999).
8   See B Rider and C Nakajima at Chapter 18 in S Archer and R Karim (eds) *Islamic Finance* (Wiley 2007) and in particular, B Rider, 'Corporate Governance for Institutions Offering Islamic Financial Services' in C Nethercott and D Eisenberg (eds), *Islamic Finance, Law and Practice* (Oxford University Press 2012).

position does take an unauthorised benefit from his position, then he should be held accountable whatever his state of mind. While such a draconian approach might be appropriate in the case of trustees in the strict sense, there are many situations involving those in a fiduciary or analogous position where the courts have considered that proof of lack of probity is a material factor.[9]

2.7   In the business and financial world, those in a fiduciary position will, it seems, be allowed to enter into situations where there is a possible and even, on occasion, real conflict of duties, provided they act with integrity. On the other hand, where there is a conflict between a duty to another and the self-interest of a fiduciary, the courts will be far more prepared to examine what has in fact taken place. Self-interest has been considered to be almost presumptive of abuse. The greater the degree of self-interest or benefit, the stronger will be the inference of corruption. On the other hand, it must be recognised that even in the case of conflict of duties, an intermediary will often expect to receive a benefit, be it in terms of commission or simply the retention of a business relationship. Consequently, it will rarely be the case that there is absolutely no element of self-interest in the equation.

SECRET PROFITS

2.8   Let us turn to a rule that is perhaps even more clear in its articulation than the 'no conflict rule'. Those in a fiduciary relationship must not derive from their position, or rather by virtue of the relationship, a 'secret profit'. In other words, any calculable benefit that comes into their possession that has not been expressly approved or permitted by the principal must be handed over to the principal.[10] This is an important rule of stewardship and is a core principle in any system of good governance. It strikes at the very root of self-dealing. Furthermore, it is one of the few rules that can be applied to directors and certain other corporate fiduciaries who have taken advantage of inside information.[11] Indeed, section 175 of the Companies Act 2006 specifically provides that 'a director ... must avoid a situation in which he has, or can have, a direct or indirect interest that conflicts, or possibly may conflict, with the interests of the company' and 'this applies in particular to the exploitation of any ... information ... and it is immaterial whether the company could take advantage of the ... information or ...'. Section 176 of the Companies Act recognises the duty on directors not to accept benefits from third parties that might reasonably be regarded as likely to give rise to a conflict of interest. Sections 177 and 182 also impose a duty to disclose interests in a proposed or existing transaction with a director's company. Chapter 4 of Part 10 of the Act contains additional and somewhat stricter rules in regard to substantial property transactions between a director and his company and certain other sensitive arrangements. There are civil, and in certain cases criminal, implications for noncompliance.

---

9   See, for example, *Royal Brunei Airlines Sdn Bhd v Philip Tan Kok Ming* [1995] 2 AC 378 and *Gwembe Valley Development Co Ltd v Koshy* [2003] EWCA Civ 1048.

10   See *Regal (Hastings) Ltd v Gulliver* [1942] 1 All ER 378, *Ross River Ltd v Waveley Commercial Ltd* [2013] EWCA Civ 910 and *FHR European Ventures LLP v Cedar Capital Partners LLC* [2014] UKSC 45; *Industrial Development Consultants Ltd v Cooley* [1972] 2 All ER 162 and *Bhullar v Bhullar* [2003] 2 BCLC 241.

11   See, for example, *Nanus Asia Co Inc v Standard Chartered Bank* [1990] 1 HKLR 396.

2.9 The justification for the common law imposing such strict obligations on those who accept positions of trust is essentially pragmatic. The legal system cannot be expected to detect and monitor every transaction and therefore strict and pragmatic rules are required for the ordering of all dealings between the fiduciary and his principal and with third parties on matters in which the principal has a legitimate interest. The rule, therefore, requires all remuneration and benefits to be agreed and, therefore, strikes at self-dealing, abuse of position and the diversion of opportunities that in good conscience should have gone to the principal. The rule against taking unauthorised profits works reasonably well in the context of principal and agent, but when applied to the position of fiduciaries whose relationship is with a company, it gives rise to a number of difficulties. As the company is a separate legal person, this fiduciary obligation is owed directly to the company and to no other person. The statutory provisions in the Companies Act 2006 do not change this. Consequently, if a director uses information that he obtains as a director to deal in the securities of another company, his liability to account for his profit is to his own company and not to the issuer in whose securities he has traded. When the insider remains involved in the management of the company, there are serious practical and occasionally legal difficulties in bringing him to account. It is his company that has the right to sue for breach of the duty of good faith and the more specific duties, such as those set out in the Companies Act.[12] In practice, this will mean that the action is to be commenced by his colleagues on the board or in senior management. The possibilities for minority shareholders to intervene and bring an action on behalf of their company are, in reality, severely limited.[13]

2.10 The law relating to the circumstances in which minority shareholders may maintain an action on behalf of their company in the face of opposition from the management and majority shareholders has, over the years, attracted a great deal of comment and discussion.[14] While the courts have been prepared to assist shareholders to bring derivative actions based on the company's cause of action against persons who have seemingly engaged in fraud and misappropriation of the company's property, there has been uncertainty as to what amounts to fraud and what can be regarded as corporate property. For example, some of the cases involving allegations of equitable fraud include misconduct, such as the taking of a secret profit, in circumstances where there is no dishonesty in the common law sense.[15] The courts have, in deciding

---

12   Section 178(2) specifically provides 'the duties in those sections ...are ... enforceable in the same way as any other fiduciary duty owed to a company by its directors' and see AJ Boyle, *Minority Shareholders' Remedies* (Cambridge University Press 2002), E Boros, *Minority Shareholders' Remedies* (Oxford Univeristy Press 1995) and in particular V Joffe *et al*, *Minority Shareholders, Law, Practice and Procedure* (4th edn) (Oxford University Press 2010).

13   Note however, in certain circumstances it may well be that such conduct amounts to unfair prejudice to the minority shareholders, see s 994 of the Companies Act 2006 and *Maidment v Attwood* [2012] EWCA Civ 998, but see also the restrictions indicated by Richards J in *McKillen v. Misland (Cyprus) Investments Ltd* [2012] EWCH 2343 (Ch).

14   This is the so called rule in *Foss v Harbottle* (1843) 2 Hare 461. See in particular Boyle, note 12 above.

15   See *Armitage v Nurse* [1998] Ch 241 at 252. Millett LJ stated that equitable fraud included 'breach of fiduciary duty, undue influence, abuse of confidence, unconscionable bargains and fraud in powers'. See also for an early discussion of this B Rider, 'Amiable Lunatics and the Rule in Foss v Harbottle' (1978) *Cambridge Law Journal* 270. In *Item Softwear (UK) Ltd v Fassihi* [2005] 2 BCLC 91, it was held that a director is under a duty derived from his obligation of loyalty to disclose to his company his own wrongdoing even if it does not amount to fraudulent misconduct and see also *Tesco Stores Ltd v Pook* [2004] IRLR 618. The dishonest failure to do this might well render the law of fraud relevant. See **7.33** below.

whether the alleged misconduct is such as to justify permitting minority shareholders to proceed, at possibly considerable expense to all concerned, referred to indications of lack of good faith on the part of those responsible for the wrongdoing. Thus, attempts to hide what has occurred or frustrate the company itself proceeding, possibly by the wrongdoers or those associated with such using their votes as shareholders in general meeting, have been weighed in the balance by judges. The abuse of inside information presents real issues viewed purely from the standpoint of company law in this context. If the information can be considered, as it has in some instances, as belonging to the company, then it is possible a court will consider its misuse a misuse of corporate property.[16] Purely in the context of insider dealing there is little authority in point.[17] It is more probable that the courts would consider the taking advantage of such information as rather more akin to the taking of a secret profit. Whether from the standpoint of the company this inevitably justified a different approach is questionable.[18] The circumstances in which a minority shareholder may now assert a derivative action have been clarified, at least to some degree, in Part 11, Chapter 1 of the Companies Act 2006.[19] While the new statutory provisions almost entirely reflect the pre-existing case law, the position of a minority shareholder is arguably made easier as a result of increased clarity and the endorsement in statute, or what might be considered the more robust approach to wrongdoer influence. The practical hurdles before getting before a judge and much of the financial burden, however, remain.

LOSS TO THE INSIDER'S COMPANY

2.11   While the cases indicate that liability to account for a 'secret profit' arises notwithstanding there is no quantifiable loss to the principal,[20] the possible 'injustice' of such a strict rule has been questioned.[21] While it is necessary to sanction breaches of good faith and the company to whom the insider owes his fiduciary duty not to make secret profits is better placed than most to enforce this obligation, it is often difficult to identify any specific loss. Even in those jurisdictions in which issuers are allowed to trade in their own securities in certain circumstances, it is hard to show that an insider's misuse of inside information has occasioned quantifiable loss to the company. The company may contend that its confidence in the fair dealing of its agent has been undermined. It might also be argued that if it becomes known that a particular company's directors engage in insider dealing, the reputation of the company for integrity will diminish. It will be seen as an 'insider's company'.

16   See 2.30 and 14.12 *et seq* below.
17   See *Nanus Asia Co Inc v Standard Chartered Bank* [1990] 1 HKLR 396 and 2.29 below.
18   But see *Attorney General for Hong Kong v Reid* [1994] 1 AC 324 discussed at 2.30 below.
19   See generally *Boyle and Birds' Company Law* (9th edn) (Jordan Publishing 2014), Ch 18 and at 2.10 above.
20   In *United Pan-Europe Communications NV v Deutsche Bank AG* [2000] 2 BCLC 461, the Court of Appeal emphasised '... it is not in doubt that the object of the equitable remedies of an account on the imposition of a constructive trust is to ensure that the defaulting fiduciary does not retain the profit; it is not to compensate the beneficiary for any loss' per Morritt LJ. Reference might also be made to *Guinness plc v Saunders* [1990] 2 AC 663 and also *New Zealand Netherlands Society 'Oranje' v Kuys* [1973] 2 All ER 1222.
21   See, for example, G Jones, 'Unjust Enrichment and the Fiduciary's Duty of Loyalty' (1968) 84 *LQR* 472.

This may have implications for its business, financial and employment relations.[22] While there is little, if any, empirical evidence to support this, anecdotal evidence abounds. On the other hand, in many developing markets, even quite significant enterprises are manifestly insiders' companies. It is often said that it is the very fact that their promoters remain in control which indicates to the market that the company is a good investment opportunity. Whether it is thought to be a good or bad thing for promoters to remain in control of their companies, it is hardly appropriate that this be determined by laws designed to inhibit insider dealing. It might be said that companies that allow their insiders to speculate on the basis of their inside information are permitting their management to, at best, waste time or, at worst, subordinate management to the ends of short-term market speculation. There is also a real danger that management will manipulate or at least influence the timing of corporate disclosures to facilitate their own trading. It is perhaps more sensible simply to recognise that corporate issuers do have a proper and real interest in the market for their shares and consequently allegations of abuse in this market are of concern to them. Where dealing takes place in shares other than those issued by the insider's corporation, it may be more convincing to argue that the insider is competing with his own company in the relevant market. However, in most cases, the impact that insider dealing is likely to have in such circumstances, even accounting for the use of derivatives trading, is hardly likely to result in calculable loss.

2.12   While it is probable that an insider who is in a fiduciary position and makes a profit through using inside information may be accountable to his principal, it is not clear whether a fiduciary could be required to account to his principal for 'negative profits', that is, where he uses his privileged position to avoid a loss that he would otherwise have sustained. For example, could a director be held to account for 'profit' that he makes through avoiding a loss by selling out his shareholding on the basis of unpublished, price-sensitive information that he has obtained by virtue of his fiduciary position? Although there is no English authority directly on the point and the courts have been reluctant to allow what are essentially compensatory claims for breach of a mere fiduciary duty,[23] it is obviously desirable that someone who abuses his position by avoiding a more or less certain loss should be held accountable to the same extent as one who has benefited by making a profit. The Court of Appeal, with which the House of Lords agreed, in *A-G v Blake*,[24] while hesitating to award damages for a breach of what might in other circumstances have been regarded as a fiduciary relationship, held that, in exceptional circumstances, the court has power to award a 'restitution' measure of damages for breach of contract even if, according to ordinary principles, there would be no basis for a claim to

---

22   The new statutory obligation on directors under s 172 of the Companies Act 2006 to in good faith promote the success of the company may have relevance in this context. It is also generally recognised that directors have a responsibility to promote and protect the reputation of their company and some have argued that reputation should be protected as any other corporate asset. See for example, In *Plus Group Ltd v. Pyke* [2002] EWCA Civ 370. See also discussion at 8.9 below.

23   See, however, the comments of Mummery LJ in *Gwembe Valley Development Company Ltd v Koshy* [2003] EWCA Civ 1048 indicate that at least some judges may be prepared to be a little more imaginative. See also in this regard *Multi-Installations Ltd v Varsani* [2008] EWHC 657 (Ch).

24   [1998] 1 All ER 833; affirmed [2000] 4 All ER 385.

compensation.[25] Of course, where there is a viable claim based upon something other than the fiduciary taking advantage of his privileged position to avoid a loss, such as in *Coleman v Myers*,[26] since the fusion of the administration of law and equity, damages may be awarded for breach of a fiduciary obligation, at least where there is a parallel claim for negligence. We explore the issue of remedies in rather more detail below.

A NARROW OBLIGATION

2.13   When we contemplate the duty that a corporate fiduciary owes to his company not to take advantage of his position or, for that matter, information that comes to him by virtue of his privileged position, we must recognise the narrowness of the relationship within which this duty operates. Directors and other corporate fiduciaries owe their duties to the company and, as the company has a separate legal personality, only to that entity. They do not, as fiduciaries, owe duties to other, albeit related, enterprises, shareholders, creditors, employees or anyone else. Of course, if they step into another legal relationship, they might well find themselves owing duties directly to such persons as well as to their company. For example, as we shall see, there have been cases[27] where a director has stepped into a special relationship with one or more of the shareholders and by virtue of this has been held liable for taking advantage of privileged information in his dealings with them. Such cases, outside the United States, are, however, exceptional. It is important to remember that, while as a matter of good governance, directors are required to have regard to the interests of different constituencies, as a matter of law their duties are owed to and are enforceable by their company. Thus, while members of the board both collectively and individually must act in what they consider to be the best interests of the company and in doing this they should consider the interests of all those 'represented' in the enterprise, their duties of stewardship are owed to the company.

2.14   Consequently, the shareholders, individually or collectively as the providers of capital, have no right to sue on a claim based on an infraction of a duty owed to the company. The company's property is not theirs and it has been decided that even conduct on the part of directors which damages the share price does not give individual shareholders or even the general body of shareholders the standing to sue.[28] The claim is that of the company's for the misconduct in question. To allow the issuer to sue and also give shareholders a right of action to recover for the diminution in the value of their investment might result in them recovering twice over for essentially the same wrong, as although a share does not represent a divisible part of the corporate assets, its

25   See also the statement of Lord Reed in *Re Lands Allotment Co* [1894] 1 Ch 616 cited with approval in *AIB Group (UK) plc v Redler* [2014] UKSC 58 and *Target Holdings v Redfern* [1996] AC 421. There is, however, little support for the award of compensation where there is no loss as such but mere infidelity. See Tipping J's comments in *Bank of New Zealand v New Zealand Guardian Trust Ltd* [1999] 1 NZLR 664 cited with approval by the Supreme Court in *AIB*, in regard *inter alia* to the availability of equitable compensation for a breach of the duty of loyalty resulting in loss.
26   [1977] 2 NZLR 225 and see 2.18 below.
27   See, for example, *Allen v Hyatt* (1914) 30 TLR 444; *Briess v Woolley* [1954] AC 333 and, in particular, *Peskin v Anderson* [2001] 1 BCLC 372. *Stein v Blake (No 2)* [1998] 1 All ER 724 at 727 and 729 (per Millett LJ) and *Gadsden v Bennetto* (1913) 9 DLR 719 (Man).
28   *Prudential Assurance Co v Newman Industries Ltd (No 2)* [1982] Ch 204.

value is tied, or at least should be, to the aggregated value of the enterprise, including all those assets belonging to the company. While there are examples in a number of countries where shareholders have successfully pursued directors and other corporate insiders for essentially insider dealing, their suit has been firmly based on breach of a relationship other than to the company. In all cases, liability has been based on the breach of a special relationship that has come into existence because of the special facts of the case. In other words, the insiders have come into another external relationship with the shareholders which has given the shareholders a legitimate expectation of fair dealing.

2.15 There are other reasons why individual shareholders have not been permitted to pursue insiders with whom they happen to deal on the market. Although an insider taking advantage of unpublished, price-sensitive information in circumstances where the other party did not have or could not have had access to it may be characterised as 'unfair', the courts have, in most jurisdictions, appeared reluctant to recognise a cause of action. Their caution is based on a concern not to disrupt the proper operation of bargaining in the markets. While equality of access to information may be desirable, it is rarely, if ever, attainable. The law has long recognised that disparities or imbalances in information, let alone the ability to interpret or apply the information, cannot justify intervention in a bargain that has been completed without fraud.[29]

2.16 The mere failure to reveal information, even when it is appreciated that the other party does not have that information or could not obtain it with the exercise of reasonable diligence, does not give rise, in the ordinary course of events, to a duty to disclose or refrain from dealing. It matters not how significant or material that information might be to the decision of the other to deal and upon what terms. The notion of *caveat emptor* reflects more than a *laissez faire* approach to the market. It is based on a host of considerations that have developed over time and which are at the very heart of how we do business. The law does, of course, make exceptions. Perhaps, apart from statutory intervention, the most significant is where there exists a pre-existing relationship between the parties in which there is an expectation on the part of at least one of the parties of fair dealing.

2.17 Where a fiduciary relationship can be found, it is probable that the obligation of fair dealing will import a duty of full disclosure.[30] Where such a relationship exists between an insider and the person with whom he is dealing, it is likely that the law will provide a remedy. However, the fiduciary obligation must generally arise from a pre-existing fiduciary relationship as it is far less clear that such obligations can arise, other than in the most exceptional circumstances, by virtue of the transaction in question. While it is possible that directors may be in a contractual relationship with shareholders by virtue of their shareholding, this is not a fiduciary relationship so as to give rise to the fiduciary obligation of fair dealing. A director who deals with someone who becomes a shareholder by virtue of that very transaction is in no pre-existing relationship, whether contractual or otherwise. The traditional attitude of English law, and for that matter all common law jurisdictions, is that

---

29 *Bell v Lever Bros* [1932] AC 161, see also at 6.40 and 6.41 below.
30 It is not in all cases that those in a fiduciary relationship will be considered to have a duty of care. Indeed, it has been argued and to some degree accepted by the courts that obligations relating to care are not essentially fiduciary in nature. See P Millett, 'Equity's Place in the Law of Commerce' (1998) 14 *LQR* 214.

a director owes his fiduciary duties to his company which is a separate legal person. He does not owe duties directly, or for that matter even indirectly, to the shareholders who also have no legal interest in the company's property.[31] The rule established by Swinfen-Eady J in *Percival v Wright*[32] that directors do not owe duties as directors to members of their company either individually or collectively has been criticised, particularly in the context of insider dealing, but it remains a cornerstone of company law.

2.18 On the other hand, whilst the courts are not generally receptive to arguments that they should discover new fiduciary relationships, they are prepared to reconsider the factual circumstances in which duties can arise and in particular take account of changes in social and perhaps moral views. Thus, the High Court of New South Wales in *Glandon Pty Ltd v Strata Consolidated Pty Ltd*[33] expressed the view that as attitudes to insider dealing had changed since 1902, a court faced with the issue today might not be as unwilling as Swinfen-Eady J was to discover a fiduciary obligation. In practice, what the New South Wales court was alluding to was a long-established approach, namely the recognition that in special and exceptional circumstances the facts of a particular case might well persuade the court that an unusual fiduciary relationship arises on the particular facts of the case. Although there are a number of examples of the courts being prepared to find that, for example, directors have stepped outside their normal corporate relationship into a special relationship with their shareholders, or for that matter third parties, perhaps the most dramatic illustration is *Coleman v Myers*.[34] Although, at first instance, Mahon J was prepared to hold that *Percival v Wright* was simply *per incuriam* and should not be followed in New Zealand, the Court of Appeal, while taking the view that Swinfen-Eady J had been correct on the facts before him, held there were circumstances which could, and did in the present case, justify the court in finding that a relationship of fair dealing, involving both a duty of good faith disclosure and also one of care, arose as a legitimate expectation on the particular facts. In this case, the closely held nature of the company, the exceptional materiality of the information in question, the dishonesty of the insiders and the fact that the relevant shareholders had, over a long period, come to rely upon their probity, all served to justify the implication of a fiduciary obligation of fair dealing.

---

31 In *Heron International Ltd v Lord Grade* [1983] BCLC 244 the Court of Appeal considered that directors of a target company in a takeover may, on the facts, owe duties of a fiduciary nature to the shareholders. The finding of such a duty was, however, exceptional – see *Dawson International plc v Coats Paton plc* [1988] 4 BCC 305.The Australian High Court has also held that directors are also under a duty to act fairly between different classes of shareholders in the exercise of their powers as directors, see *Mills v Mills* (1938) 60 CLR 150.

32 [1902] 2 Ch 421 and see also Lord Lowry in *Kuwait Asia Bank v National Mutual Life Nominees Ltd* [1990] BCLC 868 at 888. In *Peskin v Anderson* [2001] 1 BCLC 372 Mummery LJ observed, referring to *Percival v Wright*, that 'the apparently unqualified width of the ruling has, over the course of the last century, been subjected to increasing judicial, academic and professional critical comment; but few would doubt that, as a general rule, it is important for the well-being of a company (and of the wider commercial community) that directors are not overexposed to the risk of multiple legal actions by dissenting minority shareholders ...'.

33 (1993) 11 ACSR 543.

34 [1977] 2 NZLR 225 and see B Rider, '*Percival v Wright* – per incuriam' (1977) 40 *Modern Law Review* 471 and B Rider, 'A Special Relationship on the Special Facts' (1978) 41 *Modern Law Review* 585.

2.19   The approach of the New Zealand Court of Appeal was in line with earlier English decisions[35] and has been followed by the Court of Appeal of New South Wales in *Brunninghausen v Glavanics*.[36] The circumstances in which an English court would be prepared to find a specific duty of disclosure to an existing shareholder, let alone a person buying into the company for the first time, are not entirely clear. It is probable that the insider would have to be in possession of highly relevant and material information which the other party could not have obtained even with the exercise of diligence. Furthermore, the situation must, it would seem, be such as to raise on the part of the person dealing with the insider a reasonable expectation of fair dealing.[37] The comment of Newberger J in *Peskin v Anderson*[38] seeking to summarise the English law after *Brunninghausen* may well go too far.[39] The learned judge observed:

> 'I am satisfied, both as a matter of principle and in light of the state of the authorities [including *Brunninghausen*], that *Percival v Wright* is good law in the sense that a director of a company has no general fiduciary duty to shareholders. However, I am also satisfied that, in appropriate and specific circumstances, a director can be under a fiduciary duty to a shareholder ... So far as the authorities to which I have referred on this issue are concerned, the decisions ... in which a duty was held to arise were cases where a director with special knowledge was buying the shares ... for his own benefit from shareholders, where the director had special knowledge which he had obtained in his capacity as a director of the company, and which he did not impart to the shareholders, and where the special knowledge meant that he knew that he was paying a low price.'

2.20   For a special relationship to develop giving rise to an obligation of fair dealing, it is most likely that the parties will be engaged in direct and personal negotiations. In the Court of Appeal in the *Peskin* case, it was emphasised that 'these duties may arise in special circumstances which replicate the salient features of well established categories of fiduciary relationships ... those duties are, in general, attracted by and attached to a person who undertakes, or who, depending on all the circumstances, is treated as having assumed, responsibility to act on behalf of, or for the benefit of, another person'.[40] Even in those states

---

35   See *Allen v Hyatt* (1914) 30 TLR 444 PC and *Briess v Woolley* [1954] AC 333. In exceptional circumstances the courts have found specific duties that directors may owe to shareholders directly as directors, for example, in the allotment of shares directors must act for a proper purpose, *Re a Company* [1987] BCLC 82 and *John Crowther Group plc v Carpets International plc* [1990] BCLC 460 and the unusual case of *Gething v Kilner* [1972] 1 WLR 337 where at 341, Brightman J said that directors were under a duty not to mislead shareholders.

36   (1999) 32 ACSR 294.

37   See for a similar approach *Re Chez Nico (Restaurants) Ltd* [1992] BCLC 192; *In Re A Company* [1986] BCLC 382 and *Platt v Platt* [1999] 2 BCLC 745, but note the reservations of the Court of Appeal [2001] 1 BCLC 698.

38   [2000] 2 BCLC 1 at 14.

39   See *Peskin v Anderson* [2001] 1 BCLC 372 and in particular Mummery LJ at 378 and 383. The Court of Appeal emphasised that the special circumstances must be such as to create essentially a 'fiduciary duty' of disclosure. Mere inequality of information cannot create a fiduciary relationship justifying fair dealing and disclosure. See also *Platt v Platt* [2001] 1 BCLC 698.

40   Per Mummery LJ (2001) 1 BCLC 372 at 397. See also *Stein v Blake (No 2)* [1998] 1 All ER 724 at 729.

in the United States that have developed the so-called 'special facts' doctrine,[41] remedies, are in practical terms, confined to non-market transactions. It is also likely that in most cases the company will be closely held. Indeed, there are cases where the company resembles a partnership in which the courts have been prepared to view the relationship between shareholders and directors as analogous to that of partners[42] bound by obligations of mutual good faith.

2.21   It is not, however, just shareholders who might feel that they should be able to bring insiders to account either for their breach of 'duty' to the enterprise or as counterparties to an objectionable transaction. Those who invest in corporate bonds, who are not shareholders in the sense of being members of the company, may consider that they have been disadvantaged by an insider utilising privileged information in a trade with them on the market. Trading in bonds and other financial paper may be just as attractive to an insider as more conventional dealing in corporate shares and options. In most jurisdictions, the duties, if any, that the board, let alone individual directors of a company, may owe to creditors is even more under-developed than in regard to the position of directors to shareholders.[43] There is little chance of an insider who trades in debt securities, on the basis of privileged information, being liable to any counterparty unless exceptional circumstances give rise to a special relationship along the lines we have discussed.

BENEFITING ANOTHER – A BREACH OF DUTY?

2.22   We must also remember in our present discussion that the remedies available for a breach of the fiduciary's duty of loyalty are rather limited. Where the fiduciary allows another to benefit in place of himself the law has been less robust. What if a director passes on to another the relevant inside information in the expectation that the other person will use it for dealing? The person who uses the inside information, in many legal systems, will not be liable to the insider's company as he is not in a fiduciary relationship. The position of the insider who passes on the relevant information is also problematical.[44] As

---

41   See *Strong v Repide* 213 US 419 (1909). Before the Court of Appeal in the Philippines interesting English cases were cited as support for a special facts doctrine (41 Phil 947), see B Rider and HL Ffrench, *Insider Trading* (Macmillan 1979), p 363 and B Rider, 'The Regulation of Insider Trading in the Republic of The Philippines' (1977) 19 *Malaya Law Review* 355. The special facts doctrine has been confused with the so called minority rule which recognises a fiduciary duty of disclosure between directors and shareholders, see *Van Shaack Holdings Ltd v Van Schaack*, 867 P.2d 892 Col. 1994 and the US Supreme Court has observed that the Court in *Repide* did little to avoid confusion, *Chiarella v US* 445 US 222 (1980).

42   For example, *Ebrahimi v Westbourne Galleries* [1973] AC 360 see generally also B Rider, 'Partnership Law and its Impact on Domestic Companies' (1979) *Cambridge Law Journal* 148.

43   Section 172(3) of the Companies Act 2006 imposes on directors an obligation to consider, in good faith among others and in the context of what is best for the company, the interests of creditors. While there is authority for the proposition that directors are under an obligation to consider the best interests of creditors as an insolvency approaches, *Winkworth v Edward Baron Development Co Ltd* [1987] BCLC 193 at 197, the better view is that this is owed to the company and probably not the creditors generally let alone to individuals, *Re Pantone 485 Ltd* [2002] 1 BCLC 266 at 285 and *Westpac Banking Corporation v. The Bell Group Ltd (In Liquidation) (No 3)* [2012] WASCA 157.

44   Note, for example, the position of the chairman in *Regal (Hastings) Ltd v Gulliver* [1942] 1 All ER 378.

the profit is not his, can it be said that he has taken advantage of his position? Of course, if the person to whom he has given the information and who has profited through its use can be regarded as his agent or alter ego, the position may be different.[45] However, the courts have been reluctant to attribute the profit made by, for example, a wife[46] or a company associated with the insider to the director.[47] Provided the profit is that of a separate person who is not acting on behalf of the director, then it seems that the fiduciary law is powerless. In no small measure, this may well be due to the difficulty that the law has in finding a suitable remedy. There is no profit in the hands of the fiduciary that the company can call to account.[48] In some respects this raises similar issues as to where a person in a fiduciary situation utilises inside information to avoid a loss rather than make a gain. We have seen that while the law is becoming rather more realistic and is prepared to consider ordering equitable compensation where there is a loss, it is very debatable if in such cases the courts would accept that the beneficiary of the fiduciary obligation has in fact sustained a loss. Of course, if the information in question can be considered as a species of property then the analysis, as we shall see, might be rather different. It might also be arguable, as it has in the US, that to the extent that, for example, the company's reputation has been harmed there is a loss that can be properly assessed.

2.23   Judges have understandably been reluctant to stand by and see insiders facilitate the looting of their companies by others with whom there is often a fair suspicion that they are in cahoots. A series of relatively recent decisions has underlined the significance of the constructive trust as a means of reaching out and imposing an obligation to make restitution on those who receive the benefits of a breach of trust or who knowingly facilitate the breach. Whilst the principles are by no means new, the way in which the judges have applied them has often been dynamic. Having said this until very recently the courts have not been good in providing clarity. As Lord Goff remarked in *Westdeutsche Landesbank Girozentrale v London Borough of Islington*,[49] 'ever since the law of restitution began ... to be studied in depth, the role of equitable proprietary claims ... has been found to be a matter of great difficulty'. He referred to the desire of restitution lawyers to mould the law relating in particular to constructive trusts into an effective remedy for unjust enrichment and the caution of traditional equity lawyers to see that 'the trust concept should not be distorted'. Indeed, while concerned to see that there is proper justice on the

---

45 The courts have always been prepared to look through companies and nominees that have been used to conceal fraud and misconduct. See in particular *VTB Capital plc v Nutritek International Corp* [2013] 2 WLR 398 and *Prest v Petrodel Resources Ltd* [2013] UKSC 34 discussed at 15.14 below.

46 See *Daniels v Daniels* [1978] Ch 406. In the case of *Ryan Willmott* (FCA, 26 June 2015), the defendant had opened an account in the name of his girlfriend, who he did not inform, and traded in her name. The FCA's Acting Director of Enforcement stated, 'this case shows that using others to try to cover up a breach of trust does not prevent detection'. Of course, it does significantly make detection more difficult. In this case the defendant pleaded guilty to the offence of insider dealing.

47 See *Ultraframe (UK) Ltd v Fielding* [2005] EWHC 66 rejecting the view of Lawrence Collins J in *CMS Dolphin Ltd v Simonet* [2001] 2 BCLC 704 who considered *Cook v Deeks* [1916] 1 AC 554 and *Canadian Aero Services v O'Malley* (1973) 40 DLR (3s) 371 as authority for the proposition that both the wrongdoer and the company which benefits are liable.

48 Note, however, that a person who receives the benefits of a breach of fiduciary duty or dishonestly assists in such a breach might well be liable as if they were a constructive trustee. See generally 2.52 below.

49 [1996] 2 All ER 948 at 969.

facts of each case, he emphasised that 'it is not the function of your Lordships' house to rewrite the agenda for the law of restitution, nor even to identify the role of equitable proprietary claims in that part of the law'. Notwithstanding this judicial reticence in a series of cases the courts have been prepared to fashion a more or less effective remedy against those who inter-meddle in and/or assist breaches of trust. Consequently there is now the prospect of restitution against those who, appreciating the facts that amount to a breach of trust, knowingly participate in it or facilitate the laundering of its proceeds, in circumstances where an ordinary person would consider what they have done, or perhaps not done, to be dishonest. The liability in such cases is not that of a constructive trustee in the conventional sense of the word – their liability is as an accomplice and the monetary liability that they are exposed to is to make restoration as if they were a constructive trustee. Having said this, it is interesting that Lord Browne-Wilkinson in the *Westdeutsche* case observed that the distinction between the concept of remedial constructive trusts, as developed in US law and the traditional and conservative approach of the English law, remains – despite judicial ingenuity and the judges dislike of crooks. He pointed out that the essentially institutional constructive trust under English law arises by operation of law and that it is for the court merely to recognise and give effect to it and it is not open to the judge simply to impose such a device to afford a remedy which would not otherwise exist.[50]

2.24   The view has been expressed that this area of the law is of little practical significance in addressing insider dealing as before a trust can be found, it is necessary to identify property which can in the contemplation of the law, be considered viable as trust property. The distinction between a person who has merely the obligations of a fiduciary and one who is under the more onerous and strict obligations of a trustee has traditionally been that the trustee holds property on behalf of another. While this nice distinction has been questioned at least on the basis that the obligations and their performance may be much the same if not actually indistinguishable – particularly in the commercial world, there has been a significant difference of opinion between commercial and restitution lawyers. In *Lister v Stubbs*,[51] the Court of Appeal established the rule that a bribe, in so far as such involved only a personal obligation to account, could not be the basis of a tracing claim and was not susceptible to being regarded as trust property. Of course, there has always been a substantial grey area in company law in regard to what the textbooks refer to as the 'corporate opportunity' cases. In one or two Commonwealth cases, the courts have seemingly regarded the benefit of a contract which in fairness should have gone to a company,[52] but which has been wrongfully diverted to another person, as a form of corporate property. As we have seen, this discussion has had a role in deciding whether a minority shareholder might be able to bring a derivative action. Where there has been a misappropriation of corporate property, the argument is that as the majority of shareholders cannot approve or ratify such conduct, a derivative action cannot be denied or frustrated.

2.25   In *A-G for Hong Kong v Reid*,[53] the Privy Council, on an appeal from New Zealand, following the approach of the Court of Appeal of Singapore in

---

50   See generally A Burrow, *The Law of Restitution* (3rd edn) (Oxford University Press 2010).
51   (1890) 45 Ch D 1.
52   *Cook v Deeks* [1916] 1 AC 554; *Canadian Aero Service Ltd v O'Malley* (1974) 40 DLR (3d) 371 and see *CMS Dolphin Ltd v Simonet* [2001] 2 BCLC 74.
53   [1994] 1 AC 498.

Sumitomo Bank Ltd v Kartika Ratna Thahir,[54] opined that the rule in *Lister v Stubbs* was inappropriate in the modern world. The robust attitude of the Board of the Privy Council may be justified given the extremely serious allegations of misconduct on the part of the defendant and as we have noted where there is clear evidence of dishonesty judges can be more easily persuaded to be imaginative. In this case the Privy Council considered that on the basis that equity looks as done that which should be done, there was a sufficient basis in law for tracing into the proceeds of a bribe. Furthermore, their Lordships' comments and particularly those of Lord Templeman were wide enough to include the proceeds of a 'secret profit'. If the proceeds of, for example, insider trading can be traced and justify the imposition of a constructive trust, the law in this area would be radically changed. For example, it would mean, as was in effect held by the High Court of Hong Kong in *Nanus Asia Inc v Standard Chartered Bank*,[55] that the proceeds of insider dealing could be traced into the hands of a recipient who took otherwise than as a bona fide purchaser without notice. It would also follow that accomplice liability could be imposed on those who facilitated the insider dealing, provided they had the requisite degree of knowledge and were, objectively speaking, dishonest. It would also be arguable that in so far as the proceeds were the 'property' of the company, the exception to the rule in *Foss v Harbottle*, placing beyond the reach of the majority of shareholders the ability to ratify or excuse cases – where there had been a misappropriation, might be available. While it was assumed that the observations of, in particular, Lord Templeman, in all probability were not necessarily intended to be applied broadly to all breaches of fiduciary duty resulting in unjust enrichment, recent cases, now endorsed by the Supreme Court,[56] have shown that some judges are willing to throw the net very widely. In *United Pan Europe Communications NV v Deutsche Bank AG*,[57] the Court of Appeal had no difficulty in applying such reasoning to the misuse of confidential information obtained within a duty of loyalty and imposing a constructive trust on shares bought by the bank. With respect, however, in *Reid*, their Lordships clearly did not have these wider issues in mind when they showed so much determination in ensuring that the unsavoury Warwick Reid should not be allowed to magic his ill gotten gains, as Lord Templeman remarked, 'to some Shangri-La which hides bribes and other corrupt moneys in numbered bank accounts'. Indeed, this is one of the real problems in this area of the law. As we have already noted the judges, once they sniff fraud and abuse, are prepared to go some way in ensuring that the crook's ill-gotten gains are taken away from him and are not always too concerned with traditional jurisprudence. In looking at some of the decisions, particularly those relating to directors' duties, it is important to remember that it is probable the end has justified the means and a search for all prevailing and entirely rational principles of restitution may well be a search in vain.

2.26   Notwithstanding important developments in the law which we examine later[58] it is still the law that not all breaches of fiduciary duty are capable of giving rise to a constructive trust relationship. In *Nelson v Rye*,[59] Laddie J followed Sir Peter Millett's view expressed extra-judicially in his

---

54   [1993] 1 SLR 735.
55   [1990] HKLR 396.
56   See *FHR European Ventures LLP v Cedar Capital Partners LPC* [2014] UKSC 45.
57   [2000] 2 BCLC 461.
58   See above at note 56 and 14.12 below.
59   [1996] 2 All ER 186.

influential article 'Bribes and Secret Commissions' published in the *Restitution Law Review*.[60] Sir Peter took the view that a constructive trust is appropriate when an agent receives property himself in circumstances where it should have gone to his principal. This is a principle which has long been recognised in the company law cases. The Australian High Court in *Warman International Ltd v Dwyer*[61] also threw some light on this issue by distinguishing situations where a fiduciary benefits by use of his principal's property or an opportunity coming to him by virtue of acting for his principal – where a constructive trust might be appropriate and other cases where he is merely guilty of a breach of his duty of loyalty. In the latter case, while there may well be an obligation to account for all or part of the 'secret profit', the more exacting relationship of a trustee may well be inappropriate particularly vis à vis the rights of third parties. However, the Court of Appeal in *United Pan Europe NV* took the view that a constructive trust might be an appropriate remedy to deprive a fiduciary of his ill gotten gains when 'the conduct complained of falls within the scope of the fiduciary duty' to exhibit loyalty and it need not be shown that the profit resulted 'by virtue of his position'. Furthermore, the Court of Appeal did not accept that a constructive trust 'will only be granted where the applicant can trace into the property over which it is sought'. The remedy would depend upon the circumstances.[62] Furthermore, in this context, it must also be remembered that the Privy Council has also shown a greater degree of flexibility in dealing with that old inflexible rule that a fiduciary should not place himself in a position where his interest and duties conflict.[63] Disclosure with assent and contractual delimitation of the scope of duties and expectations may well render what would otherwise be a conflict of interest, nothing objectionable to the law.[64]

2.27   As we have already mentioned there is debate as to whether inside information can be considered to be a form of property, thereby more easily and traditionally invoking the law relating to constructive trust and all this might entail. The law is unclear as to in which circumstances the courts will protect information of a confidential nature in a manner which is analogous to property. The Divisional Court has decided that confidential information is not property for the purposes of the law of theft in England.[65] Whether such a view adequately takes account of the civil law and can in any case stand after the view expressed by the Privy Council in *Reid*[66] remains seriously open to doubt. In *Reid*, Lord Templeman certainly regarded the majority of their Lordships in *Boardman v Phipps*[67] as imposing a constructive trust on the defendants on the basis that they had misused confidential information. In *United Pan Europe NV*,[68] the Court of Appeal had no difficulty in considering a proprietary remedy, namely a constructive trust, might well be an appropriate remedy to impose on

60   (1993) RLR 7.
61   (1995) 128 ALR 201.
62   *United Pan-Europe Communications NV v Deutsche Bank AG* [2000] 2 BCLC 461.
63   *New Zealand Netherlands Society 'Oranje' v Kuys* [1973] 2 All ER 1222.
64   See *Kelly v Cooper* [1993] AC 205 and *Clarke Boyce v Mouat* [1994] 1 AC 428 discussed at 8.16.
65   *Oxford v Moss* (1978) 68 Cr App R 183. Another issue in regard to the English law of theft is the need to establish that the defendant has an intention to 'permanently deprive' the owner of the information of its use or value. This is highly problematic in the ordinary case of insider dealing. Of course, this is not to say that the circumstances of a misappropriation of confidential information might not involve the commission of other offences.
66   [1994] 1 All ER 1.
67   [1967] 2 AC 46.
68   [2000] 2 BCLC 461.

shares purchased by a fiduciary who had used confidential information. Indeed, as we have seen, Morritt LJ did not think it an issue whether the applicant could trace into the relevant property; what was at stake was depriving a fiduciary who had stepped into a conflict of interest of its 'secret profit'.

2.28   Whilst it might well be appropriate to protect confidential information as if it were a form of property in certain circumstances,[69] it would be pushing the boat out far too far to contend that most inside information is properly regarded as property for the law of trusts. It must also be remembered that considerable care needs to be taken in setting the limits for the use of information – including other people's, in any society – there will be significant issues of public policy. In many instances, inside information may not have the qualities often associated with confidential information. On the other hand, as the Court of Appeal in *United Pan Europe NV* appears to have accepted, it would be somewhat illogical if the courts allowed one to trace the proceeds of a 'secret profit' obtained in breach of the general obligation of loyalty and yet did not allow such protection for the misuse of the actual information which gave rise to the profit in the first place. Perhaps the answer is to separate the issues of tracing into the proceeds of a profit made in breach of a fiduciary duty and the imposition of a constructive trust as an appropriate remedy to deprive a fiduciary of his illicit profit. Notwithstanding the uncertainty whether the principles relevant to the law relating to constructive trusts and the tracing remedy can be applied to all 'secret profits' and the misuse of information, it is useful to refer to a series of relatively new cases which impose liability on those who receive the benefits or assist in the laundering of the proceeds of a breach of fiduciary duty.

2.29   The 'flood' of cases seeking to impose civil liability on those which might broadly be described as 'fiduciary facilitators' or accessories are based on a principle of law set out by Ungoed-Thomas J in *Selangor United Rubber Estates v Craddock*.[70] In this case, the learned judge referred to an established principle of equity that where a person knowingly participates in another's breach of trust, he will be regarded as standing in the same place as the trustee. While there has been much discussion in the books and cases as to the exact nature of this liability and whether it is properly considered a constructive trust relationship in all cases,[71] suffice it to say in this context there would appear to be *only* two problems in fashioning this rule to become a most effective weapon against insider abuse.

2.30   The first is simply what sort of misconduct on the part of a fiduciary will be sufficient to bring the principle into play? Most of the cases have involved either a conventional trust relationship or at least something so close

---

69   See *Dunford and Elliot Ltd v Johnson and Firth Brown Ltd* [1977] 1 Lloyds Rep 505; *Indata Equipment Supplies Ltd v ACL Ltd* [1998] 1 BCLC 412 and *A-G v Blake* [1997] Ch 84.

70   [1968] 1 WLR 1555. Note also the classic formulation by Lord Selborne in *Barnes v Addy* (1874) LR 9 Ch App 244, '… strangers are not to be made constructive trustees merely because they act as agents of trustees … unless (they) receive and become chargeable with some part of the trust property or unless they assist with knowledge in a dishonest and fraudulent design on the part of the trustees'. Note, however, the law has moved on and now focuses on the dishonesty of the accessory: *Williams v Central Bank of Nigeria* [2014] UKSC 10.

71   In *Williams v Central Bank of Nigeria* [2014] UKSC 10 Lord Sumption pointed out that the basis of liability is not the willing or accidental assumption of the status of a trustee but the fact that a person's participation in the unlawful misapplication of a trust asset or property over which there are fiduciary obligations. It is this which renders the accountable as if they were constructive trustees, albeit they are not.

as to make little practical difference. It would seem, however, that the property diverted or misappropriated by the trustee must be capable of sustaining a proprietary or tracing claim.[72] This point arose in *Nanus Asia Co Inc v Standard Chartered Bank*.[73] In this case, the Hong Kong court was required to determine whether Standard Chartered was in a position analogous to that of a constructive trustee with regard to profits from insider dealing in the United States made by a Taiwanese citizen who, with an employee of Morgan Stanley, had misappropriated price-sensitive information from Morgan Stanley and then traded on it on the New York Stock Exchange. There was no problem with establishing the bank's state of knowledge as it had already been joined in civil enforcement proceedings in New York.

2.31   The Hong Kong High Court held that proceeds of the abuse of inside information were 'held' by Standard Chartered on trust for the US authorities and various other claimants in the United States. At the time, some thought this decision, although welcome, went somewhat further than the English law, as it was considered unlikely that the misuse of confidential information, let alone mere inside information, was capable of sustaining a trust relationship, which was then thought to be a prerequisite for a viable tracing claim in equity. With the rather more robust approach of the Privy Council in *Attorney General of Hong Kong v Reid*[74] now approved by the Supreme Court,[75] it is probable that an English court would today take much the same approach as the learned judge in Hong Kong. A welcome development of the law.[76] It is also worth pointing out that the courts have been prepared to take a very broad view as to what types of assistance may properly justify liability as an accessory. Clearly assisting in hiding the proceeds of a breach of fiduciary duty will suffice, but so will giving support and even advice.[77]

2.32   There has been also considerable discussion as to the requisite state of knowledge for liability. In cases involving the knowing receipt of property transferred in breach of a fiduciary obligation where the recipient asserts that he has received the property in question beneficially, he will nonetheless be liable if he knew that the property is traceable to a breach of fiduciary duty so as to render it unconscionable for him to retain it against the claims of others. The cases have indicated two basic standards, one requiring subjective knowledge and the other a rather more objective or a constructive standard. It was thought

---

72   In *Royal Brunei Airlines Sdn Bhd v Tan* [1995] 2 AC 378, Lord Nicolls at p 392 cast the potential liability of the accessory sufficiently widely to catch assisting in 'a breach of trust or fiduciary obligation'. A proprietary element was required for accessory liability by Nourse LJ in *Satnam Investments Ltd v Dunlop Heyward* [1999] 1 BCLC 385 at 404, but this view has been criticised and doubted, see *Goose v Wilson Sandford & Co (No 2)* [2001] 1 Lloyd's Rep PN 189 and *JD Wetherspoon plc v Van de Berg* [2009] EWHC 639 and is probably no longer tenable, *Novoship (UK) Ltd v. Mikhaylyuk* [2014] EWCA Civ 908 and not the availability of tracing in *FHR European Ventures LLP v Cedar Capital Partners LCC* [2014] UKSC 45, in any case.
73   [1990] HKLR 396.
74   *Attorney General for Hong Kong v Reid* [1994] 1 AC 324.
75   See *FHR European Ventures LLP v Cedar Capital Partners LCC* [2014] UKSC 45, contra *Sinclair Investment (UK) Ltd v Versailles Trading Finance* [2011] EWCA Civ 347 and at 14.12.
76   See B.Rider, 'A Simple approach to justice!' (2014) 21 *Journal of Financial Crime* 379.
77   See for example *Madoff Securities International Ltd (In Liquidation) v Raven* [2013] EWHC 3147 and even turning a blind eye to the fraud of a colleague or superior might be sufficient, see *Fayers Legal Services & Taylor v Howard Day* ChD (unreported) 11 April 2001 and discussed in this context in A. Stafford and S. Ritchie, *Fiduciary Duties* (2nd edn) (Jordan Publishing 2014) at p 343.

that the distinction could be justified in terms of whether the third party who facilitates the breach of trust comes into possession of the relevant property or simply facilitates its control or retention by another. In the first case, a more objective standard was considered appropriate and knowledge of facts which would put a reasonable man on notice that something dishonest was afoot would be sufficient to justify liability akin to that of a trustee. On the other hand, where the participation of the third party does not extend to possession of the property, it was thought that the requisite degree of *scienter* should be if not actual knowledge something approaching it. In the view of recent cases, it would seem that the question of knowledge is rather more bound up with the remedy that is sought rather than any pre-existing relationship or obligation. Where the third party does not come into possession of the trust property or its proceeds, then it is difficult to conceive of him as a constructive trustee or, for that matter, as having any status which would involve a proprietary nexus and today the term accessory is preferred. The liability of such a person for participating in the breach of trust will be personal and today is justified by his dishonesty and not necessarily as in the older law on his participation in a pre-existing dishonest design.[78] In *Agip (Africa) Ltd v Jackson*,[79] the Court of Appeal found no difficulty in regarding a chartered accountant who had facilitated laundering the proceeds of a fraud by incorporating companies and opening bank accounts in the names of these companies liable as if he were a constructive trustee and thereby holding him personally liable to restore the funds in question. In such cases, the liability is personal to the defendant and does not involve a propriety liability. In this case, the court found that the person concerned had acted dishonestly. He knew of facts which in the circumstances made him suspicious, but he then deliberately refrained from making the enquiries which an honest man would have made and which would easily have uncovered the fraud. Although the cases do indicate varying qualities of knowledge, it would seem the better view today is that before a third party can be held liable as a facilitator, the court will have to be shown that he knew the facts or deliberately turned a blind eye and then acted with a lack of probity.

2.33   In *Royal Brunei Airlines Sdn Bhd v Philip Tan Kok Ming*[80] the Privy Council handed down an opinion which does bring some clarity to this area of the law. The Privy Council emphasised that the liability of a person who assists or procures a breach of trust, but does not himself actually receive the property in question, is based on his dishonesty. It is a personal liability

---

78   See for example, Lord Selborne at 2.28 above, note 70 and *Belmont Finance Corporation Ltd v Williams Furniture Ltd* [1979] Ch 250. Whether the defendant need have knowledge of the trust or fiduciary obligation has been questioned. For example, in *Agip (Africa) Ltd v Jackson* [1990] Ch 265 at 295, Millett LJ held 'a man who consciously assists another by making arrangements which he knows are calculated to conceal what is happening from a third party takes the risk that they are part of a fraud practised on that party'. In *Madoff Securities International Ltd v Raven* [2007] EWHC 3147, Popplewell J considered 'a dishonest participant in a transaction takes the risk that it turns out to be a breach of trust or fiduciary duty. It is not necessary for the assistant to know, or even suspect, that the transaction is a breach of trust, or the facts which make it a breach of trust, or even what a trust means; it is sufficient if he knows or suspects that the transaction is such to render his participation dishonest'. See also *Grupo Torras SA v Al-Sabah* [1999] CLC 1469, at 1665 per Mance J. On the other hand, Rimmer J in *Brinks Ltd v Abu-Saleh* [1999] CLC 133 took the view that the defendant must be shown to have had knowledge of the facts which gave rise to the fiduciary obligation in the first place.

79   [1991] Ch 547.

80   [1995] 2 AC 378.

that arises from his dishonest assistance in another's breach of duty.[81] The Privy Council considered it matters not whether the trustee in breach of his fiduciary obligations has himself been dishonest. Furthermore, the probity of the facilitator is to be judged by reference to the honesty of others. The test is whether he had acted in a way otherwise than an honest man would have in the circumstances. This would invariably involve conscious impropriety on the part of the facilitator, rather than mere negligence, let alone simple inadvertence. However, a person might well be considered to be acting dishonestly for the purpose of imposing liability where he recklessly disregarded the rights of others. The Privy Council underlined that in determining whether a facilitator had acted dishonestly, his actual knowledge at the relevant time had to be considered by the court and this was a subjective issue. What might have been known by a reasonable man in the position of the facilitator might be probative, but was not conclusive. Furthermore, the personal and professional attributes of the facilitator must also be considered in determining what he did and for what reason.

2.34   The issue was further discussed in *Heinl v Jyske Bank (Gibraltar) Ltd*.[82] In this case, the judges used, as the basis of their reasoning, the judgment of Lord Nicholls in *Brunei* and concluded that it was not enough that on the whole of the information available to him he ought, as a reasonable man, to have inferred that there was a substantial probability that the funds originated from the bank in question, but that the inference had, indeed, been drawn. This clearly supports the idea that a high level of suspicion will be needed to incur liability in these cases. Another relatively recent case bearing on the issue of liability in these circumstances is *A Bank v A Ltd (Serious Fraud Office Interested Party)*.[83] This again saw the probability of liability of those who negligently participate in money laundering reduced as the court held that banks did not become constructive trustees merely because they entertained suspicions as to the provenance of money deposited with them. The level of dishonesty needed for dishonest assistance was not satisfied by a general suspicion; there needed to be substantial suspicion pertaining to the specific transaction with which they were involved for liability to be incurred. In *Twinsectra v Yardley*[84] the House of Lords endorsed the trend away from the imposition of liability on the basis of an essentially objective determination. Instead, referring to Lord Nicholls in *Brunei*, their Lordships adopted what Lord Hoffmann described as a combined test, having both a subjective and an objective element. First, it must be shown that the defendant acted in a manner in which reasonably honest people would not have. Secondly, it must be shown that the defendant actually appreciated that this conduct would be considered dishonest by other people.

2.35   There are situations where, to establish the requisite state of mind for liability under the civil and criminal law, it will be necessary to attribute knowledge from one person to another.[85] Where companies are involved, as has already been pointed out, this involves a number of issues. A similar problem arises in fixing a company with a particular state of mind or

---

81   Lord Nicholls considered that a person who had no reason to suppose that they were dealing with a trustee or other fiduciary acting in breach of his obligations should not be held accountable: [1995] 2 AC 378 at 387.
82   [1999] 34 LS Gaz R 33.
83   (2000) *Times*, 18 July.
84   [2002] 2 All ER 377.
85   See at 15.13 *et seq* below.

knowledge. In *R v Rozeik*,[86] the Court of Appeal, referring to the earlier case of *El-Ajou v Dollar Land Holdings plc*,[87] accepted that whether a company is fixed with the knowledge acquired by an employee or officer will depend on the circumstances and it is necessary to identify whether the individual in question has the requisite status and authority in relation to the particular act or omission. Therefore, it does not follow that information in the possession of even a relatively senior official will be attributed to the company if that employee is not empowered to act in relation to the transaction in question. On the other hand, as was dramatically illustrated in the House of Lord's decision in *Re Supply of Ready Mixed Concrete (No 2)*,[88] an employee who acts for the company within the scope of his employment, even if against the express instructions of his employer, may well expose the company as he is the company for the purpose of the transaction in question. A similar view was expressed by the Privy Council in *Meridian Global Funds Management Asia Ltd v Securities Commission*.[89]

2.36   As the decision of their Lordships in *Ready Mixed Concrete* clearly shows, a company may be liable to third parties or be guilty of the commission of an offence even though the relevant employee was acting dishonestly and/ or in breach of his contract of service or even against the interests of the company. In that case, the House of Lords accepted that the management had gone to considerable lengths to ensure compliance with their instructions, but once a transaction had been entered into by an employee who had the power to deliver on behalf of the company, such considerations went merely to the issue of mitigation. Whilst the Privy Council recognised in *Meridian Global Funds Management* that it is a matter of interpretation as to whether a particular statute seeks to 'fashion a special rule of attribution for the particular substantive rule', both the Privy Council and the House of Lords were quite prepared to adopt this notion of 'merger' of minds in the case of restrictive trade practices law and securities regulation, given the discerned public policy in avoiding a result which might defeat the purpose of the legislature.

2.37   Where the employee in question is perpetrating a fraud against his employer, then it is obviously inappropriate to take his knowledge of the fraud as being that of the victim company. This much is clear from *Re A-G's Reference (No 2 of 1982)*.[90] In such situations, the employee cannot be both a party to the deception and represent the company for the purpose of it being deceived.

2.38   When the company is the victim, the person or persons who may be taken to represent its state of mind may well differ from those whose state of mind will be attributed to the company in cases where it is the company that is charged with an offence. In *Rozeik*, the Court of Appeal thought that in this latter situation such persons are more likely to represent what Viscount Haldane called 'the directing mind and will of the corporation'.[91]

---

86   [1996] 1 BCLC 380.
87   [1994] 2 All ER 685.
88   [1995] 1 AC 456.
89   [1995] 2 AC 500 and see at 15.4 below.
90   [1984] 2 All ER 216. See also generally Cheong-Ann Png, *Corporate Liability* (Kluwer 2001).
91   See *Lennard's Carrying Co Ltd v Asiatic Petroleum Co Ltd* [1915] AC 705 discussed further at 16.15 below.

SHADOW DIRECTORS AND OTHERS

2.39   In our discussion of the civil law we have focused on those who are in what is generally recognised to be a fiduciary relationship with the relevant principal or company. The courts have been prepared to hold persons who are *de facto* directors albeit they have not been properly appointed to the same obligations as a duly appointed director.[92] Persons in accordance with whose instructions the directors are accustomed to act notwithstanding that they may not be formally appointed as directors, are known as 'shadow directors'.[93] Section 170(5) of the Companies Act 2006 provides that 'the general duties apply to shadow directors where, and to the extent that, the corresponding common law rules or equitable principles apply'. In *Ultraframe (UK) Ltd v Fielding*,[94] Lewison J held that shadow directors who were not formally appointed as director or who were not *de facto* directors, do not generally owe fiduciary duties to the company whose directors they have influence over. The Court took this view as, unlike directors, *de jure* or *de facto*, they had not assumed a fiduciary obligation to the company. While in many respects an unfortunate decision, other cases have emphasised the distinction between *de facto* directors, who are directors in all but name, and shadow directors who do not claim or purport to act as directors – indeed, they 'lurk in the shadows, sheltering behind others who (they) claim are the only directors of the company to the exclusion of' themselves.[95] However, in the most recent case to consider this issue Newey J departed from the view of Lewison J in *Ultraframe* and considered that shadow directors would to some degree own fiduciary duties to their company.[96] While it remains uncertain as to the extent to which the obligations relating to avoidance of conflicts of interest and the taking of secret profits apply to such persons, it is clear under both the restrictive and wider view that on the facts of a particular case, there might well be fiduciary obligations. It is also the case that the Companies Act 2006 does impose certain statutory duties on shadow directors, for example in regard to the disclosure of interests in existing transactions under section 187.

2.40   The position of officers and senior employees of companies, who are not *de facto* directors, is also not entirely certain. In English law while it is clear that the duty of fidelity that an employee owes to his or her employer is not a fiduciary duty as such,[97] fiduciary obligations can arise, directly or indirectly, by virtue of contract and from the special facts of a case.[98] It is

---

92   See *Secretary of State for Trade and Industry v Tjolle* [1998] 1 BCLC 333 and In *Re Canadian Land Reclaiming and Colonzing Co* (1880) 14 Ch D 660.

93   Section 251 of the Companies Act 2006.

94   [2005] EWHC 1638.

95   See *In Re Hydrodam (Corby) Ltd* [1994] 2 BCLC 180, but see *Yukong Line Ltd v Rendsburg Investments Corporation of Liberia* [1998] 1 WLR 294.

96   *Vivendi SA v Richards* [2013] EWHC 3006. It is possible that this might have serious implications for members of Shari'a boards in companies offering Shari'a compliant financial services and products. See generally on this B Rider, Chapter 5 in C Nethercott and D Eisenberg (eds), *Islamic Finance, Law and Practice* (Oxford University Press 2012) and B Rider, Ch 3, *Strategies for the development of Islamic Capital Markets* (Islamic Financial Services Board 2011), and B Rider, Ch 5, *The Changing Landscape of Islamic Finance* (Islamic Financial Services Board 2010).

97   *Customer Systems plc v Ranson* [2013] EWCA Civ 841 and see also *Concut Pty Ltd v Worrell* [2000] HCA 64.

98   See generally *Helmet Integrated Systems Ltd v Tunnard* [2007] IRLR 126, *Customer Systems plc v Ranson* [2013] EWCA Civ 841 and in particular Elias J. in *University of Nottingham v. Fishel* [2000] ICR 1462.

probable that the misuse of price sensitive information acquired by virtue of such employment would justify liability based on breach of the contract of employment.[99] In *Canadian Aero Services Ltd v O'Malley* the Canadian Supreme Court considered that the general duties of directors applied to officers of the company and senior employees 'who are authorised to act on the company's behalf and in particular to those acting in a senior management capacity'.[100] In the majority of cases abuse of inside information would be considered gross misconduct justifying dismissal of an employee.

2.41   Finally, it is clear that fiduciary obligations are finite. Generally speaking, they start in the case of a director on appointment and terminate on relinquishing office. However, there are exceptions and these are preserved by section 170(2) of the Companies Act 2006. Generally speaking, where the opportunity to profit has arisen while in a fiduciary relationship, the obligation of fair dealing applies to the subsequent drawing down of the relevant benefit.[101]

THE POSITION OF INVESTORS

2.42   Investors who subscribe directly or indirectly through an issuing house to a new issue of securities may suffer a loss if the securities in question are sold at a price in excess of their 'real' worth. While this is not really insider dealing in the conventional sense, the issuer and its agents are in a privileged position in that they are aware that the securities are worth less than the market thinks. In many jurisdictions, the law has long recognised that such conduct is highly damaging to the market. Indeed, a special commission appointed by the House of Commons in 1697[102] described such practices, when compounded by insiders dumping their shares on the market, as undermining the 'trade and wealth' of the country. Consequently, in cases of the new issue of securities, most legal systems, as we have seen, impose strict disclosure obligations on those involved in promoting the issue. Consequently, a failure to disclose material information would be unlawful and result in civil and possibly criminal liability. Of course, if those privy to the relevant information seek to use it in their own dealings, then this would be insider dealing. The justification for imposing onerous disclosure obligations on a company at the time it issues securities to the public is that all the facts pertaining to the nature and extent of the investment risk are exclusively in the possession of the issuer and its insiders. It has also been argued in South Africa[103] that the sale of over-priced securities in such circumstances is akin in legal terms to selling chattels that have latent defects.

99   See *Industrial Development Consultants Ltd v Cooley* [1972] 1 WLR 443 and see the *Attorney General v Blake* [1998] Ch 439 in regard to the duty of loyalty that an employee has to his employer. Employees that receive brides are considered to have breached a fiduciary obligation or at least something analogous thereto, see *Thompson v Havelock* (1880) 1 Camp 527, *Reading v The King* [1948] 2 KB 268 and *National Grid Electricty Transmissions plc v McKenzie* [2009] EWHC 1817.
100   (1973) 40 DLR (3d) 371.
101   See *CMS Dolphin Ltd v Simonet* [2001] 2 BCLC 704 and *Industrial Development Consultants Ltd v Cooley* [1972] 1 WLR 443.
102   *Commission Appointed to Inquire into the Trade of England*, House of Commons Journals, 20 November 1697.
103   *Pretorius v Natal South Sea Investment Trust Ltd* 1965 (3) SA 410 (W) 418.

2.43 On the other hand, the courts have been concerned to limit the scope and extent of the issuer's liability. Consequently, in most jurisdictions, there is a reluctance to afford market purchasers' and sellers' actionable claims against those whose action might influence the price of securities already in the market. Thus, it will often only be those who have transacted directly with the relevant issuer that will be able to sue. Those who deal in the market with other parties will have no right to complain. By the same token, it has been held that auditors only owe their duty of care to the company for which they are appointed to act. They do not owe a duty in the ordinary course of events to those investors in the market who may well be influenced in their investment decisions by what the auditors say in their reports.[104] Although often expressed in terms of principle, the court's decision in such cases is clearly based on policy considerations. The need to consider the proportionality as to the possible extent of liability, when compared with the wrong in question, is recognised in other areas of the law. For example, in the United States, Congress enacted legislation limiting the exposure that insiders dealing on the market might have to contemporaneous market traders.

2.44 In the case of investors who are already in the market, the question as to whether they suffer loss or not from insider abuse is more problematic. They are not, as in the case of those who subscribe for securities in a new issue, left with over-priced securities that the market has had no opportunity to evaluate. In most organised markets, the matching of parties is essentially random and in the case of an active and relatively deep market there will be willing sellers or purchasers at whatever the market price happens to be. In the majority of situations, this price will be wholly uninfluenced by the insider's conduct. Consequently, the mere failure of an insider to 'share' his information with whoever happens to end up as his counterparty, cannot really be said to have misled that person into dealing at that price or with the insider on the terms he has. Therefore, the insider's failure to disclose has not in any real way caused that particular individual to deal on the terms he has. Thus, in market transactions, the elements that are usually required for a viable civil action are either absent or can only be found as fictions.

2.45 On most markets, the securities that are traded represent capital that was contributed to the relevant company in the past. Therefore, it is not unlikely that modern investors operating on the market will be primarily concerned with current valuations and returns rather than the longer term fortunes of the enterprise. Consequently, a relatively high proportion of trading on the markets will be dictated by the current price. With the advent of computer assisted trading programs and the development of related and derivative markets, trading will be far more responsive to price fluctuations. Therefore, it is argued that the only 'real' price is that currently on offer and there is no way in which an investor can logically complain that he has been harmed by the existence of information outside the market. It has also been said that it is only those investors who trade in the time lapse between the insider's transaction and the disclosure of the relevant information who have any real complaint. Longer term investors who remain in the security in question will reap the rewards or suffer the consequences of the information when it does come to the market, regardless of the insider's conduct. While derivatives may have the effect of gearing gains or losses, essentially the same considerations apply. If we cannot

104   See, for example, *Caparo Industries plc v Dickman* [1990] 2 AC 605.

attribute price movements to the action of the insider, then it is difficult to claim that, whatever way the price moves, it is caused by, or is the fault of, insider dealing.

2.46 While the above discussion has centred on dealings in equity securities or rights derived from or related to equity securities, we need to consider whether loss arises when insider dealing occurs in dealings in debt securities. Those holding debt securities may be regarded as standing in the position of creditors to the relevant issuer. In most cases, this will be a somewhat indirect relationship. The attitude of holders of debt securities to the activities of management will be influenced by the extent to which the relevant borrowings are secured. A significant difference between an equity and a debt security is that the latter is likely to have a relatively determined life expectancy. Of course, given the complexity of structuring corporate finance today, this may be a distinction without a difference. However, in the case of securities with fixed maturity or, for that matter, any pre-determined right or obligation, their very sensitivity to time renders them a more attractive instrument for certain forms of insider manipulation.

2.47 The attitude of those who provide capital to a company to the conduct of management will be influenced by many other factors. The emphasis that has been placed around the world on the benefits of good governance and ethical management has no doubt had some effect on the way in which management operates and their conduct is assessed. Small investors may well be annoyed that those in positions of trust have abused inside information, but in most legal systems there is little they can do about it. In the vast majority of jurisdictions, even if they were contemporaneous traders, the chances of their being able to frame and pursue any claim for compensation or rescission are remote. Larger institutional investors may be in a rather different position. An institutional investor may not have the same degree of flexibility that a smaller private investor has. For example, an institutional investor with a significant holding in a particular company may find that it is almost 'locked in'. This may result not only from the size of its holding, but also from the knowledge that it acquires by virtue of its position. Although most systems of regulation tend to focus attention on protecting the weak rather than assisting the strong to ensure better treatment for all, institutional investors have been encouraged to take more interest in the proper management of the issuers in which they invest. Some, in furtherance of their own policies of good governance and ethical investment, have been prepared to stand up to those suspected of committing abuses. It must always be remembered that institutional investors are not spending their own money in pursuing those that they suspect of bad management practices and abuse. Therefore, it is necessary for institutional investors to consider the balance carefully between the costs and benefits of such a course of action.

2.48 While it is difficult to demonstrate the sort of loss resulting from insider dealing that legal systems would normally be willing to compensate, where the insider does more than trade on the basis of the information or encourages another to do so, the position may be very difficult. If the insider engages in acts of fraud or manipulation, then his actions may well result in quantifiable losses for which most systems of law would provide remedies. As has been pointed out, there must be some justification for allowing the investor to transfer the loss that has resulted in the movement of the market price on to the insider. In virtually every legal system, this can only be done if it can be established that the investor's loss was in some way caused by the insider's actions or default.

2.49   Much of what has been said with regard to the position of those who happen to be matched as the counterparty to an insider transaction is on the basis that the dealing takes place on a market. In the case of most developed markets, the dealing will be indirect, impersonal and anonymous. Consequently, as we have noted, the matching of counterparties will be essentially random. Where, however, the transactions take place in circumstances where the parties are known to each other and there is therefore an opportunity for negotiation, it is possible that the legal position may be somewhat different. For example, in direct and personal transactions, it is rather more likely that a court might be persuaded that the conduct of the insider amounts to a misrepresentation. Of course, in such cases, it is still necessary to impose on the insider an obligation to disclose so as to convert his failure to speak into a misrepresentation. Nonetheless, where the parties are contracting with each other directly, it is easier for a court to find an implied undertaking of fair disclosure than in the context of market transactions. Having said this, however, except in rather special circumstances, there is little, if any, jurisprudential authority directly on the point. On the other hand, it is no doubt true that a judge may well be rather more sympathetic to a plaintiff who has been disadvantaged in dealings with an insider who has acted in a manner that most people would have no difficulty in regarding as dishonest.[105]

2.50   It is hard to find in the law or, for that matter, the institutional structures of modern enterprise, a concern for inhibiting insider abuse, other than on the basis that it undermines the time honoured notion of stewardship. While it is true that investors and other 'stakeholders' may deplore and feel personally aggrieved by the abuse of inside information, in the vast majority of jurisdictions, the law has not recognised this by imposing any duty on insiders that could be enforced, otherwise than through the company. However, as we have seen, even this cause of action is based not so much on logic, but the notion that those who are placed in positions of trust should not be allowed to abuse them.

ILLEGALITY AND PUBLIC POLICY

2.51   It is provided in section 63(2) of the Criminal Justice Act 1993 that 'no contract shall be void or unenforceable by reason only' that it violates section 52 which, as we shall see, renders the misuse of inside information a criminal offence.[106] The intention behind the enactment of this provision was to exclude the operation of the common law doctrine of illegality and the prospect of attempts to unravel transactions in the market. As a general rule, where the performance of a contract involves the commission of a crime or other act that is regarded as contrary to public policy, the law will consider the contract void and unenforceable.[107] It is important to note that section 63(2) does not seek to prevent an innocent party seeking to challenge the validity of a transaction on some other basis than illegality, such as misrepresentation.[108] It may also be possible for an innocent party dealing with an insider to argue that an objectionable transaction should be considered void on the wider basis

---

105   See, for example, Lord Lane CJ in *Re A-G's Reference (No 1 of 1988)* [1989] BCLC 193.
106   See Chapter 3.
107   See generally *Euro-Diam Ltd v Bathurst* [1988] 2 All ER 23 and particularly Kerr LJ at 28.
108   See Chapter 6.

that insider dealing is against public policy. The subsection only refers to the transaction being impugned as a result of the specific offence. It is probable that without section 63(2) the courts would have no difficulty in striking down a contract which resulted from a criminal misuse of information. This is clear from the judgment of Knox J in *Chase Manhattan Equities v Goodman.*[109] In this case Knox J, while accepting that the almost identical provision to section 63(2) in the earlier statute[110] rules out the civil consequences that might otherwise arise from the commission of an insider dealing offence, refused to make available the powers of the court to enforce a transaction which was still incomplete, on the basis that to do so would be tantamount to ordering the enforcement of an objectionable transaction. The court considered that the misuse of inside information was against public policy whether it amounted to a crime or not and therefore a transaction so tainted would not, in the discretion of the court, be enforced.

REMEDIES

2.52   It is important to recognise that the issue as to whether a cause of action exists is a different, albeit in practice related issue to whether an appropriate remedy is available. The courts do not like to find themselves in a situation where they are powerless to provide a remedy which will give effect to their determination as to the merits of a matter. In many ways the common law has developed around the existence of remedies and perhaps historically the courts have not focused as much as they might have on the issue of rights as opposed to remedies. As we have seen, it used to be said that damages were a common law remedy and could not be awarded for merely a breach of fiduciary duty. Of course, in many cases the breach of a fiduciary obligation will not stand alone and there may well be causes of action in tort and contract. While the award of damages is not traditionally a remedy of the Courts of Equity, Chancery Courts were prepared to make financial orders. For example, as we have seen, a fiduciary who makes a secret profit or receives a bribe can be ordered to account for this and hand it over to his principal. In appropriate cases, interest will be ordered or an account surcharged, and in cases of fraud this interest might be compounded. It is also possible in some situations to put the parties on terms. In other words, condition the award of an equitable remedy such as specific performance or rescission, by the undertaking of one party to make financial contribution to another. Section 50 of the Supreme Court Act 1981 provides that the English courts may award damages in addition to or in substitution for, an injunction or specific performance. It should be noted that it is only in regard to such a provision, that it is appropriate to speak in terms of equitable damages as opposed to equitable compensation. Equity is also able in certain cases to impose trusts, and in effect charges, on money and other property and demand that such be delivered up to those entitled to it. Consequently, it has never been the case that equity is powerless in providing financial compensation. In many common law countries the merger of the common law and equitable jurisdictions, at least in the making of orders to

---

109   [1991] BCLC 897. However, in the Hong Kong case of Innovisions Ltd v Chan Singchuk, Charles and Others (1992) 1 HKLR 71 affirmed (1992) 1 HKLR 255, Kaplan J did not consider insider dealing would 'shock the ordinary citizen or affect the public conscience'. Nazareth JA in the Court of Appeal strongly disagreed with Kaplan J and his colleagues.

110   Company Securities (Insider Dealing) Act 1985, s 8(3).

facilitate the administration of justice, has led to cases in which it is unclear whether an award of damages is being made by the judge wearing his common law or equitable hat. Many jurisdictions in effect allow their courts to award what passes for damages in cases of breach of fiduciary duty. In some cases this is pursuant to statutory provisions. It has been said, for example, by the Court of Appeal of New Zealand, that there is no difference in the rules of remoteness in the award of damages or compensation for breaches of, for instance, the common law duty of care or the fiduciaries' obligation to exercise care and prudence.[111] This is not the case in every jurisdiction and the availability of a financial order in cases of a breach of fiduciary duty – standing on its own – cannot be taken for granted.

2.53 The law of restitution has developed significantly over the last 30 years. It might be claimed with some accuracy that until the 1980s, the law of restitution was a best a rag bag of specific remedies, mostly of an equitable nature, that could be used only in very specific circumstances. While other common law jurisdictions and, in particular Australia and New Zealand forged ahead, the English courts showed rather more caution. We have already noted that there is, at least traditionally, no claim for damages in equity, albeit there is a reasonably expansive and perhaps ever expanding jurisdiction to award compensation. Where there is a trust and a misapplication of funds, whether capital or income, the beneficiary has an election to simply take over the investment into which the money has been placed or reject it. The trustee in breach is required to make good any depreciation in the value of the trust as a result of his breach and he can be charged interest and surcharged. Where there is no trust, those to whom the fiduciary obligation is owed may seek equitable compensation. In English law it seems that the principles behind the court's discretion to award equitable compensation, in terms of causation, remoteness and measure are the same as in damages claims.[112] The object of any award is to place the trust or beneficiaries in the position, at the day of trial, they would have been in had the breach of duty not occurred. While this approach appears to be correct where the relevant breach of duty is essentially a common law duty, such as the duty to act with diligence or care, it has been authoritatively doubted whether it is appropriate where what is in issue is the breach of a purely fiduciary obligation. In such cases the obligation to make restoration occurs at the time of breach and the common law approach to causation is irrelevant. To hold otherwise would be to undermine the special obligations of a fiduciary. Where the beneficiary rejects a misapplication of funds, what has happened after the breach is irrelevant. The fiduciary is under an obligation to make good the trust or fund as it was at the time of breach. This approach was taken in a case of equitable fraud and the directors or a company had to make full restoration to the company and could not simply pay over the difference between the value of the unlawful dividend and the value of a lawful dividend that they could and would have in fact paid.[113] In this case the Court of Appeal emphasised that they were stewards and had acted dishonestly. In another case involving an allegation of fraud in equity, the court held that the defendant 'is liable to restore the plaintiff to the situation he was in when the defendant did him wrong' much in the same way as the courts treat common law fraud.[114]

---

111   See at 2.18 above and see B Rider, 'A Special Relationship on the Special Facts' (1978) 41 *Modern Law Review* 585.
112   See Lord Browne-Wilkinson in *Target Holdings Ltd v Redferns* [1996] AC 421.
113   *Bairstow v Queen's Moat Houses plc* [2001] 2 BCLC 531.
114   *Swindle v Harrison* [1997] 4 All ER 705.

2.54   It is open to debate whether the basis for awarding equitable compensation is the breach of fiduciary duty, the obligation of stewardship, or the loss that is occasioned as a result of the wrongdoing. It is interesting that in the *Swindle v Harrison* case Mummery LJ stated 'in considering the extent of liability for breach of fiduciary duty it is not always necessary to consider all the matters which may be relevant in determining' a claim based on negligence. 'Forseeability and remoteness of damage are, in general, irrelevant to restitution remedies for breach of trust or breach of fiduciary duty. The liability is to make good the loss suffered by the beneficiary of the duty.'[115] He added, however, that it is necessary to consider the issue of causation.

2.55   One of the most important equitable remedies is the imposition of a constructive trust on property or money. We have already considered the circumstances where this might be relevant in the context of insider abuse. In so far as the imposition of a trust establishes a proprietary relationship between the relevant funds and those entitled, which can have significance in cases of insolvency, it is questionable whether at least in English law it is appropriate to regard the constrictive trusts as remedial. Until very recently largely as a result of the desire on the part of judges to be cautious in relation to third party rights, we have noted the significance of establishing a proprietary nexus. Where there is a misappropriation or wrongful disposal of trust property, the property in which the money is invested may be subjected to the original trust or the beneficiaries may reject this and petition the court for equitable compensation. If they take the property, there may still be a claim for any shortfall. Fiduciaries as we have seen may also be liable for secret profits and other unauthorised benefits that they have received by virtue of their fiduciary position. In such cases it is said that the imposition of a trust on those benefits is a constructive trust. It is a new trust, whereas in the case of a misapplication, equity reaches out and brings the property that now represents the diverted funds as the original trust. Until relatively recently, it was not clear whether all benefits obtained by virtue of a fiduciary relationship, could be subject to a constructive trust or traced. As we have seen, the decisions appeared to distinguish between secret profits tainted because of lack of authority and the potential for conflicts of interest and the receipt of a bribe.[116] In the case of a bribe there was merely a personal obligation to account. The Privy Council in *Attorney General for Hong Kong v Reid* disapproved of such a distinction and considered that applying one of the maxims of equity – equity looks as done that which should be done – a constructive trust could be recognised in regard to properties purchased with the proceeds of a bribe.[117] The reasoning adopted by the Privy Council was considered in depth and rejected by the Court of Appeal in *Sinclair Investments (UK) Ltd v Versailles Trade Finance Ltd*[118] and the sharp distinction between proprietary and personal liability ordained in the earlier Court of Appeal decision in *Lister & Co v Stubbs*[119] reaffirmed. However, within a very short space of time the Supreme Court adopted if not the reasoning in the *Reid* case, its result and held that unauthorised profits and bribes held by a fiduciary will be held in constructive trust.[120]

---

115   [1997] 4 All ER 705.
116   See at 2.24 above.
117   [1994] 1 AC 324.
118   [2011] EWCA Civ 347.
119   (1890) 45 Ch D 1.
120   [2014] UKSC 45.

2.56 We have referred to the personal obligation of a fiduciary to account for secret profits and, indeed, any benefit that he receives in breach of his duty of loyalty to his principal. We have already seen that calling a fiduciary to account and demanding the disgorgement of profits that he has made by virtue of his fiduciary status, in no way depends upon establishing loss to the principal. It is enough that he has violated his fiduciary obligation. We have also seen in our discussion of the possible use of this restitution remedy in cases of insider abuse that it only applies to profits and not the avoidance of losses. It is also probably limited to benefits that arise, directly or at least traceably, in the hands of the fiduciary himself. While an account for profits is properly an equitable device, recent cases have indicated that a similar liability may be invoked in common law actions. In *Attorney-General v Blake*, a former British spy profited from the publication of a book in breach of among other things his contract of employment with the British Government. The House of Lords recognised that there existed a power to call the defendant to account for his profits, as the Government 'had a legitimate interest in preventing the defendant's profit- making activity and, hence, in depriving him of his profit'.[121] While the boundaries of this remedy are unclear, it is necessary to show that the normal action for contractual damages would not be adequate or fair. It should also be noted that the English courts have allowed the award of damages and in many cases an accounting of profits where there has been a misuse of confidential information and particularly intellectual property rights.[122] Of course, it would rarely be the case that the sort of information that is relevant in cases of insider abuse would be protected in this way.[123]

2.57 We have also referred, in the context of liability for misrepresentation, to the remedy of rescission. While this may be asserted independently of the court, it is usual to obtain an order of rescission. Generally speaking it may be asserted in cases of equitable fraud, including where a fiduciary has made an unauthorised profit from his fiduciary position. Where there is a breach of fiduciary duty then any resulting transaction will be voidable in law. By asserting a right to rescind, the parties are placed back in the position they were before the misconduct or misrepresentation. There are, as we have seen, many other orders that can be obtained from the courts requiring restitution of property, whether these be in the form of decrees for specific performance or an injunction. It must not be forgotten that there are also powers in the criminal courts to order the return of property and restitution.[124]

---

121   [2001] 1 AC 268.
122   See *Seager v Copydex (No 2)* [1969] 1 WLR 809.
123   But see Dunford and Elliot Ltd v Johnson & Firth Brown Ltd [1977] 1 Lloyd's Rep 505.
124   See generally the Powers of Criminal Courts (Sentencing) Act 2000. Section 148 empowers the courts to order a convicted person to restore certain property and, possibly of more relevance; s 130 enables the court to order the payment of compensation for '... loss or damage resulting from the offence' or any other offence taken into consideration. The courts in cases of fraud have been encouraged to use this power.

Chapter 3

The main offences of insider dealing – dealing on the basis of inside information

THE LAW BEFORE 1980

3.1 In the United Kingdom insider dealing can be relatively simply defined as trading on organised securities markets by persons in possession of material non-public information. While in practice insider dealing can take many forms the misuse of privileged information in the context of take-overs and mergers during the 1970s and 1980s convinced most people that legislation was needed to curb it.[1] Of course, taking advantage of information that you obtain in privileged circumstances is nothing new and there has been considerable debate over the years as to whether this is sufficiently wrongful so as to justify rendering it a criminal offence.[2] We do not, however, propose to discuss here whether in fact insider dealing causes harm or the policy reasons for policing it. The reality is that anti-insider dealing laws are here to stay and debate on exactly what they should be about or are in fact designed to achieve is at best academic. Notwithstanding the widely held view that insider dealing is still a very real issue for the markets and given all the concerns as to the ability of the traditional criminal justice to secure convictions, there is no appetite in government for a radical re-evaluation of the current law. Indeed, at the international level and certainly within the European Union, insider dealing has been demonised to such an extent that it is often regarded as one of the more serious forms of economically motivated crime. Perhaps because it invokes notions of unfairness in the markets which capitalism has hitherto proved unable to reconcile with progress. Insider dealing becomes the very

---

1   See generally G Gilligan, *Regulating the Financial Services Sector* (Kluwer 1999), Chapter 4; J Davies, 'From gentlemanly expectations to regulatory principles: a history of insider dealing in the UK' (2015) 36 *The Company Lawyer* 132, continued at 163. See also B Rider, 'The role of the City panel on Take-overs and Mergers on the regulation of insider trading in Britain' (1978) 20 *Mal. L.R.* 315 and generally B Rider and HL Ffrench, *The Regulation of Insider Trading* (Macmillan 1979), and B Rider 'Policing the city – combating fraud and other abuses in the corporate securities industry' (1988) 41 *Current Legal Problems* 47.

2   See for example, B Rider and HL Ffrench, 'Should Insider Trading be regulated – Some initial considerations' (1978) 95 *South African Law Journal* 79; B Rider, 'The Control of Insider Trading – Smoke and Mirrors', (2000) 7 *Journal of Financial Crime* 227 and S Clark, *Insider Dealing Law and Practice* (Oxford University Press 2013), Ch 1.

noticeable wart on the face of capitalism to misquote Prime Minister Edward Heath and one that brings the sanctity of the market into issue.

3.2 The general criminal law has long sought to protect the integrity of public markets.[3] Indeed, there were very early common law offences which criminalised attempts to interfere with the proper operation of the markets. In the eighteenth century, Parliament and the City of London introduced a number of measures aimed at promoting the integrity of intermediaries and those engaged in stock-jobbing.[4] While the effectiveness of many of these initiatives may be questioned, there has always been a realisation that manipulative and fraudulent conduct has far more serious and greater implications for the markets, than the direct harm that it causes to individual investors. The protection and advancement of confidence in the integrity, fairness and efficiency of the markets, particularly the financial markets, has long been accepted as a serious matter. As we have already indicated, however, the use of information obtained in privileged circumstances has not always been considered objectionable, let alone unfair.

3.3 Until 1980, the restrictions on insider dealing in the United Kingdom were extremely limited. There was no specific legislation other than the requirements in the Companies Acts for directors, members of their families and substantial shareholders to report dealings in the shares of their companies. While these disclosure obligations were justified on a number of grounds, a significant one was that this would discourage the abuse of inside information. Whether reporting such transactions does in fact discourage abuse is open to debate. In any case, these provisions were poorly policed. Mention has been made elsewhere of the argument that the dishonest concealment of material information might constitute an offence under what was then section 13 of the Prevention of Fraud (Investments) Act 1958.[5] We have also seen that the common law provided no real possibility for those who dealt with those who abused inside information to seek recovery in the civil courts.[6] The use of inside information, absent some affirmative obligation to disclose it, did not and probably in most cases still does not give rise to a cause of action in the civil law. The most significant element of regulation was that provided by a range of self-regulatory and professional bodies in the City of London. For example, the City Panel on Takeovers and Mergers[7] and the London Stock Exchange[8] had adopted rules and guidelines that restricted insider dealing and the 'tipping' of inside information in the early 1970s.[9] However, there was considerable scepticism as to how effective they were in practice.[10] The

---

3   See BAK Rider and M Ashe, *Insider Crime – the New Law* (Jordan Publishing 1993), at 20. Reference should also be made to Chapter 6.
4   See 6.5 below.
5   Now s 89 of the Financial Services Act 2012, repealing s 397 of the FSMA 2000; see Chapter 6.
6   See for example *Percival v Wright* [1902] 2 Ch 421 and at 2.18 *et seq* above.
7   City Code on Takeovers and Mergers, Rule 4.1.
8   LSE, Model Code for Securities Transactions by Directors of Listed Companies, in Annex 1 to Listing Rule 9.
9   For a detailed discussion see B Rider, *Insider Trading* (Jordan Publishing 1980), Ch 3
10   See B Rider, C Abrams and TM Ashe, *Financial Services* (CCH/Butterworths 1996), Chs 1,2 and 3; B Rider and C Nakajima (eds); *The British Financial Services Reporter* (3 vols) (Sweet & Maxwell 1998), Chs 1 and 2; B Rider (ed), *The Regulation of the British Securities Industry* (Oyez 1979) particularly D Sugarman, Ch 4; B Rider, 'Self-regulation: The British approach to policing conduct in the securities business with particular reference

self-regulatory bodies in the City of London increasingly recognised that for effective enforcement, particularly where there was an international element in the transaction, statutory powers were required. Consequently, by 1980 many in the City recognised the need for insider dealing to be made a specific criminal offence.[11]

3.4   After two unsuccessful legislative attempts to outlaw insider dealing in the 1970s,[12] in 1980 Parliament amended the Companies Act to make insider dealing a criminal offence.[13] These provisions were consolidated in 1985 when the Companies Act was revised. The insider dealing provisions of the Companies Act 1985 became known as the Company Securities (Insider Dealing) Act 1985.[14] There were further amendments the following year in the Financial Services Act 1986 that were intended primarily to strengthen the government's enforcement powers.[15]

3.5   The Insider Dealing Act 1985 prohibited persons who had access to material non-public information by virtue of their position with a company (including directors, officers, employees and various kinds of agents of the company) from trading in the securities of the company while in possession of such information. These insiders were also prohibited from making selective disclosure of such information to others ('tipping') and it prohibited their tippees from trading on the basis of such inside information. The Act also prohibited persons in possession of non-public information about a proposed takeover of a company from trading in that company's stock.

3.6   The Insider Dealing Act 1985 provided for only criminal liability and its prohibitions applied only to individuals who acted while knowingly in possession of inside information. Although the Insider Dealing Act was an important step in outlawing the practice of insider dealing, the scope and impact of the British legislation was rather narrow. In fact, despite the fact that insider dealing had been an offence since 1980, there were no convictions under the Act's provisions until the late 1980s. The general view was that the law was not effective.

to the role of the City Panel on Take-overs and Mergers in the regulation of insider trading' (1978) 1 *Journal of Comparative Corporate Law and Securities Regulation* 319 (also published as an occasional paper by the City Panel on Takeovers and Mergers/Bank of England); B Rider and E Hew, 'The structure of regulation and supervision in the field of corporation and securities laws in Britain,' (1977) *Revue de la Banque* 83; B Rider and E Hew, 'The Regulation of corporation and securities laws in Britain – The beginning of the real debate' (1977) 19 *Mal Law Rev* 144; B Rider, 'The British Council for the Securities Industry' (1978) *Revue de la Banque* 303; B Rider, 'Policing the International Financial Markets' and 'Policing Insider Dealing: The International Perspective' in BT Tan, *The Regulation of Financial and Capital Markets* (Singapore Academy of Law 1991).

11   See generally B Rider and HL Ffrench, *The Regulation of Insider Trading* (Macmillan 1979) and B Rider and E Hew, 'The Regulation of corporation and securities laws in Britain – The beginning of the real debate' (1977) 19 *Mal LR* 144.
12   In 1973, the Conservative Government published a Companies Bill that would have outlawed insider trading, but it failed when the Government was defeated in the February 1974 General Election. The Companies Bill that was proposed by the Labour government in 1978 suffered a similar fate after that Government was defeated in the May 1979 General Election. See generally B Rider and HL Ffrench, *The Regulation of Insider Trading* (Macmillan 1979) and B Rider, *Insider Trading* (Jordan Publishing 1980).
13   Companies Act 1980, ss 68–73.
14   Company Securities (Insider Dealing) Act 1985 (hereinafter the 'Insider Dealing Act').
15   Financial Services Act 1986, ss 173–178.

3.7 In the following sections we will analyse the legislation that makes insider dealing a criminal offence. This is now found in Part V of the Criminal Justice Act 1993. The Financial Services and Markets Act 2000 (FSMA) imposes criminal and civil liability for market abuse which includes activity which would also fall within the scope of the Criminal Justice Act. The market abuse regime is discussed in Chapter 4. Over the years responsibility for investigating and prosecuting crimes involving insider trading has proved to be something of a 'hot potato'. In the early years the Department of Trade and Industry did attempt to prosecute a small number of cases with mixed results. For a time this power was held by the Treasury, which distinguished itself no better. The Crown Prosecution Service has often been left holding the file and has done its best. The Serious Fraud Office has been reluctant to take cases of insider trading and for a number of years dismissed such offences as being of a 'technical and regulatory' nature. As with the police, attitudes have changed. The SFO and in particular the City of London Police, which is the lead police force in the UK for economic crime, have both realised, albeit belatedly, the impact that allegations of insider abuse can have on the reputation of the City of London and its financial markets. With the realisation that 'real' criminals may engage in the deliberate gathering and exploitation of price-sensitive information, even the National Crime Agency's Economic Crime Command has exhibited some interest. However, given the Financial Conduct Authority's (FCA) exclusive responsibility for policing the market abuse regime it is sensible that the FCA is now the lead prosecutor for cases under Part V of the Criminal Justice Act.[16] The FCA's predecessor, the Financial Services Authority (FSA) was criticised among other things for what was perceived, perhaps unfairly, as a rather laid back attitude to policing insider dealing and other rules relating to integrity. The FCA's initial Director of Enforcement and Financial Crime promised that there would be a much more robust approach to the investigation and prosecution of such cases. She stated in late 2012 at a conference 'our current work to tackle insider dealing is a world away from where it was five years ago. Since 2009 we have seen 21 convictions, confiscation orders totalling more than £ 2.2 million, prison sentences up to forty months…This tough approach will continue'.[17] and on the whole it has. It should also be remembered that serious cases of insider abuse will often involve other criminal conduct and more general offences,

---

16 Section 402(1) of the FSMA provides that the FCA is authorised to institute proceedings for an offence under Part V of the CJA. Section 61 of the CJA provides that proceedings for an offence in England and Wales can only be instituted with the consent of the Secretary of State, the Director of Public Prosecutions, in Northern Ireland, the DPP for Northern Ireland and in Scotland the Scots Law Officers. The courts have held that the FCA has concurrent authority to prosecute and does not need to seek authorisation as this is covered by FSMA, s 402(1), see *R (on the application of Matthew Uberoi and Neel Uberoi) v City of Westminster Magistrates Court* [2008] EWHC 3191 (Admin).

17 T. McDermott, (Acting Chairperson of the FCA 2015 to 2016) conference speech, 15 November 2012. Lord Thomas LCJ, rejecting the appeal of Tom Hayes in regard to convictions on eight counts of conspiracy to defraud relating to the rigging of the LIBOR rate, emphasised (as did the trial judge Cooke J at Southwark Crown Court) the importance of sending out a message to those in the financial sector, and in particular banking, that failures of integrity will not be tolerated and deterrent sentences will be passed. In the present case, despite the defendant returning to the UK voluntarily and pleading guilty, he was initially sentenced to 14 years imprisonment. This was reduced on appeal to 11 years on account of his age (36), his non-managerial position in the relevant banks and his mild Asperger's condition (*R v Hayes*, Court of Appeal, 21 December 2015).

which we address in Chapter 6. Proceeds of crime and anti-money laundering law might also be relevant and reference should also be made to Chapter 7.[18]

THE OFFENCE OF INSIDER DEALING

The Criminal Justice Act 1993, Pt V

3.8 The Criminal Justice Act 1993 (CJA 1993), Part V came into force on 1 March 1994. It, apart from drawing on the experience of earlier legislation, seeks to implement the European Insider Dealing Directive.[19] Part V provides for the offence of insider dealing. This seeks to prohibit individuals from engaging in three classes of conduct in particular circumstances. First, the Act prohibits dealing in price-affected securities on the basis of inside information.[20] Secondly, it prohibits the encouragement of another person to deal in price-affected securities on the basis of insider information and, thirdly, it prohibits knowing disclosure of insider information to another.[21] To prove an offence under section 52, it is necessary to demonstrate two elements: (a) the status of the person charged as an insider and (b) the type of information in its possession to be inside information.

3.9 Section 52 provides:

'(1)   An individual who has information as an insider is guilty of insider dealing if, in the circumstances mentioned in subsection (3), he deals in securities that are price- affected securities in relation to the information.

(2)   An individual who has information as an insider is also guilty of insider dealing if –

(a)   he encourages another person to deal in securities that are (whether or not that other knows it) price-affected securities in relation to the information, knowing or having reasonable cause to believe that the dealing would take place in the circumstances mentioned in subsection (3); or

---

18   Note that the FCA is competent to pursue other offences related to insider dealing. For example, it can also prosecute money laundering under ss 327 and 328 of the Proceeds of Crime Act, see *R v Rollins* [2010] UKSC 39 and see Chapter 8. In addition to offences related to money laundering there are offences in the Fraud Act 2006 which might be very relevant and there is the possibility of conspiracy under s 1 of the Criminal Law Act 1977, as were laid in *R v Richard Joseph*, Unreported, Southwark Crown Court, 30 January to 11 March 2013 and FSA/PN/023/ 203.

19   Council Directive 89/592/EEC, 13 November 1989. This Directive provides for minimum standards for harmonisation and was the product of prolonged discussion and negotiation within the Community. European regulation was first seriously considered in the Segre Report, *The Development of a European Capital Market, Report of a Group of Experts*, EEC Commission, November 1966. Reference might also be made to the recommendation of the Commission, *The European Code of conduct for transactions in transferable securities*, 25 July 1977, OJ L212/37. For a discussion of the *Segre Report* and the Code see generally B Rider and HL Ffrench *The Regulation of Insider Trading* (Macmillan 1979), B Rider (ed), *The Regulation of the British Securities Industry* (Oyez 1979) particularly R Pennington, Ch 8 and K Hopt and Eddy Wymeersch, *European Insider Dealing* (Butterworths 1991). For a comprehensive discussion of the implementation of the directive, see R Alexander, *Insider Dealing and Money Laundering in the EU: Law and Regulation* (Ashgate 2007).

20   CJA 1993, Pt V, s 52(1).

21   CJA 1993, Pt V, s 52(1) and (2).

(b)   he discloses information, otherwise than in the proper performance of the functions of his employment, office or profession, to another person.

(3)   The circumstances referred to above are that the acquisition or disposal in question occurs on a regulated market, or that the person dealing relies on a professional intermediary or is himself acting as a professional intermediary.'

3.10   Criminal liability for each offence may only attach to an individual because the term 'individual' is defined to exclude corporations and other entities such as public authorities. This is a significant point of difference with the civil offence of market abuse under the FSMA, as we shall see. The definition of individual does cover, however, unincorporated partnerships or firms comprising a collection of individuals. Moreover, it should be noted that a company could be liable for insider dealing by committing the secondary offence of encouraging another person to deal.[22]

INSIDERS

3.11   To commit the offence of insider dealing, an individual must have information 'as an insider', which is defined in the CJA 1993, section 57:

'(1)   ... a person has information as an insider if and only if –

(a)   it is, and he knows that it is, inside information, and

(b)   he has it, and knows that he has it, from an inside source.

(2)   For the purposes of subsection (1), a person has information from an inside source if and only if –

(a)   he has it through

(i)   being a director, employee or shareholder of an issuer of securities; or

(ii)   having access to the information by virtue of his employment, office or profession; or

(b)   the direct or indirect source of his information is a person within paragraph (a)'.

3.12   The CJA 1993, section 57 creates a distinction between a primary insider (a person who has direct knowledge of inside information) and a secondary insider (a person who learns inside information from an inside source).[23] The primary insider obtains inside information through being a director, employee or shareholder of an issuer of securities or any person who has information because of his employment, profession or office. A secondary insider obtains inside information either directly or indirectly from a primary insider. For example, section 57 would impose liability on brokers or analysts as secondary insiders if they act on 'market intelligence' that comes from a primary insider.[24]

3.13   The insider dealing offence can only be committed if the acquisition or disposal of securities occurs on a regulated market or if the person dealing

---

22   See an analysis of the encouragement offence at 3.67 below, and 3.24 below in regard to secondary offences.

23   This terminology was first adopted in B Rider, *Insider Dealing* (Jordan Publishing 1983). See also B Rider and HL Ffrench, *The Regulation of Insider Trading* (Macmillan 1979).

24   See the discussion of 'tippee' liability at 3.77 *et seq* below.

relied on a professional intermediary or is himself a professional intermediary.[25] The CJA 1993 defines 'professional intermediary' as a person who carries on a business of acquiring or disposing of securities (whether as principal or agent) or a business of acting as an intermediary between persons taking part in any dealing in securities, or who hold himself out as willing to do so.[26] Individuals employed by such a person to carry out these activities are also defined as 'professional intermediaries'. The definition of professional intermediary does not include a person whose activities are merely incidental to other activities or if those activities are only conducted occasionally.[27]

3.14 The CJA 1993, section 59 defines professional intermediary as follows:

'(1) ... a professional intermediary is a person –

    (a) who carries on a business consisting of an activity mentioned in subsection (2) and who holds himself out to the public or any section of the public (including a section of the public constituted by persons such as himself) as willing to engage in any such business; or

    (b) who is employed by a person falling within paragraph (a) to carry out any such activity.

(2) The activities referred to in subsection (1) are –

    (a) acquiring or disposing of securities (whether as principal or agent); or

    (b) acting as an intermediary between persons taking part in any dealing in securities'.

3.15 Under this definition, a person will rely on a professional intermediary only if the professional intermediary either acquires or disposes of securities (whether as principal or agent) in relation to the dealing or acts as intermediary between persons taking part in the dealing.[28] If deals in securities do occur on a regulated market (that is an investment exchange), the insider dealing offence will be relevant unless the transaction is truly a private deal off the market without the intervention of a market professional. This section therefore confines the scope of the offence to organised markets and where professional intermediaries are involved reflecting the concern to protect confidence in the operation of markets rather than address private direct transactions.[29]

3.16 The offence of insider dealing cannot apply to anything done by an individual acting on behalf of a public sector body in pursuit of the government's economic policies such as, for example, managing monetary policy through the adjustment of exchange rates, interest rates or the public debt or foreign exchange reserves.[30] The purpose of these exclusions is to permit government

---

25   CJA 1993, s 52(3). The dealing will be caught therefore if a professional intermediary is involved even though the securities are not traded on a regulated market (see *R v Sanders*, Unreported, Southwark Crown Court, 20 June 2012, where Simon J. ruled it is sufficient 'if the prosecution can show that the person dealing relied on a professional intermediary, it does not matter whether or not the dealing occurred on a regulated market'). It is only dealings outside a regulated market that do not involve in any way a professional intermediary that fall outside the offences.

26   CJA 1993, s 59(1)(a).

27   CJA 1993, s 59(3)(a)–(b).

28   CJA 1993, s 59(4).

29   'The purpose of the legislation is to ensure confidence in the market in the broadest sense. So only transactions in securities that are market related are to be caught.' HC Deb, Standing Committee A & B, *Official Report*, Session 1992–93, vol 11, col 166.

30   CJA 1993, s 63(1).

policymakers to have sufficient discretion to manage the economy in the public interest. However, these exclusions would not apply to the government's sale of shares in a privatisation. Nor would they cover the private transactions of officials.

We have already noted that section 63(2) also provides that no contract shall be void or unenforceable by reason only that an offence may have been committed under section 52.[31]

The elements of the dealing offence

3.17 The two essential requirements for the dealing offence are that (a) an individual must have information as an insider, and (b) the insider must deal in securities that are price-affected securities in relation to the information.[32] Securities are price-affected securities for the purposes of this offence if the information if made public would be likely to have a significant effect on the price of the securities. Therefore there must be a causal link between the relevant information and its likely impact on the price of the securities in which the insider deals or encourages another person to deal. By the same token, price-sensitive information in relation to securities must be such as to have similar impact.[33] Accordingly, if an insider has inside information, he must not deal in the securities to which that information relates. The CJA 1993 adopts a broad definition of 'dealing in securities' to cover any acquisition or disposal of a security, including an agreement to acquire or dispose of a security and the entering into a contract which creates the security or the bringing to an end of such a contract.[34] Moreover, such acquisitions or disposals are within the definition irrespective of whether they are made by an individual as principal or as agent.

3.18 Section 54 provides that the securities covered by the anti-insider dealing offences are those included within the list in Schedule 2 of the Act and which satisfy the conditions set out in the relevant statutory instruments.[35] This approach was designed to avoid catching all shares including those of private companies. The securities referred to in the list include shares, debt securities,[36] warrants, options, depository receipts, futures and contracts for differences. They also include gilts and local authority stock (even of foreign public bodies) and their derivatives. The list conforms to the EC Directive on Insider Dealing[37] so that not only corporate securities and instruments based on such securities are included, but also that other contractual rights in other futures and derivatives markets are covered. While spread bets are not specifically included in Schedule 2 the better view is that they are also covered.[38] The Treasury, has effectively implemented the requirement of the Directive to restrict the offence to securities that are 'officially listed in a State

31 See 2.51 above.
32 CJA 1993, s 52(1).
33 CJA 1993, s 56(2). See generally *Hannam v Financial Conduct Authority* [2014] UKUT 0233 (TCC).
34 CJA 1993, s 55(3)(b).
35 Insider Dealing (Securities and Regulated Markets) Order 1994 (SI 1994/187).
36 See generally *Fons Hf v Corporal Ltd* [2014] EWCA Civ 304.
37 Council Directive 89/552/EEC, Article 1(2).
38 *R v Butt and others* (Unreported) Southwark Crown Court, 17 March 2004 and see also *Spreadex v Battu* [2005] EWCA Civ 855 and *City Index Ltd v Balducci* [2011] EWHC 2562 (Ch).

within the European Economic Area, or admitted to dealing on, or have its price quoted on or under the rules of, a regulated market'.[39]

3.19 The relevant time at which to consider whether or not an offence has been committed would appear to be at the time of agreement to acquire or dispose the security in question. At that time, if the individual had inside information about these securities, he will have committed an offence. However, if he received inside information only after making the agreement, he will probably not have violated the provision if he completes the deal and actually acquires or disposes of the securities. On the other hand, if the individual had the inside information at the time when he agreed to acquire or dispose of the security, it would seem that he will still have committed an offence, even if he does not complete the bargain.

3.20 The acquisition or disposal may be made by an individual acting either as principal or agent. Accordingly, if an agent has inside information, he will be within the scope of the offence if he deals in the relevant securities even though, in a direct sense, he will not gain from the transaction. This has special relevance to a trader who is engaged in a transaction as agent, to benefit his principal. The fact that the individual deals as agent and not principal is irrelevant. However, where the agent deals on an execution basis only, such an approach hardly seems justified and is unfair to the principal who gave the instruction if the agent then feels inhibited from processing the order. Fortunately, it appears that a defence in this situation would allow the agent to act on instructions notwithstanding that, incidentally, he has inside information.[40]

3.21 A person is also regarded as dealing in securities if he procures, directly or indirectly, an acquisition or disposal of the securities by another person.[41] Such procurement may occur in a number of ways, including where the person who actually acquires or disposes of the security is acting as an agent, nominee or at the direction of another in relation to the acquisition or disposal of a security.[42] This aspect of the definition of 'dealing in securities' is designed to cover transactions through an agent or nominee where the principal has relied on inside information without purchasing or selling the securities himself. We have already noted that only the most optimistic and naïve director would today risk dealing directly himself on inside information. For example, in *R v Goodman*[43] the company's chairman, aware that the company was about to announce a significant loss, gave his substantial shareholding to his girlfriend to off load. The court had no difficulty in holding that he has procured her

---

39 Council Directive 89/552/EEC, Article 4. Section 60 defines a regulated market as any market, however operated, that is identified as a regulated market by the Treasury. The Insider Dealing (Securities and Regulated Markets) Order 1994 as amended by the Insider dealing (Securities and Regulated Markets) (Amendment) Orders (SI 2000/1923 and SI 2002/1874) provides that a regulated market is any market which is established under the rules of an investment exchange specified in Sch 2. This list is now quite out of date and contains several anomalies. For example, NASDAQ is included in the Schedule although the NYSE is not. Of course, with multiple listings and cross quotation this does not result in the lacunae that might be thought. See also *R v Sanders and others* (Unreported) Southwark Crown Court, 20 June 2012 and FSA/PN/060 2012 and FSA/PN/ 067 2012.

40 CJA 1993, s 53(1)(c).

41 CJA 1993, s 55(1)(b).

42 CJA 1993, s 55(4). In section 55(5) it is made clear that subsection (4) is not exhaustive as to the circumstances in which one person may be regarded as procuring an acquisition or disposal of securities by another.

43 Unreported, but see *Financial Times* 1 May 1991 and 16 June 1992 and refer to *Chase Manhattan Equities Ltd v Goodman* [1991] BCLC 897 discussed at 2.51 *et seq* above.

disposal. Transactions are also covered that are undertaken at the direction of a sole shareholder who uses its influence over a company to deal in its shares.[44]

3.22   The broad scope of the procurement prohibition was recognised in debates in the House of Commons Standing Committee during passage of the Criminal Justice Bill in which the phrase 'a person who is acting at his direction' may likely result in liability for a principal who has inside information, but whose investment portfolio is handled by someone else on a discretionary basis. For example, this might occur in the case of a fund manager who had the authority to deal in a discretionary manner in securities to which his principal's insider information relates, thus resulting in liability for the principal, despite the principal's lack of knowledge of the specific transaction.

3.23   The government's Economic Secretary responded by stating that whilst it was possible for a person who had transferred its holdings of a portfolio to an investment manager to be exposed to liability as a procurer, 'it may well be that'[45] a person who gives a general direction to another to manage its affairs would not be considered to have directed and, therefore, to have procured dealings in securities which were undertaken by the person with responsibility for managing the fund. Moreover, the minister stated that in cases where there were circumstances to suggest that a person had procured a transaction, the holder of the shares would have a statutory defence if the holder had not genuinely influenced the dealing.[46]

3.24   We have already emphasised that Part V needs to be considered in the context of the general criminal law. For example, while the offence of primary insider dealing does not extend to companies as the statute refers to individuals rather than persons, there is nothing to stop a charge alleging liability as a secondary offender. In the case of *R v Neel and Matthew Uberoi*[47] the Crown Court accepted that on the facts it was appropriate to charge the accused for aiding and abetting the dealing of his father rather than allege procurement. The accused had imparted the relevant information to his father who then dealt with the accused's complete knowledge and agreement, albeit no evidence was put before the court that the accused had benefited personally. Judge Testar had no difficulty considering that the accused was liable as a joint principal in this joint enterprise. He rejected the argument that section 55(4) determined the way in which a person could deal referring to section 54(5) which makes it clear that the circumstances set out in subsection (4) are not exhaustive. Furthermore, he accepted the prosecution's view that section 55(4) was meant to catch those who procured another to deal in circumstances where that other person was not aware that they were engaged in insider dealing. In cases where they were, then it was appropriate to charge a joint enterprise and impose liability as an accessory. Of course, this does not mean that the accused on the facts of this case could not have been just as well charged with procuring the fact that his father was complicit would not have been a defence.[48]

---

44   See HC Deb, Standing Committee B, *Official Report*, 10 June 1993, vol 11, col 171 per the Economic Secretary.
45   See HC Deb, Standing Committee B, *Official Report*, 10 June 1993, vol 11, col 171 and 172 (per Mr Peter Ainsworth MP).
46   See the CJA 1993, s 53(1)(c).
47   (Unreported) Southwark Crown Court, 28 October to 6 November 2009 and see FSA/PN/149/ 2009 and 10 December 2009, FSA/PN/170/2009.
48   *Attorney-General's Reference (No 1 of 1975)* [1975] 61 Cr App R 118 where the Court of Appeal emphasised that it could be appropriate to charge procurement 'even though there is no sort of conspiracy between the two'.

The characteristics of insider information

3.25 Each of the three offences provided for in the CJA 1993 and the FSMA 2000 require that insider information be an essential element of the offence. Commentators have acknowledged, however, that, notwithstanding the statutory definition, inside information is a difficult concept to define in practice. For example, at any one time, a substantial amount of information will be generated within a company and be available to its directors, employees and advisors. Much of this information will be confidential and may have some impact on share prices. Generally, insider dealing law should not be concerned with this type of information, but rather it should focus on information that is essentially extraordinary in nature and which is reasonably certain to have a substantial impact on the market price of securities.[49] Indeed, during debate over the original UK insider dealing law, ministers acknowledged that the kind of knowledge they were concerned with was that of dramatic events and major occurrences that would transform a company's prospects.[50] Over the years it has often been emphasised that the purpose of the law is certainly not to discourage those in an insider relationship with a company from investing in that company. If they act properly then their relationship as an investor is entirely acceptable.[51]

3.26 The CJA 1993 and the FSMA 2000 both assess the quality of information to determine whether it is inside information by use of criteria that seek to ascertain whether or not information has a 'significant effect' on the market price of the security. It is important to remember that in real cases there are likely to be more than one item of information and the prosecution must establish, beyond a reasonable doubt, that each item of information that it seeks to rely on to prove guilt meets all the criteria. In many cases and certainly most of those in which action has been taken under the market abuse regime in the FSMA the information has been relatively sensational and related to take-overs or other major corporate events.[52] Indeed, it is these cases that are often the easiest to detect as the very event when it takes place, operates as a red flag to those interested in market surveillance. Interestingly, however, in the case of prosecutions under Part V other types of information have often been the basis for the allegations. For example, in *R v McQuoid and Melbourne*[53] the inside information was serious negative trading results and in *R v Neel and Matthew Uberoi*[54] the prosecution was based on very positive results from test drillings by an exploration company.

---

49 See 1.15 *et seq* above and in particular *SEC v Texas Gulf Sulfur Co* 401 F 2d 833, 848 (2nd Cir, 1968).
50 Parliamentary Debates, House of Commons, Standing Committee A (debates on the Company Bill), 6 December 1979, col 394.
51 See for example, Herbert Smith Freehills, *A Practical Guide to the UK Listing Regime* (3rd edn) (ICSA 2015), Ch 5 in regard to the Model Code.
52 See in regard to the handling and disclosure of such information Chs 5, 8 and 9 in Herbert Smith Freehills, *A Practical Guide to the UK Listing Regime* (3rd edn) (ICSA 2015).
53 (Unreported) Southwark Crown Court, 9 to 17 March 2009 and FSA/PN/042 2009 see also *R v Neil Rollins* (Unreported) Southwark Crown Court, 16 to 26 November 2010 and FSA/PN/168 2010.
54 (Unreported) Southwark Crown Court, 28 October to 6 November 2009 and FSA/PN/149 2009. In others it has been take-over related, see for example, *R v Malcolm Calvert* (Unreported) Southwark Crown Court, 16 February to 11 March 2010 and FSA/PN/041 2010 and *R v Mustafa and others* (Unreported) Southwark Crown Court, 5 March to 23 July 2012 and FSA/PN/080 2012 and *R v Richard Joseph* (Unreported) Southwark Crown Court, 30 January to 11 March 2013 and FSA/PN/023 2013.

3.27   The CJA 1993 defines inside information by reference to four characteristics as provided in the CJA 1993, section 56:

> '(1)   ... inside information means information which –
>
>> (a)   relates to particular securities or to a particular issuer of securities or to particular issuers of securities and not to securities generally or to issuers of securities generally;
>> (b)   is specific or precise;
>> (c)   has not been made public; and
>> (d)   if it were made public would be likely to have a significant effect on the price of any securities.
>
> (2)   ... securities are "price-affected securities" in relation to inside information, and inside information is "price-sensitive information" in relation to securities, if and only if the information would, if made public, be likely to have a significant effect on the price of the securities'.[55]
>
> (3)   For the purposes of this section 'price' includes value.

The FSMA has also adopted this meaning of the term 'inside information'.

3.28   The characteristics and elements of inside information are such that they should cover information which relates to a specific sector as well as to a specific security, while excluding general information. General information has been defined, for example, under the FSMA, as information which can be obtained by research or analysis conducted by or on behalf of users of a market.[56]

3.29   The approach of the CJA 1993 and the FSMA 2000 conforms with that of the European Directive on Insider Dealing[57] and even seems to accomplish the objective of promoting an efficient market through the timely disclosure of information more effectively than the Directive, which has been criticised on the grounds of obscurity.

Particular securities and particular issuers of securities

3.30   The first of these four characteristics as set out in the CJA 1993 makes clear that information which relates to a specific sector is included, as well as that which relates to a specific security. Accordingly, information may still be inside information, although it has nothing specifically to do with a particular company or its shares, but rather relates to the industry in which that company operates.[58] Similarly, inside information relating to an issuer will include information which comes directly from the issuer. Thus, for example, information about a substantial increase or reduction in profits of a

---

55   CJA 1993, s 56. Under the Company Securities (Insider Dealing) Act 1985, inside information was referred to as 'unpublished price-sensitive information' that contained the following elements:
- the information was not generally to be known to those persons accustomed or likely to deal in the company's securities;
- the information should be likely to affect the price of the securities; and
- the information was such that it would be reasonable to expect a primary insider not to disclose it, except in the proper performance of its functions.

56   FSMA, s 118(7).

57   Council Directive 89/592/EC, Article 1(1).

58   See BAK Rider and M Ashe, *Insider Crime* (Jordan Publishing 1993) at p 30 *et seq.*

company, which clearly has its source within the organisation, will certainly be information which relates to an issuer. The information, however, referred to in the CJA 1993 also includes information that arises from a source outside of the issuer. This may occur in a takeover bid where the proposal to acquire the company's shares emanates from the bidder. Similarly, information relating to securities may be internal, such as dividends, but may be external, such as a decision by the company to be listed on the Stock Exchange.

3.31   There are situations, however, when the question will not be so straightforward regarding when information relates to a particular security or particular issuer or issuers. Although it is clear that the definition does not include information which relates to securities generally or to issuers generally, there is much information which, although not of that general quality, is not related to a particular security, but may, nonetheless, have a significant effect on its price if disclosed to the public.

3.32   If, for example, an employee of Microsoft has, in the course of her employment, gained knowledge that Microsoft is about to submit a bid for the shares of another publicly-held company, this information is likely to be advantageous if she were to purchase shares in the other company. Undoubtedly, the information has its most direct relationship with Microsoft and, because the employee has the information as an insider (and assuming it to be price sensitive, negatively, in relation to Microsoft's shares) she should not deal in Microsoft's shares by selling them before the news becomes generally available with the likely result that their price will drop. Similarly, the information may also have been considered to relate to the target company. It would be curious, if not illogical, if the employee, having obtained the information as an insider, had committed an offence by selling the shares in Microsoft, but not have committed an offence by purchasing shares in the target company. In both cases, the employee was acting on the same information obtained as an insider and in both cases that information would have a significant effect on the prices of each share. Yet, it is arguable that the information did not relate to the target company, rather it only related to Microsoft. It would seem, however, that such a result would offend common sense.

3.33   The CJA 1993, section 60(4) provides clarification on this issue by stating:

> 'For the purposes of this Part, information shall be treated as relating to an issuer of securities which is a company not only where it is about the company but also where it may affect the company's business prospects.'

This provision appears to apply to the above example by ensuring that the information relates not only to Microsoft, but also to the target company, because it will affect the target company's prospects, that is Microsoft's proposed purchase of the shares will likely enhance the value of the target company's shares.

3.34   The statutory provision was criticised as being too broad because of its inclusion of the term 'business prospects' in the definition of insider dealing. The statute's inclusion of the term 'business prospects' was defended by the Earl of Caithness on behalf of the government in debate in the House of Lords when he said:

> 'It is included because the government believes that it is essential our insider dealing legislation catches as inside information, information which, while not relating directly to a company, would nonetheless be likely to have

a significant effect on the price of its shares. An example of information in this category might be important regulatory decisions and information about a company's major customer or supplier'.[59]

3.35   It is generally accepted that the CJA 1993 adopts a broad-based approach to the definition of inside information, together with an expanded approach to who is an insider,[60] but the exclusion from the definition of information which relates to securities generally, or to issuers of securities generally, appears to mean that, for example, confidential information of a particular government economic policy which will impact on the market generally is outside the definition of inside information. In this regard, the CJA 1993 appears to be less strict than the European Directive on Insider Dealing, Article 1(1), which places no such restriction and specifically includes such general news. The Directive, therefore, has a broad scope, as compared to the narrower approach of the CJA 1993. The FSMA 2000 seeks to address this discrepancy by adopting an approach that includes information that affects the market generally, but which may have a specific effect on the issuers of specific securities.

'Specific' or 'precise'

3.36   Inside information must also be characterised by the terms 'specific' or 'precise'. The CJA 1993 includes the word 'specific' because the word 'precise', by itself, may not have covered, for example, information that there will be a huge dividend increase if the quantum of that increase is not indicated. In Australia directors were exonerated from an allegation that they had violated the stock exchanges' timely disclosure policy when they failed to make an announcement that the company was facing significant losses, when the actual amounts had yet to be assessed. The inspectors appointed to inquire into this took the view that a premature statement might, with the benefit of hindsight, have appeared, if wrong, manipulative.[61] Of course, this is a somewhat different issue than whether the information might have been considered inside information.[62] Information is precise when it is exact. The word 'specific' is intended to ensure that information that, for example, involves a large drop in a company's earnings would be considered inside information, while mere rumour and untargeted information cannot.[63]

3.37   Moreover, the use of the word 'specific' may eliminate more than mere rumour and untargeted information. An Australian case held that the phrase 'specific information' meant not merely that the information was precisely definable, but that its entire content can be precisely and 'unequivocally expressed and discerned'.[64] The court concluded that specific information had to be specific in itself and not based on a process of deduction.[65] On this approach, a company that was prepared to purchase a large amount of shares

59   *Parliamentary Debates*, House of Lords, 3 December 1992, col 1501 (The Earl of Caithness).
60   CJA 1993, s 57(2)(a)(ii).
61   Mr PD Connolly QC in his *Report into the affairs of Queensland Syndication Management Pty Ltd and Ors* (1974), see B Rider and HL Ffrench, *The Regulation of Insider Trading* (Macmillan 1979) and B Rider, *Insider Trading* (Jordan Publishing 1980). See also in this regard *Thorold Mackie v HM Advocate* 1994 JC 132, 1995 SLT 110.
62   See generally in regard to the position today in the UK, Herbert Smith Freehills, *A Practical Guide to the UK Listing Regime* (3rd edn) (ICSA 2015) at Ch 8.
63   *Parliamentary Debates*, House of Lords, 3 December 1992, col 1501 (The Earl of Caithness).
64   *Ryan v Triguboff* [1976] 1 NSWLR 588 at 596 per Lee J.
65   *Ryan v Triguboff* at 597.

from several persons would not be considered specific in relation to a similar purchase from one person. Although this view may be attractive, it is often inferences drawn from facts which affect market price and, theoretically, if the facts are not made public, the insider who has them also needs to be restrained from trading on inferences made from those facts as we have indicated above.

3.38 Whatever the correct approach for inferences, information may still be specific even though, as information, it has a vague quality.[66] Thus, information concerning a company's financial problems has been held to be specific.[67] Moreover, information as to the possibility of a takeover may be regarded as specific information[68] and will likely rank as precise, given that it is more than a mere rumour. In cases of secondary insider abuse regard must be had to the facts and in particular the sophistication and knowledge of those involved.[69]

The House of Commons Standing Committee that was considering the Criminal Justice Bill provided some examples of what the words 'specific' and 'precise' would cover.

Example 1

3.39 As the chairman of a company and an analyst walked into a car park, they saw the chairman's battered BMW. The analyst said to the chairman, 'Isn't it time you got a new car?' The chairman replied that he would not buy a new car that year.

3.40 The Economic Secretary considered that these circumstances would lead neither to specific nor precise information in relation to the company, given that there could be many reasons for the statement, including the fact that the chairman may have been experiencing personal financial troubles.[70]

Example 2

3.41 In contrast, if the chairman had remarked that 'Our results will be much better than the market expects or knows' it would not be precise information because there was no disclosure of the company's results, but it would likely be specific information because the chairman would have disclosed information about the company's result, whilst making it clear that the information was not public.[71]

---

66 See *R v Staines and Morrissey* [1997] 2 Cr App E 426 under the earlier provisions.
67 *Public Prosecutor v Choudhury* [1980] 1 MLJ 76 at 78 (Singapore).
68 See *Green v Charterhouse Group of Canada Ltd* (1976) 12 OR (2d) 280. The Ontario Court of Appeal held such information to be specific even though it may not have been worthy of credence or not have been of sufficient weight to justify any positive action by the board.
69 See in particular *R v Staines and Morrissey* [1997] 2 Cr App R 426 in which it was considered information that was imparted during a guessing game was nonetheless sufficiently precise as it was relatively easy for those involved to put two and two together. Lord Bingham LCJ stated 'The most obvious case of insider dealing plainly occurs where a connected person tells a friend that he is advising a client who is prepared to make a bid for the share capital of named Company B. But there will doubtless occur less obvious cases where a connected person supplies a friend with information which enables the friend to identify Company B. It all depends upon what is said and to whom. Material which may be meaningless to a hearer ignorant of the operation of the securities market may be of great significance to a sophisticated city analyst.'
70 HC Deb, Standing Committee B, *Official Report*, 10 June 1993, vol 11, col 171.
71 See the comments of the Economic Secretary, HC Deb, Standing Committee B, *Official Report*, 10 June 1993, vol 11, col 175.

3.42 Some commentators have also noted that the section 56 of the CJA 1993's requirement that information be specific or precise was drafted more broadly than EC Directive 89/592, which required in Article 1 that the information be of 'a precise nature' only.[72]

3.43 While there have in practice been relatively few problems in the case of primary insider abuse X problems have arisen in meeting the criteria on cases of secondary insider dealing. In cases where the information is transmitted through another, complicit or otherwise, then in the nature of things it is likely that it will suffer some distortion. In many ways this is simply a manifestation of the old parlour game 'Chinese Whispers'. It is also the case that the more information is relayed down a line of communication, possibly involving a number of individuals it becomes rather more difficult for the prosecution to establish the insider nexus.[73]

'Made public'

3.44 Perhaps the most important criteria that must be met before information will be considered inside information is that it has not been made public. Indeed, this goes to the very heart of the matter and is set out in section 56. This section provides that it has to be established by the prosecution that the information has not been made public.[74] This is a relatively rare example in the criminal justice system of the prosecution having to prove a negative.[75] In many cases that have come before the courts and have been the basis of FCA proceedings under the market abuse provisions in the FSMA, the defence has contended that in fact the relevant information has all or in part been in the public domain before the trading that is complained of took place. It is clear,

---

72 See the discussion in J Fisher and J Bewsey, *The Law of Investor Protection* (Sweet & Maxwell 1997) p 291 and generally R Alexander, *Insider Dealing and Money Laundering in the EU: Law and Regulation* (Ashgate 2007).

73 Compliance systems which record certain communications and conversations may prove to be invaluable as they would have done in *R v Sanders and others* (Unreported) Southwark Crown Court, 20 June 2012 and FSA/PN/060/ 2012 and FSA/PN/067/ 2012 if the defendants had not decided to plead guilty. Of course, there may well be legal and in particular privacy related issues in recording conversations outside a compliance system.

74 As in the case of many other issues, in a prosecution under Part V expert evidence will often play an important part for both the defence and prosecution. Having said this, it has not always proved particularly easy to identify expertise. In the early days of anti-insider dealing regulation it was not uncommon for the prosecution to experience considerable difficulty in persuading competent experts to testify on acceptable City practice. There appeared to be a perception that to do so was letting the 'side' down. For a good discussion of the responsibilities of the prosecutor in regard to discharging the burden of showing the information in question has not been made public, see S Clark, *Insider Dealing, Law and Practice* (Oxford University Press 2013) at p 79 *et seq*. See also *Madhavan v Public Prosecutor (Singapore)* [2012] SGCA 49.

75 The original drafts of the Criminal Justice Bill that were introduced in the House of Lords provided no guidance for defining what was meant by the phrase 'made public'. See BAKRider and M Ashe, *Insider Crime* (Jordan Publishing 1993) at p 34. The previous law provided that the information should 'not be generally known to those persons who are accustomed or would be likely to deal in those securities (Company Securities (insider Dealing) Act 1985, s 10(b)). The Government (Mr Anthony Nelson MP) in introducing Part V emphasised that s 58 is intended 'to bring a good deal more clarity and a good deal more understanding on the part of those who will have to operate within the law ...' (HC Deb, Session 1992-93, Standing Committee B, 10 June 1993, col 182). Indeed, the Government claimed that it was this issue upon which it had received the most comment and expressions of concern.

however, that it is not sufficient for the defence to assert merely that there is general information in the market or speculative rumours, or even some in the market have made what appear to be recommendations,[76] as section 56(1) needs to be considered as a whole and all the criteria met.

3.45   Under the CJA 1993, section 58(2) inside information is made public or is to be treated as made public in the following circumstances:

• if the information is published in accordance with the rules of a regulated market for the purpose of informing investors and their professional advisors;
• if the information is contained in records which, by virtue of any enactment, are given to inspection by the public;
• if the information can be readily acquired by those likely to deal in any securities to which the information relates or of an issuer to which the information relates; or
• if the information is derived from information which has been made public.

3.46   In addition, CJA 1993, section 58(3) provides five circumstances when information may be treated as having been made public and it is important to note that these are not exhaustive.[77] These are where information:

• can only be acquired by persons exercising diligence or expertise;
• is communicated to a section of the public and not to the public at large;
• can only be acquired by observation;
• is only communicated on payment of a fee; or
• is only published outside the UK.[78]

3.47   The above definitions state that information may be treated as public, even though further efforts have to be made to obtain the information. This accords with the broad scope of the definition of 'made public' in European Directive 89/592, which provides that information derived from publicly available data cannot be regarded as inside information and any transaction executed on the basis of such information would not constitute insider dealing under the broad definition of the Directive.

Information published according to the rules of a regulated market

3.48   Publication of information will not necessarily deprive insiders of their advantages because markets often take time to absorb information. There prior knowledge allows them to steal a march on the rest of the market by trading the instant the information becomes public. We have referred to this in our preliminary discussion of what may be properly considered to be insider dealing.[79] It is generally accepted in the vast majority of financial markets that prices do not adjust immediately upon the release of material information. There needs to be a period for digestion. Accordingly, US securities law recognises this market reality by imposing liability on insiders for transactions undertaken before the market has assimilated the information.[80] Indeed, there are US cases

---

76   See for example *R v Neel and Matthew Uberoi* (Unreported) Southwark Crown Court, 28 October to 6 November 2009.
77   CJA 1993, s 58(2).
78   CJA 1993, s 58(3).
79   See at 1.39 *et seq* above.
80   *SEC v Texas Gulf Sulfur Co* 401 F 2d 833 (2nd Cir, 1968); and *SEC v MacDonald* 699F 2d 47 (1st Cir, 1983).

which suggest that even proximity to the market may create unfair advantage. However, it is also true in the USA that the authorities have declined to set out clear guidelines and have relied instead on the judges to do justice on the facts of each case.[81]

3.49 With computer assisted trading systems the potential for reaping the benefits through almost instantaneous dealing are so much greater. Prior to the enactment of the present law, the Company Securities (Insider Dealing) Act 1985 would arguably have prohibited insiders from immediately dealing on insider information after announcement until prices had adjusted to the information. Insiders were therefore strongly advised if not actually required to wait for the market to assimilate the information. The European Directive on Insider Dealing has also been given this interpretation.[82] However, considering how notoriously difficult it is to assess at what point in time a market has fully digested information there was an unfortunate degree of uncertainty.[83]

3.50 Section 58(2)(a) of the CJA 1993 clarifies the procedure for insiders to know when they can trade on information just released to the market. It adopts a procedure for notifying information to the Stock Exchange[84] that contains the following requirements: (a) the information which issuers wish to release to the public must be delivered in the form of an announcement to the Company Announcements Office; (b) the Stock Exchange then arranges for the prompt publication of announcements through its Regulatory News Service; and (c) at this point, for example, there could be an announcement on that the information will be 'made public' for the purposes of the CJA 1993.

3.51 We address the obligations on companies to make proper and timely disclosures in Chapter 9. The FCA Listing Rules provide that no information may be released to a third party before such information is released to the

---

81 In *Dirks v SEC* 463 US 646 (1983) Blackmun J. stated 'the SEC has been less than helpful in its view of the nature of disclosure necessary to satisfy the disclose or refrain duty. The Commission tells persons with inside information that they cannot trade on that information unless they disclose; it refuses, however, to tell them how to disclose. This seems to be a less than sensible policy ...'. On the relevant US law see W Wang and M Steinberg, *Insider Trading* (3rd edn) (Oxford University Press 2010), Ch 4.

82 See Klaus J Hopt, 'The European Insider Dealing Directive' (1990) 27 *CMLR* 51. The recital to the Directive states that investors should be 'placed on equal footing'.

83 There was also a concern to reduce the scope for essentially economic argument on the efficiency of markets. According to the market efficiency theory it is possible to determine the strength of markets and sectors of markets by virtue of their ability to draw in and discount in the price of traded securities various types of information. In a highly efficient or strongly efficient market there should be no significant items of information, inside or otherwise, that have not already at a moment in time, been fully discounted in the actual price of a security. In such an ideal market there is no room for asymmetrical information and therefore what might be described as inside information has no value. Of course, in reality no such perfect market exists, although it is true that technology, albeit a two edged sword, has made a contribution both to efficiency and the exploitation of asymmetrical information balances. See generally W Wang and M Steinberg, *Insider Trading* (3rd edn) (Oxford University Press 2010), Ch 2.

84 See generally The Listing Rules, Chapter 9 and Herbert Smith Freehills, *A Practical Guide to the UK Listing Regime* (3rd edn) (ICSA 2015), Chs 4 and 9, and the Traded Securities (Disclosure) Regulations 1994 (SI 1994/188) giving effect to Article 7 of the European Directive 89/592 [1989] OJ L334/30. This is a complex area of practice and is one where the law relating to insider dealing, market abuse and transparency particularly in regard to companies with securities traded on recognised investment exchanges overlap. In particular note the impact of the European Union Market Abuse Regulation (EU 592/2014) which takes effect in July 2016 and introduces new rules and guidance in particular in relation to the delaying of disclosure and insider lists. The Regulation is directly applicable and does not require implementation in English law.

Company Announcements Office. If announcements are made outside the operational hours of the Regulatory News Service, however, the information must be given to two or more UK national newspapers and to two news services to ensure adequate coverage. This information must also be lodged with the Company Announcements Office no later than it is given to the other parties. In these circumstances, the information would appear to have been made public on publication of the newspapers. The CJA 1993 definition of 'made public' provides the advantage of clarity because it avoids the uncertainty of waiting for the market to absorb the news by providing a clearer set of standards as to the time when insiders may deal.

Information contained in public records

3.52 By virtue of section 58(2)(b) information will be regarded as being made public if it is contained on records which, by virtue of any enactment, are open to inspection by the public. This covers registers set up under the statute, such as companies' or patents' registers or in publications such as the Official Gazette.[85]

Information readily acquired by people 'likely to deal' in securities

3.53 Information will be considered 'public' when it can readily be acquired by those likely to deal in any securities to which or to whose issuer the information relates (1).[86] The phrase 'likely to deal' in securities is a term of art having its origin in the Company Securities (Insider Dealing) Act 1985, which defined it as 'unpublished price-sensitive information' (2).[87] Although it could be argued that the phrase only embraces the market professionals who deal in securities, such as market makers who are clearly 'likely to deal', it is also possible that it refers to the market in the shares itself. If information can readily be acquired by the market, that information is already likely to have made its price impact and is, therefore, not properly to be regarded as inside information. Thus, it is treated as having been 'made public'.

Information derived from information made public

3.54 Information is considered 'public' if it originates from information which has been 'made public'.[88] As we have noted it is in the public interest that information is sifted and analysed by professional experts to facilitate good investment decisions by others. Of course, problems may well arise when not all the facts let alone inferences upon which a report is written are publicly available. The CJA 1993 addresses the problem posed by an analyst who has knowledge of the company and industry and who can put together seemingly inconsequential data with public information into a mosaic which reveals material non-public information. Whenever managers, advisors and analysts meet in non-public places, there will be a risk that the analysts will

---

85   HC Deb, Standing Committee B, *Official Report*, 10 June 1993, vol 11, col 184 (per the Economic Secretary). The Minister pointed out that this would not cover for example, material in obscure public documents that are not governed by statute.
86   CJA 1993, s 58(2)(c).
87   Company Securities (Insider Dealing) Act 1985, s 10(b) and see above.
88   CJA 1993, s 58(2)(d).

take away knowledge of material information which is not publicly available. This should not be a violation of UK law so long as the mosaic, which contains inside information, is derived from information which has been made public.

3.55   It is not entirely clear what information that is 'readily available' actually means. As in regard to the other tests it will be a question of fact. Information that is only available through subscription may qualify, but much will depend on how available the service actually is and its cost. It has been questioned whether publication in an obscure newssheet would be acceptable. This has been an issue in certain other jurisdictions, particularly where there is a diversity of languages.[89] Obviously developments in technology and the internet have rendered even quite obscure publications reasonably readily available. Consequently, perhaps today the test is rather more relaxed than when it was initially provided in the legislation. This is certainly the view of many professional analysts and journalists. It is also arguable that the fact that the information may belong to another person who might consider it to be confidential, would not stop a court considering that it is in fact readily available to the public.[90]

3.56   It might also be appropriate here to consider two other issues to which reference has been made in Chapter 1. Firstly, it is the situation when a person has knowledge that an analyst is about to recommend a particular security but does not have access to the detail of the analyst's report. Is this inside information? In such cases the pre-knowledge relates to likely market impact. In the USA the courts have generally accepted that there should be liability, provided that the information is material and it is appreciated that it is improperly obtained or used.[91] In the United Kingdom knowledge that a company is going to act in a certain way in regard to securities should be sufficient basis for liability, provided the information meets the criteria that we have discussed. A related issue involves journalists who, having written on a particular event that is price sensitive in relation to particular security or who like an analyst write up a security or issuer, trade prior to the article's publication. Again we have discussed this in the context of insider dealing.[92] It is probable that under Part V journalists could not be considered to have possession of inside information justifying a conviction for insider dealing.[93]

---

89   See for example the discussion in B Rider, 'The regulation of Insider trading in the Republic of South Africa', (1977) 94 *South African Law Journal* 437.

90   Information may cease to be confidential if it is disclosed by its owner, *Mustad & Sons v Dosen* [1964] 1 WLR 109 or by a third person, although in such cases there may be a financial claim, see *Attorney General v Guardian Newspapers Ltd (No 2)* [1990] 1 AC 109, but note the caution of Lord Neuberger in regard to the conscience of those who receive information and then use it in *Vestergaard Frandsen A/S and others v Bestnet Europe Ltd* [2013] UKSC 31. In *The Observer and Guardian v UK*, Application No 13585/88, 26 November 1991 the availability of material overseas prevented the UK Government obtaining an injunction to prevent its publication in the UK.

91   See generally W Wang and M Steinberg, *Insider Trading* (3rd edn) (Oxford University Press 2010) and see in particular *US v Winans* 612 F Supp (1985) 827 and *US v Carpenter* 791 F 2d 1024 (end Cir 1986) and from the perspective of the Hong Kong courts *Nanus Asia Co Inc v Standard Chartered Bank* [1990] 1 HKLR 396.

92   See 1.37 above and for an example of this see the City Press case discussed in B Rider, *Insider Trading* (Jordan Publishing 1980) at p 121 *et seq* and for an early discussion of the issues B Rider and HL Ffrench, *The Regulation of Insider Trading* (1979) Ch 6.

93   See *R v Hipwell, Bhoyeul and Shepherd* (Unreported) Southwark Crown Court 7 December 2005 involving charges for conspiracy to commit an offence under what today would be Part 7 of the Financial Services Act 2012. Of course, bodies such as the Panel on Take-overs and Mergers and various professional bodies have long taken a dim view of such practices.

However, this would not mean that they might not be liable in the civil law and for other offences. If a journalist in writing his article or in the conduct of his research receives inside information the matter would be very different.

Information obtained as a result of diligence and expertise

3.57 So far our discussion of the circumstances where information that otherwise satisfies the criteria for being considered inside information, becomes public, are mandatory in the sense that if the court finds that the circumstances fall within the provisions the information will loose its liability. Section 58(3) sets out, as we have seen, five situations in which the court may but does not have to regard the information as being publicly available. It has been noted that the statement in section 58(1) that the list of circumstances are not exhaustive seemingly applies to both following subsections. However, in the case of those discussed above under section 58(2) this would seem to be in practical terms meaningless. Under section 58(3)(a) a court may regard information as sufficiently publicly available if it can be acquired only by persons exercising diligence or expertise. This allows the court to protect the highly diligent and resourceful analyst or investor, which is in the interests of the market. It also addresses the problem of highly specialised, esoteric and obscure publications and sources of information. It is important to remember that each case will be judged on its facts.

Information communicated to only a section of the public

3.58 Section 58(3)(b) provides that the court may consider information to be public even if it is communicated to only a section of the public and not the general public. It is thought that this was included to allow the court discretion where the information is, for example, only available through an expensive or restricted service. Again it is going to be a question of fact. Of course, given that the court has discretion - issues of fairness and public policy will no doubt play a role.

Observed information

3.59 The third situation in which the court may consider that information is sufficiently in the public domain is when it can be acquired by observation.[94] The example given in the debate introducing this legislation is not particularly helpful or for that matter sensible. It was suggested that one could observe that a factory was working overtime if smoke was billowing from its factory chimneys at night time! On another occasion a minister referred to insiders looking affluent – again not particularly helpful as neither inference would be sufficiently specific and precise. The City panel on Take-overs and Mergers has had cases involving alleged violations of its rules on the misuse of privileged information involving site visits to businesses where it has been observed the employees appear to be exceptionally busy.[95] It has also been suggested that

---

94 CJA 1993, s 58(3)(c).
95 See B Rider, 'Self-regulation: The British approach to policing conduct in the securities business with particular reference to the role of the City Panel on Take-overs and Mergers in the regulation of insider trading' (1978) 1 *Journal of Comparative Corporate Law and Securities Regulation* 319. Without additional information the Panel in most cases involving mere observation, while emphasising the need for caution in giving privileged and possibly unfair access, did not consider that Rule 30 had been violated.

information observed from a document that was intended to be confidential but has been publicly exhibited might also fall within this test. An example of this might be the case of the senior police officer being photographed entering Downing Street to meet the Prime Minister holding highly classified papers. When enlarged the front page was easily readable and was widely carried in the media.[96] Although on the facts such a case might be better dealt with under one of the other statutory tests, it might be in not dissimilar circumstances possible to claim that the relevant information was clearly observable. Perhaps a better view is that the knowledge should be obtainable by mere observation and not require the intervention of others. A better example, might therefore be seeing a serious fire in the main plant of a company.[97]

Information that is available for a price

3.60   Section 58(3)(d) makes it clear that information that is communicated only on the payment of a fee may nonetheless still be considered sufficiently public. Of course, this also relates to the publication of information through services and in publications which are only available on subscription or for a specific charge. Where the cost of acquiring the information is very significant or disproportionate then it may well be that the court will consider that the relevant information is not public. An interesting point is that for this provision to be relevant the information should conform to the criteria for inside information. Therefore, the provision would seemingly apply to circumstances where a person with what is inside information is making it available to others for a fee. Indeed, it has long been though that one of the most insidious types of insider abuse is where inside information is obtained, possibly in unlawful circumstances, and then retailed or exchanged.[98] There is some evidence of this occurring in the UK, France[99] and the USA, but to a much greater extent in places such as Hong Kong[100] and particularly Japan.[101] Of course, deeming the information not inside information for those who acquire it on payment of a fee, would not prevent a prosecution of the informer. To avoid liability as a tippee the court would need to be persuaded by the recipient that the information was not offered to only a very limited number of individuals.

Information that has been published outside the UK

3.61   Section 58(3)(e) provides that information that is published only outside the United Kingdom may still be considered to be publicly available for the purposes of Part V. This provision is mean to address the issue that we

---

96   Mr Bob Quick, then head of counter-terrorism in the Metropolitan Police, *Guardian* 9 April 2009. A similar incident occurred in regard to the Secretary of State for International development, Mr Andrew Mitchell MP, *Guardian* 30 August 2011.
97   See S Clark, *Insider Dealing, Law and Practice* (Oxford University Press 2013) at p 77.
98   See B Rider and TM Ashe (eds) *Money Laundering Control* (Sweet and Maxwell 1996) at Ch 3. See also *Report on Organised Crime in the U.K.*, Home Affairs Committee, House of Commons (1993 and 1994).
99   B Rider and HL Ffrench, 'The Regulation of Insider Trading in Corporate Securities in France' (1977) 26 *International and Comparative Law Quarterly* 619.
100 B Rider 'The Regulation of Insider Trading in Hong Kong' (1975) 17 *Mal Law Review* 310, continued 18 *Mal Law Review* 157.
101 See B Rider and TM Ashe (eds) *Money Laundering Control* (Sweet and Maxwell 1996) at Ch 11 (C Nakajima) and B Rider and HL Ffrench, *The Regulation of Insider Trading* (Macmillan 1979).

have already raised about publications that are available predominantly outside the UK. Obviously much will depend upon the nature of the publication and how likely it is to be picked up internationally. With the development of the internet and specialised search engines, giving the court a discretion is not unreasonable. In practice attempting to show what information might have been available on the internet, had one searched competently, several years after the relevant event is not an easy task and is one which will often involve the use of expert witnesses.[102]

3.62   Finally, it is worth again emphasising that these tests are not exhaustive and it is open to the court to rule that information has become public albeit none of the above tests are satisfied. Having said this, it is difficult to imagine a scenario which could not be justified under one of the relevant subsections.

Price sensitivity

3.63   The final aspect of the definition of 'insider information' is the price sensitivity of the information. The test is that if the information were made public, it would be likely to have a significant effect on the securities. This is the most essential feature of the statutory definition of inside information. This criterion, rather than the issue of how qualitative the information actually is, is what really matters and which, ultimately, will be the determining factor when a jury considers whether information is inside information. While there is little debate as to the utility of a market impact test, there has been some degree of controversy primarily in the USA and particularly in the academy, as to whether given the nature of the misconduct any degree of impact should be considered to be an unfair and therefore potentially unlawful advantage. It is further contended that today with the ability to engage in high volume computer assisted trading, miniscule price impacts can result in vast fortunes being made. Certainly recent investigations in the USA would tend to support the view that this does occur. Having said this, the approach in the UK and the rest of Europe has traditionally been to focus on significant and major events which clearly have noticeable market impact. This was made clear in the Parliamentary debates on the bill that became Part V and is reflected in the history of the European Directive. While in theory the ability of market surveillance systems is far greater today, the reality is that technology has also developed to serve those who wish to obscure their activities and hide their identities.

3.64   Price sensitivity can only be determined at the moment of the deal when, by definition, the information is not known to the public and can have no impact on the price. Indeed, the information that the insider uses may subsequently not have any significant impact on the market. For example, in *R v Sanders and others*, the anticipated take-over did not in fact materialise.[103] Nonetheless at the time that the transactions took place the information would have impacted on the price of the shares had it been known. In cases where the insider has dealt close to the time when the information was made public, the

---

102   See for example, *R v Mustafa and others* (Unreported) Southwark Crown Court, 5 March to 23 July 2012. In this case the expert witness was able to assist the court with the sources that may have been available at the relevant time. In practice given the nature of the cases that come to trial this is not the hurdle that it might at first seem for the prosecution.

103   (Unreported) Southwark Crown Court, 20 June 2012 and see FSA/PN/060 2012.

courts may rely on evidence that measures price sensitivity by the effect of the information on the market.[104] It is, however, a decision of fact for the jury and this is to be made to the best evidence available and this may be that of expert witnesses.[105]

3.65   Because the CJA 1993 provides no further guidance, the UK courts in considering the evidence have set it against what a reasonable investor would have done. In other Commonwealth jurisdictions judges have adopted a reasonable investor test and held that information will be price sensitive if it is information which would influence the ordinary reasonable investor to buy or sell the security in question. In *R v Sanders and others*[106] Simon J seemingly accepted the expert view of the prosecution that if a movement of about 10% in the price of a security could be reasonably anticipated then it would be significant. While the defence did not challenge this and a similar approach appears to have been accepted in subsequent cases, it would be dangerous to assume that this is a hard and fast rule. The courts have also accepted the proposition that it is necessary to show that the movement in price is not accounted for by normal market movements, in other words it has to be exceptional.[107]

Territorial scope of the offence

3.66   The territorial scope of the offence of insider dealing is clearly set out in section 62(1) of the Act. It provides that an individual is not guilty of an offence under section 52(1) unless he is in the UK at the time he is alleged to have done any act constituting or forming part of the alleged dealing or the dealing took place on a regulated market or the professional intermediary was within the UK at the time of the alleged dealing. As we have seen regulated markets are those designated as such by statutory instrument.[108] This territorial limitation cannot be avoided by alleging that an individual who is not at the time of the dealing in the UK, and did not trade on a UK regulated market or with or through a UK based professional intermediary, is in a joint enterprise with someone who does meet the territorial qualifications.[109] It is important to note as has been pointed out elsewhere purely private deals, even involving securities covered by the CJA 1993, fall outside the scope of the offence. By contrast, the FSMA market abuse regime covers both transactions by regulated persons and dealing by private persons off regulated exchanges.

---

104   *Chase Manhattan Equities Ltd v Goodman* [1991] BCLC 897 at 931 (per Knox J).
105   See for example *R v Neel and Matthew Uberoi* (Unreported) Southwark Crown Court, 28 October to 6 November 2009; *R v Calvert* (Unreported) Southwark Crown Court, 16 February to 11 March 2010 and *R v Gray* (1995) 2 Cr App R 100.
106   See above at note 103.
107   See for example, the prosecution evidence in *R v Mustafa and others* (Unreported) Southwark Crown Court, 5 March to 23 July 2012, FSA/PN/080/ 2012 and *R v Richard Joseph* (Unreported) Southwark Crown Court, 30 January to 11 March 2013, FSA/PN/023/203.
108   As we have seen regulated markets in the UK for the purposes of Part V are those which are those markets established under the rules of the regulated markets set out in art 10 of the Insider Dealing (Securities and Regulated Markets) Order 1994, as amended by further orders in 2000 and 2002. The names of some of the markets have changed and there have also been mergers and de-recognitions. The most important regulated market is the London Stock Exchange Ltd, but effectively the all organised formal markets in the UK are included.
109   *R v Ammann, Weckwerth and Mang* (Unreported) Southwark Crown Court, 24 May 2012.

ENCOURAGING INSIDER DEALING

3.67   As we have seen there are many practical reasons why primary insiders might choose not to abuse the relevant information themselves. The English law in accordance with the European Directive throws the net of criminal liability over situations where the primary insider encourages another to deal or actually discloses the privileged information to another person. It should be noted that in both cases the statute uses the word person[110] and therefore the individual who is a primary insider will commit an offence if he encourages a company to deal or discloses, without proper authority, inside information to a company or individual. Section 52(2)(a) provides that an individual is guilty of insider dealing if he encourages another person to deal in securities that are, whether or not that other person knows, price-affected securities in relation to the relevant information. The individual encouraging the other to deal must know or have reasonable grounds to believe that the dealing would take place on a regulated market or through or with a professional intermediary. Of course, if that person is himself a professional intermediary this is sufficient for the offence.

3.68   It is not a requirement of the offence for the individual who has the information as an insider to pass this information to the other person, nor is it necessary that the other person should know that the securities he or it is encouraged to buy, are price-affected securities. The offence covers the classic situation where a tip is given by an insider to another, for example, 'sell as many shares of XYC plc as you can before tomorrow's profit report'. Obviously, this could also include a number of other situations.

3.69   If the insider knows or has reasonable cause to believe that the other person will deal on a regulated market or through a professional intermediary, the offence will be committed even if, in fact, the other person does not undertake a transaction. In practice, however, it is probable that a transaction will have taken place as otherwise it may be extremely difficult to identify the crime.[111] A defence is available where no dealing was expected or anticipated.[112] It is also important to appreciate, as we have seen, that if deals in securities do not occur on a recognised investment exchange, they will only be within the insider dealing legislation if the person dealing relies on a professional intermediary or is himself a professional intermediary. A person will rely on a professional intermediary only if the professional intermediary either acquires or disposes of securities (whether as principal or agent) in relation to the dealing or acts as intermediary between persons taking part in the dealing.[113]

DISCLOURE OF INSIDE INFORMATION

3.70   A primary insider will, as we have pointed out, also be guilty of insider dealing if he discloses the relevant information to another person, including a company, without proper authority. Section 52(2)(b) provides that an individual who has information, as an insider, is guilty of the offence of

---

110   See the Interpretation Act 1978 (Sch 1).
111   See for example, *R v Sanders and others* (Unreported) Southwark Crown Court 20 June 2012, where the defendant pleaded guilty to encouraging clients and fellow professional traders to deal in a certain security, while in possession of inside information.
112   CJA 1993, s 52(3).
113   CJA 1993, s 59(1)(a).

insider dealing if he discloses the relevant information, otherwise than in the proper performance of the functions of his employment, office or profession to another person. The Take-over Panel has over the years had many cases where information has been disclosed or tips given that are not necessarily motivated by any direct financial interest on the part of the informant. In one case highly price-sensitive information was disclosed to friends and relatives at a wedding party by way of an excuse for the late arrival of the insider. In another case information was disclosed to a girlfriend to impress her. In another investigation colleagues were given tips again for the primary purpose of impressing them. Under section 52(2)(b) for the offence to be proven it does not have to be shown that the primary insider had any particular reason let alone motive for disclosing the information. Indeed, in contradistinction to the encouragement offence he does not have to know or have reason to believe that any dealing, let alone on a regulated market or with a professional intermediary, is likely to take place. The offence is complete on disclosure. It follows that the recipient need not be shown to have either understood it or acted upon it.

3.71 Part V is silent as to what 'otherwise than in the proper performance of the functions of his employment, office or profession' means. In some respects this is similar to section 57(2)(a)(ii) which defines insiders as *inter alia* those who have access to the relevant information 'by virtue' of employment, office or profession. Debate has taken place in regard to this subsection in the context of an employee acquiring the information in breach of their duties as an employee – for example, obtaining access to a colleague's office or computer without proper authority. It has been argued that it is the opportunity to obtain access to the information that is critical and if this is in fact given to an individual by virtue of his employment it matters not that in the circumstances he may be in breach of his employment contract.[114] Of course, in practice this is not a major problem as he will in any case be aware that he is taking the information from an inside source and will therefore be a secondary insider. Determining in the case of section 57(2)(b) what is meant by the proper performance of his functions has possibly more significant implications as it could well determine guilt. What of a senior broker who discloses information to a colleague, in accordance with what he and perhaps even his compliance officer considers to actually be the proper function of his position? What about a lawyer who, with the benefit of hindsight, told the client too much detail? While this is essentially a question of fact, there is room for argument as a matter of law as to what is and is not the proper performance of an obligation.[115]

3.72 Debate has also centred on exactly what needs to be disclosed to justify criminal liability. The former law had the offences of counselling and procuring which perhaps more clearly addressed the situation where an insider

114 See 1.11 above.
115 In *Grongaard and Bang* the European Court interpreted Article 3(a) of the European Directive upon which s 52(2)(b) is based. The ECJ considered that the requirement that the information be disclosed in the 'normal course of the exercise of his employment, profession or duties' should be strictly construed. The disclosure would only be acceptable if it was directly pursuant to the discharge of a specific obligation arising by virtue of employment or a professional duty and this was to be determined by the relevant domestic law. The ECJ referred to the objective of the Directive in promoting investor confidence and therefore thought that a narrow interpretation of this exception was justified, *C-384/02 Grongaard and Bang* [2006] ECR I-9939, [2006] IRLR 214.

simply tips someone else that a particular security would be a good buy.[116] In such cases today a charge of encouraging would be appropriate and it is important to remember that these offences operate within the general criminal law.[117] It should also be emphasised that the definition of dealing in section 55 also catches procurement as we have seen. Section 55(1)(b) provides that a person deals on securities if he procures, directly or indirectly, an acquisition or disposal of the securities by any other person. For liability under section 52(2)(b) the insider must disclose 'the information' and therefore what is imparted must count as inside information under the various criteria that we have discussed above. Consequently the prosecution will need to establish that exactly what was disclosed would be sufficient to charge the insider with dealing under section 52(1) if in fact he had dealt rather than tipped.

TERRITORIAL SCOPE OF OFFENCES RELATING TO ENCOURAGEMENT AND DISCLOSURE

3.73   Under section 62(2) of the Act an individual is not guilty of the offence of encouraging another to deal or of disclosing inside information to another person unless he was within the United Kingdom at the time when it is alleged he made the disclosure or encouraged the dealing, or the alleged recipient of the information or encouragement was in the United Kingdom at that time.

TIPPEE LIABILITY

3.74   The third type of insider liability[118] created by the CJA 1993 and expanded upon and applied in the market abuse regime of the FSMA is tippee liability.[119] Tippee liability arises when a person who has information, as an insider, obtains such information, either directly or indirectly, from a person who falls within one of the other two categories of insider, namely, directors, employees or shareholders of issuers or those who have access to inside information, by virtue of their employment, office or profession.

3.75   The essential elements of tippee liability are that the tippee must know that the information is inside information and that such information is derived from an inside source. In many cases, tippees and sub-tippees will not know that information is inside information. Indeed, the classic tip will involve a statement such as, for example, 'sell XYZ plc' or 'buy ABC plc'. Under these circumstances, no inside information will have been conveyed because, although the individual who gave the tip will have committed the offence

---

116   See Company Securities (Insider Dealing) Act 1985, s 1(7) discussed in B Rider, C Abrams and C Ferran, *Guide to the Financial Services Act 1986* (2nd edn) (CCH 1987), Ch 7.
117   See generally Serious Crime Act 2007, Part 2 in regard to the offences of encouraging and assisting crime and D Ormerod and R Fortson, 'Serious Crime Act 2007; the Part 2 Offences' (2009) *Crim LR* 389.
118   CJA 1993, s 57(2)(b).
119   In fact, when the word 'tippee' was included in the Criminal Justice Bill in 1992, it drew strong opposition from their Lordships and the word was eventually withdrawn before the Bill was approved in the House of Lords; see Parliamentary Debates, House of Lords, 19 November 1992, cols 756–767 and 3 December 1992, col 1496. See the discussion in BAK Rider and M Ashe, *Insider Crime* (Jordan Publishing 1993) at p 46.

of encouragement, the tippee will not have obtained the 'information as an insider' (even though the tippee knows the tip came from an inside source) and would, therefore, appear to be outside the scope of the provision's coverage.

3.76   The CJA 1993 significantly expanded the scope of the criminal law in defining 'insider' to include primary and secondary insiders, such as tippees who did not have a connection with the company whose securities were traded. Primary insiders, as we have seen, are those individuals who have inside information through being a director, employee or shareholder of an issuer of securities or by having access to the information by virtue of their employment, office or profession.[120] The latter category of primary insider could include an individual who obtains inside information and thereby becomes a primary insider by virtue of his or her employment, office or profession, without necessarily having any direct professional, fiduciary or contractual connection with the company whose securities were traded.[121] The category of persons having access to inside information by virtue of their employment, office or profession is potentially large and includes professional advisers such as lawyers, merchant bankers, accountants, public relations specialists and the like. Whilst it would not be unreasonable to expect such persons to assume the responsibilities of insider status on a temporary basis, the section's language is wide enough to cover many others performing rather more peripheral services to an issuer. These examples of temporary insiders might be office cleaners, temporary secretarial staff, postmen and couriers who have access to inside information by virtue of their employment. Although these groups would certainly have the opportunity to acquire inside information by engaging in the activities of their employment, it is questionable, as we have seen, whether the scope of insider liability should be cast so widely.

SECONDARY PERSONS AND TIPPEE LIABILITY

3.77   The CJA 1993 defines a person as having information as an insider if, and only if, the person subjectively knows that it is inside information and possesses such information, and subjectively – in other words actually knows that he has it, from an inside source.[122] As we have seen before a person can be convicted of the offence of insider dealing, the prosecution must prove beyond all reasonable doubt that the individual concerned was fully aware that the information was 'inside information' as defined under the CJA 1993, section 56 and that the individual received the information from an inside source. It is proving these elements to the criminal standard of proof that has render insider dealing cases one of the most difficult types of economic crime to obtain convictions.[123]

---

120   CJA 1993, s 57(2)(a).
121   See for example *R v Holyoak, Hill and Morl*, Financial Times 28 October 1989 where the defendants (who were in fact acquitted) were employees of a firm of accountants which was acting for one of the parties in a takeover negotiation.
122   The better view is that in a prosecution under s 52 the prosecution must establish actual knowledge and reckless indifference or wilful blindness will not be sufficient. The European Directive in Article 2(1) refers to liability being predicated on 'full knowledge of the facts'.
123   In some cases it will be necessary to rely on circumstantial evidence, see for a good example of this, *R v Rupinder Sidhu* (Unreported) Southwark Crown Court, 28 November to 15 December 2011 and FSA/PN/114/ 2011.

3.78   The CJA 1993, section 57(2) provides the legal basis for tippee liability as a criminal offence. It describes the ways in which tippee liability may arise as follows:

'(2)   For the purposes of subsection (1), a person has information from an inside source if and only if –

(a)   he has it through –(i)being a director, employee or shareholder of an issuer of securities; or (ii)having access to the information by virtue of his employment, office or profession; or

(b)   the direct or indirect source of his information is a person within paragraph (a).'

3.79   The CJA 1993, section 57(2)(b) thus creates tippee liability or secondary liability for someone who receives inside information directly or indirectly through as opposed from, a director, employee, shareholder or other insider of an issuer. Secondary insiders are essentially persons who know that the 'direct or indirect source' of that information is a primary insider. Some uncertainty exists as to whether the recipient must know the exact identity of the source and the circumstances under which the disclosure occurred or must merely be aware that the disclosure came from a primary source. This has implications where for example, information is obtained from a listening device or is simply overheard, where the recipient is fully aware that the source is privileged, but does not know the specific identity of the person making the statement. The better view is that in such circumstances the test would be satisfied. It is not necessary to show that the secondary insider actively sought the information or that the primary insider discloses the information in an unlawful manner.

3.80   A person can only be charged with the offence of being a secondary insider or tippee, if it can be proved that the person was aware that the source of the information was one of these primary insiders or someone who had access to non-public, price-sensitive information.[124] If the informant and the recipient are both charged and the prosecution claims that the information was provided by the particular informant, it is not necessary for the prosecution to establish that no one other than the informant could have provided the information to the secondary insider. It is enough that the prosecution establish a case that the informant did in fact provide the information.[125] It is not necessary to prove that the secondary insider did anything to obtain the relevant information as we shall see. Before the CJA 1993, the Company Securities (Insider Dealing) Act 1985, sections 1(3), (4) and 8 made it a criminal offence, subject to exceptions and conditions, where 'an individual has information which he knowingly obtained (directly or indirectly) from' a person connected with a company and then deals on the Stock Exchange in the shares of that company knowing that the information is confidential and unpublished price-sensitive information in relation to those shares. The CJA 1993 differs from the Company Securities (Insider Dealing) Act 1985 by eliminating the requirement of a connection

---

124   See for example, *R v Littlewood and others* (Unreported) Southwark Crown Court, 10 January 2011 and 2 February 2011 and FSA/PN062/ 2011 and *R v Mustafa and others* (Unreported) Southwark Crown Court, 5 March to 23 July 2012 and FSAQ/PN/080 2012 which both involved the disclosure of information to family and friends who became secondary insiders.

125   See *R (on the application of the Financial Services Authority) v MM, AR and AK* [2010] EWCA Crim 1151.

between the insider and the issuer. Moreover, the CJA 1993 makes it clear that tippee liability may arise even if the recipient of the information received it passively and did not attempt actively to obtain it.[126]

3.81   The wider scope of liability is based on a philosophy that seeks to penalise the exploitation of informational advantages that arise from insider access. Discussion has taken place as to whether a journalist or analyst who deals before the release of his own recommendations will be guilty of insider dealing. As we have seen some commentators, however, argue that such dealing is not an offence under the CJA 1993 because a precondition for liability requires the relevant information to be from an inside source. For example, a director or employee may obtain inside information from an inside source if the information was received by virtue of the director's or employee's position with the issuer. Based on this analysis, information created by an employee would not be regarded as information to which the employee had access by virtue of employment. Thus, having access to information would appear to require that the information in question exists independently of the person seeking to obtain it or to access it. The recommendations of a journalist or analyst would not therefore be inside information in so far as that individual is concerned because he is not allowed to access his own information. If this is not so, then a person who dealt in the market prior to his making further and substantial acquisitions or disposals might be guilty. It is hard to see how one's own intentions can be considered 'inside information' in this context.

3.82   It should be emphasised that under UK law the establishment of tippee liability does not necessarily depend on the liability of the individual who tips. For example, if, in the course of negotiations, inside information is passed *bona fide* to another person and the recipient then deals on the basis of that information, the tippee who dealt will be likely to have committed an offence, even though the tipper passed the information in a lawful manner. Thus, for example, if a partner of a large law firm that is advising a corporation on a takeover overhears inside information during negotiations, the lawyer will possess that information as an insider if he knows it is inside information and knows that the information is derived from an inside source. Similarly, an individual who knowingly becomes aware of inside information and knows it to be from an inside source, but who is not an insider (by virtue of employment, office or profession), will incur tippee liability as well.

3.83   Where the information has passed through several hands it may have lost some of the qualities that made it inside information such as its precision and specificity, with the result that it may be difficult to establish that the tippee has inside information. Aside from proving the tippee's state of knowledge, it may be difficult to prove that the information is in fact inside information because at this stage it may have lost much of its accuracy and novelty. Moreover, even if the information, after passing through several hands, still retains these qualities it may be difficult to show that the sub-tippee knew that the inside information was from an inside source.

---

126   See *Re A-G's Reference (No 1 of 1988)* [1989] AC 971 at 973–77 and 986, HL holding that the defendant, who had been given unsought, unpublished, price-sensitive information, had 'obtained' that information within the meaning of the Company Securities (Insider Dealing) Act 1985, s 1(3) on the basis that the term 'obtained' in s 1(3) meant no more than 'received' and thereby had a wider meaning than 'acquired by purpose and effort'. See also *R v Fisher* (Unreported) Southwark Crown Court 14 April 1988.

THE FSMA 2000 AND TIPPEE LIABILITY

3.84   The CJA 1993 extended the scope of tippee liability so that, unlike the Company Securities (Insider Dealing) Act 1985, the inside source need have no connection with the issuer whose securities are involved. This extension of tippee liability is also reflected under the civil liability regime for market abuse under the FSMA 2000. While this is discussed in more detail in Chapter 4 it is convenient to note here that the FSMA 2000 civil liability for market abuse covers insider trading and applies to any person whose behaviour is based on inside information. Under the FSMA 2000 market abuse regime, the FSA may impose civil sanctions on any person or firm who engages in market abuse through insider trading. The FSMA 2000 makes no distinction between primary and secondary insiders, nor requires the alleged insider to be linked directly or indirectly to the company whose securities are traded. Thus, under both the CJA 1993 and the FSMA 2000, where the person disclosing the information has access to it through their employment, it is not necessary to show that the person was in a position (by virtue of employment, office or profession) which might reasonably be expected to give him access to such inside information as under the old law.

DEFENCES TO ALLEGATIONS OF INSIDER DEALING

Introduction

3.85   The best defence to a charge of insider dealing is simply that one of the elements of the offence that needs to be established by the prosecution is not proved beyond a reasonable doubt. However, given the complexity of the subject area, the legislation provides a number of specific defences. These defences will succeed only if, after the prosecution has proved all the ingredients of the offence, the defendant proves on a balance of probabilities that the offence was not committed.[127]

General defences to insider dealing under the CJA 1993

3.86   It is for the prosecution to make out its case by proving the constituent elements of the offences that we have discussed above. Of course, if the defence is able to introduce a significant doubt and the prosecution is not able to rebut it, then the defendant will be entitled to an acquittal. At the end of the day, the judge or jury must be satisfied that the prosecution has proved all that is required to establish the offence beyond a reasonable doubt. The Act, however, goes further on introducing a number of statutory defences, which must be raised and established by the defence. The prosecution need only address them if raised by the defence.

3.87   It is clear from the wording of the various defences provided in Part V that the defence has a legal burden of proof and not merely an evidential one.[128]

---

127   CJA 1993, s 53. See also *R v Cross* [1991] BCLC 125, upholding the general principle that the burden is on the accused to raise a statutory defence and see below.

128   See *R v Cross* [1990] 91 Crim App R 115. It is the better view that the reverse burden of proof in regard to s 53 (including Sch 1) is compatible with Article 6(2) of the European Convention on Human Rights and the Human Rights Act 1998, see *Sheldrake v DPP* [2005]

In other words it is not enough for the defence to simply adduce some evidence. It is necessary for it to achieve the civil burden of proof – namely satisfying the court to a balance of probabilities as to all aspects of the defence.[129]

3.88   Section 53(1) sets out three general defences to a charge of insider dealing. An individual will not be guilty if he shows that he did not at the time expect the dealing to result in a profit attributable to the fact that the information in question was price sensitive information in relation to the relevant securities. He will also have a defence if he can show that at the time he believed on reasonable grounds that the information had been disclosed widely enough to ensure that none of those taking part in the dealing would be prejudiced by not having the information. Finally, if he can show that he would have done what he did even if he had not had the information then he will also be entitled to an acquittal. Let us examine these three defences which need to be raised specifically by the defence in a little more detail.

3.89   Under section 53(1)(a) if the defence can show that at the time of the transaction the defendant did not expect to make a profit or avoid a loss from the inside information then he is entitled to a defence. Indeed, section 53(6) makes it clear that this also extends to not expecting to make a loss as well. It should be emphasised that the offence is committed at the time the agreement is made and not on completion of the transaction and it must be remembered that dealing is defined in sections 55(2) and 55(3) to agreeing to acquire or dispose a security. Thus, the statutory language does not appear to provide a defence in the situation where the transaction, on which the agreement to deal was based, does not in fact take place. Precluding a defence on this basis in respect of the encouragement offence seems to be appropriate because the encouragement will have factually occurred, whether or not a deal takes places, so the expectation of the parties at that time is clearly important. This approach, however, has raised some concern regarding its application to the dealing offence,[130] where it is argued that if the transaction does not take place, the deal itself will not have occurred so that the expectations at the contract formation stage seem less important. Prosecutions will probably be rare where completion has not taken place. While the subsection does not require the defendant to show that his expectation was reasonable, the less reasonable that in fact it is the greater will be his task in persuading the jury or judge that in fact he did have such a belief.

3.90   It is hard to imagine the circumstances where a defendant could establish that he had absolutely no expectation of making a profit or avoiding a loss attributable to the price sensitivity of the information. Sarah Clark in

---

1 AC 264. As a general proposition if the legal burden is properly cast on the defence it will only require proof to the civil standard. The Government in justified this at the time of the introduction of the bill that became Part V on the basis that the facts that could establish one of the statutory defences were peculiarly within the knowledge of the accused, see generally B Rider and TM Ashe, *Insider Crime – The New Law* (Jordan Publishing 1993).

129   See *R v Mustafa and others* (Unreported) Southwark Crown Court, 5 March to 23 July 2012 and FSA/PN/080/ 2012; note the direction of Judge Pegden that once the prosecution established beyond a reasonable doubt the elements of the offence, here the unauthorised disclosure of inside information, it was for the defence to prove to a balance of probabilities the constituent elements of the statutory defences that they raised, namely s 53(3)(a) and (1)(c) discussed below.

130   See BAK Rider and M Ashe, *Insider Crime – The New Law* (Jordan Publishing 1993) at p 54.

Insider Dealing, Law and Practice[131] refers to one possible example, namely
the case of *R v Gooding*.[132] In this case the accused claimed that at the time he
purchased shares in a company that he knew to be in takeover negotiations he
genuinely believed that they would not succeed.

3.91   The second defence in section 53(1)(b) is that the defendant on
reasonable grounds thought that the information had been sufficiently widely
disseminated so that no one would be prejudiced. It should be noted that this
is a lesser threshold than providing that it was publicly available and therefore
not inside information. This defence could be raised when two or more parties
are in contact with each other and although they are in possession of inside
information that information cannot be disclosed. The defendant essentially has
to prove that there is a level playing field and no unfairness. The Government
in introducing this provision, which it was acknowledged would have very
restricted relevance, thought that it could be useful in underwriting transactions
where both parties know or are aware of the information.

3.92   The CJA 1993, section 53(1)(c) also provides defences to the dealing
offence where the defendant can show that he would have acted in the same
way without the inside information. In such a case, after the prosecution has
proved all the ingredients of the offence, the defendant must show that, on a
balance of probabilities, his possession of the inside information did not affect
his decision to deal or encourage another to deal. The policy rationale seems to
be that an individual who is planning either to deal or to encourage someone
else to deal should not be inhibited from doing so because they then acquire
inside information. It would follow that a defence is available for an individual
who has come into possession of inside information after making a decision
to deal. A defence may also be available in circumstances where an investor
who possesses inside information was forced to sell because of economic
circumstances. For example, economic compulsion may provide a defence
for a person who was forced to sell in the face of no other readily realisable
property.[133]

3.93   Moreover, it would be more difficult to prove that possession of the
inside information had had no relevance to a decision to deal, in the absence of
any economic pressure to sell. An important factor for maintaining a defence
will be the timing of the deal, unless the defendant can show that the timing
of the deal was not related to the inside information. For example, a defence
may be available for a trustee who, whilst possessing inside information about
securities, dealt in them on the basis of independent advice and for the benefit
of the trust.

3.94   Section 53(2) with much the same wording provides for defences in
regard to the offence of encouraging another person to deal in price affected
securities. Section 53(2)(a) mirrors section 53(1)(a) and provides a defence
if the person charged with encouraging can show that at the time he did not
expect the dealing to result in a profit or avoidance of a loss in regard to the
inside information. Section 53(2)(b) reflects section 52(2)(b) by providing a
defence if the encourager can show that on reasonable grounds that he believed
that the information had been sufficiently disclosed not to prejudice anyone.
There is a slight difference in the wording in that the defence will also be

131   (Oxford University Press 2013) at p 121.
132   See *The Financial Times* 2 March 1990.
133   See B Rider and TM Ashe, *Insider Dealing* (Jordan Publishing 1993) at p 54.

available if he believes that at the time the person he seeks to encourage to deal, the information will be disclosed widely enough to ensure that none of those taking part in the dealing would be prejudiced by not having the information. This might apply, for example, to information which is in the course of coming out or has been time embargoed. Section 53(2)(c) is exactly the same as section 52(1)(c).

3.95   Section 53(3) addresses the offence of disclosing inside information. Under section 53(3)(a) no individual will be guilty of this offence if he shows that he did not at the time expect any person, because of the disclosure, to deal in securities in the circumstances set out in section 52(3). By virtue of section 53(3)(b) he will also be entitled to a defence if he can show that although he had an expectation at that time, he did not expect the dealing to result in a profit or avoidance of a loss attributable to the fact that the information was price-sensitive in relation to the securities. Section 53(3)(a) is straightforward and reflects the similar defences that we have already discussed. Section 53(3)(b) is perhaps of more interest. We have already mentioned that there are cases that have come to light where inside information has been disclosed for purely social and domestic reasons. For example, the uncle who was late for his niece's wedding because he had been kept in the office or the chap who wanted to impress his girlfriend with how important he is.[134] Again it is not necessary for the expectation that the information would not be abused to be reasonable. It is necessary for the defence to prove, however, that the accused did in fact believe that the information would not be used for dealing.[135] As we have noted the more unreasonable this belief is the more difficult it will be for the court to convince a jury or judge. However, even unauthorised disclosures of inside information might be exonerated in circumstances in which the insider knows that the recipients are highly honest and professional people who are unlikely to break the law.

Special defences under the CJA 1993

3.96   The CJA 1993 provides three special defences to the dealing and encouragement offences. These defences may be described generally as 'market defences'. Two of these defences are specific, covering market makers and those involved in price stabilisation. The third defence relates to what has become known as 'market information'. The defences are authorised under section 53(4) of the Act and are set out in Schedule 1 to the Act. The Treasury under section 53(5) is empowered to amend the Schedule in this regard.[136]

---

134   See for example the facts of *R v Staines and Morrisey* [1997] 2 Cr App R 426 where information was disclosed over drinks during a social evening with friends.
135   See *R v Mustafa and others* (Unreported) Southwark Crown Court, 5 March, 23 and 27 July 2012 and FSA/PN/080 2012.
136   There is in fact an additional defence, to which reference has already been made under s 63(1) which provides that the offences do not apply to anything done by an individual acting on behalf of a public sector body in pursuit of monetary policies or polices with respect to exchange rates or the management of public debt or foreign exchange reserves. As has also been pointed out this defence would not be available if the public servant is not acting on behalf of a public sector body. Indeed, some of the earliest cases of insider abuse that came to light involved senior officials and even ministers taking advantage of their inside knowledge in regard to public securities, see B Rider and HL Ffrench, *The Regulation of Insider Trading* (Macmillan 1979) Ch 1.

Market related defences

3.97 Market makers are recognised under the rules of a regulated market or an approved organisation[137] as performing an essential market function, buying or selling securities to assist in ensuring adequate liquidity in the market. Market makers are ordinarily required to comply with the rules of the regulated market or an approved organisation and to be willing to acquire or dispose of securities according to these rules.[138] Given the nature of their responsibilities and business they might well find themselves in possession of price-sensitive information.

3.98 Paragraph 1(1) provides that a market maker may raise a defence where he can show that he acted in good faith in the course of his business, or in his employment, as a market maker).[139] It is important to note that in the original Criminal Justice Bill this defence would have applied to any employee of a market maker. This was later amended so that the defence would only apply to an employee of a market maker who was engaged in market making activity.[140] Most commentators agree that it is not clear whether this defence is available to a market maker who, after becoming aware of inside information by mistake, continues to deal in the securities in question. In such circumstances, obvious difficulties would arise for a market maker who, for example, was employed by a corporate broker with responsibility for dealings in a particular share and who would arouse suspicions amongst traders if he suddenly withdraws from the market. In this situation, the dealing offence would appear to cover the market maker who stayed in the market and dealt.

3.99 Paragraph 1(2) of Schedule 1 sets out the defence and provides that an individual is not guilty of the dealing or encouraging offences if he can show that the information which he had as an insider was market information and it was reasonable for an individual in his position to have acted as he did despite having that information as an insider at that time. In determining whether it was reasonable, the Schedule requires three issues to be taken into account. First, the content of the information; secondly, the circumstances in which the market maker first had the information and in what capacity and finally, the capacity in which he now acts.

3.100 The market maker's defence in the CJA 1993, Schedule 1, paragraph 1 is arguably narrower than the equivalent defence that had been available under the Company Securities (Insider Dealing) Act 1985. The counterpart provision of the 1985 Act prohibited the market maker from dealing whilst in the possession of inside information if the inside information on which the market maker dealt had been obtained by the market maker in the course of its business and was of a type for which it was reasonable for the market maker to have obtained in the ordinary course of that business.[141] The CJA 1993 sought to do away with these requirements in order to impose liability on a broader basis, but does provide a defence in the CJA 1993, section 53(1)(c) for a market maker who was wrongly exposed to inside information and continues to deal. Section 53(1)(c) provides, as we have seen, an individual is not guilty if he can

---

137 An approved organisation is under para 1(3) of Sch 1, an international securities self-regulating organisation approved by the Treasury under s 22 of the FSMA 2000 as amended.
138 CJA 1993, Sch 1, para 1(2).
139 CJA 1993, Sch 1, para 1(1).
140 HC Deb, Standing Committee B, *Official Report*, 15 June 1993, vol 11, col 216.
141 Company Securities (Insider Dealing) Act 1985, s 3(d).

show that he would have done what he did even though he had possession of inside information.

3.101   In this context it is also important to note the defence provided in paragraph 1(3) of the Schedule which is to some extent based on the old law and which facilitates the completion of acquisitions or disposals. It is provided that an individual will not be guilty of the offences of dealing or encouraging if he shows that he acted in connection with an acquisition or disposal which was under consideration or negotiation, or in the course of a series of such transactions and that what he did was with a view to facilitating the accomplishment of the transaction or series of transactions. Furthermore, he must also show that the information which he had as an insider was market information arising directly out of his involvement in the acquisition or disposal or series of such transactions. This defence overlaps with that in paragraph 1(2) but is specifically although not exclusively aimed at potential take-over bidders who wish to acquire a foothold in the securities of another company.

3.102   What may be considered to be market information is set out in paragraph 4 of Schedule 1. Here it is provided that it will involve one or more of the following facts: the actual or contemplated disposal or acquisition of securities; that securities are not going to be acquired or disposed of or have not in fact been traded; the number, price, including price range of such securities and the identity of the persons involved.

3.103   It is necessary for the individual seeking to make out this defence that notwithstanding his insider status he acted in good faith and that it was reasonable for him to have acted in the way that he did. Good faith is essentially a subjective test, whereas reasonableness is objective. Much will depend upon the market maker being able to show that he acted in compliance with the market rules and good practice.

3.104   The price stabilisation defence is available for an individual who deals in securities, or encourages another to deal in securities on the basis of inside information, if the individual can show that the dealings were in conformity with the price stabilisation rules or those of the European Commission's Regulation.[142] Stabilising the price of securities in the context of new issues is seen as entirely acceptable in terms of market stability. The price stabilisation rules are enforced by the FCA.[143] The purpose of these rules is to permit a manager of an issuance of securities to enter the market (usually by purchasing shares) in order to stabilise or maintain the market price of those securities. A defence is available for price stabilisation if such activity is carried out in conformity with the rules. For example, the FCA's price stabilisation rules, adopted pursuant to the FSMA, section 144(1) and (3), contain safe harbour provisions to the effect that behaviour conforming to those rules will not amount to market abuse.[144] These safe harbour provisions for price stabilising activity

---

142   CJA 1993, Sch 1, para 5 and Commission Regulation (EC) No 2273/2003, 22 December 2003 implementing Directive 2003/6/EC.

143   See Price Stabilisation Rules, MAR 2, FCA Handbook. These rules were originally adopted by the Securities and Investments Board in 1990 and, under the Financial Services Act 1986, s 48(7), conformity with these rules provided a defence against the offence of market manipulation under the Financial Services Act 1986, s 47(2).

144   MAR 1.7.2. Other FSA rules containing provisions to the effect that behaviour conforming to that rule does not amount to market abuse will be discussed below and include the rules relating to Chinese Walls, certain parts of the Listing Rules in MAR 1, Annex 1G and rule 15.1(b) of the Listing Rules.

are available to any person, whether that person is a firm or not, who can show one of the following: they acted in conformity with the price stabilisation rules for the purposes of the CJA 1993, Schedule 1, paragraph 5(1), their conduct conformed with the price stabilising rules for the purposes of Part 7 Financial Services Act 2012 (misleading statements and practices) or their behaviour conforms with the rules in accordance with the FSMA, section 118(8) (market abuse).[145]

3.105   The price stabilising safe harbours would cover any person concerned with an offer of securities for cash. For instance, there is no legal restriction on the appointment of stabilising managers to whom the FSMA 2000 price stabilising rules would apply. The main focus, however, is on lead managers when they are considering or undertaking an offer of securities for cash. These safe harbours could also apply to agents appointed by lead managers.[146] The safe harbours would cover both initial public offers and public offers of additional securities, along with securities already in issue.[147] The FSA observes that an offer is likely to be public in character where it is made in a prospectus.[148]

---

145   See the *FCA Handbook*, Chapter 2, Price Stabilising Rules, MAR 2.1.2(1)(a)–(c).
146   MAR 2.1.2(2).
147   MAR 2.1.3(R).
148   Other offers may be regarded as public when they are made to a section of the public, such as distributions and placements that are not essentially private (see MAR 2.1.4), but the requirement that there must be a public announcement means that some offers for sale of securities, for example by means of block trade, would not be covered.

Chapter 4

The market abuse regime

INTRODUCTION

4.1   The market abuse provisions of the Financial Services and Markets Act 2000 (FSMA) were designed to preserve the criminal and regulatory aspects of the previous market misconduct regime, but were also intended to address weaknesses in the enforcement of the civil regulatory framework and criminal law by creating a civil offence of market abuse.[1] The market abuse regime applies to all persons, whether or not authorised or approved under the FSMA. The market abuse offence attracts civil liability that can take the form of unlimited fines or public censure by the Financial Conduct Authority (FCA) or a court order for restitution to compensate investors who have suffered losses as a result of market abuse. The regime was designed to curb the misuse of information in prescribed financial markets and to combat market operators who sought to manipulate and distort those markets. The overriding policy objective was to ensure that participants in regulated markets were using and disseminating information that related to qualified investments in a way that did not undermine market confidence or the integrity and good governance of those markets.[2]

4.2   FSMA 2000 contained a market abuse regime creating a civil offence for market abuse and enhanced criminal penalties for insider dealing and three criminal offences for misleading statements and practices.[3] In respect of the criminal offence of insider dealing, the market abuse regime supplemented,

---

1   The market abuse regime became effective on 1 December 2001. Before the UK adopted secondary legislation implementing the EU Market Abuse Directive in 2005, s 118(2)(a)–(c) of FSMA contained the three main categories of market abuse defined as: (1) misuse of information; (2) creating false or misleading impressions; and (3) market distortion. These three types of behaviour constituted market abuse if they satisfied a regular user test and were related to qualified investments that were traded on a UK-prescribed exchange or market.

2   The International Organisation of Securities Commissions (IOSCO) recognises market abuse and insider dealing to be a threat to the integrity and good governance of financial markets and can, in certain circumstances, undermine systemic stability in those markets. Accordingly, IOSCO has adopted international standards for the efficient regulation of securities markets that contain recommended prohibitions on market abuse and insider dealing. IOSCO, 'Objectives and Principles of Securities Regulation' (IOSCO, 2010), paras 33–38 (p 12), see www.iosco.org/library/pubdocs/pdf/IOSCOPD323.pdf.

3   FSMA, ss 118–123 ('Penalties for Market Abuse'), s 402 (authorising FSA to bring insider dealing prosecutions which may result in a fine or seven years of imprisonment under Part V of the Criminal Justice Act of 1993).

rather than superseded, the existing provisions of the criminal law of insider dealing (Part V, CJA 1993) and created criminal offences for misleading statements and misleading practices intended to manipulate prescribed financial markets.[4] In 2012, Parliament enacted the Financial Services Act 2012 which broadened the scope of the market abuse regime by replacing section 397 with three separate offences, namely: 'Misleading statement' (section 89), 'Misleading impressions' (section 90) and 'Misleading statements etc in relation to benchmarks' (section 91).[5] The Financial Services Act 2012 also, among other things, eliminated the Financial Services Authority and replaced it with the Prudential Regulation Authority responsible for regulating banks, certain investment firms, and insurance firms and a Financial Conduct Authority responsible for regulating conduct and market practice issues. In contrast to the criminal offence of insider dealing, the scope of the market abuse offence is much broader, prohibiting not only the misuse of privileged ('inside') information by company insiders, but also 'behaviour' by persons who create false or misleading impressions, or distort the demand and supply, of qualifying investments on prescribed markets.

4.3   The FCA (formerly the 'FSA') is under a statutory obligation to issue a Code giving guidance to those determining whether or not behaviour amounts to market abuse.[6] The FSMA empowers the FCA to punish both regulated and unregulated market participants whose market conduct falls below acceptable standards of market conduct as defined by a reasonable user of the market.[7] Significantly, the market abuse offence expands the prohibition on market misconduct regarding the misuse of legally privileged and market sensitive information belonging to issuers of listed securities to include behaviour that could undermine confidence on prescribed markets covering transactions in a wider range of qualifying investments. The market abuse offence was designed to enhance market confidence and investor protection by prohibiting *any* person – not just insiders who owed a duty to corporate issuers not to benefit from the use of inside information – from misusing information (ie legally privileged information), or creating false or misleading impressions

---

4   See FSMA, s 397(1)–(3) creating three criminal offences for misleading statements and practices.
5   See FSMA, ss 89, 90, 91 (as amended).
6   Section 119. As discussed at 4.5 below, the Code of Market Conduct (MAR) was issued by the FSA in 2001 and has since been amended to take account of the implementation of the EU Market Abuse Directive. Sections 119 and 122 authorise the FCA to carry out a primary role in implementing and enforcing the regime.
7   The reasonable investor standard derives from the regular user test, which was set forth in the amended FSMA, s 130(3). The regular user test required that for market abuse liability to attach the behaviour in question had to be regarded by a regular user of the market as falling below an acceptable standard. The EU Market Abuse Directive, however, did not provide for a regular user test and the UK was only permitted to retain the regular user test for its original three types of market abuse – misuse of information, false or misleading impressions, and market distortions – as expressly recognised in the amended section 118(4) and (8) was subject to a sunset clause. See the Financial Services and Markets Act 2000 (Market Abuse) Regulations 2005, SI 2005/381 as from 1 July 2005. Regulations 3(2) and 3(3) amend ss 118(9) and 118A(6) of the FSMA to change the date by which the provisions affected by those sections will cease to have effect. The sunset clause was extended three times while the EU Market Abuse draft Regulation was pending. The offence under s 118(4) expired on 31 December 2014, while the offence under s 118(8) was extended again and will remain in effect until July 2016, the deadline for EU Member States (including the UK) to have adopted legislation giving effect to the new Market Abuse Regulation (replacing the Market Abuse Directive of 2005).

in the market, or distorting the market concerning qualified investments traded on prescribed markets or exchanges. By defining the offence in broad terms, the regulatory authority could police the market for behaviour that was not only abusive to particular issuers, but also undermined confidence in the market as a whole.[8]

THE EU MARKET ABUSE DIRECTIVE AND THE UK MARKET ABUSE REGIME

4.4   The FSMA market abuse regime was significantly amended with the implementation of the European Union Directive on Insider Dealing and Market Manipulation[9] ('Market Abuse Directive' or 'MAD 1'). The Market Abuse Directive introduced a common EU approach for preventing and detecting market abuse and ensuring that the flow of information to the market is equally accessible to all market participants.[10] Significantly, the regular user of section 118(10) of the original FSMA did not appear in the Directive and was retained only for those types of market abuse offences which pre-exist the Directive.[11] MAD 1 required all Member States to create an administrative or civil offence for market abuse that was modelled in part on the UK market abuse regime.[12] MAD 1 prohibited or restricted trading on the basis of inside information, creating false or misleading impressions, or taking positions that would distort the demand or supply of qualifying investments on regulated markets.[13] MAD 1 applied to a broad array of qualifying investments that are traded on regulated markets (ie exchanges) or on multilateral trading facilities (MTFs) *and* to financial instruments (ie derivatives) which are traded off exchange but derive their value from investments traded on regulated markets (but not on MTFs).

4.5   The Market Abuse Directive significantly extends the definition of market abuse under UK law.[14] Market abuse is now defined in section 118 as:

(1)   'behaviour (whether by one person alone or by two or more persons jointly or in concert) which: (a) occurs in relation to a qualifying investment traded or admitted to trading on a prescribed market or in respect of which a request for admission to trading on such a market

---

8   See discussion in B Rider, K Alexander and L Linklater, *Market Abuse and Insider Dealing* (Butterworths 2002), pp 73–74.

9   Council Directive 2003/6/EC of 28 January 2003 on insider dealing and market manipulation (market abuse) [2002] OJ L 96/16. The Market Abuse Directive 2003 was later supplemented by three Commission Directives: Council Directive 2003/124/EC [2003] OJ L 339/70; Directive 2003/125/EC [2003] OJ L 339; Directive 2004/72/EC [2004] OJ L 162/70, and a Commission Regulation 2273/2003/EC [2003] OJ L 336. providing implementing measures in relation to exemptions for buy-back plans and stabilisation of financial instruments.

10   See FSA, FSA publishes rules implementing Market Abuse Directive (22 March 2005), FSA/PN/029/2005.

11   See Financial Services and Markets Act 2000 (Market Abuse) Regulations 2005, SI 2005/381.

12   MAD 1 was implemented by all EEA/EU states on or before 2006.

13   The scope of MAD 1 was limited to activity relating to financial instruments admitted to trading on a regulated market or for which a request for admission to trading on such a market has been made.

14   See Financial Services and Markets Act 2000 (Market Abuse) Regulations 2005, SI 2005/381 and the Investment Recommendation (Media) Regulations 2005, SI 2005/382. See also discussion in Freshfields Bruckhaus and Deringer, *Financial Services Investigations and Enforcement* (Tottel 2005); p 625.

has been made, and (b) falls within any one or more of the types of behaviour set out in subsections (2) to (8) as follows';[15]

(2)   an insider who deals, or attempts to deal, in a qualifying investment or related investment on the basis of inside information relating to the qualifying investment; or

(3)   an insider who discloses inside information to another person other than in the proper course of his employment, profession or duties; or

(4)   behaviour not falling within subsections (2) or (3)(a) but which is based on information which is not generally available to those using the market but which, if available to a regular user of the market, would be, or would likely be, regarded by him as relevant when deciding the terms on which transactions in qualifying investments or related investments should be effected, and (b) is likely to be regarded by a regular user of the market as a failure on the part of the person concerned to observe the standard of behaviour reasonably expected of a person in his position in relation to the market;[16] or

(5)   behaviour which consists of effecting, or participating in effecting, transactions or orders to trade (other than in conformity with accepted market practices) which give a false or misleading impression as to the supply of, or demand for, or as to the price or value of, one or more qualifying investments or related investments, or to secure the price of one or more of such investments at an abnormal or artificial level; or

(6)   behaviour which consists of effecting, or participating in effecting, transactions or orders to trade which employ fictitious devices or any other form of deception or contrivance; or

(7)   disseminating information by any means which gives, or is likely to give, a false or misleading impression as to a qualifying investment or related investment by a person who knew or could reasonably be expected to have known that the information was false or misleading; or

(8)   misleading behaviour or distortion of the market where the behaviour falls below the standard of behaviour reasonably expected by the alleged abuser.

Subsections 2 and 3 are known as the EU insider dealing prohibitions, while subsections 4 and 8 are 'super-equivalent' provisions which are not found in the Directive, but were retained from the original UK market abuse regime and represented a kind of gold-plating that contains a regular user test and prohibitions[17] on misuse of information and behaviour that misleads or distorts the market.[18] However, subsections (4) and (8) were the subject of a 'sunset clause' according to which the offences would expire unless legislation was introduced to maintain them. The sunset clause was extended three times while the review of the EU market abuse framework was pending. The offence in subsection (4) expired on 31 December 2014, whilst the offence in subsection (8)

---

15   As noted above, s 118(2)–(8) applies to any financial instrument and also makes an offence of requiring or encouraging acts that are market abuse.
16   The regular user test was established in the original FSMA at s 118(10), but as discussed above was not incorporated in the Market Abuse Directive. Subsection (4) lapsed on 31 December 2014, while subs (8) will lapse on 3 July 2016 when the Market Abuse Regulation is given effect under UK law.
17   The Financial Services Authority had referred to these prohibitions as 'super-equivalent' in relation to the original regime.
18   The relevant provisions under the original UK market abuse regime (prior to the amendments introduced by the EU Market Abuse Directive) were s 118(2)(a)–(c).

88

will expire on 3 July 2016 when the EU Market Abuse Regulation is given effect under UK law.

THE PRESCRIBED MARKETS

4.6   The market abuse offence is triggered when behaviour occurs in relation to qualifying investments or related investments that are traded on a prescribed market. The essential elements of the offence can be broken down into four categories: (1) what are the prescribed markets; (2) which investments are qualifying; (3) what are related investments; and (4) when does behaviour occur in relation to these investments.

4.7   The UK Treasury has the authority to prescribe markets to which the market abuse regime will apply.[19] The FSMA provides no limit on how many markets which the Treasury can prescribe. Generally, the Treasury has prescribed all markets that are listed under the rules of a UK recognised investment exchange and the OFEX. Moreover, the Market Abuse Directive requires the UK to prescribe all regulated markets and exchanges prescribed by the other EEA States.[20] According to article 4 of the Financial Services and Markets Act 2000 (Prescribed Markets and Qualifying Investments) Order 2001 (the 2001 Order),[21] the UK-prescribed markets were initially the following exchanges: COREDEAL, the London Stock Exchange, the International Petroleum Exchange, Jiway, the London Metal Exchange, OM London Exchange, Euronext-LIFFE, Virt-x, and EDX London. HM Treasury can amend this list, but the list is generally amended when the FCA recognises other recognised investment exchanges or revokes their recognition.[22] As of April 2014, the following are new UK recognised investment exchanges or regulated markets: ICE Futures Limited, BATS Trading Limited, CME Europe Limited, ICAP Securities & Derivatives Exchange Limited, The London International Financial Futures and Options Exchange (LIFFE). Furthermore, a list of the other prescribed EEA/EU markets can be obtained from the relevant EEA/EU supervisory authority.

4.8   The HM Treasury has authority to prescribe markets[23] which are located in other jurisdictions, and is now required by the Market Abuse Directive to prescribe all regulated markets that are listed by other EEA states. This raises the important issue of extraterritorial jurisdiction that has been created under the regime. Section 118(5) provides that '[b]ehaviour' may attract liability under the market abuse regime if:

'it occurs –

(a)   in the United Kingdom; or

(b)   in relation to qualifying investments traded on a market to which this section applies which is situated in the United Kingdom or which is accessible electronically in the United Kingdom.'

---

19   FSMA, s 130A(1). The Treasury has prescribed markets and specified qualifying investments by the Financial Services and Markets Act 2000 (Prescribed Markets and Qualifying Investments) Order 2001, SI 2001/996 (as amended by the Financial Services and Markets Act 2000 (Market Abuse) Regulations, SI 2005/381, reg 10(2)).

20   See the Market in Financial Instruments Directive. See the FSMA 2000 (Prescribed Markets and Qualifying Investments) Order 2001, SI 2001/996 (as amended), art 4(1)(c).

21   SI 2001/996.

22   SI 2001/996 (as amended).

23   FSMA, s 130A(1).

The test for a prescribed market is that it may either be located within the UK or be accessible electronically from within the UK. This potentially creates extraterritorial jurisdiction because it applies to behaviour whether in the UK or abroad in respect of financial instruments traded on prescribed markets based in the UK. Moreover, under the Market Abuse Directive, the scope of the regime has been expanded to include behaviour occurring in the UK in respect of financial instruments admitted to trading on regulated markets based in other EEA countries.[24] A market therefore does not necessarily need to be situated in the UK; it merely has to be accessible electronically in the UK, or be a prescribed market in a Member State of the EEA.

QUALIFYING INVESTMENTS

4.9   The market abuse offence may only apply to behaviour that occurs in relation to qualifying investments admitted to trading on a prescribed market and/or related investments to such qualifying investments.[25] HM Treasury is also authorised by FSMA to prescribe which investments are qualifying in relation to the prescribed markets. In doing so, in Article 5(1) of the 2001 Order the Treasury has referenced the investment instruments that are listed in article 1(3) of the Market Abuse Directive, which covers a broad number of financial instruments, which include:

- Company shares and securities equivalent to company shares.
- Bonds and other forms of securitised debt.
- Any other securities giving right to acquire shares or bonds.
- Derivatives on commodities.
- Units in collective investment undertakings.
- Money market instruments.
- Financial futures contracts.
- Forward interest rate agreements.
- Options.
- Interest rate, currency/equity swaps.

4.10   Also covered are any other investments admitted to trading on a regulated market in an EEA state or for which a request for admission to trading has been made for such a market. The Directive effectively applies the insider trading laws to financial instruments that are traded or capable of being traded on a EEA regulated market. The Directive, however, contains important differences from the previous UK insider dealing legislation. For example, it applies not only to securities, but also to all financial instruments, including derivatives over commodities. The commentary to the Directive provides that 'the scope of financial instruments significantly affected by privileged

---

24   This means that extraterritorial application of the regime is now required within the European Union's 28 Member States and the three states of the European Economic Area not in the EU.

25   FSMA, s 118A(3). For example, contracts for difference (CFDs) are covered by the market abuse regime. In *re Shevlin*, the then FSA imposed a penalty of £85,000 on John Shevlin for trades he made in CFDs that referenced the share price of Body Shop International plc, a company whose ordinary share capital was traded at the relevant time on the London Stock Exchange. Shevlin's trades were made on the basis of inside information which he had obtained while an employee at the Body Shop. FSA Final Notice, *John Shevlin* (1 July 2008).

information is not limited to those of the issuer, but enlarged to related derivative financial instruments (eg options on equity, futures and options on an index)'. As discussed below, the new EU Market Abuse Regulation (which replaces MAD 1 and must be implemented into UK law by July 2016) applies the market abuse offence to a much broader range of financial instruments in the OTC derivatives markets even if the referenced assets are not traded on an EEA exchange or UK prescribed market.

4.11   The market abuse offence covers all investments for which the prescribed UK recognised investment exchanges (RIEs) are the primary traded markets (ie domestic listed securities and on exchange derivatives, and also investments only incidentally traded on these exchanges (for example, on the London Stock Exchange's international equity or fixed income markets)). In addition, it applies to conduct relating to derivatives on those 'qualifying investments' (for example, OTC derivatives on securities), and applies to conduct relating to instruments that underlie exchange traded derivatives or structured notes or warrants. These financial instruments are what the FCA calls 'relevant products'.

RELATED INVESTMENTS

4.12   As discussed above, market abuse can be classified into one of seven types of behaviour.[26] Two of these types of behaviour involve insider dealing and the improper disclosure of insider information in respect of qualifying investments, or related investments on a prescribed market.[27] Unlike the other types of market abuse, these two types of market abuse apply to related investments of qualifying investments that are traded on prescribed markets.[28]

The breadth of the term 'related investments' should be emphasised: it could be any *financial instrument* admitted to trading (or where a request for admission to trading has been made) on a *regulated market* situated or operating in the UK or other EEA state. It applies to all transactions concerning those instruments, whether undertaken on regulated markets or elsewhere (eg spreadbets).[29]

4.13   The breadth of the term 'related investments' can be demonstrated by the following. Regarding misuse of information, it would not be necessary to show any nexus with the UK at all, other than the behaviour that relates to a UK traded investment in the broad sense described above. Compliance with local standards in another jurisdiction will not necessarily be a defence in a civil enforcement action for market abuse or to a criminal prosecution for misleading market conduct.

4.14   In addition, the term 'related investments' also has a potential application to behaviour which is less directly connected or indirectly related

---

26   FSMA, s 118(2)–(8) (as amended).
27   Section 118(2).
28   Section 118(3).
29   Insider dealing law also applies to financial instruments not admitted to trading on a regulated market, but whose value depends on a security traded on a regulated market. The EU Market Abuse Regulation applies the market abuse offence, including insider dealing, to all investments traded in multi-lateral trading facilities (MTFs) and organised trading facilities (OTFs) and to all financial instruments (ie, OTC derivatives) referencing these investments. See 4.47–4.50 below.

to the qualifying investments on the relevant prescribed market. Essentially, behaviour is covered which directly involves or affects the investments themselves.

PRESCRIBED MARKETS, QUALIFYING INVESTMENTS AND THE *JABRE* CASE

4.15 The Financial Services Authority enforcement action against the hedge fund manager Phillipe Jabre and his employer GLG partners raised an important issue regarding the scope of the term 'qualifying investments'. In the *Jabre* case,[30] Jabre had entered into agreements to short sell the stock of the Japanese bank Sumitomo Mitsui Financial Group (SMFG) a few days after receiving price-sensitive information about the bank from a Goldman Sachs salesman. Jabre argued that his conduct in short selling SMFG stock was not, as a matter of law, market abuse contrary to section 118 because his trades in SMFG shares occurred on the Tokyo Stock Exchange and therefore were not qualifying investments on a prescribed market. He argued that it would violate the 'territoriality' principle for a market abuse penalty to be imposed in the exercise of the FSA's power under section 123. The FSA found, however, that Mr Jabre's behaviour did occur in relation to qualifying investments (SMFG shares) that were traded on a prescribed market. SMFG's shares were qualifying investments of a corporate body (SMFG) and, crucially, those shares were quoted at the relevant time on the London Stock Exchange's SEAQ International Trading System, which was a market to which section 118 applied.[31] Jabre contended that the actual shares he shorted were not traded by him on the London market, but rather on the Tokyo market, and that the term 'qualifying investments' applied only to the shares actually traded, and not to all the shares of the same kind. Moreover, he argued that the purpose of section 118 (prior to the Market Abuse Directive) was to regulate conduct in relation to UK markets, and not in respect of markets outside the UK which were not prescribed by the UK Treasury; and that his conduct on the Tokyo market had no effect on the shares listed on the London market and therefore could not constitute market abuse simply because the shares in question were listed on both markets.

4.16 The Tribunal rejected this argument by reasoning that the statutory phrase 'traded on a market to which this section applies' in subsection (1)(a) does not mean that the actual shares traded were the same shares that were subject to the abusive behaviour. The Tribunal held that behaviour constituting market abuse 'does not require the identification of any particular shares as being the qualifying investments to which the behaviour relates'.

---

30 See *Philippe Jabre and the Financial Services Authority (Decision on Market Abuse)*, The Financial Services and Markets Tribunal (10 July 2006), hearing on appeal by Mr Jabre of the Financial Service Authority's Decision Notice to Philippe Jabre and to GLG Partners (28 February 2006).

31 The Tribunal observed that SEAQ International (the Stock Exchange Automatic Quotation System for International equity market securities) is a quote-driven trading service in which securities traded on SEAQ International required at least two market makers registered with the London Stock Exchange and that two-way prices must be displayed on the LSE system for the security in question. SEAQ International was a prescribed market because of its link with the LSE and SMFG's shares, which were listed on the LSE system through SEAQ, were qualifying investments.

Indeed, the Tribunal reasoned that, if Jabre's argument were accepted, it would be nearly impossible for a regulator in market abuse cases involving, for example, disclosing inside information or disseminating false rumours, to identify any particular share or group of shares which were the subject of wrongful behaviour. Moreover, Jabre's assertion that his conduct on the Tokyo market did not have an effect on the London market was inapposite because the real issue was whether Jabre's behaviour on the Tokyo market could be reasonably expected to undermine confidence in the shares traded on the London market. The Tribunal held that Jabre's insider dealing by shorting the shares of the Japanese bank, wherever it occurred, had the effect of destroying confidence in the global market for the bank's securities and therefore constituted market abuse with respect to qualifying investments on UK prescribed markets.

THE DUTY TO THE MARKET

4.17   The *Jabre case* also highlights the duty that market participants have to the market to maintain transparency and overall market confidence. An important aspect of the market abuse offence was that, unlike the criminal offence of insider dealing, it established a duty to the market for anyone whose conduct – whether on or off market – was defined as being market abuse. This meant that it was not necessary for prosecutors to prove that the defendant breached a duty to an investor or to the company or firm whose financial instruments were being traded. It was sufficient for the regulator to show on a balance of probabilities that the behaviour in question in respect of qualifying investments had impacted the market itself by undermining investor confidence and the integrity of the market as perceived by regular users of the market. In imposing liability, however, the FCA may still under certain circumstances need to show that the state of mind of the alleged abuser was relevant for committing the offence.[32]

4.18   Market abuse is therefore defined as behaviour which occurs in relation to qualifying investments admitted to trading on a prescribed market, or in respect of which a request for admission to trading has been made. It also applies to qualifying investments and to investments that are related to qualifying investments.[33] These related investments can be traded on exchanges that are not prescribed UK exchanges. For instance, related investments could be traded on prescribed exchanges or off exchange in other EEA jurisdictions, or on or off exchange outside the EEA, if they relate to qualifying investments on a UK prescribed market. Although relevant in some circumstances, the state of mind of the market abuser is not necessarily relevant for a successful prosecution of the civil offence.

---

32   Although the FCA is primarily concerned with the impact on the market, the purpose of the behaviour will be relevant for determining how a reasonable investor should act under certain circumstances. See Section 1.2.5 of the MAR.

33   It is worth noting that recently the UK Court of Appeal held that effecting an order to trade in such investments as contracts for difference (CFD), which would not fall under the definition of 'qualifying investments' pursuant to Order 2001/996, may nonetheless be regarded as market abuse even when the orders are effected through intermediaries, see *7722656 Canada Inc (formerly Swift Trade Inc) v Financial Services Authority* [2013] EWCA Civ 1662.

WHAT CONSTITUTES MARKET ABUSE

4.19   The statutory framework creating the market abuse offence is very broad, covering 'behaviour' that is both on market and off market, including trading activity and disseminating false or misleading information. As discussed in 4.4 above, MAD 1 extended the three categories of market abuse under the original section 118(2)(a)–(c) – misuse of information, creating false or misleading impressions, and market distortion – to seven categories as set forth in section 118(2)–(8):

(1)   insider dealing; or

(2)   improper disclosure of inside information;[34] or

(3)   misuse of relevant information where the behaviour falls below the standard of behaviour reasonably expected by a regular user of the market or a person in the position of the alleged abuser;[35] or

(4)   manipulating transactions in the relevant market unless for legitimate reasons[36] and in conformity to accepted market practices on the relevant market; or

(5)   manipulating devices;[37] or

(6)   information dissemination that gives or is likely to give a false or misleading impression;[38] or

(7)   misleading behaviour or distortion of the market where the behaviour falls below the standard of behaviour reasonably expected by a regular user of the market or an alleged abuser;[39]

unless such behaviour:

•   conforms with a rule which expressly provides that behaviour which conforms with the rule will not amount to market abuse; or

•   conforms with Commission Regulation 2273/2003/EC which implements the Market Abuse Directive in relation to exemptions for buy-back plans and stabilisation of financial instruments; or does not amount to market abuse under the Code of Market Conduct, or some other FCA position.

In addition, the UK regime maintains its separate civil offence of requiring or encouraging another to commit market abuse if the act in question would

---

34   See Section 1.4.2 of the MAR: The following behaviours are, in the opinion of the FCA, market abuse (improper disclosure): (1) disclosure of inside information by the director of an issuer to another in a social context; and (2) selective briefing of analysts by directors of issuers or others who are persons discharging managerial responsibilities.

35   This refers to subs (4) which ceased to have effect as of 31 December 2014.

36   See Section 1.6.6 of the MAR: In the opinion of the FCA, the following factors are to be taken into account when considering whether behaviour is for 'legitimate reasons', and there are indications that it is: (1) if the transaction is pursuant to a prior legal or regulatory obligation owed to a third party; (2) if the transaction is executed in a way which takes into account the need for the market or auction platform as a whole to operate fairly and efficiently; (3) the extent to which the transaction generally opens a new position, so creating an exposure to market risk, rather than closes out a position and so removes market risk; and (4) if the transaction complied with the rules of the relevant prescribed markets or prescribed auction platform about how transactions are to be executed in a proper way (for example, rules on reporting and executing cross-transactions).

37   See MAR sections 1.7.2 and 1.7.3.

38   See Sections 1.6.2 and 1.6.9 of the MAR.

39   See Section 1.2.21 of the MAR: 'The regular user is a hypothetical reasonable person who regularly deals on the market and in the investments of the kind in question or bids on the auction platform in relation to investments of the kind in question'. However, this refers to subs (8), which will cease to have effect on 3 July 2016 when the Market Abuse Regulation becomes effective under UK law.

have amounted to market abuse if committed by the requirer or encourager.[40] It states in relevant part that the requirement or encouragement offence can be committed if 'by taking or refraining from taking any action, a person has required or encouraged another person or persons to engage in behaviour which if the person themselves engaged in such behaviour would amount to market abuse'. In considering whether to bring an action for this offence or the market abuse more generally, the FCA will take account of factors such as acceptable market practices and level of knowledge and skill of person concerned.

MANIPULATING DEVICES

4.20   The FCA has demonstrated that it will prosecute firms and individuals involved in using manipulating devices that create false or misleading impressions of qualified investments. In 2011, the FCA brought an enforcement action[41] obtaining an interim injunction against Da Vinci Invest Ltd, Mineworld LtD, Mr Szabolcs Banya, Mr Gyorgy Szabolcs Brad and Mr Tamas Pornye restraining them from committing market abuse in relation to 186 UK-listed shares and freezing the assets of the mentioned companies.[42] The FCA's action was based on the grounds that the defendants were alleged to have committed market manipulation of a type known as 'layering'. This involved the entering and trading of orders relating to shares traded on the electronic trading platform of the London Stock Exchange and multi-lateral trading facilities which gave, or were likely to give, a false or misleading impression as to 'the supply of, or demand for, or as to the price of, shares listed on the LSE, contrary to section 118(5) of FSMA'. The FCA gave evidence of violation of section 118(5) of the FSMA and imposed penalties in the following amounts: Da Vinci Invest Ltd £1.46 million; Mineworld £5 million; Mr Banya and Mr Pornye £410,000; and Mr Brad £290,000.[43] The case was also of interest because the High Court decided on 12 August 2015 that the FCA had the right to impose permanent injunctions under section 381 of the FSMA and penalties under section 129 of the FSMA (totalling £7,570,000) against the defendants. The court observed that '[t]his is the first case in which, in addition to seeking an injunction under section 381, the FCA has invited the court to impose a penalty for market abuse under section 129: such penalties are more usually imposed by the FCA itself, subject to review by the Upper Tribunal (Tax and Chancery Chamber)'. The case shows that the FCA will use not only regulatory proceedings to impose fines on defendants for using manipulating devices under section 118(5) but also use the High Court to restrain assets and impose further penalties for such violations.

INSIDER AND INSIDE INFORMATION

4.21   The EU Insider Dealing and Market Manipulation Directive[44] has defined insider dealing as a form of market abuse which can constitute both a

40   FSMA, s 123.
41   [2015] EWHC 2401 (Ch), [2015] WLR(D) 475.
42   See [2011] EWHC 2674 (Ch).
43   The defendants were granted the right to apply for permission to appeal, a hearing is to be fixed to determine the terms of the final injunction. See http://www.fca.org.uk/news/fca-secures-high-court-judgment-awarding-injunction-and-over-7-million-in-penalties.
44   See FCA Final Notice 2014 *Ian Charles Hannam*, RF ICH01012, see https://www.fca.org.uk/your-fca/documents/final-notices/2014/ian-charles-hannam.

civil and a criminal offence.[45] The Directive expanded the scope of personal liability for primary insiders by excluding any requirement that they have 'full knowledge of the facts' in order for criminal or civil liability to be imposed. The repeal of this requirement recognises the market reality that primary insiders may have access to insider information on a daily basis and are aware of the confidential nature of the information they receive. In addition, the Directive adopted an 'information connection' requirement to the definition of secondary insider. According to this definition, a secondary insider would be any person, other than a primary insider, 'who with full knowledge of the facts possesses inside information'.[46] They would be subject to the same prohibitions on trading, disclosing and procuring as primary insiders.[47]

4.22   The UK regulations implementing the Directive replaced the original section 118(2)(a)–(c) with new definitions of who are the 'insiders' and of what constitutes 'inside information'.[48] Rather than having three definitions of abusive behaviour in section 118, there are now six categories which provide more specific definitions of prohibited or restricted behaviour.[49] This includes 'behaviour', 'where an insider deals, or attempts to deal, in a qualifying investment or related investment on the basis of inside information relating to the investment in question.' By section 118A, behaviour is taken into account only if it occurs 'in the United Kingdom'[50] or is taken outside the UK with respect to a qualifying investment (or related investment) on a prescribed UK market or a qualifying investment (or related investment) on a market prescribed by another EEA state. This provides extraterritorial jurisdiction for the FCA or other EEA authorities to enforce their market abuse legislation against parties who engage in behaviour outside their territory that amounts to market abuse if it relates to qualifying investments on prescribed markets in an EEA Member State.

4.23   Section 118B defines *insiders* as any person who has inside information, amongst other things, 'as a result of having access to the information through the exercise of his employment, profession or duties'.[51] In

45   See also Article 8 of Regulation (EU) No 596/2014 of the European Parliament and of the Council of 16 April 2014 on market abuse (market abuse regulation) and repealing Directive 2003/6/EC of the European Parliament and of the Council and Commission Directives 2003/124/EC, 2003/125/EC and 2004/72/EC [2014] OJ L 173/1. See for the criminal offence **3.25** *et seq* above.
46   Articles 2, 3 and section A of the Annex.
47   Article 2.
48   Under the pre-Directive UK legislation, the definition of market abuse was broadly defined in three categories: misuse of information, creating false or misleading impressions, or market distortions in relation to qualifying investments on prescribed markets. FSMA, s 118(2)(a)–(c).
49   FSMA, s 118(2)–(8).
50   FSMA, s 118A(1)(a).
51   FSMA, s 118B(c). Insiders who acquire inside information in relation to their professional and employment duties were subject to FSA enforcements in the cases of Richard Ralph (FSA Notice, 12 Nov 2008/Ralph) and Filip Boyen (FSA Notice, 12 Nov 2008/Boyen). In the action against Mr Ralph, the UK's former Ambassador to Belgium, it was proved that, at the relevant time, Mr Ralph was the executive chairman of AIM-listed, Monterrico Metals plc (Monterrico) when he asked Mr Boyen to buy £30,000 worth of shares on his behalf. At the time, it was public information that the company was in takeover talks, but Mr Ralph also knew that a takeover had been agreed in principle at a premium price that substantially exceeded the then share price. Mr Ralph was involved in the takeover discussion and knew he was not allowed to deal in the company's shares while the material information on the takeover had not been disclosed. He nevertheless directed his broker to execute trades on his behalf before the material information was disclosed. He agreed a fine with the FSA of £117,691.41, and Mr Boyen agreed a fine of £81,982.95.

this respect, the FCA in 2012 fined Ian Charles Hannam (at that time Chairman of Capital Markets at JPMorgan and Global Co-Head of UK Capital Markets at JPMorgan Cazenove) £450,000 for violating section 118(3) of FSMA because he leaked inside information through two emails to a third party foreign government official.[52] Mr Hannam argued that the information was not inside information and, alternatively, if it was, he was acting legitimately according to his employment and professional duties. In May 2014, the Upper Tribunal upheld the FCA's decision imposing liability for market abuse and the fine because Mr Hannam had in fact leaked inside information by sending two emails to an unauthorised third party. Even though both the FCA and the Tribunal acknowledged that Mr Hannam did not act deliberately or recklessly and that no profit was generated consequently to the disclosure, it was claimed that because of his senior position and experience he could not ignore the 'inside' nature of the disclosed information. Hence, he should have taken the necessary measures to keep it confidential.[53]

4.24   The term *insiders* also applies to any person who has inside information as a result of his membership of the administrative, management, or supervisory bodies of an issuer of qualifying investments, or as a result of his holding in the capital of an issuer of qualifying investments, or as a result of his criminal activities, or obtained by other means and which he knows, or could reasonably expect to know, is inside information.[54] In this respect, the FCA Code of Market Conduct (MAR) sets out the factors as indicators of whether a person is an insider: (1) if a normal and reasonable person in the position of the person who has inside information would know or should have known that the person from whom he received it is an insider; and (2) if a normal and reasonable person in the position of the person who has inside information would know or should have known that it is inside information.[55]

4.25   Section 118C defines 'inside information' for the purposes of Part VII of the Act as the following:

'(2)   In relation to qualifying investments, or related investments … inside information is information of a precise nature which –
(a)   is not generally available;[56]

---

52   See FCA Final Notice 2014 *Ian Charles Hannam*, RF ICH01012, see https://www.fca.org.uk/your-fca/documents/final-notices/2014/ian-charles-hannam.
53   *Ian Charles Hannam v The Financial Conduct Authority* [2014] UKUT 0233 (TCC).
54   See FCA Final Notice 30 March 2015/Carver, see https://www.fca.org.uk/your-fca/documents/final-notices/2015/kenneth-george-carver. In the action against Kenneth George Carver, the FCA gave evidence of violation of s 118(2) of the FSMA. Mr Carver had purchased 62,000 shares in Logica Plc based on inside information obtained from a family friend Ryan Willmott, employed by Logica Plc. The information was concerned with a possible takeover of Logica by CGI Inc. On 31 May 2012, CGI Inc made public its intention to acquire Logica at a significant premium. Because of the announcement, the share price increased by 59.8%. Mr Carver promptly sold all his shares and made a profit of £ 24.206.70. According to the FCA, 'Carver knew that there was a risk of market abuse and traded anyway. He used his own funds to place a trade on Willmott's behalf and knew that Willmott had a financial incentive to persuade him to trade'. Consequently, the FCA imposed on Mr Carver a financial penalty of £35,212. Ryan Wilmott faced prosecution before the Crown Court and was finally sentenced to a 10 month custodial sentence for insider dealing, see FCA Press Release, https://www.fca.org.uk/news/ryan-willmott-sentenced-to-imprisonment-for-insider-dealing.
55   See Section 1.2.8 of the MAR.
56   Section 1.2.12 of the MAR specifies the factors which should be taken into account to determine whether or not information is generally available and are indications that it is (or not) 'inside information: (1) whether the information has been disclosed to a prescribed market or a prescribed auction platform through a regulatory information service or RIS

(b)   relates, directly or indirectly, to one or more issuers of the qualifying investments or to one or more of the qualifying investments; and

(c)   would if generally available, be likely to have a significant effect on the price of the qualifying investments or on the price of the related investments ...'

This broad definition of 'inside information' derives from the Directive's definition of inside information as 'precise, not been made public, relates directly or indirectly to issuers, and if made public, would have a significant effect on price of qualifying investments (ie financial instruments actually issued by issuer)'. Information is regarded as generally available to users of the market if it can be 'obtained by research or analysis conducted' by or on their behalf. Furthermore, by way of referring to the definition of section 118 and the MAD, the MAR lists additional behaviour which amounts to insider dealing. This includes: (1) dealing on the basis of inside information which is not trading information; (2) front running/pre-positioning – that is, a transaction for a person's own benefit, on the basis of and ahead of an order (including an order relating to a bid) which he is to carry out with or for another (in respect of which information concerning the order is inside information), which takes advantage of the anticipated impact of the order on the market or auction clearing price; (3) in the context of a takeover, an offeror or potential offeror entering into a transaction in a qualifying investment, on the basis of inside information concerning the proposed bid, that provides merely an economic exposure to movements in the price of the target company's shares (for example, a spread bet on the target company's share price); and (4) in the context of a takeover, a person who acts for the offeror or potential offeror dealing for his own benefit in a qualifying investment or related investments on the basis of information concerning the proposed bid which is inside information.[57]

INFORMATION THAT IS 'PRECISE' AND HAS AN 'EFFECT' ON PRICE

4.26   Section 118C(5) defines information to be precise if it:

'(a)   indicates circumstances that exist or may be reasonably expected to come into existence or an event that has occurred or may be reasonably expected to occur, and

(b)   is specific enough to enable a conclusion to be drawn as to the possible effect on the price of those qualifying investments or related investments.'

Section 118C(6) defines information as likely to have an effect on price if the '[i]nformation would be likely to have a significant effect on price

---

or otherwise in accordance with the rules of that market; (2) whether the information is contained in records which are open to inspection by the public; (3) whether the information is otherwise generally available, including through the Internet, or some other publication (including if it is only available on payment of a fee), or is derived from information which has been made public; (4) whether the information can be obtained by observation by members of the public without infringing rights or obligations of privacy, property or confidentiality; and (5) the extent to which the information can be obtained by analysing or developing other information which is generally available.

57   See Section 1.3.2 of the MAR.

if and only if it is information of a kind which a reasonable investor would be likely to use as part of the basis of his investment decisions'. Nonetheless, the MAR provides that consideration should be given to the following factors to determine whether or not a person's behaviour is deemed to be on the basis of inside information: '(1) if the decision to deal or attempt to deal was made before the person possessed the relevant inside information; or (2) if the person concerned is dealing to satisfy a legal or regulatory obligation which came into being before he possessed the relevant inside information; or (3) if a person is an organisation, if none of the individuals in possession of the inside information: (a) had any involvement in the decision to deal; or (b) behaved in such a way as to influence, directly or indirectly, the decision to engage in the dealing; or (c) had any contact with those who were involved in the decision to engage in the dealing whereby the information could have been transmitted.' According to the FCA, such factors should be regarded as indications that the 'person's behaviour' is not 'inside information'.[58]

BEHAVIOUR

4.27   The term 'behaviour' has been interpreted broadly by the FCA to include action and inaction,[59] and the Code of Market Conduct states the following factors shall be taken into account in determining whether inaction amounts to behaviour that is market abuse:

(1)   if the person concerned has failed to discharge a legal or regulatory obligation (for example to make a particular disclosure) by refraining from acting; or

(2)   if the person concerned has created a reasonable expectation of him acting in a particular manner, as a result of his representations (by word or conduct), circumstances which give rise to a duty or obligation to inform those to whom he made the representations that they have ceased to be correct, and he has not done so.[60]

Moreover, behaviour can be undertaken by one person acting alone or two or more persons acting jointly or in concert.[61] Unlike the criminal offence of insider dealing which applies only to natural persons, the market abuse regime defines a person as not only an individual or natural person, but also as a business entity or non-profit organisation. The offence of market abuse therefore can be committed by a single person or any combination of natural and legal persons acting jointly or in concert.

THE CODE OF MARKET CONDUCT (MAR)

4.28   Essential to determining whether behaviour amounts to market abuse is the MAR issued by the FCA.[62] The Code has guided market participants in

---

58   See Section 1.3.3 of the MAR. See also FCA Final Notice to Steve Harrison (8 September 2008) at p 3.
59   FSMA, s 130(3).
60   Code, MAR 1.2.6 (1) & (2).
61   FSMA, s 118(1).
62   The provisions of the MAR can be accessed at: http://fshandbook.info/FS/html/handbook/MAR/1.

identifying practices which do or do not amount to market abuse. The Code has played an important role in determining what conduct is acceptable.[63] The MAR is helpful to persons who: (1) want to avoid engaging in market abuse or to avoid requiring or encouraging another to do so; or (2) want to determine whether they are required by to report a transaction to the FCA as a suspicious one.[64] The FSMA recognised that the adoption of the Code was necessary given the breadth of the statutory definition of market abuse.[65]

4.29   The Code provides guidance on what the statutory provisions of the market abuse regime mean and on the FCA's views regarding what behaviour or conduct is acceptable. For authorised firms, the Code has been praised for adding greater transparency in determining what does and does not amount to market abuse and therefore has clarified compliance objectives and promoted legal certainty.[66]

4.30   The main provisions of FSMA governing the Code provide as follows:

'119. –

(1)   The Authority must prepare and issue a code containing such provisions as the Authority considers will give appropriate guidance to those determining whether or not behaviour amounts to market abuse.

(2)   The code may among other things specify –

   (a)   descriptions of behaviour that, in the opinion of the Authority, amount to market abuse;

   (b)   descriptions of behaviour that, in the opinion of the Authority, do not amount to market abuse;

   (c)   factors that, in the opinion of the Authority, are to be taken into account in determining whether or not behaviour amounts to market abuse;

   (d)   descriptions of behaviour that are accepted market practices in relation to one or more specified markets;

   (e)   descriptions of behaviour that are not accepted market practices in relation to one or more specified markets.

and

'122. –

(1)   If a person behaves in a way which is described (in the code in force under section 119 at the time of the behaviour) as behaviour that, in the Authority's opinion, does not amount to market abuse that behaviour of his is to be taken, for the purposes of this Act, as not amounting to market abuse.

(2)   Otherwise, the code in force under section 119 at the time when particular behaviour occurs may be relied on so far as it indicates whether or not that behaviour should be taken to amount to market abuse.'

---

63   Section 122(2) provides that the code 'may be relied on so far as it indicates whether or not that behaviour should be taken to amount to market abuse'.
64   See Section 11.2 of the MAR.
65   The definition of market abuse is found at ss 118 and 118A.
66   See Freshfields Bruckhaus and Deringer, *Financial Services Investigations and Enforcement* p 622 (Tottel 2005).

THE MAR SPECIFYING BEHAVIOUR

4.31   The MAR may specify behaviours which, in the FCA's view, amounts to market abuse and the related penalties; or which, in its view, does not amount to market abuse. It may also specify factors which should be taken into account in determining whether, in the FCA's view, behaviour should amount to market abuse; and it may specify behaviour which is accepted market practice in relation to one or more specified markets, and which is not accepted market practice. The MAR's provisions are neither conclusive nor exhaustive.[67] However, the Code is commonly regarded by market participants as a quasi-rule book.

BEHAVIOUR WHICH DOES NOT AMOUNT TO MARKET ABUSE

4.32   Section 118(1)(c) states that where behaviour does amount to market abuse, it will not give rise to a penalty or remedy if the person accused of market abuse believed on reasonable grounds that its behaviour did not amount to market abuse; or it took all reasonable precautions and exercised all due diligence to avoid committing market abuse. The FCA applied this reasonable person test in the *Harrison* case involving a portfolio manager who was given inside information about the refinancing plans of a company whose shares he later bought before the information became public.[68] The FCA acknowledged that Mr Harrison, a fund manager with Moore Credit Fund, did not realise that he was given inside information at the time, but that he should have realised it was inside information, and because he profited from it, he was required to provide restitution of £44,000 which included his employer's profits from the transaction, to cover the FCA's enforcement costs and he was suspended as a fund manager for one year. The case shows the importance of investors taking reasonable care to recognise inside information when they see it and not to misuse it. It was the first FCA market abuse case involving fund managers in the credit markets and is applicable to hedge fund managers who are often provided legitimately with inside information in the course of their business. The FCA expects fund managers in receipt of such information to observe high standards of conduct and not to profit from their privileged access to inside information.

4.33   The MAR is intended to provide more clarity to the definition of market abuse and greater flexibility in applying that definition to changing market conditions and thus serves as a source of regulatory innovation. Nevertheless, under the FSMA, the MAR has a limited role in determining whether market abuse has occurred. The only legal certainty it provides is its description of

---

67   See Section 1.1.6 of the MAR: 'The Code does not exhaustively describe all types of behaviour that may or may not amount to market abuse. In particular, the descriptions of behaviour which, in the opinion of the FCA, amount to market abuse should be read in the light of: (1) the elements specified by the Act as making up the relevant type of market abuse; and (2) any relevant descriptions of behaviour which, in the opinion of the FCA, do not amount to market abuse. Likewise, the Code does not exhaustively describe all the factors to be taken into account in determining whether behaviour amounts to market abuse. If factors are described, they are not to be taken as conclusive indications, unless specified as such, and the absence of a factor mentioned does not, of itself, amount to a contrary indication'.

68   FCA Final Notice (08 September 2008), FSA/PIN/101/2008.

behaviour as *not amounting* to market abuse.[69] In contrast, the MAR only plays an evidentiary role in determining whether or not behaviour amounts to market abuse.[70] In both situations, the MAR provides an important set of definitions and guidelines for behaviour that does not amount to market abuse, but its evidential factors that suggest that certain behaviour could constitute market abuse are subordinate to the statutory definition of market abuse.

SAFE HARBOURS

4.34   Section 122(1) provides that if a person behaves in a way that is determined by the MAR not to be market abuse, then the person cannot be taken to have committed market abuse. This occurs, for example, if a person's behaviour has conformed to the safe harbour conditions described in the MAR. The Market Abuse Directive enumerates an exhaustive list of safe harbours which a Member State must incorporate into its market abuse regime. The implementation of the Directive into UK law had the effect of reducing the number and scope of safe harbours which the FSA had originally incorporated into the MAR. The FSA had resisted eliminating the safe harbours that were not enumerated in the Directive on the grounds that they were merely descriptions of practices that did not constitute market abuse and therefore irrelevant to implementation of the amended regime under the Directive.[71] The Committee of European Securities Regulators (now ESMA), however, took a strict position prohibiting the FSA from adopting express 'safe harbours' in the MAR that were not enumerated in the Directive or the Regulation.[72] Accordingly, the FCA has amended the MAR to include the following safe harbours that are required in the Directive.

Share buy-backs

4.35   This is the buying back of shares from a corporation to reduce the number of shares on the market. It is carried out in the interest of investors to improve shareholder dividends or strengthen the demand for an issuer's equity capital. By allowing corporate management to decide whether to buy-back shares while in possession of relevant information that has not been disclosed to the market, an important exception to the market abuse regime is created that is justified on the economic rationale that management should not have unnecessary regulatory restrictions on their efforts to maintain or enhance the value of shares held by investors. Share buy-back plans are nevertheless heavily regulated under EU company law directives to prevent issuers from using these programmes to engage in abuse through buying back shares before the relevant disclosure to the market is made with a potential impact on the price of the

---

69   FSMA, s 122(1).
70   FSMA, s 122(2).
71   HM Treasury and FSA, 'UK Implementation of the EU Market Abuse Directive' (Directive 2003/6/EC), *A Consultation Document*, June 2004, p 3 [HM Treasury].
72   This approach has been criticised on the grounds that the original safe harbours in the UK Code added clarity for practitioners and therefore by limiting those safe harbours under the Directive the Code's guidance may create further uncertainty, especially in view of the fact that the Directive has been often criticised for providing vague definitions of offences and the conditions for those offences. See CESR (December 2002) *Feedback statement for Level 2 Implementing Measures CESR/02–287b* (CESR, Paris).

shares.[73] Furthermore, in order to guarantee an adequate level of harmonisation across Member States in the context of stabilisation, the EU issued a Buy-Back and Stabilisation Regulation[74] which was taken into consideration in the provisions of the Code to draw a line between what amounts (or not) to market abuse.[75]

4.36   The safe harbour is limited to share buy-back programmes and has restrictions upon the price and volume allowed. For instance, not more than ten per cent (10%) of the subscribed share capital can be repurchased; a maximum of twenty five per cent (25%) of the average daily volume can be purchased, but it cannot be purchased at a price higher than the value for which it was bought.[76]

4.37   Industry representatives have expressed the concern that the scope for permitted buy-backs in the safe harbour is too limited, particularly in relation to price and volume restrictions, and many believe the safe harbour should have been expanded to include debt repurchases and sales of own shares.[77] In any case, as the MAR specifies: 'The effect of article 8 of the Market Abuse Directive and section 118A(5)(b) of the Act is that behaviour by any person which conforms with the stabilisation provisions in the Buy-back and Stabilisation Regulation will not amount to market abuse.'[78]

Price stabilisation

4.38   This is an important economic mechanism to maintain the price of securities during an initial public offering. As in the UK Code, this is included in the Buy-back and Stabilisation Regulation as a safe harbour, and is subject to strict rules rather than forming part of a blanket exemption.[79] The rationale is that stabilisation measures taken over an extended period of time could be used as a form of market manipulation to increase or maintain share prices at an artificial level.[80] A stabilisation programme must meet a number of conditions before safe harbour status can be granted. Stabilisation may only occur during a certain period that has been disclosed to the market in advance. For example, during an IPO, the period will begin when the security is traded on a regulated market and end no later than 30 days after allotment, while the price may not exceed the offering price.[81] There must also be adequate levels

---

73   Procedurally, share buy-back schemes must accord with the Second Company Law Directive 77/91/EEC and CESR (December 2002) *Advice on Level 2 Implementing Measures for the Market Abuse Directive* CESR/02–089d (CESR, Paris), p 34.

74   Regulation (EC) No 2273/2003 of 22 December 2003 implementing Directive 2003/6/EC of the European Parliament and of the Council as regards exemptions for buy-back programmes and stabilisation of financial instruments (2003) OJ L 336/33.

75   See Chapter 2 of MAR.

76   See Article 5 of Regulation (EC) No 2273/2003; see also CESR Advice (Dec 2002), p 36.

77   CESR's Feedback Statement (Dec 2002), p 30. CESR responded to these criticisms by saying that its discretion for expanding the scope of the safe harbour is limited due to the prescriptive requirements of the Directive.

78   See Section 2.2.4 of MAR.

79   See Chapter III Regulation No 2273/2003.

80   See discussion in G A Ferrarini, 'The European Market Abuse Directive' (2004) 41 (3) *Common Market Law Review* 711–741, p 735.

81   CESR's Advice (Dec 2002), pp 39–40.

of disclosure, including disclosure of possible risk factors.[82] Again, behaviour which conforms to the FCA's stabilisation safe harbours is not regarded as market abuse and is not subject to the insider dealing prohibitions set out in the Criminal Justice Act 1993.

Accepted market practice

4.39   The final safe harbour involves an exemption if behaviour complies with accepted market practices, as established by the competent Member State regulatory authority.[83] This is defined as 'practices that are reasonably expected in one or more financial markets and are accepted by the competent authority'.[84] As specified in the MAR:

'1. An accepted market practice features in section 118 in the following ways:

(1)   it is an element in deciding what is inside information in the commodity markets;

(2)   it provides a defence for market abuse (manipulating transactions).

2. The FCA will take the following non-exhaustive factors into account when assessing whether to accept a particular market practice:

(1)   the level of transparency of the relevant market practice to the whole market;

(2)   the need to safeguard the operation of market forces and the proper interplay of the forces of supply and demand (taking into account the impact of the relevant market practice against the main market parameters, such as the specific market conditions before carrying out the relevant market practice, the weighted average price of a single session or the daily closing price);

(3)   the degree to which the relevant market practice has an impact on market liquidity and efficiency;

(4)   the degree to which the relevant practice takes into account the trading mechanism of the relevant market and enables market participants to react properly and in a timely manner to the new market situation created by that practice;

(5)   the risk inherent in the relevant practice for the integrity of, directly or indirectly, related markets, whether regulated or not, in the relevant financial instrument within the whole EEA;

(6)   the outcome of any investigation of the relevant market practice by any competent authority or other authority mentioned in Article 12(1) of the Market Abuse Directive, in particular whether the relevant market practice breached rules or regulations designed to prevent market abuse, or codes of conduct, be it on the market in question or on directly or indirectly related markets within the EEA; and

---

82   See Section 2.3.5 of MAR.
83   Although we focus primarily on acceptable practices in the UK financial markets, UK and non-UK issuers with securities trading on prescribed exchanges in other EU/EEA states should be cognisant of the different practices in those markets.
84   CESR (August 2003) 'Advice on the second set of Level 2 Implementing Measures for the Market Abuse Directive' CESR /03–212c, (CESR, Paris), p 6.

(7)   the structural characteristics of the relevant market including whether it is regulated or not, the types of financial instruments traded and the type of market participants, including the extent of retail investors participation in the relevant market.'[85]

4.40   The FCA has not produced a definitive list, however, of accepted market practices, most probably because it wants to retain its discretion to approve a variety of covered practices. By not being too prescriptive with this requirement, the FCA leaves adequate room for market and regulatory innovation in how it addresses appropriate market practices. ESMA has provided advice, however, but has avoided using prescriptive approaches that would inhibit market innovation in this area.[86] The discretion afforded Member State regulators to approve acceptable market practices, though necessary to respond quickly to changing practices in financial markets, compromises the aim of harmonisation of regulatory approaches across EU states, as different regulators will interpret it in their own way to reflect the needs of practitioners in their markets. This has led to a diversity of approaches amongst EU state regulators in determining what acceptable market practices should be for this safe harbour.

Implications for practitioners

4.41   The Market Abuse Directive's amendments to the UK market abuse safe harbour rules have important consequences for practitioners. The cost and effort to revise risk management practices for firms has been significant. This is compounded by the fact that compliance practices were redesigned just after the first UK market abuse regime came into effect in 2001, which was a costly adjustment for many firms.[87] Most of these additional costs of complying with the Market Abuse Directive will be borne by the financial services and listed company sector which will have to pass the costs on to consumers and investors. The consolidation of the Code that has occurred because of the Directive's implementation has meant greater reliance on the Directive's prescriptive requirements and less discretion for the regulator to craft rules that are more sensitive to market practice. This has arguably limited FCA efforts to develop safe harbours that reflect appropriate market practices in the UK financial markets. Also, a stricter EU regime, due to the UK policy of super- equivalence and elimination of the regular user test, has meant that some EEA jurisdictions have only implemented the Directive's minimum standards, which may mean that the UK could become less competitive with other EEA jurisdictions because of the more stringent requirements of their super- equivalent provisions that are vestiges from the earlier regime. On the other hand, the UK should not lose its competitiveness if the super-equivalent requirements, not required in the Directive, have actually increased investor confidence by making it more difficult to engage in market misconduct without legitimate market efficiency justification. This is the tension confronting UK policymakers and regulators. Moreover, it has become more difficult for practitioners with large cross-border firms in Europe to settle upon acceptable

---

85   See Annex 2 of MAR.
86   CESR (August 2003) 'Feedback Statement for Level 2 Implementing Measures' CESR/03–213b, (CESR, Paris), p 5.
87   See J Coffey, *The Market Abuse Directive—the first use of the Lamfalussy Process.*

practices that comply with the rules of those jurisdictions, while simultaneously complying with the super-equivalent requirements of the UK regime or similar super-equivalent practices in other EEA states.

SANCTIONS

4.42   FSMA 2000[88] requires the FCA to issue a statement of its policy with respect to the imposition of penalties for market abuse and the amount of the penalty. The FCA's policy regarding sanctions is contained in Chapter 6 of the Decision Procedures and Penalties (Manual).[89] In deciding whether to exercise its enforcement power under section 123 regarding any particular behaviour, the FCA must have regard to this statement. The FCA will also take into account any relevant provisions of its Enforcement manual as they are in force at any particular time. The FCA can impose penalties, including fines and public censure, against a person who commits market abuse *or* against persons who require or encourage others to engage in behaviour which would have amounted to market abuse had it been engaged in by that first person.[90] The FCA can also petition a court of law for remedies against those engaged in market abuse or those who encourage or require behaviour that amounts to market abuse by seeking injunctions to freeze the assets of the abuser or other third parties or petition the court for restitution and/or compensation.

REGULATORY POLICY AND THE MARKET ABUSE DIRECTIVE

4.43   The Market Abuse Directive's objectives were to consolidate and update previous legislation and expand the scope of conduct subject to liability to include both civil and criminal offences under the general offence of market manipulation. It also required each Member State to establish a single regulatory authority with responsibility for both investigating and enforcing the requirements of the Directive. The creation of the single authority was intended to increase certainty, accountability and transparency regarding which agency has responsibility for investigating and enforcing the civil offence of market abuse. This means that under the UK market abuse regime the FCA has sole responsibility for investigating and enforcing the market abuse civil offence regime, whilst the FCA and several other UK government agencies, including the Serious Fraud Office, have responsibility for investigating and enforcing the criminal offences of misleading statements and impressions, and the manipulation of benchmarks under sections 89–91 of the FSMA and insider dealing under the Criminal Justice Act 1993 (Part V).[91]

4.44   Implementation across EU Member States was criticised as not being consistent or uniform due to differences in governmental institutions, legal traditions and business culture.[92] Generally, the Directive provided two broad descriptions of the market abuse offence: (1) the insider uses inside information

88   FSMA, s 124(1).
89   See Chapter 10.
90   FSMA, s 123.
91   See 5.5–5.6 below.
92   Charlie Pretzlik (10 May 2004) 'UK warned not to obey EU's rules too strictly', *Financial Times*, p 21.

that is not publicly available to his/her advantage, and (2) he/she attempts to distort or manipulate the demand for, or supply of, financial instruments or the underlying assets on which their value is derived, or provides false or misleading impressions about financial instruments or their underlying assets. This could potentially involve disturbances of the broader financial system without involving a breach of fiduciary duty to a shareholder or other company official. In the aftermath of the 2007–2009 financial crisis, the European market abuse framework was subject to review and significantly expanded in application and coverage. Accordingly, in June 2014 the MAD was replaced by the Market Abuse Regulation (EU MAR)and its related directive imposing criminal sanctions for market abuse (CSMAD).[93]

UK IMPLEMENTATION

4.45   HM Treasury's implementation approach[94] has always aimed to maintain its 'super-equivalence' in parts of the regime that exceeds the Directive's minimum requirements, while amending portions of the regime that do not meet the Directive's minimum standards.[95] The policy objective was to allow the provisions of the UK market abuse regime to remain unaltered where it met the Directive's minimum standards. As the Market Abuse Regulation replaces the Directive (MAD 1), the UK regime will be subject to a maximum harmonisation framework that is much more prescriptive at the EU level. This has potentially created greater compliance costs because of the perceived complexity by business professionals who would be expected to have in depth knowledge of the previous UK civil regime as well as understanding how the EU MAR amends and changes practice under the current regime. The FCA has reduced some of the complexity by amending the Code of Market Conduct and publishing guidance that assists firms in complying with the new requirements of the Directive.

4.46   Nevertheless, when adopting the 2005 Market Abuse implementation regulations, the Treasury decided to reduce what it had perceived to be the broad scope of the offence under the original section 118(2)(a)–(c), which had defined market abuse as misuse of information, creating false or misleading impressions and market distortion based on the application of a regular user test, in order to comply with the Directive's more precisely drafted classifications of market abuse. This complicated policy manoeuvre was described by the Treasury in an explanatory note as:

'[The 2005 Market Abuse] Regulations amend sections 118 and 118A of the Financial Services and Markets Act 2000 (c.8) ("the 2000 Act") which were substituted, together with sections 118B and 118C, for the original section 118 by the Financial Services and Markets Act 2000 (Market Abuse) Regulations 2005, SI 2005/381 as from 1 July 2005. Such Regulations implemented, in part, Directive 2003/6/EC of the European Parliament and of the Council of 28 January 2003 on insider dealing and market manipulation ("the Market Abuse Directive").

93   Directive 2014/57/EU of the European Parliament and of the Council of 16 April 2014 on criminal sanctions for market abuse (market abuse directive) [2014] OJ L 173/179. See 4.47–4.50 below for analysis of EU Market Abuse Regulation.
94   HM Treasury and FSA, 'UK Implementation of the EU Market Abuse Directive' (Directive 2003/6/EC), *A Consultation Document*, June 2004, p 3.
95   *Ibid*, p 15.

Subsections 118(4), 118(8), 118A(2) and 118A(3) of the 2000 Act retain the definitions of market abuse which are broader than those in Articles 1 to 5 of the Market Abuse Directive and were already in the original section 118. Section 118(9) provides that these provisions will cease to have effect on 30 June 2008; section 118A(6) does the same for the related provisions in section 118A.

Regulations 3(2) and 3(3) amend sections 118(9) and 118A(6) of the 2000 Act to change the date on which the provisions affected by those sections will cease to have effect. The result of these amendments is that subsections (4) and (8) of section 118 of the 2000 Act and related ancillary provisions will remain in force until 31 December 2009.'[96]

One of the important effects of the Market Abuse directive, therefore, has been to define the market abuse offence in a more precise way, and to limit what the UK government had perceived to be its broad application through the three types of market abuse in section 118(2)(a)–(c) combined with the regular user test. Nevertheless, it is submitted that the overall effect of the Market Abuse Directive has been to make the UK market abuse regime stricter by providing more precision to the definitions of the relevant offences and removing many of the safe harbours under the previous regime with a view to enhancing investor confidence in the UK market and across European markets. As discussed below, the new European market abuse framework represents an important overhaul of the previous regime incorporated in the MAD. Most of the MAR provisions are expected to come into force by 2016 and they will be directly applicable in EU Member States. In the UK, the government has decided not to opt in to CSMAD. In any case, further changes are expected in the UK market abuse regime consequently to the direct applicability of MAR.

EU MARKET ABUSE REGULATION (EU MAR)

4.47   EU policymakers sought to address the problem of market abuse in the over-the-counter (OTC) derivatives markets by extending the scope of the Market Abuse Directive (MAD 1) to apply to a wider range of financial instruments, including all OTC derivative contracts traded by EU counterparties or on EU markets or trading platforms.[97] The EC published its first formal legislative proposal for a new market abuse regulation and a new market abuse directive in October 2011. An updated proposal was published in July 2012, reacting primarily to the LIBOR scandal and extending the market abuse regime to cover directly also any manipulation of benchmarks. Somewhat amended text was endorsed by the European Parliament in September 2013 and final version of the EU Regulation on market abuse, No 596/2014 (EU MAR) entered into force on 2 July 2014.[98] EU MAR (other than the provisions dealing with the exemptions for the share buy-back program and stabilization

---

96   Financial Services and Markets Act 2000 (Market Abuse) Regulations 2008, SI 2008/1439.
97   In this regard, it should be recalled that the G20 Heads of State 2009 Pittsburgh communique provided that one of the three pillars of the international regulatory reform agenda should include "protecting against market abuse". The G20 Pittsburgh Summit. Heads of State Communication providing that one of the three pillars of the international regulatory reform agenda included "protecting against market abuse".
98   Council Regulation (EU) 596/2014 of 16 April 2014 on Market Abuse (Market Abuse Regulation) and repealing Council Directive 2003/6/EC and Commission Directives 2003/124/EC, 2003/125/EC and 2004/72/EC [2014] OJ L 173/1 (the 'MAR').

which have already entered into force on 2 July 2014) will become directly applicable in July 2016 and will replace MAD 1. Its stated purpose is to establish a more uniform and stronger framework in order to preserve market integrity, avoid potential regulatory arbitrage and provide more legal certainty and less regulatory complexity for market participants.[99]

4.48   EU MAR replaces the Market Abuse Directive (MAD 1),[100] and was also accompanied by a separate Directive imposing an obligation on all Member States to create criminal sanctions for market abuse (MAD 2).[101] MAD 2 was introduced to harmonise administrative sanctions in each EU Member State and also to introduce for the first time a requirement to establish criminal offences for market abuse in Member States where market abuse has so far been only enforced with administrative sanctions.

EU MAR's Scope

4.49   The scope of MAD 1 was limited to activity relating to financial instruments admitted to trading on a regulated market or for which a request for admission to trading on such a market has been made. The view taken now by the EU authorities is that financial instruments are increasingly traded on other venues and the scope of EU MAR should therefore cover these new trading facilities. The new trading facilities have been defined in Article 4 of the Markets in Financial Instruments Directive (MiFID 2) which was published at the same time as the Markets in Financial Instruments Regulation (MiFIR).[102] As a result, EU MAR applies not only to financial instruments admitted to trading on a regulated market but also to any financial instruments traded on a multilateral trading facility (MTF),[103] admitted to trading on an MTF or for which a request for admission to trading on an MTF has been made and to financial instruments traded on an organised trading facility (OTF).[104] It also applies to financial instruments not covered by any of the above, the price or value of which depends on or has an effect on the price or value of a financial instrument otherwise covered by EU MAR. This effectively broadens the scope of EU MAR to various instruments traded over the counter (such instruments, 'OTC instruments') such as credit default swaps and contracts for differences. In addition, EU MAR now also covers behaviour which occurs outside any of these trading venues, acknowledging the fact that a financial

---

99   Reg 596/2014, Recital 4.
100   Directive 2003/6/EC (MAD 1).
101   Council Directive 2014/57/EU of 16 April 2014 on criminal sanctions for market abuse (market abuse directive) [2014] OJ L 173/179 (MAD 2).
102   Council Directive 2014/65/EU of 15 May 2014 on markets in financial instruments [2014] OJ L 173/349 (MiFID 2) and Council Regulation 600/2014 of 15 May 2014 on markets in financial instruments (MiFIR). MiFID 2 and MiFIR together replace Directive 2004/39/EC of the European Parliament and Council of 21 April 2004 on markets in financial instruments (MiFID 1) which had been in force since November 2007.
103   An MTF is defined in Article 4 of MiFID 2 as: 'a multilateral system, operated by an investment firm or a market operator, which brings together multiple third-party buying and selling interests in financial instruments – in the system and in accordance with non-discretionary rules – in a way that results in a contract in accordance with Title II of this Directive'.
104   An OTF is defined in Article 4 of MiFID 2 as: 'a multilateral system which is not a regulated market or an MTF and in which multiple third-party buying and selling interests in bonds, structured finance products, emission allowances or derivatives are able to interact in the system in a way that results in a contract in accordance with Title II of this Directive'.

instrument may be manipulated through behaviour that does not occur on any of the trading venues.[105] By broadening the scope to cover instruments traded on an MTF or OTF, the EU market abuse rules now apply to very diverse markets and instruments. While the regulated market and multilateral trading facility (MTF) are categories covering markets where financial instruments are traded continuously, an OTF is a category that covers a number of fixed income broker crossing systems, wholesale interdealer markets and voice-hybrid systems that do not rely on continuous trading. By extending the application of the rules to other trading venues, the European market abuse rules now apply to a number of securities that are listed on markets outside the EU as many of them are also traded on an EU MTF. This significantly extends the extra-territorial reach of the market abuse regulation to insider dealing and market manipulation taking place entirely outside the EU simply because the trading relates to an instrument which happens also to be admitted to trading on a trading facility in the EU. There is no need for any EU entity to be involved or for there to be any impact on the markets in the EU.

4.50   The EU MAR's approach was to extend the application of the concepts developed in MAD 1 to be applied to instruments traded on a regulated market. The regulation, however, does not seem to make any distinction between the equities markets, the bond markets and the commodities markets although it is generally understood that for example the pricing of bonds is less dependent on the issuer itself than is the case with pricing of shares. Equities are priced based on expectations regarding the issuing company, expectations of future earnings and overall expectations regarding the industry. In contrast, bond markets are dependent on a number of other factors such as interest rate levels, volatility, inflation and liquidity. By focusing on the differences in how these markets operate, the regulator could tailor different approaches to applying and enforcing the market abuse rules for different instruments traded in different markets. The EU MAR's approach was however to apply concepts developed primarily in the context of equity markets and apply them broadly to the debt markets and to all other covered financial instruments and commodities. The regulation also does not distinguish between different products when referring to the 'issuer' of a financial product. Derivatives, for example, do not have an 'issuer' so applying EU MAR to derivatives remains problematic where the regulation refers to an 'issuer' of a financial product.

---

105   Regulation (EU) 596/2014, Art 2(3).

Chapter 5

FSMA criminal offences of market manipulation

INTRODUCTION

5.1   An intrinsic characteristic of financial markets is that prices move in response to individual transactions and to supply and demand factors in the market. An efficient market for securities can often lead to volatile price movements that might reflect sharply changing investor preferences based on the dissemination of price sensitive information. Volatile movements in securities prices might also reflect significant adjustments in demand and supply of the relevant assets. Nevertheless, more sinister motivations of market participants can create distortions from the regular patterns of demand and supply which can undermine the efficiency and integrity of the market. Some commentators would agree that a price is likely to be distorted when price movements deviate from the norms expected by a regular user of the market. This could potentially lead to some forms of legitimate behaviour attracting civil liability for market abuse because of the sudden movement of asset prices that respond to different information in the market. Indeed, Keynes noted that changing investor sentiments regarding their perception of average investor opinion in the market could suddenly change based on rational and irrational factors which could result in a liquidity shock to financial markets.[1] The Financial Services Authority recognised that distortion as a form of market abuse was very controversial. There was a concern that some types of legitimate behaviour would be restricted or prohibited by the market abuse regime. The civil and criminal law should acknowledge and make exception for market users who legitimately trade at times and in sizes most beneficial to them in maximising profit, but yet with a potentially volatile impact on the market. The criminal law of market distortion or manipulation accepts that where prices are trading outside of their normal range, this will not necessarily indicate that they are trading at a distorted or manipulated level. For the criminal law to impose liability, a person's 'purpose' or 'intent' is particularly relevant to whether they are engaged in distortion or manipulation of the market. This chapter addresses the Financial Services and Markets Act 2000 (FSMA) criminal law of market manipulation and examines some of the challenges for the Financial Conduct Authority (FCA) in determining

---

1   JM Keynes, *The General Theory of Employment, Interest, and Money* (1936), Chapter 12.

whether behaviour manipulates the market, given that market transactions inherently affect the price of the market. The chapter will also address the relevant provisions of the EU Market Abuse Regulation that prohibit market manipulation of most financial instruments – both off exchange and in the OTC derivatives markets.

MANIPULATION

5.2   The term 'manipulation' in the context of financial markets has pervaded markets from the Dutch tulip bulb mania in the early seventeenth century to the collapse of the share prices of internet dotcom companies and Enron and WorldCom in the early 2000s. Some major jurisdictions, such as the United States, do not define 'manipulate' or 'manipulation'.[2] The US Securities and Exchange Commission has adopted rules, instead, that describe 'manipulation' by relating it to specific acts or activities that are then proscribed as 'manipulation' or 'manipulative'. The term 'manipulate' or 'manipulative' is often described as involving 'motive' or 'intent' to punish a result that is socially undesirable. A strict interpretation of the term would lead one to deduce that many types of acts could be characterised as manipulation, including activities regularly engaged in by securities professionals and others, but not necessarily in contexts predetermined to be undesirable. A less than rigid standard may be used to define 'manipulation' as it could cover many activities in the marketplace that are not viewed as harmful or socially undesirable. Indeed, the concept of manipulation is a constantly evolving one that takes on a less than objective standard that is similar to the 'he knows it when he sees it' definition used by former US Supreme Court Justice Potter Stewart. For instance, the Seventh Circuit Court of Appeals adopted a definition of 'manipulation' as 'the creation of an artificial price by planned action'.[3] The Eighth Circuit utilises a definition that describes manipulation to occur when a price does not 'reflect basic forces of supply and demand',[4] yet no agreement exists regarding the types of behaviour that would qualify as market manipulation. Some agreement has coalesced around certain conduct that can be termed as artificial factors that result in manipulation in financial markets, such as 'corner', 'squeeze', 'domination and control', 'rumour manipulation', 'investor interest' manipulation and even 'price effect' manipulation, but these criteria appear to be hard to define in practice as the US courts have been contradictory in the application of these terms to conduct that is allegedly manipulative. In contrast, UK policymakers have since 1986 defined market manipulation, first under the Financial Services Act 1986, s 47(1) and (2), and later under the FSMA, s 397. This chapter examines sections 89, 90 and 91 of the Financial Services Act 2012 (FSA 2012) and which define the criminal offence of market manipulation, including section 91's criminalisation of the manipulation of financial benchmarks, such as Libor. The chapter then discusses how the EU Market Abuse Regulation defines market manipulation as a form of market abuse that attracts civil liability.

2   The US Securities and Exchange Act 1934 does not define 'manipulative' or 'manipulation'.
3   *General Foods Corpn v Brannon* 170 F 2d 220, 234 (7th Cir, 1948).
4   *Cargill Inc v Hardin* 452 F 2d 1154 at 1163 (8th Cir, 1971).

UK CRIMINAL OFFENCES FOR MISLEADING STATEMENTS AND PRACTICES

5.3   As of 2012, some of the world's largest banks came under regulatory scrutiny in the UK and USA because of their role in the London Interbank Offered Rate (LIBOR) scandal. Investigations revealed that, between 2008 and 2013, the banks manipulated the LIBOR rates to their own advantage. Investigations are still ongoing and the concerned financial institutions have been facing civil lawsuits and regulatory fines. In the UK, prior to the LIBOR scandal, conduct such as misleading statements and misleading practices were criminal offences under section 397 of FSMA.[5] The LIBOR facts led to the repeal of section 397 through Part VII of the Financial Services Act 2012, which came into force on 1 April 2013. To have a better understanding of the new provisions, it is desirable to revisit the old section 397 regime. Section 397 of the FSMA established two criminal offences. First, it created an offence of making false or misleading statements in relation to market activity.[6] Misleading statements could be made in one of three ways: (1) making a misleading statement whilst knowing that it is false; (2) concealing facts about such statements with dishonest intent; or (3) recklessly making (dishonestly or otherwise) a misleading statement. In practice, to commit the offence, it was necessary that a person, whether dishonestly or recklessly, made the statement or concealed the facts with a view to inducing another person to enter into an investment agreement.[7] In this context, evidence should be given that the person in question either acted dishonestly and was therefore fraudulent in making the particular statement or was reckless in doing so. On the other hand, in the case of recklessness, evidence should be given as to the fact that there was a high degree of negligence in the absence of fraud and dishonesty.[8] Secondly, it punished the creation of false or misleading impressions in relation to the value of investments. In this respect, section 397(3) stated: 'Any person who does any act or engages in any course of conduct which creates a false or misleading impression as to the market in or the price or value of any relevant investments is guilty of an offence if he does so for the purpose of creating that impression and of thereby inducing another person to acquire, dispose of, subscribe for or underwrite those investments or to refrain from doing so or to exercise, or refrain from exercising, any rights conferred by those investments.' Significantly, individuals or firms could be liable of an offence

---

5   The statutory predecessor of the market manipulation provisions of section 397 is section 47 of the Financial Services Act 1986 (FSA 1986). Section 47(1) prohibited misleading statements, while section 47(2) prohibited misleading practices. Under the FSA 1986, the number of prosecutions for violations of section 47 was less than 10. The conviction rate was 50%. The FSA has had little more success with section 397, while bringing few prosecutions

6   Section 397(1) states that it applies to a person 'who – (a) makes a statement, promise or forecast which he knows to be misleading, false or deceptive in a material particular; (b) dishonestly conceals any material facts whether in connection with a statement, promise or forecast made by him or otherwise; or (c) recklessly makes (dishonestly or otherwise) a statement, promise or forecast which is misleading, false or deceptive in a material particular.'

7   Section 397(1)(c).

8   Unlike previous criminal offences for insider dealing, the making of false and misleading statements may be committed either within or outside the market and applies to all natural persons including legal persons, such as companies, limited partnerships, limited liability partnerships (LLPs), limited liability companies (LLCs), or other business organisations. The aim of this particular offence was to prevent deliberate market manipulation by inducing investors to enter transactions based upon false statements.

under section 397 if they made false statements with the intention of inducing or preventing another person from entering into an agreement or exercising (or refraining from exercising) particular rights in relation to an agreement. In each of the two criminal offences, recklessness was sufficient *mens rea* – with the exception of section 397(1)(b) which required the accused to have acted dishonestly in concealing material facts, involving recklessness as to whether it induced a person to enter into an investment agreement.

5.4 Unlike the actual knowledge standard for the insider dealing offence under Part V of the Criminal Justice Act 1993, recklessness is an objective test. The objective test of recklessness involves the following question: did the accused make the statement while recklessly disregarding the known risks?[9] The making of reckless or grossly negligent statements which attracted criminal liability under section 397 could also be a concern for a person engaging in financial promotions, whether as an authorised or unauthorised person. Furthermore, it could be relevant to firms or individuals involved in making public statements during takeovers and in other circumstances governed by the FSMA regime. The old regime also set out proper defence mechanisms. Under both sections 397(2) and 397(3), the accused could assert that its conduct was in conformity with price stabilisation rules, or other acceptable market practices, such as control of information rules. These defences were similar to defences which could be asserted for committing the market abuse offence. Moreover, under section 397(3), the accused could assert the defence that it believed reasonably that its conduct would not create a false or misleading impression. This required active conduct to corroborate its belief that its conduct did not create false or misleading impressions, not simply subjective perceptions.

5.5 The two-offence framework of section 397 has been replaced by three separate offences in sections 89 ('misleading statements'), 90 ('misleading impressions') and 91 ('misleading statements etc in relation to benchmarks') of the FSA 2012. As to the misleading statement offence, pursuant to section 89(1), this is to be identified in the conduct of a person who: (1) makes a statement which [the person] knows to be false or misleading in a material respect; (2) makes a statement which is false or misleading in a material respect, being reckless as to whether it is; or (3) dishonestly conceals any material facts whether in connection with a statement made by [the person] or otherwise. Such conduct concretises the offence in question where they influence a person's decision as to the stipulation of an agreement or exercise of rights relating to investments. Even though there are some slight changes in wording, section 89 substantially replicates section 397(1).[10] The same applies to section 90 on 'misleading impressions'. However, section 90 strengthened the scope of the offence originally set out in section 397(3). Not only does it punish those who create impressions to induce another person to make investments or refrain from doing so, but it also outlaws impressions created with the view to making *gain* for oneself or causing *loss* to another person. In this respect,

---

9   Some practitioners have interpreted this to mean section 397 criminalises 'grossly negligent' statements and conduct. See Charles Marquand *Comments on FSMA market abuse and market manipulation requirements* (2003) (London).

10 The only difference is that s 397 outlawed misleading promises and forecasts in addition to misleading statements. Both promises and forecasts are not included in s 89. Moreover, s 397 provided for reckless statements 'dishonestly made or otherwise'. This wording has not been included either.

recklessness as to whether the impression is false or misleading, or awareness that the impression is likely to result in gain or loss, are the thresholds that section 90 sets out to create criminal liability.[11] Both 'misleading statements' and 'misleading impressions' under sections 89 and 90 are subject to the same defences, as illustrated above.

5.6 In addition to misleading statements and misleading impressions, section 91 criminalises the offence of 'misleading statements etc in relation to benchmarks'. Its provisions incorporate both the offences of false or misleading statements and false or misleading impressions in relation to the setting of a 'relevant benchmark' (eg, Libor). The former offence is committed when three situations occur: (1) a false or misleading statement is made during the arrangements for the setting of a relevant benchmark; (2) the statement will influence the setting of the benchmark; (3) the person who makes the statement knows, or is reckless as to whether, this is false or misleading.[12] On the other hand, the latter offence arises in relation to a misleading impression as to the price of any investment or interest rate of any transaction. Other than the awareness or recklessness as to whether the impression is false or misleading, section 91 also requires the intention to create a false or misleading impression and awareness that this may affect the setting of a relevant benchmark.[13] From a jurisdictional perspective, the new offence does not change the scope of the previous section 397: misleading statements must be made in the UK or to a person in the UK; likewise, misleading impressions and the course of conduct must be respectively created or take place in the UK. Furthermore, like in the event of offences pursuant to sections 89 and 90, charges under section 91 are balanced through the possibility of defence. This includes, for instance, giving evidence that statements were made in compliance with price stabilising rules or for the purpose of stabilising the price of investments.[14] Finally, pursuant to section 93(4), relevant benchmarks for the offence set out in section 91 were only those known as LIBOR. However, in light of the new scandal concerning the manipulation of the closing spot rate in foreign exchange (Forex) transactions and consequent criminal and regulatory investigations in the UK and elsewhere, calls have been made to widen the UK criminal regime for market abuse so as to include additional financial benchmarks. To this end, in June 2014, the UK government announced the Fair and Effective Market Review (the Review) jointly led by the HM Treasury, the Bank of England and the FCA.[15] Following the recommendations issued by the authorities in their report, seven other benchmarks are now designated as 'relevant benchmarks' under section 91 of the Act.[16] Consequently, in addition to LIBOR, the FCA's enforcement powers under section 91 are now extended to other benchmarks the manipulation of which constitutes criminal offence.

---

11   See s 90(3)(4).
12   See s 91(1).
13   See s 91(2)(d).
14   See s 91(3)(a), (b), (c).
15   Fair and Effective Markets Review (FEMR), 'Recommendations on Additional Financial Benchmarks to be Brought into UK Regulatory Scope' (August 2014) Report to HM Treasury.
16   See FEMR Final Report (June 2015), these include, in addition to LIBOR, Sterling Overnight Index Average (SONIA), Repurchase Overnight Index Average (RONIA), LBMA Gold Price, LBMA Silver Price, WM/Reuters London 4pm Closing Spot Rate, ICE Brent Index and ICE Swap Rate.

MARKET DISTORTION AND MARKET MANIPULATION

5.7 If the behaviour engaged in interferes with the proper operation of market forces with the purpose of positioning prices at a distorted level, then such behaviour could attract criminal liability for market manipulation. The necessary *mens rea* may be shown even if the defendant had other objectives for entering into the transaction so long as the manipulative practice was the actuating purpose of the transaction, and that there was a real and not fanciful likelihood that the behaviour in question will have such an effect, though the effect need not be more likely to occur than not. The 'behaviour' may, or may be likely to, give rise to more than one effect, including the manipulative behaviour in question.

5.8 A type of market distortion or manipulation can be caused by price positioning. For example, price positioning can occur if a person enters into a transaction or series of transactions with the purpose of positioning the price of a 'qualifying investment' or 'relevant product' at a distorted level. The positioning need not be the sole purpose for entering into the transaction or transactions, but must be an 'actuating purpose', defined as a purpose which motivates or incites a person to act.

5.9 In considering whether to bring a criminal action for market manipulation based on price positioning, the FCA will examine the legitimate commercial rationale and how the transaction could have been implemented in a proper way. Some of the factors that are taken into account in considering whether price positioning has taken place are much more detailed and can provide more certain guidance to market users, but there is a recognition that market practices evolve and the notion of what is acceptable market conduct can evolve to influence a determination by the regulatory authority of whether to bring an action.[17]

ABUSIVE SQUEEZES

5.10 Two particular types of market distortion identified by the Code of Market Conduct under the original market abuse regime were price positioning and abusive squeezes. These practices could also constitute market manipulation under section 397 and would not be prohibited by FSA 2012, ss 89 and 90. Although the statutory conditions governing the market manipulation offences do not specifically refer to distortions of supply and demand in market, the FCA could potentially bring a criminal action against those engaging in such behaviour.

5.11 An abusive squeeze is behaviour which could amount to both market abuse and market manipulation. For instance, the Code of Market Conduct defined an abusive squeeze as occurring when (Code at MAR 1.6.13) a person had a significant influence over the supply of or demand for, or delivery mechanisms for, a 'qualifying investment' or 'relevant product'; and had a position (directly or indirectly) in an investment under which quantities of the 'qualifying investment' or 'relevant product' in question are deliverable. Abuse would occur if the person engaged in behaviour with the purpose of

---

17   Specific examples of price positioning that could potentially be market distortion or market manipulation were listed in the Code at MAR 1.6.12.

positioning at a distorted level the price at which others have to deliver, take delivery or defer delivery to satisfy their obligations (the purpose need not be the sole purpose for such conduct, but must be an actuating purpose).

5.12   Moreover, it should be emphasised that a significant influence over supply, for instance where there is market tightness, is not in itself abusive.[18] Regulators and enforcement authorities might rely on several factors that will be taken into account when considering whether a person has engaged in an abusive squeeze. These factors include: the extent to which a person is willing to relax his control or other influence in order to help maintain an orderly market and the price at which he is willing to do so; and the extent to which the person's activity causes or risks causing settlement default by other market users on a multilateral basis and not just a bilateral basis. The more widespread the risk of multilateral settlement default, the more likely that the market has been distorted.[19]

FCA PROSECUTION

5.13   FSMA subjects market manipulation and the offences relating to financial services to a civil and criminal penalties regime. In general, section 150 of the FSMA confers a private action right for certain breaches of FSMA, such as the market abuse regime. With specific regard to the FCA's powers, under section 380 of the FSMA, the FCA can apply to court for an injunction to restrain a breach of the relevant requirement (or against a person 'knowingly concerned' in a violation). Furthermore, section 382 authorises the FCA to apply to court for a restitution order against a person who has violated a 'relevant requirement' of FSMA. The FCA may also seek a court order to require a defendant to disgorge profits or pay compensation to any party suffering losses arising from a breach of FSMA, including for market abuse and market manipulation.[20] From a criminal perspective, it is worth mentioning that in 2005 the FCA enforced the market manipulation offence based on misleading statements *in R v Rigby, Bailey, and Rowley* case.[21] The new offences in Part VII of the FSA 2012 do not modify the previous regime

---

18   See discussion of factors as it relates to market distortion for the civil offence of market abuse in MAR 1.6.14.

19   The Code of Market Conduct gives a specific example of an abusive squeeze at MAR 1.6.18 to assist market users. It seems likely that the FCA will give specific examples of price positioning when giving guidance to market users.

20   Although a private right of action exists for those who suffered losses because of market abuse, no private right action exists for persons who have suffered losses as a result of market manipulation.

21   The facts of the case were as follows. On 2 May 2002, AIT directors Rigby & Bailey issued a statement via the Regulatory News Service that both turnover and profit were in line with expectations. The forecasted profit depended on revenue from three contracts worth £4.8 million. The announcement was rendered false because the contracts did not exist. Rigby and Bailey were found guilty by a jury in August 2005 of one count of recklessly making a statement, promise or forecast which was misleading, false or deceptive. Rigby was chairman & CEO of AIT and Bailey was AIT's finance director. Rigby served a custodial sentence of three and a half years, while Bailey served a custodial sentence of two years. Defendant Rigby was convicted of one count of recklessly making a statement to the market which was misleading, false or deceptive in a material particular; and Bailey was convicted of one count of recklessly making a statement, promise or forecast which was false, misleading or deceptive in a material particular, and Rowley was convicted on all counts. See FSA/PN/106/2005 (7 October 2005).

under section 397, that is, a fine or a maximum of seven years' imprisonment following a trial on indictment.[22]

5.14   Nonetheless, the repeal of section 397, and its replacement by three separate offences, must be analysed in the context that the Financial Services Authority, among other things, was tightly circumscribed under section 397 in its ability to bring criminal prosecutions against individuals involved in the manipulation of LIBOR. Such limitations in the power to prosecute were underlined during the regulatory debate over LIBOR: 'we [the FCA] are not a general fraud prosecutor. We have specific powers to prosecute particular offences, and I am sure that you will be aware that we have spent quite a lot of time and energy on prosecuting both section 397 offences and indeed insider dealing offences in recent years. What we do not have is a remit to prosecute false accounting, conspiracy and soon in a general sense. We could prosecute it as ancillary to one of our main offences, so if there was a markets offence, you could throw in money laundering as well, but our investigative powers are limited to the offences that we have the ability to prosecute'.[23] At the outbreak of the LIBOR scandal, the Financial Services Authority and later the FCA did exercise their civil enforcement powers.[24] However, no individuals were held criminally liable by the Financial Services Authority or FCA because both bodies believed that they did not have the power to prosecute in relation to the manipulation of benchmarks. Consequently, the new offences, in particular section 91, have been created against the backdrop of these jurisdictional limitations. According to some data provided by the UK authorities issued in June 2015, trials and investigations are still ongoing in relation to LIBOR and Forex manipulation. Currently, the FCA is liaising with the Serious Fraud Office and the National Crime Agency to properly address crimes in Fixed Income, Currency and Commodities (FCCI) markets. The FCA has been active through regulatory enforcement actions for market abuse practices committed between 2003 and 2015.[25] In this context, it has imposed numerous fines in relation to LIBOR, Forex and gold fixing cases.[26]

EU MARKET ABUSE REGULATION AND MARKET MANIPULATION

5.15   EU Mar strengthens civil offence of market abuse involving market manipulation. Article 12 of MAR sets out what constitutes market manipulation and Annex 1 provides details of indicators that shall be taken into account when transactions or orders to trade are examined. Most importantly, due to

22   See FSA 2012, s 92. The FCA's authority to prosecute the criminal offences of insider dealing, misleading statements and market manipulation is provided in section 402. Civil and criminal sanctions could be imposed on those who violated section 397.
23   House of Common Treasury Committee, 'Fixing LIBOR: Some Preliminary Findings' (18 August 2012) Second Report of Session 2002-13 HC 481-I.
24   As of February 2013 there were three relevant cases of enforcement actions taken by the FCA against major investment banks: Barclays (£59.5m fines), UBS (£160m fines) and RBS (£89.5m fines), see FCA, 'Enforcement Annual Performance Account 2012/13',: http://www.fca.org.uk/static/documents/annual-report/fsa-enforcement-performance-account-2012-13.pdf.
25   See www.fca.org.uk/your-fca/documents/final-notices/2014/mark-stevenson.
26   See www.fca.org.uk/static/documents/benchmark-fines.pdf.

the broadened scope of MAR, the market abuse provisions now apply to any financial instruments traded, admitted to trading, or for which a request for admission to trading on a RM or MTF has been made, any financial instrument traded on an OTF, OTC derivatives (including CDS and CFDs) and spot commodity contracts (if the price of such a commodity contract is based on that of a derivative or if certain financial instruments are referenced to such spot commodity contracts). Following the information on LIBOR rigging, the initial MAR proposal was amended in 2012 to also cover manipulation of calculation of benchmarks.[27] ESMA has prepared in the final report containing its final technical advice on possible delegated acts concerning MAR (the 'FR 2015/224'[28]) a non-exhaustive list of examples of practices that could be considered as market manipulation, linking the examples to the indicators set out in Annex 1. It has been clarified that market manipulation can occur across products if for example a transaction in a derivative may result in undue influence on the price of the underlying financial instrument.

5.16 Notwithstanding such non-exhaustive list, ESMA did confirm that an example of a practice that is deemed illicit could be justified by legitimate reasons if otherwise in compliance with the applicable rules and regulations. A person entering into a transaction that could be deemed to constitute market manipulation may be able to establish that his reasons for entering into such transaction were legitimate and in conformity with accepted practice on the relevant market.[29] However, the current proposal in FR 2015/224 does not give any further guidance on what would constitute 'legitimate reasons' in this context.

5.17 On the other hand, ESMA did state that absence of an intent to manipulate the market does not necessarily imply that particular conduct may not still fall within the scope of market manipulation. A person may therefore commit market abuse unintentionally by engaging in practices that have certain manipulative effects even without realising that such activity may have such consequences.

5.18 MAR also extends the discretion afforded to Member States under MAD 1 to decide what are accepted market practices in the OTC markets and thus do not constitute market manipulation. Under MAD 1, accepted market practice (AMP) is a specific market practice that could fall under the definition of market manipulation but is accepted by the competent authority of a Member State if carried out for a legitimate reason and therefore does not constitute market manipulation. Since MAR applies also to OTC transactions, AMP may be also established in the context of the OTC markets. ESMA left to the competent authority to decide when approving an AMP whether such AMP can be conducted only by regulated entities or also by any unregulated entities participating in the market.

BUYBACKS AND PRICE STABILISATION

5.19 Buy-backs and stabilisation activities are designed to increase price of securities or maintain prices for such securities at an increased level.

---

27 Regulation (EU) 596/2014, art 12(1)(d).
28 ESMA, 'Final Report: ESMA's technical advice on possible delegated acts concerning the Market Abuse Regulation'; see www.esma.europa.eu/system/files/2015-224.pdf.
29 Reg (EU) 596/2014, Recital 42.

In order for such activity not to be considered as market manipulation, it has to be carried out within limitations set out by a 'safe harbour'. Initially, this safe harbour was set out in Regulation No 2273/2003, implementing the buy-back and stabilisation measures in MAD 1. MAR details the framework for the exception from the overall prohibition of market manipulation granted to certain buy-back transactions in Article 5.

5.20 Interestingly, ESMA concludes on the basis of the fact that Article 5(1) and (3) and Article 3(17) refer to 'shares' that buy-backs using derivative instruments should not benefit from the safe harbour set out in Article 5 of MAR.[30] This would be a significant limitation of scope of the safe harbour compared to the approach in MAD 1 and the Implementing Regulation 2273/2003 which expressly recognises in Article 5(1) that the purchase of own shares can be effected through a derivative financial instrument. Since the wording in Article 8 of MAD 1 and Article 5 of MAR is identical, there seems to be very little ground for such a significant departure from the existing approach.

5.21 In order for a buy-back programme to be within the safe harbour, the issuer must publicly disclose information regarding any purchase transactions within seven trading days. It also has to provide detailed information about such transactions to each relevant competent authority (ie if the shares are listed on multiple markets, it has to report to each competent authority for the market on which the transactions have been executed). There seems to be no limitation in the proposed Article 5(3) of the draft RTS set out in Annex IV of the *Consultation Paper* 809 that would only require information to be provided to a competent authority of an MTF or an OTF with respect to which the issuer has approved trading of its financial instruments. This may mean that in practice an issuer will have to report to each relevant competent authority if its instruments happen to be traded on an OTF even if the issuer has not approved such trading. Any purchases cannot be made at a price higher than the highest price of the last independent trade or the highest current bid on the relevant trading venue. The safe harbour is not available to any transactions during an auction (such as the closing auction) if the instrument is otherwise traded on a trading venue on a continuous basis. Any purchase transactions are limited to 25% of the daily volume traded on the relevant venue.[31]

ANALYSIS AND CONCLUSION

5.22 Manipulation of the price of securities is a form of securities fraud that undermines the efficiency and integrity of financial markets. Today, market manipulation occurs across national borders through a variety of means, including the use of the internet to manipulate stock prices by, among other things, disseminating information that is false and negative about an

---

30 ESMA, 'Consultation Paper: Draft Technical Standards on the Market Abuse Regulation', (2014/809, ESMA 2014) para 9, see www.esma.europa.eu/system/files/esma_2014809_ consultation_paper_on_mar_draft_technical_standards.pdf.

31 Ibid, Article 4 of the proposed RTS attached as Annex IV to CP 809. see www.esma.europa. eu/system/files/esma_2014-809_consultation_paper_on_mar_draft_technical_standards. pdf.

issuer in an effort to drive down the price of its securities, or, alternatively, disseminating false information in order to drive a company's share price higher. UK authorities have brought few prosecutions of market manipulation as defined in section 397 or insider dealing as defined under Part V of the Criminal Justice Act 1993, as a number of obstacles, including high evidentiary standards of proof and the complexity of bringing enforcement actions against white collar criminals, have made it difficult for UK authorities to show much success in this area. Indeed, the low number of prosecutions brought since FSMA became effective in 2001 can be explained in part by inefficient use of resources and poor training and skills of UK enforcement authorities. Moreover, inadequate pre-trial criminal procedures and the absence of effective negotiation mechanisms (eg plea bargaining) have also undermined the effectiveness of UK enforcement authorities.

5.23 FSMA supplemented the market abuse regime by creating a broad market manipulation criminal offence of making misleading statements, both dishonestly or recklessly, with a view to inducing a person to enter into an investment agreement.[32] The market manipulation offence also included engaging in misleading conduct for purpose of inducing another to acquire investments.[33] This regime was regarded as inadequate in the wake of the LIBOR scandal and replaced with the new framework in Part 7 of the FSA 2012 which, in addition to misleading statements and impressions, sets out the new offence of 'misleading statements etc in relation to benchmarks'.

5.24 The FCA, however, is only now beginning to initiate enforcement actions to impose criminal sanctions for the market manipulation offences. The previous poor record of the FSA and other UK enforcement authorities in prosecuting criminal market manipulation has now changed where the FCA has begun to bring more criminal cases which could have also been brought as regulatory enforcement actions for market abuse.[34] Even in civil enforcement actions, the FSA had little success in reaching substantial settlements and admissions of wrongdoing by firms acting in concert with sophisticated trading strategies that resulted in arguably unlawful market distortions.[35] Other regulatory and enforcement complexities arise from the liberalisation and globalisation of financial markets and the associated cross-border dimension of market manipulation and the need to coordinate national investigations and enforcement actions with other national authorities, especially with EEA states whose prescribed exchanges and regulated markets attract the jurisdiction of the FCA and other EEA states. Finally, in light of the 2007–2008 financial

---

32   FSMA, s 397(1) and (2).
33   Section 397(3).
34   For example, under the pre-2012 FSMA, a number of FSA regulatory enforcement actions for market abuse could have been brought as criminal enforcement actions for making material misstatements or engaging in manipulative conduct. The FSA's enforcement action against Royal Dutch/Shell Group for making knowingly false statements and other misrepresentations about its oil and gas reserves that had a significant impact on the group's share prices could also have been brought as a case of criminal misstatements to the market about Shell's future prospects. FSA Final Notice, *The Shell Transport and Trading Company and the Royal Dutch Petroleum Company* NV (October 2005).
35   The FSA investigation into the activities of certain fund managers and brokers operating in the split capital investment trust sector led to settlement that was inadequate to compensate most of the claims of investors who had invested in zero-dividend preference shares and other unit trusts and financial products that invested in these risky instruments. See FSA Release (24 Dec 2004) 'FSA and firms announce details of Split Capital Investment Trust Settlement', FSA/PN/114/2004.

crisis, it can also be argued that securities market regulators need to adopt a broader view of what market manipulation or market abuse is. Indeed, the financial crisis teaches us that effective cross-border regulation in Europe and at the global level should address not only traditional sources of market manipulation such as spreading false rumours and manipulative practices (eg abusive squeezes) in the market, but also follow a global approach to monitoring the level of leverage and related positions in the UK and European financial markets which can be manipulated by firms to achieve illicit gains or avoid losses.

Chapter 6

Fraud and financial crime

INTRODUCTION

6.1 While it has long been recognised that one of the most important justifications for regulating conduct in the financial markets and financial services industry is the protection of investors, there has been surprisingly little discussion as to what this really means. For example, should all investors, no matter how professional or sophisticated they are, be given the same level of protection, and what type or quality of risk should this cover? There has been a tendency in the more sophisticated and developed regulatory systems to move to a position where investors are treated much in the same way as consumers and thereby entitled the same sort of protection.[1] In the context of our present discussion of insider dealing and market abuse, however, it is widely accepted that all investors should be protected from the risk of being defrauded. To the extent that we regard insider dealing and market abuse as a form of 'fraud',[2] we can be reasonably confident that most would agree that it is reasonable for the law to intervene to protect investors. While some legal systems appear to be quite happy to regard those who abuse inside information as 'defrauding' at least the market, if not individual investors, in the United Kingdom, we have tended to adopt a rather different analysis. In English law, before we characterise something as 'fraudulent', we generally require some kind of representation made with knowledge that it is materially false, together with the intention that some identified person will rely upon it to their harm. We would normally describe such conduct as 'dishonest'. While, as we have seen, in certain and generally exceptional circumstances, it is possible to regard an omission to disclose information as amounting to a form of representation, in the context of most instances of insider dealing, a failure to disclose the information in question will not be so regarded. When we consider the civil offences of market abuse, in some respects we are closer to the normal conception of fraud, but in others even further away. When the market abuse involves the commission of an act intended to create a false or misleading impression or where a statement is actually made with the same intention, we are in the realm of fraud. Where, however, there is merely a taking

---

1   Note in particular the amendments introduced to the FSMA 2000 by the Financial Services Act 2012.
2   The Court of Appeal in *R v McQuoid* [2009] EWCA Crim 1301 stated 'we ... emphasise that this kind of conduct does not merely contravene regulatory mechanisms ... when done deliberately, insider dealing is a species if fraud; it is cheating'.

advantage of privileged information, it is difficult to conceive this as fraud in any sense known under traditional English law.[3]

6.2   It is obviously the case that investors' legitimate interests may be harmed by conduct which is not undertaken with the intention that it should cause harm or in circumstances where the person concerned appreciates that it could, but just does not care whether in fact it does or not. Indeed, it is probable that investors are more likely to be harmed by negligent rather than fraudulent conduct in most developed markets.[4] While there are many laws and procedures designed to address this problem, this chapter focuses on what might be described as 'sharp practice' and not the competence of financial intermediaries. We are concerned here with what the Financial Services and Markets Act 2000 (FSMA) describes as 'financial crime'.[5] There has been considerable concern, over many years, as to whether the law and the various agencies that are required or rather expected to enforce it, have or for that matter can, adequately police 'sharp practice' in the financial sector. Despite the early development of laws and even the recognition that specialised enforcement machinery might be necessary,[6] the general view is that the traditional criminal justice system has not delivered. The Fraud Trial Committee, sitting under Roskill LJ, observed in 1986:

> 'the public no longer believes that the system … is capable of bringing the perpetrators of serious fraud expeditiously and effectively to book. The overwhelming weight of evidence laid before us suggests that the public is right'.[7]

6.3   One of the driving forces behind the restructuring of the supervision of the financial sector and the FSMA was the concern to address financial crime and deal with it on a broader basis than the ordinary criminal justice system. Consequently, the FSMA, before the amendments in the wake of the financial crisis[8] provided in section 2(2) that the reduction of financial crime was one

---

3   But see the approach in the USA under Rule 10b-5 of the Securities Exchange Act 1934 in regard to fraud on the market, *Affiliated Ute Citizens v US* 406 US 128 (1972) and in *Basic v Levinson* 485 US 224 (1988) the US Supreme Court held 'because most publicly available information is reflected in the market price, an investor's reliance on any public material misrepresentations … may be presumed for the purposes of a Rule 10b-5 action …'. As we shall see in *Scott v Brown, Doering, McNab & Co*, AL Smith LJ observed in holding that an agreement to purchase shares in excess of their real value thereby creating a false market was a criminal conspiracy, 'test it in this way. Suppose a purchaser induced to purchase shares … by means of the fictitious premium created by (the parties) solely for the purpose of inducing such purchaser and other to buy, could he or not have successfully sued either or both for a false and fraudulent misrepresentation? I say that he could': [1892] 2 QB 724 at 734. Of course, the US law also employs other devices and arguments to justify liability, see generally W Wang and M Sreinberg, *Insider Trading* (3rd edn) (Oxford University Press 2010).
4   JK Galbraith famously observed 'I have never adhered to the view that Wall street is uniquely evil, just as I have never found it possible to accept with complete confidence the alternative view … that it is uniquely wide': *The Great Crash 1929* (Penguin 1992) at p 27.
5   See generally B Rider (ed), *International Financial Crime* (Edward Elgar 2015).
6   See for example Report of the Royal Commission on the Stock Exchange (1878) Govt. Printer under Lord Penzance and see generally, B Rider, 'Policing the City – combating fraud an d other abuses in the corporate securities industry' (1988) 41 *Current Legal Problems* 47 and B Rider, C Abrams and M Ashe, *Guide to Financial Services Regulation* (3rd edn) (CCH 1997) Chs 1 and 2.
7   Report of the Fraud Trial Committee (1986, HMSO), para 1.
8   See generally N Ryder, The Financial Crisis and White Collar Crime – The Perfect Storm (Edward Elgar 2014) and J McGrath, *Corporate and White Collar Crime in Ireland, A New Architecture of Regulatory Enforcement* (Manchester University Press 2015).

of the four objectives that the then Financial Services Authority (FSA) should pursue in the discharge its various statutory and regulatory functions. This objective was 'fleshed out' in section 6, where it was made clear that the FSA was to be concerned with reducing the extent to which financial intermediaries can be 'used for a purpose connected with financial crime'.[9] Furthermore it was made clear that the FSA must have regard to ensuring that financial intermediaries are aware of the risks of being used in connection with financial crime and the importance of installing and adequately maintaining systems designed to prevent, detect and monitor the incidence of financial crime. The meaning of 'financial crime' was spelt out in section 6(3) as including any offence involving fraud or dishonesty, misconduct in, or misuse of information relating to, a financial market. It also included 'handling the proceeds of crime', whatever that crime may be. The notion of handling is wide enough to include laundering the proceeds of crime and the FSA was given and now the FCA retains specific authority to promulgate rules on this by the FSMA, section 146. It should also be noted that section 6(4) made it clear that an 'offence' includes an act or omission which would be an offence if it had taken place in the United Kingdom, even if it actually occurred overseas. Given the financial regulator such statutory obligations was at the time novel not just in the United Kingdom but internationally. Until relatively recently the view was taken by many that it was not appropriate for supervisory organisations to get their hands' dirty dealing with real criminals and crimes other than rather technical and regulatory offences. Indeed, many in regulatory bodies argued that to give them a specific role in fighting financial crime would undermine the relationship of confidence and candour that such bodies need to maintain with those whom they regulate and oversee.

6.4   The extent to which the FSA took its statutory mandate to facilitate the fight against financial crime at all seriously may be debated. Until the about 2009 there was little evidence that at senior levels within the FSA there was any great desire for the Authority to be seen as having any profile in this regard. At least one chairman of the FSA was prepared to say that financial crime was not as far as he was concerned a priority area for the FSA. Very few specialists were recruited and retained and persons with no obvious experience in addressing issues related to financial crime were put in key positions of authority. Most inside and outside the law enforcement community considered that the FSA had little appetite and perhaps even less ability to address financial crime in any meaningful sense. The financial crisis associated with the sub-prime debacle and the systematic revelations of widespread abuse and misconduct in the financial sector convinced many including the politicians that the FSA had at least in terms of its enforcement and policing responsibilities been asleep. To be fair this indictment could just as easily be levelled at the US Securities Exchange Commission and many other custodians of the public's trust in overseeing the financial sector.[10] This is not the place to enter into a wider discussion of the restructuring of the supervisory regime in the United

---

9   FSMA 2000, s 6(1) (unamended).
10   It is reported that of some 81,631 reports of suspected fraud by businesses in London in 2013 to 2014 there were only nine successful convictions. Of some 103,000 suspected cases of business related crime only 758 were considered solvable by the police, H. Warrell, 'Police urged to crack down on business crime' *Financial Times* 23 July 2014. The UK police also fail to identify a suspect in three-quarters of property related crimes, R Ford, *Times* 18 July 2014, albeit the Homes Secretary asserts 'criminal gangs are running swathes of Britain': R Ford, *Times* 12 June 2014.

Kingdom and frankly, there are those who take the view, in substance not much has changed in regard to financial crime and misconduct. While there have been a constant flow of cases, both sides of the Atlantic, in which various financial regulators, including the Financial Conduct Authority (FCA), have imposed very large financial penalties on financial institutions and the odd individual for an array of misconduct most relating to failures of compliance, relatively few have involved substantive criminality and prosecutions remain exceptional.

6.5   The FCA appears to be doing rather more than its ill-fated predecessor and there is evidence that it is acquiring the resources to be able to make a difference. The Government and various other public bodies have re-emphasised the importance of addressing financial crime and restoring the reputation of the City of London which has been serious damaged. The Economic Crime Command of the new National Crime Agency which replaced the Serious Organised Crime Agency (for reasons not too dissimilar to those employed against the FCA), appears to be interested in attacking economically relevant crime across a broad spectrum. Indeed, in its first few months of existence it focused its attention on insider abuse and in particular the involvement of professionals in the financial and legal communities. It is also the case that greater efforts are taking place to focus resources through the timely exchange of intelligence and better interface with compliance. Having said this, however, many within the criminal justice system today see the disruption of crime as the priority and traditional prosecutions are but one aspect of this.[11]

6.6   The Financial Services Act 2012, passed to address the weaknesses exposed during the financial crisis and restructure supervision over the financial sector, recasts the FCA's statutory mandate to emphasise its responsibilities to protect investors and place them much in the position of consumers. Of particular interest to us, however, is the recasting of the mandate to be concerned with financial crime. Under section 1B(1) of the amended FSMA, the FCA must as far as is reasonably possible advance one or more of its new operational objectives along with its strategic objectives. The FCA's operational objectives are to promote consumer protection, integrity and competition (1).[12] However, in discharging the first two of these it should have regard to the promotion of effective competition in the interests of consumers. Section 1B(5) provides that in discharging its general functions the FCA must have regard to the regulatory principles set out in section 3B[13] and the importance of taking action intended to minimise the extent to which it is possible for a business carried on by an authorised person or recognised investment exchange 'to be used for a purpose connected with financial crime'.[14] Financial crime is now defined in section 1H(3) in almost identical words to was section 6(3) of FSMA,[15] which

---

11   B Rider, 'Intelligent investigations: the use and misuse of intelligence – a personal perspective' (2013) 20 *Journal of Financial Crime* 293. See also S Keene, *Threat Finance, Disconnecting the Lifeline of Organised Crime and Terrorism* (Gower 2012). See also B Rider (ed), *International Financial Crime* (Edward Elgar 2015). Note also the creation of a new and specific offence in s 45 of the Serious Crime Act 2015 of participating in the criminal activities of an organised crime group.

12   See s 1B(3).

13   In addition to emphasising that 'consumers should take responsibility for their decisions' s 3B points out that 'a burden or restriction which is imposed on a person, or on the carrying out of an activity, should be proportionate to the benefits, considered in general terms which are expected to result from the imposition of that burden or restriction.'

14   See s 1B(5).

15   Section 1H(4) also makes it clear that this extends to any act or omission which would be an offence if it had taken place in the United Kingdom as did s 6(4) of the FSMA before the Financial Services Act 2012.

we have already considered. The new provision, however, also specifically includes offences relating to the financing of terrorism.[16]

6.7   Section 1D(1) elaborates on the FCA's integrity objective. It states that this is protecting and enhancing the integrity of the UK financial system. Subsection 2 goes on to explain that in this context integrity includes the following:

(a)   its soundness, stability and resilience,
(b)   its not being used for a purpose connected with financial crime,
(c)   its not being affected by behaviour that amounts to market abuse,
(d)   the orderly operation of the financial markets, and
(e)   the transparency of the price formation process in those markets.

Although worded in a rather more convoluted manner this boils down to much the same as provided for in the original provisions. Of course, the promotion of integrity places a wider burden on the FCA to address malpractice, but in terms of addressing financial crime and preventing authorised persons becoming victims of or vehicles for fraud and abuse there is no real change. It is important to appreciate that these provisions do not require the FCA to do anything other than in the exercise and discharge of its powers to pursue the reduction of crime as an objective. They do not mandate the FSA to pursue financial crime outside its limited statutory remit. The only other amendment that is worth pointing out here is the specific obligation on the FCA to consider the needs that consumers may have for the timely provision of information and advice that is accurate and fit for purpose in section 1C(c).

6.8   In this chapter we address a variety of offences mostly related in one way or another with fraud which have some relevance to insider abuse and the circumstances in which the offence of insider dealing might occur.[17] Of course, in a book of this nature we need to draw lines somewhere and we accept that these might appear arbitrary. In the US and increasingly in the UK the offences related to money laundering and proceeds of crime law are relevant in addressing insider dealing and the UK law is dealt with in the following chapter.

THE CREATION OF FALSE MARKETS

6.9   The early English law recognised that certain forms of conduct could undermine the efficient and fair operation of markets and there were common law offences, such as 'forestalling, re-grating and cornering', as early as the eleventh century.[18] These were later superseded by statutory offences and today survive, to some degree, within the offence of conspiracy to defraud. While scandals were certainly not unknown in the financial markets, it was not until the early part of the last century that legislation was introduced specifically to

16   See s 1H(3)(d).
17   See generally B Rider (ed), *International Financial Crime* (Edward Elgar 2015) and A Arlidge, A Milne and P Springer. *Arlidge and Parry on Fraud* (4th edn) (Sweet & Maxwell 2014) and K Harrison and N Ryder, *The Law Relating to Financial Crime in the United Kingdom* (Ashgate 2013).
18   See WS Holdsworth, *A History of English Law* (Little Brown1922–1938), IV at 375, T Plucknett, *A Concise History of the Common Law* (Liberty Fund 2010) and B Rider, C Abrams and M Ashe, *Guide to Financial Services Regulation* (3rd edn) (CCH 1997), Ch 1.

outlaw certain frauds in the context of investments. The Prevention of Fraud (Investments) Act 1939, which was replaced and slightly amended by the Prevention of Fraud (Investments) Act 1958, made it a serious offence to induce an investment transaction by making a false statement, either dishonestly or recklessly, or by dishonestly concealing a material fact. This provision was more or less re-enacted in the Financial Services Act 1986, section 47(1) and with some useful redrafting as the FSMA, section 397. It has been further refined and is now in Part 7 of the Financial Services Act 2012 as section 89 which has been discussed in the previous chapter. A legislative history if ever there was one!

6.10   While few prosecutions were successfully brought under these provisions, until the Financial Services Act 1986, there was no attempt to address, through legislation, attempts to manipulate the market, other than through making false statements. Before the Financial Services Act 1986, section 47(2) – now section 90 of the Financial Services Act 2012 – creating a false market by conduct was left to the general criminal law and various self-regulatory provisions. Consequently, the statutory control of manipulative practices, as opposed to the inducement of transactions by fraudulent misrepresentation, is relatively new in the United Kingdom. It follows that English law does not have the wealth of experience in addressing the many problems that arise from attempting to curb and control the creation of false markets that, for example, US law has.

THE COMMON LAW

6.11   The most significant area of law in England with regard to manipulation was, prior to the enactment of the Financial Services Act 1986, section 47(2), the common law. The judiciary have rarely shown much sympathy for those involved in manipulating public markets. For example, in *Rubery v Grant*,[19] Sir Robert Malins VC considered that to allege that a person was a member of a share rigging syndicate amounted to an allegation that they were dishonest. He added:

> 'going into the market pretending to buy shares by a person whom you put forward to buy them, who is not really buying them, but only pretending to buy them, in order that they may be quoted in the public papers as bearing a premium, which premium is never paid, is one of the most dishonest practices to which men can possibly resort.'

The learned judge went on:

> 'there is a class of people who think it is a legitimate mode of making money, but if they would only examine it for a moment they would see that a more abominable fraud, and one more difficult of detection, cannot be found.'

6.12   Perhaps the first English case to be decided by the English courts, or at least reported, is that of *R v De Berenger*.[20] This case involved one of the most audacious frauds ever perpetrated on a stock market. The United Kingdom had been at war with France for over two years and the price of British government stock was naturally depressed. The conspirators sought to raise the price of stock on the London Stock Exchange, enabling them to dump securities that

19   (1871–1872) LR 13 Eq 443.
20   (1814) 105 ER 536.

they had already acquired, by spreading rumours that Napoleon had been killed and that peace was certain. The London Stock Exchange appointed a committee of inquiry which discovered the relevant facts. De Berenger and seven others were indicted of:

> 'unlawfully contriving by false reports, rumours, acts and contrivances, to induce the subjects of the King to believe that a peace would soon be made ... thereby to occasion without any just or true cause a great increase and rise of the public government funds and the government securities of the Kingdom ... with a wicked intention thereby to injure and aggrieve all the subjects of the King who should, on 21 February, purchase or buy any part or parts, share or shares of and in said public government funds and other government securities'.[21]

The defendants contended that seeking to raise the price of securities in the market was not of itself a crime and that there was no criminal conspiracy without some allegation that they had intended to cheat certain investors or cause harm to the government. Indeed, it was argued that it was in the government's interest that the price of its securities should be kept high.

6.13   The court, however, had little sympathy for such arguments and held that it was not necessary for the Crown to allege, let alone prove, that anyone had in fact been misled and injured. Both the means used, along with the object of the enterprise, were unlawful. The public had the right to expect that the market had not been interfered with by wrongful means. Lord Ellenborough stated:

> 'A public mischief is stated as the object of this conspiracy; the conspiracy is by false rumours to raise the price of the public funds and securities and the crime lies in the act of conspiracy and combination to effect that purpose and would have been complete although it had not been pursued to its consequences, or the parties had not been able to carry it into effect. The purpose itself is mischievous, it strikes at the price of a vendible commodity in the market and if it gives a fictitious price, by means of false rumours, it is a fraud levelled against all the public, for it is against all such as may possibly have anything to do with the funds on that particular day. The excuse is that it was impossible that they should have known, and if it were possible, the multitude would be an excuse in point of law. But the statement is wholly unnecessary, the conspiracy being complete independently of any persons being purchasers. I have no doubt it must be so considered in law according to the cases'.

The decision in *De Berenger* does not address directly, however, the issue as to whether it is an indictable conspiracy to interfere with the proper operation of the markets, not through the circulation of false rumours and information, but by a course of dealing. Under the ordinary law, it is possible to make a statement

21   (1814) 105 ER 536. Lord Thomas LCJ, rejecting the appeal of Tom Hayes in regard to convictions on eight counts of conspiracy to defraud relating to the rigging of the LIBOR rate, emphasised 'this court must make it clear to all in the financial and other markets in the City of London that conduct of this type, involving fraudulent manipulation of the markets, will result in severe sentences of considerable length, which depending on the circumstances, may be significantly greater than the present total sentence' of 11 years imprisonment: *R v Hayes* (Court of Appeal, 21 December 2015). The Court of Appeal had reduced Hayes' term from 14 years because of his circumstances and the fact that he was in a relatively junior position. At trial Cooke J emphasised the importance of a deterrent sentence to send out a message on the fundamental importance of integrity to the financial sector. It should be noted, however, the five defendants accused of conspiring with Hayes were in fact acquitted by a jury, Southwark Crown Court, 27 January 2016.

by word or by conduct, so, as a matter of principle, manipulative conduct could be regarded as constituting a false and misleading representation. Nonetheless, in *De Berenger*, one of the learned judges said:

> '... the raising or lowering the price of the public funds is not per se a crime. A man may have occasion to sell out a large sum, which may have the effect of depressing the price of stocks, or may buy in a large sum, and thereby raise the price on a particular day, and yet he will be guilty of no offence. But if a number of persons conspire by false rumours to raise the funds on a particular day, that is an offence and the offence is, not in raising the funds simply, but in conspiring by false rumours to raise them on that particular day.'

6.14   In a subsequent civil case involving an action for rescission against a stockbroker who had agreed to purchase shares on the Stock Exchange on behalf of the plaintiff for the sole purpose of creating trading on the market at a premium in order to create the impression that there was a thriving market and thereby induce other investors to purchase, in denying rescission, the court expressed the view that the relevant agreement amounted to a criminal conspiracy to defraud the public.[22] The view was expressed by Lopes LJ that there is 'no substantial distinction between false rumours and false and fictitious acts'.

THE FAIR PRICE

6.15   On the other hand, it is also clear that not every concerted intervention into the market to hold a price will be considered manipulative. In *Sanderson and Levi v British Westralian Mine and Share Corpn*,[23] a contract was enforced pursuant to which a jobber on the Stock Exchange had made a market at a fair price, while the defendant distributed a substantial block of shares. In the rather less authoritative decision in *Landon v Beiorly*,[24] where a new trial was ordered,[25] the court also denied rescission of an allotment on the basis that the pegging of share prices during the launch of the company was to prevent 'undue depreciation below their actual worth'.

6.16   Thus, it is clear on the English authorities that there is a distinction between manipulation and what we describe today as stabilisation. It is not without interest, however, that the courts of other jurisdictions have not always been prepared to accept such a distinction. For example, in *Harper v Crenshaw*,[26] the US Court of Appeals for the District of Columbia went further than the English Court of Appeal in *Scott v Brown*[27] and held that an agreement to stabilise the price of shares, while a large block of shares was brought onto the market, was illegal and unenforceable. There was no evidence that the agreement sought to create a fictitious price for the securities in question or to raise the price higher than the real value of the relevant securities. In *Bigelow v Oglesby*,[28] an Illinois appellate court declined to enforce a syndicate agreement

22   *Scott v Brown, Doering, McNab & Co* [1892] 2 QB 724.
23   (1898) 43 Sol Jo 45.
24   (1849) 10 LTOS 505.
25   (1849) 13 LTOS 122.
26   82 F 2d 845 (DC Cir, 1936).
27   [1892] QB 724.
28   303 Ill App 27, 36, 23 NE 2d 382 (1939).

among underwriters because it contained what was then a standard clause for stabilisation. The court distinguished the English case of *Sanderson & Levi* on the basis that in the present case the agreement was to stabilise the price of the relevant shares at a level which had not already been determined by the market itself.

CONSPIRACY

6.17 It is important to remember when considering these authorities that the law might not necessarily be the same in the case of a criminal and a civil conspiracy and different considerations apply as to whether the persons concerned are being prosecuted for a criminal offence, are seeking to enforce an agreement inter-party or are being sued before the civil courts by an innocent third party. Unfortunately, the judges, in categorising certain conduct as illegal, do not always observe these distinctions. It would seem that a conspiracy to influence the price of shares or other securities on a market by making false statements or by engaging in purposeful conduct, such as a series of transactions with the intention of misleading the market, will be a conspiracy at criminal law. Conspiracy to create a public mischief no longer exists, but the facts in the relevant cases could fall within the scope of conspiracy to defraud today.[29] Generally speaking, however, it would be appropriate for the prosecution to allege a statutory conspiracy to breach sections 89 or 90 of the Financial Services Act 2012, which are discussed in the preceding chapter.[30]

6.18 Considerable discussion has taken place over the years as to the proper scope of conspiracy in the criminal law. The Law Commission's working party published a consultation document in 1973[31] in which it concluded that the crime of conspiracy should be confined to an agreement to commit a specific offence. In other words, the mere agreement to engage in a course of conduct, no matter how malicious, should not of itself constitute a crime, unless the conduct in question was itself a specific offence. The Law Commission took the

---

29 It is, however, proper to enter a caution after the House of Lords decision in *Norris v Government of the USA* [2008] UKHL 16. Lord Bingham held that a cartel agreement does not amount to a conspiracy to defraud in the absence of some aggravating factor such as 'fraud, misrepresentation, violence, intimidation or inducement of breach of contract' at paragraph 17. This decision was followed in *R v Goldshield Group plc* [2008] UKHL 16. Their Lordships were particularly concerned about extended the criminal law into uncertain areas and the arrangements that had hitherto not been considered to amount to a conspiracy and the impact of Article 7 of the European Convention on Human Rights. On the other hand in *R v Rimmington* [2005] UKHL 63, Lord Roger stated 'where Parliament has not abolished the relevant area of the common law when it enacts a statutory offence, it cannot be said that the Crown can never properly frame a common law charge to cover conduct which is covered by the statutory offence'. He added, 'where nothing would have prevented the Crown from charging the defendant under the statute and where the sentence imposed would have been competent in proceedings under the statute, the defendant is not prejudiced by being prosecuted at common law and can have no legitimate complaint'.
30 Or in the case of misleading statements in regard to benchmarks, s 91 of the Financial Services Act 2012; see note 21 above. See *R v Cooke* [1986] AC 909 modifying the strict rule in *R v Ayres* [1984] AC 447 to the effect that a conspiracy to defraud could not be charged where a substantive offence could be made out. A count of conspiracy would not normally be appropriate in cases of insider dealing. The substantive offence should be the basis of the prosecution, see generally S Clarke, *Insider Dealing Law and Practice* (Jordan Publishing 2013) at p 136 *et seq*.
31 Working Paper 50, *Inchoate Offences*.

view, however, that there were situations covered by the crime of conspiracy to defraud which might not be susceptible to this approach.[32]

6.19 The Criminal Law Act 1977, section 1 enacted a statutory offence of conspiracy to replace the common law offence of conspiracy. This reflected the Law Commission's view that the crime of conspiracy should be limited to circumstances where the object of the agreement is to commit an act which would itself be a substantive offence already known to the criminal law. However, the Criminal Law Act 1977, section 5(2) excepted the common law offence of conspiracy to defraud which remains outside section 1. Discussion has taken place as to whether conspiracy to defraud should remain an exception to the general rule. The Law Commission report Criminal Law: *Conspiracy to Defraud*[33] takes the view that it still has a role to play. This is illustrated in *Adams v R*.[34] The Privy Council was of the opinion that an agreement to conceal transactions with regard to which there was a fiduciary duty of disclosure, so that those responsible might avoid being called to account for their unauthorised profits, amounted to an indictable conspiracy to defraud.

ENFORCING THE BARGAIN

6.20 The agreement between the parties to the conspiracy would generally be unenforceable before the civil courts as being contrary to public policy. Indeed, Sir Frederick Pollack[35] referred to *Scott v Brown*[36] in which an attempt was made to enforce such an agreement, describing it as reminiscent of the 'well-known legal legend … of a highwayman coming into equity for an account against his partner'. Indeed, some US courts have taken this approach quite far and refused to enforce agreements involving the touting of shares, such as *Ridgely v Keene*.[37] In England, the courts have certainly declined to allow a wrongdoer to enforce such a transaction against the other party when that party is innocent and where both parties are involved in the wrongdoing. The general rule is that the courts should remain aloof. Losses and profits remain where they fall.

6.21 As we have seen in a case involving insider dealing, Knox J, despite a statutory provision to the effect that breach of the then insider dealing law did not make the relevant contract void or voidable, declined to lend the court's support to the enforcement of a partially completed transaction.[38] It has long been the English law that an innocent party can seek rescission or cancellation of a fraudulent transaction and the courts will not be keen to allow formalities or technical arguments to stand in the victim's path.[39] It is rather less likely that the courts would be prepared to see such an agreement enforced rather than rescinded by an innocent party. This is particularly so when the purpose of the agreement is to achieve something which is contrary to the public interest. In such circumstances, an innocent party would generally have other remedies than those based on the relevant agreement.

32 Working Paper 56, *Conspiracy to Defraud*.
33 1994, HMSO.
34 [1995] 1 WLR 52.
35 In an article published in the *Law Quarterly Review* in 1893 (9 LQR 105).
36 [1892] 2 QB 724.
37 134 AD 647, 119 NYS 451 (2nd dept, 1875).
38 *Chase Manhattan Equities Ltd v Goodman* [1991] BCLC 897.
39 See *Gillett v Peppercorne* (1840) 3 Beav 78.

6.22   It is unclear to what extent a 'third party' such as an investor in the market, who claims to have been harmed by the manipulation, can pursue those responsible in the civil courts for deceit. In *Bedford v Bagshaw*, Pollock CB, stated:

> 'all persons buying shares upon the Stock Exchange must be considered as persons to whom it was contemplated the representations would be made … I am not prepared to lay down a general rule, that if a person makes a false representation, everyone to whom it is repeated and who acts upon it may sue him. But it is a different thing where a director of a company procures an artificial and false value to be given to shares which he professes to offer to the public'.[40]

6.23   The Chief Baron thought that where the person responsible contemplated that the plaintiff was 'one of the persons' to whom the representation could be made or 'ought to have been aware he was injuring or might injure', a cause of action might be found. Of course, in this case, the defendant had effectively procured a false value for stock by fraudulently securing a quotation and settling date. The plaintiff reasonably assumed that the sufficient shares had been taken up to justify the quotation. In *Barry v Croskey*,[41] while agreeing with Pollock CB's comments, Page Wood VC, referring to the contention that 'every person, who in consequence of (the defendant's) frauds on the Stock Exchange, was induced to purchase stock at an advanced price in reliance on the false rumour he had circulated, was entitled to maintain an action against (the defendant)' questioned whether 'such consequences' would not be too remote to form grounds for action. In *Peek v Gurney*,[42] Lord Chelmsford also thought it highly dubious that those who had made an assumption on the basis that, according to the rules and practices of the market, certain underlying facts must exist or have been represented to exist, had a viable complaint. In *Salaman v Warner*,[43] a remedy was denied to a jobber who had acted on his 'own judgment' as to a presumed state of affairs, rather than on a direct representation to himself. Of course, these cases are primarily concerned with false representations made to the market authorities, which result in securities being traded at an inflated price. Where there is a direct representation, such as the issue of a false statement directly to the market, then it is not unlikely, at least in the case of fraud, that all those who can establish direct loss will be able to sue for the full extent of that loss.

6.24   The real problem in cases of manipulation, in particular by conduct, is whether it is possible to contend that the market price is itself a representation of, for example, compliance with all the rules and procedures which contribute to the availability of the market and, thus, price. Where a market has been manipulated and a 'false price' achieved, all those who come to the market or rely upon the market, at the relevant time, are harmed. In the leading US case of *US v Brown*,[44] Woolsey J, at first instance, referring to some of the English decisions, observed:

> 'when an outsider, a member of the public, reads the price quotations of a stock listed on an exchange, he is justified in supposing that the quoted

40   (1859) 4 H & N 538.
41   (1861) 2 John & H 1.
42   (1871) LR 13 Eq 79.
43   (1891) 7 TLR 484, CA.
44   5 F Supp 81 (SDNY, 1933).

price is an appraisal of the value of the stock due to a series of actual sales between various persons dealing at arm's length in a free and open market on the exchange.'

In other words, the investor is entitled to assume that the price is a true reflection of the proper interaction of supply and demand. While similar sentiments can be found in cases such as *Scott v Brown*,[45] it is questionable whether an English court would, on the basis of the common law, find liability to market participants for their loss. The twin hurdles of reliance and causation are likely to prove insurmountable.

6.25 To what extent it may be possible to base an action for manipulation on some other cause of action than fraud is debatable. The courts have not been particularly sympathetic to arguments that seek to invoke allegations of conspiracy. At the end of the day, for a civil claim based on this particular tort, it is necessary to show that the plaintiff's legitimate interest has been harmed. In the context of our present discussion, this would be problematic to say the least. While it may well be appropriate to frame an action in the tort of negligence, the courts are notoriously reluctant to contemplate open-ended liability and in most cases that can reasonably be conceived of as manipulation, it is most unlikely the courts would find sufficient proximity between the wrongdoer and a person who simply comes into the market. The most likely civil claim for conduct that violates the FCA's rules and, in particular, the market abuse provisions, is under the FSMA, section 138D.[46] This creates a right of action[47] for 'private persons' who suffer loss as a result of such a contravention of FCA and in certain circumstances the Prudential Regulatory Authority's (PRA) rules by an authorised person. A plaintiff may recover simply by showing a breach of the rules which has resulted in him suffering loss. Of course, as with the earlier provisions in the Financial Services Act 1986, sections 62 and 62A, it has to be shown that the loss in question occurred as a result of the violation. This remains a major stumbling block. It is, however, important to remember that the cause of action under section 138D is in addition to any rights that may exist at common law.

FRAUD (BY REPRESENTATION OR CONDUCT)

6.26 The early common law recognised the importance of punishing conduct that involved fraud and also providing those harmed by it, with recompense. However, in common with many other legal systems the law has had difficulty in determining exactly what is fraud. In the context of the civil law one of the leading works on the subject (*Kerr on the Law of Fraud and Mistake*)[48] states 'It is not easy to give a definition of what constitutes fraud in the extensive signification in which the term is understood by the Civil Courts of Justice. The Courts have always avoided hampering themselves by defining or laying down as a general proposition what shall be held to constitute fraud.

---

45 [1892] 2 QB 724.
46 This provision replaces s 150 of the FSMA although as far as FCA rules are concerned there is no substantive change, See Financial Services Act 2012, Financial Services (Banking Reform) Act 2013 and the FSMA (Rights of Action) Regulations 2001, SI 2001/2256.
47 See *R (British Bankers' Association) v Financial Services Authority* [2011] EWHC 999.
48 (7th edn) by Denis Lane McDonnell and John George Monroe (Sweet & Maxwell 1952), at p 1.

Fraud is infinite in variety. The fertility of man's invention in devising new schemes of fraud is so great, that the courts have always declined to define it ... reserving to themselves the liberty to deal with it under whatever form it may present itself. Fraud, in the contemplation of a Civil Court of Justice, may be said to include properly all acts, omissions, and concealments which involve a breach of legal or equitable duty, trust or confidence, justly reposed, and are injurious to another, or by which an undue or unconscientious advantage is taken of another. All surprise, trick, cunning, dissembling and other unfair way that is used to cheat any one is considered fraud. Fraud in all cases implies a wilful act on the part of anyone, whereby another is sought to be deprived, by illegal or inequitable means, of what he is entitled to.'

6.27   In the context of the criminal law there has been concern as to the fairness of such vagueness and in many countries attempts have been made to provide what passes for a definition. In reality most do little more than recite the ways in which the courts have identified something as fraudulent. Paradoxically, in Britain after much discussion and an extensive *Fraud Review*[49] ordered by the Attorney General in July 2006, a new law was enacted which in many respects broadens the crime of 'fraud'. Judge Alan Wilkie QC, then one of the Law Commissioners of England and Wales in referring to an earlier report by the English and Welsh Law Commission on *Fraud*, published in July 2002, stated that the objectives of a new law should be 'to make the law of fraud clearer and simpler ... (and) as a result all concerned whether jurors, police, victims, defendants or lawyers, will be better placed to understand who has committed a crime and who has not'.[50] In so far as the new Fraud Act 2006 bases liability on the concept of 'dishonesty' it remains to be seen whether there is any greater certainty.

6.28   In the United Kingdom there is only one offence of fraud in this new Act. It may be committed in three broad ways under section 1. First, by a false representation.[51] Secondly, by failing to disclose information in regard to which there is a legal duty to disclose[52] and thirdly, by abuse of a position in which one is expected to safeguard, or not to act against, the financial interests of another person.[53] The offence is committed if what is done is done dishonestly with a fraudulent intention. Thus, it is the state of mind that is the determinant factor in liability.

REQUISITE STATE OF MIND – MENS REA

6.29   Dishonesty is a core and, indeed, protean concept, in fraud. Dishonesty is a question of fact, not law. Thus, the appropriate instruction, according to English law, to the jury is – where the prosecution has proved that what the defendant did, was dishonest by the ordinary standards of reasonable and honest people, must the defendant have realised that what he was doing

---

49   Reference should be made generally to S Farrell, N Yeo and G Ladenburtg, *The Fraud Act 2006* (Oxford University Press 2007) and D Ormerod and D Williams, *Smith's Law of Theft* (9th edn) (Oxford University Press 2007).
50   See generally the *Fraud Report No 276*, Law Commission, http://www.lacom.gov.uk/docs/lc276.pdf; *Law Commission, Legislating the criminal Code: Fraud and Deception* (Consultation paper No 155, 1999).
51   Section 2.
52   Section 3.
53   Section 4.

would be regarded as dishonest by those standards?[54] It is important to note that it is for the jury to decide what the relevant standards of honest behaviour are. Furthermore, in considering whether the defendant actually appreciated that what he was doing violated these standards, the jury must consider the defendant's own state of mind at the relevant time.

6.30 The second element that must be established is that of fraudulent intent. In establishing that a fraud has been committed, it must be proved that in making the false representation, failing to disclose information, or abusing the position, the defendant intended to make a gain for himself or for another, or to cause loss to another, or expose another to a risk of loss. It is important to note that the offence is complete if what is done is done with the requisite intention, the fact that a gain or loss occurred or did not, is irrelevant.[55] It is the defendant's intention that is determinant. It is not without interest that the English Law Commission in its *Report on Fraud* (2002, paragraph 7.53) stated that 'fraud is essentially an economic crime, and we do not think the new offence should extend to conduct which has no financial dimension'. Thus, gain or loss is stated in the Act only to apply to 'money or other property'. However, gain or loss does extend to a temporary gain or loss. There is no need for the defendant to intend to achieve a permanent gain or loss.

PROOF OF DISHONESTY AND FRAUDULENT INTENTION

6.31 Establishing dishonesty to the satisfaction of the court has been said to be one of the main stumbling blocks to securing more convictions. Juries have been criticised for not having the expertise and understanding to properly understand the facts that are placed before them and on occasion a similar complaint has been made about judges. The complexity of information and in particular documents placed before the court is often perceived to be a significant hurdle in achieving the level of appreciation upon which a sound determination of the facts can be made. On the other hand in common law jurisdictions it is often said that once the jury or judge 'sniffs' the stench of dishonesty, it is not difficult to find it. Given that the determination as to what amounts to dishonest conduct is in most cases an issue for the jury, proof of intention is probably more problematic. It is important to distinguish the question as to what the defendant's intention was, from what his motive may have been. Generally speaking, motive is an irrelevant issue in the determination of criminal liability. While it may be of significance, for other reasons such as classification, profiling and detection, motive is generally no concern of the court until sentencing. Intention is generally a straightforward issue, as a person intends something if he acts with the purpose of causing that result. Thus, juries will often be instructed to be sure that the defendant did the act he intended.

6.32 Intent may, however, not always be so simple. In many systems of law, the courts distinguish between direct and indirect or oblique intent. Direct intent is as we have set out, that is where the consequence is desired and the

---

54   See *R v Ghosh* (1982) 75 Cr App R 154 and see *R v Cornelius* [2012] EWCA Crim 500, but also *R v Atkinson* [2004] EWCA Crim 3031.
55   See *R v Gilbert* [2012] EWCA Crim 2392 and also *R v Jeevarajah* [2012] EWCA Crim 1299.

defendant seeks to bring it about, or, at least strives to. Indirect intent is where the defendant realises that the consequence is certain, or virtually certain, as a result of what he does or does not do, but he does not in any positive sense desire it, and yet proceeds. Oblique intention would normally be sufficient for a determination that the defendant has the required fraudulent intention. Thus, a result is intended when it is the defendant's purpose to cause it, or though it is not the defendant's purpose to cause it, the result is a virtually certain consequence of the act or omission, and he knows that it is a virtually certain consequence. It is necessary, however, to distinguish intention from recklessness. If the defendant foresees a consequence as likely or even possible as a result of his actions and yet proceeds, and in the result that consequence does in fact occur, the defendant can be said to have caused the result recklessly. It is important to note that even a very high degree of foresight as to a given consequence is not the same thing, in law, as an intention. Nevertheless, if the jury accept that the defendant was virtually certain that a specific result would occur and it did, it would not be unreasonable for the jury to conclude that the defendant did in fact intend it.

MISREPRESENTATION BY WORDS OR CONDUCT

6.33   The offence of fraud will be committed if the defendant, with the requisite *mens rea*, makes a false representation. The representation may be made by word or conduct, express or implied, in regard to any fact, including the state of mind of the person making the representation or another. It may also, unlike generally in the civil law, be a representation as to the law. It will be a false representation if it is untrue or misleading and the person responsible for the representation knows that it so. The Fraud Act also provides that a representation may be regarded as made if it, or anything implying it, is submitted in any form to any system or device designed to receive, convey or respond to communications, with or without human intervention. It should be noted that under the new English law the offence is based on the making of a misrepresentation by the defendant and not the deception of the victim. The focus for liability is the conduct of the defendant and not the effect of that on the mind of the victim.[56]

6.34   This is important in the case of, for example, the unauthorised use of a payment card. It may well be that the merchant who takes the card, does not rely in any way on the implied representation of the person presenting the card for payment that he has authority to use it in that transaction, as the merchant will normally be reimbursed either way. Under the new provisions it is not necessary for the prosecution to allege, let alone prove, that the merchant was misled. It is enough that the defendant falsely represented that he had authority. By the same token, a merchant participating in a 'sting' operation, having been warned by the police, need not be deceived. It is enough that the defendant made the relevant false representation.

6.35   Returning to the issue of what is a representation, the English criminal law is based very much on the law of contract. A representation in the law of contract is a statement, by word or conduct, of material fact, made by one person to another during the negotiations leading up to contract, which was

---

56   But see *UAE v Allen* [2012] EWHC 1712 (Admin).

intended to be relied upon, and was in fact relied upon, but which was not intended to be a binding contractual term. Where that representation is false or misleading it is properly termed a misrepresentation. The state of a man's mind is according to the law, as much a statement of fact as the state of a man's digestion.[57] It follows that a false statement as to one's current intention is a misrepresentation of fact. By the same token an assertion of belief in the existence of certain facts, even the likelihood of future events, may be a misrepresentation of the fact that the person making the statement actually had, at that time, such a belief.

SILENCE

6.36   Attributing responsibility for mere silence is always a problem in the law. Generally speaking there is no duty to disclose material facts and therefore mere silence cannot be considered to amount to a representation. There is no indication in the Fraud Act that the law has changed. Having said this, it has been argued that where an ordinary and honest person would consider it right to speak out, and such a person appreciating this, does not – then the very dishonesty of his conduct might justify liability. The problem with this argument is that there is still no representation as such. It is highly doubtful whether dishonesty can in itself create an obligation of disclosure. This issue has arisen in the context of whether a failure to disclose price sensitive information might amount to a dishonest concealment within the scope of section 397 of FSMA (now section 89 of the Financial Services Act 2012), which is discussed in more detail in the previous chapter. In the context of the predecessor provision, section 13 of the Prevention of Fraud (Investments) Act 1958, prosecutions were considered but not initiated. In other jurisdictions, cases have been brought under similar provisions. The argument in Britain against proceeding was that it cannot be dishonest not to disclose information which you may well be under a duty to treat with confidence. However, this is debateable, and is in any case a question of fact for the jury.

6.37   In the general law of contract, there are only three situations where silence may be regarded as being tantamount to a representation. First, where there is a half-truth. If only half the truth is told, and the result is misleading, then the civil law normally imposes on the person responsible for the half-truth an obligation to correct the false impression. Thus, a statement by a lawyer that he was not aware of any adverse provisions in a draft contract was held a misrepresentation, because he omitted to say that he had not examined it. Secondly, a representation that is true when made, but is later falsified by events or in some cases a change of intention, would normally require correction. This reflects the notion that a representation continues to operate as an inducement to contract until the contract is entered into. Thirdly, there is a special category of contracts of utmost good faith – *uberrimae fide*. In these exceptional circumstances the law, by tradition, imposes an obligation to affirmatively disclose all material facts relating to the contract. Fiduciaries are under duty in dealing with their principals and beneficiaries to act in good faith and this, while not entirely accurate, may be considered to be to all intents and purposes within the scope of the duty of *uberrimae fide*. However, in the

---

57   *Edgington v Fitzmaurice* (1885) 29 Ch D 459 at 483 per Bowen LJ and *British Airways Board v Taylor* [1976] 1 All ER 65 at 68, per Lord Wilberforce.

case of fraud by persons in a fiduciary position, it would probably be better to resort to the provisions in the new statute imposing liability for fraudulently taking advantage of one's special position. Indeed, it was partly because of the uncertainties as to the scope of the obligation to disclose in the course of fair dealing that justified the enactment of these specific provisions. Having said this, the dishonest failure to disclose information that should be disclosed, even on the basis of a fiduciary relationship, such as between a director and his company, may amount to a conspiracy to defraud.

6.38   For liability, the representation must be untrue or misleading. Under the English law it would seem that there might be liability in the criminal law for the making of an untrue statement, which the defendant does not know is untrue, but does appreciate might in the circumstances be misleading. Misleading means less than wholly true and capable of an interpretation to the detriment of the victim. In the case of the criminal law, where it is not necessary, at least in the United Kingdom, to consider whether it actually influenced the mind of the person to whom it was addressed, issues of reliance are irrelevant. Of course, where what is said is so ridiculous no reasonable person would rely upon it, the jury or court may find the defendant's conduct does not fail to meet the standards of ordinary and honest people. Of course, this is all rather subjective.

6.39   As we have pointed out, the reformed criminal law in the United Kingdom in regard to fraud has a different emphasis than in many other jurisdictions. One point that is worthy of note is that the United Kingdom law does not require proof of materiality. This is an important issue in many provisions relating to false statement in other countries. A good example in the US Federal law is section 1001 of Title 18 USC. This makes it a criminal offence to falsify, conceal or cover up by any trick, scheme or device a material fact, the making of any materially false, fictitious, or fraudulent statement or representation or making or using any false writing or document knowing that it contains any materially false, fictitious, or fraudulent statement or entry. In determining whether a false statement or concealment is material the US courts examine whether the statement has a natural tendency to influence, or be capable of influencing, the decision of the other party. It is not necessary to prove that the victim was actually influenced let alone that the victim relied on it. The Supreme Court considers that the issue of materiality involves questions of both fact and law and should therefore be submitted to the jury.

CONCEALMENT

6.40   We have already noted that section 3 of the Fraud Act in the United Kingdom provides that the offence of fraud may be established if a person dishonestly fails to disclose to another person information which he is under a legal duty to disclose, intending thereby to make a gain for himself or another, or to cause loss to another or to expose another to a risk of loss. We have already seen that generally the law does not place an obligation on a person, even during the negotiation of a contract, to disclose information that he appreciates would be material to the other party's decision. However, there are situations where by statute, contract, custom and fiduciary obligation a duty to disclose facts arises. We have also seen that in certain circumstances there may be a duty to correct the misleading impression resulting from a half-truth or the falsification of a continuing representation. Where the person failing to disclose is not under a specific legal duty to disclose the relevant information, then it may still be possible to find liability, but based on the notion of an implied representation. For example, in one case a defendant who asked a bureau de change to exchange obsolete foreign currency for sterling was convicted on the basis that he impliedly represented that the relevant currency was still in circulation. He was under no legal obligation to inform the cashier, but by tending the money he made a representation.[58]

6.41 We have already raised the issue of whether a mere moral obligation to disclose information should be enough to provide a basis for liability. It is important to remember that legal rules do not operate in isolation of each other and there is an interaction between the civil and criminal law. Generally speaking the civil law does not obligate persons to disclose information simply because it would be the right thing to do. For example, the information might well have a proprietary value, which the owner would not wish to share. A duty to disclose information, simply because the other party is unaware of it or maybe could not have acquired it, would, for example, undermine the valuable role of research in the financial markets. Indeed, it was partly for this reason that the American courts somewhat pragmatically developed the so called 'abstain or disclose' rule in regard to price sensitive information in the USA. It is not without interest, however, that the English Law Commission[59] did recommend that the offence be wide enough to cover information of a kind that the defendant knows or is aware that the other party trusts him to disclose and that in the circumstances it would be reasonable for him to disclose it. The Government rejected this as it considered to impose liability where there is not a pre-existing duty under the civil law would have far reaching implications for the general approach of *caveat emptor*. On the other hand, for liability under the Fraud Act it is not necessary for the prosecution to establish, as the Law Commission also suggested, that the defendant is aware that he is under a legal duty to disclose the information in question. Of course, if he did not, it may well be that he is not dishonest.

CRIMINAL BREACH OF TRUST (CBT)

6.42 Before the enactment of the Fraud Act it has been claimed that English law did not recognise the offence of criminal breach of trust. Interestingly, this is an important offence in combating financial and other misconduct in many other Commonwealth jurisdictions. In the various Criminal Codes drafted and implemented during Imperial rule, it is not without interest that specific provisions were included in regard to dishonest breach of trust. Of course, it is true that most situations covered by such laws, would have been offences in Britain, but almost certainly not all. The Fraud Act 2006 now specifically addresses this in section 4. A person will be guilty of fraud if he occupies a position in which he is expected to protect or safeguard, or at least not act against, the financial interest of another person and he dishonestly abuses that position, intending thereby to make a gain for himself or another, or to cause loss to another, or to expose another to a risk of loss. It is expressly provided that a person may be regarded as having abused his position even though his conduct consists of an omission rather than an affirmative act.

---

58   *R v Williams (Jean Jacques)* [1980] Crim LR 589.
59   The Fraud Report No 276, Law Commission, http://www.lacom.gov.uk/docs/lc276.pdf.

6.43   The real issue revolves around who can properly be said to occupy a position where he is expected to safeguard, or not act against, the financial interests of another. It is clear that the formulation is wider than those in a conventional trust relationship, or for that matter fiduciary relationship. It is unclear whose expectation is relevant. Is it the expectation of the victim or a more objective determination? It is also unclear whether the expectation must be reasonable. It seems that it is the intention of the Government that this is a question of fact to be determined by the jury, in the same way as the issue of dishonesty. On the other hand there is a strong argument for contending that it is a question of mixed law and fact as it is in the USA. For example, should not the court rule as to whether in law the relationship is capable of giving rise to such expectations?

6.44   The concept of fiduciary obligation, as we have seen in Chapter 2, was authoritatively set out by Millet LJ in *Bristol and West Building Society v Mothew*.[60] The learned judge stated 'a fiduciary is someone who has undertaken to act for or on behalf of another in a particular matter in circumstances which give rise to a relationship of trust and confidence. The distinguishing obligation of a fiduciary is the obligation of loyalty. The principal is entitled to the single-minded loyalty of his fiduciary ...'. Therefore company directors in their dealings with the company, partners in dealing with each other, an agent in dealing with his principal, a trustee in dealing with his beneficiary, a public official in regard to his office and a professional adviser in dealing with his client would all be included. It is also probable that an employee in his dealings with his employer would also be covered. While employees are not generally considered to be fiduciaries,[61] they are within a duty of fidelity which has much in common with the obligations cast upon a fiduciary. An employee is 'trusted' by his employer not to make use of the employer's property or premises for the employee's benefit. It is important to note, however, that unlike an ordinary fiduciary relationship, the obligations, albeit different, flow both ways. As we have seen directors of a company owe fiduciary duties, arising by virtue of their office, only to the company and not its shareholders.[62] Whether it could be argued that the shareholders have a reasonable expectation that directors will not act against their financial interests, such as by insider dealing, remains to be seen. It has been accepted that in the context of a takeover, directors are under a duty to shareholders to act honestly and shareholders therefore might well have a reasonable expectation that they, as directors, would not act contrary to the advice and information that they have given to the members.[63] It is also clear that there are family, domestic and other personal relationships, even within a business context[64] that might also give rise to such expectations and therefore be within the scope of the offence. It is probable that the criminal and civil law will not be entirely matched on such issues.

---

60   (1998) Ch 1 at 118.
61   Employees who in senior management positions act on behalf of a company, may well be considered to owe fiduciary obligations much the same as the company's directors, see *Canadian Aero Services Ltd v O'Malley* (1973) 40 DLR (3d) 771 and 381.
62   See 2.18 *et seq.*
63   See *Heron International Ltd v Lord Grade* [1983] BCLC 244. The expectations of other 'stakeholders' such as employees and creditors are rather more problematic in this regard, see generally *Winkworth v Edward Baron Development Co Ltd* [1986] 1 WLR 1512.
64   See *Peskin v Anderson* [2001] 1 BCLC 372, *Re Chez Nico (Restaurants) Ltd* [1992] BCLC 192 and *Platt v Platt* [1999] 2 BCLC 745 and in particular *Coleman v Myers* [1977] 2 NZLR 225. See 2.19 *et seq.*

6.45   In the past there have been problems with imposing criminal liability for diverting so called corporate opportunities and the taking of secret profits. As we have seen, corporate opportunity is a contract or other advantageous arrangement that should in fairness have gone to a particular company, but which has been diverted by insiders, typically the directors, for their own personal benefit. The approach of the courts differs and may have rather more to do with the perceived integrity of what has occurred rather than any underlying jurisprudence. There are decisions which treat the opportunity as some kind of expectant property which in good conscience belongs to the company. Therefore, when directors divert it they are in effect stealing or at least misappropriating an asset that belongs to the company. Other courts have been reluctant to treat this as property and have simply sought to impose personal obligations based on conflict of interest on the relevant insiders. There are very few cases where it has ever been thought appropriate to consider a charge theft. Such conduct does, however, in most instances amount to a breach of trust. Directors are under an obligation to safeguard the financial interest of the company and the dishonest diversion or such opportunities would be an offence under the Fraud Act.

6.46   We have also seen in Chapter 2 that those in a fiduciary position are forbidden from making a 'secret profit'. This is essentially a profit that arises in the course of the fiduciary obligation and which has not been specifically authorised or consented to by the person to whom the fiduciary obligation is owed. In most legal systems, the secret profit is owed much in the same way as a debt to the principal, but is not owned by him. In other words, the taking of a secret profit does not involve the misappropriation of another person's property. Provided the taking of a secret profit is now dishonest, it may well amount to a criminal breach of trust. This is important as the law relating to the taking of secret profits is potentially onerous. For example, in *Regal (Hastings) Ltd v Gulliver*,[65] Lord Russell of Killowen, stated 'the rule of equity which insists on those, who by the use of a fiduciary position make a profit, being liable to account for that profit, in no way depends on fraud, or absence of bona fides; or upon such questions or considerations as whether the profit would or should otherwise have gone to the plaintiff, or whether the profiteer was under a duty to obtain the source of the profit for the plaintiff, or whether he took a risk or acted as he did for the benefit of the plaintiff, or whether the plaintiff has in fact been damaged or benefited by his action. The liability arises from the mere fact of the profit having, in the stated circumstances, been made. The profiteer, however, honest and well intentioned, cannot escape the risk of being called to account'. It must be remembered in this case the issue was one of civil liability and not criminal liability. Nonetheless, it does indicate how wide the 'duty' not to profit from one's position is.

MISAPPROPRIATION (INCLUDING THEFT)

The offence of theft

6.47   Theft in English law is rendered an offence under section 1 of the Theft Act 1968. This provides that a person is guilty of theft if he dishonestly appropriates property belonging to another with the intention of permanently

---

65   [1942] 1 All ER 378.

depriving the other of it and it is immaterial whether the appropriation is made with a view to gain, or is made for the thief's own benefit. There are those who have argued that a charge for theft would have been rather more appropriate in a number of cases of misconduct in the City than the way in which the authorities in fact proceeded. This contention is based on the view, that has some justification, that traditionally those responsible for the integrity of the markets and financial services industry have been reluctant, for a variety of reasons, to treat those whose engage in misconduct as 'real criminals'.

6.48   There is a fundamental difference between the offences of theft and fraud, although in some situations there may be a potential overlap. In the case of fraud the victim is deceived into handing over property and therefore the notion of misappropriation is inappropriate. The victim thus, effectively 'consents' to the taking of the relevant opportunity or property. This 'consent' albeit based on a misapprehension will continue to operate in law until steps are taken to rescind the contract. However, there are cases which show that the effect of a fraud can be to induce a mistake which renders the contract void *ab initio.*[66] Consequently, in such circumstances the law of theft may well be relevant. Having said this, the Courts have become increasingly reluctant to accept that fraud operates other than within the law of misrepresentation.[67] Of course, fraud involves rather more than the dishonest appropriation of property. Issues have arisen not so much as to the nature of an appropriation, but in regard to what is capable of being appropriated. In the context of corporate law, for example, we have already mentioned the issue as to whether an opportunity that should in good conscience have been delivered up to a company, can be regarded as a form of expectant property capable of belonging to the company. There is also an issue in regard to bribes and secret profits. Do they belong to the person who can assert a right to their recovery? Until relatively recently it was thought that in such cases the law of theft was irrelevant. However, in the civil law, it has been held that as equity looks as done that which should be done, it will regard the bribe or secret profit as having been transferred, thereby justifying property based remedies.[68] The issue as to whether confidential information can amount to property and therefore be capable of being misappropriated, is also a potentially important issues. In the USA the courts have attempted to develop the law penalising the abuse of inside information largely on the basis of misappropriation. Those who acquire price sensitive information in circumstances where they appreciate it 'belongs' to another are not allowed to misappropriate it for their own or another person's benefit.[69] The English Courts have held that confidential information is not property for the purposes of the law of theft[70] although in the civil law, it can be protected almost as if it is a form of property. It has been said in Britain 'it is not too much to say that we live in a country where … the theft of the boardroom table is punished far more severely than the theft of the boardroom secret'.[71] It is interesting that both the Law Commission and the Government decided not to include trade secrets and confidential information as a species of property in the Fraud Act 2006.

---

66   *Cundy v Lindsay* (1878) 3 App Cas 459.
67   *Phillips v Brooks Ltd* [1919] 2 KB 243 and *Lewis v Averay* [1972] 1QB 198.
68   The availability of proprietary remedies or what appear to be such, does not necessarily or even logically create property see for example, *Armstrong DLW GmbH v. Winnington Networks Ltd* [2012] 3 All ER 425.
69   See *US v O'Hagan* 117 S.Ct 2199 (1997) and *Carpenter v US* 484 US 19 (1987).
70   *Oxford v Moss* (1979) 68 Cr App R 183.
71   Sir Edward Boyle MP, *HC Debates* 13 December 1968, vol 775, col 806, and see **2.28**.

REQUISITE STATE OF MIND – MENS REA

6.49   Theft requires proof of two mental elements, dishonesty and an intention to permanently deprive the person of possession of the relevant property. We have already discussed what dishonesty means in this context. However, the relevant statutes have gone further, by setting out circumstances in which as a matter of law a person does not act dishonestly for the purposes of the law of theft. For example, section 2(1) of the Theft Act 1968 provides that a person is not dishonest if he believes he has in law the right to deprive the other person of the property; where he believes that the other person would have consented to the appropriation if he had known of the appropriation and the circumstances, and, except where he is a trustee or personal representative, he acts in the belief that the true owner cannot be found by taking reasonable steps. The section does, however, make it clear in subsection (2) that a person can be found to be dishonest notwithstanding his willingness to pay for the property in question. Thus, generally speaking a genuine belief of right or consent, will exonerate a person from allegations of dishonesty. It is important to appreciate that in English law the belief of the accused need not be reasonable. However, the more unreasonable it is, the more difficult it will be for him to convince the jury that he had a genuine belief and was not therefore subjectively dishonest. If a jury does consider that the accused did in fact have a genuine belief in his right or the consent of another, as a matter of law – in England, this is an end of the matter. He is entitled to an acquittal and the issue of dishonesty will not be put to the jury. This is not the case in regard to a prosecution for fraud under the Fraud Act 2006. In the case of fraud, the Act does not include similar provisions as in the Theft Act and therefore, even if the jury consider that the accused did in fact genuinely believe he had a right, the issue of dishonesty is not resolved. It is in law possible for the jury to still find that he was dishonest for the purposes of the fraud law. In practice it is difficult to conceive of a situation where it would be reasonable for a jury to find dishonesty in such a case.

6.50   In theft cases, as we have noted, it must also be shown that the accused has the intention to permanently deprive the owner of the property in question. Merely taking a briefcase and examining its contents to see if there is anything worth stealing is not in English law theft. Under section 6 of the Theft Act it is provided 'a person appropriating property belonging to another without meaning that other permanently to lose the thing itself is nevertheless to be regarded as having the intention of permanently depriving the other of it if his intention is to treat the thing as his own to dispose of regardless of the other's rights; and borrowing or lending of it may amount to so treating it if … the borrowing or lending is for a period and in circumstances amounting to an outright taking or disposal'. It has long been held by the English courts that a person in possession or control of another person's property who, dishonestly and for his own purpose, deals with the property in such a manner that he knows he is risking its loss, may be guilty of theft.

What can and cannot be stolen

6.51   While there are differences in the law from one country to another, generally speaking the law of theft is quite comprehensive in what is considered to be property. Section 4 of the Theft Act provides that property, for the purposes of theft, may include real and personal property, money and intangible property, such as the credit in a bank account. Thus, in one case the accused, a builder, dishonestly over-billed for work which he had undertaken. The owner of the house gave the accused a cheque for this amount which was paid in to his account. In paying this cheque into his account the accused was held to have dishonestly appropriated part of the credit standing in his customer's bank account.

6.52   For a charge of theft the property must 'belong to another'. Section 5 of the Theft Act provides that property is regarded as belonging to anyone having possession or control of it or having a proprietary right or interest in it. Thus, merely an equitable right in property will be sufficient. It should also be noted that the owner of property can be guilty of stealing his own property from someone with a lesser interest, such as a lien for an unpaid bill. There may be circumstances where full legal ownership passes to the accused, but nonetheless, for the purposes of theft the law deems the original owner as still entitled. For example, section 5(3) of the Act provides that 'where a person receives property from or on account of another, and is under an obligation to that other to retain and deal with that property or its proceeds in a particular way, the property or proceeds shall be regarded, as against him, as belonging to the other'. This provision is, of course, particularly important when money is given to a person to pay certain expenses and is used for something else. Given the required state of mind, the crime of theft will have occurred. It is important, however, to note that the money or other property must be entrusted for a specific purpose.

6.53   As we have seen[72] in cases where a person receives property by virtue of another's mistake and is under an obligation in the civil law to make restoration in whole or in part, of the property or its proceeds, then to the extent of this obligation, the relevant property or proceeds will be regarded, in English law, as belonging to the person entitled to restoration.[73] Thus a person who receives property or payment by mistake, at the point when they form the necessary state of mind – which is to dishonestly and permanently deprive the owner of the relevant amount, they are guilty of theft. Of course, this means that they must actually be aware of the mistake and that they are under a legal obligation to make restoration. If they had a genuine belief in their right to retain it, as we have seen, they would not be dishonest, as a matter of law.

Unjust enrichment

6.54   The common law has not been eager to base liability on the unjust acquisition of wealth in circumstances where a specific wrong has not been committed. Indeed, there are cases in the English courts which affirm that characterising something as unfair or even unjust does not of itself establish a cause of action or enable the court to intervene. Of course, where there is an obligation such as in a fiduciary relationship to act fairly, the situation is different. The imposition of criminal liability for the acquisition of unexplained wealth, while controversial, is not as radical as some would suggest. Britain imposed in many of its territories and dominions[74] provisions relating to the

---

72   See 6.52 above.
73   Section 5(4) of the Theft Act 1968.
74   One of the best examples of the criminalisation of unexplained wealth is to be found in the Prevention of Bribery Ordinance (Cap 201) in Hong Kong. Section 10(a) provides that any person who is or has been a Crown Servant who maintains a standard of living above

acquisition of unexplained wealth, particularly in the case of public officials. These have been adopted in other jurisdictions and now the United Nations Convention against Corruption 2006 urges all countries to enact such laws. Article 20, provides:

'Subject to its constitution and the fundamental principles of its legal system, each State Party shall consider adopting such legislative and other measures as may be necessary to establish as a criminal offence, when committed intentionally, illicit enrichment, that is a significant increase in the assets of a public official that he or she cannot reasonably explain in relation to his or her lawful income.'

6.55   It is important to remember that many officials are in a position in which they are expected to safeguard or not to act against the financial interests of another person, including the public at large or the state. Consequently, many cases of abuse of office would be potentially an offence under the Fraud Act 2006. In cases where a public official, without reasonable excuse or justification, wilfully neglects to perform his public duty or wilfully misconducts himself, to the extent that he abuses the public's trust in the office, he is guilty of the common law offence of misfeasance in public office.[75] The collapse of the Bank of Credit and Commerce International (BCCI) led to allegations in Britain and elsewhere that the authorities and in particular the Bank of England had been 'wilfully negligent' in their duty to protect depositors. Suits were brought alleging that the Bank of England and certain officers were guilty of the tort of misfeasance.[76] These actions failed in part because it could not be established that the Bank of England had acted with wilfulness in the breach of its duties. However, in the USA and certain other jurisdictions, this liability has become an important factor in the policing of misconduct, both in attributing responsibility and rather less commendably in inhibiting the authorities.

FALSE STATEMENTS AND MANIPULATION

6.56   We have already discussed in Chapter 5 the offences in section 89 of the Financial Services Act 2012 relating to the inducement of investment transactions by false statements and the dishonest concealment of material facts. The law has long recognised that those responsible for promoting new issues of stock have a special responsibility to ensure that those who are likely to subscribe are given all the information that they need to make an informed decision. In addition to requiring full disclosure of material facts, there are statutory obligations on those responsible for promoting new issues

that which is commensurate with his present or past official emoluments or is in control of pecuniary resources or property disproportionate to his present or past official emoluments, shall be guilty of an offence, unless 'he gives a satisfactory explanation to the court as to how he was able to maintain such a standard of living or how such pecuniary resources or property came under his control'. Furthermore, under subsection 2 of this section, where a court is satisfied in proceedings for an offence under the first subsection, that 'having regard to the closeness of his relationship to the accused and to other circumstances, there is reason to believe that any person was holding pecuniary resources or property in trust for or otherwise on behalf of the accused or acquired such resources or property as a gift from the accused, such resources or property shall, in the absence of evidence to the contrary, be presumed to have been in the control of the accused'.

75   *Attorney General's Reference (No 93 of 2003)* (2004) 2 Cr App R 23.
76   *Three Rivers District Council v Bank of England (No 3)* [2003] 2 AC 1.

and placing securities in the market to ensure that due care is exercised in complying with the relevant disclosure requirements. For example, under the FSMA, section 90,[77] persons responsible for a false or misleading statement or omission in listing particulars will be liable to compensate any person who has acquired the securities in question for any loss that they have suffered unless it can be proved by them that they had reasonable grounds for believing what was said was not false or misleading. Indeed, under the FSMA, section 91, the FCA can impose financial penalties on the issuer or its directors if they were 'knowingly concerned' in the breach.

6.57   When discussing the common law's stand against the deliberate creation of false markets, mention was made of the fact that, apart from some very ancient statutes relating to the integrity of markets, it was not until the enactment of the Financial Services Act 1986, section 47(2) that there were UK statutory provisions specifically designed to outlaw the manipulation of markets other than by the making of false statements. It is possible, of course, to make a representation by conduct, but in the context of the financial markets, seeking to establish a charge or claim on such a basis would in practice be exceedingly difficult, albeit not impossible. Section 47(2) was re-enacted as the FSMA, section 397(3) and is now section 90 of the Financial Services Act 2012 and is discussed in detail in Chapter 5.

HIGH PRESSURE SELLING

6.58   The high pressure selling of securities at a greater price than they are worth has long been identified as a major issue in investor protection. High pressure selling operations, sometimes referred to as 'boiler room' operations, are often associated with other fraudulent schemes and this form of crime has attracted organised criminals. As early as 1936, the government established a committee under Sir Archibald Bodkin 'to consider operations commonly known as share pushing and share hawking and similar activities'. The result of the committee's recommendations was the enactment of the Prevention of Fraud (Investments) Act 1939 which, in addition to addressing fraudulent statements, as we have seen, regulated the selling practices of share dealers and the dissemination of investment related information and, in particular, advertisements. The Financial Services Act 1986, section 56 went somewhat further than this and in effect made it a 'civil offence' to make unsolicited calls to procure an investment agreement, to or from the UK, unless such were made in conformity with rules drawn up by the Securities and Investments Board. In *Alpine Investments BV v Minister van Financien*,[78] the European Court accepted that while such rules curbing 'cold calling' were a restriction on a person's freedom to offer cross-border services, they could be justified on the basis that a member state had the right to ensure the protection of investors and the integrity of its markets.

6.59   The Financial Services Act 1986, section 56 has been replaced by the FSMA, section 30. At the cornerstone of the new regulatory regime is the FSMA, section 21 which prohibits a person, in the course of business, communicating an invitation or inducement to engage in investment activity unless that person is an authorised person or the communication is approved

---

77   But see also ss 90ZA and 90A.
78   Case C-384/93: [1995] All ER (EC) 543.

by an authorised person. The rules promulgated by the FCA on financial promotion by authorised persons achieve more or less the same result as the earlier regime. If a person enters into 'controlled agreement' (that is one within the purview of section 21) as a result of an 'unlawful communication', then, subject to the discretion of the court, the customer is entitled to compensation for any loss or restitution of any moneys or property transferred and the agreement is unenforceable against him. Where the other party to the claimant is not the communicator, that person will be liable for any losses, subject to the discretion of the court. It must also be remembered that activity in breach of the prohibition in section 21, in addition to amounting to a criminal offence, will also bring into play the full enforcement powers of the FCA under the FSMA, section 25.

FRAUDULENT TRADING AND INSOLVENCY RELATED OFFENCES

6.60   It is sadly too often the case that a fraud will only be discovered once an insolvency occurs. While to some the insolvency provisions may appear to be 'shutting the stable door after the horse has bolted', they have an important role in attributing responsibility, tracing misappropriated funds and facilitating compensation and restitution. The procedures provided for by these laws also assist in attempting to resolve the conflicts which inevitably arise between various parties when there is not enough money to meet every obligation. Perhaps the most important in the control of fraud and sharp practice are those provisions which address misconduct on the part of those who manage insolvent enterprises and which enable the authorities to intervene. For example, under the UK's FSMA, section 367 as amended by the Financial Services Act 2012, the FCA may petition the court for a winding up, not only of an authorised person, but also any unauthorised person who is engaged in activity in contravention of the general prohibition on conducting unauthorised investment business. Of course, these statutory provisions are in addition to those in the general law relating to companies and insolvency.

6.61   In most systems of law there will be a number of specific offences relating to malpractice and abuses before and during liquidation. Obviously it is not possible here to give more than a brief indication of their nature. Frauds against creditors may be divided into three broad categories. Firstly, there are cases where debts are incurred, albeit there is no intention of making payment. Long firm frauds are a good example. Here crooks will form a company or create some other form of trading vehicle, establish some degree of credibility and then place orders on credit for goods for which they have no intention of paying. These will then be sold, often at a discount, and the criminals will abscond with the proceeds leaving the creditors to pursue a mere shell. The second situation is the fraudulent evasion of debts and obligations that have already been incurred. Here assets may be transferred and siphoned off to prevent creditors getting their hands on them. The third situation, involves the concealment of the true state of affairs and perhaps the resurrection of the insolvent company's business in a 'phoenix company' to which the insolvent company's undertaking has been transferred at an undervaluation – thereby leaving the creditors with a shell. Of course, in all three categories it is probable that numerous non-insolvency specific offences may be committed.

6.62 The Fraud Act 2006 creates a new offence which is of particular relevance. It provides that 'a person is guilty of an offence if he is knowingly a party to the carrying on of a business' otherwise than as a company with intent to defraud creditors or for any other fraudulent purpose. Section 993 of the Companies Act 2006, provides that whether or not a company has been or is in the course of being wound up, if any business of the company is carried on with an intent to defraud creditors of that company or creditors of any other person, or for any fraudulent purpose, 'every person who is knowingly a party to the carrying on of the business in that manner commits an offence'. These two offences effectively catch all those who engage in fraudulent trading in the course of business. While fraudulent trading has a long history in the company laws of most countries, in Britain it became increasingly evident that there was widespread use of business forms other than companies engaging in bogus trading and long firm frauds. As we have seen, it is also not uncommon to discover that what appear to be companies are in fact phantoms – never having been properly incorporated. As the Law Commission observed (Law Commission No 277) 'it is anomalous and illogical that fraudulent trading should be an offence where it is done through the medium of a … company, but not where the individual who is trading fraudulently does not do so through the medium of such a body'.

6.63 For these offences a single fraudulent transaction is sufficient, provided 'it can properly be described as fraud on a creditor perpetrated in the course of carrying on business'.[79] The notion of being 'a party' to the fraudulent trading has caused some difficulty in the courts. Some judges have indicated that at least in the case of companies the person must have a relatively senior position in 'running the business' whereas other courts have held that the term 'must on its natural meaning indicate no more than 'participates in' 'takes part in' or 'concurs in' and involve some positive steps of some nature in the carrying on of the company's business in a fraudulent manner'.[80] Indeed, it has been held that the person who it is claimed is 'a party' to the fraud might even be an outsider. The breadth and scope of these provisions should not be underestimated and in particular it should be noted that they are not, as are most of the provisions that we are about to discuss, relevant in or near an insolvency.

6.64 A convenient starting point in our analysis of the insolvency law is section 89(1) of the Insolvency Act 1986. This provides that a majority of the directors of a company can make a statutory declaration, affirming that after their inquiries, they are satisfied that the company is solvent. The company can then, within a year, be subject to a members winding up as a solvent company. However, section 89(4) provides that if a director made such a declaration without having reasonable grounds for his opinion, he is guilty of an offence. It is important to note that it need not be proved that he knew the situation, his negligence is sufficient for criminal liability and if, indeed, within five weeks of the making of the declaration or such reasonable time as set out in the declaration, the company's debts are not discharged, it may be presumed that the directors did not have reasonable grounds for their opinion.

6.65 It is also provided in the Insolvency Act 1986, section 206 that a present or former officer of a company in liquidation who, within the previous year, conceals, fraudulently removes or pawns any of the company's property

---

79   Templeman J in *Re Cooper Chemical Ltd* [1978] Ch 262.
80   Pennycuick VC, *In Re Maidstone Building Supplies* [1971] 1 WLR 1085.

or conceals or falsifies any records[81] relating to the company's property, will be deemed to have committed an offence. By the same token, an officer or former officer who is privy to any of these actions will also be deemed to have committed an offence. It should be noted that the term 'officer' includes shadow directors. Section 206 not only applies to things done prior to and in anticipation of a liquidation, but also to things done during a winding up. The defendant is entitled to a defence if he can establish that he had no intent to defraud, conceal information from the company or defeat the law. Section 207 provides when a company is being wound up, a person is deemed to have committed an offence if he, being at the time an officer of the company, has made or caused to be made any gift or transfer of, or charge on, or has caused or connived at the levying of any execution against, the company's property, unless the transaction in question took place more than five years before the commencement of winding up or if he proves that, at the time of the conduct constituting the offence, he had no intent to defraud the company's creditors. There has been debate as to whether the defendant has a legal burden of proof – that is to a balance of probabilities, or merely an evidential burden. In *Attorney-General's Reference (No 1 of 2004)*[82] the House of Lords considered that 'it can be tempting to those involved in the management of a company or a bankrupt to conceal or dispose of ... assets to the disadvantage of creditors. Furthermore, such concealment or disposal may be done by a person alone and in private. a failure to record or disclose an asset, or a disposal of stock at an under value or the making of a disposal for nil consideration, may be known only to those involved in the transaction. There will be no independent witnesses to the act in question. Whether there has been fraud will often be known only to the individual, or individuals who are alleged to have committed the fraud'. Given the considerable benefits of incorporation and the operation of the personal bankruptcy laws to debtors, the House of Lords considered it was not unreasonable that the defendant has the full legal burden of proof – which is, of course, even in criminal matters, the civil burden.

6.66 There are further offences that are worth considering. Section 211(1) provides that a past or present officer of a company that is being wound up, commits an offence if he makes any false representation or commits any other fraud for the purposes of obtaining the consent of the company's creditors to an agreement concerning the company's affairs. Furthermore, he is deemed to have committed such an offence, if prior to the winding up, he has made any false representation, or committed any other fraud, for this purpose. False representations require that the accused either knew the representation was false or that it might be. However, proof of dishonesty is not required. Under section 210(1) a past or present officer of a company that is being wound up, commits an offence if he makes a material omission in any statement relating to the company's affairs. He will also be deemed to have committed this offence, as in the case of section 211, if the company is ordered to be wound up by the court or passes a resolution for voluntary winding up, and he has previously made any material omission in any such statement. The scope of this offence is unclear. It has been argued that it cannot extend to all omissions that are or

---

81   Records in this context is to be widely construed and includes computer records see *R v Taylor* [2011] EWCA Crim 728.
82   [2004] 1 WLR 2111 and see *R v Johstone* [2003] UKHL 28, *Sheldrake v DPP* [2004] UKHL 43 and *R (on the application of Griffin) v Richmond Magistrates Court* [2008] EWHC 84 (Admin).

could become material. The better view, is that only omissions which render what has been said misleading are caught. It should be noted, however, there is no way to establish that the omission is fraudulent or even deliberate. However, if the defendant can show that he has no intent to defraud, he is entitled to an acquittal. Another potentially useful provision is found in section 208. This states that a person will be guilty of an offence if a company is being wound up and, being a present or past officer of the company, he 'does not to the best of his knowledge and belief fully and truly discover to the liquidator all the company's property' and how and to whom and for consideration and when the company disposed of any part of that property. Property that has been disposed of in the course of the company's ordinary business is excluded from this obligation. Such a person also commits an offence if he does not deliver up to the liquidator all the company's property and books and papers under his control. He is also obliged, 'knowing or believing that a false debt has been proved' by any person in the winding up to notify the liquidator. As in the case of the other offences, if the defendant proves that he had no intent to defraud he is not guilty. It is also an offence under section 208(2) if after the commencement of a winding up, any past or present officer 'attempts to account for any part of the company's property by fictitious losses or expense'. He is deemed to have committed this offence, if he is proved to have attempted to do this at any time within a year of the commencement of the winding up.

6.67   Perhaps one of the most important provisions is, however, the Insolvency Act 1986, section 213. This provides that if in the course of a winding up it appears that any business of the company has been carried on with the intent to defraud creditors of the company or creditors of any other person, or for any fraudulent purpose, the court on the application of the liquidator, may declare that any person who was knowingly party to the carrying on of the business in the manner mentioned, is liable to make such contributions to the company's assets as the court thinks proper. Given the requirement of intent to defraud, as in the case of a prosecution brought under the Insolvency Act 1986, section 206, and see *Re Patrick and Lyon Ltd*,[83] it is necessary to prove 'actual dishonesty, involving real moral blame'. Consequently, the provision is of limited use and proceedings for wrongful trading under the Insolvency Act 1986, section 214 are usually far more efficacious.

6.68   This section empowers the court to declare that a person who is or has been a director, of the company in certain circumstances, must make a contribution to the assets of the company as the court considers proper. The circumstances in which an order can be made are, that that company is in insolvent liquidation, and at some time before the commencement of the winding up, the relevant person knew or ought to have concluded that there was no reasonable prospect that the company would avoid going into insolvent liquidation, and that at that point in time, he was a director of the company. However, the court should not make an order if it is satisfied, that after those circumstances occurring, the relevant person 'took every step with a view to minimising the potential loss to the company's creditors, assuming that he knew that there was no reasonable prospect that the company would avoid insolvent liquidation, which he ought to have taken. In section 214(4) it is provided that the facts which a director ought to know or ascertain, the conclusions which he ought to reach and the steps which he ought to take

83   [1933] Ch 786.

are those 'which would be known or ascertained, or reached or taken, by a reasonably diligent person having both: (a) the general knowledge, skill and experience that may reasonably be expected of a person carrying out the same functions as are carried out by that director in relation to the company, and (b) the general knowledge, skill and experience that that director has'. It should be noted section 214 applies with equal force to shadow directors.

6.69 In addition to these provisions, there are others facilitating investigation and recovery. For example, section 212 provides for summary proceedings in cases of misfeasance. Where, in a winding up, it appears that a person involved in the management or promotion of the company has misapplied or retained, or become accountable for, any money or other property of the company, or been guilty of any misfeasance or breach of any fiduciary or other duty in relation to the company, the court may, on the application of the liquidator or a creditor, examine the person concerned and make an order requiring restoration or contribution.

6.70 Our above discussion has focused on offences, primarily by those involved in the management, of a company that has become insolvent and is being wound up. Of course, it is important to remember that these offences operate in the context of the general criminal law and in particular the relevant corporate law. There may well be other proceedings. In our brief discussion of insolvency related financial crimes it is desirable to also refer to crimes involving the bankruptcy of an individual. In practice those involved in insolvency proceedings might also be involved in personal proceedings for their own bankruptcy.

6.71 Generally speaking, the relevant crimes apply to an individual who has been declared a bankrupt. Such a person will under section 352 of the insolvency Act 1986 be entitled to a defence if he can establish, in most cases to a balance of probabilities, that he at the material time had no intent to defraud or conceal the state of his affairs. However, where the offence is worded so widely as to catch conduct that would not normally be dishonest, the courts have taken the view that the burden imposed on the defendant is only evidential. Let us now look at two substantive offences which illustrate this. Section 357(1) renders it a crime if the bankrupt makes or causes to be made, or has in the five years ending with the commencement of his bankruptcy made or caused to be made any gift, or transfer of, or any charge on, his property. Under section 357(3) he is guilty of an offence if he conceals or removes, or has at any time before the commencement of the bankruptcy concealed or removed, any part of his property after, or within two months before, the date on which a judgment or order for payment has been made against him. Given the breadth of these offences, it is not unreasonable that the defendant has only to introduce evidence that he had no intention to defraud.[84] On the other hand, it is arguable that the defendant would have the full legal burden if he made the relevant dispositions after being declared a bankrupt and in regard to the offence under section 357(3) of concealing property after such a declaration. As in so many areas of the law, it is possible to find similar offences in other statutes. Section 13 of the Debtors Act 1869 makes it a criminal offence for any person with intent to defraud his creditors to make a gift or dispose or conceal his property. It should be noted that for this offence it is not necessary for the defendant to be bankrupt.

---

84   See *Attorney-General's Reference (No 1 of 2004)* [2004] 1 WLR 2111.

6.72   A declared bankrupt might also be charged with offences under section 354 if he conceals any debt that is due to or from him or any other property which he is required to deliver up to the receiver or trustee in bankruptcy. If he removes such property he also commits an offence. Furthermore, if he does any of these acts within a year before the petition for his bankruptcy, he commits an offence. Again he is entitled to a defence if he proves he had no intent to defraud. Under section 358 a bankrupt who leaves or attempts or makes preparations to leave the jurisdiction with any property that he is required to hand over, commits an offence. The same is true in regard to such conduct within six months before the petition, but as in regard to the other offences, he has the defence that he had no intent to defraud. The falsification, alteration and hiding of records is rendered a specific offence under section 355. Section 356 mirrors the provisions in the case of officers of insolvent companies in sections 210 and 211 discussed above. There is also a similar duty under section 353, to disclose property to the receiver or trustee.

6.73   In the case of insolvent companies the company will, at the end of the legal process, cease to exist. It may well be that proceedings will be initiated against the director of the company under the Company Directors Disqualification Act 1986 which has the effect of banning under criminal penalties former directors from being involved in the management of a company. There are many other grounds for such an order than being involved in the affairs of an insolvent company. Section 11 of this Act, however, renders it an offence, without the leave of the court, for an un-discharged bankrupt to serve as a director or become directly or indirectly involved in the management of a company. Section 360 of the Insolvency Act renders it a crime for a declared bankrupt to engage in any business in a name other than that in which he has been adjudged bankrupt. Merely operating behind a sham company will not assist him. In *R v Doubleday*,[85] the Court of Appeal thought that the offence was committed where the prosecution established that the accused was 'in fact the proprietor of a business set up under another name'. The courts will, as we have seen in the misuse of companies, look at the reality of the situation. By section 360 an offence is also committed by a bankrupt if he obtains credit without disclosing his status. Finally, section 362(1) is of some interest in that it makes an offence for the bankrupt in the two years before the petition, to have 'materially contributed to, or increased the extent of, his insolvency by gambling or by rash and hazardous speculation ...'. In determining whether any speculation was rash 'the financial position of the bankrupt at the time when he entered into' the relevant activity 'shall be taken into consideration.'

RECKLESS MANAGEMENT OF BANKS

6.74   With the caveat that we seek to address only in general terms offences other than those in Part V of the CJA 1993 in so far as they might be of relevance in a case of insider abuse, it would be remiss not to mention the new offence created to address the reckless management of banks and building societies. This offence was a direct result of the concern of many that the law was not adequate in addressing the conduct of some bank insiders

---

85   (1964) 49 Cr App R 62.

before and during the financial chaos following the so called sub-prime crisis.[86] The Government's implementation in large measure of the recommendations of the Parliamentary Commission on Banking Standards needs to be viewed in the context of its other initiatives to create a Senior Persons Regime replacing the Approved Persons Regime and the emphasis that is now placed on taking personal and individual responsibility particularly in regard to compliance.[87] Section 36 of the Financial Services (Banking Reform) Act 2013 provides that a person commits an offence if when at a time that person is a senior manager in relation to a financial institution, he takes or agrees to take any decision or fails to take steps to prevent such a decision being taken, being aware at that time of a risk that implementation of the decision may cause a failure of the institution, and in fact that decision does cause the failure. However, it must also be proved that in the circumstances that person's 'conduct in relation to the taking of the decision falls far below what could reasonably be expected of a person' in his position. It was the element of *mens rea* that proved to be the most controversial in the drafting of this provision. Obviously, it is necessary for the prosecution to prove that the relevant person was guilty of rather more than mere negligence. On the other hand the test is essentially objective it does not require the prosecution to show that he was conscious that his conduct or inaction in fact fell 'far below' that which can be reasonably expected of a person in his position. It is not necessary to show that there was any intention to benefit personally. While many commentators, particularly in the City of London consider that this offence requires proof of recklessness, the better view is that what the criminal law sometimes regards as gross negligence[88] would be sufficient. It would not seem necessary to show recklessness in the sense that the person was aware of the relevant issues but nonetheless acted with indifference to what he appreciated was a likely consequence. Of course, proof of this would be sufficient for establishing gross negligence.

6.75 Furthermore, it is important to note that the failure need not relate directly to the company of which the person is a senior manager, but to any financial institution within the group. The financial institutions to which this offence relates are essentially those that are allowed under the FSMA to accept deposits or those regulated by the PRA with permission to carry on the regulated activity of dealing in investments as principal. Consequently, the offence is primarily concerned with banking institutions.

6.76 Senior managers are defined in section 37(7) as being persons 'under an arrangement entered into by the institution, or by a contractor of the institution,

---

86   See Changing Banking for Good, Report of the Parliamentary Commission on Banking Standards, First Report of Session 2013–14, June 2013 and The Government's Response to the Parliamentary Commission on Banking Standards, July 2013 Cm 8661 and HM Treasury, Sanctions for the directors of failed banks, July 2012 and see in regard to the provisions introduced by the Financial Services Act 2012 to create the specific offences of making false statements or misleading submissions in connection with the determination of financial benchmarks, discussed in Chapter 5.

87   See 14.46 *et seq* below.

88   See, for example, the similarly worded provision in the law of dangerous driving, Road Traffic Act 1988, s 2A and *R v Bateman* (1925) 19 Cr App R 8 and in relation to manslaughter, *R v Akomako* [1994] UKHL 6. In *R v Misra and Srivastava* [2005] 1 Cr App R 328 it was said that to qualify as falling well below the standard that would reasonably be expected the conduct must be reprehensible. It is submitted that a similar test would be appropriate in regard to s 36 of the Financial Services (Banking Reform) Act 2013. As we have seen in regard to prosecutions in related areas of the law, expert evidence is likely to play a significant role.

in relation to the carrying on by the institution of a regulated activity' requiring that person to perform a senior management function spelt out in subsection (8). A senior management function is essentially what the FCA or PRA say it is.[89] The failure of an institution is set out in subsections (9) and (10) and in broad terms means that it cannot pay its debts as they fall due. The offence is punishable under section 36(4) on indictment to a term of imprisonment of not more than seven years and or an unlimited fine. Prosecution can, however, only be commenced by the FCA, PRA, the Secretary of State or with the consent of the Director of Public Prosecutions.

BLACKMAIL AND EXTORTION

6.77   The FSA and the Serious Organised Crime Agency (SOCA) emphasised the risks facing those engaged in the financial services industry as a result of the activities of organised crime and other professional criminals. The successor to SOCA has been equally vocal. We address the issues presented by the misuse of financial institutions and intermediaries for the laundering of the proceeds of crime in Chapter 7. However, in recent years evidence has come to light of criminals deliberately penetrating financial institutions not merely to facilitate the laundering of money, but to facilitate other crimes against the financial sector and others. Indeed, Sir Cullum McCarthy, the former Chairman of the FSA issued a warning to the financial services industry specifically about this threat in November 2005.[90] Consequently, in the context of our discussion of the offences relating to the financial sector, it is necessary to consider extortion and blackmail. While such crimes are often motivated by greed, they have another and more sinister aspect. It is the preying on persons, making unjustified threats to them or their loved ones that gives these crimes a particularly unpleasant character. It is also the case that such crimes are often used by organised crime and in particular criminal groups who would not stop at extreme violence.

6.78   The crime of blackmail is set out in section 21 of the English Theft Act 1968. It provides that a person commits the crime 'if with a view to gain for himself or another or with intent to cause loss to another, he makes any unwarranted demand with menaces.' For the purposes of this offence 'a demand with menaces is unwarranted unless the person making it does so in the belief: (a) that he has reasonable grounds for making the demand; and (b) that the use of the menaces is a proper means of reinforcing the demand'. The concept of gain or loss in this context is confined to money or property. A demand is made for the purposes of the offence when it is spoken or mailed. The better view, on the authorities, is that it need not be heard, understood or even received.[91] The issue as to whether the demand is unwarranted or not is subjective, the accused does not have to be reasonable. On the other hand if the way in which an accused has acted is not proper, then even a reasonable belief in his right to, for example, pursue a debt, is criminal.

89   See FSMA, s 59(6A) in regard to the FCA and subs (6B) in regard to the PRA.
90   See 'warning over mafia gangs infiltrating British banks', *Times*, 16 November 2005. This led to the European Commission initiating a five-country study of this problem with the assistance of the City of London Police under its AGIS Programme. See also R Ford, 'Criminal gangs are running swathes of Britain' *Times* 12 June 2014.
91   *Treacy v DPP* [1971] AC 537.

6.79   The term menaces is not defined in the Act, but one judge has said that it involves conduct or a threat of conduct 'of such a nature and extent that the mind of an ordinary person of normal stability and courage might be influenced or made apprehensive'.[92] It is to be noted that a threat to reveal another person's criminal activity, if made with a view to gain, can be sufficient for liability. The moral obligation to report crimes to the authorities should not be capable of being 'bought off' – indeed, in the United Kingdom, accepting payment, other than as compensation, for not reporting a crime is an offence under section 5 of the Criminal Law Act 1967. Thus, a threat to expose the crime or other wrongdoing of another unless payment is made would be a crime. But so would a threat to attack a company in a newspaper article to depress price of its shares[93] or the threat to disclose sensitive commercial information[94] or probably the threat to initiate civil proceedings.

COMPUTER-RELATED CRIME

6.80   In the modern world it is difficult to imagine a situation where a significant financial crime can be perpetrated without the use or misuse of a computer. While the advent of technology has greatly facilitated the commission of many forms of fraud and abuse, the essential crimes remain much the same. Computers are used to assist in the execution of crime. Of course, it may be that threats are made against the security and integrity of computer systems; however, this is in essence no different than crimes involving criminal damage against any other form of property. It should also be noted that under section 13 of the Theft Act there is a specific offence of dishonestly abstracting or diverting electricity, which may well be technically relevant. However, the more significant law is found in the Computer Misuse Act 1990 as amended by the Police and Justice Act 2006. This Act created three new and specific offences. Section 1 makes it an offence to access without authority computer material that is a programme or data; section 2 renders it an offence to access without authority a computer system with intent to commit or facilitate the commission of a serious crime; and section 3 provides that it is an offence to without authority modify computer material. While the computer and hardware might be adequately protected by the law relating to criminal damage, information is, as we have seen, not so easily protected. Section 3 seeks to address this, by providing that anyone who does any act which causes an unauthorised modification of the contents of a computer and has the requisite intention and knowledge, which includes recklessness, commits a crime. A modification is defined to include alteration or erasing any program or data on the computer. The requisite intention is an intention to impair the operation of any computer, to prevent or hinder access to any program or data, or impair the operation of any program or the reliability of any data. It is enough for the knowledge element that the accused knows that what he is doing is unauthorised. It is immaterial whether the alteration is merely temporary, the offence is still committed. The 1990 Act was amended in 2006 to make it clear that section 3 covers conduct designed to disrupt and deny computer related services. A new section 3A also, much in the same way as section 6 of the Fraud Act 2006, renders it a criminal

---

92   *R v Clear* [1968] 1 QB 670.
93   *R v Boyle and Merchant* [1914] 3 KB 339.
94   *R v Cox and Jenkins* (1979) 1 Cr App R(S) 190.

offence to have or distribute 'tools' to be used for hacking computer networks. Part 2 of the Serious Crime Act 2015 further amends section 3 to criminalise unauthorised acts causing, or creating a risk of, serious damage. This offence is committed if a person does any knowingly unauthorised act in relation to a computer which causes serious damage of a material kind or the risk of such occurring and is reckless as to whether such damage is caused.

6.81 Of course, one of the serious problems in addressing computer crime is the fact that it may often be perpetrated from overseas. As we have seen under section 2 of the Computer Misuse Act 1990 in the UK it is a crime to cause a computer to perform a function with intent to secure unauthorised access to programs or data with the intention of committing or facilitating the commission of some other offence. An offence under section 1 which simply renders it an offence to access without authorisation may be committed abroad provided that there is a 'significant link' with the UK. Thus, if the defendant does what he does to secure access from abroad, if the computer is physically in the UK there would be an offence. However, in the case of section 2, it is enough that the offence that it is intended to facilitate is within the jurisdiction of the UK. Thus, both the defendant and the computer could be outside the UK provided crime that he intends to facilitate is in the UK.[95]

CORRUPTION

6.82 In earlier editions of this work we have bemoaned the then state of English criminal law in regard to bribery and other corrupt practices.[96] The UK law was considered deficient and failed to meet the various international obligations on the United Kingdom.[97] The Law Commission and Home Office had for a number of years striven with varying degrees of enthusiasm to develop acceptable legislative proposals[98] and there had been considerable criticism of the manner in which the British Government dealt with certain high profile cases.[99] The Bribery Act 2010 is regarded as if not quite the 'gold standard' in anti-corruption legislation, pretty close to it. The various offences in the Act, which replace the old law[100] are comprehensive and wide ranging. The heart

---

95 Note also the amendments introduced by the Serious Crime Act 2015 in regard to the territorial scope of the offences in sections 4 and 5.

96 See generally B Rider (ed), *Corruption: the enemy within* (Kluwer 1997) and B Rider 'Corruption the Sharp End of Governance' in SA Ali (ed), *Risky Business, Perspectives in Corporate Misconduct* (Caribbean Law Publishing Company 2010), Ch 1.

97 See, for example, United Kingdom: Phase 2bis: Report on the Application of the Convention on Combating Bribery of Foreign Public Officials in International Business Transactions and the 1997 Recommendation on Combating Bribery in International Business Transactions (2008) OECD.

98 See Legislating the Criminal Code: Corruption (1998) Law Com No 248; Joint Committee on the Draft Corruption Bill, Session 2002–2003, HL Paper 157, HC 705 (2003); The Government's Reply to the Report of the Joint Committee on the Draft Corruption Bill, Session 2002–2003, HL Paper 157, HC 705 (2003) Cm 6086 and Reforming Bribery: A Consultation Paper (2007) Law Com Consultation Paper No 185 and Reforming Bribery (2008) The Law Commission Law Com No 313.

99 See *R (on the application of Corner House Research) v Director of the Serious Fraud Office* [2008] 4 All ER 927.

100 See B Rider, K Alexander, L Linklater and S Bazley, *Market Abuse and Insider Dealing* (2nd edn) (Tottel 2009), at 6.74 et seq. It should also be noted that the offence of criminal breach of trust under the Fraud Act 2006 might also be very relevant in some cases of bribery. See generally A Arlidge, A Milne and P Springer, *Arlidge and Parry on Fraud* (4th edn) (Sweet & Maxwell 2014).

of the offence of bribery is offering, promising or giving a financial or other advantage to another person where he intends the advantage to induce a person, whether this is the same person related to the advantage or another, to perform improperly a relevant function or activity or to reward him for so doing.[101] It is also an offence where a person offers, promises or gives a financial or other advantage to another person and he knows or believes that the acceptance of that advantage would itself constitute the improper performance of the relevant function.[102] In both cases it matters not whether the advantage is offered or given directly or through a third person, innocent or otherwise.

6.83   The offence of being bribed is set out in equal clarity in section 2 of the Act. A person will be guilty of this offence where he requests or agrees to receive, or accepts a financial or other advantage intending that in consequence, a relevant function or activity, should be improperly performed whether by himself or another.[103] The offence is also made out where the request itself constitutes the improper performance of the relevant function.[104] A person will also be guilty of taking a bribe if he requests, agrees to receive or accepts an advantage as a reward for the improper performance by himself or another.[105] Indeed, the offence also catches a person who in anticipation of or in consequence of his request, agreement or acceptance of an advantage, a relevant function is improperly performed by him or another person at his request, asset or acquiescence.[106] Again it does not matter whether for this offence, the advantage is to be received directly or through a third party or the benefit is for the person making the request or another.[107]

6.84   The functions or activity referred to in the offences must be of a public nature, or connected with a business, trade or profession, or performed in the course of a person's employment, or be performed by or on behalf of a body of persons, whether incorporated or not, such as a partnership. In addition, one or more of the following conditions must also be satisfied. First, that the person performing the function is expected to perform it in good faith. Secondly, that it is expected to be performed impartially or thirdly, that a person performing the function or activity is in a position of trust by virtue of performing it. Obviously, many of the issues that we have already examined in the context of fiduciary obligations may well be relevant in this context.[108] Section 3(6) makes it clear that a function or activity is still relevant even though it has no connection with the UK and is performed outside the UK.

6.85   For the purposes of the Act a function or activity is improperly performed if it is performed in breach of a relevant expectation or the failure to perform is a breach of such expectation.[109] The expectation is tied to the conditions set out above and therefore relate to good faith, impartiality and the proper discharge of a fiduciary obligation. It is also made clear in section 4(2)

---

101   See s 1(2) Case 1.
102   Section 1(3) Case 2.
103   Section 2 (2) Case 3.
104   Section 2(3) Case 4.
105   Section 2(3) Case 5.
106   Section 2(4) Case 6.
107   Except in case 3. Furthermore, in cases 4, 5 and 6, it does not matter whether the person making the request knows or believes that the performance of the function is improper and in case 6, where a person other than the person making the request is performing the function or activity, it does not matter whether that person knows or believes that the performance is improper: s 2(7) and (8).
108   See Chapter 2 and also Chapter 9.
109   Section 4.

that anything that a person does or omits to do arising from or in connection with that person's past performance of a relevant function or activity is to be treated for the purposes of the Act as being done or omitted by that person in the performance of that function or activity. In regard to these provisions in sections 3 and 4 the test of what is expected is a test of what a reasonable person in the UK would expect in relation to the performance of the type of function or activity in question.[110] Furthermore, in applying this test any local custom or practice is to be disregarded unless it is permitted or required by the written law, including case law, of the overseas country concerned.

6.86   Perhaps the offence that attracted most interest is that contained in section 6 of the Act which makes it a crime to bribe foreign officials anywhere. A person is guilty of an offence if in bribing a foreign official if his intention is to influence that individual in his capacity as a foreign public official and that he has the intention of obtaining or retaining business or an advantage in the conduct of business. In this context, business includes a trade or profession in line with the more general offences. Will not be an offence, however, if the person receiving the bribe in such circumstances is permitted or authorised to act in the way intended, by virtue of a relevant local written law.[111] On the other hand, the notion of influencing the performance of an overseas official's duty is wide enough to encompass not an act or omission in the discharge of his functions, but also any use of his position even if outside his actual authority. Section 6(5) provides that a foreign public official includes any individual who holds a legislative, administrative or judicial position of any kind outside the UK and who exercises a public function for or on behalf of a foreign country or for any public agency or public enterprise of a foreign country or is an official or agent of a public international inter-governmental organisation.

6.87   Section 7 is of particular interest as it introduces into this area of law the notion of control liability, which has been developed with considerable effect in the USA. It provides that a relevant commercial organisation will be guilty of an offence if a person associated with it bribes another person in the circumstances set out in sections 1 and 6. Section 12(5) makes it clear that it does not matter whether the relevant acts or omissions took part in the UK or elsewhere.[112] However, the prosecution must prove the individual did so intending to obtain or retain business for the commercial organisation or to obtain or retain an advantage in the conduct of its business. For the purposes of this provision, a relevant commercial organisation includes any company incorporated in the UK or one incorporated overseas which carried on business in the UK. The same also applies to partnerships. Although the Government is under a duty to give guidance[113] as to the meaning of being associated with the company or partnership, section 8 makes it clear that the test is whether the person performs services for or on behalf of the business, albeit the capacity in which he does so is irrelevant. Therefore a person may be associated as an employee, agent or subsidiary of the relevant business. Where the test is met is to be determined by reference to all the relevant circumstances and not merely by the nature of the relationship. On the other hand, if the relevant person is an employee of the business it is to be presumed, unless it is shown

---

110   Section 5.
111   See also s 6(7).
112   See generally on the territorial application of the Act, s 12.
113   See *Ministry of Justice Bribery Act 2010; Guidance to help Commercial organisations prevent bribery* (March 2011).

to the contrary that he is associated in regard to the relevant activity. A specific defence is provided for businesses if they can prove that it had in place adequate procedures designed to prevent persons associated with it from engaging in the prohibited conduct. In other words, if the firm can show that it has taken steps through compliance and training to address the risk of corruption then it is entitled to a defence. Under section 9 a duty is placed on the Government to publish guidance as to what might be considered by a court as adequate in this regard. In the Ministry of Justice's *Guidance*[114] six principles are propounded with the intention of assisting commercial organisations from avoiding or at least minimising the risk of bribery. First, the organisation should design and implement procedures to prevent bribery which are proportionate to the risk in relation to the business. Secondly, there must be commitment to preventing corruption by those at the top. Thirdly, there should be periodic and thorough risk assessments. Fourthly, the business is to engage in due diligence in regard to the assessment and control of risk related to those who are associated with it. Fifthly, the policies that the firm has must be properly embedded and understood by all concern and reinforced with appropriate training. Finally, there needs to be a continuing process of monitoring and review. The FCA has endorsed these principles and they reflect its own attitude to suitable compliance and accountability.

6.88   Finally, section 14 provides that if an offence is committed by a company under sections 1, 2 and 6, a director, manager or the secretary, including a person who purports to act in such a capacity, may also be guilty of an offence if it can be shown that the crime was committed with their consent of connivance.

FALSE REPORTING

6.89   It is of fundamental importance to the proper operation of so many aspects of the legal and regulatory systems that information is properly and accurately recorded and reported. Indeed, in recent years, some of the most dramatic financial scandals have involved misconduct in this process. Under the English law, directors of a company must prepare accounts for each financial year and also a directors' report. The accounts must be audited and under section 499(1)(b) of the Companies Act 2006 an auditor can require various persons including the directors, officers and employees of the company to provide him with such information and explanations as he thinks necessary for the proper performance of his duties. Under section 501(1) of the Act a person who knowingly or recklessly makes an oral or written statement to an auditor that conveys or purports to convey information or explanations which the audit requires, or is entitled to require, and is misleading, false or deceptive in a material particular, commits an offence. It is also provided, much in line with the Sarbanes-Oxley provisions in the USA, that a director is required to state, in the directors' report, that so far as he is aware, there is no information needed by the auditor of which the auditor is unaware and that he has taken all the steps that he ought to have taken to make himself aware of any information needed by the auditor and to establish that the auditor is aware of it. It is sufficient for this purpose that he has made such enquiries

---

114   See *Ministry of Justice Bribery Act 2010; Guidance to help Commercial organisations prevent bribery* (March 2011).

of his fellow directors and of the auditors, and taken such other steps, as are required by his duty to exercise reasonable care, skill and diligence. If such a report is approved and the statement turns out to be false, the director commits a crime under section 418(5). Furthermore, the offence is committed by every director who knew that the statement was false or was recklessly indifferent as to whether it was true or false, and failed to take reasonable steps to prevent the report being approved. This places an affirmative obligation on directors to ensure that auditors are placed in a position to discharge their own duties in verifying the information that the company is required to disclose to the shareholders and other stakeholders. It is not now possible for directors to hide behind a veil of ignorance.

6.90   Every company, under section 386(2) of the 2006 Act, is required to keep and maintain proper accounting records. In particular, they must be sufficient to show and explain the company's transactions, be such as to disclose with reasonable accuracy, at any time, the company's financial position and be such as to enable the directors to ensure that the accounts comply with the statutory requirements. Furthermore, detailed information to be included in the records is set out in other provisions of the Act. If the company fails to discharge its obligations in this regard, every officer of the company who is in default commits an offence under section 387(1). It is a defence for a director to show that he acted honestly and in the circumstances in which the company's business was carried out his default was excusable. In like terms, there is a statutory obligation to ensure that such records are kept available in the UK for officers of the company to inspect by virtue of section 388(2).

6.91   These provisions do not stand alone. Section 17(1) of the Theft Act 1968 renders it an offence for any person, 'dishonestly, with a view to gain for himself or another or with intent to cause loss to another to (a) destroy, deface, conceal or falsify any account or any record or document made or required for any accounting purpose; or (b) in furnishing information for any purpose produces or makes use of any account, or any such record or document as aforesaid, which to his knowledge is or may be misleading, false or deceptive in a material particular'. This offence covers documents 'if it is made for some purpose other than an accounting purpose, but is required for an accounting purpose as a subsidiary consideration ...'.[115] If a document is required for an accounting purpose it matters not what it was created for. Furthermore, it should be noted that this is in no way confined to companies or established businesses, an individual may have accounting purposes. It is further provided in section 17(2) that for the purposes of the offence, 'a person who makes or concurs in making in an account or other document an entry which is or may be misleading, false or deceptive in a material particular, or who omits or concurs in omitting a material particular from an account or other document, is to be treated as falsifying the account or document'.

6.92   Section 18(1) of the 1968 Act provides that where an offence under section 17 is committed by a company and 'is proved to have been committed with the consent or connivance of any director, manager, secretary or other officer' of the company, or any person purporting so to be, that individual will also be guilty of the offence. It would seem from this that once knowledge is established, then passive acquiescence would be enough for liability. By section 19 'an officer of a body corporate or unincorporated association, or

115   *Attorney-General's Reference (No 1 1980)* [1981] 1 WLR 34.

person purporting to act as such, with intent to deceive members or creditors of the body corporate or association about its affairs, publishes or concurs in publishing a written statement or account which to his knowledge is or may be misleading, false or deceptive in a material particular ...' commits an offence. This offence does not extend to oral statements. However, if, for example, a director orally made a false statement to the press which is then written up this would be sufficient. Section 1(1) of the Prevention of Corruption Act 1906 also includes a provision of interest. It provides that 'if any person knowingly gives to any agent, or if any agent knowingly uses with intent to deceive his principal, a receipt, account, or other document in respect of which the principal is interested, and which contains any statement which is false or erroneous or defective in any material particular, and which to his knowledge is intended to mislead the principal' is guilty of an offence.

6.93   Of course, there are many other provisions and procedures concerned with the integrity of disclosure and the reporting of information. In the case of companies that have their securities listed or registered for trading on an organised securities market, there will be many additional and specific reporting and disclosure obligations. We have already discussed the significance of these and in particular the obligation to make continuous and timely disclosure in the context of insider dealing. These obligations may give rise to liability at many levels within the legal system. The obligation to disclose will bring in fraud and possibly anti-manipulation laws. These may well result in criminal and civil liability. Those who are harmed by false and misleading information may also have a civil claim against those responsible, including the company. Those responsible for the false or misleading statements in the company may find that they are in breach of their duties to the company and be liable accordingly in the civil courts. In certain cases, in some jurisdictions, they might also be liable to anyone, including dealers in the market, who relied on this false information. The securities exchange upon which the relevant securities are listed or traded may also have grounds for complaint. In many countries the listing agreement is regarded as a contract and even where it is not, there are usually legal devices under which those responsible for the market can initiate injunctive and other actions against those responsible for each of the terms of listing and possibly misleading the market. It is also probable that the market regulator will also have powers to intervene and pursue those responsible. Finally in this regard, it is important to note that failure to disclose information as it should be, may well result in other problems for those in management. Insiders in such circumstances will generally not be able to deal.

FORGERY AND THE RELIABILITY OF DOCUMENTATION

6.94   The significance of documentation in the perpetration of so many financial crimes need not be laboured here, suffice it to say that in the commercial and financial sector documentation is vital and therefore a fraudster or money launderer will need to be able to manipulate and control the documents which establish his credibility and ability to operate. Section 1 of the Forgery and Counterfeiting Act 1981 provides 'a person is guilty of forgery if he makes a false instrument, with the intention that he or another shall use it to induce somebody to accept it as genuine, and by reason of so accepting it to do or not to do some act to his own or any other person's prejudice'. In the context of this offence 'instrument' includes any document whether formal or informal in character, stamps and any disc, tape, sound track or other device on or in which information is recorded or stored by mechanical, electronic or other means. In *Attorney-General of Hong Kong v Pat Chiuk-Wah*[116] the Privy Council stated that it includes 'any document intended to have some effect, as evidence of, or in connection with, a transaction which is capable, or giving rise to legal rights and obligations ...'. The notion behind forgery is that the instrument must not only tell a lie, but a lie about itself. The English Law Commission said, 'the primary reason ... for ... the law of forgery is to penalise the making of documents which, because of the spurious air of authenticity given to them, are likely to lead to their acceptance as true statements of the facts related in them' (Law Commission No 55). Section 9(1) sets out what is meant by a false instrument. Basically an instrument will be false if it purports to be made in a form in which it was not in fact made, or in a form, or on terms that the person did not have authority to make, or has been altered, or made on a date or place or in other circumstances where it was not, or by a person who does not exist. Thus, the document may lie about itself in terms of the identity of the person making or authorising the statement, the circumstances of its making and the circumstances of any alteration.

6.95 It must be remembered that the wrongful conduct – the so called *actus reus* of forgery – is the making of a false instrument. This includes making an instrument which is false when it is made, altering a genuine instrument to render it false and altering an instrument which is already false by making it false in some additional way. The maker of this false instrument must intend that he or another shall use it to induce someone to accept it as a genuine instrument and that the person so accepting it by reason of so accepting it will do or not do some act and that act or omission shall be to his or another person's prejudice. It should be noted that the offence of forgery is complete on the making of a false instrument with the relevant intention. It matters not that no one was in fact prejudiced. It follows that an accused cannot escape liability '... merely because at the time when he is creating the document he has not made up his mind about the method of despatch ...'.[117] Section 10(3) provides that 'references to inducing someone to accept a false instrument as genuine ... include references to inducing a machine to respond to the instrument ... as if it was genuine'. Furthermore, section 10(4) adds that 'the act or omission intended to be induced by the machine responding to the instrument ... shall be treated as an act or omission to a person's prejudice'. The notion of prejudice is set out in section 10(1) where it is provided 'an act or omission intended to be induced is to a person's prejudice if, and only if', it is one which, if it occurs will result in his temporary or permanent loss of property, or deprivation of an opportunity to earn remuneration or to gain a financial advantage, or will result in somebody being given an opportunity to earn remuneration or gain a financial advantage or will be the result of his having accepted a false instrument as genuine in connection with his performance of any duty.

6.96 The offence of forgery is extended to the copying of a false instrument by section 2 of the 1981 Act. It is an offence 'for a person to make a copy of an instrument which is, and which he knows or believes to be, a false instrument, with the intention that he or another shall use it to induce somebody to accept it as a copy of a genuine instrument, and by reason of so accepting it to do or not to do some act to his own or any other person's prejudice'.

---

116   [1971] AC 835.
117   *R v Ondhia* [1998] 2 Cr App R 150.

6.97   Section 3 of the Forgery and Counterfeiting Act 1981 provides that 'it is an offence for a person to use an instrument which is, and which he knows or believes to be, false, with the intention of inducing somebody to accept it as genuine, and by reason of so accepting it to do or not to do some act to his own or any other person's prejudice'. It should be noted that if the person uttering or using the false instrument knows or believes that the instrument is false and in fact it is false, it matters not that the person actually making the instrument has not been guilty of forgery. It is necessary, however, to establish some kind of nexus between the user and the instrument. It is not sufficient that someone acts in a manner where he knows someone else will supply a forged document, he must himself use it. Section 4 creates a similar offence in regard to use of a copy of a false instrument.

6.98   Given the ease with which forged documents can be transferred and hidden, it is under the English law an offence to merely be in possession of certain specified forged instruments. These include forged money and postal orders, postage stamps, share certificates, cheques and other bills of exchange, travellers' cheques, bankers' drafts, promissory notes, cheque, debit and credit cards and certificates relating to entries in official registers. It is an offence under section 5(1) of the Act 'for a person to have in his custody or under his control an instrument' to which this provision applies, 'which is, and which he knows or believes to be, false, with the intention that he or another shall use it to induce somebody to accept it as genuine and by reason of so accepting it to do or not to do some act to his own or any other person's prejudice'. It should be noted, however, that there is a lesser offence where the person will be guilty, if he has 'in his custody or under his control without lawful authority or excuse' a false instrument within the scope of this provision and 'which is and which he knows or believes to be false'. It is also an offence to have in possession 'a machine or implement, or paper or any other material' which to that person's 'knowledge is or has been specially designed or adapted for the making of an instrument' to which this provision applied with the intention that he or another will in fact make such an instrument and use it to another's prejudice (section 5(3)). The accused must actually know that the equipment has been so adapted or designed, but it is important to note that they need not have been adapted or designed to create a 'false' document. Section 5(4) creates an offence of merely being in possession of such equipment or materials without lawful excuse.

6.99   Suppression of documents in the commission of fraud is addressed in the English law under section 20 of the Theft Act 1968. This provides that 'a person who dishonestly, with a view to gain for himself or another or with intent to cause loss to another, destroys, defaces or conceals any valuable security, any will or other testamentary document or any original document of or belonging to, or filed or deposited in, any court of justice or any government department shall' be guilty of an offence. The notion of defacement is broad and might extend to altering a document and thus, this might be an alternative charge to one of forgery.

ACTS PREPARATORY TO FRAUD

6.100   Most frauds require the assistance of others and a considerable amount of preparation. However, generally speaking there is a reluctance in the law to punish mere acts of preparation other than in the context of terrorist related crime. While fraud is a crime of intent and the offence is complete whether or not the accused actually manages to dupe someone, there may be situations where all the requirements for a charge of fraud are not present and yet justice demands intervention. On the other hand the current English law is in regard to the relationship between inchoate offences and secondary liability is confused. Under section 1(4)(b) of the Criminal Attempts Act 1981 there cannot be an attempt to aid, abet, counsel; and procure an offence by another person. The position is, however, uncertain as to whether this amounts to a conspiracy,[118] although as we shall see the Serious Crime Act 2007 now impacts on this.

6.101   Where a person agrees with another to carry out a course of conduct that would amount to the crime of fraud, he may as we have seen be guilty of conspiracy to defraud.[119] We have already referred on a number of occasions to the important offence of conspiracy and noted that it remains in England a common law conspiracy although it may also be charged as a conspiracy to commit the substantive crime of fraud as a statutory conspiracy. Section 1 of the Criminal Law Act 1977 renders it a statutory offence if a person agrees with any other person, including a company, that a course of conduct shall be undertaken, where if the agreement is carried out in accordance with their intentions it will amount to or involve the commission of a specific crime. Before a conviction can take place the jury must be satisfied that there was in fact an agreement between two or more persons to commit the crime in question; that the particular accused was a party to that agreement in the sense 'that he agreed with one or more of the other persons that the crime should be committed and at the time of agreeing to this, he intended that they (and he) should carry it out'.[120] It is not necessary that the agreement be to commit a specific offence under a statute. For example, an agreement to launder the proceeds of insider dealing or another crime, may be charged as a single conspiracy. The Criminal Law Act in section 1(2) provides that a person shall not be guilty of conspiracy under the Act unless he and at least one other party to the agreement intend or know that the facts necessary to the commission of the offence shall or will exist at the time of the conduct. This would seem to have the effect of blocking charges for conspiracy to commit crimes under, for example, the Fraud Act and the anti-money laundering provisions, where the accused might in the substantive offence be liable for reckless conduct or in the case of certain money laundering offences 'having reasonable grounds to suspect ...'.

6.102   The common law conspiracy to defraud is preserved by the Act, as we have seen.[121] It was said by Buckley J in *London and Globe Finance Corporation*[122] that 'to defraud is to deprive by deceit; it is deceit to induce a man to act to his injury'. It would seem on the authorities that an agreement by two or more persons by dishonesty to deprive a person of something which he is or to which he is or would be or even might be entitled and an agreement by which two or more by dishonesty to injure some proprietary right of another is a conspiracy at common law. Furthermore an agreement to deceive a public official, as we have seen, into doing something, or not doing something, that he would not have done but for the deceit is also a conspiracy to defraud.[123]

---

118   See *R v Hollinshead* [1985] AC 975. Sections 45 and 46 of the Serious Crime Act 2007 would now be the appropriate offences.
119   See at 6.17 *et seq* above.
120   Judiciary Studies Board, England and Wales, *Specimen Direction* 2005.
121   See 6.19 above.
122   [1903] 1 Ch 728.
123   See generally *Scott v Metropolitan Police Commissioner* [1975] AC 819 and *DPP v Welham* [1961] AC 103.

It is important to appreciate that it is the risk of prejudice not actual prejudice that is necessary for the offence. Thus, in *Attorney General of Hong Kong v Wai Yu-Tsang*,[124] the fact that the bank accountant covered up bad cheques passing through the bank to prevent a run on the bank still amounted to a conspiracy to defraud the bank. The Privy Council stated 'it is …important to distinguish a conspirator's intention or immediate purpose … from his motive (or underlying purpose.) The latter may be benign in that he does not wish the victim … to suffer harm; but the mere fact that it is benign will not of itself prevent the agreement from constituting a conspiracy to defraud'. The scope and arguable vagueness as to the perimeters of this offence have resulted in criticism over many years. Where it is possible to charge a conspiracy to commit a specific statutory offence – such as fraud under section 1 of the Fraud Act 2006, then the common law should not be used as we have noted. There are situations, however, where the crime of conspiracy to defraud is wider than the statutory law. For example, in the case of a statutory conspiracy to commit fraud, it would need to be shown that at least one of the parties to the agreement was intended to commit the fraud. In a situation where the agreement is to enable or facilitate someone else to commit the fraud, who is not a party to the agreement, the only charge would be conspiracy to defraud at common law. The creation of a general false impression over a period of time, such as in a long firm fraud along the lines we have already discussed, might be charged as a conspiracy to defraud.

6.103   If a person does an act which is more than merely preparatory to the commission of a crime then he or she may well be guilty of an attempt to commit that crime and generally punished in the same manner, under section 1 of the Criminal Attempts Act 1981. He or she must have moved beyond the stage of planning and preparation to that of starting to implement his or her intention. Merely putting oneself in a position to commit a crime is different from actually trying to commit it. In the case of fraud, given what has been said above, there is relatively little scope for the offence of 'attempt' to operate. It might be relevant where, for example, the accused makes a representation which he or she intends to be false, but which as a result of a mistake of fact, is true, or where he or she tries to communicate a false representation but this fails. However, in regard to other financial crimes there is rather more scope for charging attempt.

6.104   The Serious Crime Act 2007 has made a significant impact on the relevant law.[125] Under section 44 a person commits an offence if he does an act which is capable of encouraging or assisting the commission of an offence and can be shown to have intended to encourage or assist in its commission. Section 45 provides that a person commits an offence if he does an act capable of encouraging or assisting the commission of an offence, and he believes that the offence will be committed and that his acts will encourage or assist its commission. Section 46 further provides that a person commits an offence if he does an act capable of encouraging or assisting the commission of one or more of a number of offences and he believes that one or more of those offences will be committed, but has no belief as to which, and that his act will encourage or assist the commission of one or more of them.[126] Section 50

---

124   [1992] 1 AC 269.
125   See *Inchoate Liability for Assisting and Encouraging Crime*, Law Commission (2006) Law Com No 300, Cm. 6878.
126   These offences are not objectionable under article 7 of the European Convention on Human Rights, see *R v Sadique* [2012] 1 WLR 1700.

provides a defendant with a defence of acting reasonably in two situations. Firstly, where the defendant knew that certain circumstances existed and it was reasonable for him to act as he did in those circumstances and secondly, where he reasonably believed certain circumstances to exist and it was reasonable for him to act as he did in the circumstances as he believed them to be.

6.105 The law will in certain specific contexts punish the mere possession of certain substances, articles and equipment. In the context of burglary, for example, section 25 of the Theft Act 1968 renders it an offence for an accused to be found at a place 'other than his place of abode' with 'any article for use in committing a burglary or theft …'. Furthermore, 'proof that he had with him an article made or adapted for us in committing a burglary or theft shall be evidence that he had it with him for such use'. In the case of fraud, under section 6 of the Fraud Act 2006 a person will be guilty of an offence if he has in his possession or under his control any article for use in the course of or in connection with any fraud. Under this offence the accused can be charged for possession of equipment, such as skimmers and letters used for 'flash' purposes, in his home. It should also be noted that section 8 makes it clear that 'article' includes 'any program or data held in electronic form'. It is only necessary for the prosecution to prove that the accused was in possession and intended the article to be used by himself or another, in the commission of a fraud or merely in connection with a fraud. It is interesting to compare the breadth of this provision with section 16 of the Terrorism Act 2000. This renders it a crime to possess money or other property but only if 'he intends that it should be used, or has reasonable cause to suspect that it may be used, for the purpose of terrorism'. This provision has been used effectively against those engaged in various frauds and other fund raising activities in support of terrorists. Finally, in this regard, section 7 of the Fraud Act 2006 makes it a crime for a person to make, adapt, supply or offer to supply any article 'knowing that it is designed or adapted for use in the course of or in connection with fraud, or intending it to be used to commit, or assist in the commission of a fraud'.

PERJURY AND FALSE DECLARATIONS

6.106 From our discussion above, it is clear that a number of abuses have occurred as a result of the 'crooks' misleading the market authorities and other regulators into permitting a state of affairs to come about or continue, which of itself creates an impression that certain underlying and justifying events have satisfactorily taken place. In *R v Aspinall*,[127] it was held that it is an indictable conspiracy at common law to obtain a listing of securities on the Stock Exchange by falsely representing that the required number of shares have been allotted and paid for. In this case, it was emphasised that it was enough for the prosecution to show that the defendants' purpose was to mislead the Stock Exchange's officials; it was not necessary to prove that the defendants intended to injure investors by securing a higher price for the shares they were floating than would otherwise have been obtainable. It might also amount to the crime of conspiracy to defraud, to agree with others to induce, by false statements, made by word or conduct, a public official to do, or not to do, an act in the course of his official duties. For example, it has been argued that furnishing the

---

127   (1876) 1 QBD 730; affd (1876) 2 QBD 48, CA.

executive of the City Panel on Takeovers and Mergers with false information designed to mislead it in exercising its responsibilities under the Code might well fall within the scope of this offence. The FSMA, section 398, as amended by the Financial Services Act 2012, makes it a criminal offence for a person knowingly or recklessly to give 'in purported compliance with any requirement imposed by or under this Act' false or misleading information to the Authority or, under the FSMA, section 399, to the Competition and Markets Authority.[128] This provision is somewhat narrower than the offence which was created under the Financial Services Act 1986, section 200 and which was not confined to misleading officials of the Securities and Investments Board.

6.107 There are many situations where documents and statements are required to be made under oath or pursuant to some solemn legal undertaking to tell the truth. For example, section 5 of the Perjury Act 1911 renders it a crime to 'knowingly and wilfully make (otherwise than on oath) a statement false in a material particular' if the statement is made in a statutory declaration, 'in any abstract, account, balance sheet, book, certificate, declaration, entry, estimate, inventory, notice, report, return, or other document' which the person concerned is authorised, or required to make, attest, or verify by an 'public general Act of Parliament' and in any oral declaration or oral answer which he is required to make by, under, or in pursuance' of any such law. The statement must be intentionally false and under section 13 of the Act its falsity must be corroborated.

6.108 There are, however, many other statutory offences under various Acts imposing liability for false statements made in purported compliance with statutory obligations to tell the truth or affirm the veracity of certain facts or the genuineness of certain documents. For example, section 1112(1) of the Companies Act 2006 provides for an offence where a person for any purpose knowingly or recklessly delivers or causes to be delivered to the Registrar of Companies a document or makes to the Registrar a statement that is misleading, false or deceptive in a material particular.

6.109 Finally, it is important to remember that there are numerous and quite diverse provisions making it a criminal offence to disclose information in certain circumstances and usually without appropriate authority. Obviously, these offences have some degree of relevance in the policing of insider abuse. There are, of course, offences under the Official Secrets Act 1989, but also many statutes establishing regulatory and specialised agencies contain specific offences criminalising the unauthorised disclosure and in some cases misuse of information obtained in an official capacity.

CIVIL FRAUD

6.110 When examining the law relating to the manipulation of markets, reference was made to the possibility of suing in the civil courts for compensation. Mention has also been made of the statutory tort action that is expressly provided for under the FSMA, section 150 in relation to violations of the various rules promulgated by the FCA. In the context of restitution and compensation, it is also important to remember the various powers that the FCA has to initiate civil actions. None of the statutory provisions, however, displaces

---

128 Amended by Enterprise and Regulatory Reform Act 2013.

the traditional common law remedies based on fraud. It is therefore worthwhile examining briefly the civil law relating to fraudulent misrepresentation.

6.111 The dividing line between the criminal and civil law with regard to fraudulent conduct has never been entirely clear in English law. Indeed, one of the earliest causes of action, that of deceit, involved considerations of almost a penal nature. Given the harm that allegations of dishonesty can cause to individuals, particularly if they are in business, the courts have always been concerned by way of procedure and proof to ensure as far as is practical that such allegations are not made and pursued wantonly. Therefore, as a matter of pleading in the civil law, averments of fraud must be specially pleaded with all the relevant facts establishing the specific averment set out. While there is a difference between the standard of proof in an ordinary criminal trial and one for fraud in the civil law, judges have often emphasised that as the seriousness of the allegation increases in criminal proceedings, the standard of proof that is required to be met will be more exacting. Therefore, in practice, there may not be a great deal of difference between the standards of proof required to establish fraud in the civil and criminal law, particularly when it is remembered that in most cases considerable reliance will need to be placed on documentary evidence. Where allegations of fraud or deliberate misconduct involving moral turpitude are made and persisted with in circumstances which the court considers unjustified, there will be serious cost implications for the plaintiff and on occasion judges have expressed their disapproval of counsel.

6.112 The issue of fraud may arise in the civil law in a number of ways. However, since *Paisley v Freeman*,[129] it has been the rule that if a person knowingly or recklessly – that is not caring whether it is true or false, makes a statement to another with the intention that it shall be relied upon by that person, who in fact does rely on it and as a consequence suffers harm, then an action in deceit will be available. It is the need for the plaintiff to establish that the defendant acted with actual knowledge or could not care less whether what he said was true or not, which distinguishes liability in fraud from, for example, liability in the tort of negligence.[130] In the case of negligent misstatement, the defendant will be liable if an ordinary reasonable person would have known that what was said was untrue, the standard being objective. Where a person has been induced to enter into a contract as a result of a fraudulent misrepresentation, the law provides remedies or rescission and damages. While rescission may be a more attractive remedy in the case of investment transactions, it will not always be available. There is a strict rule which requires full restoration of property transferred under the relevant contract. In other words, the parties must be restored to their original position. It follows that if the victim of the fraud, rather than run the risk of a further, perhaps unrelated, diminution in the value of his securities, disposes of them, he will have lost his right to rescind. In *Smith New Court v Scrimgeour Vickers*,[131] Nourse LJ observed that, in the case of a fungible asset like quoted shares, the rule which requires restitution *in specie* is a hard one and in cases of fraud it was clear that the court had little sympathy with it, although in the circumstances it was not appropriate to depart from it. The rule works harshly, particularly in the case of an omission to disclose information which does not give rise to an independent cause of action for damages.[132]

---

129 (1789) 3 TR 51.
130 See *Derry v Peek* (1889) 14 App Cas 337.
131 [1994] 4 All ER 225.
132 See *Banque Keyser Ullman v Skandia* [1989] 2 All ER 952.

6.113   In an action for damages while the traditional approach is to compensate the innocent party for his loss many courts have been concerned to ensure that a fraudster takes no benefit from his fraud or the false circumstances that he has created. In *Clark v Urquhart, Stracey v Urquhart*,[133] Lord Aitkin emphasised that the measure of damages is the 'actual damage directly flowing from the fraudulent inducement' and this includes consequential loss.[134] On the other hand, depreciations of the value of shares by market forces operating after the date of acquisition do not flow directly from the fraudulent inducement, but from the purchaser's decision to retain the shares and accept the hazards of the market rather than sell at once.[135] The measure of damages will therefore be the difference between the price that the plaintiff paid and the 'true value' of the securities at the time he was fraudulently induced to acquire them. Valuation is always a difficult task and determination of the price depends upon a number of assumptions, one of the most important being what assumption should be made about the information which was available to the market.[136] In *Smith New Court v Scrimgeour Vickers (Asset) Management*,[137] the Court of Appeal considered that there were only two plausible possibilities in determining what assumption should be made as to information in the case of fraud. First, to assume that the market knew everything it actually did know, but was not influenced by the misrepresentation itself or, secondly, to assume that the market was omniscient. The Court of Appeal thought that the first approach was rational, but the second arbitrary and therefore disagreed with Chadwick J who at first instance appeared to have assumed that the market was omniscient. In the result, the Court of Appeal held that the correct measure of damages in a case where a person is induced to acquire shares by deceit is the difference between the price that was actually paid and the price which, in the absence of the misrepresentation, the parcel of shares would have fetched on the open market at that time. In the House of Lords, their Lordships emphasised that the plaintiff is entitled to recover the amount by which it is out of pocket but not for the loss of the bargain, which would be a measure of damages appropriate for a contractual claim rather than one based on the tort of deceit.[138]

6.114   The relationship between actions based on the torts of deceit and negligence have already been alluded to. As it is not necessary for a plaintiff in an action for damages to specify the particular tort which he is seeking to rely on for a remedy, provided he asserts and establishes the facts required for liability under at least one accepted cause of action, there may in practice be little lost in not alleging to being able to prove dishonesty, given the court's attitude to allegations of fraud. Apart from the desire to brand a person as a fraudster, it remains possible to obtain exemplary damages in cases of proven fraud and the statute of limitation may be more favourable,[139] but in the majority of cases plaintiffs are well advised to refrain from specific averments of fraud. In the case of a misrepresentation inducing a contract between the parties, the statutory remedies for negligent statements provided by the Misrepresentation Act 1967, section 2(1) are, in practical terms, superior to an action in tort. Under section 2(1), the person responsible for the misrepresentation has the

133   [1930] AC 28 at 68.
134   See *Doyle v Olby (Ironmongers) Ltd* [1969] 2 All ER 119.
135   See *Waddell v Blockley* (1879) 4 QBD 678.
136   See *Lynall v IRC* [1971] 3 All ER 914 and with regard to insider trading.
137   [1994] 4 All ER 225.
138   See [1997] AC 254 and Lord Browne Wilkinson at 267.
139   Limitation Act 1980, s 32.

burden of establishing that he had reasonable grounds for believing and did in fact believe what he said to be true.

6.115 As we have seen, the issues of fraud may also be relevant in other actions such as conspiracy and under specific statutory provisions giving rise to a civil remedy. Equity follows the law and will not enforce a bargain that has been procured by fraud. Furthermore, as we have seen the courts have developed a form of restitution liability for those who receive property transferred in breach of trust or who facilitate the laundering of such property with the requisite degree of dishonesty.[140] It must also be remembered that whilst there have been significant developments in the criminal law facilitating the taking and receipt of evidence from overseas, the civil law provides far greater weapons in obtaining evidence and discovery, in freezing funds and in enforcing orders of the court. Whilst the criminal courts possess statutory power, in certain circumstances, to order restoration and even compensation, as we have seen in the context of insider dealing, such orders are rarely appropriate in the case of securities related fraud.

DISCLOSURE ORDERS AND FREEZING ORDERS

6.116 The range of orders that the court can make in theory may be limited only by the judge's imagination, but in practice orders tend to follow precedents and in most countries the law has been settled into recognised procedures and orders. Perhaps the most significant from our perspective are orders for the freezing of monies in bank accounts or the immobilisation of wealth. Section 37 of the Supreme Court Act 1981 enables the High Court to grant injunctions 'in all cases in which it appears to the court to be just and convenient to do so' and within this wide power the courts are prepared to issue a freezing injunction to restrain a party from removing from the jurisdiction assets located there or dealing with any assets whether located in the jurisdiction or not. Freezing orders were previously referred to as Mareva injunctions. In *Mareva Compania Naviera SA v International Bulkcarriers SA*,[141] the court issued an injunction restraining the defendant from improperly disposing of his assets or concealing or moving them overseas and thereby making himself 'judgement proof'. A freezing order may be obtained in the English Court and most other common law jurisdictions whenever there is a real risk of dissipation of assets. Such orders play a most significant role in fighting financial crime and render the courts of common law jurisdictions attractive to those who wish to pursue the assets of fraudsters and their confederates. While many non-common law jurisdictions may order the interdiction of property, few have procedures as effective and as wide reaching in terms of their personal jurisdiction. It is important to remember that in so far as the order enjoins individuals to whom it is addressed or who have proper notice of it, it is in no way confined, unless it so provides, to territorial jurisdiction. The order may have world-wide application. A considerable amount of law has been developed as to the availability, reach and terms of such orders given the devastating impact that they can have on a person's business and life.

---

140 See *Agip (Africa) Ltd v Jackson* [1992] 4 All ER 385 at 451; *El Ajou v Dollar Land Holdings plc* [1993] 3 All ER 717 and *Royal Brunei Airlines Sdn Bhd v Tan* [1995] 2 AC 378.
141 [1975] 2 Lloyd's Rep 509.

6.117   Application is usually made without notice possibly before the action has even commenced. There will be three primary issues for the High Court judge hearing the *ex parte* application. First, whether there is a good arguable case; secondly, whether the claimant can adduce sufficient evidence as to the existence and location of assets which the injunction, if made, would affect; and whether there is a real risk that the defendant may deal with those assets so as to render nugatory any judgment which the claimant may obtain. The application must identify as precisely as possible the bank accounts or other assets that the injunction is to be aimed at. Generally speaking if there is sufficient wealth within the jurisdiction to satisfy a likely judgment, the order will be confined to the jurisdiction. It might apply to bank accounts and other wealth in the name of other people if there is evidence that in fact it belongs to the defendant.[142] If the defendant is the majority shareholder in a company than an order can be made against the assets of that company and the company will become a co-defendant in the cause.[143] The risk of dissipation will be decided on the facts of each case. However, dishonesty or any proof of lack of integrity on the part of the defendant will be relevant, as will the use of offshore banking facilities in suspect jurisdictions.

6.118   Section 25 of the UK Civil Jurisdiction and Judgments Act 1982 empowers the court to grant all forms of interim relief in aid of foreign courts unless 'in the opinion of the court, the fact that the court has no jurisdiction apart from this section in relation to the subject matter of the proceedings in question makes it inexpedient for the court to grant it'. Thus an application can be made to an English High Court judge to freeze assets relevant to a proceeding in any foreign court. The Courts have been careful to in effect issue a world-wide freezing order when the foreign proceedings have nothing to do with the UK and the parties are not resident here. However, in *Motorola Credit Corporation v Uzan (No 2)*[144] the court was prepared to uphold on appeal certain orders in regard to various defendants based in Turkey, who were accused of participating in an international fraud and who were subject to local freezing orders in New York. While the court accepted that the requirements for an order on behalf of a foreign applicant in foreign proceedings were much the same as those for an application in regard to proceedings in the English courts, it recognised the need for caution. For example, in the present case the New York court did not have the 'unusually wide powers against a foreign defendant' that the English courts had, Furthermore, there was sensitivity in Turkey and an order had been obtained in the Turkish Courts attempting to restrain the claimants from resorting to the New York and UK courts.

6.119   It is important to realise that the making of an order gives the claimant no property rights in the relevant monies and he does not become a secured or preferential creditor. He will also have to give undertakings in damages, as in the case of any interim injunction. The applicant will have to undertake to indemnify any person upon whom notice of the order is served in respect of expenses and liabilities they may incur in seeking to comply with the order. This is in addition to the claimant's cross undertaking to compensate the defendant if the case is not substantiated. Of course, these undertakings present a serious hurdle to the claimant. However, in *RBG Resources PLC v Rastogi*,[145]

---

142   *SCF Finance Co v Masri* [1985] 1 WLR 876.
143   *TSB Private Bank International SA v Chabra* [1992] 1 WLR 231.
144   [2004] 1 WLR 113.
145   (2002) LTL May 31 2002.

Laddie J accepted a limited cross undertaking where there was strong evidence of the defendant's wrongdoing and the claimant was financially weak.

6.120   A curious feature of freezing orders is that although it is made against the defendant it may be effective only if notice of it is given to the relevant bank or person in possession of the assets. It would seem on the authorities that a claimant cannot sue a bank or other person for failing to preserve the relevant assets, even after proper notice has been served, as they do not owe him a duty of care.[146] Nonetheless, it may be that such a person would be subject to a tracing claim or liable to pay compensation if they dishonestly assisted the defendant to transfer assets. Their primary liability is, however, to the contempt jurisdiction of the court. If they knowingly ignore an order of the court they will stand in contempt. However, to be guilty of contempt it must be shown that the bank or other person had notice of the probability that the monies would be disposed of in breach of the terms of the injunction.[147] It should be noted that the courts in such cases have the power to order the person in contempt to pay compensation. Of course, if the parties are outside the jurisdiction and the order has been made without notice, then it is unlikely foreign courts would give effect to an order of the English Courts, as in like circumstances in all probability an English court would not. The issue of enforceability is a real one, as the courts will not act in vain and if there is no real prospect of an order being obeyed or enforced out of jurisdiction the courts will be reluctant to issue one.

6.121   Once an order has been made, the claimant is under an obligation to forge ahead with his claim. He is also under a continuing duty of disclosure to the defendant in regard of any matter which may render his cross undertaking unreliable. Of course, it is always open to the defendant to seek discharge or variation of the order. While the courts will generally allow release of monies for living expenses, outstanding debts and legal fees, the courts will be alert to any attempt to use up the monies within jurisdiction. They will be prepared to inquire into the financial resources of the defendant on a world-wide basis. Of course, it is also open to third parties to intervene in regard to relevant assets and obligations.

6.122   Perhaps as important as freezing orders in dealing with financial misconduct are civil search orders. This is in addition to the various systems that operate in different legal systems to require parties in civil litigation to make proper disclosure and respond to interrogatories. It may well be that one party will suspect that the other is about to destroy or conceal information. Consequently in some countries the civil courts have authority to authorise essentially a civil search. It is important to appreciate that this is not the same as a search warrant as it gives no authority to force entry on to private property. The sanction for non-compliance is the court's contempt power. A search order compels the defendant to permit the claimant's agents, usually his solicitor, to enter the defendant's property to search for and in most cases seize certain documents or property. In England this is a special form of mandatory injunction the object of which is to preserve evidence. While some commonwealth jurisdictions have similar procedures most civilian countries do not, nor do the US courts. These injunctions used to be referred to as Anton Piller orders after the case *Anton Piller KG v Manufacturing Processes Ltd.*[148]

---

146   *Commissioners of Customs and Excise v Barclays Bank PLC* (2006) 3 WML 1.
147   *Bank Mellat v Kazmi* [1989] QB 541.
148   [1976] Ch 55.

The order must be made by a High Court judge and the applicant must make a cross undertaking in damages as in the case of a freezing order. In the nature of the case, the application will normally be made without notice and the applicant must show that there is a strong case that serious harm or injustice will occur.

6.123 Of course, the court may order the defendant in proceedings, even interim proceedings, to disclose information. In the case of an application for a freezing order the defendant can be required to disclose immediately and then subsequently in affidavit, for example, the whereabouts of his assets. An issue that has arisen in this context is whether the defendant is bound to disclose information that might incriminate him in future criminal proceedings.[149] If the defendant does assert the privilege against self-incrimination and the court considers it is not made out, then he will be in contempt. Furthermore, there is no privilege against exposure to criminal proceedings in other jurisdictions. The courts have also held that even threats of violence overseas do not justify refusal to disclose information that has been ordered to be revealed. Courts in the UK and USA have also held that where a question is properly put to a defendant it is still contempt if he refuses to answer on the ground that to do so would constitute a criminal offence under the secrecy or blocking laws of another state. In cases where information can only be disclosed under the relevant laws of another state with the consent of the person to whom the information 'belongs', certain US courts have been prepared in both civil and criminal cases to order the defendant or another within their jurisdiction to furnish this authorisation for disclosure to the appropriate person. Failure to do so is treated as contempt. Of course, it goes without saying that furnishing false or misleading information to the court is contempt and it may constitute a specific offence, as we have seen. It might also result in the court deciding a matter against the interests of that party. In *Canada Trust Co v Stolzenberg*,[150] Neuberger J held that where a foreign defendant, with no assets in the UK, failed to comply with an order for disclosure and there was a strong case against him, it may be appropriate to debar him from defending the case, if he persisted in his failure to comply with the terms of the injunction. His contention that compliance with the order would involve a breach of the laws of another jurisdiction was, while a factor to be taken into account, not determinative.

6.124 There will always be a temptation for those under investigation to flee the jurisdiction. While there have been significant developments facilitating co-operation and mutual assistance, particularly within the European Union, it is always more problematic to ensure justice is served once a suspect or material witnesses leaves the jurisdiction. In criminal cases arrest will effectively prevent this, at least, in regard to those suspected of a criminal offence. In civil cases the position is more difficult. The courts are not, however, without power. In *Bayer AG v Winter*[151] an injunction was issued against the defendant ordering him to deliver up his passport and restraining him from leaving the jurisdiction of the English courts. The courts have, as we have seen, significant powers over property and can make a wide range of orders including the appointment of receivers to get in property and monies. In *International Credit and Investment Co (Overseas) Ltd v Adham (Appointment of Receiver)*[152] the court held that it could pierce the veil of incorporation of a

149   See *Coca-Cola Company v Gilbey* [1995] 4 All ER 711.
150   *The Times*, November 10 1997.
151   [1986] 1 WLR 497.
152   [1998] BCC 134.

company and appoint a receiver over property in a case where a world-wide freezing order had been granted over property and where there was a real risk that the order would be breached.

DISQUALIFICATION PROCEDURES

6.125 While fraud does not always involve the use of a company, it often does. Consequently, it is sensible to deprive those who have committed fraud and other misconduct, of the opportunity to misuse the privilege of using a company as a vehicle for their dishonesty. This is one of the justifications for disqualifying certain persons from being involved in the management of companies. Disqualification proceedings under the Company Directors Disqualification Act 1986 play an important role in preventing further abuses and constitute an additional sanction with regard to conduct that has already taken place.[153]

6.126 It should be noted that in certain circumstances an order may be made with regard to a foreign citizen in relation to conduct taking place outside the United Kingdom. In construing the Company Directors Disqualification Act 1986, section 6, Arden J decided that the fact that modern communications enabled companies to be controlled across frontiers, given Parliament's intention to create an effective and integrated response to misconduct, justified an interpretation of the provisions which could extend to foreigners and conduct out of the jurisdiction.[154] An order made under the Act against a director or, in many cases, a shadow director makes it unlawful for him to be a director, liquidator, administrator or receiver of a company or be in any way, either directly or indirectly, concerned with the promotion, incorporation or management of a company in the United Kingdom during the currency of the order.

6.127 There are a number of statutory grounds upon which an application can be made by the Secretary of State, or in some instances the liquidator or even a creditor, to the court under the Company Directors Disqualification Act 1986. Conviction for an indictable offence in connection with the promotion, formation, management or liquidation of a company is a ground under the Company Directors Disqualification Act 1986, section 2. It has been held that a conviction for insider dealing, when the conduct in question clearly had a relevant factual connection with the management of the company, was sufficient to justify a disqualification order.[155] Under the Company Directors Disqualification Act 1986, section 3, a court may make a disqualification order where there has been persistent default in making returns or delivering accounts and other documents required under the Companies Act 1985. The Company Directors Disqualification Act 1986, section 5 empowers the court to make an order on summary conviction for failing to comply with the statutory provisions relating to the filing of returns where there has been three such convictions within a period of five years.

6.128 The Company Directors Disqualification Act 1986, section 4 empowers the courts to make an order where it appears to the court in the

---

153 See generally A Walters and M Davis-White, *Directors' Disqualification and Insolvency Restrictions* (Sweet & Maxwell 2010).
154 See *Re Seagull Manufacturing Co Ltd (No 2)* [1994] 1 BCLC 273.
155 See *R v Goodman* [1994] 1 BCLC 349, and see 2.51 above.

course of insolvency proceedings, which need not necessarily end in a determination of insolvency, that there has been fraudulent trading or a breach of duty to the company. It should be noted that a conviction is not a prerequisite to the court exercising its powers under this section. The Company Directors Disqualification Act 1986, section 5 gives the court power to disqualify a person.

6.129   The Company Directors Disqualification Act 1986, section 6 relates to the disqualification of a director who has been associated with an insolvent company and is found to be unfit to be a director. It has been accepted by the courts that deliberately concealing transactions from the company and its shareholders is sufficient for the court to determine that a person is unfit to be a director.[156]

6.130   By the Company Directors Disqualification Act 1986, section 8, the Secretary of State is empowered to seek an order for disqualification when he has received a report from inspectors appointed under the companies' legislation or FSMA, or information pursuant to his own powers of investigation, indicating that it is in the public interest that an individual should be so disqualified. Before the court can make an order, it must be satisfied that the conduct in relation to the company makes the person concerned unfit to be involved in corporate management under the Company Directors Disqualification Act 1986, section 9. In determining the issue of unfitness, it is further provided that the court has regard to the matters set out in the Company Directors Disqualification Act 1986, Schedule 1, Part 1 which relates to the question of unfitness in cases brought under the Company Directors Disqualification Act 1986, section 6. Thus, a director who abuses his power in circumstances indicating a lack of commercial probity was held to be unfit.[157] The House of Commons Select Committee on Trade and Industry severely criticised the refusal of the Secretary of State to initiate such proceedings against the Fayed brothers following a recommendation by inspectors appointed to inquire into the House of Fraser affair. Although there was evidence that the Fayeds and their advisers had misled the City Panel on Takeovers and Mergers, the Department of Trade and Industry took the view that their conduct was not related to the management of a company, albeit that it is arguable that their misconduct facilitated the acquisition of the House of Fraser.[158]

6.131   Finally, with regard to the grounds for disqualification, the Company Directors Disqualification Act 1986, section 10 permits a court to disqualify a person against whom it decides to make an order under either the Insolvency Act 1986, section 213 for fraudulent trading or the Insolvency Act 1986, section 214 for wrongful trading.

6.132   Breach of a disqualification order constitutes a criminal offence under the Company Directors Disqualification Act 1986, section 13, as well as contempt of court. Under the Company Directors Disqualification Act 1986, section 15, a person who is involved in the management of a company in violation of an order made under the Act, or a person who acts or is willing to act as a 'front man' for a person whom he knows to be subject to disqualification,

---

156   See *Re Godwin Warren Control Systems plc* [1993] BCLC 80.
157   See *Re Looe Fish Ltd* [1993] BCLC 1160.
158   See *Company Investigation*, Third Report of the Trade and Industry Committee (HMSO 1990).

will be personally liable for all debts of the company. It should be noted that the same rules apply with regard to un-discharged bankrupts.[159]

6.133   Under the FSMA as amended by the Financial Services Act 2012, section 56, the FCA is empowered to issue 'a prohibition order' prohibiting an individual from performing a specified function or any function falling within a specified description if it appears to the Authority that the individual 'is not a fit and proper person to perform' the relevant functions in relation to regulated activity carried on by an authorised person. Before the Authority makes such an order, it is necessary for the individual concerned to be given a warning notice and he may request that the decision is referred to the Financial Services Tribunal. While the notion of 'fit and proper' is open textured, it is clear that fraud and many of the other forms of misconduct described in this chapter would justify the Authority in concluding that the person responsible is not a fit and proper person to be involved in investment business. The same may well also apply to those responsible for supervising that person's activities. It is a criminal offence under section 56(4) to perform or agree to perform a function in breach of a prohibition order, although it is a defence to show that the person concerned took all reasonable precautions and exercised all due diligence to avoid committing the offence. Furthermore, under section 56(6), an authorised person must take reasonable care to ensure that no function of his, in relation to the carrying on of a regulated activity, is performed by a person who is prohibited from performing that function pursuant to a prohibition order. If an authorised person violates this, any private person who suffers loss as a result has a right of action against him under the FSMA, section 71.

6.134   In this context, it is also important to note the provisions in the FSMA as amended, Part XII relating to control over authorised persons. Obviously, the safeguards that have been put in place to ensure that only fit and proper persons become authorised, or employ persons that are fit and proper, would count for very little if authorised persons could come under the control of unscrupulous individuals. The obligations to give notice and comply with orders by the FCA are reinforced by the criminal law under the FSMA, section 191.

OFFENCES BY BODIES CORPORATE

6.135   Mention has already been made of the use that fraudsters make of companies as a vehicle for fraud. While the common law is well able to cut through corporate personality and fix liability directly on the individuals responsible when the corporate form is a sham or has been employed merely as an engine of fraud, the position is more difficult when a 'real' company that is not purely a device for the fraudster is involved. The law is able to attribute knowledge and even a guilty intent to a company, provided that knowledge or intent reposes in an individual who is sufficiently senior to be regarded as the company's mind or at least determinant over the function in question.[160] Indeed, in some cases, the courts have gone even further and held that the acts of an individual may be attributed to the company, even if that person is acting outside the duties of his employment and in breach of his employer's instructions, if acts are carried out in the course of his employment. In such

---

159   See the Company Directors Disqualification Act 1986, ss 11 and 15.
160   See generally Cheong-Ann Png, *Corporate Liability* (Kluwer 2001) and see 16.5 *et seq* below.

cases, the attempts that the employer has gone to in ensuring compliance with the law are merely an issue for mitigation.

6.136   The FSMA, section 400 addresses the reverse problem when it is appropriate to hold individuals responsible for offences committed by a company. It is necessary that the company be guilty and thus has the requisite state of knowledge before this issue arises. The section states that if an offence under the Act committed by a company is shown to have been committed with the consent or connivance of an officer or to be attributable to any neglect on his part, that officer, as well as the company, will be guilty of the offence in question. The concept of 'officer' is defined to include all those who have managerial responsibility, including directors and 'an individual who is a controller' of the company. Similar rules are applicable to partnerships. The exact implications of this provision are difficult to state. Provided a company could be given the requisite degree of culpability to justify a charge under the FSMA, section 397(2) or (3), it is possible that charges could be brought against an 'officer' who was only guilty of 'neglect'.

CONCLUSION

6.137   Given the emphasis that has been placed on the protection of investors, the need to maintain confidence in the integrity of the markets and the desirability of reducing financial crime, the policing of fraud and other abuses will inevitably attract a great deal of attention. The FCA cannot complain that it has not been given the weapons to police at least those offences within its statutory purview. The civil enforcement powers that have been entrusted to it are considerable and there has been a significant 'tidying up' of the relevant legislation which will no doubt render enforcement less hazardous. On the other hand, experience has shown in the UK and elsewhere that the problems in dealing effectively with serious fraud are far ranging and intractable.[161] Obviously, much will depend upon the level of co-operation and collaboration that the FCA is able to achieve, not only with other authorities in the UK, but also with its counterparts overseas. A great deal will also depend upon how much it can rely upon those in the industry and in particular those working in compliance to get their own houses in order and work effectively with the authorities. While civil enforcement by or through the FCA is destined to become a more significant feature of policing the markets, it remains very doubtful whether private litigants will become the champions of integrity to the extent that some think they are in the United States.

---

161   See B Rider (ed), *International Financial Crime* (Edward Elgar 2015).

Chapter 7

Anti-money laundering and proceeds of crime

THE CORPORATE AND FINANCIAL DIMENSION

7.1   In 2013, the Government's Serious and Organised Crime Strategy[1] confirmed that organised crime in the United Kingdom misuses the privilege of incorporation to assist in financial crimes.[2] The report referred, in particular, to the estimated more than £1 billion laundered through money service businesses and informal value transfer systems each year. It was said that illicit profits are often laundered through cash-rich overt businesses, which very often operate on the high street. The strategy report set out that money was sometimes physically transferred outside the UK using not only MSBs but also front companies and offshore services and that complicit, negligent or unwitting professionals in the financial, accountancy and legal professions in the UK facilitate money laundering on behalf of organised criminals.

7.2   There can be little doubt that criminals have found the organisational advantages of the corporate form beneficial in their illicit enterprises. More importantly the ability to hide behind corporate nominees and obscure the ownership and control of business, whether legal or illegal, has proved invaluable. While the Courts have long been prepared to look at the real purpose for which a company has been incorporated[3] and will not allow criminals and fraudsters to hide behind the legal fiction of incorporation, to distort responsibility and avoid accountability,[4] it is in the context of the relatively recent significance that has been attached to pursuing the proceeds

---

1   *Serious and Organised Crime Strategy* (Command Paper 8715).
2   A point that had been raised as far back as evidence was presented in 1995 to the Home Affairs Select Committee.
3   See *Bowman v Secular Society Ltd* [1917] AC 406. Normally incorporation should be denied, *R v Registrar of Joint Stock Companies* [1931] 2 KB 197. Once incorporated, it should be wound up, rather than struck down – *Princess of Reuss v Bos* (1871) LR 5 HL 176, Lord Hatherley LC at 193. For the current principles in this area, see *Prest v Petrodel Resources Ltd* [2013] 2 AC 415 (SC) in which Lord Sumption JJSC found that the 'concealment' and 'evasion' principles should be applied.
4   *Smith v Hancock* [1894] 2 Ch 377; *Gilford Motor Co Ltd v Horne* (1933) Ch 935 and *Jones v Lipman* [1962] 1 WLR 832. In the context of confiscation under the Proceeds of Crime Act 2002 (POCA 2002), see *R v Sale* [2014] 1 WLR 663 (CA) in which the principles of *Prest v Petrodel Resources Ltd* were applied.

of crime, that concern about the misuse of incorporation has become most pressing. The facility that easily incorporated business forms offer those engaged in hiding the proceeds of crime, or at least seeking to sever the nexus between the predicate crime that produces the illicit sum its present location, has been recognised throughout the world. While there has always been a variety of reasons why those in possession of wealth, whatever its source, may wish to hide it,[5] the development of laws that allow the proceeds of crime, actual or even presumptive, to be seized by the authorities, has given a real incentive to those capable of laundering wealth. In this process the company plays a vital role. Consequently, there are a number of legal issues thrown up directly by these new laws and perhaps more importantly, in terms of risk, indirectly, by virtue of the shift of responsibility to fight serious crime, on to those who in the ordinary course of their commercial and financial business mind other peoples' wealth. Indeed, such is the concern that section 1D of the Financial Services Act 2002, which created the Financial Conduct Authority (FCA), states that the integrity of the UK financial system includes 'its not being used for a purpose connected with financial crime' and 'its not being affected by behaviour that amounts to market abuse'. Section 1B ensures that the 'integrity objective' is one of three operational objectives for the FCA.[6] The impact of anti-money laundering laws on the way in which financial and wealth business is conducted, in many respects has probably been greater than any other substantive body of law. In assisting in the interdiction of the proceeds of serious crime and the flow of funds to terrorist organisations, company law clearly has a role to play.

7.3   Having regard to the risks both legal and otherwise, that can arise for those involved, innocently or not, in the laundering of the proceeds of crime or the transfer of terrorist funds, ensuring proper and effective compliance with the statutory and other obligations is an important task of management. Oversight in terms of the establishment and support of such systems is an important issue in governance. In certain situations the failure of management and those responsible for governance might well result in legal and regulatory liability. It is also important to note the complex web of law and regulation thrown up by anti-money laundering laws often has the effect imposing obligations with the risk of legal consequences, internationally. For example, generally speaking under most laws, the offences relating to money laundering apply to conduct within jurisdiction, even if the criminal activity generating the property in question took place entirely out of jurisdiction. It is also the case that some provisions operate on wider notions of jurisdiction than would traditionally be encountered in most criminal justice systems. The significance that governments and, in particular inter-governmental organisations, now attach to combating serious crime, corruption and the funding of terror, through inhibiting the transfer and concealment of funds associated or representing such activity, means that regulators and indeed, even the courts, have been robust in the administration and application of relevant laws and procedures. A powerful illustration of the importance now attached to depriving criminals of their illicit wealth is provided in the new United Nations Convention Against

5   See generally B Rider, Memorandum 15, Organised Crime, Minutes of Evidence and Memoranda, Home Affairs Committee SI Session 1994–95, HMSO and B Rider and M Ashe (eds), *Money Laundering Control* (Sweet & Maxwell 1996), Ch 1.
6   The Financial Conduct Authority also has the power to prosecute money laundering offences, see *R v Rollins* [2010] 1 Cr. App. R. 14 (CA), a case that determined this issue for the FCA's predecessor, the Financial Services Authority.

Corruption.[7] Article 51 states that pursuing the proceeds of corruption is a fundamental principle of the Convention. It should be noted that many of the Convention's provisions might well have impact on the business world.[8] Furthermore, it must also be borne in mind that as it has proved in practice difficult to interdict property associated with crime and terror, law enforcement and regulatory authorities have adopted strategies designed rather more to disrupt criminal and subversive enterprises than interdict specific property. The National Crime Agency (NCA) noted in its Annual Report for 2014–15[9] that 'The Government's first priority of the Serious and Organised Crime Strategy is the highest priority for the NCA: to identify and disrupt serious and organised crime'. The problem with this approach is that the perimeters of what is acceptable, let alone lawful, disruptive conduct are not clear. It is also the case that often those being used knowingly or otherwise in the processes of disruption will be individuals and companies engaged in business or the financial sector. The legal risks in placing such persons in the 'front line' have not been sufficiently determined, or for that matter considered.

7.4   Few laws can or do operate in a legal vacuum and the inter-relationship of rules is not always predictable or does not always produce desirable results. A serious problem, in many jurisdictions, is that those laws relating to the imposition of criminal and increasingly, what might be described as administrative, penalties for misconduct, impact on the way business is conducted. The laws facilitating and controlling business and in particular financial business may not adequately or comfortably interface with these essentially criminal laws. A good example is the obligation not to reveal, to anyone other than the appropriate public authority, one's suspicion of money laundering. In the United Kingdom the unauthorised disclosure of this information may well amount to the serious crime of 'tipping off'. While this offence is intended to facilitate effective law enforcement by allowing the secret monitoring of transactions by the authorities, the relationship of this crime with the obligations occasionally imposed under the civil law were not sufficiently recognised. For example, there are situations where a person, in a fiduciary relationship or in a position which may result in the imposition of fiduciary obligations, is under a duty, in the proper discharge of those fiduciary responsibilities, to search out and inform those who may, in line with the suspicions that he has properly formed, have a claim against the property in question.[10] There are other situations, in which, there would be a duty in the civil law, to take steps on protect the relevant property, which might have the effect of 'tipping off' those under suspicion.[11] The Courts have been required to consider such situations, but have not always found it possible to provide a degree of guidance, let alone protection, that would meet the expectations of those engaged in legitimate business.[12] Again, while it is clear, under the

---

7   See generally B Rider, 'Recovering the Proceeds of Corruption', (2007) 10 *Journal of Money Laundering Control* 5.
8   See, for example, Article 12 in regard to anti-corruption initiatives in the private sector; Article 20 on unjust enrichment and Articles 21 and 22 in regard to bribery and embezzlement in the private sector.
9   National Crime Agency Annual Report and Accounts 2014–15 at page 7.
10   See for example, *Finers v Miro* [1991] 1 WLR 35. See generally, *Banking on Corruption, The Legal Responsibilities of those who Handle the Proceeds of Corruption* (Sir Richard Scott and Lord Steel of Aikwood, 2000), Society of Advanced Legal Studies.
11   See for example *Bank of Scotland v A Ltd* [2001] EWCA Civ 52.
12   See *C v S* [1999] 2 All ER 343, *Amalgamated Metal Trading Ltd v City of London Police Financial Investigation Unit* [2003] EWHC 703 (Comm) and *Hosni Tayeb v HSBC and Al Farsan International* [2004] EWHC 1529 (Comm).

relevant statutory provisions, that liability for breach of contract or disclosure of confidential information, when reporting a bona fide suspicion to the proper authorities, is unlikely, although in certain cases not entirely unthinkable, there are real and unresolved issues in the law of defamation. Therefore, in seeking to comply and ensure proper compliance, with these laws and the various rules they have spawned, care needs to be taken in regard to the general law as well. It is often the case that compliance systems and advice focus almost exclusively on the criminal and administrative laws and ignore the legal environment within which the relevant transactions or conduct occur. This is particularly important in the context of corporate life given the many relationships that, for example, a director will find himself in, both to his company and others. This is not a simple or straightforward area of law.

MONEY LAUNDERING IN CONTEXT

7.5   Given the significance, for various reasons, that has been attached to attacking the proceeds of crime and now the wider concept of 'criminal property' as a means of disrupting criminal enterprises, all legal systems have complex laws facilitating the identification, pursuit, seizure and then either confiscation or forfeiture[13] of the property in question. This is not the place to enter into a discussion of these provisions. Suffice it to say, that in the vast majority of cases, by the time that these statutory powers are properly invoked by the appropriate authorities, the situation in terms of the probable legality of the relevant transactions or conduct, will be sufficiently obvious. A director or officer acting in good faith in the proper performance of his duties would not normally be at risk. Having said this, the expansion of these powers, which are often very far reaching, to cases where no crime has actually been proven and their re-casting into the civil law,[14] has increased the potential for uncertainty. The relevant provisions whether in the criminal or the civil law do not, however, present a major problem for those who act and continue to act within the scope of, for example, the traditional duties of directors. Of rather greater impact, in practice, is the use of the civil law in essentially a restitutory role.[15] The perimeters of liability for receipt of property that is subject to a fiduciary obligation, and providing assistance in the handling and concealment of such property, are far more uncertain and potentially dangerous.[16] This important and dynamic area of the law, has in recent years had a significant impact on the law relating to directors duties and in particular the recovery of the proceeds of fraud and breaches of fiduciary duties.[17] It is not without interest that the United Nations' Convention Against Corruption places significant emphasis on the ability of litigants, public and private, to pursue the proceeds of corruption

---

13   See generally T Millington and M Sutherland Williams, *The Proceeds of Crime, Law and Practice of restraint, Confiscation, Condemnation and Forfeiture* (4th edn) (Oxford University Press 2013).

14   See generally the POCA 2002 and in particular Part 5. Note in particular the ability to recover unlawful property, by civil process, irrespective of criminal guilt. See also the civil forfeiture case of *Gogitidze v Georgia* [2015] ECHR 475, in which the Chamber found that reversing the burden of proof after the unexplained wealth had been identified accorded with internationally accepted standards and was A1P1 proportionate.

15   See for example *Attorney General of Hong Kong v Reid* [1994] 1 AC 324.

16   Reference should be made to, for example, G Virgo, *The Principles of the Law of Restitution* (2nd edn) (Oxford University Press 2006), at Ch 20.

17   See 2.23 and 6.115 above and note 42 in Chapter 9.

and fraud and impose liability to make restoration on those who facilitate, with the requisite degree of culpability, the laundering of such property. It is this area of the law that has created issues for banks and other financial institutions in attempting to comply with the criminal law and in particular the offence of 'tipping off'.[18] It must also be born in mind that invariably cases that do arise, involve a number of different jurisdictions with differing legal standards. The vitality of civil law in ensuring integrity on the part of those who are stewards of other peoples' wealth is increasingly being recognised around the world and private actions in pursuit of fraudsters and in particular corrupt officials and those complicit in such crimes are likely to increase significantly.

7.6   Before we examine the specific offences relating to the laundering of criminal wealth, it is also important to flag the importance of other areas of the criminal law. It has been held that conspiring to evade a civil duty of disclosure, such as might arise under statute or, for example, the fiduciary obligations of director to his company, can amount to a conspiracy to defraud in the criminal law.[19] Indeed, dishonesty may well be established, simply by the desire of those involved to act in secret.[20] After all, secrecy is the badge of fraud! Charges for handling stolen property may also be appropriate.[21] It is important to remember that this offence is not confined merely to the property that is stolen in the narrow legal sense. Money or other property that results from fraud or even blackmail may well be handled in the criminal sense. Many money laundering operations will involve fraudulent conduct. Indeed, in some cases those involved in laundering might well be susceptible to a substantive change of theft. There is also the prospect of offences under the insolvency law, in appropriate cases, and invariably implications under the relevant tax laws. Indeed, the significance of the role of Her Majesty's Revenue and Customs (HMRC)[22] in pursuing the proceeds of crime and in particular the disruption of criminal enterprises has been clear in a number of major cases. Finally in this context, the level of international co-operation,[23] at all levels, in this area is second to none. The law enforcement authorities, regulators and courts have been zealous in providing assistance to the authorities of other jurisdictions in the tracking of funds and their interdiction.

7.7   The law relating to money laundering suffers from having been developed on an ad hoc basis without a great deal of regard to the different characteristics of the laundering process in relation to the nature of the underlying criminal or subversive activity. The process of laundering will be rather different in the case of a continuing criminal enterprise, than in, for example, an isolated case of fraud, insider dealing or corruption. The law relating to money laundering has also been adopted and applied, more

---

18   See below at 7.26.
19   See for example *R v Adams* [1995] 1 WLR 52.
20   *Norris v Government of the United States* [2007] EWHC 71 (Admin), 25 January 2007, QBD.
21   See s 22 of the Theft Act 1968.
22   It is important to remember that HMRC, under a number of statutory provisions, have considerable powers to identify, interdict and charge funds and property that is or may be subject to taxation in one form or another. The proceeds of crime are, of course, taxable income in the hands of the criminal or anyone in control thereof. Note that the Revenue and Customs Prosecutions Office merged with the Crown Prosecution Service in 2010 and the position of Director of Revenue and Customs Prosecutions has since been abolished by virtue of the Public Bodies (Merger of the Director of Public Prosecutions and the Director of Revenue and Customs Prosecutions) Order 2014.
23   See generally T Millington and M Sutherland Williams, above, Ch 19.

or less without modification, to those who provide financial support for terrorist activity. The processes involved in channelling such funds to terrorist organisations are different in character from most cases involving profitable crime. While there is disappointment in most jurisdictions that the amounts of money and other property seized, let alone actually confiscated or forfeited, are relatively small compared with the guesstimates as to the amount of wealth that could be subject to such procedures,[24] the offences relating to money laundering have proved rather useful. The regime of reporting, recording and monitoring suspicious funds, has generated useful intelligence and has served to place a hurdle in front of those who seek to conceal their ill-gotten gains. The use of the regime has been increasing.[25] It has created additional risk and cost for criminals, particularly organised crime. It has also fostered a greater degree of awareness of the dangers of serious crime, and co-operation among those who, in the ordinary and legitimate course of their business or profession mind or assist in the minding of other peoples' wealth. To some extent it has placed such persons in the forefront of the 'financial war' against organised crime and even terrorism. Whether the use to which intelligence has been deployed justifies the considerable costs and risks, legal and otherwise, to those in the financial community, remains to be seen. The effect of the law and the various systems of compliance that have been developed, is to facilitate the reconstruction of financial transactions by providing a 'paper trail' and assist in the financial profiling of suspects. Of course, the laws also have the effect of essentially criminalising those who facilitate profitable and enterprise crime, thereby placing yet another risk and financial hurdle in the path of organised crime. Prosecutions simply for breach of the substantive offences of money laundering are not common. In most jurisdictions a charge of money laundering is added to other substantive charges. However, it is noticeable that in the USA prosecutors appear to prefer charges for money laundering than basing prosecutions on the so called predicate offence in many cases of securities and corporate related fraud and abuse. Having said this, however, it is important to recognise that in the USA laws relating to integrity, whether in the corporate or market context, tend to be enforced through civil enforcement proceedings rather than the traditional criminal law. As has already been emphasised, in this area of law, the environment and in particular the institutional aspects of law enforcement, in particular jurisdictions, play a very significant role in the way matters are brought before the courts and are disposed of.

---

24   See for example the opening comments of Margaret Hodge to the Committee of Public Accounts on 15 January 2014, in which she stated 'if we are really getting only 26p or 35p in every £100 that criminals are benefiting from in their activity, it is pathetic. It is ludicrously small. The other fact – maybe this is where I should start – is that you are spending between you, in the NAO assessment, about £100 million, and in 2012–13 you only got back £130 million. That is dismal. What do you feel about that as a cost-benefit?' at Public Accounts Committee, available at http://www.publications.parliament.uk/pa/cm201314/cmselect/cmpubacc/942/150114.htm.

25   In 2013–14 more than 350,000 SARs were raised, of which more than 14,000 were seeking consent to proceed. In the year to October 2014, 82% of SARs were raised by banks, 12% by credit or other financial institutions, and the remainder from a range of regulated organisations. In 2015, the government began a consultation process to identify how, in collaboration with partners in the regulated sector, a more efficient model can be developed that takes into account the increasing number of SARs and the demands placed upon companies and the NCA in operating the regime, with the intention to reduce the burden on businesses in complying with the reporting obligations. See Home Office 'Suspicious Activity Reports regime: call for information' (2015).

PROCEEDS OF CRIME

7.8   Money laundering is defined in the Explanatory Notes to POCA 2002 as 'the process by which the proceeds of crime are converted into assets which appear to have a legitimate origin, so that they can be retained permanently or recycled into further criminal enterprises'.[26] The law in the United Kingdom relating to money laundering developed after the creation of statutory powers to seize the proceeds of particularly profitable crimes. Indeed, there is a view that the failure to criminalise the laundering of the proceeds of crime at the time such statutory powers were given to the courts, may have constituted another incentive for criminals to develop money laundering in Britain. In common with most legal systems, the early law focused exclusively on the proceeds of illicit drug related crime. The difficulty in law and practice of establishing that particular property was related to specific drug offences rendered these provisions of relatively little value. Consequently, the offences were extended to the proceeds of all serious crime and even such crimes committed overseas.[27]

7.9   There are a number of international instruments relating to the criminalisation and control of money laundering, including no less than four EU Directives specifically on the subject.[28] Generally speaking, the English law has run ahead of the various international obligations and therefore, in this brief discussion we will not refer to the various and many international documents.[29] The importance of the international community in developing this area of the law, should not, however, be underestimated. For example, almost a third of the provisions in the United Nations Convention Against Corruption relate directly or indirectly to the identification, interdiction, recovery and laundering of wealth related to corruption. In addition, States that are party to the Financial Action Task Force are required to implement the FATF Recommendations and these are often adopted by other regional bodies.[30] It is also important to appreciate the strength of the political imperative, largely set by the US Government, but taken up by many others, to foster 'stability' through integrity of the financial system. Of course, cynics may argue that all this has rather more to do with fostering and strengthening western banking and facilitating the recovery of tax, than promoting integrity and frustrating organised crime.

---

26   A statement that was approved by the Supreme Court as the ordinary meaning of the expression, in *R v GH* [2015] 1 WLR 2126.

27   See generally on the initial development of the law, T Graham, E Bell and N Elliott, *Money Laundering* (Butterworths 2003); K Hinterseer, *Criminal Finance*, (Kluwer 2002); S Savla, *Money Laundering and Financial Intermediaries* (Kluwer 2001); P Alldridge, *Money Laundering Law* (Hart 2003) and S Bazley and C Foster, *Money Laundering – Business Compliance* (LexisNexis 2004).

28   The fourth directive was agreed in 2015 and must be implemented by 26 June 2017: Directive (EU) 2015/849 of the European Parliament and of the Council of 20 May 2015 on the prevention of the use of the financial system for the purposes of money laundering or terrorist financing, amending Regulation (EU) No 648/2012 of the European Parliament and of the Council, and repealing Directive 2005/60/EC of the European Parliament and of the Council and Commission Directive 2006/70/EC, published at OJ L 141/73.

29   P Schott, *Reference Guide to Anti-Money Laundering and Combating the Financing of Terrorism* (2nd edn) (World Bank/IMF 2006). Reference should also be made to the relevant websites of the Financial Action Task Force, United Nations, European Union, World Bank and International Monetary Fund.

30   For a recent examination of money laundering from an international perspective see Bryant 'Money Laundering Offences' in B Rider (ed) *Research Handbook on International Financial Crime* (Edward Elgar 2015).

7.10   The principal legislation relating to money laundering is now the POCA 2002. However, there are also important provisions in the Terrorism Act 2000, the Anti-terrorism, Crime and Security Act 2001 and the Terrorism (United Nations) Order 2001. The POCA 2002 has also been amended on many occasions; most recently in the Serious Crime Act 2015. As the relevant statutory provisions have been brought into effect in stages, by Order, care needs to be taken in ascertaining, at any point in time, exactly what provisions are pertinent. The Money Laundering Regulations 2007[31] are of particular significance. Our analysis and discussion here needs to be general and cannot descend to the considerable detail that is required for proper compliance with the many and varied obligations. Of course, given the significance of authoritative guidance from such bodies as the FCA, British Bankers Association and the Law Society, which have an impact on the determination of liability, businesses engaged, in particular, in regulated activities and especially in the financial sector, will need to have specific regard to industry standards and advice. Having said this, here we will focus rather more on the substantive law.

7.11   Part 7 of the POCA 2002 establishes three basic crimes. These offences are 'parasitic', because they are predicated on the commission of another offence yielding proceeds, which then become the subject of a money laundering offence.[32] Section 327 makes it a criminal offence to conceal, disguise, convert or transfer criminal property, or remove it from the jurisdiction. Section 327, renders it criminal to make an arrangement to facilitate the acquisition, retention, use or control of criminal property, by, or on behalf of, another person. Section 329 makes it an offence to acquire, use or have possession of criminal property.

7.12   In regard to all three basic offences, a person does not commit a crime if an authorised disclosure is made to the relevant authority and when appropriate, the necessary consent to continue the relevant transaction is given, pursuant to section 338. By the same token, there is no offence if the person concerned intended to make such a disclosure, but had a reasonable excuse for not doing so. Nor does a person commit a section 327–329 offence if he knows, or believes on reasonable grounds, that the relevant criminal conduct[33] occurred in a particular country or territory outside the United Kingdom, and the relevant criminal conduct was not, at the time it occurred, unlawful under the criminal law then applying in that country or territory, and is not of a description prescribed by an order made by the Secretary of State.[34] In regard to all the substantive offences, it is also a defence to establish that what has been done is in fact merely carrying out a function that the accused has in relation to enforcing any provision in the Act or other statute relating to the benefits of criminal activity. Given the panoply of provisions allowing the interdiction of property that is suspected or proven to be the proceeds of criminal conduct, the burden placed on officials and others charged with preserving and managing it, before final determination by the courts, is considerable and would present certain risks of prosecution under the anti- money laundering laws, but for such a defence. By section 329, in the case of the offence under section 329, namely

---

31   SI 2007/2157.
32   See *JSC BTA Bank v Ablyazov* [2010] 1 WLR 976 (CA).
33   The 'relevant criminal conduct' is the criminal conduct by reference to which the property concerned is criminal property, see ss 327(2B), 328(4) and 329(2B), added by the Serious Organised Crime and Police Act 2005.
34   See ss 327(2A), 328(3) and 329(2A), added by the Serious Organised Crime and Police Act 2005.

acquisition or use of property, no offence will be committed if this has been done for 'adequate consideration'. The substantive offences are supported by a number of provisions which oblige certain persons to ensure that they know for whom they act and the character of their business and transactions. As we have already seen, other provisions require disclosure of suspicions to the authorities and outlaw 'tipping off'.

7.13   While we are concerned essentially with the proceeds of crime, the legislation is concerned to impose criminal responsibility on any person who benefits from property derived from criminal conduct or uses or comes into possession of such. It is important to note that this responsibility applies whenever or wherever the crime 'creating' the property is committed and it is irrelevant whether the 'launderer' is aware of who was involved in that original criminal activity. The Act defines property extremely widely as it does the concepts of obtaining, possession and use. Any involvement in the use, possession or realisation of the property or any interest in such will be caught. Under section 340(3) of the Act, property is 'criminal property' if (a) it constitutes a benefit from criminal conduct, whether directly or indirectly, in whole or in part[35] and (b) the alleged offender knows or suspects that it constitutes or represents such a benefit. Where the allegation is a conspiracy or an attempt, then knowledge or belief is required and suspicion is not sufficient.[36] By section 340(5), a person benefits from conduct if he obtains property as a result of or in connection with the conduct. If a person obtains a pecuniary advantage as a result of or in connection with conduct, then by section 340(6) he is to be taken to obtain as a result of or in connection with the conduct a sum of money equal to the value of the pecuniary advantage. A pecuniary advantage is obtained when cheating the revenue, but profits from trading in legitimate goods without declaring the profits do not however become criminal property simply by reason of the failure to declare profits.[37] In a tax evasion case where turnover was falsely represented the criminal property was the entirety of the undeclared turnover and not merely the tax due.[38]

7.14   Regarding knowledge or suspicion, it relates to the legitimacy of the property in issue, not those creating it.[39] Of course, knowledge that

---

35   In *R v Smallman* [2010] EWCA Crim 548, it was held that the breadth of the definition of (a) must be given its full weight. In this case, gambling winnings were mixed with criminal property at the time of the transfers made to the defendant. Kay LJ found that 'notwithstanding that the transfers were made as and when he won at gambling, it was open to the jury to conclude that the money transferred represented, in part at least, MS's benefit from criminal conduct'.

36   See *R v Saik* [2007] 1 AC 18 (HL) for conspiracies and *R v Pace and Rogers* [2014] 1 WLR 2867 (CA) for attempts. The reason for this is that the act of conspiracy or attempt requires a higher mens rea than suspicion. Mistakes on the *Saik* point are still being made by the Crown Court see eg *R v Thomas* [2014] EWCA Crim 1958 or *R v Tree* [2008] EWCA Crim 261. Where a defendant can, however, be shown deliberately to have turned a blind eye to the provenance of goods and deliberately to have failed to ask obvious questions, then that can be capable, depending on the circumstances, of providing evidence going to prove knowledge or belief, see *Pace and Rogers*.

37   See *R v IK* [2007] 1 WLR 2262 (CA) and *R v Yip* [2010] EWCA Crim 1381. *R v Gabriel* [2007] 1 WLR 2722 (CA) was distinguished by *R v IK* upon this basis.

38   See *R v William and Others* [2013] EWCA Crim 1262.

39   Suspicion goes further than the UK's international obligations. This is noted by Lord Toulson in *R v GH* [2015] 1 WLR 2126 (SC), 'As the Court of Appeal explained in *Bowman v Fels (Bar Council intervening)* [2005] EWCA Civ 226, [2005] 1 WLR 3083, POCA gave effect to Council Directive 91/308/EEC on prevention of the use of the financial system for the purpose of money laundering (as amended by Council Directive 2001/97/EC), but the Directive set minimum requirements and in some respects POCA was more stringent.

those individuals are engaged in crime would be sufficient, but such is not necessary. The law focuses on the status in law of the property and rights in it. The concept of criminal conduct is set out in section 340(2) of the Act. It is broad in every respect. It includes offences in the United Kingdom, or conduct overseas, whether criminal there or not, which had it occurred in the United Kingdom would constitute such an offence. Under section 340(4) of the Act, it is immaterial who carried out the conduct, who benefited from it or whether the conduct occurred before or after the passing of the Act.

7.15   The substantive offence of concealment is contained in section 327 of the Act, as we have seen. This section sets out five types of concealment which are potentially criminal; namely concealment, conversion, transfer, removal and disguising the property in question. Receiving criminal property from another into a bank account that the defendant controls, with the appropriate *mens rea*, does constitute the conversion of that criminal property even if the defendant did not himself make the deposit.[40] Where a huge number of small transactions are made there is no requirement to specify each and every transaction in separate counts.[41] Concealing and disguising the property's nature, source, location, disposition, movement, ownership or any right in regard to it, are potentially an offence. For liability all that need be proved is that such took place in regard to criminal property and the person concerned knew or suspected that it constituted the benefit of criminal conduct. The property must be criminal property at the time of the transfer etc.[42] This can be shown either directly or by an irresistible inference that the property can only be derived from crime; ie the prosecution do not need to establish precisely what crime or crimes had generated the property in question.[43] In civil recovery or cash forfeiture proceedings, an irresistible inference is not enough and the claimant must show that the property seized was obtained through conduct of

For example, money laundering as defined in POCA includes dealing with property known 'or suspected' to constitute or represent a benefit from criminal conduct; by contrast, the definition in the Directive required knowledge. The current version of the Directive is 2005/60/EC. This repealed and replaced 91/308/EEC."

40   See *R v Fazal* [2010] 1 WLR 694 (CA) and *The Queen v HO Ling MO* [2013] NICA 49. In *Fazal*, Lord Justice Rix held that 'The reference to converting criminal property in this statute is not necessarily a reference to the civil tort of conversion, but it cannot be far removed from its nature and, of course, conversion in the civil law is a broad tort which is essentially concerned with the taking or receiving or retaining or parting with someone else's property. When that is wrongfully done, it is a strict offence and requires no mens rea at all in the civil law, but only requires a dealing with someone else's property so as to question, deny or interfere with the owner's title to it. So it is seems to us that not only when these monies were lodged but also when they were credited to the appellant's account, when they were retained in it, and when they were withdrawn from it, all of which occurred with the full co-operation, knowledge, approval and authority of the appellant, there were successive acts of converting criminal property'. These cases can be contrasted with *R v Loizou* [2005] 2 Cr App R 37 (CA) in which it was held that 'Section 327(1) does not create an offence of receiving criminal property', though this comment was made in the context of a case involving receipt of cash and the nature of the receipt is therefore different.

41   See *R v Middleton* [2008] EWCA Crim 233.

42   The transfer of monies not obtained through crime to a criminal will not be sufficient even where that property becomes criminal property by virtue of the transaction, see *R v Loizou* [2005] 2 Cr App R 618 (CA).

43   See *R v Anwoir* [2009] 1 WLR 980 (CA); *Ahmad v Her Majesty's Advocate* [2009] HCJAC 60 and *R v Craig* [2007] EWCA Crim 2913. It is of note that the Court of Appeal has treated *R v Anwoir* as having settled this issue and despite previous conflicting case law, the Court of Appeal has refused to consider whether *Anwoir* was wrongly decided, see *R v MK and AS* [2009] EWCA Crim 952.

one of a number of kinds each of which would have been unlawful conduct.[44] Of course, it should be noted that this offence will invariably be committed by the perpetrator of the crime that gives rise to the criminal benefit. Prosecution guidance from the Crown Prosecution Service states that where there is any significant attempt to transfer or conceal ill-gotten gains money laundering should normally be considered as an additional charge, in part because the purpose of the concealment will be to defeat or avoid prosecution and confiscation.[45]

7.16   Under section 327(2C), a deposit taking body that converts or transfers criminal property will not commit an offence, provided it does the act, in the context of operating an account that it maintains, and the value of the criminal property does not exceed the relevant threshold amount. Similar provisions exist for section 328 and 329 offences. At present this threshold is only £250, see section 339A.

7.17   Section 328 is concerned with assisting another to retain the benefit of his or another person's criminal conduct. So far as this section affects financial institutions, the purpose of this section is not to turn innocent third parties into criminals but to put them under pressure to provide information to the relevant authorities to enable the latter to obtain information about possible criminal activity and to increase their prospects of being able to freeze the proceeds of crime.[46] The actus reus of the offence is entering into or being concerned in an arrangement which in fact facilitates the acquisition, retention, use or control of criminal property. The property must therefore be criminal property and mere suspicion that it might be will not be enough for a section 328 arrangement offence. The criminal property does not, however, need to exist or be criminal at the time the arrangement is made. What matters is that the property should be criminal at a time when the arrangement operates on it.[47] It is not enough

44   For civil recovery see *Director of Assets Recovery Agency v Green* [2005] EWHC 3168 (Admin); *Director of Assets Recovery Agency v Szepietowski* [2007] EWCA Civ 766. For cash forfeiture see *Angus v UK Border Agency* [2011] EWHC 461 (Admin); *R (on the application of Bavi) v Snaresbrook Crown Court* [2013] EWHC 4015 (Admin); and *Wiese v The UK Border Agency* [2012] EWHC 2019 (Admin). A cash forfeiture case making a separate point is *Fletcher v Chief Constable of Leicestershire* [2013] EWHC 3357 (Admin), where the innocent finder of s 327 concealed cash was held not to be entitled to keep the cash, which was subsequently forfeited as recoverable property.

45   http://www.cps.gov.uk/legal/p_to_r/proceeds_of_crime_money_laundering/#Charging_practice_plea. A similar point was made in *R v GH* [2015] 1 WLR 2126 (SC) in which it was said that it would be bad practice for the prosecution to add additional counts of that kind unless there is a proper public purpose in doing so. The Court of Appeal has discouraged the charging of a defendant with money laundering rather than handling stolen goods in *R (Wilkinson) v Director of Public Prosecutions* [2006] EWHC 3012 (Admin) and *R v Rose* [2008] 1 WLR 2113 and the Supreme Court in *R v GH* [2015] 1 WLR 2126 stated that 'courts should be willing to use their powers to discourage inappropriate use of the provisions of POCA to prosecute conduct which is sufficiently covered by substantive offences'. It would also be an abuse to prosecute money laundering when strikingly in conflict with a defendant's previously accepted basis of plea in relation to a predicate offence, see *Crown Prosecution Service v Mattu* [2009] EWCA Crim 1483. Any finding in relation to a defendant's benefit, however, does not prevent a subsequent court from finding against a different defendant that they laundered a greater sum of money from that offence, see *R v Y and ZSB* [2013] 1 WLR 2014 (CA).

46   *Squirrell Ltd v National Westminster Bank Plc* [2006] 1 WLR 637 (Ch).

47   See *R v GH* [2015] 1 WLR 2126 (SC), where the appellant H opened an account for B; victims paid monies into the appellant's account and the Supreme Court found that H had agreed to retain property which became criminal upon entering the account. See also *R v Amir and Akhtar* [2011] 1 Cr App R 464 (CA) and *R v Montila* [2004] 1 WLR 3141 (HL). The Supreme Court's position in *R v GH* conflicts with the High Court's comments

that the arrangement will facilitate the acquisition of criminal property by another.[48] The mens rea required is knowledge or suspicion. Merely suspecting that one might be entering into an arrangement to acquire etc criminal property is insufficient for the offence to be committed.[49]

7.18   It is the section 328 offence that is most likely to be of concern to those involved in business and advising those in business. However, section 328 is not intended to cover or affect the ordinary conduct of litigation by legal professionals or to override legal or litigation privilege.[50] A bank employee or professional adviser, however, who suspects that the property they are dealing with has resulted from criminal activity would be at risk. Of course, as we have already seen, such a person would also, in many instances, be under certain duties in the civil law. The assistance that is provided may be for personal reward or not. The crime is committed whether the benefiting from the criminal property is by the person who committed the original criminal activity, or others. No offence is committed if the accused makes an authorised disclosure of his knowledge or belief to the authorities and receives permission to proceed, or where he does not disclose before acting and has a reasonable excuse for not having done so.[51] An authorised disclosure is defined in section 338 as disclosure to a constable, a customs officer or nominated officer on the individual's own initiative as soon as it is reasonable for him to do so. The term constable is defined in section 340(13), as amended, to include any person authorised by the Director General of the NCA. In the case of a person who is employed, and this includes persons whether remunerated or not, then disclosure to a person nominated by his employer, according to certain procedures within the organisation of company, will amount to disclosure to a constable. Of course, that person must then pass the information on. Under section 339 of the Act the Secretary of State is authorised to prescribe the form and manner of the disclosure. It should be noted that by virtue of section 335 of the Act, if after proper disclosure consent is not refused within seven working days, or if a restraint order is not obtained 31 calendar days thereafter, then no offence would be committed under section 328 in continuing the transaction. Of course, this would not absolve the person concerned and in appropriate circumstances his employer and organisation from civil liability. Indeed, in the civil law his head is already on the block, as he has documented the fact that he suspects that the relevant property may well be subject to legal claims by third

---

in *Squirrell Ltd v National Westminster Bank Plc* [2006] 1 WLR 637 in which Laddie J stated in relation to a bank account that 'Even if it does not contain funds which are, in fact, criminal property and no offence has been committed, section 328(1) bites if NatWest has a relevant suspicion'. See also *K Ltd v National Westminster Bank Plc* [2007] 1 WLR 311. *Squirrel Ltd* was not a case cited in the judgment of *GH* and *Montila* was not cited in *Squirrel Ltd*. The decision in *R v GH* can be contrasted with the case of *R v Geary* [2011] 1 WLR 1634 (CA), where property did not become criminal if merely being transferred to conceal them from matrimonial proceedings. The fact that the arrangement involved a conspiracy to pervert the cause of justice did not mean that the money had a criminal quality independent of the arrangement. Similarly, see *R v Gillies* [2011] EWCA Crim 2140. *R v GH* should also be contrasted with *In Kensington International Ltd v Republic of Congo* [2008] 1 WLR 1144 where no section 328 office was committed by the giving of a bribe as the property was not criminal at the time of the arrangement becoming operative.

48   See *Dare v Crown Prosecution Service* [2012] EWHC 2074 (Admin).
49   See *R v Saik* [2007] 1 AC 18 (HL).
50   See *Bowman v Fels* [2005] 1 WLR 3083 (CA).
51   An example of an authorised disclosure being made after the act and of having good reason for not disclosing before the act can be seen in *Sarwar v Her Majesty's Advocate* [2011] HCJAC 13.

parties. To proceed, without regard to the obligations that the civil law may on the facts impose, would be rash.

7.19   As has already been pointed out, the transmission of 'suspicion based' reports to the Financial Intelligence Unit of the NCA is at the very heart of the Government's initiative to disrupt organised crime and discourage career criminals.[52] Unlike the obligation to report all transactions above a certain amount in value, as exists in most jurisdictions, reports based on a reasonable suspicion, particularly those that have already gone through a process evaluation within a financial institution, by experts, are of particular value to the police. They often provide real and valuable intelligence. Of course suspicions, no matter how reasonable and well founded, are not evidence. Action based on such may need to be justified in the end before a court, and it is the ability to convert information into intelligence and then into evidence which presents the biggest challenge to law enforcement, and for that matter regulatory agencies. The emphasis that is now being placed on intervention and disruption of criminal activity may be, in practice, justified by intelligence, but those who are exposed to legal risk and possible claims will need the reassurance of evidence behind their actions. It is also important, in the context of disclosure of suspicious activity, to consider the impact of the general law relating to 'whistle blowing' and, of course, data protection.

7.20   The third substantive money laundering offence is provided for in section 329 of the Act. This renders the acquisition, use and possession of the proceeds of criminal activity a specific crime. There is no definition of the word acquisition; however, it is right to concentrate on ownership rather than possession.[53] However, section 329(2) states that the offence is not committed if the person concerned makes an authorised disclosure as in the case of section 328, or has acquired or used or had possession of the property, albeit criminal property, for adequate consideration. The notion of adequate consideration is explained in section 329(3). A person acquires property for inadequate consideration if the value of the consideration is significantly less than the value of the property; or in the case of use or possession, the value is significantly less than the consideration.[54] Consideration has its ordinary meaning in contract law.[55] Once the defendant has raised the issue of consideration, the burden is on the Crown to show that there was not adequate consideration.[56] It is also provided under section 329(3) that the provision by a person of goods or services which he knows or suspects may help another to carry out criminal conduct is not consideration. Indeed, in the case of the civil law it is probable that such would not be considered good consideration. It is, of course, necessary for the prosecution to establish that the accused knew or suspected that the property in question is criminal property. In practice, the manifest inadequacy of the consideration required, might itself indicate this. However, with all three substantive offences, it must be remembered that the

---

52   See *Proceeds of Crime: Consultation on Draft Legislation*, (2001), Home Office, Cm 5966 and in particular *One Step Ahead, A 21st Century Strategy to Defeat Organised Crime*, (2004), Home Office. Reference should also be made to FIU's *In Action*, (2001), Egmont Group.

53   See *R v Heera* [2010] EWCA Crim 1779.

54   This means that if adequate consideration has been given for the acquisition of property, then no offence is made out under the Act, even if the defendant who has acquired the property knows that it was stolen, see *Hogan v DPP* [2007] 1 WLR 2944 (CA).

55   See *R v Kausar* [2009] EWCA Crim 2242 and *R v Nawaz* [2010] EWCA Crim 819.

56   See *Hogan v DPP* [2007] 1 WLR 2944 (CA).

knowledge or suspicion of the accused is subjective. It must be proved beyond a reasonable doubt that the accused did in fact have knowledge of the status of property in question or at least a suspicion.

7.21 The three substantive offences apply to everyone. There are, however, offences which apply only to those in what is termed the regulated sector set out in Schedule 9, as amended, of the Act. The scope of this sector is ever expanding, but the notion justifying the imposition of a greater responsibility on such persons, is that they engage usually for remuneration in a specific activity which gives rise to a reasonable expectation of professionalism. Consequently, it is reasonable to hold such persons to a standard of greater diligence in the provision of their essentially facilitative services and impose an objective standard of culpability upon them. Thus, in regard to certain offences, it will not be necessary for the prosecution to establish that the accused did actually have knowledge or was suspicious, it will be enough for criminal liability that an ordinary and reasonable person in their line of work would have known or, more likely, have been at least suspicious. Of course, it is rare in crimes based on a state of mind, that objective knowledge or belief is sufficient for the imposition of criminal liability. The scope of these provisions is those engaged in 'relevant financial business' as set out in Schedule 9 of the Act.

7.22 Section 330 imposes an obligation on those in the regulated sector to report to the authorities their suspicions of laundering activity. Unlike section 328,[57] there is no requirement, in fact, for the property in question to be criminal property.[58] Where a person fails to make the required disclosure as soon as is practicable, when he knows or suspects, or has reason for knowing or suspecting, another person is engaging in money laundering, and this information or other matter came to him in the course of his trade, profession, business or employment within the regulated sector, he commits a crime, provided that the person known or suspected to be engaged in money laundering, or the whereabouts of any of the laundered property, can be identified; or where there is belief or a reasonable expectation thereof that the information or other matter will or may assist in identifying the other person or the whereabouts of any of the laundered property.

7.23 A suspicion that property represents the benefit of criminal conduct committed overseas, including from inchoate offences such as conspiracy, would be caught under this provision. There is some protection, although not much, in that a person who does not in fact know or suspect that laundering is taking place, and has not had the benefit of the training that is required to be given the Regulations, will not be guilty of an offence.

7.24 There are other limited defences. Where there is a reasonable excuse for non-disclosure then no offence is committed. Furthermore, a professional legal adviser or other relevant professional adviser[59] will not be guilty for

---

57 Following *R v GH*, above.

58 See *Ahmad v Her Majesty's Advocate* [2009] HCJAC 60, at para 30: 'There is nothing in the language of section 330(2) which states or requires that money laundering is in fact taking place. It is plain that the obligation thereunder can arise if a person suspects or has reasonable cause for suspecting that it is.'

59 See s 330(14): 'A relevant professional adviser is an accountant, auditor or tax adviser who is a member of a professional body which is established for accountants, auditors or tax advisers (as the case may be) and which makes provision for (a) testing the competence of those seeking admission to membership of such a body as a condition for such admission; and (b) imposing and maintaining professional and ethical standards for its members, as well as imposing sanctions for non-compliance with those standards.'

failing to disclose information that comes to him in privileged circumstances, provided such information is not in furtherance of criminal activity. Of course, under the general law, privilege is restricted in that it cannot serve to hide and facilitate crime. However, in this context it should also be noted that in *Bowman v Fels*,[60] the Court of Appeal confirmed that the obligation to report, in that case as a defence under section 328, did not override the common law legal professional privilege in the ordinary course of litigation. In addition, a disclosure to a professional legal adviser for obtaining advice about making a disclosure and not intended to be a disclosure to a nominated officer, is not to be taken as a disclosure.[61] An offence is also not committed if the person knows, or believes on reasonable grounds, that the relevant criminal conduct occurred in a particular country or territory outside the United Kingdom, and the relevant criminal conduct was not, at the time it occurred, unlawful under the criminal law then applying in that country or territory, and is not of a description prescribed by an order made by the Secretary of State.

7.25   Section 331 of the Act imposes responsibility on nominated officers commonly referred to as Money Laundering Reporting Officers (MLROs) to pass on information that they receive in consequence of a disclosure made under section 330, in circumstances similar to that already described above in relation to section 330.[62] They are under an obligation to forward this information, in the prescribed manner, to the authorities as soon as practicable. However, in considering whether an offence has been committed, courts are required to consider whether the officer in question followed guidance issued, with the approval of the Treasury, by appropriate designated bodies under Schedule 9 of the Act. Thus, compliance with, for example, the Guidance Notes of the Joint Money Laundering Steering Group of the British Bankers Association, the Law Society or the FCA would be relevant in the determination of guilt. In the case of the non-regulated sector, section 332 imposes similar obligations on other nominated officers to report, as soon as practicable, knowledge or suspicion based on information that they have received, in a similar manner to section 331; however, as we have seen here the test for liability is only subjective rather than section 331 in which either subjective or objective knowledge or suspicion is sufficient for the offence to be made out. For both sections 331 and 332 there are similar territorial defences in as found in section 330 and under both sections no offence is committed if the person has a reasonable excuse for not making the required disclosure.

7.26   Reference has already been made to the offence of 'Tipping off' contained in section 333A of the Act. This crime involves disclosing any matter already disclosed to a constable, Revenue and Customs officer, nominated officer or an authorised NCA officer that is likely to prejudice any investigation[63] that might be conducted following the disclosure, where the information on which the disclosure is based came to the person in the course of a business in the regulated section. It is not just the fact of disclosure but also the information disclosed which is forbidden.[64] It is also an offence

---

60   [2005] EWCA Civ 226. See also s 106 of the Serious Organised Crime and Police Act 2005.
61   See s 330(9A)
62   Knowledge or suspicion that another person is engaged in money laundering, with similar provisions about the identification of the other person or property.
63   Where the person does not know or suspect that the disclosure is likely to have this effect, no offence is committed, see s 333D(3).
64   See *Becker v Lloyds TSB Bank Plc* [2013] EWHC 3000 (Ch).

to disclose that such an investigation is being contemplated or carried out, where the disclosure is likely to prejudice that investigation[65] and where the information on which the disclosure is based came to the person in the course of a business in the regulated sector. This second offence applies to everyone, including professional advisers.

7.27   Section 333B provides that a section 333A offence is not committed in respect of disclosures to employees, officers or partners of the same undertaking; or if in respect of a disclosure by a credit institution or financial institution if to a similar institution in the EEA or in a country or territory imposing equivalent money laundering requirements if both institutions are part of the same Group. Section 333B also ensures that a professional legal or relevant professional adviser commits no section 333A offence if to another similar person, where both persons carry on business in the EEA or in a country or territory imposing equivalent money laundering requirements, and where both persons perform their professional activities within different undertakings that share common ownership, management or control.

7.28   Section 333C provides that a Section 333A offence is also not committed if the disclosure is to a client, former client, a transaction involving them both or the provision of a service involving them both, where the disclosure is for the purpose only of preventing an offence under this Part of the Act, where the institution or adviser to whom the disclosure was made is in an EEA State or another country or territory imposing equivalent money laundering requirements, and where both parties to the disclosure are subject to equivalent duties of professional confidentiality and protection of personal data.

7.29   Section 333D provides that a section 333A offence is not committed if the disclosure is to the authority that is the supervisory authority for that person by virtue of the Money Laundering Regulations 2007, or for the purpose of the detection, investigation or prosecution of a criminal offence, an investigation under this Act or the enforcement of any order of a court under this Act, eg a restraint or confiscation order. Section 333D also provides that a professional legal adviser or a relevant professional adviser does not commit an offence under section 333A if the disclosure is to the adviser's client, and is made for the purpose of dissuading the client from engaging in conduct amounting to an offence.

7.30   Under section 342 of the Act, a person commits an offence if he knows or suspects that a money laundering investigation is being or is about to be conducted and he makes a disclosure which is likely to prejudice the investigation. There are defences rather similar to those relating to an offence under section 333A. Of course, where there is a deliberate interference with the administration of justice or destruction, concealment or falsification of evidence, then there would be the prospect of prosecution for offences under the general criminal law.[66]

---

65   Where the person does not know or suspect that the disclosure is likely to have this effect, no offence is committed, see s 333D(4).
66   The justification would be similar to that in *R v Kenny* [2013] 3 WLR 59 in which a prosecution for perverting the course of justice was upheld for a serious breach of a restraint order. A perverting charge is appropriate when sensibly applied. This may be where it is appropriate to reflect the gravity or complexity of the wrongdoing in question and where it may be thought (whatever the ultimate outcome) that the maximum sentence for contempt may prove insufficient.

7.31 Mention has been made of the possibility of liability resulting from the disclosure of information, pursuant to the statutory obligations in the Act, under the general law. Section 337 provides that a disclosure which satisfies the following three conditions is not to be taken to breach any restriction on the disclosure of information (however imposed). First, the information or other matter disclosed must have come to the discloser in the course of his trade, profession, business or employment. Secondly, the information or other matter must have caused the discloser to know or suspect, or given him reasonable grounds for knowing or suspecting, that another person is engaged in money laundering. Thirdly, the disclosure must be made to a constable, a customs officer or a nominated officer as soon as is practicable after the information or other matter comes to the discloser. A disclosure to a nominated officer is a disclosure which is made to a person nominated by the discloser's employer to receive disclosures under section 330 or under section 337 and is made in the course of the discloser's employment.

7.32 Section 338 extends protection to all authorised disclosures made under the provisions of the Act, whether by persons in the regulated sector or not, but with slightly different criteria. For the purposes of section 338, a disclosure is authorised if it is a disclosure to a constable, a customs officer or a nominated officer by the alleged offender that property is criminal property, and one of the following three conditions are satisfied. If authorised, the disclosure is not to be taken to breach any restriction on the disclosure of information (however imposed). If authorised and made in good faith, no civil liability arises in respect of the disclosure on the part of the person by or on whose behalf it is made. The disclosure to a nominated officer is a disclosure which is made to a person nominated by the alleged offender's employer to receive authorised disclosures, and is made in the course of the alleged offender's employment.

7.33 The three conditions for the section 338 disclosure are as follows: first, if the disclosure is made before the alleged offender does the prohibited act. Secondly, the disclosure is made while the alleged offender is doing the prohibited act; he began to do the act at a time when, because he did not then know or suspect that the property constituted or represented a person's benefit from criminal conduct, the act was not a prohibited act; and the disclosure is made on his own initiative and as soon as is practicable after he first knows or suspects that the property constitutes or represents a person's benefit from criminal conduct. Thirdly, the disclosure is made after the alleged offender does the prohibited act; he has a reasonable excuse for his failure to make the disclosure before he did the act; and the disclosure is made on his own initiative and as soon as it is practicable for him to make it.

7.34 It is important to note that sections 337 and 338 are capable of protecting against liability, based on a breach of any restriction on the disclosure of information, however imposed. Thus, there would be no liability for breach of confidentiality arising, for example, by contract or a fiduciary relationship. However, this protection does not extend to, for instance, liability in the law of defamation. While it would be possible in most cases to assert a defence of qualified privilege, the threat of suit is a significant inhibition. Furthermore, it must not be forgotten that these statutory defences under the Act can only apply to proceedings within jurisdiction.

7.35 Another matter which affects both section 337 and 338 disclosures is that if made to a constable or an officer of Revenue and Customs, then section

339ZA requires the constable or officer of Revenue and Customs to disclose it in full to a person authorised by the Director General of the National Crime Agency as soon as practicable after it has been made.

7.36   As far as penalties are concerned, section 334 provides that, anyone convicted on indictment of an offence under sections 327 to 329, is liable to a prison term of up to 14 years and an unlimited fine. In the case of sections 330 to 332, on conviction on indictment, the maximum penalty is five years imprisonment and an unlimited fine. Of course, in the case of summary convictions the maximum term of imprisonment is six months and a level 5 fine. In the case of an offence under section 333A, the maximum penalty is two years imprisonment and an unlimited fine if convicted on indictment and for a summary conviction the maximum term of imprisonment is three months and a level 5 fine. It is also an offence under section 339(1A) to make a disclosure in a manner other than in the form prescribed by the Secretary of State, absent reasonable excuse. The summary only penalty for a breach of section 339(1A) is a fine not exceeding level 5 on the standard scale. Offences under all these provisions might well be suitable for triggering proceedings for confiscation, for which see later in this chapter.

7.37   Before finishing this section, we refer briefly to the Money Laundering Regulations 2007.[67] These Regulations are substantial – there are 51 Regulations and 6 Schedules to the regulations, so the examination here is cursory. As the Explanatory Note to the Regulations explain: 'These Regulations implement, in part, Directive 2005/60/EC of the European Parliament and of the Council on the prevention of the use of the financial system for the purpose of money laundering and terrorist financing (the Third Directive). The Regulations require the financial, accountancy, legal and other sectors to apply risk-based customer due diligence measures and take other steps to prevent their services being used for money laundering or terrorist financing.'

7.38   Regulation 3 sets out that the Regulations apply, subject to certain exclusions, to credit institutions, financial institutions, auditors, insolvency practitioners, external accountants and tax advisers, independent legal professionals, trust or company service providers, estate agents, high value dealers and casinos.

7.39   It is an offence pursuant to regulation 45(1)[68] to fail to comply with any requirement in relation to some of the regulations relating to:

- 7(1)–(3) Application of customer due diligence measures
- 8(1) or (3) Ongoing monitoring
- 9(2) Timing of verification
- 10(1) Casinos
- 11(1)(a)–(c) Requirement to cease transactions etc
- 14(1) Enhanced customer due diligence and ongoing monitoring
- 15(1)–(2) Branches and subsidiaries
- 16(1)–(4) Shell banks, anonymous accounts etc
- 19(1), (4)–(6) Record-keeping
- 20(1), (4)–(5) Policies and procedures
- 21 Training
- 26 Requirement to be registered

---

67   SI 2007/2157.
68   In addition, there is a further offence at reg 45(1A) relating to auction platforms.

196

- 27(4) Applications for registration in a register maintained under regulation 25
- 33 Requirement to be registered

7.40 Company officers, partners in partnerships and officers of unincorporated associations can also be liable under regulation 47 for a regulation 45 offence, where committed with the consent or the connivance that person or body corporate; or attributable to any neglect on his part

7.41 Proceedings for an offence under regulation 45 may be instituted by order of the Commissioners, a local weights and measures authority, DETI, the Director of Public Prosecutions or the Director of Public Prosecutions for Northern Ireland. The penalty for a breach of the above is on indictment up to two years imprisonment and/or a fine; and on summary conviction, a fine not exceeding the statutory maximum.

7.42 Regulation 45(2) ensures that in deciding whether a person has committed an offence, the court must consider whether the person followed any relevant guidance which was at the time issued by a supervisory authority or any other appropriate body, approved by the Treasury, and published in a manner approved by the Treasury as suitable in their opinion to bring the guidance to the attention of persons likely to be affected by it.

7.43 There is a defence at regulation 45(4) to ensure that a person is not guilty of an offence under this regulation if he took all reasonable steps and exercised all due diligence to avoid committing the offence.

7.44 The Money Laundering Regulations 2007 will need to be updated as the UK brings into force the 4th Money Laundering Directive.[69] This directive must be brought into force by 26 June 2017. The purpose of the directive is set out at Article 1(1) and 'The Directive aims to prevent the use of the Union's financial system for the purposes of money laundering and terrorist financing'. The new Regulations to be brought into force are substantial and are beyond the scope of this text, however among the developments introduced by the new Directive is a requirement for each State to hold a central register of beneficial ownership in relation to corporate entities, trusts and legal entities and arrangements similar to trusts. In addition, although this will not affect the UK as such provision has already been in force in POCA 2002 for the same, tax crimes must now be included as a predicate offence for money laundering. Gambling services are also caught by the new Directive, including internet gambling.

MONEY LAUNDERING LIABILITY IN THE CIVIL LAW

7.45 We have already referred to liability in equity for breach of trust and other fiduciary obligations.[70] While every breach of trust will amount to a breach of fiduciary duty, not every breach of a fiduciary relationship will

69 Directive (EU) 2015/849 of the European Parliament and of the Council of 20 May 2015 on the prevention of the use of the financial system for the purposes of money laundering or terrorist financing, amending Regulation (EU) No 648/2012 of the European Parliament and of the Council, and repealing Directive 2005/60/EC of the European Parliament and of the Council and Commission Directive 2006/70/EC, Official Journal of the European Union L 141/73.
70 See 2.29 above and at 14.14 below.

amount to a breach of trust. Trusts, even remedial constructive trusts, involve property and rights in property. The relationship between the trust and the trustee is a proprietary relationship. It is upon this basis that trustees are under a strict obligation that does not depend upon culpability or a state of mind, to replace property that has been improperly removed or diverted from the trust.[71] Trustees are also held to the general and strict fiduciary obligations to avoid all conflicts of interest, to act in good faith in the best interests of their beneficiaries and to act with prudence and diligence. They have an overall obligation of loyalty and fair dealing. While the obligations of a trustee are expressed in proprietary terms, many of the obligations are also personal, and the remedies that are applied may well be compensatory. One area which has caused difficulty is the situation where a person receiving property, including rights in or to property, appreciates that it is being transferred to him in breach of trust. Generally speaking in terms of priorities a *bona fide* purchaser of such property, without actual knowledge, will be able to take the property unencumbered. The original owner's rights in the property, which are equitable, will be defeated by the stronger right of the so called 'equity's darling'. The position may be different if the 'original' owner has been able to re-establish his legal ownership in the property. For example, in cases of theft, or fraud where there has been an effective rescission of the contract, the legal ownership remains in or reverts in full to the owner and even 'equity's darling' will, save in exceptional circumstances, in most common law as opposed to most civilian jurisdictions, have no right to the property against the owner. Of course, in such cases as where the original owner's equitable interest is defeated, the remedy will be in damages against the fraudster – who sadly is likely to have disappeared. Where a third party takes property with knowledge of a breach of trust, then in many legal systems he will become a constructive trustee and hold the property on much the same terms as the trustee in breach. There are cases which indicate that in such circumstances, actual knowledge of the breach does not need to be established. Knowledge of facts that would put a reasonable man on inquiry would be sufficient to create the obligation of trustee. Reckless indifference to the rights of another would be enough, but whether negligence is an appropriate standard has been questioned. Deliberately refusing to make inquiries in circumstances where you are suspicious is generally considered to place on you the risk of what you might have found had you made proper and reasonable inquiry. Of course, if the person who takes the transfer is a volunteer, that is, does not provide consideration, then he will not be considered a *bona fide* purchaser and the issue of knowledge is irrelevant. He will not be able to resist a claim by the beneficial owner and may well be considered to possess the property as a constructive trustee. While the courts as a matter of contract law generally do not consider the adequacy of consideration, in cases such as we are discussing a wholly inadequate consideration might not be considered as dealing in good faith.

7.46   The circumstances where a fiduciary obligation is imposed are not fixed. The courts may be prepared to find that in the circumstances of a case, a person has stepped into a fiduciary relationship and is thus subject to fiduciary obligations. There are many factors influencing the courts in this regard, but issues such as reposing confidence in another and reasonably expecting

---

71   See *Clough v Bond* (1838) 3 My & C 490; *Target Holdings v Redferns* [1996] 1 AC 421 and *Attorney General for Hong Kong v Reid* (1994) 1 AC 324.

fairness and good faith play a role.[72] As do deliberate taking advantage of an imbalance of opportunity in unfair circumstances. Having said this, given the onerous obligations attaching to fiduciary status, the courts do not find such a relationship easily. Where a person is a fiduciary, however, then the obligations are strict and remedies generally do not depend upon the state of mind of the fiduciary in breach. If a fiduciary enters into a conflict of interest or takes a secret profit he will be liable irrespective of whether he was dishonest or not. His breach of stewardship is sufficient harm and justification for a remedy.[73] The state of mind of the fiduciary may, however, have an impact on the way in which the court deals with him and in regard to such issues as ratification and indemnity. The more dishonest a person is the less easy will it be for him to persuade a court that there has been agreement, express or implied, to his conduct.

7.47   Mention has been made of the liability that equity has developed for those who assist others in the breach of their fiduciary obligations. Where the trust property is actually transferred to the third party, then it is often appropriate to talk in terms of liability based on a constructive or resulting trust, as we have just seen. There is a proprietary relationship. Of course, there are issues as to what can be considered trust property for the purposes of imposing or rather finding a trust relationship. In equity it seems that confidential information and opportunities to profit, such as by virtue of an embryo contract, may be considered, unlike in the criminal law, to be a form of property.[74] We have already seen that in certain circumstances secret profits and bribes may be considered to amount to trust property on the basis that equity looks as done that which should be done and will look to the stage after the fiduciary has been ordered to account for the illicit benefit.[75] However, what is the position of a third person who does not actually receive into their control or possession, property that can be the basis of a tracing claim, but nonetheless assists the fiduciary to breach his duties or launder the proceeds of such? It is misleading to describe such a person as coming into a constructive trust relationship with the ultimate beneficiary as there is no proprietary nexus – there is no property upon which equity can focus. Of course, imaginative lawyers and occasionally sympathetic judges – who do not like to see fraudsters retaining their ill-gotten gains, invent arguments by which rights to call to account or even sue, are transmuted into something resembling a right in property. However, this is not really good law and creates uncertainty and potential unfairness, particularly for relatively innocent third parties.

7.48   Rather than bend property law, in many common law jurisdictions the courts have found liability for culpable third parties on the basis of their dishonest assistance in the breach of another. This form of accessory liability is based purely on their dishonesty and not upon notions of property or for that matter the viability of a tracing claim. In a number of cases the courts in many Commonwealth and even some non-common law jurisdictions, have imposed personal liability on those who dishonestly assist others to breach their fiduciary duties, including the laundering of the proceeds of such. In providing assistance it is not necessary that the accessory has at any time control over or possession of the illicit wealth. On the other hand, the assistance must be

---

72   See 6.44 above.
73   See 6.46 and Chapter 2 above.
74   See *Boardman v Phipps* [1967] 2 AC 46 and *Cook v Deeks* [1916] 1 AC 554.
75   *Attorney General for Hong Kong v Reid* [1994] 1 AC 324 and see 2.29 *et seq.*

material. There has been debate as to the state of knowledge that the accessory must be proved to have to justify his personal liability. Actual knowledge of the facts relating to the breach of duty by the fiduciary is obviously sufficient.[76] It has also been held that the reckless disregard of the rights of another might well be sufficient.[77] It is on this level of knowledge that dishonesty can be found. Of course, unlike in the criminal law, the test is in civil cases objective.[78] Thus, the defendant will be taken to know or appreciate what a person in his position, with his knowledge and skill, would appreciate. It has, for example, been held that an accountant who refrains from asking why his client wants companies registered in England with bank accounts, might well be taken to know the facts that would have come out if he had received answers.[79] By not asking, he deliberately put himself in a position of ignorance. He had what has been termed 'Nelsonian' knowledge. When Admiral Nelson was asked if he saw his commander's flag signals requiring that he withdraw from a navel engagement he held his spyglass to his blind eye and asserted he saw nothing!

NAUGHTY KNOWLEDGE AND MENS REA

7.49   It is useful here to briefly consider in the context of the criminal law what the prosecution needs to prove, beyond a reasonable doubt, in the case of a prosecution under the relevant statutory provisions. It will be noted that most of the substantive offences require either knowledge or suspicion.

7.50   Knowledge is a straightforward word that does not need judicial explanation.[80] As we have seen in the case of certain of the offences relating to terrorist finance, it will suffice to prove that the accused has reasonable cause to suspect. In other words an ordinary reasonable man, in the position of the accused, would have formed a suspicion. Of course, it has to be proved even under this objective standard, that the accused knew such facts as would have properly grounded such a suspicion. In the case of handling charges, under section 22 of the Theft Act 1968, it is necessary to prove that the accused knew or believed that the relevant goods were stolen or were the proceeds of fraud. Some of the commentaries on the anti-money laundering provisions refer to belief as suspicion. This is certainly wrong in the criminal law and probably misleading in the civil law. Knowledge in the criminal law is certain knowledge of the relevant facts.

---

76   By way of example, see *Frank Houlgate Investment Co Ltd v Biggart Baillie LLP* [2015] SC 187 (Court of Session (Inner House, Extra Division)). In this case a solicitor's firm was liable for £100,000 advanced to their client when the solicitor knew that their client was not the title holder of the property that was to be the security and that their client was committing fraud. Lord McEwan noted that the solicitor did not tell the money laundering reporting officer in his firm and found that the solicitor should have stopped acting for his client, told his partners why and also advised the solicitors on the other side as to the reason for it and that the security too was a fraud and worthless.

77   *Royal Brunei Airlines v Tan* [1995] 1 AC 378 and *Selangor v Cradock (No 3)* [1968] 1 WLR 1555; see also at 2.33 above.

78   But it has been held that the defendant must realise that his actions would be considered dishonest by ordinary reasonable people, see *Twinsectra Ltd v Yardley* [2002] 2 All ER 377.

79   *Agip (Africa) v Jackson* [1991] Ch 547.

80   See *R v Afolabi* [2009] EWCA Crim 2879. An example of the issue of knowledge being at issue can be found in *Sarwar v Her Majesty's Advocate* [2011] HCJAC 13, in which it was found that the managing director of a company did not have access to the details of the transactions with the customer and in such circumstances could not be found to have the requisite knowledge.

7.51 Belief is something less than certain knowledge and the presence of uncertainties does not prevent there being reasonable cause to believe.[81] Nor is there, when assessing reasonable cause to believe, any need to reach a final conclusion even to the civil standard as to any liability on the part of the defendant at an interim stage.[82] A stricter definition is taken during a criminal trial where belief is an inherent element, for example in a handling stolen goods case, belief is when a person might say to himself: 'I cannot say I know for certain that those goods are stolen, but there can be no other reasonable conclusion in the light of all the circumstances, in the light of all that I have heard and seen.'[83] A suspicion would not be sufficient. However, it has been accepted that wilful blindness, that is deliberately not acquiring knowledge, is sufficient to establish a belief.[84]

7.52 Suspicion is defined in the Oxford Dictionary to include: an impression of the existence or presence of; belief tentatively without clear grounds; being inclined to think; being inclined to mentally accuse or doubt innocence and to doubt the genuineness or truth of a suspected person. In *R v Da Silva*, the Court of Appeal, in regard to an earlier provision, thought that the accused must be shown to think that there is a 'possibility, which is more than fanciful, that the relevant facts exist'; neither a vague feeling of unease nor gross negligence was sufficient as the suspicion had to be firmly grounded and targeted on specific facts.[85] The definition of suspicion in *R v Da Silva* applies equally to civil cases.[86] However, in *Squirrell Ltd v National Westminster Bank plc*[87] Laddie J rather unhelpfully noted that there was no direct authority on what 'suspect' means under the anti-money laundering provisions. He did recognise that there is no need for the suspicion to be reasonable.[88] The definition in *R v Da Silva* has though since been followed in the courts in a number of subsequent cases.[89] In practice, it may well be possible to establish the requisite state of mind from circumstantial evidence, although this is problematic. The conduct of the accused may well indicate, beyond a reasonable doubt, that he or she was in fact suspicious. It is clear that negligence is not sufficient. While culpable and gross negligence are terms that rather distort the criminal law, it may well be that self-interested negligence[90] may be a sufficient basis. Wilfully shutting one's eyes to what would have been obvious,[91] would be sufficient in

---

81   See *Windsor and Hare v Crown Prosecution Service* [2011] 1 WLR 1519 (CA).
82   See *Re Al Zayat* [2008] EW Misc 3 (CCC).
83   *R v Hall* (1985) 81 Cr App Rep 260.
84   *R v Moys* (1984) 79 Cr App Rep 72 and see also in regard to a 'great suspicion' and a refusal to believe, *R v Forsyth* [1997] 2 Cr App Rep 299.
85   [2006] EWCA Crim 1654.
86   See *K Ltd v National Westminster Bank Plc* [2007] 1 WLR 311 (CA).
87   [2005] EWHC 664 and also *K Ltd v National Westminster Bank Plc* [2006] EWCA Civ 1039. In *Hussein v Chong Fook Kam* [1970] AC 942, Lord Devlin, observed 'suspicion in its ordinary meaning is a state of conjecture or surmise where proof is lacking'. He also added that suspicion did not require admissible evidence or, for that matter, evidence.
88   Note the contrast between the subjective standards in the substantive offences in ss 327 to 329 as compared with the objective standard in the reporting obligations imposed under POCA 2002, ss 330 and 331.
89   Not just in *K Ltd v National Westminster Bank Plc*, ibid, but also *Shah v HSBC Private Bank (UK) Ltd* [2010] 3 All ER 477 (CA); *R v Afolabi* [2009] EWCA Crim 2879; and *Parvizi v Barclays Bank plc* (Unreported) 1 May 2014, QBD case number HC13A02291). In *K Ltd*, the Court also noted in the context of s 328 that 'the existence of suspicion is a subjective fact'.
90   See for example, albeit in a rather different context, *Daniels v Daniels* [1978] 2 WLR 73 discussed in B. Rider 'Amiable Lunatics and the Rule in Foss v Harbottle' (1978) CLJ 270.
91   See for example Millett J's comments in *AGIP v Jackson* (1990) Ch 265, affirmed (1991) Ch 547, see at 7.48 above.

most cases. An accused who deliberately prevented himself acquiring certain knowledge, would, in the vast majority of situations, be doing so because he suspected the truth. Having said all this, the notion of suspicion is a difficult one, especially for the criminal law.[92]

COMPLIANCE

7.53 Mention has been made of the importance of secondary legislation in this area of the law, particularly in regard to what might be described as compliance issues. The legislation requires those within the regulated sector and in many respects those outside, to establish procedures for identifying and knowing clients (Know Your Client – KYC) and others with whom one deals, the recording or relevant information, training of staff and the development and implementation of procedures for monitoring, reporting and handling suspicions.[93] As has already been pointed out, the actual requirements differ, at least in emphasis, from one business or profession to another. It is also the case that the requirements, in law and good practice, differ in regard to whether one is considering, for example, serious crime, market abuse,[94] corruption, tax fraud or terrorist related activity. Added to this is the need to incorporate into such systems and procedures provisions to address other areas of legal and other risk, such as that presented by restitutory actions or proceedings for the interdiction of property.[95] There has been concern that the burdens placed on particularly financial institutions are not cost effective and produce little of real value in discouraging crime or in assisting law enforcement. This was a concern that was taken up by the Financial Services Authority.[96] The FSA abandoned its detailed and prescriptive rules relating to money laundering in favour of a risk-based approach, which placed the burden on particular businesses to identify and address the peculiar risks facing them. Consequently, while the FCA (the FSA's successor for this part of the FSA's role) was concerned to take action, including enforcement action,[97] where records are not adequately maintained, or there is a failure of KYC, in practice it is concerned with failure to establish and adequately operate and supervise systems.

---

92   While Courts generally take the view that it is wrong to try and define concepts such as knowledge and belief for juries (see *R v Harris* (1986) 84 Cr App Rep 75 and in particular *R v Smith* (1976) 64 Cr App Rep 217), 'where much reference is made to suspicion, it will be prudent to give (a direction)' to the jury, *R v Toor* (1986) 85 Cr App Rep 116.

93   See Chapter 12 and S Bazley and A Haynes, Financial Services Authority Regulation and Risk-based Compliance, (2nd edn) (Tottel 2007), and Money Laundering and Terrorist Financing, Reporting Officer's Reference Guide 2007 (British Bankers Association), in particular the Joint Money Laundering Steering Group Guidelines, www.jmlsg.org.uk, and the website of the International Compliance Association www.int-comp.com.

94   In particular note FSMA, s 131A in regard to protected disclosures.

95   See generally P Birks (ed), *Laundering and Tracing* (Oxford University Press 1995) and J Ulph, *Commercial Fraud* (Oxford University Press 2006), Part B.

96   See for example, P Robinson, *The Fight Against Money Laundering; Promoting Effectiveness*, 22 June 2005. Reference should be made to the FSA website www.fsa.gov. uk. See also *Anti-money Laundering current customer review cost benefit analysis: Report prepared by Pricewaterhouse Coopers for the FSA* (2003), *FSA and Anti-Money Laundering Requirements; Costs, Benefits and Perceptions* (X/Yen, 2005), Corporation of the City of London.

97   See for an early example, Final Notice: The Governor and Company of the Bank of Ireland, 31 August 2004, FSA.

7.54   A tension that financial institutions face under the POCA 2002 regime is that on the one hand they have a contractual duty to their client and on the other they have a duty not to tip their client off, as set out above. How should a financial institution deal with this tension and what can they say to their client if freezing their account for 7 working days or 31 calendar days thereafter? This question has been looked at in a succession of cases.

7.55   In *Squirrell Ltd v National Westminster Bank Plc*,[98] the claimant lodged an application nine days after its account was frozen pursuant to a SAR made by the bank. The legal action was taken after the bank declined to unblock the bank account, providing the claimant with no explanation for its decision. The claim was for an order that the bank accounts be unfrozen. The bank stated that it wished to comply with its client's instructions but it was forced to block them because of the provisions of section 328(1) and because of the anti-tip off provisions, it could not explain its actions. HMCE intervened in the proceedings. It was investigating possible VAT offences. Before examining the law in his judgment, Laddie J noted that: 'I should say that I have some sympathy for parties in Squirrell's position. It is not proved or indeed alleged that it or any of its associates has committed any offence. It, like me, has been shown no evidence raising even a prima facie case that it or any of its associates has done anything wrong. For all I know it may be entirely innocent of any wrongdoing. Yet, if POCA 2002 has the effect contended for by Natwest and HMCE, the former was obliged to close down the account, with possible severe economic damage to Squirrell.' Despite finding that on the material before the court, there was nothing to justify concluding that the bank account held criminal property, Laddie J found that the course adopted by NatWest was 'unimpeachable. It did precisely what this legislation intended it to do'.

7.56   The rationale behind and proportionality of the legislative position was explained by Longmore LJ in *K Ltd v National Westminster Bank Plc*,[99] who found that:

> 'The truth is that Parliament has struck a precise and workable balance of conflicting interests in the 2002 Act. It is, of course, true that to intervene between a banker and his customer in the performance of the contract of mandate is a serious interference with the free flow of trade. But Parliament has considered that a limited interference is to be tolerated in preference to allowing the undoubted evil of money-laundering to run rife in the commercial community. The fact that the interference lasts only for 7 working days in what we were told were the majority of cases and a further 31 days only, unless the relevant authority goes to the length of applying to the court for a Restraint Order when all cards will have to be on the table in any event, shows that the interference with freedom of trade is limited. Many people would think that a reasonable balance has been struck".

7.57   In *K Ltd*, the claimant raised more developed arguments than those in *Squirrell Ltd*. It was submitted that if the bank was going to rely on any suspicion that the money in the customer's account was criminal property, it should have given admissible evidence to the court of any such suspicion. It was argued that a solicitor's letter which baldly stated that the Bank had made a disclosure was insufficient and that if there had been admissible evidence

98   [2006] 1 WLR 637 (Ch).
99   [2007] 1 WLR 311.

before the court, the maker of the statement could be cross-examined on the question whether he did actually entertain a suspicion and (perhaps) whether there were any grounds for such suspicion. Otherwise, it was argued, a customer's account could be effectively frozen even if a suspicion had not been entertained. It was further submitted that the claimant was deprived of access to a court in breach of Article 6 of the ECHR and deprived of his possessions under Article 1 Protocol 1.

7.58 On these submissions, Longmore LJ again found that the bank complied lawfully and properly complied. It would be a fruitless exercise to cross-examine the solicitor about the existence of the bank's suspicion. There was no mechanism whereby any officer of the bank can be required to attend for cross-examination since there was no provision enabling the relevant person to give evidence of his suspicion. It may well have been the intention of the statute to protect those having a suspicion and reporting that suspicion to the authorities from being identified and any cross-examination of a bank employee would, in fact, be almost as pointless as cross-examination of a bank's solicitor. Once the employee confirmed that he had a suspicion, any judge would be highly likely to find that he did indeed have that suspicion. Any cross-examination would be bound to decline into an argument whether what the employee thought could amount in law to a suspicion, which is not a proper matter for cross-examination at all. From an ECHR perspective, the limited interference was found to be proportionate and in the public interest.

7.59 The law in this area developed further in the case of *Shah v HSBC Private Bank (UK) Limited*.[100] In this case the claimant and his wife sought damages against the bank for failure to comply with his instructions and for other breaches of duty. Unlike most previous decisions, this case raised for the first time the question as to whether the same considerations applied to an action for damages for breach of contract or duty which fell to be resolved well after the time within which consent to transact had to be given or a restraint order applied for. Longmore LJ held that in these circumstances, the claimant could require the bank to prove its case that it had the relevant suspicion and be entitled to pursue the case to trial so that the bank can make good its contention in this respect and that: 'By the time of any trial the dust will have settled and it is most unlikely that the tipping-off provision will continue to be relevant. It will also almost certainly be known whether any investigation is or might be taking place which any disclosure by admissible evidence in court proceedings would be likely to prejudice within section 333(1). If any such investigation is occurring (or is likely to occur) the court can be informed of that matter in an admissible manner.' The difficult position of the bank was, however, acknowledged, namely that 'the 2002 Act has put banks in a most unenviable position. They are at risk of criminal prosecution if they entertain suspicions but do not report them or, if they report them, and then nevertheless carry out their customer's instructions without authorisation. If they act as instructed, their customers are likely to become incensed and some of those so incensed may begin litigation. But it cannot be right that proper litigation should be summarily dismissed without any appropriate inquiry of any kind. The normal procedures of the court are not to be side-stepped merely because Parliament has enacted stringent measures to inhibit the notorious evil of money-laundering, unless there is express statutory provision to that effect'.

---

100 [2010] 3 All ER 477 (CA). See also 14.16 note 64 below.

7.60   Two years later, this matter was put to the test in further litigation between the same parties[101] and the bank's nominated officer had to give evidence for six days, being cross-examined at length. Supperstone J found that he was 'left in no doubt' that the nominated officer 'honestly and genuinely suspected that the funds were criminal property when he submitted his report'. He did not act in bad faith and was a patently honest witness. There was an implied term in the contract permitting the defendant bank to refuse to execute payment instructions in the absence of appropriate consent under section 335 where it suspected a transaction constituted money laundering. So far as providing the claimant with information was concerned, there was a further implied term between the claimant and the defendant bank, permitting the defendant to refuse to provide information where it might, in providing that information, contravene the banks duties under sections 333 and 342 of the POCA 2002, so the bank was not under a duty to provide the information sought.

7.61   Finally, in *Parvizi v Barclays Bank Plc*,[102] the relevant bank employee was again cross-examined in court outside of the relevant period where tipping off might have been in issue. Master Bragge dealt with the burden of proof in such cases, accepting that:'a claim by a customer that its bank has failed to carry out instructions will be usually a strong claim in contract. The burden of proof that the implied term, which effectively is what is in issue here, operates because a suspicion is on the bank, because, as I observed in the course of argument, only the bank can explain its position.' A frontline monitoring analyst in the anti-money laundering team gave made a witness statement. This type of material had not been made available in the *Shah v HSBC Private Bank (UK) Ltd* and although there was an arguable lack of reasoning in some of what the analyst said, the evidence still established a clear belief by her of a relevant suspicion that was not simply fanciful. There was no real prospect of the case being made out at trial and the claim was struck out.

7.62   In summary, these cases highlight the tensions that the bank faces between when complying with its statutory and contractual obligations. It is clear that once a suspicious activity report is made, that during the period before consent is granted or a restraint order is made, then the bank is required to give its client no reason for suspending his account should this constitute a tipping off offence. This does not, however, absolve the bank of being challenged as to its actions or as to why it held such a suspicion and these matters can be contested at a trial after the Bank is no longer at risk of committing an offence in defending its actions.

CONFISCATION

7.63   It is essential to remove from defendants the value of their proceeds of crime, as the incentive to commit the crime must be removed upon conviction. Without powers to confiscate at the end of a criminal trial, defendants may often be able to retain their proceeds of crime[103].

---

101   *Shah v HSBC Private Bank (UK) Ltd* [2009] EWHC 79 (QB).
102   (Unreported) 1 May 2014, QBD case number HC13A02291.
103   The power to confiscate goes much further than the power to compensate. For example, in confiscation proceedings, the value of any tainted gifts made by the defendant can be recovered from the recipients of those gifts, whereas a compensation order can only be based upon the defendant's means to pay.

7.64   The purpose of the confiscation regime is to resolve this issue. It is to ensure that criminals (and especially professional criminals engaged in serious organised crime) do not profit from their crimes, and it sends a strong deterrent message to that effect.[104]

7.65   The effectiveness of the confiscation regime has been questioned in recent years. In particular, there has been considerable concern about recovery levels and the Parliamentary Accounts Committee[105] and the National Audit Office[106] have both been at the forefront of these discussions. Since these discussions, there has been significant legislative change to strengthen the confiscation regime.[107] What effect these changes will have remain to be seen.

7.66   The process for making a confiscation order is as follows:

7.67   Confiscation proceedings can be initiated either by the prosecutor or the court.[108] The court has a discretion as to whether or not it institutes proceedings but when initiated by the prosecutor, the court is obliged to follow the statutory process[109] and can only reduce the amount of a confiscation order where it is necessary to do so to make the confiscation order proportionate.[110]

7.68   The first question that the court must ask itself is whether or not the defendant has a criminal lifestyle.[111]

7.69   A defendant has a criminal lifestyle if (a) he is convicted of a Schedule 2 offence;[112] (b) if the defendant is convicted of four offences or more on the indictment from which the defendant has benefited, cumulatively having a value of £5,000 or more;[113] or (c) if the offence is committed over a period of at least six months and the defendant has benefited in the value of £5,000 or more.[114]

7.70   If applying the above test, the court finds that the defendant has a criminal lifestyle then the court must decide whether the defendant has benefited from his general criminal conduct.[115] If the defendant does not have a criminal lifestyle then the court must decide whether the defendant has benefited from his particular criminal conduct.[116]

---

104   *R v Waya* [2013] 1 AC 294 (SC).
105   Public Accounts Committee "Confiscation Orders: Forty-ninth Report of Session 2013–14" (2014) House of Commons, available at http://www.publications.parliament.uk/pa/cm201314/cmselect/cmpubacc/942/942.pdf
106   For the 2013 National Audit Office report, see http://www.nao.org.uk/wp-content/uploads/2013/12/10318-001-Confiscation-Book.pdf in which the key facts were headed by the following: '26p estimated amount confiscated for every £100 of criminal proceeds in 2012–13', '£133m collected by enforcement agencies from confiscation orders in 2012–13' and '£102m our estimated annual cost of the end-to-end confiscation order process'.
107   Part 1 of the Serious Crime Act 2015, allowing for third party disputes to be resolved earlier at the confiscation stage rather than at enforcement, increasing default terms and removing early release for the offenders with the largest orders, reducing the period that can be given for time to pay and lowering the test for a restraint order to be imposed.
108   POCA 2002, s 6(3). All statutory sections referenced in the confiscation section of this chapter are in relation to POCA 2002 unless otherwise stated.
109   Sections 6(1) and (5).
110   See *R v Waya* [2013] 1 AC294 (SC).
111   Section 6(4).
112   Which include ss 327 (concealment etc) and 328 (arrangement) money laundering offences.
113   This is referred to as conduct forming part of a course of criminal activity.
114   Section 75.
115   Ibid.
116   Ibid.

7.71 Benefit in particular criminal conduct cases includes benefit from the offences the defendant was convicted of and offences which the court will be taking into consideration in deciding his sentence.[117]

7.72 In particular criminal conduct cases, the court must first ask what has the defendant obtained as a result of or in connection with his criminal conduct[118] and then go on to assess the value of the property obtained.[119] This may produce some interesting results. Take by way of example a case involving market abuse, where the defendant gave inside information to his son so that his son could make a profit trading shares. The son may have benefited from his trading, but may not have realised that the information was inside information. The father will argue that he obtained nothing from his offence; he committed the offence so that his son could benefit, not so that he could. In this situation, it may be that no confiscation order can be made against the father in relation to his son's gains.[120]

7.73 A similar issue may arise where a company is involved in an offence. It is trite law that a company has separate legal personality to its shareholders[121] and that shareholders do not own company property. Where a defendant has been convicted of an offence which his company has benefited from, it is necessary to apply the 'concealment principle'.[122] A court may treat company property as if it were the defendant's property in confiscation proceedings where an offender: (a) attempts to shelter behind a corporate façade, or veil to hide his crime and his benefits from it; (b) does acts in the name of a company which constitute a criminal offence which leads to the offender's conviction; or (c) the transaction or business structures constitute a 'device', 'cloak' or 'sham', ie an attempt to disguise the true nature of the transaction or structure so as to deceive third parties or the court.[123]

7.74 It is also important to note that 'obtains' does not mean 'retains'. It makes no difference if the property is subsequently lost, destroyed or damaged.[124] Once the defendant has obtained the property he benefits from it and the value of that benefit[125] is the higher of its value when first obtained[126] and its value at the date of the confiscation hearing.[127] Again, this can produce some interesting results. In *R v Rigby and Bailey*,[128] a company's share price rose after a false trading statement was made. Rigby's shares rose in value

---

117 Section 76(3).
118 Whether that is the obtaining of property or the obtaining of a pecuniary advantage (such as the evasion of a tax liability). For the relevant provisions see s 75(4)–(5), (7),
119 These are simplifications of the first two questions that the court is required to ask taken from the Endnote to *R v May* [2008] 1 AC 1028 (HL).
120 It may be that civil recovery is an option against the son's profits, by way of an action against criminal property.
121 See *Salomon v A Salomon and Co Ltd* [1897] AC 22 (HL) and see 2.42 et seq above and at 15.14 below.
122 See *R v Sale* [2014] 1 WLR 663 (CA) which applied the principles of the civil law case *Petrodel Resources Ltd v Prest* [2013] 2 AC 415 (SC).
123 See *R v Sale*, ibid, in which it was found that the activities of both the company and the appellant (who corruptly procured a contract for the benefit of the company which he owned 100%) were so interlinked as to be indivisible.
124 See *R v Islam* [2009] 1 AC 706 (HL).
125 See s 80.
126 Adjusted to take account of later changes in the value of money.
127 Including the value of any property that might directly or indirectly represent the property obtained.
128 [2006] 1 WLR 3067 (CA).

by around £250,000. The FSA argued that Rigby benefited by this sum even though he did not sell any of the shares and even though the share price subsequently collapsed. The Court of Appeal found that there was no proper sense in which Rigby obtained a benefit or derived a pecuniary advantage constituted by the temporary unrealised increase in the share price. The increase in value was, for Rigby, purely notional and soon disappeared. The Court of Appeal also quashed the finding that the defendant's benefited by their salaries. They were 'employed despite the offence, not because of it. There was a narrative connection between the offence and their continued employment, but no sufficient causal link'.

7.75 Where property is obtained as a result of a joint criminal enterprise, it will often be appropriate for a court to hold that each of the conspirators 'obtained' the whole of that property.[129] A paid hand in the enterprise, eg cash courier, custodian or other minor contributor; or a latecomer to a conspiracy in which nothing was obtained after his arrival, will not however have jointly obtained the whole of the property.[130] The facts of each case must therefore be carefully analysed.

7.76 General criminal conduct includes all a defendant's criminal conduct committed at any point in time.[131] This will include the indictment benefit, any benefit that can be proven using the assumptions and any other criminality that the prosecution can prove.

7.77 Section 10 sets out the assumptions that can be made. Any property transferred to the defendant or expended by the defendant at any time after the relevant day, can be assumed to be obtained by him as a result of his general criminal conduct. In addition, any property held by the defendant at any time after the date of conviction can be assumed to have been obtained by him as a result of his general criminal conduct. Finally, when valuing any property obtained by the defendant, it can be assumed that he obtained it free of any other interests in it. The assumption will be made unless incorrect or unless there would be a serious risk of injustice if the assumption were to be made.[132]

7.78 The relevant day for the property transferred and expenditure assumptions is six years before the proceedings for the offence started.[133] If there are two or more offences and proceedings for them were started on different days, then the relevant day is the earliest of those days. If, however, a confiscation order has already been made against the defendant during the six year period, the relevant day is the day when the defendant's benefit was last calculated and the assumptions do not apply against any property held on or before the previous confiscation order date.

---

129 See *R v Ahmad* [2015] AC 299 (SC). Apportionment as a general principle was rejected in the linked case of *R v Fields*.
130 See *R v May*, above, though a courier putting monies through his bank account will benefit because unlike a cash courier there is a thing in action in favour of the defendant rather than him being a mere bailee, see *R v Allpress* [2009] 2 Cr App Rep (S) 58 (CA).
131 Section 76(2).
132 Section 10(6). The defendant must produce clear and cogent evidence; vague and generalised assertions will not suffice, see *R v Williams* [2007] EWCA Crim 1768. The application of the assumptions is not incompatible with the ECHR, see *R v Benjafield and Rezvi* [2003] 1 AC 1099 (HL); *Phillips v United Kingdom (41087/98)* 11 BHRC 280.
133 Section 10(8).

7.79 When looking at general criminal conduct, it is important to take into account the varying standards of proof.

(a) The indictment offences will already have been proved to the criminal standard by virtue of the convictions.

(b) For criminal offences not on the indictment, the prosecution must prove the offence to the criminal standard[134].

(c) The criminal standard of proof does not however apply to the assumptions. When the court makes the statutory assumptions, the prosecution need only show that the defendant has received, expended, or held property to the civil standard.[135] The burden is then on the defendant on the civil standard to displace the assumptions.

So differing standards need to be applied to differing parts of the general criminal conduct.

7.80 After determining the defendant's benefit, the court must then consider the 'available amount'.[136] The available amount is the total value of all the free property[137] held by the defendant (minus priority obligations[138]), plus the value of the tainted gifts that the defendant has made.[139]

7.81 The 'recoverable amount'[140] is then made in the value of the defendant's benefit unless defendant can show that the available amount is less than his benefit.[141] This is because whatever the defendant's benefit, the defendant cannot be expected to repay monies that he does not have.

7.82 The court must then make a confiscation order in the value of the recoverable amount,[142] unless (a) a victim has started or intends to start civil proceedings against the defendant in relation to the criminal conduct, in which case the duty to make a confiscation order in the recoverable amount becomes a discretionary power; or (b) it would be disproportionate to make a confiscation order in the recoverable amount, in which case the court should refuse to make a confiscation order in that sum but accede only to an application for such sum as would be proportionate.[143]

---

134 See *R v Briggs-Price* [2009] 1 AC 1026 (HL).
135 See *R v Whittington* [2010] 1 Cr App R (S) 83 (CA).
136 Section 9.
137 Pursuant to s 82, free property is property not already subject to certain other court orders, eg forfeiture or deprivation orders. Property includes property in which the defendant merely has an interest, see s 84.
138 A priority obligation is the amount due in respect of a previous fine or court order as well as well as any sum that would be a preferential debt if bankrupt. This importantly *includes* secured loans, but *excludes* unsecured loans.
139 A gift is any transfer of property by the defendant for significantly less consideration than the value of the property at the time of the transfer, see s 78. The gift is tainted if made at any time after either (a) six years before criminal proceedings began in criminal lifestyle cases or (b) the offence in particular criminal conduct cases, see s 77. There is no requirement for a tainted gift to be the proceeds of crime. A tainted gift includes a gift of property not derived from criminal conduct.
140 Section 7.
141 Section 7(2). This reverse burden upon the defendant is to the civil standard. The imposition of the reverse burden regarding the available amount is ECHR compatible, see *Grayson and Barnham v United Kingdom* (2009) 48 E.H.R.R. 30.
142 Section 6(5).
143 See *R v Waya*, above.

7.83   The issue of proportionality, introduced by *R v Waya*[144] and now imposed on a statutory basis,[145] is one that has brought a wave of litigation in the appeal courts where every tenet of confiscation law is being re-tested to see if it is proportionate to confiscate the amount of the benefit determined under the Act.[146]

7.84   The Supreme Court has made it clear however that the introduction of proportionality is not the reintroduction of discretion into the confiscation process.[147] What then is proportionality? To answer this one must consider the purpose of confiscation proceedings, which is to recover the financial benefit that the offender has obtained from his criminal conduct. A confiscation order must bear a proportionate relationship to this purpose and a confiscation order should not operate as if it were an additional fine.[148]

7.85   A confiscation order might be disproportionate where property has already been restored to the victim,[149] if joint obtainers each have to repay the value of the amount jointly obtained,[150] where a corruptly procured contract is properly performed,[151] or where the underlying activity is lawful.[152]

7.86   In regulatory offences, the critical question is as follows: what is the conduct made criminal by the statute – is it the activity itself; or is it the failure to register, or obtain a licence for, the activity? There is a narrow but critical distinction to be made between an offence that prohibits and makes criminal the very activity admitted by the offender or proved against him and an offence in failing to obtain a licence to carry out an activity otherwise lawful. In the former case, the defendant benefits by the proceeds received. In the latter case, the defendant does not benefit at all by his offending.[153]

7.87   The confiscation hearing can be postponed until after sentence, however any postponed hearings must take place within two years of conviction

144   See *R v Waya*, above.
145   Introduced into s 6(5) by virtue of para 19 of Sch 4 of the Serious Crime Act 2015.
146   See eg *R v Ahmad*, above, which was in the Supreme Court on whether it is proportionate to confiscate from multiple defendants; *R v Kakkad* [2015] EWCA Crim 385 (whether it is proportionate to confiscate in the value of drugs that have already been seized by the police); *R v Harvey* [2014] 1 WLR 124 (CA), now in the Supreme Court with judgment awaited as to whether or not it is proportionate to confiscate in the value of sums since accounted for to the government by way of VAT. Another key case citing *Waya* was *Paulet v United Kingdom (6219/08)* 37 BHRC 695, looking at whether or not it was proportionate to confiscate the wages of an illegal immigrant who properly performed the work his contractual (but fraudulently obtained) work. These are just a select few of the cases that have since been before the appeal courts.
147   See *R v Waya*, above.
148   See *R v Waya*, above.
149   See *R v Waya*, above.
150   See *R v Ahmad*, above.
151   See *R v Sale* [2014] 1 WLR 663 (CA).
152   See *R v Beazley* [2013] 1 WLR 3331 (CA); *R v Parsons* [2014] EWCA Crim 2500; *R v King* [2014] 2 Cr App R (S) 54 and *R v Hussain* [2014] EWCA Crim 2344, as well as the cases in the footnote below.
153   See *R v McDowell and Singh* [2015] 2 Cr App R (S) 14 (CA). The former conviction related to trading in arms without the appropriate licence and the underlying activity was unlawful. The latter conviction was scrap metal dealing without registering and the underlying activity was said to be lawful, although this conclusion is not one easily distinguishable on the facts or reconcilable with the principle; see also *R v JGE Commercials Limited* [2015] EWCA Crim 1048, a breach of the money laundering regulations case where the failure to cease the transaction without complying with customer due diligence was said to be on the McDowell side of the line, ie underlying activity was unlawful. These three cases are difficult to reconcile with each other.

without there being exceptional circumstances.[154] Confiscation hearings may also be postponed pending an appeal against conviction; however, any postponed hearing for an appeal must take place within three months of the determination of the appeal without there being exceptional circumstances.[155]

7.88 Confiscation hearings are more civil than criminal. Thus, the judge can decide issues on the balance of probabilities, compel the defendant to disclose documents, draw adverse inferences from the absence of evidence, and rely on hearsay evidence.[156]

7.89 Where compensation is an issue for the court, it must first of all make the confiscation order.[157] Having made the appropriate confiscation order, the court then ignores it when deciding the appropriate compensation order.[158] If, having made both orders, the defendant has not got the means to pay both compensation and confiscation orders, the court must direct that compensation be paid out of confiscation in the amount of the shortfall.[159] If on the other hand, the defendant does have the means to pay both orders, then he is at risk of paying the same sum twice for the same offence; once in compensation and once in confiscation and it would be disproportionate to have the certainty of double payment.[160] To avoid this outcome the defendant must guarantee payment at the confiscation hearing, but there may be some limited exceptions requiring a brief adjournment, for example where there is a genuine dispute about the amount to be confiscated which requires a judicial ruling. What a court should not entertain, because there is no need to do so, are expressions of well-meaning intentions on behalf of a defendant which are not backed by assurance of repayment. Still less is a court likely to be receptive to pleas to adjourn the confiscation hearing for the defendant to seek ways of making repayment.

7.90 The court must also make the confiscation order before making a fine or an order for costs.[161]

7.91 Once a confiscation order is made, a default sentence of up to 14 years can be imposed, consecutive to the defendant's substantive term of imprisonment, to be activated in default of payment. The default sentence lengths have recently been strengthened.[162] There are a number of other options available to the prosecutor and courts to enforce the confiscation order, including the appointment of a receiver.[163] There is also the power to vary the benefit and available amount findings at a later date.[164]

7.92 Finally, in order to preserve assets that might be needed to satisfy a confiscation order that has or which may be made, the prosecutor may apply to the Crown Court for a restraint order to be imposed.[165] A restraint order has

154 Section 14.
155 Ibid.
156 See *R v Ahmad*, above.
157 Sections 13(2) and 13(3)(a).
158 Section 13(4).
159 See section 13(5)–(6)
160 See *R v Jawad* [2014] 1 Cr App R (S) 16 (CA) for this point and the remainder of the points in this paragraph.
161 See s 13(2).
162 Section 10 of the Serious Crime Act 2015.
163 Sections 54–57.
164 Sections 19–25.
165 Sections 40–47. A restraint order may be imposed from the outset of a criminal investigation and there must be reasonable cause to suspect that the defendant has benefited from his criminal conduct. This is a lower test introduced under s 11 of the Serious Crime Act 2015, before which the test was reasonable cause to believe.

the effect of prohibiting any specified person from dealing with any realisable property held by him.[166] Realisable property is any free property held by the defendant as well as any free property held by the recipient of a tainted gift.[167] Restraint orders can have worldwide effect *in personam* and can bite on assets whether or not the realisable property is specified in the restraint order or held in the name of the defendant.

TERRORIST FINANCE

7.93   It has long been recognised, particularly in the context of terrorist activity in Northern Ireland and more recently in the context of the Global War on Terror, that there is value in attempting to disrupt the flow of funds to terrorist organisations. There is also value in being able to subject such organisations to financial investigation and profiling. There is, however, an important difference between attempting to interdict the funds of terrorist organisations and those of organised crime. Generally speaking a significant proportion of the funding for criminal and other activity by organised crime will be derived from criminal activity. In other words, it will be the proceeds of crime. However, while terrorists may be indistinguishable from organised crime in what they do, some organisations derive their financial support from legitimate sources. To take action against such funds, it is necessary to 'taint' them by virtue of the purpose for which they are given. Thus, it is the intention or at least, knowledge of the donor that renders the property 'criminal property'. This is an important difference.

7.94   The principle offences in regard to terrorist funds are found in the Terrorism Act 2000 (TA 2000), as amended.[168] Section 1 defines terrorism as having three parts. First there must be the use or threat of action involving serious violence against a person, serious damage to property, which endangers a person's life other than that of the person committing the action, which creates a serious risk to the health or safety of the public or a section of the public, or which is designed seriously to interfere with or seriously to disrupt an electronic system. Secondly, the use or threat must be designed to influence the government or an international governmental organisation or to intimidate the public or a section of the public, however where the action involves the use of firearms or explosives it is terrorism whether or not the use or threat is designed to have such influence. Thirdly, the use or threat must be made for the purpose of advancing a political, religious, racial or ideological cause. It is of note that action, person, property, public and government are all given extra-territorial definitions.[169]

---

166   Section 41(1).
167   Section 83.
168   SI 2001/3365. See also *Review of Safeguards to Protect the Charitable Sector from Terrorist Abuse; A Consultation Document*, (2007), Home Office. There are provisions in the anti-terrorist law that may be relevant in the context preparatory activity and investigation, see generally C. Walker, *The Anti-Terrorism Legislation* (Oxford University Press 2002) and A. Jones, R. Bowers and H. Lodge, *The Terrorism Act 2006* (Oxford University Press 2006). See also R. Cranston, *The Funding of Terror, The Legal implications of the Financial War on Terror* (Society of Advanced Legal Studies 2002).
169   See TA 2000, s 1(5). As a result, it is important to note that s 1 'does not specify that the ambit of its protection is limited to countries abroad with governments of any particular type or possessed of what we, with our fortunate traditions, would regard as the desirable characteristics of representative government. There is no list or Schedule or

7.95   There are offences in relation to proscribed organisations. Section 11 of the Act makes it an offence to belong to a proscribed organisation. Section 12 of the Act makes it an offence to provide support for a proscribed organisation. Section 13 of the Act makes it an offence to wear the uniform of a proscribed organisation, whether in the form of clothing or by means of a badge or something of that kind implying membership or support.

7.96   There are further offences that relate generally to terrorist property and are not limited to proscribed organisations. Section 14 defines terrorist property as '(a) money or other property which is likely to be used for the purposes of terrorism (including any resources of a proscribed organisation), (b) proceeds of the commission of acts of terrorism, and (c) proceeds of acts carried out for the purposes of terrorism'. This definition is wider that that under sections 327–329 of POCA 2002 as it includes forward looking acts whereas the definition of criminal property under section 327 looks backwards.[170] Section 14(2)(b) further provides that any money or other property which is applied or made available or is to be applied or made available for use by such an organisation is also included. It is also made clear that the proceeds of the commission of acts of terrorism as well as the proceeds of acts carried out for the purposes of terrorism will be considered to be terrorist property. In this context, the proceeds of such crimes have a similarly wide meaning to that of 'criminal property' in the general anti-money laundering law.

7.97   Raising funds and providing property for terrorism is outlawed in section 15 of the Act. Under section 15(1) a person commits an offence if he invites another to provide money or other property and intends that it should be used, or has reasonable cause to suspect that it may be used for the purposes of terrorism. Section 15(2) renders it a crime[171] to receive money or other property with the intention that it will be used for the purposes of terrorism. It is also an offence to receive funds or property where there is reasonable cause to suspect that it will be so used. Section 15(3) renders the financing of terror a crime, in that a person commits a crime if he provides money or other property and knows or has reasonable cause to suspect that it will or may be used for the purposes of terrorism. It is made clear that a reference to the provision of funds or other property includes it being lent or otherwise made available, whether or not for consideration. The objective aspect to this crime should be noted.

7.98   Section 16 provides that a person commits an offence if he uses money or other property for the purposes of terrorism. The section 16 offence

statutory instrument which identifies the countries whose governments are included within section 1(4)(d) or excluded from the application of the Act. Finally, the legislation does not exempt, nor make an exception, nor create a defence for, nor exculpate what some would describe as terrorism in a just cause. Such a concept is foreign to the Act. Terrorism is terrorism, whatever the motives of the perpetrators', see *R v F* [2007] QB 960 (CA). Also of note is *R v Gul* [2012] 1 WLR 3432 (CA), in which it was held that 'there is nothing in international law which would exempt those engaged in attacks on the military during the course of an insurgency from the definition of terrorism'. In *Gul* the Court of Appeal also found that 'although it is clear that in all forms of armed conflict civilians should not be attacked, that does not amount to state practice or opinio juris that those who attack military personnel in non international armed conflict cannot be designated as terrorists'.
170   See *R v GH* [2015] 1 WLR 2126 (SC).
171   It is not a crime under this Act for council tax to be raised. The applicant in *The Queen on the Application of Coverdale v Hastings Magistrates Court* [2014] EWHC 2348 (Admin) had argued that the money when collected would be transferred to central government and then reallocated to the councils and that in this way, the council tax supported the Government in waging wars.

is committed if a person possesses money or other property, and intends that it should be used, or has reasonable cause to suspect that it may be used, for the purposes of terrorism. The Section 16 offences are not incompatible with the right to freedom of expression[172].

7.99   Section 17 makes it an offence to enter into or become concerned in a funding arrangement where there is reasonable cause to suspect that the funds will or may be used for the purposes of terrorism.[173] The test is objective and 'the proper approach is to examine the evidence in relation to the appellant's actings and state of knowledge and ask whether a reasonable person in the position of the appellant would suspect that the payments would or might be used for the purposes of terrorism'.[174]

7.100   Section 17A makes it an offence for insurers under insurance contracts to make certain payments in respect of any money or other property that has been, or is to be, handed over in response to a demand made wholly or partly for the purposes of terrorism, and where the insurer or the person authorising the payment on the insurer's behalf knows or has reasonable cause to suspect that the money or other property has been, or is to be, handed over in response to such a demand. A director, manager, secretary or other similar officer of the body corporate may also commit an offence if a Section 17A offence was committed with their connivance or if attributable to their neglect.

7.101   Section 18 provides that it is a crime to become concerned in an arrangement which facilitates the retention or control of terrorist property by or on behalf of another whether this is done by concealment, removal from the jurisdiction, transfer to nominees, or in any other manner. However, an accused is entitled to a defence if he can prove that he did not know and had no reasonable cause to suspect that the arrangement related to terrorist property. It should be noted that it is not enough for the defence to raise this issue it must actually be proved, albeit to the civil standard of proof.

7.102   Section 19 imposes a duty on those who acquire information, as a result of it coming to their attention in the course of a trade, business, profession or employment. Where such a person believes or suspects that another person has committed an offence under sections 15 to 18 of the Act and bases his belief or suspicion on information which comes to his or her attention in the course of a trade, profession or business, or in the course of his employment (whether or not in the course of a trade, profession or business, then the person commits an offence if he or she does not report his or her belief or suspicion and the information upon which it is based as soon as is reasonably practicable to the police or an officer of the NCA authorised for this purpose.[175]

---

172   It was held in *O'Driscoll v The Secretary of State for the Home Department* [2003] ACD 35 that 'If there is no question about the terrorist nature of the organisation it is difficult to see why section 16 should be regarded as disproportionate, bearing in mind the need for proof of a guilty mind and the extent of the criminal court's powers in relation to sentence. This section is not about freedom of expression. It is about knowingly providing money or other property to support a proscribed organisation, and so long as the organisation has been properly proscribed the section cannot in my judgment be regarded as disproportionate.'
173   It is not a crime under this Act for council tax to be raised, see *The Queen on the Application of Coverdale v Hastings Magistrates Court*, above.
174   See *Nasserdine Menni v Her Majesty's Advocate* 2014 SCL 191 (HCJ).
175   In *Malik v Manchester Crown Court* [2008] EMLR 19 (Admin), a journalist judicially reviewing a production order could not rely upon the ground that the judge failed to take into account the privilege against self-incrimination with regards to s 19 if he did not raise that issue before the judge.

This section does not apply if the information came to the person in the course of a business in the regulated sector. It is a defence for an accused to prove that he had a reasonable excuse for not making a report or that he did in fact report his suspicions to his employer in accordance with an established compliance procedure. The obligation to disclose does not extend to professional legal advisers, in regard to information obtained in privileged circumstances, or a belief or suspicion based upon such. Of course, information relevant to furtherance of criminal activity would not be privileged, as we have seen in regard to the general law on anti-money laundering. The scope of section 19 is significantly extended by virtue of section 19(7), which provides that for the purposes of determining whether a person has committed a crime activating the obligation to report, if that person has taken an action or been in possession of a thing, and he or she would have committed an offence under sections 15 to 18 if that had taken place in the United Kingdom, he or she will for the purpose of section 19 be considered to have committed the relevant crime. There is protection from any liability arising from the restriction on the disclosure of information, for disclosures to the authorities, or in accord with compliance procedures, both generally and in regard to section 19. Of course, as we have seen, this would only provide legal protection within jurisdiction and not from actions based on, for example, the law of defamation or malicious prosecution.

7.103 Section 20 permits disclosures to a constable or an authorised NCA officer. Section 21 provides that no offence is committed under sections 15–18 if disclosure is made to a constable before he becomes involved and the authorities consent, or afterwards, on his own initiative as soon as is reasonably practicable, along the same lines as in the general anti-money laundering law. There are also similar penalties for breach of these provisions as discussed above under section 334 of the POCA 2002.

7.104 Defences are contained in sections 21ZA–21ZC to the sections 15 to 18 offences. Section 21ZA ensures that no offence is committed where there has been an arrangement with prior consent from an authorised officer. Section 21ZB ensures that no offence is committed where disclosure took place to an authorised officer after becoming involved in the arrangement and where there was a reasonable excuse for failing to make the disclosure before and where the disclosure was of the person's own initiative and as soon as reasonably practicable to be made. Section 21ZC ensures that no offence is committed where the person intended to make a disclosure and where there was a reasonable excuse for not doing so.

7.105 At sections 21A and 21D, there are similar provisions to those found at sections 330 and 333A of the POCA 2002, discussed above, creating, respectively, offences for non-disclosure in the regulated sector and for tipping off. The *mens rea* is similarly knowledge or suspicion. Section 21B contains the section on protected disclosures akin to section 337 of the POCA 2002.

7.106 Section 21C requires a constable to whom a disclosure has been made to disclose it in full as soon as practicable after it has been made to a NCA officer. Section 21C also requires a constable to whom a disclosure has been made under section 21 to disclose it in full as soon as practicable after it has been made to an authorised NCA officer.

7.107 Section 21E ensures that it is not an offence under section 21D to disclose to an employee, officer or partner of the same undertaking.

7.108   It is also not an offence by virtue of section 21E for a credit financial institution to disclose to another credit or financial institution in the same group in the European Economic Area or in a country or territory imposing equivalent money laundering standards. Similar protection applies between professional legal advisers or relevant professional advisers where those persons perform their professional activities within different undertakings that share common ownership, management or control. Section 21F ensures that these persons also do not commit section 21D offences if the disclosure relates transactions with clients or former clients or provision of services involving them both, provided the disclosure is for the purpose only of preventing an offence under the terrorist property part of the Act, where the institution or adviser to whom the disclosure is made is situated in an EEA State or in a country or territory imposing equivalent money laundering requirements; and where the institution or adviser making the disclosure and the institution or adviser to whom it is made are subject to equivalent duties of professional confidentiality and the protection of personal data (within the meaning of section 1 of the Data Protection Act 1998).

7.109   Section 21G ensures that it is not an offence under section 21D if the disclosure by a person is to the supervisory authority for that person by virtue of the Money Laundering Regulations 2007 and where the purpose of the disclosure is the detection, investigation or prosecution of a criminal offence, an investigation under the POCA 2002, or the enforcement of any order of a court under that Act. In addition, a professional legal adviser or a relevant professional adviser does not commit an offence under section 21D if the disclosure is to the adviser's client, and is made for the purpose of dissuading the client from engaging in conduct amounting to an offence.

7.110   There is a definitions section for sections 21D to 21G at section 21H, dealing with 'credit institution', 'business in the regulated sector' and other words and phrases referred to in those sections.

7.111   Section 23 permits a court to make a forfeiture order where a defendant is convicted of an offence under sections 15 to 18. The money or property must have been under the person's possession or under their control or be the property that the arrangement related to. The property must also have been used for the purposes of terrorism or intended for such use, or in sections 15(1)–(3) and 16 cases, it is enough for there to have been reasonable cause to suspect the property might have been used for those purposes. For insurance cases under section 17A, the court may order the forfeiture of the amount paid under, or purportedly under, the insurance contract. For money laundering cases under section 18, the court may order the forfeiture of the money or other property to which the arrangement in question related. Finally, where a person is convicted of an offence under any of sections 15 to 18, the court may order the forfeiture of any money or other property which wholly or partly, and directly or indirectly, is received by any person as a payment or other reward in connection with the commission of the offence.

7.112   Section 23A deals with forfeiture for other specified terrorism offences and offences with a terrorist connection. Forfeiture of money or property make be ordered after conviction if under the possession or control of the person convicted and where it had been used for the purposes of terrorism, was intended by that person that it should be used for the purposes of terrorism, or where the court believes that it will be used for the purposes of terrorism unless forfeited.

7.113   Whether forfeiting under section 23 or 23A, a court must give third parties an opportunity to be heard where they are claiming to be the owner or otherwise interested in anything which can be forfeited. The court must have regard to the value of the property, and the likely financial and other effects on the convicted person of the making of the order.

7.114   Finally, it is noted that there are civil proceedings available for the forfeiture of terrorist cash pursuant to section 1 of and Schedule 1 to the Anti-terrorism, Crime and Security Act 2001.

Chapter 8

Conflicts of interest

A FUNDAMENTAL RULE

8.1   The significance of the law relating to conflicts of interest in the control of abuse and in particular insider dealing has already been emphasised on several occasions in this work.[1] We have seen that much of the traditional fiduciary law is based on the fundamental obligation to avoid conflicts of interest and account for any benefit that results from an actual conflict of interest.[2] In this regard it is probably worth quoting Lord Herschell LC in *Bray v Ford*[3] that 'it is an inflexible rule of a Court of Equity that a person in a fiduciary position ... is not, unless otherwise expressly provided, entitled to make a profit; he is not allowed to put himself in apposition where his interest and duty conflict'. And Lord Russell of Killowen in *Regal (Hastings) Ltd v Gulliver*:[4] 'The rule of equity which insists on those, who by the use of a fiduciary position make a profit, being liable to account for that profit, in no way depends on fraud, or absence of bona fides; or upon such questions or considerations as whether the profit would or should otherwise have gone to the plaintiff, or whether the profiteer was under a duty to obtain the source of the profit for the plaintiff, or whether he took a risk or acted as he did for the benefit of the plaintiff, or whether the plaintiff has in fact been damaged or benefited by his action. The liability arises from the mere fact of the profit having, in the stated circumstances, been made. The profiteer, however, honest and well intentioned, cannot escape the risk of being called to account'. This strict rule has recently been underlined by the Supreme Court in *FHR European Ventures LLP v Cedar Capital Partners LLC*.[5] We have already considered the liability of those who abuse unpublished price sensitive information in the civil law[6] and now let us consider the 'codification' of these principles, in so far as they relate to company directors, in the Companies Act 2006.

---

1   See 2.3 *et seq* and generally C Nakajima and E Sheffield, *Conflicts of Interest and Chinese Walls* (Butterworths 2002) and L Thevenoz and R Bakar (eds), *Conflicts of Interest, Corporate Governance and Financial Markets* (Kluwer 2007).
2   See generally Chapter 2.
3   [1896] AC 44.
4   [1967] AC 152 and see 2.8 and 6.46 *et seq* above.
5   [2014] UKSC 45 and see also *In Plus Group Ltd v Pyke* [2002] EWCA Civ 370 and *Lee v Futurist Developments Ltd* [2010] EWHC 2764 (Ch).
6   See Chapter 2.

DIRECTORS AND THEIR DUTY OF LOYALTY

8.2   Section 175(1) of the Companies Act 2006 provides that 'a director of a company must avoid a situation in which he has, or can have, a direct or indirect interest that conflicts, or possibly may conflict, with the interests of the company'. It is made clear in section 175(7) that the 'no conflict rule' applies also to conflicts of duties.[7] It has been argued that all the relevant fiduciary obligations are based on this fundamental principle. Consequently, the obligation to account for secret profits is but a manifestation of this strict obligation of loyalty. This is, however, an over simplification.[8] Indeed, it is clear even in the context of directors' duties that there are at least three relatively distinct, albeit often related, situations. This is underlined by the fact that section 175(3) states that the duty set out in section 175(1) 'does not apply to a conflict of interest arising in relation to a transaction or arrangement with the company'. Self-dealing in such transactions, on the part of a director, is governed by a specific set of rules relating to disclosure, control and approval.

8.3   The common law imposed a very strict obligation on directors. Lord Cranworth LC in *Aberdeen Railway v Blaikie*[9] stated 'it is a rule of universal application that no one' having duties of a fiduciary nature 'shall be allowed to enter into engagements in which he has, or can have, a personal interest conflicting, or which possibly may conflict with the interests of those whom he is bound to protect' and 'so strictly is this principle adhered to that no question is allowed to be raised as to the fairness or unfairness of a contract so entered into ...'. To hold directors to the duties of a trustee was not practical, or perhaps in many cases in the commercial interests of the company. Consequently, despite the strict law, the courts permitted directors to deal with their own companies provided the shareholders, after full disclosure, ratified what had occurred. Indeed, in the case of prior authorisation by the shareholders, it is arguable that the potential conflict is avoided. The exigencies of business led to the courts going somewhat further and accepted that provided adequate disclosure was made to an appropriate body, determined by the company's constitutional documents, which may be merely the board of directors, the so called 'universal' rule of Lord Cranworth was effectively avoided. Commercial practice went perhaps too far and since the Companies Act 1929 there has been a statutory obligation of disclosure to the board which cannot be excluded or modified by the articles of association.[10] Section 177(1) of the Companies Act 2006 places a statutory obligation on a director who is 'in any way, directly or indirectly' interested in a proposed transaction or arrangement with his company to declare to the other directors the 'nature and extent' of the interest before the relevant arrangement is entered into. It is important to note that this obligation goes beyond contract and includes non-contractual arrangements. The purpose of this provision is to alert the

---

7   See also s 176(5) in regard to benefits from third parties.
8   See for example, *Bhullar v Bhullar* [2003] 3 BCLC 241. But note also that the courts have increasingly taken note of whether a director actually does have responsibility for the issue in hand. If there is no responsibility and influence then the courts have questioned whether equitable supervision is necessary, see *Framlington Group plc v Anderson* [1995] BCC 611, *Plus Group Ltd v Pyke* (2002) 2 BCLC 201 and *Halcyon House Ltd v Baines* [2014] EWHC 2216.
9   (1854) 2 Eq Rep 1281 and *Parker v McKenna* (1874) 10 Ch App 96 and *CMS Dolphin Ltd v Simonet* [2001] 2 BCLC 704.
10   See generally AJ Boyle *et al*, *Boyle and Birds' Company Law* (9th edn) (Jordan Publishing 2014), Chs 16 and 17.

board to the existence of a conflict and therefore obligate it to address it in the interests of the company. It follows that changes in the nature and extent of the relevant interest must also be disclosed and recorded. While the scope of this obligation is wide in so far as it includes 'indirect' interests such as a shareholding in another company with which a transaction is proposed, section 177(6)(a) provides that a director need not declare an interest 'if it cannot reasonably be regarded as likely to give rise to a conflict of interest'. Furthermore, he need not disclose any interest that his fellow directors are already aware of and 'the other directors are treated as aware of anything of which they ought reasonably to be aware' under section 177(6)(b). A similar obligation to disclose interests is imposed on directors and shadow directors by section 182 in regard to existing transactions or arrangements. It should be noted that failure to disclose existing interests, usually upon appointment, is made a specific criminal offence under section 183.

8.4 Section 180 of the Companies Act 2006 provides that compliance with the disclosure obligation means that the director will not be in breach of his duty to the company if the relevant transaction is then entered into. Compliance will also ensure that 'the transaction or arrangement is not liable to be set aside by virtue of any common law rule or equitable principle requiring the consent or approval of the members of the company'.[11] While section 178(1) of the Companies Act 2006 provides the consequences of breach of section 177 are to be the same as under the corresponding common law or equitable rules,[12] it should be noted that the imposition of a statutory obligation to disclose may well render the law of fraud relevant.[13] A dishonest failure to disclose might well constitute the offence of fraud, and connivance on the part of others might well amount to a conspiracy to defraud.[14]

8.5 The Companies Act 2006, as the previous legislation, recognises that there are certain situations where the temptation and consequent risks of self-dealing are of such significance that mere disclosure to the board is not enough. Consequently in regard to substantial property transactions[15] and loans to directors[16] and those connected with them,[17] and certain aspects of their service contracts,[18] there must be full disclosure to the shareholders and a vote in general meeting. While of importance in promoting and ensuring the integrity of directors and in certain respects other insiders, we need not address these provisions here in detail. The Act provides specific civil remedies, which while resembling the general law, are specifically honed to deal with the involvement of persons connected with the director.[19]

8.6 The other two areas of liability that arguably flow from the general rule against conflict of interest, in the context of corporate law, relate to the misuse of corporate property, information and opportunities and the making

---

11 Section 180(1). Note, however, 'this is without prejudice to any enactment, or provision of the company's constitution, requiring such consent or approval'.
12 Section 178(2) provides: 'the duties … are, accordingly, enforceable in the same way as any other fiduciary duty owed to a company by its directors'.
13 See 6.40 *et seq* above.
14 See 6.17 above.
15 See ss 190 to 196. Note in particular s 194, which excludes transactions on a recognised investment exchange through an independent broker.
16 See s 197 *et seq*.
17 See ss 252, 253 and 254.
18 See ss 188 and 189 and generally Part 10, Chapter 5.
19 See s 195 and also s 213.

of secret profits. In our discussion of civil liability we have already noted that section 175(2) specifically refers to the misuse of information.[20] It also refers to the exploitation of property and so called corporate opportunities.[21] We have examined the liability that can arise where a person in a fiduciary relationship, without proper consent or approval, derives profit from the exploitation of information or property, including expectant property[22] or receives a benefit from a third party. It has been argued that the strict obligations of stewardship should render any risk of a conflict of interest or duty unacceptable. However, in the case of directors who are in the commercial world, the law is less exacting. Section 175(4) in regard to the avoidance of conflicts of interest, in the context of exploiting information, property and opportunity, states 'the duty is not infringed if the situation cannot reasonably be regarded as likely to give rise to a conflict of interest'. By the same token section 176(4), in the context of outlawing benefits from third parties, provides 'this duty is not infringed if the acceptance of the benefit cannot reasonably be regarded as likely to give rise to a conflict of interest'. Consequently, theoretical and unrealistic conflicts actual as well as potential should not expose a director to the prospect of liability.[23]

MULTIPLE APPOINTMENTS

8.7   An issue that has caused controversy is the position of directors who hold multiple directorships. We have seen that the courts have tended to treat directors less strictly than other fiduciaries, recognising the commercial environment within which they are required to operate.[24] Indeed, there is authority, albeit not particularly strong, that a director cannot be restrained from serving as a director of another company actually competing in the same line of business.[25] Without informed consent this would not be permissible in the case of an ordinary fiduciary. The situation is complicated where the director is also an employee. While the duty of fidelity owed by an employee to his employee is less demanding than the ordinary fiduciary obligations, it has been held that an employee cannot work for a competitor even in his

20   See 2.8 above.
21   See 2.24 *et seq* above. Note that these obligations extend to the exploitation of opportunities (and information) acquired while a director, after ceasing to hold office, *CMS Dolphin Ltd v Simonet* [2001] 2 BCLC 704 and *Killen v Horseworld Ltd* [2012] EWHC 363 and *Safetynet Security Ltd v Coppage* [2012] 1 All ER 57. The important issue is whether the opportunity or information was acquired during the currency of a fiduciary relationship. Terminating such a relationship with a view to exploiting such an opportunity or information could well indicate bad faith.
22   See 2.24 *et seq* above.
23   See generally *Island Export Finance Ltd v Umunna* [1986] BCLC 460; *Framlington Group Plc v Anderson* [1995] 1 BCLC 475 and *Ultraframe (UK) Ltd v Fielding* [2005] EWHC 1638.
24   For an example of the court appearing attentive to commercial realities and in particular the impact of proprietary claims on the rights of third persons see *Sinclair Investments Holdings SA v Versailles Trade Finance Ltd* [2011] EWCA Civ 722, but see *FHR European Ventures LLP v Cedar Capital Partners LLC* [2014] UKSC 45.
25   *London & Mashonaland Exploration Co v New Mashonaland Exploration Co* [1891] WN 165 approved by Lord Blanesburgh in *Bell v Lever Bros* [1932] AC 161 at 195, but see *In Plus Group Ltd v Pyke* [2002] 2 BCLC 201 where doubts were expressed as to whether today this is appropriate. Of course, a director should not subordinate the interests of one company to another, even within the context of a group, see *Scottish Co-op Wholesale Society Ltd v Meyer* [1959] AC 324 at 366.

spare time.[26] Of course, if the director makes adequate disclosure and secures permission under section 175, which provides that the 'no conflict rule' will not be breached if the matter has been authorised by the board – presumably in such a case of both companies, he should not be at risk. However, any material change in the nature of the conflict will need to be disclosed for this to provide protection. It goes without saying that if a director does exploit information, property or opportunity belonging to another company personally or for the benefit of another, then he will be liable, as may well the company or person for whose benefit that property or information is used.[27]

MODIFICATION OF DUTIES

8.8   We have seen that in regard to the various obligations associated with the 'no conflict rule', directors are able to secure authorisation or obtain ratification of their conduct from the shareholders and in some cases simply the board. We have also referred to the practice of attempting to redefine fiduciary obligations in the company's constitutional documents and in particular articles of association. Successive legislation has intervened to curb this. Section 232(1) provides that any provision that purports to exempt a director or shadow director from any liability that would otherwise attach to him in connection with any negligence, default, breach of duty or trust in relation to the company is void. On the other hand section 232(4) states that 'nothing in this section prevents a company's articles from making such provision as has previously been lawful for dealing with conflicts of interest'.[28] The problem is that the law before the enactment of these provisions was not entirely clear. In *Movitex Ltd v Bulfield*[29] Vinelott J distinguished between the fundamental principle that directors would be accountable for any benefit resulting from a conflict of interest regardless of whether it was fair or not, and the obligation of directors to always pursue the best interests of the company. This second obligation could not be varied or excused. In the case of the obligation to yield up benefits, the articles or shareholders could essentially redefine what might be considered to be a conflict of interest. If what might otherwise have been considered to be a conflict is rendered no longer a conflict then there is nothing for the fundamental rule to bite upon and therefore there is no breach to be excused. Thus, would it be acceptable to provide that directors could exploit information that came to them in their capacity as directors? Of course, it may be difficult in practice to distinguish information from property or opportunity. We have seen that the courts, at least in the civil law, are willing, in certain circumstances, to regard information as resembling property and to protect it accordingly.[30] There is also an informational element in every case of so called 'corporate opportunity'. Indeed, some cases that have been regarded as illustrating the taking of an opportunity might equally be considered examples

---

26   See *Hivac Ltd v Park Royal Scientific Instruments Ltd* [1946] Ch 169. See also *Industrial Development Consultants v Cooley* [1972] 1 WLR 433.

27   See 2.27 *et seq* above.

28   See also s 180(4)(b) in the same vein. Consequently where a company's articles of association contain provisions for dealing with conflicts of interest, the statutory duties under s 175 will not be infringed providing the director has acted in accordance with the relevant articles.

29   [1988] BCLC 104.

30   See 2.25 *et seq* above.

of insider trading on the basis of price sensitive information.[31] It would seem that where the company has itself an interest in exploiting the information or opportunity, then a misappropriation or diversion by the directors would be contrary to their obligation to place the interests of the company first. In such a case a purported modification of their duty would be void. However, if the relevant organ of the company has made a *bona fide* decision not to use the information or pursue the opportunity then there may be no objection, as there is no actual conflict. Of course, this in the context of insider dealing may not be as simplistic. As we have seen it would not generally be in the interests of a company for its directors to be seen to be utilising unpublished price sensitive information improperly.[32]

8.9   The cases indicate that in regard to most, but not all, fiduciary obligations, the person to whom they are owed may after full disclosure decide to waive their performance or excuse their non-performance. However, in the case of companies there is a problem. We have seen that directors owe their fiduciary duties to the company. While there are situations where the board of directors is the proper organ of the company to decide on performance, there are situations where the decision falls to the shareholders in general meeting. In such cases what is the position of a director who wishes to see his duties modified or excused, if he is also a shareholder. May he vote his own shares to change or excuse performance of his duties as a director to the company? Traditionally the law has taken the view that as shares are proprietary rights and shareholders are not in a fiduciary relationship with the company, there is no inhibition on director shareholders exercising their votes in general meeting as they choose. Having said this there are cases which indicate a willingness of the courts to have regard to the actions of directors in such circumstances as an indication of their good faith.[33] If a director who is in breach of his duties is prepared to have the matter resolved by an independent majority of the shareholders, after full disclosure, this surely indicates integrity. Furthermore, an independent resolution better reflects what is in fact considered to be in the best interests of the company. Section 239(4) in regard to the *ex post facto* ratification of directors' breaches of duty and trust provides that the ordinary resolution is to be considered passed 'only if the necessary voting majority is obtained disregarding the votes in favour of the resolution by the director … and any member connected with him'. In some respects this section is narrower than the common law, which is not necessarily pre-empted. The recent approach of some judges when considering the effect of a resolution on the ability of minority shareholders to raise a challenge on behalf of the company is rather wider and more searching. The section only 'disqualifies' the votes of the specific director and those connected with him as defined in the provisions relating to substantial property transactions.[34] Thus, cronies and others who may be very interested in the wrongdoing, but who are not connected in a formal sense, will be able to vote as they choose.

---

31   See *Boardman v Phipps* (1967) AC 46 and see in this context B Rider 'The Fiduciary and the Frying Pan' (1978) *Conveyancer* 114.

32   See 2.11 above and *Diamond v Oreamuno* (1969) 248 NE 2d 910 (NY 1969) where the view was expressed that insider dealing by directors may damage the reputation of their company, although the court left open whether this would itself justify the imposition of liability.

33   See *Smith v Croft (No 2)* [1988] Ch 114. Vinelott J's more extreme view expressed in *Prudential Assurance Co Ltd v Newman Industries Ltd (No 2)* (1981) Ch 257 is probably not good law. But see also *Daniels v Daniels* [1978] Ch 406.

34   See ss 252 to 254 of the Companies Act 2006.

8.10   We have noted that it is the better view that there are certain duties which cannot be excused even after full disclosure and purported ratification. It has been argued that it would be against public policy to allow ratification of fraudulent conduct or other misconduct that amounts to a serious crime, such as, presumably, money laundering or for that matter insider dealing. The perimeters of what might be considered excusable as a matter of public policy, albeit from merely the perspective of the civil law, are unclear. We have seen that courts have taken differing views on insider dealing.[35] Perhaps assistance can be obtained from the law of insurance? Directors and Officers indemnity cover does not extend to allegations of fraud or deliberate wrongdoing. However, there has been uncertainty in regard to regulatory misconduct and civil enforcement. It is argued that a breach of duty involving the misappropriation of property belonging to the company cannot be excused. For example, in *Cook v Deeks*[36] directors who misappropriated a corporate opportunity which 'belonged' to their company were not allowed to exercise their votes, which constituted a majority, to 'make a present to themselves'.[37] Whether the position would have been different had the vote been by a disinterested majority is open to question. It is important in this regard to remember that section 239 only applies to breaches of duty and trust that the law has considered capable of ratification. The traditional interpretation of *Cook v Deeks* is that as a misappropriation of corporate property was in issue, ratification was not possible. On the other hand there are cases involving forms of self-dealing where the courts have allowed or contemplated allowing ratification. It is argued that in these cases the company's claim was simply for an account of unauthorised profits and did not involve a misappropriation of corporate property.[38] This analysis has always been open to question given the different ways in which courts have regarded the misuse of information. In some, the courts have regarded it as giving rise to a personal claim for the benefit that the fiduciary has received and in others to a proprietary claim based on the misuse of information as a species of corporate property.[39] Of course, the explanation may be rather more to do with whether the benefit remains in the hands of a fiduciary and can therefore be subjected to a personal claim. After the approach of the Privy Council in *Attorney General of Hong Kong v Reid*[40] it is doubtful whether a sensible distinction can now be made between these cases simply on the basis of the traditional approach to whether a personal and proprietary claim is in issue. Perhaps a better approach is to return to the issue of honesty, conscionability and fair dealing.[41]

8.11   Our discussion has focused on the ratification of conduct which, without such informed approval, would have amounted to a breach of fiduciary duty.

---

35   See 2.51 above.
36   [1916] 1 AC 554.
37   [1916] 1 AC 554 at 564 and see Templeman J in *Daniels v Daniels* [1978] Ch 406 discussed on this point in B Rider 'Amiable Lunatics and the Rule in *Foss v Harbottle*' (1978) *Cambridge Law Journal* 270.
38   *North West Transportation Co v Beatty* (1887) LR 12 App Cas 589 and *Regal (Hastings) v Gulliver* [1967] AC 152.
39   For example *Phipps v Boardman* [1967] AC 46; *Attorney General of Hong Kong v Reid* (1994) 1 AC 324 and *Daraydan Holdings Ltd v Solland International Ltd* [2005] Ch 119.
40   Above at note 39 and in particular *FHR European Ventures LLP v. Cedar Capital Partners LLC* [2014] UKSC 45.
41   See B Rider above at note 37. Of course, where actual dishonesty is alleged then the allegations of fraud have allowed judges to cut through procedural and other barriers, *Atwood v Merryweather* [1867] LT 5 Eq 464. Having noted this, however, the courts do not like allegations that are justified purely as procedural devices.

The effect of the ratification is to render the conduct no longer objectionable. Of course, it may well be that a particular transaction that could be avoided for breach of duty might be affirmed by the board or the shareholders, albeit the liability of those responsible for the wrong not excused. There is also the issue which we have touched upon of prior authorisation. We have noted the attempts, primarily through the articles of association, to authorise actions which would otherwise constitute a breach of fiduciary duty. The Companies Act 2006 does not as in the case of *ex post facto* ratification address the issue whether the directors as shareholders might use their votes in this context. It is probably the case that, save in exceptional circumstances, there is no objection to those who might well be interested in some other capacity – even as a potential wrongdoer, utilising their own votes to amend the articles to include a relevant provision. We have seen that there are limitations on what can be excluded or modified in terms of duty to the company.[42] Finally in this context, it is important to remember that directors who have acted honestly and reasonably and who in fairness ought to be excused from all or part of liability for a breach of duty can apply to the court under section 1157 for the judge to exercise his discretion.

8.12 Section 232 of the Companies Act 2006 prohibits any provision by which the company provides directly or indirectly an indemnity to a director or a director of an associated company.[43] However, under section 233, companies are permitted to purchase insurance cover for their directors even in regard to liability arising for breach of their duties to the company. It is most unlikely that this cover would extend to deliberate misconduct and in particular fraud, as we have seen. By the same token it is questionable whether such cover is available for secret profits as opposed to losses actually occasioned to the company. The company may also provide indemnity, directly or indirectly, in regard to liability to third parties. However, under section 234, this may not extend to fines imposed as a result of criminal proceedings, costs incurred in unsuccessfully defending a prosecution, a penalty imposed by a regulatory authority[44] and the costs of defending civil proceedings brought by the company or an associated company in which judgment is given against the director.[45] It should be noted that under this section there is no objection to a company indemnifying a director against the costs of unsuccessfully defending an action brought by a regulator, such as the FSA, although this would not extend to the penalty.

OTHER FIDUCIARIES

8.13 Our discussion has so far focused on the directors of companies and in particular the issue of conflict of interest. Of course, in the context of financial service industry the range of fiduciary relationships is somewhat wider.

---

42 See 8.8 above.
43 However, see ss 205 and 206 in regard to loans for defending civil actions and regulatory procedures.
44 See generally 12.41 *et seq* below.
45 The company cannot, by any provision, cover a director in regard to liability for any breach of duty to the company. Therefore, this provision is directed at actions where it is not the director's own breach of duty to the company that is in issue.

There will be many individuals and companies that find themselves owing fiduciary obligations who are not in the position of directors.[46] The regulatory system has, as we shall see, imposed obligations relating to the control and management of conflicts of interest and duty on persons who would not, in law be considered fiduciaries.[47] It is also the case that the regulatory system and its rules have not always been in compliance with fiduciary law[48] and certainly the reliance that some have placed on following industry practice and even regulatory guidance may as a matter of law be misplaced.[49] There are numerous conceivable situations where conflicts of interest and duty may arise in the conduct of financial business. This is not the place to try and identify these, let alone address them. It is also the case that the intervention of law on a much broader basis has made a considerable difference in resolving certain conflicts. For example, today it could not be sensibly argued that a stockbroker who learnt unpublished price sensitive information is under a duty to use it for the benefit of his client.[50] The same would also be true of a trustee in the prudent management of the trust funds.[51] However, potential conflict issues arise that have perhaps not been considered with as much thought in the past. For example, the position of members of a shari'ah council advising financial institutions on issues of shari'ah compliance in regard to different products and funds may raise issues of conflict and handling of price sensitive information.[52] It will not always be clear, where fiduciaries operate in multiple functions or for different clients, who is entitled to primacy and on what basis. The traditional rules of equity that give primacy in the discharge of a duty, to those who are first in time – subject to issues of notice – is not in the context of the realities of financial life, practicable.[53] Attempts to expand and apply rules based on simple conflicts between two principals, in the context of simple commercial transactions or agency agreements, have also proved inadequate for the task.[54] Referring to the strict rules of confidentiality and no conflict developed, for example, in the practice of law, tends to neglect the public policy issues that dictate exacting standards as a matter of justice, which are arguably inappropriate in the world of business. Reliance on so called 'Chinese walls' and other methods of segregating information, focus on liability attaching to the flow of information and knowledge rather than the issue of conflict of

---

46 See generally C Nakajima and E Sheffield, *Conflicts of Interest and Chinese Walls* (Butterworths 2002); B Rider and TM Ashe (eds), *The Fiduciary, the Insider and the Conflict* (Sweet and Maxwell 1995) and C Hollander and S Salzedo, *Conflicts of Interest* (3rd edn, Sweet and Maxwell 2008).

47 See 14.45 *et seq.*

48 See generally *Law Commission, Fiduciary Duties and Regulatory Rules, A Consultation Paper* (LC No 124) (1992) HMSO; Law Commission, *Fiduciary Duties and Regulatory Rules*, Report (LC No 236) (1995) HMSO and B Rider (ed), *The Regulation of the British Securities Industry* (Oyez 1979) Ch 5.

49 See B Rider and T M Ashe, above at note 46.

50 See G Cooper and R Cridlan, *The Law and Procedure of the Stock Exchange* (Butterworths 1971) at p 104 and also see the allegations in *Briggs v Gunner* (Unreported) Chancery Division 16 January 1979 discussed in B Rider and HL Ffrench, *The Regulation of Insider Trading* (Macmillan 1979) at 440.

51 But see *Phipps v Boardman* [1967] 2 AC 46 and B Rider 'The Fiduciary and the Frying Pan' (1978) *Conveyancer* 114.

52 See B Rider and C Nakajima, Chapter 18 in S Archer and R Karim, *Islamic Finance, the Regulatory Challenge* (Wiley 2007) and in particular B Rider, 'Corporate Governance for Institutions offering Islamic Financial Services' in C Nethercott and D Eisenberg (eds), *Islamic Finance, Law and Practice* (Oxford University Press 2012).

53 See generally C Nakajima and E Sheffield, above at note 46.

54 See *Anglo-African Merchants Ltd v Bayley* [1969] 1 All ER 421 and *North and South Trust Company v Berkeley* (1971) 1 All ER 980.

duty.[55] While as we shall see the regulators and professions have attempted to deal with some of these issues, given the complexity of the issues and vested interests, successive governments have been reluctant to resort to legislation and the matter has somewhat pragmatically been left largely in the hands of the courts.[56]

8.14   At the heart of the modern law is the colourful case of *Prince Jefri Bolkiah v KPMG*.[57] Essentially this involved the issue of whether KPMG, by constructing various informational barriers, could act for the government of Brunei in investigating the dispersal of certain funds to companies possibly associated with Prince Jefri, when KPMG has undertaken work relating to these issues on instruction from Prince Jefri. At first instance Pumfrey J granted an injunction on the basis that KPMG had not convinced the court that its arrangements would satisfactorily protect Prince Jefri's confidential information.[58] The court considered that KPMG in providing forensic services were in much the same position as a solicitor and accordingly a very high burden was upon them. Lightman J had adopted a similar stance in *Re Solicitors (A Firm)*.[59] The Court of Appeal disagreed with Pumfrey J and thought on the facts that there was no real danger of information leaking across the Chinese Wall and the matter was one for the court to take a balanced view on.[60] The House of Lords agreed with the court at first instance. It is interesting to note that the House of Lords emphasised that KPMG were under no fiduciary obligations to Prince Jefri as he had been a former client. The matter was therefore to be resolved purely on the issue of protection of confidential information. Prince Jefri's right to protection was unqualified. It was not an issue of balance and unless KPMG could persuade the court that there was no risk other than a fanciful one of disclosure, he was entitled to an injunction.[61] Lord Millett who delivered the leading speech attempted to set out principles of wider application than to the facts before the court. It is worth considering these here.

8.15   In circumstances where a person is in a fiduciary relationship with two clients at the same time he cannot discharge his duties of loyalty to both and he will be in a conflict of interest.[62] In such circumstances the issue is wider than that of the protection of confidential information. Where there is such a conflict the fiduciary must obtain the informed consent of both parties. However, Lord Millett considered that there are circumstances where the conflict is such that even written consent after full disclosure may not resolve the problem. If one of the fiduciary relationships ceases then the only issue will be protection of confidential information obtained during the currency

---

55   See for example *Financial Services in the UK, A new framework for investor protection, DTI* (1985) Cmnd 9432 HMSO para 7.4 'the Government is not convinced that total reliance can be placed on Chinese Walls because they restrict flows of information and not the conflicts of interest themselves' and see also *Dunford & Elliott Ltd v Johson & Firth Brown Ltd* [1977] 1 Lloyds Rep 505, per Roskill LJ at 515.
56   See generally above at note 46.
57   [1999] 2 AC 222.
58   (1999) BCLC 1.
59   [1997] Ch 1 and see also *Re Solicitors (A Firm)* [1992] QB 959.
60   (1999) BCLC 1.
61   (1999) 2 AC 222.
62   *Bristol & West Building Society v Mothew* [1998] 1 Ch 1 and *Clark Boyce v Mouat* [1994] 1 AC 428.

of that relationship.[63] As we have seen, the duty of loyalty exists only during the currency of a fiduciary relationship except possibly where an opportunity to exploit it continues. This is similar to the situation of a director whose office ends. As there was in the *Jefri* case and also in other cases relating to solicitors, if there is confidential information the person seeking to enter into another relevant relationship must be able to show that there is no risk of this information being misused. While the courts in practice, if not in law, probably do adopt a higher standard in cases involving privileged information in the hands of lawyers,[64] the burden of showing that there is no real risk of leakage or misuse is a very exacting one. Where it is possible to show that the information has been effectively isolated within a firm or company, the problem is not necessarily resolved. In many cases the business or professional adviser will have duties of care involving obligations to search out relevant information and use it for the benefit of other clients. While it has been accepted that in the discharge of such duties a fiduciary is under no obligation to acquire inside information,[65] it is not clear that it would have a defence to an action based on negligence.[66] Would it be acceptable to argue that the firm was not negligent because in its own commercial interests it had disabled those responsible for advising the relevant client from access to certain material information in its possession? This is not likely to be an appealing argument for most firms. It must be remembered that in many cases the action will be brought against the firm and not necessarily against individuals. Where the quality of advice is tested solely at the level it was in fact given, then it may be arguable that the individual professional could not reasonably be expected to have access to information that in any case had been acquired by the firm in confidential circumstances. The issue would be whether in the discharge of his duties the relevant professional adviser or manager should have acquired this or similar knowledge from another unobjectionable source? However, the courts have shown themselves to be relatively unsympathetic to banks and other financial institutions who for purely their own commercial reasons find themselves in a conflict of duties in money laundering cases.

CONTRACTING OUT

8.16   We have already raised the issue in the case of directors of companies seeking to redefine or exclude their fiduciary and other duties by contractual provisions.[67] In most situations involving activity in the financial services

---

63   Albeit a different issue, the court have held that an impression of impropriety will be enough to involve the 'no conflict rule' see *Supasave Retail v Coward Chance (a firm) see Lee (David) & Co (Lincoln) Ltd v Coward Chance (a firm)* [1991] Ch 259, [1990] 3 WLR 1278, [1991] 1 All ER 668 at 674, per Brown-Wilkinson VC.

64   Of course, information should be used only for the purposes for which it was given, *Barclays Bank Ltd v Quistclose Investments Ltd* [1970] AC 567. Furthermore, in certain cases it may not be appropriate to terminate the relationship, see *Young v Robinson Rhodes* [1999] 3 All ER 524.

65   See *Briggs v Gunner* (Unreported) Ch D 16 January 1979 discussed in B Rider *Insider Trading* (Jordan Publishing 1983), at 224 and see above at 8.13 note 50.

66   See generally B Rider and TM Ashe above at 8.13 note 46 and also *Jones v Canavan* [1972] 2 NSWLR 236 and *Daly v The Sydney Stock Exchange Ltd* (1986) 160 CLR 371.

67   See **8.8**. Consideration also needs to be given to the general issues that arise when attempts are made to exclude or modify legal obligations by contract. In particular, s 3 of the Misrepresentation Act 1967 and the Unfair Terms in Consumer Contracts Regulations 1999, noting that the Unfair Contract Terms Act 1977 excludes contracts relating to securities,

industry, there will be a contractual as well as fiduciary relationship. The terms of the relevant contract may well be pertinent in regard to many of the issues discussed in this book. We have already seen that contractual terms may well determine the scope of disclosure obligations there by having relevance in both the civil and the criminal law.[68] The parties may agree by contract to vary and inhibit the enforcement of other legal obligations including those arising by virtue of a fiduciary relationship. While responsibility for fraud and certain other criminal acts cannot be excluded by contractual terms, we have seen that the law is by no means certain. Much will depend upon a construction of the contractual terms. Obviously, the courts will be unsympathetic to those who seek to abuse their position or act unfairly. We have already seen that judges have indicated in certain cases a dislike for directors who seek to manipulate circumstances in furtherance of dishonest designs.[69] However, the courts must give effect to the clear and unambiguous intentions of the parties, determined objectively, unless such is contrary to statute or public policy. In *Clark Boyce v Mouat*[70] the Privy Council accepted that a solicitor could act for two parties with conflicting interests provided he had the informed consent of both. It is important to note, however, that the Board of the Privy Council were most concerned to determine exactly what the scope of the solicitor's duties were on the facts of the case. Lord Jauncey stated that 'when a client in full command of his faculties and apparently aware of what he is doing seeks the assistance of a solicitor in the carrying out of a particular transaction, that solicitor is under no duty whether before or after accepting those instructions to go beyond those instructions by proffering unsought advice on the wisdom of the transaction'. This is important in the context of fiduciaries operating in the financial sector. For example, absent a contractual provision it has been held that a stockbroker in the ordinary course of his business when instructed to execute a particular transaction is under no obligation to provide advice.[71] The express obligations imposed by a contract may not, however, be determinative. For example, additional contractual obligations may arise by implication or by virtue of a collateral contract. It is also the case that reasonable expectations may arise as a result of a course of dealing or the circumstances of the case. The obligations in the law of negligence[72] and equity are by no means confined within the precise terms of contract.

may well be relevant. There are developed rules of construction which operate against the party seeking the benefit of the exclusion or limitation of liability. It may also be relevant to consider pre-contractual negotiations in the context of the law of misrepresentation and as to whether other contractual obligations of a collateral nature have been entered into. Note also specific statutes which in certain contexts give considerable discretion to the courts, for example, s 140A of the Consumer Credit Act 2006.

68   See 6.40 *et seq* above.
69   See 8.9 above.
70   [1994] 1 AC 428.
71   *Scheder & Co v Walton and Hemingway* (1910) 27 TLR 89. However, note in this case the client's instructions were unequivocal and irrespective of whether there is an obligation to proffer advice, if it is given it must be honest, see Allun KC at 89, accepted by Ridley J at 90. Furthermore, considerable caution needs to be exercised on the impact of obligations imposed by the FCA in regard to the conduct of business, particularly in regard to vulnerable investors.
72   In the law of negligence it is rarely true that the claimant will have contracted to have received the relevant advice. There may also be concurrent and overlapping duties in contract and tort, see *Pirelli General Cable Works Ltd v Oscar Faber & Partners* [1983] 2 AC 1, and for that matter in equity. It should be noted, however, the courts are reluctant to find duties to disclose information which would not otherwise require disclosure, see *Banque Financiere de la Cite SA v Westgate Insurance Co* (1991) 2 AC 249.

INFORMED CONSENT

8.17   There has been much discussion as to the adequacy of informed consent. In *Clarke Boyce* the Privy Council appear to accept that 'consent given in the knowledge that there is a conflict between the parties and that as a result the solicitor may be disabled from disclosing to each party the full knowledge which he possesses as to the transaction or may be disabled from giving advice to one party which conflicts with the interests of the other' is sufficient.[73] The cases do indicate that where the fiduciary's conflict is as a result of a conflict with his own self-interest, the obligations to ensure proper understanding on the part of the client are somewhat more onerous.[74] Indeed, they are of the utmost good faith.[75] Disclosure must be full and complete as to the material facts and not serve merely as a warning to the client. Where the conflict arises between two or more clients, the law is not entirely certain as to exactly what needs to be disclosed. The better view is that it must be enough to allow those concerned to fully appreciate the risks. Of course, much will depend upon the circumstances and the status of the parties. Given that we are in the realm of fiduciary obligations, it is clear that the test will be subjective and take account of the circumstances and knowledge of the relevant parties. Thus, disclosure must be in a legal sense suitable to the parties. On the other hand, full disclosure might itself conflict with a specific obligation to one or more of the parties. For example, too much detail might involve a breach of confidence and even the disclosure as to the existence of a specific conflict or other party might prejudice a legitimate interest. In such cases, perhaps the fiduciary must just take the consequences of liability. As Donaldson J observed in *North and South Trust Company v Berkeley*, '… he cannot say to his principal "I have not discharged my duty to you because I owe a duty to another"'.[76] As Donaldson J. emphasised, in such a case the fiduciary has to accept the 'consequences flowing from the unlawful nature' of the position in which he has deliberately got himself into, in most cases for financial reward! Such strict principles do not sit well with the way in which business has traditionally been done in the City of London where the wearing of many hats has long been fashionable. The self-regulatory authorities and even the Securities and Investment Board took the view that these rules could be varied by practice and their own rules. The Financial Services Authority has been rather more circumspect, accepting that the law may only be changed by legislation specifically addressing the relevant issues.[77] Mere compliance with best City practice[78] or even non-statutory principles and rules will not protect a fiduciary who has breached his fundamental duty. As Donaldson J. pointed out, 'how do you train anyone to

---

73   [1993] 4 All ER 268 Lord Jauncey at 273. In *Rhodes v Macalister* (1923) 29 Com Cas 19 Atkin LJ stated: 'the remedy is a very simple one and it is well within the compass of any ordinary businessman. The complete remedy is disclosure, and if an agent wishes to receive any kind of remuneration from the other side and wishes to test whether it is honest or not, he has simply to disclose the matter and rest upon the consequences if that.' See also Jacob LJ in *Imageview Management Ltd v. Jack* [2009] EWCA Civ 63 and *Towers v. Premier Waste Management Ltd* [2011] EWCA Civ 923. Note that the FCA has expressed the view that reliance by a fiduciary on informed consent should be the last defence! See 8.21 *et seq* above.

74   *New Zealand Society 'Oranje' v Kuys* [1973] 1 WLR 1126 and *Phipps v Boardman* [1967] 2 AC 46.

75   See 6.37 above.

76   [1971] 1 All ER 980.

77   See 8.13 note 48 above.

78   See 8.22 *et seq* below.

act properly in such a situation? What course of action can possibly be adopted which does not involve some breach of duty to one principal or the other? ... Neither skill nor honesty can reconcile the irreconcilable.'[79]

8.18 It has been argued that there are situations where it is reasonable to find that the parties, because of the circumstances or the nature of the business, can be taken to have given their consent to the conflict. In *Kelly v Cooper*[80] the Privy Council accepted that an estate agent could act for a number of vendors and 'ring fence' the confidential information he received from each *vis à vis* other parties with admittedly competing interests. The Board considered that this was justified by the implication of a term in the relevant contracts and this determined the scope of the fiduciary obligations. The basis upon which the Privy Council found this implied term is not clear from their decision. In the *Jefri* case Lord Millett took the view that the Privy Council in *Kelly* based their opinion not so much on an implied term, but the deemed consent to a state of affairs on the part of the competing principals. Referring to firms of accountants engaged in audits for clients with possibly competing interests, Lord Millett stated 'their clients are taken to consent to their auditors acting for competing clients though they must of course keep confidential the information obtained from their respective clients'.[81] It would seem, however, that the courts require evidence that the relevant parties were aware of the conflicts and that such are common in the particular business or activity. While not entirely satisfactory, such a pragmatic approach has much to commend it.[82] Indeed, in *Kelly* their Lordships emphasised the advantage of such an approach, as a matter of expedience, in regard to stockbrokers with competing clients, who could not reasonably be expected to share inside information obtained in other capacities.[83]

8.19 The situation would therefore appear to be that provided the fiduciary can show that he has the informed consent of his clients, he will be at risk. The courts will, however, be prepared to examine the scope of his contractual obligations and the terms, express or implied, might well fashion the extent of other obligations including those arising in equity. The basis upon which an implied term may be found is not free from controversy and, although there is no authority particularly in point, it has been argued that this may be as a result of an established trade practice.[84] Nonetheless, this would have to be something rather more than mere common practice.[85] The extent to which it is reasonable to infer a contractual agreement to reduce the expectations of a client on the basis of his knowledge of what takes place in a particular trade or business remains unclear. It is therefore perhaps better to take the approach that where certain practices, such as the acting for multiple clients, are well established and the client appreciates this, then consent may be inferred or deemed. On the basis of the knowledge that the client has of what goes on it is reasonable to assume he will not object! Indeed, to allow him so to do would be unconscionable. As Donaldson J stated in the *Berkeley* case, 'if X, a third

79   [1971] 1 All ER 980 at 991.
80   [1993] AC 205.
81   [1999] 2 AC 222 at 235.
82   See B Rider, 'The Fiduciary and the Frying Pan' (1978) *Conveyancer* 114 at 119.
83   [1993] AC 205 at 214.
84   See generally *Hutton v Warren* (1836) 1 M & W 466 and in particular Baron Parke at 475 and *Cunliffe-Owen v Teather and Greenwood* [1967] 3 All ER 561.
85   See 8.17 above. Lord Langdale MR in *Gillett v Peppercorne* (1840) 3 Beav 81 expressed the view that the fact that something might be 'every day practice in the City' did not necessarily mean it was not a fraud.

party, knowing that A is the agent of P, the principal enters into an agreement with A involving duties which are inconsistent with those owed to P then in the absence of the fully informed consent of P, X acts at his peril'.[86] While this observation is in a somewhat different and perhaps easier context,[87] it does show that the courts have no sympathy with those who come into relationships in the knowledge that there are pre-existing obligations. Of course, much depends upon the degree of knowledge that the client has and the burden is on the fiduciary to ensure, in his own interests, that each client is aware of the circumstances.

A CASE AT LAST!

8.20 Having regard to the practical significance of many of the issues that we have raised and the implications that such have for proper legal and regulatory risk management, it is perhaps surprising that there is such a dearth of directly relevant authority pertaining to the financial services sector. The recent financial crisis did result in the threat of a great deal of litigation alleging that banks and others had acted or given advice tainted by conflicts of interest. However, with very few exceptions these matters were settled and did not reach court.

8.21 A relatively recent case[88] before the Federal Court of Australia has addressed many of the questions that we have raised in this chapter. The case was brought by the Australian Securities and Investments Commission against Citigroup Global Markets Australia Ltd on the basis that Citigroup as an adviser to another company in the context of a takeover – Toll Holdings Ltd – was in a fiduciary relationship and was therefore obliged not to violate its duty of loyalty by virtue of undertaking any activity which could amount to a conflict of interest. While Citigroup had constructed a Chinese Wall, its own proprietary trading was characterised as insider dealing. ASIC contended that to avoid allegations of breach of duty and deception it was necessary for the bank to obtain the informed consent of Toll to its own trading. The Commission maintained that the fiduciary relationship arose from the contractual arrangement between the bank and Toll despite the fact that Citigroup had inserted a term in the contract making it clear that the bank was acting 'as an independent contractor and not in any other capacity including as a fiduciary'. Jacobson J, following other Australian cases, took the view that where a contractual and fiduciary relationship co-exist, the fiduciary relationship must conform to the contractual terms.[89] He distinguished between a pre-existing fiduciary relationship and one that comes about as a result of a particular agreement of occurrence. In the latter case the relevant contract or agreement defines and determines the scope of the fiduciary duties that arise. With the exception of fraud and deliberate dereliction of duty, the court took the view that all such duties were capable of being varied

---

86   [1971] 1 All ER 993.
87   This approach as we have seen does not adequately address the situations where there are many potential principles with various expectations, perhaps changing over time. See in particular C Nakajima and E Sheffield at 8.13 note 46 above.
88   *Australian Securities and Investments Commission v Citigroup Global Markets Australia Pty Ltd* [2007] FCA 963.
89   *Hospital Products Ltd v US Surgical Corporation* (1984) 156 CLR 41 and *Breen v Williams* (1996) 186 CLR 71. See also *Chan v Zacharia* (1984) 154 CLR 178.

or excluded by the terms of the contract.[90] As there was no pre-existing fiduciary relationship between the parties, as there had been in, for example, some of the cases involving agents and solicitors, the court doubted whether it was even necessary for the bank to obtain the informed consent of Toll for its own share dealings. Jacobson J also considered that given Toll's knowledge of the banks structure and operations and its own sophistication, it had sufficient knowledge of the real possibility of proprietary trading by Citigroup to amount to an informed consent. ASIC also failed in its assertion that certain transactions amounted to inside information. While the court considered that an un-communicated supposition could constitute inside information within the relevant provision[91] it would not, on the facts, have had the required material effect.[92] Furthermore, Jacobson J held that the arrangements that the bank had put in place to reinforce its 'Chinese Wall' were adequate within the statutory test.[93] He noted, however, that such arrangements would not necessarily have addressed the conflict of interest had one actually arisen. He referred to Lord Millett in the *Jefri* case where it was emphasised that the efficacy of a Chinese Wall would depend upon the facts and it being 'an established part of the organisational structure' and not created on ad hoc basis.[94]

CONFLICTS COMPLIANCE AND THE REGULATORY ENVIRONMENT

8.22   In this part of the chapter we examine the impact of regulatory requirements for firms authorised to conduct investment business in the United Kingdom to establish internal arrangements to manage and control conflicts of interest that arise from their services or the activities they undertake. In particular, we shall identify that compliance with 'Control of Information rules' under the Financial Services and Markets Act 2000 (FSMA),[95] whilst creating challenging procedural requirements, can provide valuable defences to allegations of certain classes of market abuse. The trading on price sensitive information relies on the exploitation of a conflict of interest. Furthermore, individuals and firms can use their position of conflict in a financial market to manipulate market trading or gain an advantage at the expense of a client or other users of the market. Firms authorised to conduct investment business under FSMA carry a series of regulatory obligations intended to ensure the identification and control of conflicts that may arise within the firm's business activities.

8.23   Indicating the seriousness with which the United Kingdom's Financial Conduct Authority (FCA or Authority) views the importance of

---

90   The Law Commission, see 8.13 note 49 above, has also adopted this view and was cited with approval by Jacobson J. However, on the older authorities the position is perhaps not as clear as it seems, see for example in regard to gross negligence *Ferguson v Paterson* [1900] AC 271 at 281 and *Re Poche (1984) 6 DLR 40* at 55. We have already seen that the courts have been reluctant to allow directors to excuse themselves for self-dealing: see 8.9 at note 33 above.
91   See s 1043A of the Australian Corporations Act.
92   See s 1042D.
93   See ss 912A and 1043F.
94   [1999] 2 AC 222 at 239. Jacobson J also referred to Bryson J in *D & J Constructions Pty Ltd v Head & Ors Trading as Clayton Utz* (1987) 9 NSWLR 118 at 123 where the practical efficacy of Chinese Walls was doubted. As we have seen the English courts have in practice been reluctant to accept that Chinese Walls actually do secure confidential information.
95   FSMA 2000, s 137P (as amended).

conflicts management, it has (and when previously operating as the Financial Services Authority) taken enforcement action against authorised firms that have breached its conflict management rules. It is important to note, that the FCA's, conflict management enforcement work has not been confined to conflicts management failures associated with Market Abuse under Part 8 of the FSMA, or the criminal offences of market abuse in sections 89–91 of the Financial Services Act 2012, or the offence of insider dealing in the Criminal Justice Act 1993. Conflicts management concerning trading activities in hitherto unregulated corners of the financial markets are considered worthy of attention where they involve an authorised firm and indeed can provide useful guidance to the wider financial services sector on the characteristics of an effective conflicts management process. The FCA's Final Notice to Barclays Bank on 23 May 2014[96] set out details of failings identified by the Authority in the adequacy of Barclays arrangements to manage conflicts of interest arising from its participation in the London Gold Fixing process and activities on the Gold market. Together with additional breaches relating to the adequacy of Barclays' systems of organisation and control, the breaches identified by the Authority resulted in a financial penalty of £26,033,500. The facts of the case in their simplest sense were that Barclays participated in a process that involved it in the 'fixing' of the price for gold and also to sell products to its customers that were affected by prices set at the 'Gold Fixing'. By way of example the Final Notice refers to one occasion where a Barclays representative was able to place orders that contributed to the fixing of the price of gold at a level that resulted in the Bank not having to make a US$3.9m payment to a customer but making a US$1.75m profit. Although the aforementioned enforcement case against Barclays does not concern behaviour or investments covered by the market abuse regime in FSMA Pt 8, it does serve to illustrate the extent of the nature of conflicts of interests and the regulatory liability that can occur when conflicts of interests are not effectively managed.

8.24   As examined earlier in this chapter, conflict situations such as where a firm acts on the buy and sell side of a transaction can often be at the core of an allegation of insider dealing or present a threat or risk to the effective control of a firms market conduct. In Chapter 13, the book examines the compliance arrangements that authorised firms are required to establish and indeed many of such obligations will be based on an appropriate assessment of the risks to a firm's ability to act in compliance with its regulatory obligations. Indeed Chapter 13 will consider how the 'reasonable grounds' defence to an allegation of market abuse at section 123(2) of the FSMA along with the 'control of information rules conformity' defences in sections 89–91 of the Financial Services Act 2012 operate in such a way to raise the importance and effectiveness of a firm's internal controls and compliance arrangements.

Authorisation to conduct an investment business – the interplay between threshold conditions and conflicts management

8.25   The effectiveness of a financial institution's internal processes and controls, including its conflicts controls may be a key consideration for the

96   FCA Final Notice to Barclays Bank PLC 23 May 2014, see http://www.fca.org.uk/your-fca/documents/final-notices/2014.

firms application for authorisation and its ability to meets the 'conditions' for authorisation. Section 55B(3) of the FSMA requires the relevant regulatory authority (either the Prudential Regulation Authority or FCA) to be satisfied that the applicant firm meets (and will continue so to do) the Threshold Conditions set out in Schedule 6 of the FSMA. The conditions set out at paragraph 2E of Schedule 6 to the FSMA[97] (for firms that do not conduct any PRA regulated activity) and paragraphs 3D, 4E and 5E of Schedule 6 to the FSMA (for firms that do carry on PRA regulated activities) address issues relating to the firm's 'suitability'. (Once again, the relevance of the suitability threshold condition to a firm's wider compliance arrangements is examined in Chapter 13).

8.26 In guidance provided in the Threshold Conditions Sourcebook within the FS Handbook at COND 2.5.6G 1A, specific reference is made to the imperative of a firm's internal arrangements being able to comply with regulation, which arguably draws in consideration of a firm's conflicts management arrangements, including compliance with the provisions of the FS Handbook Senior Management Systems and Controls (SYSC) sourcebook which will be examined in further detail below. The guidance at COND sets out that in assessing the suitability threshold condition the FCA will consider whether 'the firm has made arrangements to put in place an adequate system of internal control to comply with the requirements and standards for which the FCA is responsible under the regulatory system'.

High Level Principles for Business and Fundamental Rules

8.27 Authorised firms are subject to 11 High Level Principles for Business, in essence setting out the 'spirit' of a firm's regulatory obligations, The nature of and regulatory imperative of the FCA's high levels principles was addressed in *R on the application of British Bankers Association v the Financial Services Authority*,[98] (although not a case relating to conflicts management or indeed market abuse), in which Ouseley J stated,[99] 'The Principles are best understood as the ever present substrata to which the specific rules are added. The Principles always have to be complied with. The specific rules do not supplant them and cannot be used to contradict them. They are but specific applications of them to the particular requirements they cover …'.

8.28 High Level Principle for Business 8 sets out a direct conflict management obligation stating: 'A firm must manage conflicts of interest fairly, both between itself and its customers and between a customer and another client.' As seen in the FCA's Enforcement action against Barclays[100] the obligations created by Principle for Business 8 can be used for non-market abuse regime trading activity conflicts management. Other High Level Principles for Business arguably touch upon the wider control framework in which conflicts management sits, addressing standards of business conduct (such as Principle 2: 'A firm must conduct its business with due skill, care and diligence'), the necessity to have appropriate systems of control and to

---

97 As amended by the Financial Services Act 2012.
98 *R (on the application of) British Bankers Association v the Financial Services Authority & ors* [2011] EWHC 999 (Admin), 2011 Bus LR 1531.
99 [2011] EWHC 999 (Admin) per Ouseley J at [162].
100 See note 96 above.

ensure the firm conducts its business effectively (Principle 3: 'A firm must take reasonable care to organise and control its affairs responsibly and effectively, with adequate risk management systems'), the conduct of the firm as measured by standards in the financial markets (Principle 5: 'A firm must observe proper standards of market conduct') and the firm's direct obligations to its customers (Principle 6: 'A firm must pay due regard to the interests of its customers and treat them fairly'). When considering the nature of regulatory obligations addressed as High Level Principles for Business it is important not to overlook that credit institutions and other firms covered by the EU Capital Requirements Directive[101] are additionally required to meet 'Fundamental Rules', including at Fundamental Rule 6 a requirement that 'A firm must organise and control its affairs responsibly and effectively'.

The FCA's rules on organisational systems and controls

8.29   A series of obligations addressed at the level of 'Governance' and management control within an authorised firm address amongst other things the necessity of conflicts management arrangements within an authorised firm, and are set out within the SYSC. The applicable provision of SYSC varies dependent on the class of regulated business activity undertaken by a firm, and in many cases provisions of European legislation, although arguably, despite differences in terminology, in many instances provisions in SYSC address core underlying regulatory themes.

8.30   Although many of the provisions of SYSC address matters relating to how a firm is governed and controlled, including specific provision for 'Compliance' and 'Financial Crime' at SYSC 6 and 'Risk Management' at SYSC 7 (which will be examined in Chapter 13), there can be found at SYSC 10 separate and distinct reference to conflicts of interest obligations and guidance covering matters such as conflicts identification and management and provision relating to the effect of Chinese Walls. Indeed as examined further below, the rules and guidance at SYSC 10.2 are significant in relation to how an effective Chinese Wall can operate as a defence to proceedings for 'criminal market abuse' under Pt 7 of the Financial Services Act 2012 or administrative market abuse under Pt 8 of the FSMA.

Application of the conflicts rules and conflict identification

8.31   The rules at SYSC 10 apply to certain classes of authorised persons in relation to the services they provide including those which provide services 'in the course of carrying on regulated activities or ancillary activities or provide ancillary services',[102] certain UK Alternative Investment Funds Managers and certain managers of collective investments.[103] For the purpose of SYSC 10.1

---

101   Directive 2013/36/EU on access to the activity of credit institutions and prudential supervision of credit institutions and investment firms, 26 June 2013. OJ L176/338 and Regulation (EU) 575/2013 on prudential requirements for credit institutions and investments firms and amending regulation, 26 June 2013, OJ L321/6.
102   An 'ancillary activity' is defined as 'an activity which is not a regulated activity but which is (a) carried on in connection with a regulated activity or (b) held out as being for the purposes of a regulated activity; 'ancillary services' are as set out in Section B Annex I to MiFID.
103   See SYSC 10.1.1R and SYSC 10.1.1A R for rules on application and associated defined terms.

there is no relevance in the class of customer to whom the services are being provided. (see SYSC 10.1.2R). The prime obligation within SYSC 10.1 is for the identification of conflicts of interest. The specific obligation however (see SYSC 10.1.3R) is for applicable firms to 'take reasonable steps' to identify actual and prospective conflicts of interest that may arise 'in the course of' the services they provide. The obligations at SYSC 10.1.3R address conflicts arsing between the firm (including its representatives such as 'managers, employees and appointed representatives' and 'persons linked to [the firm] by control') and the firm's client; and conflicts between clients of the firm.

Defining a conflict and identifying its characteristics

8.32   Although the rules at SYSC 10 do not provide a definition for the meaning of 'Conflict', guidance provided at SYSC 10.1.5G (derived from Recital 24 of the Markets in Financial Instruments Directive implementing measures[104]) illustrates that there needs to be more to the conflict situation than the firm gaining a benefit where the client suffers no potential disadvantage. Furthermore, provisions at SYSC 10.1.4R in essences require firms[105] to take into account certain conflict characteristics where the conflict may involve a 'material risk of damage to the interest of a client' including requiring the firm to take into account matters where it:

'(1)   is likely to make a financial gain, or avoid a financial loss, at the expense of the client;

(2)   has an interest in the outcome of a service provided to the client or of a transaction carried out on behalf of the client, which is distinct from the client's interest in that outcome;

(2A)   ...

(3)   has a financial or other incentive to favour the interest of another client or group of clients over the interests of the client

...'

8.33   The record keeping obligations at SYSC 10.1.6R essentially require applicable authorised firms to maintain a conflicts register setting out the types of services and activities they carry out that may give rise to the risk of material damage to the interest of clients. Furthermore, the general record keeping obligations imposed on authorised firms set out at SYSC 9, allow the FCA to monitor a firm's compliance with its regulatory obligations and operate to require a firm to maintain a record of all conflicts it has identified in accordance with its obligations in SYSC 10.1.3R.

The obligation to maintain a conflicts policy

8.34   The requirement for firms to 'establish, implement and maintain' a conflicts policy operates to ensure firms plan for and embed their conflicts management arrangements. The wording of the obligation set out at SYSC 10.1.10R, referring to the appropriateness of the policy by reference to the

---

104   Commission Directive No 2006/73/EC implementing Directive 2004/39/EC of the European Parliament and of the Council as regards organisational requirements and operating conditions for investment firms and defined terms for the purposes of that Directive.

105   The obligation at SYSC 10.1.4R does not apply to UK AIFM's, being addressed only to 'common platform firms' as defined and management companies.

'nature, scale and complexity' of the firm's business provides sufficient flexibility in the regulatory obligation to allow a firm to design a policy appropriate for the unique features of its business, rather than having to adopt a standardised and perhaps inappropriate policy solution.

8.35   The substantive content of the conflicts policy are as set out in SYSC 10.1.11R and cover matters such as:

(1)   '[t]he circumstances which constitute or may give rise to a conflict of interest entailing a material risk of damage to the interests of one or more clients' (these circumstances must specifically relate to the services or activities carried on by the firm. Furthermore guidance at SYSC 10.1.12G suggests that firms should address what are, it is submitted, high risk conflict services and activities such as 'investment research and advice, proprietary trading, portfolio management and corporate finance business');

(2)   'procedures to be followed and measures to be adopted in order to manage such conflicts'.

Procedural requirements for managing conflicts of interests

8.36   The conflicts policy requirement in SYSC 10.1.10 sits alongside a discrete obligation to establish conflicts procedures. Indeed the specific procedural obligation may be viewed as one complementing the operational effectiveness Principle for business (at PRIN 3) as well as the more generic governance obligations, including the obligations to have 'internal control mechanisms' (SYSC 4.1.1R) and 'adequate policies and procedures ... to ensure compliance ... with its obligations under the regulatory system and for countering the risk that the firm might be used to further financial crime' (SYSC 6.1).

8.37   SYSC 10.1.11(2) R sets out an obligation for a firm to establish procedures for managing conflicts of interest including processes to ensure that persons involved in the firm's activities that give rise to the conflict do so 'at a level of independence' albeit that the regulatory provision allows for the staff independence arrangement to be determined as necessary by reference to the firm's size and activities as well as 'the materiality of the risk of damage to the interests of clients'. Furthermore, SYSC 10.1.11(3) R provides that the 'independence procedures should include where it is necessary and appropriate' additional measures to 'ensure requisite level of independence' such as those for the (as fully described in SYSC 10.1.11(2)(b) R):

(a)   prevention or control of exchange of information;

(b)   separation of the supervision (ie management) of person involved in conflicted activities;

(c)   elimination of direct linkage in remuneration or revenue between the conflicted activities;

(d)   prevention or limitation of 'inappropriate influence' over the carrying out of the services or activities;

(e)   prevention or control of the 'simultaneous or sequential involvement of a relevant person in separate services or activities where such involvement may impair the proper management of conflicts of interest'.

8.38   Although SYSC 10.1.11(2) does not specifically refer to the incorporation of staff training into conflict procedures, it is not difficult to imply into the notion of 'prevention and control' arrangements the need to train or familiarise staff with the firm's controls and the types of conflicts that may arise in the firm's activities. The FCA in its Final Notice to Barclays[106] referred to the adequacy of the Bank's staff training arrangements in the context of its conflicts management. Training may thus be regarded as an inherent part of a firm's conflicts management procedures. In the Barclay's Final Notice the FCA stated: 'The firm's lack of specific training and guidance, given the absence of clear and sufficiently-tailored policies and procedures with respect to the Gold Fixing, meant that Barclays' personnel (including supervisors) may have been unaware of which conflicts of interest they should pay particular attention to in relation to the Gold Fixing.'[107] There can of course be found in the FCA's rules at SYSC 5 generic obligations addressing staff competence and training, which can be applied to staff knowledge of conflicts management arrangements as well as wider areas of the firm's business and compliance arrangements.

Conflicts management and disclosure

8.39   The regulator's starting point under SYSC 10.1.7R is for firms to take all reasonable steps' to prevent identified conflicts from having a 'material risk of damage to the interest of its clients'. Nonetheless, SYSC recognises that where a firm's internal arrangements are not sufficient to prevent the risk of damage to the firm's clients then before undertaking the client business and so that the client may make 'an informed decision' about the services the firm will provide and by reference to the conflict, details of the source and nature of the other client must be disclosed to the client in question.

Control of Information rules and the regulatory impact of the Chinese Wall

8.40   By virtue of section 137P of the FSMA the FCA is required to publish rules addressing the 'control of information'. These Control of Information Rules are set out at SYSC 10.2 and provides at SYSC 10.2.2R(1) that a firm maintaining a Chinese Wall may '(a) withhold or not use the information held; and (b) for that purpose, permit persons employed in the first part of its business to withhold the information held from those employed in that other part of the business'. Importantly, at SYSC 10.2.2R(4) the FCA provides that conformity with the control of information rule at SYSC 10.2.2(1) will 'for the purposes of s118A(5)(a) *[FSMA]*' will not be market abusive behaviour.

8.41   Similarly provisions within the FCA's statutory code under section 119 of the FSMA (which has been considered in Chapter 4) providing guidance on the types of behaviour the FCA considers to be abusive, includes reference to the role of conflicts management and Chinese Walls. At MAR 1.3.5E (an evidential provision), the FCA provides, that in its opinion: 'if the inside information is held behind an effective Chinese wall, or similarly effective arrangements, from the individuals who are involved in or who influence the decision to deal, that indicates that the decision to deal by an organisation is not "on the basis of" inside information.'

106   See note 96 above.
107   See note 96 above, at [2.7].

8.42 In respect of the prohibited behaviour of dissemination at MAR 1.8.5E in the FCA's opinion: 'if the individuals responsible for dissemination of information within an organisation could only know that the information was false or misleading if they had access to other information that was being held behind a Chinese wall or similarly effective arrangements, that indicates that the person disseminating did not know and could not reasonably be expected to have known that the information was false or misleading.'

8.43 The Control of Information rules at SYSC 10.2.2, along with the FCA rule book glossary, defines the term 'Chinese Wall' as '… an arrangement that requires information held by a person in the course of carrying on one part of the business to be withheld from, or not to be used for, persons with or for whom it acts in the course of carrying on another part of its business …'.

8.44 Previously this chapter has considered the notion of the 'Chinese Wall' as an arrangement that can be used for the prevention and control of the exchange of information within an organisation. The Law Commission's Consultation Paper on Fiduciary Duties and Regulatory Rules (1992),[108] considered the purpose of the Chinese Wall as '… to prevent the attribution of knowledge between the component parts of a firm on different sides of the wall'[109] and highlighted that to be considered effective it would normally involve some combination of the following organisational arrangements:

'(a) the physical separation of the various departments in order to insulate them from each other …;
(b) an educational programme … to emphasise the importance of not improperly or inadvertently divulging confidential information;
(c) strict and carefully defined procedures for dealing with a situation where it is felt that the wall should be crossed and the maintaining of proper records where this occurs;
(d) monitoring by compliance officers of the effectiveness of the wall;
(e) disciplinary sanctions where there has been a breach of the wall.'[110]

8.45 In the opinion of the House of Lords in the case of *Bolkiah v KPMG*,[111] it was observed by Lord Millet that whilst Chinese Walls are in common use, such an arrangement can only be considered effective where it is an established part of a firm's structure. Lord Millet stated: 'In my opinion an effective Chinese Wall needs to be an established part of the organisational structure of the firm, not created ad hoc and dependent on the acceptance of evidence sworn for the purpose by members of staff engaged on the relevant work …'.[112]

8.46 Whilst conflict management procedures anticipated by SYSC 10.1.11R may not necessarily have the characteristics of a 'Chinese Wall', it is certainly the case that arrangements that can legitimately be characterised as a Chinese Wall will satisfy some of the SYSC process requirements. There is recognition at SYSC 10.2 as to the effect of information control on any presumption of corporate knowledge of the controlled information. SYSC 10.2.1 provides a definition for a Chinese Wall for the purpose of identifying necessary characteristics in order for the regulatory recognition to apply. SYSC

108 Law Commission, Fiduciary Duties and Regulatory Rules. A Consultation Paper No 124 (1992) (HMSO).
109 See note 108 above, at [4.5.1].
110 See note 108 above, at [4.5.2].
111 *Bolkiah v KPMG* [1998] 2 AC 222, [1999] 1 All ER 517.
112 [1998] 2 AC 222 at p 239.

10.2.1 provides: '…an arrangement that requires information held by a person in the course of carrying on one part of the business to be withheld from, or not to be used for, persons with or for whom it acts in the course of carrying on another part of its business …'.

8.47   In conclusion, the obligations imposed on authorised firms to establish arrangements to identify and manage conflicts of interest are complex and arguably operationally challenging but can, if maintained effectively, provide protection against allegations of market abuse. In Chapter 13 we shall examine in more detail the broader compliance procedure and systems obligations imposed on authorised firms, including those aimed at financial crime, dealing and investment research.

Chapter 9

Issuer disclosure and liability

DISCLOSURE AND THE ISSUER

9.1 Issuer liability for market abuse is an important compliance concern for companies and their advisers. The UK listing rules, which are administered by the Financial Conduct Authority (FCA), were significantly amended in 2005 to incorporate the extensive disclosure and record keeping requirements imposed upon issuers by the Market Abuse Directive.[1] Most of the ongoing reporting requirements in the listing rules are similar to those required under the Market Abuse Directive. However, the scope of coverage of the listing rules and the disclosure requirements of the Market Abuse Directive are different: the listing rules are administered by the FCA under Part VI of the Financial Services and Markets Act 2000 (FSMA) and apply only to companies whose shares are admitted to the official list, while the disclosure requirements of the Market Abuse Directive (MAD) apply to all issuers whose securities are admitted to trading (or for which a request for admission to trading has been made) on a regulated market in an EEA State.[2] Moreover, the Directive extends disclosure requirements to professional third parties, such as lawyers, accountants and investment banks who advise issuers. Disclosure has been determined as the 'sole mechanism to satisfy the directive's requirements'.[3] The chapter will discuss the disclosure requirements as they relate to the market abuse offence and potential liability issues. It will also discuss related areas of issuer disclosure and liability involving takeovers and mergers.

DISCLOSURE OBLIGATIONS

9.2 The listing rules contained in Part VI of the FSMA require issuers to disclose via the Regulatory Information Service information that is not

---

1   The listing rules only cover issuers whose securities are admitted to the official list, which is a narrower set of issuers than those covered by the Directive. The FSA makes the listing rules under powers in Part VI of the FSMA. The chapter will primarily focus on those disclosure requirements for issuers and related third parties required by Articles 6(1)–(4) of the Market Abuse Directive. The Transparency Directive also imposes ongoing issuer disclosure and reporting requirements which are not addressed in this book.

2   See generally J. Hansen, 'MAD in a Hurry' (2004) 15 (2) *European Business Review* 183–221, 219.

3   Committee of European Securities Regulators (CESR) *Feedback Statement for Level 2 Implementing Measures* CESR/02–287b (CESR Paris) (Dec 2002), 'Comments in relation to Article 1 (insider dealing and market manipulation)'.

public knowledge that, if known, would lead to substantial movement in the price of their listed securities (ie price-sensitive information).[4] The disclosure requirement applies to all issuers with securities traded on regulated UK markets.[5] This requirement derives from the MAD's disclosure obligations that apply to all issuers who have securities trading, or who are seeking to have securities trading, on a regulated market in an EEA state.[6] The duty of disclosure arises when the issuer comes into possession of 'inside information.' Inside information is defined in Article 1(1) of MAD 1, which has been transposed into UK law through Article 118C of FSMA (as amended),[7] as:

> '[I]nformation of a precise nature which has not been made public, relating, directly or indirectly, to one or more issuers of financial instruments and which, If it were made public, would be likely to have a significant effect on the prices of those financial instruments or on the price of related derivative financial instruments.'

Article 1(1) defines 'inside information' by reference to four criteria: (1) the information is of a precise nature; (2) it has not been made public; (3) it relates to one or more issuers of financial instruments; and (4) if it were made public, would be likely to have a significant effect on the prices of those financial instruments, or on the price of related derivative financial instruments. Significantly, these elements must coexist for any information to qualify as 'inside information' and to trigger an issuer's disclosure obligation. However, it should be noted that the criteria of information of a precise nature and significant price effect are very much linked to each other and hence it is important not to consider each criterion in isolation. Nevertheless, it is possible to identify separately the factors which should be taken into account in respect of each criterion.[8]

9.3   Among these criteria, the interpretation of the 'precise nature' and the 'significant price effect' requirements are the most contentious. Article 1(1) of Directive 2003/124/EC (MAD's Level 2 Implementing Directive) clarifies that the precise nature requirement is met where, first, the information relates to an existing event or set of circumstances, or a future event or set of circumstances which are likely to occur; and, secondly, the event or circumstances are specific enough to allow an evaluation of their potential impact on the price of the issuer's financial instrument.[9] The precise nature test must be based on firm and

---

4   FSMA, Part VI. Pursuant to Part VI, the FSA makes the Listing, Prospectus and Disclosure and Transparency Rules. The Disclosure and Transparency Rules (DTRs) for listed companies are set out in the FSA's Handbook. The DTR rules require an issuer to publish specified inside information (FSMA, s 96A). DTR 2.2.1 states that: 'An issuer must notify a RIS [Regulatory Information Service] as soon as possible of any inside information which directly concerns the issuer unless DTR 2.5.1R applies'.

5   The listing rules set out the Listing Principles which apply to every listed company with a primary listing of equity securities. The purpose of the Listing Principles is to ensure that listed companies have regard to the important role they play in maintaining market confidence and ensuring fair and orderly markets. Listing Principle 4 provides: 'a listed company must communicate information to holders and potential holders of its listed equity securities in such a way as to avoid the creation or continuation of a false market in such listed equity securities'.

6   Directive 2003/6/EC, Article 9.

7   See s 118C of FSMA.

8   See Committee of European Securities Regulators (CESR), 2007, p 4.

9   The wording of Article 1 of Directive 2003/6/EC and Article 1 of Directive 2003/124/EC have been incorporated in Article 7 of the EU market abuse Regulation No 596/2014 (MAR) which, as of 2016, will repeal the MAD and implementing legislation. Article 7 of the MAR widens the definition of 'inside information' by combining Article 1 of the MAD and Article 1 of the Level 2 implementing directive.

objective evidence, not mere rumours or speculation, and assessed on a case-by-case basis. In this respect, in *Hannam v the Financial Conduct Authority*, the Upper Tribunal held that the likelihood of occurrence of the event or set of circumstances does not mean 'that there must be a more than even chance of the circumstances coming into existence or the event occurring. It certainly means that the prospect must not be fanciful. [and] … [w]here the communication or statement contains a mix of accurate and inaccurate information the exercise will be to establish what actual or reasonably expected circumstances and events are indicated by the information taken as a whole'.[10] In this context, when considering what may reasonably be expected to come into existence, a crucial issue will be whether it is reasonable to draw a conclusion based on *ex ante* information available at the time. This issue was recently addressed by the Court of Justice of the European Union (CJEU) in *Geltl v Daimler AG*, where questions were raised as to whether information that is part of a chain of events or a protracted decision-making process could constitute inside information and thus be disclosable. The CJEU ruled that intermediate steps that are part of a protracted decision-making process that lead to a future event can be regarded as inside information irrespective of whether the final event is reasonably expected to occur. In practice, the intermediate steps would, according to CJEU reasoning, constitute historical facts which, in turn, may be deemed as information of a precise nature and, thus, meet the first requirement of the insider dealing definition under Article 1(1).[11]

9.4   As to the 'significant price effect' requirement, Article 1(2) of the Level 2 Implementing Directive specifies that 'information which, if it were made public, would be likely to have a significant effect on the prices of financial instruments or related derivative financial instruments shall mean information a reasonable investor would be likely to use as part of the basis of his investment decisions'. This provision sets out the so-called 'reasonable investor test', according to which the determination of whether the information has an impact on the price of financial instruments depends on whether the reasonable investor would be likely to use the information as part of the basis for his investment decisions. This provision in Article 1(2) of the MAD 1 Implementing Directive has been interpreted as qualifying or substituting for the ordinary meaning of Article 1(1) of MAD 1 that does not have a 'reasonable investor test' and instead only requires that the information has a 'significant effect on the price' of the financial instruments. There is no uniform interpretation and application of Article 1(2) amongst EU Member States. In the UK, the Upper Tribunal in *David Massey v the Financial Services Authority*, interpreted the reasonable investor test based on section 118C(6) of the FSMA.[12] According to the Tribunal, the reasonable investor test was, by itself, sufficient for determining whether the information had a significant effect on the price of the securities. Consequently, regardless of whether the information may actually have had an impact on the price of the securities, it is sufficient, according to the Tribunal in *Massey*, that a reasonable investor uses the information as part of the basis of his

---

10   [2014] UKUT 0233 (TCC).
11   *Case C-19/11, Markus Geltl v Daimler AG* 28 June 2012; see also Article 7(3) of MAR stating that: 'intermediate step in a protracted process shall be deemed to be inside information if, by itself, it satisfies the criteria of inside information as referred to in this Article'.
12   [2011] UKUT 49 (TCC), Upper Tribunal reference FIN/2009/0024.

investment decision.[13] This interpretation raised doubts in some quarters that the Tribunal had given the reasonable investor test a meaning which, rather than supplementing, supplanted the significant price effect test and that it could create uncertainty and inconsistent market practices amongst market participants with regard to disclosure obligations and dealing decisions.[14]

9.5   Successive FCA decisions have followed the Upper Tribunal's broad interpretation of the reasonable investor test in *Massey*.[15] In 2014, however, in the *Hannam* case, the Upper Tribunal regarded the *Massey* approach as simplistic and ruled that the reasonable investor, in the process of making an investment decision, would only rely on information which is likely to have an impact on the price of the security. Also, once made public, this information should enable a prediction as to an upward or downward price movement.[16] Significantly, the *Hannam* case rebalanced the interaction between the reasonable investor test and the significant price effect so that the former supplements (and does not replace) the latter. It remains to be seen the extent to which the provisions of the new EU Market Abuse Regulation (MAR) will overcome the interpretative issues arising from the definition of inside information under the MAD and its Level 2 Implementing Directive. MAR Article 7(5) delegates authority to the European Securities and Market Authority (ESMA) to issue guidelines for developing a non-exhaustive list of examples of information that would be considered inside information and thus would be disclosable.[17] In any case, it is worth recalling that an issuer's disclosure obligation is triggered if all four criteria set out in Article 1(1) of the MAD occur.[18]

DELAYED DISCLOSURE

9.6   Under Article 6(1) of the MAD, Member States have to ensure that any information falling under the definition of 'inside information' be disclosed to the public by the issuer 'as soon as possible'. Indeed, Recital 4 of the Level 2 Implementing Directive clarifies that an issuer's disclosure obligation finds

13   Ibid: 'We consider next whether the information was likely to have a significant effect on the price of the shares. Mr Massey's case is that it was not likely to have such an effect. We would have considerable sympathy with his view if the phrase "likely to have a significant effect on the price" had been used in the Act in its ordinary sense. But we have to apply the specially extended meaning assigned to this expression by s 118C(6). Whether or not the information was (in the ordinary sense) likely to have a significant effect on the price, we consider it is clear that it was information "of a kind which a reasonable investor would be likely to use as part of the basis of his investment decisions".'
14   See, Financial Markets Law Committee, Issue 154 – *Analysis of Legal Uncertainties Arising From Article 6 of the Proposal for a Regulation on Insider Dealing and Market Manipulation* (30 March 2012) Appendix 2.
15   See Hartmut Krause and Michael Brellochs, 'Insider trading and the disclosure of inside information after Geltl v Daimler – A comparative analysis of the ECJ decision in the Geltl v Daimler case with a view to the future European Market Abuse Regulation' (2013) 8 *CMLJ* 3, 292.
16   *Hannam v Financial Conduct Authority*, para 105: The tribunal appears from that passage to have considered that it might be possible to find a situation where a reasonable investor would take into account, in making his investment decision, information which would not in fact have a significant effect on price; but, because of the extended definition in s 118C(6), that information would nonetheless be inside information. It is not at all clear to us why the tribunal put the matter the way it did.
17   See Article 7(5) of MAR.
18   These criteria can are now found in Article 7 of the MAR.

its rationale in the protection of investors that the EU market abuse regime aims at guaranteeing. To this end, it is necessary that the disclosure be fast, synchronised and such that all categories of investors can have equal access to it at Community level. The disclosure requirement for UK issuers is wider than the previous UK listing rules, which only applied to securities that were admitted to the Official List. UK issuers are now required to inform the public 'as soon as possible' of inside information that concerns them.[19] This means as soon as the event occurs. The requirement, however, has been criticised on the grounds that the near immediacy of the disclosure obligation would not give the issuer adequate time to assess the relevance of the information and therefore might result in issuers becoming far more reluctant to disclose information.[20] The FCA has authority to make rules governing information disclosure with respect to instruments admitted to trading in regulated markets.[21] The rules related to instruments admitted to trading on a regulated market are subject to strict disclosure requirements.[22] Issuers are required under the rules to publish and update, if necessary, any inside information. The rules also allow an issuer to delay the publication of insider information in certain circumstances, and require an issuer who discloses information to a third party to publish that information without delay with certain exceptions. It also requires an issuer to draw a list of those persons who have access to inside information that directly relates to the issuer, and requires the issuer's senior management, and those closely connected, to disclose transactions conducted on their own account in the issuer's shares.

9.7   Disclosure obligations raise the question of the extent to which the interest to ensure an adequate level of investor protection can be balanced with the issuer's interest to legitimately delay the disclosure of the information. In this respect, the European Securities Market Expert Group (ESME), in its 2007 report, providing a first evaluation of the EU Market Abuse regime, underlined that: [in the Directive] 'the public good in investors obtaining information as soon as possible is preferred to any public good in allowing companies to delay disclosure, in all but the most limited circumstances'. However, the MAD does allow issuers to delay the disclosure of information. In this respect, Article 6(2) of the MAD clarifies that: 'An issuer may under his own responsibility delay the public disclosure of inside information such as not to prejudice his legitimate interests provided that such omission would not be likely to mislead the public and provided that the issuer is able to ensure the confidentiality of that information. Member States may require that an issuer shall without delay inform the competent authority of the decision to delay the public disclosure of inside information.' While this rule sets out the possibility of delaying the disclosure, Article 3 of the Level 2 Implementing Directive indicates those (non-exhaustive) circumstances in light of which the issuer's delay is legitimate. Reference is made to negotiations in course or decisions taken on contracts by the management body. These are situations which may make a

---

19   Article 6(1).
20   CESR's 'Advice on Level 2 Implementing Measures for the Market Abuse Directive' CESR/02–89d, (CESR: Paris), p 34. This also complies with the Second Company Law Directive 77/91/EEC. HM Treasury observed that this requirement should allow for a longer period to disclose, but the FCA has implemented CESR's interpretation for immediate disclosure. See DTR 2.2.1R.
21   FSMA, s 73A. Rules made under this power and the existing power with respect to listed securities are known as Part VI rules.
22   FSMA, s 96A.

delay legitimate if the disclosure may jeopardise the interest of existing or potential shareholders. It appears that, under these circumstances, the decision of delaying the disclosure must be the result of an *ex ante* evaluation by the issuer as to the possibility of hampering the shareholders' interest through the disclosure. These are the only two mitigating circumstances as to the issuer's disclosure obligation. The list is non-exhaustive and therefore other factual scenarios might qualify to permit the issuer to delay the disclosure of inside information if doing so for a legitimate reason that is in the interest of shareholders and serves broader public policy regulatory objectives.[23] Based on CESR's advice, the FCA has accepted several examples of when delay is acceptable, such as if disclosure would harm the issuer's interests, or affect the negotiation of a deal.[24] Issuers, however, delay at their own risk and, therefore, if delay is unjustified, they may incur market abuse liability.[25] The FCA has made it clear in several enforcement actions that listed companies must carefully consider what could be inside information and their obligations to disclose. For example, it is unacceptable for a company not to disclose negative news because it believes other matters are likely to offset it. By failing to correct the negative news immediately, an investor's ability is hampered to make informed investment decisions and risks distorting the market.[26]

SELECTIVE DISCLOSURE

9.8 The sharing of information is key for efficient business transactions in modern financial markets. The internet has facilitated the dissemination of information to market participants. It can also, however, be a source of abusive behaviour. In such an environment, it is important that the distribution of information in the normal course of business is conducted in a way that does not unduly expose the firm or its agents to liability for insider dealing or market manipulation. This concern is reflected in Article 6(3)'s requirement that issuers must make prompt public disclosure when they have disclosed inside information to a third party in the course of their employment, profession or duties.[27] Cross-border disclosures to third parties must be made to the relevant authorities of the jurisdictions in question when such disclosures involve parties in EEA states.[28]

9.9 The FCA has put this in practice with Disclosure Rule 9A.7 which allows an issuer to delay disclosure of inside information provided that it does not mislead the public and provided the issuer can ensure confidentiality. The rule states, however, that any decision to delay disclosure is taken at the issuer's own risk. For instance, delayed disclosure could be limited to matters under negotiation, but is unlikely to be extended to other circumstances. When the disclosure is made, it should distinguish between an event giving rise to inside information (ie loss of a big contract) and subsequent events (ie attempting to renegotiate contract).

---

23 See Article 17(5) of the MAR which widens the range of possible scenarios for legitimate delay by referring, *inter alia*, to the need to preserve the stability of the financial system.
24 CESR's Advice (Dec 2002), p 23. See DTR 2.5.1R and 11.12.
25 Article 6(1), Directive 2003/6/EC.
26 FSA, Final Notice, Wolfson Microelectronics plc (Jan 2009). See also, FSA Final Notice *Woolworths Group plc* (12 June 2008).
27 See DTR 2.2. Pursuant to s 157 of FSMA, the FCA has published guidance on DTR obligations in the DTR.
28 Directive 2003/6/EC, Article 6(3).

MANAGERIAL DISCLOSURES

9.10　The managers of issuers and other senior officers are required to disclose their share dealings in the issuer. All managers privy to inside information are required to disclose to the RNS every time they buy or sell shares in their employers. This has had broad impact on corporate disclosure, as a large number of senior managers below board level are exposed to price-sensitive material. It should be remembered that these rules apply to spread bets and derivatives as well as to shares trading.

SAFE HARBOURS

9.11　Article 8 of the Directive exempts from the insider trading prohibitions an issuer's buy back of shares in an initial public offering and any buying and selling of securities intended to stabilise the market for an issuer's equity or debt securities in a secondary offering by insiders who have complied with the Commission's Regulation containing the stabilisation rules.[29] The Directive states in its commentary that '[t]rading in own shares and stabilisation however must be carried out transparently in order to avoid insider dealing or giving misleading signals to the markets. Trading in own shares could be used to strengthen the equity capital of issuers and so would be in investors' interests'.[30]

ISSUER DISCLOSURE AND THIRD PARTY LISTS

9.12　The FCA disclosure rules apply to all issuers who have requested or been approved admission of their financial instruments to trading on a regulated market.[31] These disclosure rules require the issuer to publish without delay in the following circumstances: when the issuer has certain price-sensitive information about the issuer's securities; when there has been any significant change concerning inside information in certain circumstances; and when an issuer or any person acting on its behalf discloses inside information to a third party.[32] Moreover, an issuer is required to maintain lists of those persons working for it (as independent advisers or employees) who have access to inside information relating directly or indirectly to the issuer.[33] Individuals discharging managerial responsibilities within the organisational structure of the issuer, and any persons connected to such persons discharging managerial responsibilities (eg family members, close associates or friends), are required to disclose transactions conducted on their own account in shares of the issuer, or derivatives or any other financial instrument relating to those shares.[34]

9.13　In addition, issuers must create lists of third parties who are likely to have access to inside information. These lists must be released to the FCA when required or requested by the FCA. This requirement has been criticised

29　Article 6, para 5.
30　Commentary to the proposed Directive.
31　FSMA, s 96A(1).
32　Section 96A(2)(a)–(d).
33　Section 96A(2)(e).
34　Section 96A(2)(f).

because of the significant compliance costs of monitoring information within a business organisation. It has been argued that the cost of maintaining these lists is disproportionate to the regulatory benefit or to the benefit of the market.[35]

ISSUER AND SENIOR OFFICER LIABILITY

9.14   As a general matter, it should also be emphasised that market abuse can be committed by individuals, legal persons (companies, businesses, LLPs, LLCs, and other business entities) where the entity commits the offence. The Directive requires all Member States to impose civil or administrative sanctions for market abuse on 'any natural or legal person'. This makes all corporations, partnerships and other business entities civilly liable for market abuse. Article 6 requires that any 'natural person, or entity, professionally arranging transactions in financial instruments shall refrain from entering into transactions, and reject orders on behalf of its clients, if it reasonably suspects that a transaction would be based on inside information'. The entity may have been deemed to have committed the offence if its senior managers or officers have engaged in behaviour that amounts to market abuse while discharging their official functions for the firm. The attribution of liability to the firm for the market misconduct of its employees was an issue in the FCA's enforcement action against GLG Partners in 2005.[36] GLG Partners was a limited partnership whose managing director, Philippe Jabre, had committed market abuse after trading on the basis of price-sensitive information which he had received from a third party bank. The issue was whether GLG Partners should be subjected to a penalty for Jabre's abuse of the market. The FCA issued a Decision Notice holding that GLG Partners had failed to maintain adequate internal controls to oversee the activities of Jabre, a leading fund manager at the firm, and that the weaknesses in its internal oversight significantly contributed to the environment in which Jabre was able to abuse the market. The FCA imposed a £750,000 penalty on GLG Partners in part to require the firm to disgorge its ill-gotten gains and to deter future poor oversight of its senior fund managers.

9.15   Officers, employees, or agents of the company or business organisation may also be held liable personally or individually for the firm's commission of the market abuse offence if certain conditions are satisfied: (a) if the offence was committed with consent or connivance of the officer, or (b) the offence is attributable to neglect on the part of the officer. The FCA would need to show that the individuals in question had in fact participated in some meaningful way – either through action or inaction – in the firm's commission of the offence.

PROFESSIONAL DISCLOSURE REQUIREMENTS

9.16   Civil liability for market abuse arises for any person professionally arranging transactions in financial instruments who reasonably suspects insider dealing or market manipulation if they fail to report the suspected behaviour to

---

35   CESR (August 2003) 'Feedback Statement for Level 2 Implementing Measures' CESR/03–213b (CESR: Paris), p 12.
36   See the Financial Service Authority's Decision Notice to Philippe Jabre and to GLG Partners (28 February 2006).

the FCA. In other words, professionals must disclose suspicious transactions.[37] For issuers, the determination of indicative factors that identify suspicious transactions is determined by guidelines set forth by the FCA. For third party professionals, indicative factors will be determined in part by professional codes and guidelines approved by the FCA.

9.17   Brokers and spread betting firms are obliged to report all transactions to the FCA if they suspect insider dealing or market manipulation. Brokers have complained about these suspicious transaction reports, as they are duplicative of existing requirements to report transactions that might be related to money laundering or terrorist financing. In addition, brokers will have to report the sources of research information and any potential conflicts of interest.

PROFESSIONALS AND CONFIDENTIALITY

9.18   The emphasis on disclosure in the market abuse regime can arguably be criticised on the grounds that it places an undue burden upon professionals, requiring them to be responsible for policing their firms and professions. Following the corporate governance scandals of the early 2000s and the subsequent weaknesses of financial institutions as demonstrated in the 2007/08 financial crisis, however, the focus on issuer disclosure and third party professional disclosure is now more favourably viewed by investors and other users of financial products.

9.19   The market abuse regime's requirements that professionals disclose suspicious transactions has raised confidentiality concerns, as they are obliged to report to the FCA if they suspect insider dealing or market manipulation in respect of a client's account. This action can potentially harm professional-client relationships, possibly undermining investor confidence, and inhibiting issuers from using third party professionals when accessing the capital markets if they fear disclosure to regulatory authorities of confidential information. On the other hand, a strict disclosure regime can reduce the likelihood of market abuse, thus promoting more transparency in the market and enhancing its integrity with the result that more investors will have confidence to invest in the market. It should be recalled that Article 6 of the Directive requires that issuers of financial instruments inform the public as soon as possible of inside information, subject to various confidentiality and other exemptions.[38]

FCA FAVOURS ENHANCED DISCLOSURE

9.20   In light of the Financial Services Authority's investigations into volatile share price movements of UK financial institutions during the 2008–09 market turbulence, the UK government has taken a stricter stance on disclosure to enhance the integrity of UK financial markets. Although most of the volatility in 2008–09 arose from a loss of investor confidence in UK equity markets and a dramatic de-leveraging in asset exposures by institutional investors and hedge funds due to limited access to liquidity, the UK government in 2008 blamed

37   This provision mirrors the UK money laundering legislation that requires disclosure of suspicious transactions. Proceeds of Crime Act 2002, s 330.
38   Article 6, paras 1–4, contains related restrictions on selective disclosure. See 9.2–9.4 above.

much of the market turbulence on short selling by institutional investors and other allegedly abusive practices.[39]

9.21   The resulting regulatory practice of both the FSA and later the FCA was to require much stricter disclosures by issuers and professional advisers of suspicious transactions that could possibly, but not necessarily, amount to market abuse. In deciding whether to take enforcement action in cases involving issuer disclosure, the FSA will have regard to specific guidance on the identification of inside information set out from DTR 2.2.3G to DTR 2.2.8G.[40]

ISSUER'S DISCLOSURE DECISION TREE

9.22   To summarise the issuer's obligations in a general context, the following decision tree could be useful. Detailed compliance, however, should always take account of the facts of each situation and the issuer involved and applicable regulatory rules and requirements.

TAKEOVERS

9.23   The Panel on Takeovers and Mergers administers the City Code on Takeovers and Mergers. The City Code (known as the 'Takeover Code') contains general principles and rules governing takeovers and mergers for companies listed on the UK market.

GENERAL PRINCIPLES

9.24   The essential requirements of the Takeover Code's general principles are the following: equality of treatment for shareholders; adequate information and advice for shareholders; the maintenance of fair and orderly markets for shares of the company during periods of the offer; and no board or management action to thwart an offer by a target company during the offer period without shareholder approval. Significantly, General Principle 7 prohibits defensive measures to frustrate bids by target companies (ie poison pills) without shareholder approval. Also important is Rule 21.1, which allows the offeror company to break through certain offeree company restrictions (eg restrictions on share voting rights and transfer of securities) and to tender for a company's shares.

THE TAKEOVER PANEL'S POWERS

9.25   The Takeover Panel has no formal sanctioning power but its decisions are respected and have been given effect by market participants and regulated persons. The Takeover Panel exercises influence in a number of ways including

---

39   See FSA limitations on short selling in the shares of financial institutions (August 2008).
40   See FSA Final Notice *Entertainment Rights plc* (19 January 2009).

Does the issuer have inside information?

Can an issuer legitimately delay disclosure of inside information?

Can an issuer selectively disclose inside information?

Does the issuer have inside information?

To be inside information the information must be:

- Precise
- Not generally available
- Relate to qualifying investments
- Price sensitive (DTR 2.2.4 G)

Can an issuer legitimately delay disclosure of inside information?

It can delay so as not to prejudice its legitimate interests provided:

- It does not mislead the public
- Selective disclosure is confidential
- Issuer can ensure confidentiality (DTR 2.5.1.R)

Can the issuer selectively disclose inside information?

- Yes as long as there is a confidentiality obligation and
- The recipient has valid reason to receive the information (DTR 2.5.7 G)

Disclosure must be made as soon as possible if the issuer is not able to ensure confidentiality of the information
(DTR 2.6.2 R)

Issuer disclosure

by making critical statements about the conduct of a bid; panel members often influence senior management which can affect a firm's commitment to follow through with a merger. Some Panel decisions may be recognised by professional bodies and by the FCA and thereby serve as a basis for sanctions to be imposed against the person in a breach of the Code. For example, the FCA can withdraw authorisation from a person or company for failing to comply with the Code which can result, for instance, in a delisting from the London Stock Exchange.

THE FCA's ROLE

9.26   Under the FSMA, the FCA has significant investigative and enforcement powers against conduct which may amount to market abuse. In the context of takeovers there can be an overlap between the FCA and the Takeover Panel which may disrupt the takeover bid process. Consequently, the two regulators issued a set of guidelines to ensure effective coordination between them. According to the 2013 'Operating Guidelines between the Financial Conduct Authority and the Panel on Takeovers and Mergers on Market Misconduct', the FCA and the Panel will liaise on market, policy, and enforcement issues of mutual interest.[41] In particular, if issues amounting to market misconduct arise during a takeover bid, the FCA and the Panel will be required to liaise as follows: (1) the FCA will not exercise its investigative and enforcement powers during a takeover bid prior to the conclusion of the procedures under the Takeover Code except in certain circumstances;[42] (2) the FCA will consult the Panel before taking any action which may affect the timetable or outcome of a takeover bid. However, the following principles apply in case the FCA decides to exercise its powers during a takeover bid: (a) the FCA will keep the Panel informed of the steps it is taking in the exercise of its powers and will give due weight to the Panel's views on any issues which arise; and (b) in cases where the Panel also has the power to take action, the matter will be reviewed regularly as it develops to determine whether the lead responsibility for dealing with the matter should be with the FCA or the Panel. Furthermore, in case of concurrent investigations and enforcement actions, the FCA and the Panel will be required to coordinate in accordance with the following principles: (1) persons should not be subject to more than one investigation or set of enforcement proceedings for the same misconduct unless it is appropriate for the FCA and the Panel to exercise different powers in relation to that person or the two sets of investigations or proceedings relate to different aspects of the suspected misconduct; and (2) cases of mutual interest will be reviewed regularly as they develop to determine whether the lead responsibility for conducting any necessary investigation should be with the FCA or the Panel.

9.27   The FCA may overrule the Panel in areas such as takeovers where they have overlapping responsibility. The Code of Market Conduct provides a defence for persons who take certain actions to comply with the Takeover Code

---

41   The guidelines can be accessed at: http://www.fca.org.uk/static/documents/operating-guidelines-takeover-panel.pdf.

42   The exceptional circumstances to be considered during a takeover bid are: (1) where the Panel requests the FCA to consider the use of any of the following powers: the FCA's power to impose penalties (s 123 of FSMA), the power of the court to impose penalties (s 129 of FSMA), injunctive powers (s 381 of FSMA) and restitutionary powers (ss 383 or 384 of FSMA; (2) where the suspected misconduct falls within sub-ss 118(2)–(4) of FSMA (misuse of information) or Part V of the Criminal Justice Act 1993 (insider dealing); (3) where the suspected misconduct extends to securities or a class of securities which may be outside the Panel's jurisdiction; (4) where the suspected misconduct threatens or has threatened the stability of the financial system.

that come within the safe harbour provisions of the Market Abuse Directive.[43] For instance, if an issuer is engaging in certain acceptable market practices as defined in the Directive and recognised by the FCA in disclosing information according to a timetable recognised by the FCA in the Takeover Code, then that behaviour – ie a disclosure (or not) that is required by Takeover Code – is protected against market abuse liability.

MARKET ABUSE

9.28   Certain Code rules if not complied with may result in market abuse liability.

Rule 2.2 requires that the offeror must announce a possible takeover when, following the approach to the offeree company, unusual movements occur in the offeree's share price, or the offeree is subject to rumour or speculation.[44] Also, the offeror must announce a takeover attempt before an approach is made to the offeree if there is an unusual share price movement and it is reasonable that such movement is attributable to the offeror's actions.[45] The offeror must also announce when negotiations are extended to include more than a restricted group of persons ('outside those who need to know in the parties concerned and their immediate advisers').[46] Breach of these rules can potentially lead to a FCA enforcement action for market abuse.

ACTUAL OR POTENTIAL OFFERORS

9.29   Rule 2.1 requires third party advisers (eg accountants) who are privy to price-sensitive inside information to keep offer discussions secret and that they should not approach additional third parties without prior approval of the Panel. According to the Rule, secret information can be passed to another person if it is necessary to do so and that person is made aware that the information must be kept secret. The FCA can enforce breach of this rule by imposing sanctions. For example, an accountant seeking to avoid market abuse liability under this rule would be required to obtain approval from the Panel before disseminating the information to other parties. This would be an example of acceptable market practices under the safe harbour of the Market Abuse Directive and the FCA would likely recognise the safe harbour by not seeking market abuse sanctions.

---

43   See discussion in Chapter 4 at 4.31–4.40.
44   See Rule 2.2(c) of the City Code on Takeovers and Mergers (the Takeover Code), available at: http://www.thetakeoverpanel.org.uk/wp-content/uploads/2008/11/code.pdf.
45   See Rule 2.2(d) of the Takeover Code.
46   See Rule 2.2(e) of the Takeover Code.

Chapter 10

Information gathering

INTRODUCTION

10.1　This chapter considers the role of information in supplying the Financial Conduct Authority with intelligence about potential abuse in the financial markets and weakness in the arrangements that firms are required to have in place to comply with their regulatory obligations. The chapter will show that even before the Financial Conduct Authority (FCA) chooses to conduct a formal investigation, information is gathered from a variety of sources including that routinely obtained from transaction reporting, reports of suspicious activity and information otherwise supplied by authorised persons. The gathering of information and market intelligence facilitates the FCA in developing and understanding the extent to which market participants are involved in, or the market itself is exposed to, abusive behaviour, thus allowing it to appropriately focus its investigation and enforcement activity. Indeed the FCA's use of information gathering is an integral part of its role as an investigator and enforcement agency. The analysis provided in this chapter thus complements Chapter 11's examination of the FCA's powers of investigation. Notably this chapter will identify that the FCA places significant reliance on firms to be open and cooperative, even to the extent of it recognising in its enforcement guide the merit, in appropriate circumstances, for an authorised person to carry out its own investigation for the purpose of supplying information to the FCA. In paragraph 3.18 of the Enforcement Guide (EG) the FCA states:

> 'A firm's report – produced internally or by an external third party – can clearly assist the firm, but may also be useful to the FCA where there is an issue of regulatory concern. Sharing the outcome of an investigation can potentially save time and resources for both parties, particularly where there is a possibility of the FCA taking enforcement action in relation to a firm's perceived misconduct or failing.

10.2　In analysing the role of information gathering this chapter considers the general reporting obligations imposed upon authorised firms, the regulatory obligation imposed upon those persons executing transactions to routinely and timely report those transactions to the FCA, and the regulatory obligation to report suspicious transactions, along with the FCA's statutory powers to gather

information including the use of skilled persons pursuant to section 166 of the
Financial Services and Markets Act 2000 (FSMA).[1]

GENERAL REPORTING AND THE OBLIGATION TO COOPERATE

10.3   The FCA provides in its rules a series of obligations requiring
authorised persons, and to an extent approved persons, to proactively disclose
matters that may be of concern to the FCA as well as to cooperate during
any FCA supervisory or investigative activity. As will be apparent from the
following analysis such obligations apply equally to concerns of market abuse
and more general issues regarding an authorised person's systems and controls.
The primary reporting and cooperation obligation applying to authorised
persons is provided in FCA Principle for Business 11, which requires 'A firm
must deal with its regulators in an open and cooperative way, and must disclose
to the FCA appropriately anything relating to the firm of which the FCA would
reasonably expect notice.' An equivelant obligation is imposed on authorised
persons at Principle 4 of the Approved Persons Code which provides: 'An
approved person must deal with the FCA and with other regulators in an
open and cooperative way and must disclose appropriately any information
of which the FCA would reasonably expect notice.' The importance attached
to compliance with Principle 11 can be found in the FCA Final Notice to
Threadneedle Asset Management Limited on 10 December 2015.[2] Although
that case is not concerned with Market Abuse but rather with Threadneedles'
trading controls and communication with the FCA about the steps it had
taken to strengthen those controls, it is clear from wording of the Final Notice
and the level of the financial penalty (£6,038,504) that the FCA treats non-
compliance with Principal 11 seriously. The FCA states in the Final Notice at
paragraph 2.10: 'TAML breached Principle 11 because it did not accurately
describe the trading processes in place on its Emerging Markets and High
Yield trading desks when it responded to the Authority in the RMP Response
on 30 June 2011 and it did not correct its response until 28 October 2011.'

10.4   Considering first the obligation of disclosure, the generality of that
obligation leaves for interpretation the nature and materiality of what the
FCA would expect to be dislcosed as well as the timliness of the disclosure.
Determining what information is required to be disclosed under Principle 11
is challenging, although what is apparent from the wording of Principle 11
is that information to be disclosed is not determined by reference to the
reasonable assessment of the authorised person but rather by reference to an
objective assessment of the FCA's expectations. Indeed the FCA's notification
expectations are to some extent likely to vary, dependent on the circumstances,
size and risks of the business of the individual authorised person. Some
assistance to this notification dilemma is provided in the FCA Supervision
sourcebook (SUP) which at SUP 15.3.8G provides guidance, by way of a non
exhaustive list, on those matters of which the FCA would expect notification

1   In addition to drawing from and updating material from B Rider *et al Market and Abuse
    and Insider Dealing* (2nd edn), this chapter includes material drawn from S Bazley, *Market
    Abuse Enforcement Practice and Procedure* (Bloomsbury Professional 2013).
2   FCA Final Notice *Threadneedle Asset Management Limited* (10 December 2015) http://www.
    fca.org.uk/your-fca/documents/final-notices/2015/threadneedle-asset-management-limited.

258

under Principle 11. However, none of the examples at 15.3.8G directly address instances of market abuse. Arguably given the existence of the market abuse suspicious transaction reporting requirement in SUP 15.10 (which is examined in 10.14–10.16 below), a Principle 11 disclosure may better serve notification of systemic failing within an authorised firm's business than addressing issues of market abuse. For example, a failure in an authorised firm's conflict management and information barrier controls (see further Chapter 8 and Chapter 13) is likely to warrant a notification to the FCA. Indeed SUP 15.3.8G(2) describes a Principle 11 notification of 'any significant failure in the firm's systems or controls, including those reported to the firm by the firm's auditor'. It is submitted, however, that when one applies the generality of Principle 11 along with the FCA's statutory 'integrity objective' (see section 1D of the FSMA which defines at section 1D(1) the FCA integrity objective as 'protecting and enhancing the integrity of the UK financial system' and at section 1D(2) where 'integrity of the UK financial system' is defined as including '… not being used for a purpose connected with financial crime' and 'its not being affected by behaviour that amounts to market abuse'. Section 1H(3) defines financial crime as including offences invloving 'a) fraud or dishonesty, b) misconduct in, or misuse of information relating to, a financial market, c) handling the proceeds of crime, or d) the financing of terrorism'), it is difficult to forsee the FCA not expecting disclosure under Principle 11 of market abuse subject matter where a disclosure is technically not required under the suspicious transaction reporting regime, such as where there has been an unsuccessful attempt at abuse. It is important to note, however, that the EU Market Abuse Regulation (2014/596/EU), which comes into force on 3 July 2016, introduces an obligation to report suspicious orders in addition to suspicious transactions.

10.5 A second tier of more specific authorised persons reporting obligations is provided by the FCA in SUP, many of which, can have an application to market abuseas well as the market abuse compliance arrangements that authorised persons are required to maintain. For instance, SUP 15.3.11R imposes a reporting obligation in the context of significant breaches of the FCA rules, breaches of financial services regulation or FSMA and prosecution for a FSMA offence, whether in relation to the authorised person or its employees, directors, officers or agents. SUP 15.3.17R addresses reporting from the perspective of fraud and misconduct, requiring reporting of significant fraud by employees against customers or by any persons against the authorised person and serious misconduct by employees. The FCA has not provided in SUP 15.3.17R a definition of the word 'fraud', although of course constituent elements of fraud offences are dishonesty and intention (for example, see the offences under the Fraud Act 2006).

10.6 It is submitted that the exploitation of information or market trading resulting in another investor suffering a loss may in certain circumstances consitite an offence of fraud (see further Chapters 3, 5 and 6). However, (as explored in Chapter 4) dishonesty and an 'actuating purpose' is not a constituent element of market abuse under section 118 of the FSMA and thus not all instances of abuse may be notifiable under the fraud notification provisions of SUP 15.3.17R.

10.7 In addition to proactive disclosure, Principle 11 also refers to an imperative to cooperate with the FCA. The FCA addresses in guidance at SUP 2.3 amongst other things the obligation for cooperation in the context of information gathering, paying particular attention to the need for cooperation

10.7   *Information gathering*

under Principle 11 when addressing (at SUP 2.3.3G) its access to an authorised person's records as well as for authorised persons to 'answer truthfully, fully and promptly all questions which are reasonably put to it'. The need for, and extent of, cooperation becomes particulalry pertinent during FCA formal investigations and enforcement. At EG 2.33 the FCA explains that an authorised person's cooperation will be taken into account when considering enforcement action, including the extent to which the substance of the enforcment action was self reported by the authorised person. The FCA states at EG 2.33 'In this respect, relevant matters may include whether the person has self-reported, helped the FCA establish the facts and/or taken remedial action such as addressing any systems and controls issues and compensating any consumers who have lost out'. Furthermore the FCA sets out in its Decision Procedure and Penalties Manual (DEPP) that a person's conduct after a breach will be taken into account in addressing whether or not to impose a penalty including: '(a) how quickly, effectively and completely the person brought the breach to the attention of the FCA ...; (b) the degree of co-operation the person showed during the investigation of the breach ...'. Further similar guidance is provided at DEPP 6.5A.3G as to its mitigating effect in step 3 of the FCA's 5-step approach to financial penalty setting. (Chapter 12 examines in detail the FCA approach to enforcement and financial penalties). Although it is important to highlight that the obligation to cooperate under Principle 11 does not apply to members of the public (who may be exposed to the market abuse regime), the provisions in DEPP are applicable to the FCA's decision in commencing a formal investigation or taking enforcement action against the public. The impact of self-reporting and cooperation by members of the public can be illustrated in decisions such as the FSA Final Notice to *Mehmet Sepil*,[3] in respect of insider dealing under section 118(2) of the FSMA, where Mr Sepil chose to notify the FCA of his trading behaviour. In that case the Final Notice states: 'The FSA has taken into account your high degree of co-operation in coming forward, providing information about your dealing and others and in co-operating with the FSA investigation.'[4]

10.8   It is also important to recognise that the FCA may also receive confidential or anonymous disclosures relating to potential market abuse made under the Public Interest Disclosure Act 1998. Indeed the FCA has been given powers under sections 71 and 72 of the Serious Organised Crime and Police Act 2005 to give so-called whistleblowers who cooperate with the FCA statutory immunity from prosecution,[5] although concern has previously been expressed about the extent to which city professionals may be willing to 'whistleblow' on their colleagues.[6] The FCA promotes the availability of confidential

---

3   FSA Final Notice *Mehmet Sepil* (12 February 2010).
4   *Mehmet Sepil* (note 3) at [3.6].
5   The FSA was given power under s 71 of the Serious and Organised Crime and Police Act 2005 (following amendment by the Coroners and Justice Act 2009 s 113(2)). For general comment on proposals for an FSA statutory immunity and commentary on the City's culture of blowing the whistle see Gary Wilson and Sarah Wilson, 'Market Misconduct, the Financial Services FSA and creating a system of "city grasses": blowing the whistle on whistle-blowing' (2010) 31(3) *Comp Law* 67.
6   See 'Whistles the City boys just won't blow' *Evening Standard*, Business Section, 1 April 2008. In addition the BBC reported at http://news.bbc.co.uk/1/hi/business/7317845.stm, 'Treasury eyes whistleblower plan', that Chris Brennan (partner at law firm Barlow Lyde and Gilbert) said 'I am not sure how much the whistleblowing provisions will help, but the plea bargaining may well incentivise individuals to plead and avoid the need for a trial'.

disclosures through confidential reporting to its intelligence department.[7] Whilst the guidance encourages (in the FS Handbook Senior Management Systems and Controls sourcebook (SYSC) 18) authorised persons to maintain internal confidential whistleblowing procedures, the UK Parliamentary Commission on Banking Standards made a series of recommendations in relation to whistleblowing, which have resulted in new rules coming into force from March 2016 applying to PRA authorised firms. These new rules at SYSC 18 and SYSC 4.5 require the appointment of a senior manager within the firm with responsibility for acting as the firm's 'whistleblowing champion'.

Transaction reporting

10.9   Those authorised persons executing transactions in qualifying investments that are admitted to trading on a regulated or prescribed market are required to report prescribed information on those transactions to the FCA. The basis for the transaction reporting obligation is derived currently from Article 25(3) of the Markets in Financial Instruments Framework Directive (MiFID),[8] which provides:

> 'Member States shall require investment firms which execute transactions in any financial instruments admitted to trading on a regulated market to report details of such transactions to the competent FCA as quickly as possible, and no later than the close of the following working day. This obligation shall apply whether or not such transactions were carried out on a regulated market.'

It is important to note that modifications will be made to the European rules on transaction reporting as a result of EU Second Markets in Financial Instruments Directive, which when in force will extend transaction reporting to cover a wider range of financial instruments, such as those where their underlying investments are traded on a venue, as well as instruments trading on Multilateral Trading Facilities and Organised Trading Facilities.

10.10   In addition to the reporting requirements the FCA is also required by the markets in Financial Instruments Directive to exchange appropriate transaction reports, such as those from the UK branches of all EEA authorised firms through the European Securities Markets Authority transaction reporting exchange mechanism to other EEA regulatory authorities. The FCA has implemented Article 25(3) transaction reporting requirements through the provisions in SUP 17, which sets out detailed technical provisions addressing the class of authorised persons required to report transactions, the type of transactions that are reportable and the content and method of reporting. The FCA has also published a Transaction Reporting User Pack (TRUP)[9] which

7   See the FCA whistleblowing section of its website at https://www.the-fca.org.uk/whistleblowing. The promotion of so called whistleblowing to encourage the reporting of financial crime has increased amongst regulatory agencies. For example in 2008 the SFO established a confidential reporting system allowing employees of legal, accountancy and financial services to report concerns about fraud and financial crime. See SFO press release 'City Insiders and advisers asked to help to prevent fraud', 15 December 2008, at http://www.sfo.gov.uk/press-room/press-release-archive/press-releases-2008/city-insiders-and-advisers-asked-to-help-prevent-fraud.aspx.
8   EU Markets in Financial Instruments Directive Council Directive 2004/39/EC OJL145/1.
9   FCA Transaction Reporting User Pack version 3.1 in force from 6 February 2015. See http://www.fca.org.uk/your-fca/documents/finalised-guidance/fg15-03.

provides essential guidance on the approaches the FCA expects firms to take in order to provide compliant reporting. The core reporting obligation arises for firms that execute transactions as provided at SUP 17.1.4R, with the term 'transaction' defined in the FCA glossary as 'only the purchase and sale of a financial instrument'. The FCA further provides a wide definition of the critical term 'execute', which covers both where a person completes a trade instruction as well as the transmission to another of an instruction to execute the transaction: '(in relation to a transaction) carry into effect or perform the transaction, whether as principal or as agent, including instructing another person to execute the transaction'. Further clarification of the term 'execution' is provided by the FCA at TRUP 9.5 where it draws a distinction between transactions and orders stating that 'there is no reporting obligation for firms that simply receive and transmit orders to another firm to execute' but the FCA clarifies such proposition by in effect explaining at TRUP 9.5 that for the purpose of reporting, order transmission only occurs where the 'executing broker ... has the relationship with the client'. This clarification in effect excludes from reporting trading introductions such as that described at TRUP 4: 'if the firm is simply receiving and transmitting a client order (and plays no role in executing the transaction), then it has no transaction reporting obligation, providing it has also transmitted the identity of the client to the executing broker ...'.

10.11   The FCA has extended the MIFID reporting obligation so that as confirmed by SUP 17.1.4R reporting is required by authorised persons which 'execute transactions' in financial instruments (which are defined to include instruments such as securities, units in collective investments, options and futures including those relating to relating to securities and commodities and financial contracts for difference[10]) and are admitted to trading on regulated or prescribed markets,[11] thus bringing within the scope of reporting the London Stock Exchange Alternative Investment Market. Reporting is also required for trade execution as described in SUP 17.1.4R as 'any OTC derivative the value of which is derived from, or which is otherwise dependent upon, an equity or debt-related financial instrument which is admitted to trading on a regulated market or on a prescribed market'. Importantly as confirmed in SUP 17.1.4R it is irrelevant for transaction reporting whether the transaction is executed on the regulated or prescribed market and thus transactions executed off market between counterparties or clients are likely to be reportable.

10.12   Strict time limits apply to when transaction reports must be made with the FCA requiring at SUP 17.2.7R that transaction reports be made 'no later than the close of the working day following the day upon which the transaction took place'. The rules in SUP 17.2 allow for transaction reports to be made on the authorised person's behalf by a third party such as the regulated market, a Multilateral Trading Facility or an Approved Reporting Mechanism (ARM), but where such third party reporting is elected, the FCA expects as set out at SUP 17.2.4G that the authorised person will takes steps to verify that the reports are being made. The accuracy of transaction reporting is vital as will be shown 10.13 below. Firms with the obligation to report are expected to establish appropriate transaction reporting systems of control to ensure both accurate and timely reporting (see further Chapter 13 which considers

---

10   The full list of financial instruments is set out in the FCA's glossary.
11   See the Financial Services and Markets Act 2000 (Prescribed Markets and Qualifying Investments) Order 2001 (SI 2001/996).

compliance procedures and systems). At paragraph 10.1 of the Transaction Reporting User Pack the FCA highlights the range of internal reporting arrangements that it considers will most likely be necessary, which include, 'a clear allocation of responsibility ... within an organisation; appropriate training for staff ... appropriate information ... to enable proper oversight; testing whether Alternative Reporting Mechanisms are used; appropriate oversight of transaction reporting by compliance, including reviews, as part of the compliance monitoring program ...'. In addition in order to enable firms to you verify that their transaction reports have been submitted accurately to the FCA, the authority offers a service allowing firms to obtain samples their submitted reports. The content of the reporting is prescribed tightly, being drawn from requirements in article 13(1) of the MiFID implementing regulations. The exact reporting data required is set out in SUP 17 annex 1 covering, in particular, information such as the names of financial instruments transacted, the amount, whether the transaction was a buy or a sell, the time of execution and the execution venue and an identification of the authorised person, client and transaction counterparty.

10.13   Given the volume of transactions that are reported to the FCA, the Authority uses the Transaction Reporting Pack to stress to firms the imperative of notifying the FCA promptly of failings in transaction reporting. Indeed, as will be explored further below, the FCA has taken tough enforcement action against firms that fail to report and thus, given the general reporting obligations discussed above, such as that arising from high-level principle for business 11 and with the regard that will be had to self-reporting confirmed at DEPP 6.2.1G(2), it is clear that prompt reporting of failings is vital. At paragraph 10.3 of TRUP the FCA sets out that in the event of a failing it expects firms to notify following items,

'The nature and extent of the reporting failure, including the volume of transactions affected and length of time the problem has persisted;

The causes of the failure and how it was identified;

Who within the firm has oversight responsibility for transaction reporting;

Your firm's plan, including a timetable, to submit corrected transaction reports;

Details of your firm's systems and controls around transaction reporting, including its processes for addressing response files from your chosen ARM(s);

Any weaknesses in your firm's systems and controls and your plans to address these; and

Any planned audit or compliance monitoring reviews of transaction reporting and the scope of these'

10.14   Since August 2011, transaction data reported to the FCA has been processed through its monitoring and surveillance system known as Zen,[12] which amongst other things, with the application of algorithms, provides the FCA with increased functionality for handling large volumes of transactions and associated market abuse monitoring. The FCA's Transaction Monitoring Unit has a variety of responsibilities covering both market abuse surveillance

---

12   See FSA Market Watch 39 March 2011 http://www.fsa.gov.uk/pubs/newsletters/mw_newsletter38.pdf which describes the FSA's transition to its Zen surveillance system.

including surveillance of wider market issues, as well as monitoring whether the transaction reporting rules have been complied with. Given this context, the FCA has routinely stressed the importance of daily transaction reporting. At paragraph 2.1 of the transaction reporting user pack the FCA highlights that the functionality of its transaction surveillance can be compromised as a result of 'inaccurate transaction reporting and poor data quality'. Additionally in *Market Watch* Issue 39, March 2011[13] it stated: 'Transaction reports are vital in detecting and investigating potential market abuse cases. Recently, where transaction reporting breaches were particularly serious, we used our enforcement tools ...' and 'We therefore encourage firms to regularly review the integrity of their transaction reports to ensure they have been successfully submitted'. Furthermore the importance of transaction reporting is also shown by the FCA's willingness to take enforcement proceedings where there have been transaction reporting failings at authorised firms. To date the FCA has taken enforcement action against 14 firms for transaction failings,[14] with the largest financial penalty to date being £13,289,900 imposed on Merrill Lynch International in April 2015. Stressing the impact of transaction reporting failings in the press release of its enforcement action against Merrill Lynch[15] the FCA's acting director of enforcement and market oversight said, 'accurate and timely reporting of transactions is crucial for us to perform effective surveillance for insider trading and market manipulation in support of our objective to ensure that markets work well and with integrity.'

Suspicious transaction reporting

10.15 The EU Market Abuse Framework Directive at Article 6(9) and its implementing measures established a regulatory framework allowing for the reporting of suspicions of market abusive. The EU-wide obligation

---

13 FSA Market Watch Issue 39 March 2011 (note 12).
14 See FCA Final Notice *Merrill Lynch International* (22 April 2015) http://www.fca.org.uk/your-fca/documents/final-notices/2015/merrill-lynch-international; FCA Final Notice *Deutsche Bank AV* (21 August 2014) http://www.fca.org.uk/news/deutsche-bank-fined-transaction-reporting-failures; FCA Final Notice *Royal Bank of Scotland plc and Royal bank of Scotland NV* (16 July 2013) http://www.fca.org.uk/your-fca/documents/final-notices/2013/rbs; FCA Final Notice *Plus500UK Limited* (17 October 2012) http://www.fca.org.uk/your-fca/documents/final-notices/2012/fsa-final-notice-2012-plus500uk-limited; FCA Final Notice *James Sharp and Company* (20 August 2012) http://www.fca.org.uk/your-fca/documents/final-notices/2012/fsa-final-notice-2012-james-sharp-and-company; FSA Final Notice *City Index Ltd* (20 January 2011) http://www.fsa.gov.uk/static/pubs/final/city_index.pdf; FSA Final Notice *Societe Generale* (25 August 2010) http://www.fsa.gov.uk/pubs/final/societe_generale.pdf; FSA Final Notice *Commerze Bank AG* (27 April 2010) http://www.fsa.gov.uk/pubs/final/commerzbank.pdf; FSA Final Notice *Credit Suisse* (8 April 2010) http://www.fsa.gov.uk/pubs/final/credit_suisse_apr10.pdf; FSA Final Notice *Getco Europe Ltd* (8 April 2010) http://www.fsa.gov.uk/pubs/final/getco.pdf; FSA Final Notice *Instinet Europe Ltd* (8 April 2010) http://www.fsa.gov.uk/pubs/final/instinet.pdf; FSA Final Notice *Barclays Bank plc (including Barclays Capital Securities Ltd)* (8 September 2009) http://www.fsa.gov.uk/pubs/final/barclays.pdf; FSA Final Notice *HSBC Bank plc* (14 December 2005) fined £100,000 http://www.fsa.gov.uk/pubs/final/hsbc_14dec05.pdf; FSA Final Notice *UBS AG* (17 November 2005) fined £100,000 http://www.fsa.gov.uk/pubs/final/ubs_17nov05.pdf; and FSA Final Notice *Bear Sterns International Ltd* (22 July 2005) fined £40,000 http://www.fsa.gov.uk/pubs/final/bearstearns_22jul05.pdf.
15 FCA Final Notice *Merrill Lynch International* (22 April 2015) (note 14). FCA press realises 'FCA fines Merrill Lynch International £13.2m for transaction reporting failures FCA press realises. http://www.fca.org.uk/news/fca-fines-merrill-lynch-international-for-transaction-reporting-failures.

is incorporated into UK regulation by the FCA at SUP 15.10.2R which provides:

> 'A firm which arranges or executes a transaction with or for a client in a qualifying investment admitted to trading on a prescribed market and which has reasonable grounds to suspect that the transaction might constitute market abuse must notify the FCA without delay.'

The EU Market Abuse Regulation (2014/596/EU), which comes into force on 3 July 2016, will establish an additional obligation to report suspicious orders. Currently, where a reporting obligation arises, the firm is required to notify the FCA pursuant to SUP 15.10.6R and Article 9 of the Market Abuse Directive with reasons for the suspicion along with the transaction's description, the nature of the order the firms capacity in executing the order, such as whether it is a proprietary or agency trade and the identification of 'the persons on behalf of whom transaction has been carried out, and of other persons involved in the relevant transaction'. The number of suspicious transaction reports received by the FCA has gradually increased year-on-year. Since 2014 the FCA has published data relating to the number of reports it receives and in its latest report published on 10 February 2015 it reported that in 2014 it had received a total of 1,626 suspicious transaction reports versus a total of 328 received in the year 2007.

10.16   The provisions at Article 6(9) and SUP 15.10.2R raise a series of technical qualifications to the core reporting proposition. Although the obligation to report is set widely in SUP 15.10.2R, applying to authorised persons that both arrange[16] or execute transactions in qualifying investments, it only applies to transactions with or for clients in investments that are admitted to trading on a prescribed market, thus excluding investments such as certain collective investments, that may nonetheless be susceptible to market abuse. Further the reporting obligation in SUP 15.10.2R and Article 6.9 relies on an objective test of where the authorised person has 'reasonable grounds to suspect that the transaction might constitute market abuse'. The obligation to report includes a duty at SUP 15.10.5R to report the matter without delay as well as an obligation at SUP 15.10.9R not to 'tip off' any other person that it has made a report of its suspicions. Arguably the single most challenging provision within SUP 15.10R is the determination of the grounds that give rise to a reasonable suspicion. The FCA presents a number of examples of possible suspicions at SUP 15 annex 5 and further explains at SUP 15.10.4G that assistance 'may be derived from the Code of Market Conduct' Nonetheless, put into the context of contemporary securities business, where firms have to evaluate suspicious activities at the same time as routinely dealing with thousands of transactions each day, the practical reality of the suspicious activity reporting obligation and the likelihood of it effectively being able to detect abusive transactions should not be underestimated. Indeed the FCA makes clear at SUP 15.10.3R that the evaluation of reasonable suspicion is to be made on 'a case-by-case basis'. Nonetheless the indicators provided at SUP 15 Annex 5 are of some assistance and provide signals of both insider dealing and market manipulation. By way of example, in relation to insider dealing at SUP 15 annex 5 section 4 the FCA provides an indicator for where,

---

16   The term 'arranging deals in investments' is a regulated activity under FSMA specified in art 25(1) of the Financial Services and Markets Act 2000 (Regulated Activities) Order 2001 (SI 2001/544).

'a client specifically requests immediate execution of an order regardless of the price at which the order would be executed ...' and in respect of market manipulation at SUP 15 annex 5 section 7, where 'an order will, because of its size in relation to the market at security, clearly have a significant impact on the supply of or demand for or the price or value of the security, especially an order of this kind to be executed near to a reference point during the trading day – e.g. near the close'. The effectiveness and viability of a firm's reporting should also take into account the arrangements which need to be in place to train staff in order for them to identify suspicious transactions as orders are passed to or executed by them. Secondly the viability and effectiveness of any automated surveillance systems established and operated by the firm for the purpose of detecting suspicious transactions do need to be enabled to take into account indications of potential abusive behaviour. Chapter 13 will further examine the compliance arrangements and systems a firm needs to establish in order to manage the risks that clients or its staff may expose it to market abuse.

10.17 Regulatory liability can occur for failings to identify the grounds for reasonable suspicion. In Chapter 14 we will examine the liability that can arise for compliance officers to report a reasonably held suspicion. For example, the then Financial Services Authority (FSA) took enforcement action against a Mark Lockwood,[17] an approved person and investment adviser with a stockbroking firm, on grounds that he had failed, despite clear warning signs, to identify that a client was placing an order on the basis of inside information. Mr Lockwood's employer was required under SUP 15.10.2.R to report to the FSA suspicious transactions and in turn, Mr Lockwood was, as recorded in the final notice, required by his employer to report to his firm's compliance department any suspicious transactions. It is not evident from this case whether the FSA considered that the failure to report had deprived it of an early opportunity to act upon the client's abusive activities, but in the final notice the FSA linked Mr Lockwood's failings to the firm's obligations under SUP 15.10 stating that: 'The impact of your failings was that the retail stockbroking firm was used to facilitate a transaction made on the basis of inside information and was prevented from considering whether to report the trade to the FSA through a STR.'[18] The case is an indication of the FSA's willingness to use its enforcement tools in cases where there has been a regulatory failure to highlight responsibilities to report activities providing evidence of levels of reasonable suspicion. In particular the FSA used the notice to set out the suspicious transaction reporting expectations it has of approved persons by stating:

'The FSA expects market participants to be alert to indications that customers are seeking to use regulated firms to facilitate financial crime, including insider dealing. Where there is a clear risk that a trade is in breach of relevant legal or regulatory requirements a market participant should refuse to execute the trade. Where it is not apparent to a broker whether or not the trade is in breach or the suspicion only becomes apparent once a trade has been executed, the trader should report the trade internally in order to facilitate the appropriate filing of a STR.'[19]

17 FSA Final Notice, *Mr Mark Lockwood* 1 September 2009.
18 *Lockwood* (note 17) at [2.3].
19 *Lockwood* (note 17) at [4.1].

THE FCA's STATUTORY INFORMATION GATHERING

Information gathering by the FCA

10.18   The FCA is given power under section 165 of the FSMA to require authorised persons (as well as certain other persons defined in section 165(7)) to disclose information or documents. Although (as discussed earlier in this chapter) there are ocassions where the FCA will routinely obtain information through its supervisory activity or from proactive reporting by authorised persons, there may be occasions when the FCA will consider it more appropriate to rely on its section 165 information gathering powers. The FCA provides a little guidance on how it determines which of its information gathering powers to use essentially recognising that it will use the most appropriate method for the case in question, stating at EG 3.1: 'In any particular case, the FCA will decide which powers, or combination of powers, are most appropriate to use having regard to all the circumstances. Further comments on the use of these powers are set out below.'

10.19   The FCA considers the variety of use that information requests may be put to, stating at EG 3.2: 'the FCA may use its section 165 power to require information and documents from firms to support both its supervisory and its enforcement functions'. The core section 165 information gathering powers as set out at section 165(1) and (3) relate to 'specified informationor information of a specified description' or 'specified documents or documents of a specified description'. The power in section 165(1) may be exercsied only upon written notice by the FCA to the authorised person and that in section 165(3) by an officer of the FCA (has defined in section 165(9) who has written authorisation from the FCA to require the provision of the information or documents. The term 'information and documents' is defined in section 165(10) as either those 'specified in the notice' (in respect of section 165(1) and (2) or specified in the authorisation (in regard to requests under section 165(3)). In relation to an equivalent provision at section 171(2) allowing an investigator to request documents of a 'specified description' in *The Financial Services Authority v Amro International SA*,[20] Lord Justice Burnton commented: 'what is important is that the person on whom the requirement is made can identify the documents he has to produce, since failure to produce them may lead to the imposition of a penalty under s177'. The terms of a formal request under section 165(1) is in part addressed by section 165(2) requiring the FCA to provide a reasonable period for provision or production of the information as well as details for where the information must be provided or produced.

10.20   Unlike section 165(1), the terms of a section 165(3) request require compliance 'without delay'. The FCA's powers under section 165 may not, however, be exercised for the purpose of a random search for information. Section 165(4) in essence establishes an information request limit by providing that the section 165 powers only apply to 'information and documents reasonably required in connection with the exercise by the [FCA] of functions conferred on it by the Act'.

---

20   *The Financial Services Authority, Elisabeth Connell, Patricia Senra v Amro International SA, Creon Management SA* [2010] EWCA Civ 123.

Information gathering by skilled persons

10.21   Sections 166 and 166A of the FSMA provide the relevant regulator with power to appoint a 'skilled person'. Section 166 is used to require the appointment of a skilled person to report on a matter and section 166A for a skilled person to collect or update information that an authorised person has failed to keep in contravention with a regulatory requirement. This section will focus on the powers to appoint a skilled person for the purpose of reporting.

10.22   The FCA is given power under section 166 to require an authorised person (or other persons described below) to provide it with a report by a 'skilled person'. The formalities of the requirement for a skilled person report are provided in section 166(1)–(4). The FCA further sets out in the Enforcement Guide its policy on the use of skilled persons and uses rules and guidance in its Supervision Manual (SUP) to define in some detail the process to be followed when it exercises its powers under section 166. In recognition that the nature of a skilled person's appointment is to provide expertise which may by its very essence not be consistent with more formal evidence gathering, the FCA's Enforcement Guide paragraph 3.5(2) provides: 'If the FCA's objectives include obtaining expert analysis or recommendations (or both) for, say, the purposes of seeking remedial action, it may be appropriate to use the power under section 166 instead of, or in conjunction with, the FCA's other available powers.'

10.23   Section 166(1)–(3) provide the core scope of the skilled person appointment. The section 166(1) in essence limits the use of section 166 to situations where the FCA can require the provision of information or documents, stating: 'This section applies where either regulator [the PRA or FCA] has required or could require a person to whom subsection (2) applies ("the person concerned") to provide information or produce documents with respect to any matter ("the matter concerned").' The provisions of section 166(2) further limit the persons that may be subject to a skilled person report requirement to authorised persons and a tightly defined group of persons connected with the approved person, namely:

'(a)   an authorised person (A);
(b)   any other member of A's group;
(c)   a partnership of which A is a member, or
(d)   a person who has at any relevant time been a person falling within paragraph (a), (b) or (c),

who is, or was at the relevant time, carrying on a business.'

Under the terms of the FSMA as originally drafted, skilled persons would be appointed by the authorised person following the issue of a requirement notice by the authority. One of the notable amendments made to section 166 by the Financial Services Act 2012 was the introduction of a power for the FCA (or PRA) itself to appoint a skilled person to make a report. Section 166(3) now provides that:

'The regulator mentioned in subsection (1) may either—

(a)   by notice in writing given to the person concerned, require the person concerned to provide the regulator with a report on the matter concerned, or
(b)   itself appoint a person to provide the regulator with a report on the matter concerned.'

The FCA provides some clues as to the circumstances when it will appoint a skilled person in SUP 5 Annex 1 which in essence cover circumstances where the FCA requires a report or information urgently or 'to assert a greater degree of control over the appointment'. Furthermore the FCA now maintains a panel of skilled person firms, from which it will select following a formal tendering process, the most appropriate firm.

10.24 Given that the reporting requirement under section 166 is restricted to the authorised person community, the value of skilled person reporting in respect of market abuse may be limited to situations when the FCA seeks to receive a report on the standard of a firm's anti-market abuse systems and controls. Section 166(4) requires that the skilled person must be '(a) appearing to the Regulator [eg the FCA] to have the skills necessary to make a report on the matter concerned'; '(b) nominated or approved by the Regulator [eg the FCA]'. The former requirement operates essentially to ensure that any person proposed as a skilled person has relevant skills. The FCA sets out at SUP 5.4.6G–5.4.9G guidance for the appointment of the skilled person, including material that addresses how it may evaluate whether the person has the necessary skill. At SUP 5.4.6G the FCA states that where it is to appoint a skilled person it '… will normally seek to agree in advance with the person … the skilled person who will make the report …'.The FCA explains at SUP 5.4.8G(1) and (2) that where it will 'nominate, approve or appoint a Skilled Person', it will consider both 'the skills necessary to make a report on the matter concerned', and 'the ability to complete the report within the time expected by the FCA'; together with other factors such as the person's 'relevant specialist knowledge' (SUP 5.4.8G(3)), 'professional difficulty or potential conflict of interest' (SUP5.4.8G(4)) and whether there may be 'enough detachment, bearing in mind the closeness of an existing professional relationship' (SUP 5.4.8G).

10.25 Ordinarily prior to a formal skilled person appointment the FCA will (as confirmed at SUP 5.4.2G) enter into a discussion with the person subject to the skilled person report about the purpose of the appointment, the scope of the report, which skilled person should be appointed and by whom, and the expected cost of the skilled person's report. The FCA will also seek to explore alternative ways in which the information could be obtained. In terms of the structural elements of the skilled persons appointment, section 166(4) allows for the FCA to specify in the requirement notice the form it requires for an individual skilled person's report. The FCA sets out in SUP 5.4.1G–5.4.5G the process it follows in setting and specifying the form of the report, including at 5.4.3G that it will set out in the section 166 written requirement notice the form the report is to meet as well as 'the purpose of the report, its scope, the timetable for completion and any other relevant matters' and also 'the matters which the report is to contain'.

10.26 The FCA traditionally utilised skilled person reporting to satisfy a variety of objectives, including as set out by the FCA at EG 3.5 'to support both its supervision and enforcement functions'. SUP 5.3 additionally explains the FCA's policy on using skilled persons and makes clear that the FCA will consider a range of matters in deciding whether to require a section 166 report such as at SUP 5.3.3G factors including 'the circumstances relating to the firm'; 'alternative tools available, including other statutory powers'; 'legal and procedural considerations'; 'the objectives of the … regulator's enquiries'; 'cost considerations'; and 'considerations relating to FCA resource'. In considering the availability of alternative tools the FCA states at

SUP 5.3.5G that it will have regard to formal requests for information under section 165 or the appointment of investigators (which will be examined further in Chapter 11). Additionally at SUP 5.3.5G(a) the FCA does consider whether it is alternatively appropriate to rely on non-statutory powers such as visiting the authorised person or requesting 'information on an informal basis'. The FCA further explains at SUP 5.3.1G four potential uses for the report requirement, namely, 'diagnostic purposes', 'monitoring purposes', 'in the context of preventative action' and 'for remedial action' each of which is provided with examples of their use at SUP 5 Annex 1. By way of example the Diagnostic purpose may be used to 'find out more about a concern ... or determine whether there may have been a breach of a rule', such as where there is an '[i]Indication of financial crime ...'. Furthermore the FCA explains at EG 3.6 that when a report is required it will 'make clear both to the firm and to the skilled person the nature of the concerns ... and the possible uses of the results of the report'. If a report is required to initially satisfy supervisory reasons, the matters reported on may be such that the FCA determines to make a reference to its enforcement division. Confirming the possibility of such an escalation of the report EG 3.6 provides: 'But a report the FCA commissions for purely diagnostic purposes could identify issues which could lead to the appointment of an investigator and/or enforcement action.' In such circumstances it appears likely that the FCA would formally appoint an investigator but that the material produced by the skilled person would be relied on by the FCA as information relevant to its enforcement decision-making.

10.27   Section 166(7) sets out a basic safeguard to ensure the efficacy of the skilled person's report by setting out an obligation of cooperation for the person concerned (the authorised person or others listed in section 166(2) as well as those persons 'providing (or who at any time has provided) services to a person concerned'. The FCA sets out in SUP additional and important safeguards to ensure an appropriate degree of assistance to the skilled person. SUP 5.5.9R imposes on authorised persons a regulatory obligation of skilled person cooperation providing: 'A firm must provide all reasonable assistance to any skilled person appointed to provide a report under section 166 of the Act (Reports by skilled persons)' together with guidance at 5.5.10G–5.5.11G on how reasonable assistance may be provided, which covers matters such as access to the firm's records, the provision of 'information and explanations ... reasonably considered necessary or desirable' and the obtaining of information directly from the firm's auditor. In addition the FCA addresses in SUP a series of other safeguards relating to both the authorised person and skilled person applying where the skilled person is appointed by the firm (rather than by the FCA under section 166(3)(b)), thus recognising in those circumstances that the FCA has no contractual relationship with the skilled person. SUP 5.5 sets out rules and guidance addressing required terms of the skilled person's contract of appointment, including, at SUP 5.5.5R(2)(a), allowing the FCA to 'enforce the provisions of the contract' and specific obligations relating to the operation of the skilled person reporting, including at SUP 5.5.1R(1) that the contract must 'require and permit the skilled person .. (a) to cooperate with the [FCA] ... in relation to the firm'; and at 5.5.1R(2) 'requiring the skilled person to prepare a report, as notified to the firm by the [FCA], within the time specified by the [FCA]'.

10.28   Furthermore given the potential that as set out in EG 3.6 the skilled person's report may result in the formal appointment of an investigator and a referral to the FCA enforcement division (as considered above at 10.26) SUP

5.5.1R(1)(b) specifies that the contract must 'require and permit the skilled person … (b) to communicate to the [FCA] information on, or his opinion on, matters of which he has, or had, become aware in his capacity as skilled person reporting on the firm …' in the following circumstances:

'(i)   the skilled person reasonably believes that, as regards the firm concerned (A) there is or has been, or may be or may have been, a contravention of any relevant requirement that applies to the firm concerned; and (B) that the contravention may be of material significance to the [FCA] in determining whether to exercise, in relation to the firm concerned, any functions conferred on the [FCA] by or under any provision of the Act other than Part VI. (Official Listing); or

(ii)   the skilled person reasonably believes that the information on, or his opinion on, those matters may be of material significance to the [FCA] in determining whether the firm concerned satisfies and will continue to satisfy the threshold conditions; or

(iii)   the skilled person reasonably believes that firm is not, may not be or may cease to be a going concern.'

10.29   The impact of a skilled person requirement can have considerable impact on an authorised person in terms of both the extent of the engagement and cost. The FCA reports that in the year 2014/15 the average cost of a skilled person review was £722,229.[21] There appears to be on-going reliance by the FCA on the use of skilled persons to gather and report information and provide opinions. Since 30 June 2012 the FCA has reported on the number of appointed skilled persons in each quarter.[22] Further, in its Annual Report for 2014/15[23] the FCA reported that during the year 53 skilled person appointments had been made with 13 of those being directly appointed by the Authority, with five of the 53 relating to financial crime and ten relating to governance, controls and risk.

21   FCA Annual Report and Accounts 2014/15 (2 July 2015) at [130] http://www.fca.org.uk/static/documents/corporate/annual-report-2014-15.pdf.
22   FCA website 'Skilled Persons Reviews (s166 and s166A) http://www.fca.org.uk/about/what/regulating/how-we-supervise-firms/reports-by-skilled-persons.
23   FCA Annual Report and Accounts 2014/15 (2 July 2015) at [130] http://www.fca.org.uk/static/documents/corporate/annual-report-2014-15.pdf.

Chapter 11

Investigations

INTRODUCTION

11.1 In this chapter detailed consideration is given to the statutory powers of investigation granted to the Financial Conduct Authority (FCA) under Part XI of the Financial Services and Markets Act 2000 (FSMA) as amended by the Financial Services Act 2012. Given the FCA's capability of prosecuting for criminal market abuse as well as undertaking administrative enforcement action the deployment of appropriate investigation powers can be vital for the determination of a successful enforcement outcome. In addition to providing analysis of the FCA's statutory powers of investigation this chapter will explore the powers granted to the FCA to enforce its powers where there has been a failure to comply with the terms of a formal investigation.[1]

11.2 The FSMA underpins the substantive law of market misconduct with a wide range of investigation and enforcement powers. Extensive powers of investigation are provided in the FSMA in respect of all types of market misconduct (ie market abuse and the criminal offences of market manipulation and insider dealing). These powers of investigation are reinforced by a number of sanctions for failure to cooperate and comply (considered below). Furthermore, as will be shown in this chapter as well as Chapter 10 on information gathering, the FCA has refined its approach to investigations and information gathering when allowing itself to select the most appropriate method to secure information and evidence in light of the circumstances of the case and person concerned. Indeed (as will be explored in Chapter 12) with market misconduct cases involving authorised persons it is not uncommon for the FCA to rely on breaches of its High Level Principles as opposed to the specific provisions of section 118 of the FSMA to secure an enforcement outcome.

INVESTIGATIONS AND TRANSPARENCY

11.3 The FCA is concerned to ensure that it conducts its investigations in accordance with principles of fairness, efficiency and transparency; in part its investigation procedures and policies are designed to meet such

---

1   See generally S Bazley, *Market Abuse Enforcement Practice and Procedure* (Bloomsbury Professional 2013).

standards. The obligation to operate such standards in its investigations can be derived from a number of sources. Certainly the need to operate efficient and transparent investigation processes can be assessed as an inherent part of the FCA's risk-based approach to regulation, being in part derived from the 'regulatory principles' under the FSMA that apply to how it discharges its 'general functions',[2] including at section 3B(1)(a) 'the need to use its resources in the most efficient and economic way, and at section 3B(1)(h) 'the principle that the [FCA] should exercise [its] functions as transparently as possible'. Furthermore, it must also be recognised that the conduct of an FCA investigation can significantly impact its enforcement decision making and as a consequence can lead to the standard of the investigation procedure being open to close scrutiny during any reference of its decision making to the Upper Tribunal[3] (see Chapter 12 for jurisdiction of the Upper Tribunal (Tax and Chancery). Standards of fairness also arise from the obligation imposed on the FCA to separate its investigatory and enforcement decision making functions; this also limits the extent to which the FCA might otherwise act as legislator, investigator and enforcer of its own rules. In this regard, section 395(2)(a) of the FSMA (as amended) requires that the FCA procedures in relation to warning and decision notices 'must be designed to secure ...' that the decision leading to the warning or decision notice is taken 'by a person not directly involved in establishing the evidence on which that decision is based, or by 2 or more persons who include a person not directly involved in establishing that evidence'.

11.4   To inject further fairness and transparency into the FCA's investigation powers, the FCA publishes an Enforcement Guide (EG), which in part describes the FCA's approach to its information gathering powers and how it conducts investigations.[4]

11.5   The EG expressly recognises the need for standards of fairness. While addressed at the FCA's investigation and enforcement process EG 2.2 recognises a series of principles underlying its approach to enforcement by making reference to the need to ensure fair treatment when exercising its enforcement powers as well as matters such as transparency and proportionality. A considerable element of fairness in any enforcement process is achieved through the consistency with which the process is applied, as without such standard the regime's application may be considered as arbitrary. The need for consistency is also referred to by the FCA in EG 2.2 and, it is submitted, is central to the role played by the FCA's investigation process in meeting its operational objectives at section 1B(3) of the FSMA.

---

2   The FCA's general functions are defined by FSMA, s 1B(6) as: '(a) its function of making rules under this Act (considered as a whole); (b) its function of preparing and issuing codes under this Act (considered as a whole); (c) its functions in relation to the giving of general guidance (considered as a whole); and (d) its function of determining the general policy and principles by reference to which it performs particular functions'.

3   See for example *Paul Davidson and Ashley Tatham v FSA cost decision*, Financial Services and Markets Tribunal, case number 40. Reported 11 October 2006, in which the the FSA's investigation report together with its decision making in the matter was considered by the Tribunal for the purpose of assessing whether the FSA had acted reasonably. It should be noted that the FSA's enforcement and decision making process applied during the Davidson and Tatham matter had been altered by the FSA as a result of its enforcement review published in July 2005.

4   The current Enforcement Guide took effect on 1 April 2014 and can be found in the regulatory guides section to the FCA Handbook https://www.handbook.fca.org.uk/handbook/EG/link/PDF.html.

11.6   The FCA's decision to commence a formal investigation is closely aligned to its policy towards commencing enforcement proceedings (which is explored further in Chapter 12). The investigation selection criteria published by the FCA on its website,[5] as confirmed by the FCA at EG 2.10 may result in the FCA utilising other of its regulatory tools to address any concerns it may have. Indeed the FCA does not take enforcement action or commence investigations in every case, partly because it does not have the resources to do so, although in instances of suspected market abuse, it may be assumed that formal investigation is more likely than not, given the presence of referral criteria such as 'Are there actions or potential actions that could undermine public confidence in the orderliness of financial markets' (FCA criteria paragraph 20(a)); and 'Is the issue to be referred relevant to an FCA strategic priority' (FCA criteria paragraph 19(a)). Additionally in the event of decisions relating to market abuse that is also a crime the principles of the Code for Crown Prosecutors will apply,as well as consideration of the criteria set out at EG 12.8, including matters such as:

'(1)   the seriousness of the misconduct: if the misconduct is serious and prosecution is likely to result in a significant sentence, criminal prosecution may be more likely to be appropriate …

(4)   the effect of the misconduct on the market: where the misconduct has resulted in significant distortion or disruption to the market and/or has significantly damaged market confidence, a criminal prosecution may be more likely to be appropriate; …

(10)   whether the person is being or has been voluntarily cooperative with the FCA in taking corrective measures; however, potential defendants will not avoid prosecution merely by fulfilling a statutory duty to take those measures; …

(11)   whether an individual's misconduct involves dishonesty or an abuse of a position of authority or trust …'.

11.7   The investigation and information gathering powers granted to the FCA under Part XI of the FSMA set out a variety of tests to ensure the FCA is satisfied there are grounds to investigate before it may invoke its powers and thus the threshold of these tests may act to restrict the FCA from commencing a formal statutory investigation. This requirement is acknowledged by the FCA at EG 2.10 where it states, 'Before it proceeds with an investigation, the FCA will satisfy itself that there are grounds to investigate under the statutory provisions that give the FCA powers to appoint investigators. If the statutory test is met, it will decide whether to carry out an investigation after considering all the relevant circumstances.'

11.8   Where the FCA wishes to formally commence an investigation it has at its disposal a range of statutory powers dealing with a variety of subject areas allowing it to formally appoint investigators, authorise them to conduct the investigation and compel the subject to cooperate with the investigator. It is usual for investigators to be FCA staff, which is confirmed by section 170(5) of the FSMA. The core occasions on which the FCA may appoint an investigator are provide in sections 167–169 of the FSMA, which are in

---

5   See the FCA's Enforcement referral criteria at http://www.fca.org.uk/firms/being-regulated/ enforcement/how-we-enforce-the-law/referral-criteria which are further considered in this chapter.

turn supported by powers of investigation set out in sections 170–173. These specific provisions, particularly relating to investigations into market abuse, are explored in further detail below.

POWERS OF INVESTIGATION

11.9   The FSMA, as amended by the Financial Services Act 2012, provides the FCA with a variety of formal powers of investigation, enabling the FCA, Prudential Regulation Authority (PRA) and the Secretary of State to appoint persons to conduct an investigation where there are concerns regarding potential breaches of regulatory obligations including market abuse. The FCA has both 'general' powers of investigation under section 167 of the FSMA as well more specific powers under section 168, which under section 168(2) can be exercised in relation to specific concerns about both administrative market abuse and criminal insider dealing and market abuse. In part, sections 167 and 168 draw a distinction between investigations into the conduct of authorised persons (section 167), and investigations relating to the conduct of unregulated persons (section 168 is unlimited as to the type of person in respect of whom such powers may be exercised). The FCA's enforcement guide at EG 3.8 and 3.9 recognises that in cases where there is both a specific concern about potential market abuse and general concerns, then it may appoint investigators under both sections 167 and 168. Indeed, where an investigator appointed in relation to general matters under section 167 has identified specific concerns such as market abuse, the investigation may be extended to cover matters within section 168.

General power of appointment of investigator

11.10   General powers to appoint a person to investigate business matters of authorised persons (and their appointed representatives) or recognised investment exchanges (as set out in section 167(1)(a)–(c)),[6] may be exercised by the FCA under section 167 of the FSMA where, as described in section 167(1), 'there is good reason for doing so'. Given the restricted scope of section 167 it is unlikely that the FCA will exercise such powers to investigate market abuse behaviour although it is submitted that a section 167 appointment could be relied on to investigate concerns about an authorised person's systems of control for countering market abuse, such as its information barriers and controls (see Chapter 13). The conduct of investigations under section 167 together with the powers available to appointed investigators are set out in sections 170 and 171 of the FSMA, and are examined at 11.21–11.28 below.

Special market abuse investigation powers

11.11   More specific powers to appoint investigators are granted to the FCA under section 168 and unlike the powers in section 167, the FCA may make an

---

6   Section 167(4) extends s 165 investigator appointments to former authorised persons and their appointed representatives but subject to s 167(4)(a): 'business carried on at any time when he was an authorised person (or appointed representative)'; or s 167(4)(b) 'the ownership or control of a former authorised person at any time when he was an authorised person'.

appointment under section 168 in relation to any person including members of the public. Investigator appointments under section 168 and their consequent powers may be made to cover a range of specially described circumstances including those relating to market abuse. Section 168(2)(a) highlights that where circumstances suggest that 'an offence under ... Part 7 Financial Services Act 2012 [criminal market abuse] or under Part V of the Criminal Justice Act 1993 [criminal insider dealing] may have been committed'; and section 168(2)(d) where circumstances suggest that 'market abuse may have taken place'. In addition to suggestions of specific market abuse an investigator may be appointed under section 168(4) in circumstances relevant to wider market misconduct, which may be relied on by the FCA as an alternative to strict market abuse enforcement or indeed an additional measure, such as where there are potential breaches of FCA rules (see section 168(4)(c)) and misconduct in regard to approved persons (see section 168(4)(i)).

11.12   The FCA has indicated that it will normally use the power pursuant to section 168 where there are 'circumstances suggesting that contraventions or offences' set out in that section may have occurred (EG 3.8). The power to appoint an investigator under section 167 is stated by the FCA to be more likely to be used where while although the circumstances 'do not suggest any specific breach or contravention covered by section 168', the FCA still has concerns relevant to the power under section 168 (EG 3.8). Further, investigators may be appointed under both provisions (EG 3.9).

Investigation powers to support an overseas regulator

11.13   The global nature of financial markets means that any investigation into market abuse may result in enquiries having to be made into trading activity in financial markets situated in different jurisdictions. The FCA extends regulatory cooperation to regulatory agencies in other jurisdictions by virtue of section 169 which enables the FCA to utilise its investigation powers for the purpose of international regulatory assistance and the more general cooperation requirement at section 354A of the FSMA which provides that: 'The [FCA] must take such steps as it considers appropriate to co-operate with other persons (whether in the United Kingdom or elsewhere) who have functions – (a) similar to those of the FCA; or (b) in relation to the prevention or detection of financial crime' and at section 354A(4): 'Cooperation may include the sharing of information which the FCA is not preveted from disclosing'.

11.14   The FCA sets out in EG 2.16 its general view that overseas regulatory cooperation is considered as 'an essential part of its regulatory function' and stating: 'In fulfilling this duty the FCA may share information which it is not prevented from disclosing, including information obtained in the course of the FCA's own investigations, or exercise certain of its powers under Part XI of the Act.' The FCA uses the Enforcment Guide to set out at EG 3.12–3.15A its policy on overseas cooperation including that it has entered into a number of Memorandums of Understanding (MoU) with overseas regulators that address the nature of cooperation between the FCA and the other regulatory agency.[7]

---

7   The FCA publishes on its website many of the MoUs it has entered into. See for example 'Memorandum of Understanding between the Securities and Futures Commission of Hong Kong and the Financial Conduct Authority' (25 February 2014) http://www.fca.org.uk/your-fca/documents/mou/mou-between-the-fca-and-hong-kong.

Many such MoUs address in particular the steps that will be followed by the respective agency for making request for assistance.

11.15 Section 169 sets out provisions which in essence permit the FCA to use its information gathering powers under section 165 of the FSMA (as examined in Chapter 10) or investigation powers to support an overseas regulator where it has been requested by the overseas regulator to do so. Section 169(1) provides:

'(1) At the request of an overseas regulator, a regulator [FCA] may–

(a)   exercise the power conferred by section 165; or

(b)   appoint one or more competent persons to investigate any matter.'

11.16 Consideration was given in Chapter 10 of the extent to which the FCA will rely on voluntary disclsoure by firms and it is evident from EG 3.15 that the FCA will consider the potential for voluntary disclosure before using its section 169 information gathering or investigation powers. It is also essential to take into account in the context of section 169(1)(a) that the FCA's powers under section 165 are restricted to information requests directed to authorised persons, persons connected with authorised persons, operators, trustees or depositories of recognised collective investment schemes and recognised investment exchanges and clearing houses. In practical terms therefore, unless the overseas regulator request for support relates to any such person the FCA will have to appoint an investigator to gather information pursuant to formal investigator powers.

11.17 Section 169(2) operates to link an investigation under section 169 to the investigator powers under section 168(3) and thus the defined powers provided in sections 171 and 172 of the FSMA (which are explored in 11.21–11.27 below). In deciding whether to exercise its information gathering powers or appoint an investigator in support of an overseas regulator, section 169(4) sets out the following matters that the FCA may take into account, although these matters do not apply if the FCA is exercising powers of investigation to comply with an EU obligation (section 169(6)):

'(a)   whether in the country or territory of the overseas regulator concerned, corresponding assistance would be given to a United Kingdom regulatory authority;

(b)   whether the case concerns the breach of a law, or other requirement, which has no close parallel in the United Kingdom or involves the assertion of a jurisdiction not recognised by the United Kingdom;

(c)   the seriousness of the case and its importance to persons in the United Kingdom;

(d)   whether it is otherwise appropriate in the public interest to give the assistance sought.'

11.18 A series of issues regarding the FCA's powers to provide support pursuant to its powers in section 169 were considered by the Court of Appeal in *The Financial Services Authority v Amro International SA, Creon Management SA*.[8] The FSA had appointed investigators pursuant to section 169 in response to a request for information made by the US Securities and Exchange Commission (SEC), in connection with US legal proceedings, in the

---

8   *The Financial Services Authority, Elisabeth Connell, Patricia Senra v Amro International SA, Creon Management SA* [2010] EWCA Civ 123.

SEC alleged that a number of persons had engaged in trading to manipulate the price in shares of a US company named Sedona Corporation. The SEC sought the FSA's support in obtaining documents from a UK based accountancy firm named Goodman Jones Chartered Accountants, which the SEC had identified had in its possession certain documents relating to persons that a were relevant to its US legal proceedings.[9] The Appeal was concerned with a number of matters specifically relating to the Authority's appointment of investigators under section 169 and the extent of the documents they could seek production of, in particular: whether the Authority 'when considering whether to exercise the powers conferred by s169(1)' was 'under a duty to investigate or to verify the information provided by the overseas regulator'; whether the Authority was required to give a written notice of the appointment of an investigator pursuant to section 170(2) when appointing an investigator under section 169; and whether the appointed investigators 'were ... confined by the terms of their appointment to seek documents relevant to the issues pleaded in the ... [US] proceedings ...'.[10] In addressing the issue relating to the appointment of investigators, the Court of Appeal considered the international nature of financial services and the importance of transnational regulatory cooperation and whether the Authority has any obligation to evaluate the 'necessity' or 'desirability' of the documents requested from the 'standpoint of the foreign regulator'. Stanley Burnton LJ noted that the Authority had considered the matters outlined in section 169(4) when considering whether to appoint an investigator. He stated 'The FSA must, and did, consider the request when deciding whether to exercise its discretion under section 169 by the exercise of its investigative powers ... it is clear that the FSA decided to exercise its investigative power having considered the matters listed in section 169(4) ...'[11] However, Burnton LJ in essence contrasted the Authority's obligation to consider the request, particularly in the context of section 169(4), with a necessity for it to 'examine the SEC's request critically'. In general, Burnton LJ set out a useful background into the nature of regulatory cooperation and the investigator appointment powers set out in section 169, stating:

> 'It would be surprising if the Act [FSMA] did not permit the FSA to accord full faith and credit (to borrow the phrase of the Constitution of the United States and applied to a judgment of a court of the State of New York by Lord Denning MR in *Colt Industries v Sarlie (No 2)* [1966] 1 WLR 1287) to a foreign regulator, particularly one as important as and of the reputation of the SEC. I can see no good reason why Parliament should have required the FSA to second-guess as to its own laws and procedures, or as to the genuineness or validity of its requirement for information or documents.'

11.19 In addressing the question of the nature of the documents that may be sought when an investigator is appointed under section 169, it is submitted that the Court of Appeal appears to have linked its conclusion that the Authority was under no obligation to evaluate the 'necessity' or 'desirability' of the documents sought together with the objective of the investigators appointment to 'assist the FSA'. Lord Justice Burnton stated: 'The FSA was exercising an investigatory power, not a power of discovery, and it was not limited to

9   *FSA v Amro* (see note 8 above) at [5]–[11].
10 *FSA v Amro* (see note 8 above) at [34].
11 *FSA v Amro* (see note 8 above) at [39].

requiring documents relating to the allegations then pleaded in the New York proceedings.'

Interaction with other investigatory authorities

11.20   In matters involving serious allegations of financial crime or misconduct it is not uncommon for the matters under investigation to fall within the jurisdiction of a number of other UK authorities. In particular, allegations of market abuse might also fall within the jurisdiction of the enforcement division of the investment exchange on which the trading activity took place. Indeed where the investigation concerns matters that may impact the authorisation of a firm authorised by the PRA, a joint FCA and PRA investigation may be necessary. Where the subject matter of an investigation strays into the jurisdiction of another, the FCA might consider it appropriate to refer some of the issues to that agency or exchange for consideration, refer the matter when it appears that the exchange is better placed to take action or investigate and perhaps ultimately take action in parallel with the exchange. In taking such a decision the FCA practice, confirmed at EG 2.15, is to consider the extent to which the relevant exchange has adequate and appropriate powers to investigate and deal with a matter itself. It also envisages that in appropriate cases that 'The FCA may investigate and/or take action in parallel with another domestic or international authority …'. The FCA has established referral and liaison guidelines set out in its Enforcement Guide at annex 2 and at 12.11 in respect of criminal offences as well as in its Decision Procedure and Penalties manual (DEPP) at 6.2.19G to 6.2.27G. These set out a framework for the liaison and cooperation between it and certain other UK authorities where each have an interest in investigating or prosecuting any aspect of a matter or where a rule breach might also result in action by other domestic or overseas regulatory authorities or enforcement agencies. The additional guidance at EG annex 2 provides in particular some broad principles on matters such as how the FCA determines which agency should investigate a particular case; cooperation where more than one agency is investigating a matter; preventing undue duplication of effort, and preventing unfair treatment of investigation subjects because of the unwarranted involvement of more than one agency. Paragraph 9 of annex 2 provides indicators of when the action is most appropriately taken by the FCA and includes matters such as:

'Where the suspected conduct in question would be best dealt with by:

- criminal prosecution of offences which the FCA has powers to prosecute by virtue of the Financial Services and Markets Act 2000 ("the 2000 Act") (See Appendix paragraph 1.4) and other incidental offences;
- civil proceedings under the 2000 Act (including applications for injunctions, restitution and to wind up firms carrying on regulated activities);
- regulatory action which can be referred to the Tribunal (including proceedings for market abuse)'.

'Where the likely defendants are authorised persons or approved persons'

and conversely provides indicators of where another agency is more appropriate such as 'Where serious or complex fraud is the predominant issue in the conduct in question (normally appropriate for the SFO) ...[and] Where powers of arrest are likely to be necessary...'.

Investigation conduct and powers

11.21   The process to be followed for the appointment of investigators as well as the powers that investigators may exercise are prescribed in sections 170–176 of the FSMA.

Notification of the appointment of investigators

11.22   When appointing an investigator under section 167 or for the circumstances described above where an investigator is appointed under section 168, the FCA is required under section 170(2) to give the subject of the investigation 'written notice of the appointment of an investigator'. The obligation to provide written notice applies at the initial appointment stage as well as in circumstances where under section 170(9) there is a change to the scope of the investigation, although in such event section 170(9) provides significant lattitude to the FCA in deciding whether or not to issue a revised notice, stating: 'If there is a change in the scope or conduct of the investigation and, in the opinion of the investigating authority, the person subject to investigation is likely to be significantly prejudiced by not being made aware of it, that person must be given written notice of the change.'

11.23   Section 170(3)(b) excludes the notice requirement for market abuse investigator appointments under sections 168(2) and similarly under section 170(3)(a) for investigations under section 168(1) or (4) where the FCA 'believes that the notice required by subsection (2) or (9) would be likely to result in the investigation being frustrated'. Despite the complete exclusion under section 170(3)(b) the FCA indicates at EG 4.3 that save where a notification might 'prejudice the FCA's ability to conduct the investigation' it will normally nonetheless provide notice 'when it becomes clear who the person under investigation is'.

The investigator's powers and conduct

11.24   Given that the decision to appoint an investigator is made by the FCA, based on identified concerns then decisions relating to the conduct of the investigation will be taken by the FCA. Section 170(7) and (8) confirm that the FCA may direct and control the scope of investigators' work, including at section 170(7) 'the scope of the investigation', 'the period during which the investigation is to be conducted', 'the conduct of the investigation' and 'the reporting of the investigation' and under section 170(8) matters such as whether to 'extend the investigation to additional matters', 'require the investigator to discontinue the investigation ...' and 'require the investigator to make such interim reports as so specified'.

11.25   Investigators are granted specific powers depending on whether the appointment is under section 167 or 168. In addition, the investigator's powers are supported by sanctions for non-compliance. Pursuant to section 171(1), the powers available to an investigator appointed under sections 167 and 168(1) or (4) (by virtue of section 172(1)), extend to both the person under investigation as well as any person connected with him (such as a member of a group or a controller of the person under investigation) and allow the investigator to interview, gather information or documents, but only where, under section 171(3), the investigator 'reasonably considers [it] relevant to the purposes of the investigation'. More specifically section 171(1) provides that:

> 'An investigator may require the person who is the subject of the investigation ("the person under investigation") or any person connected with the person under investigation–
>
> (a)   to attend before the investigator at a specified time and place and answer questions; or
> (b)   otherwise to provide such information as the investigator may require."

11.26   Further, and in relation to document production, section 171(2) provides: 'An investigator may also require any person to produce at a specified time and place any specified documents or documents of a specified description.'

11.27   Investigators appointed under section 168, are given additional powers described in sections 172 and 173, depending on the circumstances of their section 168 appointment. Thus investigators appointed under section 168(4) to investigate misconduct may extend a requirement for attendance to answer questions and provide information to any persons provided that under section 172(3) 'the investigator is satisfied that the requirement is necessary or expedient for the purposes of the investigation'. The powers available to investigators appointed to investigate market abuse under section 168(2) are more widely drafted giving the investigator significant latitude to gather investigation materials from a wide variety of sources. In such a case the powers in effect allow, under section 173(2), an investigator to interview or request information, and under section 173(3) to request 'specified documents or documents' of a 'specified description' from any person who under section 173(1) the investigator (under section 173(4)) 'considers ... is or may be able to give information which is or may be relevant to the investigation' as well as to 'give him all assistance in connection with the investigation ...'. Further provision is made in section 175 for investigators to obtain documents required under sections 161–173 that are in the possession of third parties.

Use of statements obtained in investigations: compulsory interviews

11.28   FSMA pays specific attention in section 174 to the evidential admissibility of statements made to investigators and in particular, given the investigation sanctions at section 177 of the FSMA (which are outlined below) which have the effect of compelling a person to answer an investigator's sections 170–173 requests, section 174(2) in effect provides that statements made to an investigator are not admissible in criminal proceedings (although the investigation offences in section 177 are excluded) and market abuse actions under section 123. Recognising, these admissibility issues, the FCA sets out at EG 4.17–4.27 an indication of its approach to interviews, including at EG 4.21 that 'individuals suspected of a criminal offence' are likely to be interviewed under caution, having the right to remain silent. In such circumstances in order to not create difficulties for the admissibility of any evidence obtained the FCA investigator will not be able to make a formal interview request under the statutory powers.

11.29 As noted above, the investigator has power to compel an interview whether appointed under section 167 or 168. The FCA indicates that it will not always use its statutory powers to require individuals to be interviewed and where appropriate will seek an interview on a voluntary basis possibly under caution.[12]

11.30 However, different principles are likely to apply where a statement is made voluntarily. Such statements would not attract the protection from admissibility afforded by the FSMA 2000, section 174(2) as the decision of the European Court of Human Rights (ECHR) in *Staines v United Kingdom*[13] illustrates. The applicant (who was tried in connection with insider dealing) had first given voluntary statements and then attended a formal interview where she gave evidence under oath. The prosecution later made use of the statements that she had given under compulsion. She objected on the basis that her right to a fair trial had been breached. The ECHR distinguished the renowned case of *Saunders v United Kingdom*[14] on the facts in part because the statement in the voluntary interview did not depart from the compulsory.

11.31 This distinction may account for the FCA's stated policy to prefer to question on a voluntary basis, possibly under caution, for suspects or possible suspects in criminal or market abuse investigations (EG 4.8). The FCA's guidance notes that in these circumstances 'the interviewee does not have to answer, but if they do those answers may be used in subsequent proceedings, including market abuse proceedings' (EG 4.8). However, the FCA also warns that 'an adverse inference may be drawn from the failure to attend a voluntary interview, or a refusal to answer any question at such an interview' (EG 4.19). Irrespective of whether the interview is voluntary or under compulsion, those attending are entitled to be accompanied by a legal advisor if they wish (EG 4.20).

Additional investigation measures – scoping and preliminary findings

Scoping discussions

11.32 The FCA sets out in its Enforcement Guide other measures that it will normally operate as part of an investigation, despite there being no statutory obligation to do so. The FCA explains at EG 4.12 that it will ordinarilly hold 'scoping discussions' with firms or approved persons at the beginning of an investigation into them in order to describe the reason for and scope of an investigation. Such a scoping discussion will generally take place in a meeting between the FCA investigator, its supervisor, and representatives of the firm as well as any individuals that might be under investigation. Thereafter it is usually unlikely that an authorised firm's FCA supervisor will continue to have involvement in any investigation ensuring a clear distinction between

12 EG 4.8.
13 (16 May 2000, unreported).
14 (1997) 23 EHRR 313.

the FCA's investigation and supervision activity. The FCA does nonetheless recognise the benefit in the investigation team having access to supervisory knowledge about the firm or any individuals that has been developed by the supervisor and at EG 4.14 the FCA sets out a policy on the provision of such supervisory expertise during an investigation. The FCA will in particular use the scoping discussion to provide an indication of the documents and individuals it will need access to and how the investigation is likely to proceed. The FCA provides some guidance to the role of scoping meetings within EG 4.12–4.13, but does make it clear that '[t]here is, however, a limit as to how specific the FCA can be about the nature of its concerns in the early stages of an investigation'.

Terminating the investigation

11.33 The FCA also contemplates at EG 4.6 notices of termination of investigations in circumstances where it ceases an investigation having previously issued an investigator appointment notice, despite there being no statutory requirement to issue a notification of discontinuance. Stating that, 'FCA has given a person written notice that it has appointed an investigator and later decides to discontinue the investigation without any present intention to take further action, it will confirm this to the person concerned as soon as it considers it is appropriate to do so, bearing in mind the circumstances of the case.' The extent to which the FCA may terminate an investigation has been considered by the courts. In *R (Grout) v Financial Conduct Authority*,[15] the applicant challenged an FCA decision to terminate an investigation into him on the basis that it was unlawful to do so and that the termination deprived him the opportunity to have his name cleared given the publicity. In dismissing the application, Males J stated, '… the FCA's decision to terminate its investigation of Mr Grout was entirely rational. The matters which it took into account were legitimate considerations and it was for the FCA to determine what weight to give to them …'.

Preliminary findings letter

11.34 Following the outcome of its investigation, the usual practice of the FCA is to send a preliminary findings letter, annexing a preliminary investigation report, to the subject of the investigation before submitting a report to the Regulatory Decisions Committee (EG 4.30). The recipient then has an opportunity to respond and is usually allowed 28 days for this purpose (EG 4.32). However, there is no statutory requirement that the FCA send a preliminary findings letter. The FCA has indicated that it may decide not to send such a letter, for instance where action is urgently required to restore market confidence or no useful purpose would be achieved by sending such a letter (EG 4.31).

11.35 The purpose of such letters is described by the FCA at EG 4.31 as a way of 'focussing decision making on the contentious issues in the case'. The FCA further indiates that there may be circumstances where such letters may not be issued and indeed the courts have recogised such position. In

---

15   [2015] EWHC 596.

an application for judicial review in *R (Griggs) v The Financial Services Authority*[16] following an application for judicial review of the FSA's decision not to issue a preliminary finding letter, because it had concerns that it might be unable to meet the FSMA statutory time limit for taking enforcement action against approved persons, Burnett J, expressed the view that the FSA's concern about the statutory two-year time limit was 'a good reason for it adopting a practice other than that set out in the Enforcement Guide'; and also supported the view that in any event EG did not give rise to any 'enforceable legitimate expectation', in particular because the FSA's Enforcement Guide made clear that 'issuing a Preliminary Findings letter and the opportunity to respond to it will not invariably be a practice which is followed'.[17]

Time frame for responding to information and document requirements

11.36   The FCA expects as set out at EG 4.15 that responses to information and document requests to be made in a timely manner and that any appropriate deadlines are met. A failure to meet any such deadlines can expose those concerned to investigation or regulatory sanctions (these are discussed in further detail below). Investigations into complex matters, can however, give rise to practical concerns affecting the identification and delivery of information and documents and it is not unusual, providing that there is sufficient time within the FCA's investigation timetable, for the FCA to issue a draft information or document request allowing for comment on the practicalities of meeting the request, by the proposed deadline. Once the FCA has considered such comments it will duly confirm or amend the request and thereafter, save where there are compelling reasons, the FCA will not usually agree to an extension of time for complying with the request.

CONFIDENTIALITY

11.37   In general, the FCA must not disclose 'confidential information', which includes information it receives during an investigation, unless the source of the information and, if different, the person to whom it relates, consents.[18] Disclosure of such information is a criminal offence (FSMA, s 352). One of the characteristics of 'confidential information' for these purposes is information relating to the 'business or other affairs of any person' (FSMA, s 348(2)). It should also be noted that a person obtaining 'confidential information' directly or indirectly from the FCA is also subject to these restrictions (s 348(1)). There are, however, a wide number of exceptions to this starting point. In particular, there are a range of circumstances involving 'the carrying out of a public function', both in this jurisdiction and overseas in which such information may be disclosed (FSMA, s 349). Significant detail is given in the now much amended Financial Services and Markets Act 2000 (Disclosure of Confidential Information) Regulations 2001 (SI 2001/2188).

---

16   *R (Griggs) v The Financial Services Authority* [2008] EWHC 2587 (Admin), [2009] ACD 28.
17   *R (Griggs)* at [12].
18   FSMA, s 348(1).

SANCTIONS FOR FAILING TO COMPLY WITH AN INVESTIGATION

11.38   The Act provides a series of measures to support a persons compliance with the FCA's statutory powers, including under section 176 the availabllity of a warrant for a police constable to enter and search premises and take copies of docments. Section 177 further established a series of offences arising from a failure to comply with an investigator's requirement, including under section 177(2) failing 'without reasonable excuse to comply with a requirement'; section 177(3) falsifying, concealing, destroying or disposing of documents; section 177(4) providing 'false or miselading material'; and section 177(6) the intentional obstruction of a search and seizure warrant under section 176.

CRITERIA FOR ENFORCEMENT ACTION

11.39   Having concluded an investigation and assuming that regulatory breaches have been identified, the FCA in dealing with those breaches has a number of regulatory tools at its disposal. It is not always the case that the FCA will determine to impose a disciplinary sanction even though it does view its enforcement process as a necessary element of it providing a credible deterrent. The FCA places significance on the importance of maintaining a cooperative and open relationship with firms and thus considers in appropriate circumstances that in some cases, even though a contravention has taken place, formal disciplinary or enforcement action may not be taken where it can expect the firm to act promptly in taking the necessary remedial action agreed with its supervisors. Nonetheless where a firm does not do this, the FCA makes clear at EG 2.4 that it may take disciplinary or other enforcement action in respect of the original contravention.

CASE SELECTION BY THE FCA

11.40   The FCA's selection method for cases involving authorised and approved persons and in market abuse is determined by both its strategic planning such as priority and thematic work and its decision-making on individual cases. The FCA will not, however, only take action in priority cases and underlying its case selection method is a determination, expressed in EG 2.8, to deal with particularly serious cases where enforcement action is necessary, such as those that have a particular significance in a market or involve financial crime. In respect of individual case assessment the FSA considers that the nature of its overall relationship with a firm has a bearing on whether or not the use of its enforcement powers will support its overall regulatory objectives. Confirming this point EG 2.33 provides that:

> '... using enforcement tools will be less likely if a firm has built up over time a strong track record of taking its senior management responsibilities seriously and been open and communicative with the FSA ...'

11.41   One factor that can have a material impact on whether the FCA will determine not to seek a disciplinary sanction is whether the authorised person has self-reported (such as was explored in Chapter 10 in relation to the obligation under principle 11 to be open and cooperative), helped the FCA establish the facts and taken adequate remedial action. Any such response is likely to be an indicator to the FCA that a firm is sufficiently responsible to manage its own regulatory failings in an appropriate and responsible manner. Firms, cannot, however, assume that a strong regulatory relationship will exclude them from disciplinary proceedings and the FCA will consider each case on its own merits as well as its overall regulatory priorities. We consider in more detail in Chapter 12 on Enforcement, the criteria the FCA uses to determine when it will take enforcement action in individual cases.

Non-statutory routes to achieving an outcome

11.42   Chapter 10 discussed previously circumstances where the FCA might expect voluntary disclosure of information and considered the obligations to be open and cooperative with the FCA that are imposed upon authorised firms under High Level Principle 11 and approved persons under Principle 4 of the Approved Persons Code. Such an obligation might be relied upon by the FCA in an attempt to secure the disclosure of information without the need for it to rely on the information gathering powers in the Act. The obligations within those principles might also be used by the FCA as a method of enforcing its investigatory powers against authorised or approved persons as an alternative to the sanctions contained within section 177. The FCA indicates at EG 4.11 that a failure to comply with the exercise of the FCA's statutory investigation powers can be viewed as a serious form of non-cooperation resulting in it bringing regulatory proceedings for breach of Principle 11 or Statement of Principle 4. From a strict regulatory point of view, a refusal to cooperate with the FCA is a breach of the obligation to be open and cooperative, and therefore authorised and approved persons need to weigh up carefully their motivation for not answering questions against their regulatory responsibilities. The FCA states at EG 4.10 that it will not bring disciplinary proceedings against a person under the principles simply because they choose not to attend or answer questions at a purely voluntary interview. The FCA goes on in EG 4.10 to make clear, however, that there may be circumstances in which an adverse inference may be drawn from the reluctance to participate in a voluntary interview.

11.43   In the next chapter consideration is given to whether the results of an investigation may result in a decision to take enforcement action and, if so, the nature of the FCA market abuse enforcement process.

Chapter 12

Enforcement issues

INTRODUCTION

12.1 This chapter examines the framework of law within which the FCA conducts enforcement activity under the market abuse regime along with those enforcement powers relevant to persons authorised to conduct regulated activity under the Financial Services and Markets Act 2000 (FSMA). Whilst much of the FCA's focus on market abuse enforcement is centred on its administrative law powers under the market abuse regime in section 123 of the FSMA, as well as the enforcement powers it has against authorised firms and approved persons, those powers are supported by statutory provisions allowing applications to be made to the court in order to support the FCA's enforcement activity.[1]

12.2 Although the market abuse regime extends to all users of the market, much of the FCA's work in this area involves the conduct of regulated firms. Indeed the FCA approaches its enforcement work as key to creating 'credible deterrence' indeed in its business plan for 2015/16 (at [65]) it stated: 'We will continue to pursue a strategy of credible deterrence, taking tough and meaningful action against the firms and individuals who break our rules, reinforcing proper standards of market conduct and ensuring that firms put consumers at the heart of their businesses.' It is thus essential when considering market abuse enforcement to take into account the extent to which the FCA considers whether abuse in the market impacts on a regulated firm's authorisation to conduct regulated business and how it uses its Principles for Business and its general rules when dealing with misconduct. The term 'enforcement' is used generally, applying to both the powers available to discipline persons involved in market misconduct as well as to those powers available to the FCA to secure or confiscate assets.

12.3 This chapter will explore both the statutory framework within which the FCA must operate its enforcement activity as well as the FCA handbook provisions in the Decisions Procedures and Penalties Manual (DEPP) and enforcement policy as set out in the FCA's Enforcement Guide (EG) which set out how it approaches its enforcement decision-making including its methodology for setting financial penalties and determining the most appropriate enforcement outcome.

---

1   See generally S Bazley, *Market Abuse Enforcement Practice and Procedure* (Bloomsbury Professional 2013).

SANCTIONS FOR MARKET ABUSE

12.4 The FCA has at its disposal a number of enforcement powers[2] to combat market abuse by persons that use the financial markets including the power to impose a financial penalty pursuant to section 123(1) of the FSMA, and to require restitution pursuant to FSMA, section 384(2). In addition to instances of direct market abuse, that is where a person's behaviour is contrary to one of the prohibited behaviours in FSMA, section 118 (see further Chapter 4 of this book), FSMA, section 123(1)(b) allows the FCA to take enforcement action in relation to what might be described as indirect market abuse, in that the FCA is permitted to take action if it is satisfied that a person has required or encouraged another person or persons to engage in behaviour, which, if engaged in by the first person, would amount to market abuse under any of the market abuse behaviours (see for example the FCA's Final Notice to *Rahul Shah* (13 November 2013)). Moreover, section 123(1)(b), also permits the FCA to take action where a person 'refraining from taking any action has required or encouraged another person' to engage in abusive behaviour.

12.5 Additionally and of significance, the FCA may also exercise disciplinary measures against authorised persons and approved persons by reference to its general rules including high level principles for business or the Approved Person principles (see further Chapters 14 and 15) by imposing a financial penalty or, in very serious cases, withdrawing a person's authorisation or approval, or prohibit a person from performing a controlled function. In the context of market abuse, the FCA's enforcement activity relates specifically to identified breaches of the prohibited market abuse behaviours in section 118 of the FSMA and more widely to authorised persons where abusive behaviour causes a breach of the FCA's high level principle and rules. In addition, the FCA also has power to apply to the civil courts for injunctions and restitution orders to support its enforcement activities as well as power to prosecute criminal offences of market misconduct (which has been considered in further detail in Chapters 3 and 5).[3] The decision to take enforcement proceedings, is not, however, a straightforward one. Instances of abuse in the markets do go undetected and there are indications that the market abuse cases brought by the FCA are merely the tip of the market abuse iceberg, with many abusive activities going either undetected[4] or considered inappropriate for formal enforcement activity.[5] The FCA's finite resources result in it having to apply a risk-based approach to its enforcement work and it not being able to pursue each and every identified instance of abuse. Even where it determines that enforcement action is necessary, it must select from wide ranging statutory powers a response that is most appropriate for dealing with the issues that it has identified.

---

2 Reference to enforcement applies to both disciplinary measures such as the FCA's powers to impose penalties for Market Abuse under FSMA s 123, to impose financial penalties on authorised persons under s 206 and approved persons under s 66 and its wider enforcement protectionist powers such as business permission withdrawal and restraining orders or restitution orders or requirements under FSMA, ss 381–384.

3 Each of the measures described may run in parallel with the enforcement powers of other financial regulatory agencies such as the Regulated Exchanges and The Panel for Takeovers and Mergers.

4 For comments about the existence of dealing rings see Simon English 'A Chancellor who keeps on selling himself short', *Evening Standard* (London 1 April 2008) Business 31.

5 The criteria used by the FSA to determine whether to commence enforcement proceedings for market abuse are considered at 12.7–12.8 below.

12.6   The FCA has indicated that it does not undertake enforcement action in all cases of market abuse[6] and so it can be inferred that a significant element of the FCA's case selection process and approach to market abuse enforcement is influenced by policy considerations. At the heart of any decision to take proceedings for market abuse is consideration of a number of principles and case selection criteria, some of which have been explored in Chapter 11. The FCA articulates elements of its enforcement objectives in paragraph 2.2 of its Enforcement Guide (EG), including an indication of a policy of deterrence at EG 2.2(4) which indicates a desire by the FCA to utilise enforcement to 'change the behaviour of the person who is the subject of its action, to deter future non-compliance by others, to eliminate any financial gain or benefit from non-compliance, and where appropriate, to remedy the harm caused by the non-compliance'. In addition when considering the policy considerations behind the FCA's market abuse enforcement activity it is also important to recognise that the FCA will pursue market abuse enforcement in order to demonstrate that it meets its statutory objectives, including those relating to the maintenance of market confidence and protecting the interests of consumers.[7]

Enforcement case selection

12.7   Historically, the Authority stressed that it is not an enforcement led regulator and that its Enforcement Division shares the same priorities as those of the FCA.[8] Arguably, however, the changing emphasis of financial regulation since the global banking crisis has resulted in a view that that the FCA is as much an enforcement agency as it is a regulator. For example, in its report on the Review of enforcement decision making at the financial services regulators (December 2014) HM Treasury remarked, 'The new regulators have already delivered strong enforcement action, and will continue to do so ...' (paragraph [1.3]). Prioritisation of regulatory activity not only shapes the general work of the FCA but also how each division of the FCA uses its resources. There has, however, been a growing realisation that FCA enforcement offers a significant deterrence and that greater enforcement prominence, in part accomplished through higher financial penalties, can contribute to a change of behaviour in the financial markets. The FCA has published on its website criteria it applies for selecting a case for referral to its Enforcement and Market Oversight Division.[9] The FCA stresses that the criteria are not exhaustive and thus it will consider the full circumstances of each case. The FCA states that its starting

---

6   See EG 2.3 which positions the FCA's enforcement and supervisory options and also comments by Margaret Cole, the then FSA Director of Enforcement 'The UK FSA: Nobody does it better' Fordham Law School, New York (17 October 2006), http://www.fsa.gov.uk/pages/Library/Communication/Speeches/2006/1017_mc.shtml and also Carlos Conceicao (previously Head of Wholesale Department in the FSA's enforcement division) 'The FSA's approach to taking action against market abuse' (2007) 28(2) Co Law 43–45 at [45].

7   See EG 2.1 which refers to enforcement having a role in 'pursuit of [FCA's] statutory objectives including its operational objectives of ... protecting and enhancing the integrity of the UK financial system ...' and FSMA 2000, ss 3–6 as amended which sets out the objectives.

8   For example see Margaret Cole's speech 'Enforcement priorities and issues for 2006', SII Compliance forum (18 January 2006), http://www.fsa.gov.uk/library/communication/speeches/2006/0118_mc.shtml.

9   See FCA website Enforcement referral criteria http://www.fca.org.uk/firms/being-regulated/enforcement/how-we-enforce-the-law/referral-criteria.

point is to consider: 'Overall, is an enforcement investigation likely to further the FCA's aims and statutory objectives?'. It then considers factors to assess whether an enforcement action will met its purpose including:

'Deterring wrongdoers from repeating behaviours (specific deterrence) ...'

'Changing behaviour and raising standards in the industry (general deterrence) ...'

'Holding those responsible for very serious breaches to account with proportionate penalties and sanctions (justice) ...'

'Removing wrongdoers from the industry or imposing restrictions where appropriate (protection)'

12.8 The FCA has also published in its Enforcement Guide (at section 12) a policy for selecting cases for prosecution as opposed to administrative action under section 126 of the FSMA, where market abuse behaviour may have breached the criminal law. This criteria includes:

'(1) the seriousness of the misconduct: if the misconduct is serious and prosecution is likely to result in a significant sentence, criminal prosecution may be more likely to be appropriate ...;

(4) the effect of the misconduct on the market: where the misconduct has resulted in significant distortion or disruption to the market and/or has significantly damaged market confidence, a criminal prosecution may be more likely to be appropriate ...;

(5) the extent of any profits accrued or avoided as a result of the misconduct: where substantial profits have accrued or loss avoided as result of the misconduct, criminal prosecution may be more likely to be appropriate;

(10) whether the person is being or has been voluntarily cooperative with the [FCA] in taking corrective measures; however, potential defendants will not avoid prosecution merely by fulfilling a statutory duty to take those measures ...;

(11) whether an individual's misconduct involves dishonesty or an abuse of a position of authority or trust ...'

12.9 In addition to the aforementioned general enforcement election criteria, the FCA applies additional criteria to help it determine the most appropriate action to take in individual cases. For example at DEPP 6.2.1 and more specifically for market abuse in DEPP 6.2.2 it sets out criteria to help it decide whether to impose a financial penalty or public censure (this criteria will be considered further below). Considering the FCA's wider approach to enforcement case selection, it is right to assume that the FCA applies its criteria with a view to ensuring that enforcement cases are selected and conducted consistently. However, the FCA acknowledges in EG 2.9 that its limited resource means that it has to focus its attention towards the priority given to certain types of misconduct over others and that such 'risk-based approach to enforcement means that certain cases will be subject to enforcement action and others not'. Nonetheless, the FCA does consider in EG 2.8 that enforcement action is necessary in cases of particular significance to protect markets, consumer protection, financial crime, or in 'cases that the FCA thinks are necessary to achieve effective deterrence'. Nonetheless, as is evident from analysis of the FCA's case selection, the contrasting approach between principles based and market abuse regime enforcement in cases such as *Pignatelli*[10] and *Winterflood Securities*,[11] it is sometimes difficult to determine the exact reason why certain enforcement cases are selected over others and why cases on similar facts are concluded in different ways, thus at times leading to FCA enforcement decisions appearing arbitrary.

PRINCIPLES BASED ENFORCEMENT

12.10   The market abuse regime is to an extent a unique aspect of regulation under FSMA as it applies to all persons, whether or not authorised. The regime in Part VIII of the FSMA also relies on a series of technical measures that have the effect of ruling in and excluding certain classes of financial instruments and markets from the regime (see further Chapter 4). However, it should be noted that it is not uncommon that concerns about abuse in the markets (including that outside of the provisions of Part VIII) by authorised persons are often addressed by the FCA reaching an enforcement decision about the standard of the firm's systems and controls. Many of the FCA's rules on system and controls take the form of general principles of conduct rather than detailed or prescriptive rules. Indeed significant elements of the FCA's Code of Market Conduct are 'principles based' such that the FCA and authorised persons may focus more on the outcomes gained by compliance with principles rather than how to comply with prescriptive rules. Put another way, principles based obligations encourage compliance with the spirit of regulation as opposed to the letter. The FCA believes an approach focused more on outcomes allows it to achieve its regulatory objectives in a more efficient and effective way and will lead to an increased focus on principles-based enforcement action.[12]

12.11   Previous FSA enforcement cases such as *Roberto Chiarion Casoni*[13] and the FCA's LIBOR failings enforcement case against *Deutsche Bank AG*[14] show that the Authority, when dealing with authorised and approved persons, will take enforcement action by reference to breaches of high level Principles for Business and failures in systems and controls obligations particularly where there has been misconduct that falls outside of the technical provisions of the market abuse regime.[15] In the *Deutsche Bank* case, the FCA final notice stated (at [2.1]), 'Serious misconduct by Deutsche Bank led to breaches of Principles 5, 3 and 11 of the Authority's Principles for Businesses: first, through Deutsche Bank's attempted manipulation of IBOR rates and improper influence over IBOR submissions, second, through its systems and controls failings and third, through serious deficiencies in the way Deutsche Bank dealt with the Authority in relation to IBOR matters [IBOR is a generic term for EURIBR and LIBOR]'.

12.12   In its enforcement case against *Citigroup Global Markets Limited (CGML)*[16] the FSA focused on breaches of High Level Principle 2 of due skill, care and diligence; and Principle 3 of organisation and control, highlighting

10   FSA Final Notice *Sean Pignatelli* (20 November 2006), http://www.fsa.gov.uk/pubs/final/Pignatelli.pdf.
11   FSA Final Notice *Winterflood Securities Ltd* (22 April 2010), http://www.fsa.gov.uk/pubs/final/winterflood.pdf.
12   See FCA's Enforcement Guide, paragraphs 2.18–2.19.
13   FSA Final Notice *Robert Chiarion Casoni* (20 March 2007).
14   FCA Final Notice *Deutsche Bank AG* (23 April 2015).
15   FSMA, Part 8.
16   FSA Final Notice *Citigroup Global Markets Limited* (28 June 2005).

how its high level principles can be used to good effect to deal with market conduct cases. In the Final Notice for the action it was reported that four traders on CGML's European Government bond desk had developed a trading strategy on European government bond markets involving the building up and rapid sale of long positions in government bonds resulting in a temporary disruption to the volumes of bonds quoted and traded, as well as a drop in bond prices and a temporary withdrawal by some participants from quoting on a certain trading platform. It was reported that although the traders that had developed the strategy had discussed their proposal with their head of desk, who in turn sought and gained approval of the strategy from CGML's head of interest rate trading, there was no common or clear understanding between them as to the size of the proposed trade and thus no effective communication of the arrangements CGML was to establish.

FCA's enforcement of its decision-making

12.13 Section 395 of the FSMA requires that the FCA's procedures in relation to warning and decision notices[17] (which will be explored in further detail below) 'must be designed to secure that the decision giving rise to the obligation to provide such notice is taken by a person not directly involved in establishing the evidence on which that decision is based or by two or more persons who include a person not directly involved is establishing that evidence'; in essence, requiring the FCA to maintain an operational barrier between its enforcement division and those FCA persons that make decisions leading to statutory notices. The FCA has previously expressed the view that to ensure confidence in the system, notwithstanding the statutory requirement to separate its investigation and recommendation functions from its decisions functions, it is also vital that its enforcement decision-making process is perceived as being fair.[18]

Regulatory Decisions Committee

12.14 The FCA Regulatory Decisions Committee (RDC) functions as a key ingredient for the Authority's supervision and enforcement separation obligations under section 395.[19] Provisions relating to the nature and procedure of the RDC are set out in the FCA's Decisions Procedure and Penalties Manual (DEPP) Chapter 3, which explains at DEPP 3.1 a number of points relevant to the independence of the RDC from the FCA's enforcement division, in particular at DEPP 3.1.1 that the RDC is '… a committee of the [FCA] board … it exercises certain regulatory powers on behalf of the FCA and is accountable to the FCA Board for its decisions generally'; at DEPP 3.1.2(1) that 'The RDC is separate from the FCA's executive management structure. Apart from its Chairman, none of the members of the RDC is an FCA employee'; and at DEPP 3.1.3 that 'the RDC has its own legal advisers and support staff. The RDC staff are

---

17 Each of these Notices are referred to in s 395 as 'Statutory Notices'. See further **12.17–12.22** below.
18 FSA 'Enforcement Process Review: Report and Recommendations' in particular paragraphs 1.3 and 1.16 (July 2005), http://www.fsa.gov.uk/pubs/other/enf_process_review_report.pdf.
19 For a description of the Regulatory Decision Committee and its role in the market abuse regime, see Carlos Conceicao, 'The FSA's approach to taking action against Market Abuse' (2007) 28(2) *Co Law* 43–45.

separate from the FCA staff involved in conducting investigations and making recommendations to the RDC'. Confirming the desirability of the RDC's operational independence DEPP 3.2.21 provides that after a person has been issued with a warning notice (which will be discussed below at 12.17–12.22, the RDC does not meet or discuss the case with the FCA staff responsible for the matter 'without other relevant parties being present or otherwise having the opportunity to respond'. DEPP 3.2.3 also makes clear that the composition of each committee panel is variable with the panel members being selcted based on the nature of an individual matter. In addition the FCA is also concerned to ensure that the RDC's decision-making is absent of any conflicts of interest which is, it is submitted, essential to ensure that its decision making is not exposed to complaints of bias. In relation to conflicts, DEPP 3.2.3 seeks to ensure that a committee empanelled to consider representations 'will include additional members of the RDC who have not previously considered the matter' and at DEPP 3.2.4–3.2.6 the importance of avoiding and disclosing conflicts is made clear stating that persons will not be invited to attend a panel 'in which he has a potential conflict of interest' and 'If a member of the RDC has a potential conflict of interest in any matter in which he is asked to participate he will disclose the conflict to the RDC office and disclose it to.. *[one of a number of nominated persons specified at DEPP 3.2.5(1)(a)–(c) depending on the panel member]* …'.

12.15   It can be seen from the description of the RDC's operating procedures in DEPP 3.2 that its approach to decision-making matters is not as formal as judicial adjudication, for example DEPP 3.2.7 explains that although the RDC will follow the DEPP 3.2 procedures 'it will conduct itself in a manner the RDC chairman or deputy chairman considers suitable in order to enable the RDC to determine fairly and expeditiously the matter which it is considering'. DEPP 3.2.17 and 3.2.18 make provision for persons who wish to make oral representations including the fixing of dates for meetings and at DEPP 3.2.18 to:

'… ensure that the meeting is conducted so as to enable

(1)   the recipient of the warning notice … to make representations,
(2)   the relevant FCA staff to respond to those representations,
(3)   the RDC members to raise with those present any points or questions about the matter, and
(4)   the recipient of the notice to respond to points made by the FCA staff of the RDC.'

12.16   DEPP 3.2.18 does however make clear that the RDC chairman may seek to limit the extent of a person's representations and provides, 'the chairman may ask the recipient of the notice or FCA staff to limit their representations or response in length or to particular issues arising from the warning notice …'. Notwithstanding the RDC procedures in DEPP 3.2, the FCA makes clear that the RDC is not intended to resemble a court or a tribunal and so for example, it is not possible to call witnesses or cross examine FSA staff at the meeting or indeed appropriate for the recipient of a notice that attends an RDC meeting to be cross examined about their representations.[20] Having said this, there is a competing opinion about the judicial nature of the RDC's meetings.

---

20   See information published by the FCA on its website concerning the Regulatory Decisions Committee, http://www.fca.org.uk/about/structure/committees/rdc-faqs.

In the Tribunal decisions in *Baldwin*[21] the Tribunal observed 'In taking this approach, we remind ourselves that the process leading to the FSA's decision was not a full judicial hearing of the kind conducted by the Tribunal'.[22] In *R (Christopher Willford) v Financial Services Authority*,[23] an appeal which considered the requirement for the content of a Decision Notice, the Court of Appeal considered the then FSA's enforcement process and the role of the RDC, drawing a clear distinction between it and a judicial body. Lord Justice Moore-Bick stated in his judgment (at [21]) 'Although the function of the RDC carries with it an obligation to act fairly and to give fair consideration to any representations made to it, the RDC remains an organ of the FSA and the giving of a Decision Notice is the final step in a disciplinary process conducted by the FSA.' Furthermore, Lord Justice Pill stated in his judgment (at [64]): 'While it cannot be said that the RDC is a judicial body, the statutory framework is such, in my view, that scrupulous attention to its provisions is required, including the duty to give reasons, and for fairness throughout.'

Warning Notices and Representations

12.17 Following an investigation, if FCA staff consider that action is appropriate, they will recommend to the relevant decision maker (in the case of market abuse the relevant decision maker is the FCA's Regulatory Decisions Committee) that a warning notice be given.[24] Following such recommendation, it is possible that the decision maker may decide not to take further action and in such an event if the FCA had previously informed the person concerned that it intended to recommend action, it will communicate the decision not to take further action promptly to such a person.[25] However, if instead the FCA decides to take action, it is obliged by the FSMA 2000, section 126(1) to give a warning notice to a person against whom it proposes to impose a penalty for market abuse under the FSMA 2000, section 123. Following amendments made by the Financial Services Act 2012 to section 391 of the FSMA, warning notices falling within section 391(1ZB), which includes those issued under section 126 for market abuse, may be published following consultation with the recipient of the notice. The FCA sets out at DEPP 3.2.14 the process it follows to facilitate publication, including the opportunity for the recipient to make representations.

12.18 The first stage in the notice process is the giving of a written warning notice and arises where the FCA proposes to take enforcement action. A warning notice, as its name suggests, operates as a warning that the FCA proposes to take action and notifies its recipient of their right to make representations about the proposed action. Confirmation of the requirement for a warning notice is provided in section 126(1) of the FSMA in relation to a market abuse financial penalty; section 385 regarding a market abuse restitution requirement; section 207 in relation to authorised person discipline; and section 67(1)–(3) in relation to approved person discipline. Each of the aforementioned sections together with the definition of a warning notice set out in section 387 provide that the warning notice must satisfy minimum content

21 *Timothy Baldwin and WRT Investments Limited v Financial Services Authority* (2006) FSMT Case 028.
22 *Baldwin* (note 21) at [15].
23 *R (Christopher Willford) v Financial Services Authority* [2013] EWCA Civ 677.
24 See DEPP 2.2.1G.
25 EG 4.6.

requirements including a description of the action the FCA proposes to take, the reasons for that action, the amount of any proposed penalty and the terms of any proposed statement.[26] The process adopted by the FCA in relation to the issuing of warning notices is set out at DEPP 2.2, which makes it clear that the decision to issue a warning notice will be made by an FCA decision maker on the recommendation of an FCA member of staff and that at DEPP 2.2.3G(1) the decision maker will 'consider whether the material on which the recommendation is based is adequate to support it ...' or at DEPP 2.2.3(2): 'satisfy itself that the action recommended is appropriate in the circumstances' and at DEPP 2.2.3(3) 'decide whether to give the notice and the terms of any notice given'.

12.19   The FCA's warning notice must, in order to satisfy the provisions of section 387(2) 'specify a reasonable period of no less than 14 days within which the person to whom it is given may make representations to the [FCA]'. The notice thus acts as the formal trigger for a response and the opportunity to make formal representations to the FCA (as well as any settlement negotiations, which is explored in more detail below at 12.49–12.53).

12.20   The time permitted for making representations may, as recognised by section 387(3) be extended by the FCA. A process for addressing extensions of time is embodied in the FCA Decision Procedure and Penalties Manual. DEPP 3.2.16 provides that any request for an extension of time for making representations must 'normally be made within seven days of the notice being given', with the decision about the time extension being made by the RDC chairman or deputy chairman (DEPP 3.2.16(2).

12.21   Following receipt of a warning notice, the person concerned may, in accordance with DEPP 3.2.17,[27] make representations to the FCA about the action set out in the warning notice. Making representations to the FCA following the warning notice and ensuring that these are made within the relevant time limits is a critical step in the process and provides a formal opportunity for the recipient of the notice to put forward their case. Indeed as was explored in Chapter 4 regarding the market abuse statutory defence, pursuant to section 123(2) of the FSMA, the FCA 'may not impose a penalty on a person if it is satisfied on reasonable grounds following representations by the person concerned in response to a warning notice that the person either believed on reasonable grounds that his behaviour did amount to market abuse or took all reasonable precautions and exercised all due diligence to avoid the abusive behaviour'. See *Ian Hannam v Financial Conduct Authority*[28] in which the Upper Tribunal rejected Mr Hannam's arguments that he believed he was not engaging in market abuse. Furthermore the FCA sets out at DEPP 2.3.2–2.3.3G what it refers to as a 'default procedure' whereby it may in the absence of representations treat allegations made in its warning notice as undisputed.

12.22   Even, where a person's representations do not satisfy the FCA in accordance with section 123(2), the representations may nonetheless carry sufficient force to persuade the FSA that the action set out in the warning notice should be modified or tempered. For example, the FSA's final notice to *Darren*

---

26   See FSMA, s 126(3).
27   The process for representations at DEPP 3.2.17 applies directly to where the RDC is the decision maker but a similar process is followed for executive decision making by virtue of DEPP 4.1.13.
28   [2014] (UKUT 0233).

Morton,[29] records that Mr Morton made a series of representations about practice in the bond market and the expectations of that market, which included representations that no guidance had been available to him at the time relating to his market abuse behaviour, 'which went to support his representations about general market expectations'.[30] Although in that case the FSA decided that Mr Morton's belief was not reasonably held and that he engaged in market abuse, it responded to the representation regarding guidance by stating:

> 'The FSA notes Mr Morton's representations on the market practice prevalent at the time. It also accepts that Mr Morton believed that his behaviour did not amount to market abuse. In the absence of any guidance from ICMA the only specific guidance available to Mr Morton were the interim guidelines from Dresdner where "in the past it has been determined that SCI is not routinely privy to price sensitive non-public [information]". Consequently, in these circumstances it is noted that Mr Morton was working in an environment where until a deal had closed, the accepted view was that, in the absence of information generally regarded as inside information, that information was not regarded as specific or price sensitive and therefore any activity related to such information could not be abusive.'[31]

12.23   Section 123(2) is significant for a compliance officer, as the defence to an allegation of market abuse may often rest on the compliance procedures in place within a firm. Chapter 6 of DEPP sets out the FCA's statement policy on the imposition of penalties and provides a list of factors that the FCA may take into account in determining whether to impose a financial penalty or public censure. DEPP 6.2.2G provides factors that the FCA may consider when deciding to take market abuse enforcement action, which recognises that the features of each market may differ, including in DEPP 6.2.2(1), the market user's degree of sophistication and the susceptibility of the particular market to abuse and at DEPP 6.2.2(2) the 'impact ... that any financial penalty or public censure may have on the financial markets or on the interests of consumers ...'. DEPP 6.3.2 specifically addresses penalties for market abuse in the context of the section 123(2) statutory defence and identifies matters treated as being important steps that a person should follow in assessing whether their behaviour may amount to abuse, including:

(1)   whether, and if so to what extent, the behaviour in question was or was not analogous to behaviour described in the Code of Market Conduct (see MAR 1) as amounting or not amounting to market abuse or requiring or encouraging;

(2)   whether the FCA has published any guidance or other materials on the behaviour in question and if so, the extent to which the person sought to follow that guidance or take account of those materials (see the Reader's Guide to the Handbook regarding the status of guidance). The FCA will consider the nature and accessibility of any guidance or other published materials when deciding whether it is relevant in this context and, if so, what weight it should be given;

(3)   whether, and if so to what extent, the behaviour complied with the rules of any relevant prescribed market or any other relevant market or other regulatory requirements (including the Takeover Code) or any relevant codes of conduct or best practice;

---

29   FSA Final Notice *Darren Morton* 6 October 2009.
30   *Morton* (note 29) at [5.20].
31   *Morton* (note 29) at [6.11].

(4)   the level of knowledge, skill and experience to be expected of the person concerned;

(5)   whether, and if so to what extent, the person can demonstrate that the behaviour was engaged in for a legitimate purpose and in a proper way;

(6)   whether, and if so to what extent, the person followed internal consultation and escalation procedures in relation to the behaviour (for example, did the person discuss the behaviour with internal line management and/or internal legal or compliance departments);

(7)   whether, and if so the extent to which, the person sought any appropriate expert legal or other expert professional advice and followed that advice; and

(8)   whether, and if so to what extent, the person sought advice from the market authorities of any relevant prescribed market or, where relevant, consulted the Takeover Panel, and followed the advice received.

12.24   As highlighted earlier in this chapter, it is important to take into account however, that the FCA may propose alternative or additional enforcement action to address market abuse, particularly in relation to authorised or approved persons. DEPP 6.2.1 provides a non-exhaustive list of factors that address the generic decision to take enforcement action including factors under the heading of '(1) the nature seriousness and impact of the suspected breach ...' Furthermore DEPP 6.2.4–6.2.9 sets out additional factors relevant to approved persons, including at DEPP 6.2.6G (1): 'the more senior the approved person responsible for the misconduct, the more seriously the FCA is likely to view the misconduct' and DEPP 6.2.8G:'An approved person will not be in breach if he has exercised due and reasonable care when assessing information, has reached a reasonable conclusion and has acted on it.'

Access to FCA material

12.25   Where the FCA has issued a warning or decision notice it is obliged under section 394(1) of the FSMA to provide the recipient of the notice '(a) ... the material on which it relied in taking the decision which gave rise to the obligation to give such notice and (b) ... any secondary material which in the opinion of the [FSA] might undermine that decision'. Certain material is, however, excluded from the access obligation including at section 394(3) where 'access to material (a) would not be in the public interest; or (b) would not be fair, having regard to (i) the likely significance of the material to [the recipient of the notice] ...; and (ii) the potential prejudice to the commercial interests of a person other than {the recipient of the notice] ...'.

Decision Notice and Notice of Discontinuance

12.26   If, having considered representations made regarding the content of a Warning Notice, the FCA decides to take action, it is required to issue a written Decision Notice.[32] In practical terms a Decision Notice is the communication of the FCA's determination of the matter and indicates that the enforcement action set out in the notice will take effect unless the respondent refers the

---

32   An examination of the Third Party rights provided under FSMA, s 393(7) is provided at 12.32–12.34.

matter to the Upper Tribunal (see 12.35 below). The statutory obligation to issue a Decision Notice arises under section 127(1) in relation to market abuse penalties, section 386 for market abuse restitution requirements, section 208 in relation to authorised person discipline and section 67(4) in relation to approved person discipline. The FCA sets out at DEPP 2.3 its procedure for issuing Decision Notices, making clear that the determination on whether to issue a Decision Notice as well as the content of the notice rests with an FCA 'decision maker' following, at DEPP 2.3.1G (2), the decision maker 'consider*[ing]* any representations made (whether written or oral or both) and any comments by FCA staff or others in respect of those representations ...'. The statutory minimum content of a Decision Notice is prescribed through a combination of section 388 together with the respective sections of the regime to which the action relates. In effect, a Decision Notice must set out the action the FCA has decided to take and the amount of any financial penalty or restitution,[33] the reason for the decision and give an indication of any right as well as the procedure for the respondent to refer the matter to the Upper Tribunal. At this juncture it is important to note that pursuant to the Tribunal reference rights relevant to each of the enforcement actions described above, namely: section 127(4) (for market abuse penalties); section 386(1) (market abuse restitution requirements); section 208(4) (authorised person penalties); and section 67(7) (approved person penalties). By virtue of section 133(9) (or the equivalent provision in the part of FSMA to which the decision notice relates) the FCA 'must not take the action specified in a decision notice' until the period for referral has expired or if the matter is referred 'until the reference and any appeal against the [Upper] Tribunal's decision have been finally disposed of'. In *R (Christopher Willford) v Financial Services Authority*,[34] the Court of Appeal considered the nature of the FSA's duty under the FSMA, section 388(1)(b) to set out in the Decision Notice, 'reasons for the decision to take the action to which the notice relates'. The appeal concerned an application for judicial review of the FSA's decision to issue a decision notice. The applicant had been subject to an FSA investigation into his conduct as an approved person. Having received a statutory warning notice, the applicant made written and oral representations to the then FSA's Regulatory Decisions Committee, following which the RDC decided to issue a Decision Notice. Mr Willford maintained that the committee had failed to give adequate reasons for its decision because it had not specifically addressed each of the individual submissions that he had made. He therefore brought a claim for judicial review seeking to have the Decision Notice quashed.[35] In considering the detail that a Decision Notice should provide, Lord Justice Moore Brick stated in his judgment:

> 'What is necessary, however, is that the RDC should leave the recipient of the notice in no real doubt about why it has decided to give the notice. In deciding how fully its reasons are expressed the RDC is entitled to take into account the fact that the recipient will be aware of the arguments that were presented to it on both sides. There is a tendency in some cases of this kind for relatively simple issues to be addressed at some length and with a considerable degree of elaboration. If that is the case, the RDC is entitled

---

33 See FSMA, s 127(2), for market abuse, s 208(3) in relation to authorised person discipline and s 67(5) in relation to approved person discipline.

34 *R (Christopher Willford) v Financial Services Authority* [2013] EWCA Civ 677.

35 *R (Christopher Willford) v Financial Services Authority* (note 34) at [9].

when giving its reasons to concentrate on the substance of the matter and
need not address every aspect of the arguments directed to it …'.[36]

12.27   The Court of Appeal found that the FSA's Decision Notice contained
sufficient detail and considered it in the context of a reference to the Upper
Tribunal. Lord Justice Moor Brick said in his judgment, 'The purpose of giving
reasons is to inform the recipient why the Decision Notice has been given.
The Decision Notice may be the trigger for a reference to the tribunal, but in
contrast to some other kinds of decision (e.g. planning decisions) neither the
notice itself nor the RDC's reasons play an integral part in the procedure for
challenging it. In my view the reasons given by the RDC in this case were
sufficient to comply with the requirements of section 388.'[37] Lord Justice Pill,
however, although allowing the appeal on the basis that on a consideration of
the Decision Notice as a whole, sufficient reasons were given to comply with
the statutory requirement (at [73]) was not of the view that the availability of a
Tribunal referral could overcome a Decision Notice lacking in detail, stating:
'A person subject to a decision notice is entitled to a reasoned decision. The
availability of a reference to the Upper Tribunal does not excuse failure to
comply with that requirement. There is prejudice to a respondent in being
required to embark upon a full judicial hearing of all issues and to do so
without knowing why the FSA has decided against him. The duty to give
reasons cannot be sidelined and the existence of the alternative remedy must
be considered in a context which recognises that duty and other provisions
mentioned …'.[38]

12.28   Amendments made to FSMA, section 391(4) by section 13 of the
Financial Services Act 2010 now require the FCA to publish such details of
Decision Notices as it considers appropriate, thus allowing the FCA to publish
details of an enforcement action in circumstances where a person may have
referred the matter to the Upper Tribunal and before a Final Notice has been
issued. Section 391(6) provides further, however, that the FCA cannot publish
a decision notice, 'if publication of it would, in its opinion, be unfair to the
person with respect to whom the action was taken or prejudicial to the interests
of consumers, or detrimental to the stability of the UK financial system'. The
FCA's policy approach to the publication of Decision Notices is set out in
EG 6.8. Although the FCA will determine whether or not to publish a Decision
Notice by reference to the circumstances of each case, it states at EG 6.8 that
it expects to publish the Decision Notice for every case referred to the Upper
Tribunal. In addition it states that it may also publish a Decision Notice where
there is a compelling reason to do so, giving the examples of market confidence
or where it considers that publication is necessary 'to allow consumers to avoid
potential harm arising from a firm's actions'. The FCA also uses EG 6.8A to
describe the steps it will take where it intends to publish a decision notice,
essentially providing for the giving of advance notice of its intention to publish
and allowing for the recipient of the notice to make representations. Needless
to say, the recipient of a notice will be concerned about whether publication
of a Decision Notice, might compromise their desire for confidentiality of the
matter, particularly where on referring the matter to the Upper Tribunal intend
making a privacy application. The FCA states at EG 6.8A: 'The FCA will also
not decide against publication solely because a person asks for confidentiality
when they refer a matter to the Tribunal.'

36   *R (Christopher Willford) v Financial Services Authority* (note 34) at [44].
37   *R (Christopher Willford) v Financial Services Authority* (note 34) at [48].
38   *R (Christopher Willford) v Financial Services Authority* (note 34) at [69].

12.29   It is unclear however, whether the policy statement in EG 6.8A is meant to refer to a subject's desire for confidentiality of the detailed facts of a case or where the person indicates they intend to make a privacy application. It is important to note that any decision by the FSA to publish a Decision Notice may be taken before the Tribunal reference is made, by which time it is possible that the FSA's Decision Notice will have been published. In *R (Canada Inc) v Financial Services Authority*,[39] the applicant commenced judicial review proceedings concerning the FSA intention to publish a decision notice in respect of market abuse and obtained an interim injunction restraining the FSA from publishing the notice, pending the applicant making a reference of the FSA decision to the Upper Tribunal and applying for a direction from the Tribunal that the FSA's decision notice should not be published. That application for directions was rejected. The applicants then applied for an extension to the interim injunction. In rejecting the application, the court considered the nature of the discretion given to the FSA in section 391(4) and whether the FSA had misinterpreted section 391(4) in the way it had drafted its decision notice publication policy, as well as whether that policy was irrational. Wyn Williams J stated:

> 'It does seem to me that it was the intention of Parliament to confer a broad discretion upon the Financial Services Authority, leaving it to them to consider whether it was appropriate to publish and leaving it to them to consider when it would be unfair to publish ... For my part, given the broad discretion which I believe is conferred upon the FSA, I see nothing irrational about the way it has phrased its policy ...'.[40]

12.30   The FCA is obliged to give a notice of discontinuance to a person to whom it has given a warning or decision notice if it decides not to take the action proposed in the warning notice or the action to which a decision notice relates.[41] The FCA has also indicated that it will send such notice to all persons to whom a warning notice or decision notice has been sent.[42]

12.31   In particular, a decision to discontinue, may arise following the FCA's assessment of representations from the recipient of a warning notice. The FCA decision-making process allows for the ongoing assessment of the proposed action in the context of the emergence of both information and representations and for any decision to discontinue to be taken by FCA staff. DEPP 3.2.26G provides, 'FCA staff responsible for recommending action to the RDC will continue to assess the appropriateness of the proposed action ... The decision to give a notice of discontinuance does not require the agreement of the RDC ...' When there has been a decision to discontinue, section 389(1) of the FSMA requires the FCA 'to give a notice of discontinuance to a person to whom the warning or decision notice was given'. The FCA also indicates in DEPP 3.2.26 that the decision to give a notice of discontinuance does not require the agreement of the RDC but FCA staff will inform the RDC that the proceedings have been discontinued The FCA is further required to identify in the notice 'the proceedings which are being discontinued'.[43]

---

39   *R (on the application of Canada Inc, Peter Beck, BRMS) v the Financial Services Authority* [2011] EWHC 2766 (Admin).
40   *R (Canada Inc)* (note 39) at [19].
41   FSMA, s 389.
42   DEPP 3.2.26G.
43   See FSMA, s 389(3).

Third party rights

12.32 Where a warning notice is, in the opinion of the FCA, prejudicial to a third party and such a party is identified in a warning notice to which the FSMA 2000, section 393 applies, the FCA must give a copy of the notice to that third party.[44] This section does not apply if the FCA has given him a separate warning notice in relation to the same matter or gives him such notice at the same time as it gives the warning notice which identifies him.[45] Such notice must specify a reasonable period (not less than 14 days) within which such a third party may make representations to the FCA.[46] However, this right to be informed is qualified. The FCA is not obliged to give a copy to such a third party if the FCA considers it impracticable to do so.[47] The FSMA 2000, section 394 relating to access to material, considered above, applies equally to a third party served with a warning notice.[48] The FSMA 2000, section 393 makes similar provision for decision notices.

12.33 The rights set out in section 393 ensure that third parties should not be identified and adversely criticised in a warning notice issued by the FCA without having had an opportunity to make representations in response and if they are identified and criticised in a decision notice, they should have the right to challenge such criticisms in the Tribunal.[49] In respect of the right to make a reference to the Upper Tribunal, section 393(9) makes provision for references in respect of both the FCA decision and any opinion expressed by the FCA in relation to the third party. There may be occasions where the FCA considers that it has no obligation to provide a person with a copy of a relevant notice, but the third party disagrees. In such circumstances the third party may make a reference to the Tribunal under section 393(11) which provides that:

> 'A person who alleges that a copy of the notice should have been given to him, but was not, may refer to the Tribunal the alleged failure and:
>
> (a)   the decision in question, so far as it is based on a reason of the kind mentioned in subsection (4); or
>
> (b)   any opinion expressed by the Authority in relation to him.'

12.34 In *Financial Conduct Authority v Macris*[50] the Court of Appeal considered the provisions in section 393. The case was an appeal from an Upper Tribunal decision on a preliminary issue that Mr Macris had been identified in statutory notices to JP Morgan Chase Bank NA. Gloster J concluded that the issue in the appeal was whether the 'matter' 'identifies' Mr Macris (at [36]) and considered this was addressed with a simple objective test (at [45]):

> 'As I have already said, it is clear that it is has to be the "matter" or "matters" referred to in the relevant notice which "identifies" the third party. But, as in the defamation cases, that does not mean that the third party has to be mentioned by name. As long as the relevant description in the "matters" (whether by reference to an office, a job description, or simply "Mr X") can properly be construed as a reference to an individual person, i.e. a "he" or a

---

44   FSMA, s 393(1).
45   FSMA, s 393(2).
46   FSMA, s 393(3)
47   FSMA, s 393(7)
48   FSMA, s 393(12)
49   FSMA, s 393(9).
50   [2015] EWCA Civ 490.

"she" (or, if a corporate entity, an "it"), then it seems to me that the correct test for identification is the simple objective one applied in the defamation cases adapted for the purposes of this case, viz: "Are the words used in the 'matters' such as would reasonably in the circumstances lead persons acquainted with the claimant/third party, or who operate in his area of the financial services industry, and therefore would have the requisite specialist knowledge of the relevant circumstances, to believe as at the date of the promulgation of the Notice that he is a person prejudicially affected by matters stated in the reasons contained in the notice?'"

Reference to the Upper Tribunal

12.35   Although a study of the jurisdiction of the Upper Tribunal in relation to market abuse enforcement is outside of the scope of this chapter it is worth mentioning that the role of the tribunal as providing an independent check and balance on the powers of the FCA is the responsibility of the Upper Tribunal (Tax and Chancery) which is administered by HM Courts Service. The Upper Tribunal is an independent tribunal created under section 3 of the Tribunals, Courts and Enforcement Act 2007 (the '2007 Act') and responsibility was transferred to it under art 2 of the Transfer of Tribunal Functions Order 2010.[51] In respect of market abuse, the Tribunal's jurisdiction and decision-making powers are limited, being conferred on it by sections 127 and 133 of the 2007 Act. References to the Tribunal are not appeals as the Tribunal hears the case afresh. Specifically in relation to the market abuse regime the Tribunal may receive references under section 127 of the 2007 Act to determine the FCA's decisions to impose penalties in cases of market abuse under section 123 of the FSMA.[52] The nature of the orders that can be made by the Upper Tribunals was amended by section 23 of the Financial Services Act 2012 and now, in accordance with section 133(5) of the FSMA it must determine the reference by either 'dismissing it, or remitting the matter back to the decision maker with a direction to reconsider and reach a decision in accordance with the findings of the Tribunal'.

Final Notice

12.36   If the matter is not referred to the Upper Tribunal, the FCA must give final notice to the person concerned pursuant to the FSMA 2000, section 390. Similarly, if the Upper Tribunal or a court on an appeal on a point of law (pursuant to the FSMA 2000, section 137) gives the FCA directions to take certain action, the FCA must give the person to whom the Decision Notice was given a Final Notice pursuant to section 390(2). Section 390 sets out mandatory requirements that must be included within the notice.

12.37   Pursuant to section 391(4) the FCA 'must publish such information about the matter to which a Final Notice relates as it considers appropriate', unless pursuant to section 391(6) publication would, in the opinion of the FCA, 'be unfair to the person with respect to whom the action was taken

---

51   SI 2010/22.
52   For analysis of the role of the Upper Tribunal in relation to Market Abuse Enforcement see S Bazley, *Market Abuse Enforcement Practice and Procedures* (Bloomsbury Professional 2013), Chapters 6, 7 and 8.

or prejudicial to the interest of consumers'.[53] Equally under section 390(2), the FCA is required '... on taking any action in accordance with directions given by a) the Tribunal or b) a court on appeal against the decision of the Tribunal ...' to give the person a Final Notice. Section 390(3)–(7) of the FSMA prescribes the minimum content requirements of the Final Notice, which is in part determined by the type of FCA decision being addressed in the Final Notice. In particular the Final Notice under section 390(3) must set out the terms of any statement that is to be made and 'the details of the manner' and 'the date on which the statement will be published'; and in regard to a financial penalty, it must, pursuant to section 390(5), state the amount of the penalty, the manner and period for payment as well as how the penalty will be recovered if not so paid. The Final Notice has the effect of formally concluding the FCA's enforcement action and all of the actions set out in the notice legally take effect, including payment of the financial penalty which by virtue of section 390(8) 'must not be less than 14 days beginning with the date the final notice is given'.[54]

Publication

12.38   The FCA is required by s 391(4) to publish such information about the matter to which a Final Notice relates as it considers appropriate and by s 391(7) in such manner as it thinks fit, unless publication would, in the opinion of the FCA, be unfair to the person with respect to whom the action was taken or prejudicial to the interest of consumers.[55]

STATEMENTS AND PENALTIES

12.39   The FCA has power under section 123(3) of the FSMA to publish a statement that a person has engaged in market abuse rather than impose a penalty.[56] Although the imposition of a penalty is more appropriate for serious cases, the publication of a statement as a sanction allows the FCA to deploy its disciplinary measures to varying degrees of seriousness. DEPP 6.4 sets out a non-exhaustive list of criteria applied by the FCA to determine whether a public censure alone is a more appropriate disciplinary measure than a financial penalty. On analysis, each of the factors within the DEPP 6.4.2 criteria arguably are to a significant extent the very reverse of the factors used for determining whether a financial penalty is an appropriate disciplinary outcome and indeed at DEPP 6.4.2, the FCA clarifies that it will also include in its determination of the appropriateness of a public censure, the factors that it will take into account when determining the size of a financial penalty. It is submitted that the most significant of the factors in light of the FCA's wider general enforcement policy of deterrence is that at DEPP 6.4.2(1) which in essence questions 'whether or not deterrence may be effectively achieved by issuing a public censure' and further and in the same context, the FCA

---

53   The FCA publishes copies of Final notices on its website.
54   See FSMA, s 390(8). Similar provisions apply in s 390(10) to FCA restitution requirements (see 12.62–12.66 below), which may be enforceable by way of injunction.
55   See FSMA, s 391(6).
56   FSMA, s 131 provides that 'the imposition of a penalty ... does not make the transaction in question void or unenforceable'.

clarifies at DEPP 6.4.2 (8) that where a financial penalty is appropriate, a public warning will only be used instead in exceptional circumstances and at DEPP 6.4.2(7) the importance of ensuring like cases consistently. Other factors included at 6.4.2 that might indicate that a public censure is more appropriate than a penalty include, whether a profit or loss has been avoided (at 6.4.2(2)); the seriousness of the breach (6.4.2(3)); whether the matter was self-reported by the person concerned to the FCA (6.4.2(4)); and whether there has been an admission of the breach and cooperation with the FCA (6.4.2(5)). The imposition of a financial statement alone is, however rare, occurring in only five[57] of the reported market abuse related cases. Although in three cases the justification for the public censure alone followed consideration of the wider circumstances of the case (the other two cases involving Welcome Financial Services Limited and Cheickh Tidiaane Diallo were made on the basis of financial hardship), it is submitted that the single feature in each of the cases that tends towards a public censure, is that the persons concerned committed abuse by error or mistake. For instance, in the case of *Morton*[58] the then FSA had taken action in respect of market abusive behaviour in the bond market, although identifying that there was little available industry guidance at the time addressing whether the behaviour amounted to abuse. The RDC considered in the circumstances of the case that in line with DEPP 6, it was more appropriate to issue a public statement than impose a financial penalty and pointed to the following mitigating features: '(a) that Mr Morton did not make any personal profit; (b) Mr Morton has subsequently undertaken further training in market abuse; (c) No clear guidance was provided to Mr Morton or the OTC credit markets; and (d) Mr Morton has no adverse previous disciplinary record of compliance history.'[59] In *Jason Geddis v The Financial Services Authority*,[60] where the applicant, a London Metals Exchange trader, built up a dominant position in short-terms lead contracts and caused an increase to the price of those contracts (this behaviour is often referred to as ramping up), the Upper Tribunal determined that the ramping up of the contracts price was not part of an abusive squeeze but the result of Mr Geddis getting caught up in the excitement of trading during the LME's open outcry session; the Tribunal directed the then FSA to publish a statement without a penalty or prohibition order. In reaching this determination, the Upper Tribunal pointed to both the FSA's Market confidence statutory objective (which was, prior to amendments made by the Financial Services Act 2012 at FSMA, section 2(2)) and the aims of its enforcement powers described at EG 2.2(4);[61] it considered on the facts of the case that the FSA's 'regulatory objectives will be properly advanced by a public censure'.[62]

12.40 In relation to any enforcement proceedings, the FCA takes into account a number of factors, some of which have particular relevance for market abuse cases. These factors are set out in the FCA's Decision Procedure and Penalties manual, which makes clear that the factors are not a substitute for an analysis

---

57 The three cases are FSA Final Notice *Christopher Parry* (6 October 2009); FSA Final Notice Darren *Morton* (6 October 2009); *Jason Geddis v Financial Services Authority* [2011] UKUT 344 FS/22010/0014; FSA Final Notice *Welcome Financial Services Limited* (28 March 2012), and FSA Final Notice *Cheickh Tidiane Diallo* (24 January 2013).

58 *Morton* (note 57).

59 See *Morton* (note 57) at [7.6].

60 *Geddis* (note 57).

61 *Geddis* (note 57) at [51].

62 *Geddis* (note 57) at [55].

of the full circumstances of each individual case and nor do they provide an exhaustive list of criteria. It is therefore possible that the unique features of an individual case may give rise to issues that warrant an enforcement outcome in order for the FCA to meet its Operational Objectives[63] despite not obviously being identified by any of the FCA enforcement criteria.

12.41   The criteria set out in DEPP 6.2.1 include the following:

(a)   whether the breach was deliberate or reckless;

(b)   the amount of any benefit gained or loss avoided as a result of the breach;

(c)   the impact or potential impact of the breach on the orderliness of markets including whether confidence in those markets has been damaged or put at risk;

(d)   the degree of cooperation the person showed during the investigation of the breach;

(e)   whether the person concerned has complied with any requirements or rulings of another regulatory authority relating to his behaviour (for example the Takeover Panel or a Recognised Investment Exchange; and

(f)   the previous disciplinary record and compliance history of the person.

Determining the level of financial penalty

12.42   The FCA's approach to the imposition of financial penalties for market abuse has, since the market abuse regime was first introduced, experienced significant procedural advancement, including in 2005 the development of a more transparent approach to financial penalty settlement discounts and in 2010 the publication of a more structured approach to the calculation of penalties.[64] The FCA sets out in DEPP 6.5 a series of factors used to determine in all cases the appropriate level of a financial penalty and highlights at DEPP 6.5.2 three principles underlying the imposition of a penalty, namely: (a) 'disgorgement', that is 'a firm or individual should not benefit from any breach', (b) 'discipline', and (c) 'deterrence'. Although the FCA does not operate a penalties tariff, it has adopted a five-step approach to penalty calculation which include special provisions at DEPP 6.5C adapting the steps for penalties against individuals in market abuse cases.[65] In essence the five-step approach operates in a formulaic manner, adding and then deducting amounts calculated by reference to the subject areas identified by the FCA.

12.43   The first step in a five-step approach looks to deprive the person concerned of the financial benefit derived from the market abuse behaviour and as made clear at DEPP 6.5A.1 and 6.5C.1 the FCA will seek to disgorge any loss avoided as a result of the market abuse. The disgorgement under Step 1 is an approach distinct from any restitution requirement under section 384 of the FSMA (which is considered further below.) Cases such that of *Mehmet Sepil*,[66] where the FSA imposed a financial penalty of £967,005 inclusive of

---

63   FSMA, s 1B(3).
64   Financial Services Authority 'Enforcement Financial Penalties: Feedback on CP 09/19', Policy Statement 10/4 (March 2010), http://www.fsa.gov.uk/pubs/policy/ps10_04.pdf.
65   See DEPP 6.5.3 which outlines the 5-step approach.
66   FSA Final Notice *Mehmet Sepil* 12 February 2010.

£267,005 disgorgement of profit, and *David Einhorn*[67] where the FSA imposed a financial penalty of £3m plus a penalty of £638,000 for disgorgement, illustrate the FSA's use of its power to impose a financial penalty to recover any profits made from abusive behaviour. Furthermore in circumstances where the FCA determines that a financial penalty is inappropriate, as in the FSA case of *Stewart McKegg*,[68] it will nonetheless disgorge profits made from the activity in question. Moreover, illustrating the FSA utilisation of its power to impose a financial penalty creatively and in a way that advances its purpose in bringing the action, in the case of *Bertie Hatcher*,[69] who agreed to cooperate with the FCA as part of the insider dealing criminal prosecution in *R v Calvert*,[70] the penalty imposed on Hatcher comprised only a profit disgorgement, showing the value the FSA placed on the assistance and cooperation that persons can provide to its wider investigations. In the *Hatcher* Final Notice the FSA stated that it 'had regard to Mr Hatcher's level of culpability and the value of the evidence that he has provided and considered that the penalty imposed is appropriate in all the circumstances'.[71]

12.44 The second step allows for a penalty to be calculated by reference to a person's revenue or as the case may be, income. In so doing the FCA will apply a 'seriousness level' multiplier, where level 1 is the least serious and level 5 the most. DEPP 6.5A.2 shows that for firms, the multiplier operates in a sliding scale of 0–20% and DEPP 6.5B (for non-market abuse penalties for individuals) a sliding scale of 0%–40%. This multiplier approach is made complicated by the approach taken by the FCA to market abuse penalties for individuals as set out in DEPP 6.5C, which attempts to recognise a difference in penalty calculation for persons committing market abuse by virtue of their employment (perhaps where the abuse is designed to benefit another), and abuse committed by members of the public. The basic principle set out in DEPP 6.5C is to allow the FCA at Step 2 to calculate a penalty as a multiplier of the profit or loss avoided (at DEPP 6.5C.2(8) it shows a sliding scale of multipliers of 0–4) as well as an additional percentage of their income if they commit the abuse as part of their employment, (at DEPP 6.5C.2(8) it shows a sliding scale of 0%–40%). In either circumstance, the FCA outlines at DEPP 6.5C.2(2)(c) and 6.5C.2(3)(b), that for individuals it expects in instances of deliberate market abuse it will assess the seriousness at either its level 4 or 5 and the starting point for the penalty will be £100,000. The FCA goes on to set out a series of tests that it applies in determining which seriousness level is appropriate for an individual case, which include at DEPP 6.5C.2(10) factors relating to the impact and nature of the market abuse and whether the abuse was deliberate or reckless. The FCA highlights the typical factors that tend to show that cases are the most or less serious. At 6.5C.2(15) it highlights level 4 or 5 factors as including matter such as at (a) 'the level of the benefit gained of loss avoided ...was significant'; at (b) 'the market abuse had a serious adverse effect on the orderliness of or confidence in the market'; at (d) 'the individual breached a position of trust'; at (e) 'the individual has a prominent position in the market'; and at (f) the market abuse was committed 'deliberately or recklessly'.

---

67   FSA Final Notice *David Einhorn* 15 February 2012.
68   FSA Final Notice *Stewart McKegg* (16 October 2008), http:///www.fsa.gov.uk/pubs/final/stewart_mckegg.pdf.
69   FSA Final Notice *Bertie Hatcher* (13 May 2008), http:///www.fsa.gov.uk/pubs/final/bertie_hatcher.pdf.
70   See *R v Calvert* (2010) (Southwark Crown Court Trial Unreported).
71   FSA Final Notice *Bertie Hatcher* 13 May 2008 (published in March 2010) at [4.11].

12.45   To illustrate the third FCA step in the calculation of a financial penalty let us consider DEPP 6.5C.3 which applies to individuals in market abuse cases. This provision allows for an adjustment to the financial penalty calculated under step 2 in light of any mitigating or aggravating factors, although a step 3 adjustment will not affect the disgorgement figure arrived at under step 1. The factors included under DEPP 6.5C.3(2) cover matters relating to the person's dealings with the FCA about the market abuse case, the person's previous regulatory and compliance history and whether the person has agreed 'to undertake training subsequent to the market abuse'. Step 4 in relation to an individual at DEPP 6.5C.4 makes provision for a further upward adjustment for deterrence in appropriate cases where the FCA considers that the penalty arrived at by steps 2 and 3 'is insufficient to deter the individual who committed the market abuse or others, from committing further or similar abuse …'. Finally Step 5 (set out at DEPP 6.5C.5) recognises that the FCA may in appropriate cases allow a settlement discount (save in respect of the disgorgement amount). The FCA policy towards settlement is examined further at 12.48–12.53 below. Although the five-step approach provides for the calculation of the financial penalty, the FCA provides at DEPP 6.5D.1 allowance for cases where there is serious financial hardship, providing at DEPP 6.5D.1(2) that:

> 'Where an individual firm claims that payment of the penalty proposed by the FCA will cause them serious financial hardship, the FCA will consider whether to reduce the proposed penalty only if:
>
> a)   the individual or firm provides verifiable evidence that payment of the penalty will cause them serious financial hardship; and
>
> b)   the individual or firm provides full, frank and timely disclosure of the verifiable evidence, and cooperates fully in answering any questions asked by the FCA about their financial position.'

12.46   In *Scerri v The Financial Services Authority*,[72] (although in the context at the time of a prior version of DEPP) the Upper Tribunal was required to consider whether the applicant lacked the means to pay the financial penalty sought by the FSA. The Tribunal confirmed that where a person's lack of means has been raised in a case (in line with the burden now provided DEPP 6.5D.1) 'it is for the Applicant in question to establish by "verifiable evidence" that he lacks the means to pay …'. In respect of individuals the FCA reveals at 6.5D.2 that it will consider permitting a penalty to be paid over a period of up to three years (including at DEPP 6.5D.2(3) an instalment arrangement) and consequently will only consider financial hardship 'if during that period his net annual income will fall below £14,000 and his capital fall below £16,000 as a result of the payment of the penalty …'. Applicants for a serious financial hardship reduction should exercise care, as the FCA does not provide an automatic and formulaic approach to the reductions, presumably as a matter of policy the FCA explains at DEPP 6.5D.2(7) that in serious cases such as instances of fraud or dishonesty, or where 'the individual has spent money or dissipated assets in anticipation of FCA or other enforcement action with a view to frustrating or limiting the impact …' it may not be appropriate to reduce a penalty. There are a number of instances of the Authority permitting a serious financial hardship penalty reduction in market abuse cases. For example in the decision against *Jay Rutland*[73] the FSA reduced its penalty from £160,000

72   *Andre Scerri v the Financial Services Authority* [2010] UKUT (Penalty decision) Fin/2009/0016.

73   FSA Final Notice *Jay Rutland* 9 July 2012.

to £30,000 and in *Oluwole Fagbulu v The Financial Services Authority*,[74] the Upper Tribunal reduced the financial penalty from £350,000 to £100,000. In *Fagbulu* the Tribunal identified that even where there is evidence of financial hardship in certain circumstances the deterrence component of a penalty is still important; it stated: 'This is not a case in which we think, the penalty should be fixed without regard to the bankruptcy it might cause, yet it is one in which even a reduced penalty must be large enough to make clear that conduct of the kind in which Mr Fagbulu engaged will be severely punished …'.[75] In contrast, in the matter of *Swift Trade Inc v Financial Services Authority*,[76] the Upper Tribunal determined that a penalty of £8m was acceptable, Judge Bishop stating (at [142]):

> 'We do not, therefore, approach determination of the penalty from the viewpoint of ability to pay, nor by reference to the profits made by Swift Trade or the losses sustained by others. What is clear, as we have said, is that this was a prolonged, cynical course of market abuse committed by a company which, as the OSC Settlement Agreement shows, exhibited a wholesale disregard of regulatory requirements …'.

12.47 The approach to determining an appropriate penalty in market abuse was addressed by the Tribunal in *Parker*[77] which confirmed that by virtue of the language in the FSMA, section 124, the question of imposition of a penalty is discretionary and the Authority is under no obligation to impose a financial penalty.[78] It held that the FSA's statutory penalties policy (now contained in DEPP) was 'fair and reasonable'[79] and 'that any penalty should be proportionate to the gravity of the offence it is designed to punish and discourage'.[80] It further stated, 'A significant factor must be the financial advantage the person committing the abuse set out to obtain, which will not necessarily be the same as the gain actually made or the loss actually avoided.'[81] The Upper Tribunal in *Visser and Fagbulu*[82] stated, however, that it was not bound to follow the FSA penalties policy in DEPP: 'We are not bound by the policy or guidance, but they are a convenient and useful starting point.'[83] Having said that, in referring to specific provisions of DEPP then in force and relevant to the calculation of an appropriate financial penalty, the Tribunal commented: 'In our view they constitute proper guidance to the determination of the level of a penalty, in conjunction with a close consideration of an individual applicant's own circumstances.'

Settlement

12.48 Step 5 allows for a discount to be applied to a financial penalty in the event that the enforcement case can be settled between the FCA and the person under discipline. The FCA's settlement policy is described in Chapter 5

---

74   *Michael Visser and Oluwole Fagbulu v the Financial Services Authority* [2011] UKUT FS/2010/0001 and FS /2010/0006.
75   *Visser and Fagbulu* [n 74] at [125].
76   [2012] (UKUT FS/2011/0017 & 0018).
77   *Parker v Financial Services Authority* (2006) FSMT case 37.
78   *Parker* (note 77) at [148].
79   *Parker* (note 77) at [155]–[156].
80   *Parker* (note 77) [172].
81   *Parker* (note 77) at [172].
82   *Visser and Fagbulu* (note 74).
83   *Visser and Fagbulu* (note 74).

of DEPP.[84] It is important to note that a settled solution is not reserved for those enforcement cases involving a financial penalty, and applies equally to proposed public censures and private warnings. It is not uncommon for the FCA to put forward an enforcement settlement proposal at the end of an investigation and prior to it formally issuing a statutory notice. Furthermore, DEPP 5.1.3 makes it clear that settlement discussions can take place at all stages throughout the enforcement process even following a referral to the Upper Tribunal or during Court proceedings as was the case in the FSA's case of *Barnett Michael Alexander*.[85] Furthermore, the FCA recognises that to encourage early settlement, discussions or negotiations between it and the person concerned will often be required on a without prejudice basis and thus at DEPP 5.1.4 it provides that there may be agreement 'that neither the FCA nor the person concerned would seek to rely against the other on any admissions or statements made in the course of their settlement discussions if the matter is considered subsequently by the RDC or the Tribunal'. The FCA decision maker in cases of market abuse is the FCA's Regulatory Decisions Committee; however, the FCA's settlement process at DEPP 5.1.1(3) allows for settlement discussions and agreement (including market abuse cases) to be conducted by two members of FCA senior management as settlement decision makers, requiring that one decision maker must be at director level and the other at head of department level and further providing at DEPP 5.1.1(4) that although one of the settlement decision makers may be from the FCA's enforcement and financial crime division, the second must not be.

12.49 In practice, settlement discussions may begin between the person subject to enforcement (or that person's representative) and FCA staff (usually from the FCA enforcement division). Any such discussion may not (as recognised by DEPP 5.1.5(1) include the 'settlement decision makers'. It is common in such circumstances for the FCA staff conducting the settlement discussions to make recommendations to the settlement decision makers and in such circumstances, in accordance with DEPP 5.1.7(1) and (2), the settlement decision makers may accept or decline the proposed settlement terms. In addition to the substantive components of an enforcement settlement, such as the terms of the FCA Decision Notice, level of penalty and wording of a public statement, the FCA requires at DEPP 5.1.6 that the terms be in writing and waive any statutory rights that the person may have in relation to the warning or decision notice, such as the right to make representation to the RDC or rights of referral to the Upper Tribunal.

12.50 Although the FCA is given statutory powers to impose enforcement sanctions for market abuse, many of the administrative cases brought by the FCA are concluded following an early managed settlement. The benefits offered by early settlement apply to both the FCA and those against whom the action is brought both in financial terms (by reducing cost and a recognised discount on any financial penalty) and by affording the opportunity to acknowledge any regulatory failing at an early stage, permitting rectification of any such failing. Indeed the FCA's settlement process is supported by a mediation facility to assist the parties to negotiate an agreed settlement.

---

84   Increased enforcement settlement transparency was introduced following the FSA's enforcement process review: Report and recommendations, July 2005.
85   FSA Final Notice *Barnett Michael Alexander* (14 June 2011) and *The Financial Services Authority v Barnett Alexander & ors* (2011) (unreported) HC 10C01696. A copy of the consent order in the case is appended to the FSA's final notice.

12.51 *Enforcement issues*

12.51 The FCA has introduced increased transparency supporting a formal settlement process which is set out at Chapter 5 of DEPP. That process allows for the subject of enforcement to enter into settlement discussions with the FCA at any stage of the enforcement and in addition to setting out a formalised settlement process, Chapter 6.7 of DEPP also sets out a clear discount scheme for financial penalties that is applied to the stage at which during the FCA enforcement process settlement might be achieved.

12.52 Turning to the impact that early settlement may have on financial penalties, DEPP 6.7 articulates a penalty discount scheme applied at the stage of the enforcement process that settlement is reached. In essence the earlier that settlement is reached the greater the percentage penalty discount. In essence the following discounts are applied:[86]

- Stage 1 – A 30% discount. The FCA describes stage 1 at DEPP 6.7.3(1)(a) as, 'the period from the commencement of an investigation until the [FCA] has (i) a sufficient understanding of the nature and gravity of the breach to make a reasonable assessment of the appropriate penalty; and (ii) communicated that assessment to the person concerned and allowed a reasonable opportunity to reach agreement as to the amount of the penalty';
- Stage 2 – A 20% discount. The FCA describes stage 2 at DEPP 6.7.3(1)(b) as 'the period from the end of stage 1 until the expiry of the period for making written representations or, if sooner, the date on which the written representations is sent in response to the giving of a warning notice';
- Stage 3 – A discount of 10%. The FCA describes stage 3 at DEPP 6.7.3(1)(C) as 'the period from the end of stage 2 until the giving of a decision notice';
- Stage 4 – No discount. The FSA describes stage 4 at DEPP 6.7.3(1)(d) as 'the period after the end of stage 3, including proceedings before the Tribunal and subsequent appeals'.

12.53 Since the introduction of the market abuse regime in 2001, the Authority's level of financial penalty has steadily increased, arguably in line with the evolution of its policy of credible deterrence. During this period, the levels of financial penalty have varied considerably, with the largest market abuse penalty currently standing at £17m[87] and the smallest at £1,000.[88] A more detailed analysis of Final Notices reveals very little distinction between the market abuse penalties imposed on members of the public with the highest penalty against a member of the public standing at £4m imposed on *Remeshkumar Goenka* in 2011,[89] as compared with a penalty of £4m imposed on Winterflood Securities,[90] an authorised person, and £2.8m imposed on *Simon Eagle*, an approved person.[91]

---

86 See DEPP 6.7.3 for an outline of the FCA's penalties discount scheme.
87 FSA Final Notice *Shell Transport and Trading Company plc and The Royal Dutch Petroleum Company NV* (24 August 2004), http://www.fsa.gov.uk/pubs/final/shell_24aug04.pdf.
88 FSA Final Notice *Michael Davies* (28 July 2004), http://www.fsa.gov.uk/pubs/final/davies-mt_28jul04.pdf and FSA Final Notice *Brian Taylor* (16 August 2008), http://www.fsa.gov.uk/pubs/final/brian_taylor.pdf.
89 FSA Final Notice *Remesshkumar Satyanarayan Goeenka* (17 October 2011).
90 FSA Final Notice *Winterflood Securities Limited* (22 April 2010).
91 FSA Final Notice *Simon Eagle* (18 May 2010), http://www.fsa.gov.uk/pubs/final/simon_eagle.pdf.

ENFORCEMENT AND THE IMPACT ON BUSINESS PERMISSIONS

12.54   In market misconduct cases against authorised persons or approved persons, the FCA may determine that the facts of the misconduct are so serious that it has to take action to withdraw or vary a firm's business permissions or prohibit an approved person. Part IV of the FSMA contains powers granted to the FCA to cancel or vary a firm's business permissions and section 63 of the FSMA grants power to withdraw approved person status (see further Chapters 14 and 15. The severity of the situation might reveal that the firm ceases to satisfy the threshold conditions[92] for authorisation or that the interests of consumers are at risk to such an extent that the FCA considers it desirable to impose limitations or restrictions on the firm's regulated activities. Indeed the FCA might have concerns that the facts of the matter show that an approved person ceases to be a fit and proper person.[93] If as a result of a withdrawal of a firm's business permission there remains no regulatory activity for which the firm has permission, then the FCA may under section 33 of the FSMA withdraw the firm's authorisation.

12.55   Furthermore pursuant to section 56, the FCA may prohibit an individual under section 56(2) 'from performing a specified function' if under section 56(1) 'it appears to the Authority that an individual is not a fit and proper person' (see further Chapters 14 and 15). As an alternative to withdrawal of authorisation, following amendments to FSMA by the Financial Services Act 2010 the FCA has power under FSMA, section 206A to suspend or impose limitations on a person's authorisation or under section 66(3) approval. The FCA sets out at DEPP 6A.2 the factors it will take into account in deciding whether to impose a suspension, including at 6A.2.3 'whether it believes that such action will be a more effective and persuasive deterrent than the imposition of a financial penalty alone'. Further at DEPP 6A.3 the FCA sets out a non-exhaustive lists of factors it will apply in deciding the appropriate period of suspension, including at 6A.3.2 the 'deterrence' effect of the suspension, 'the seriousness of the breach', 'aggravating and mitigating factors' and 'the impact of suspension or restriction on the person in breach'. The FCA uses it enforcement guide to set out its approach to the variation of business permissions and withdrawal of approval, stating at EG 8.1B that when considering how to address concerns, it 'will have regard to it statutory objectives and the range of regulatory tools that are available to it'. The FCA provides at EG 8.3(1) that it may take formal action to vary permissions in particular where it, 'has serious concerns about a firm, or about the way its business is being conducted', and at EG 8.5 examples are provided of scenarios when the FCA may consider varying a permission, including at 8.5(1)(b) where 'the firm appears not to be a fit and proper person to carry on a regulated activity because (i) it has not conducted its business in compliance with high standards which may include putting itself at risk of being used for the purpose of financial crime or being otherwise involved in such crime'. Analysis of market abuse enforcement cases against approved persons shows that the FCA is increasingly determining that abusive behaviour by approved persons is inherently lacking in integrity and thus, without any mitigating circumstances, it appears likely that an approved

92   FSMA, Sch 6 together with the Financial Services and Markets Act 2000 (Threshold Conditions) Order 2013 (SI 2013/555).
93   FSMA, s 60 and the Fit and Proper Test for Approved Person FCA sourcebook (FIT).

person engaging in abusive behaviour will face a prohibition order. Indeed EG 9.9(4) specifically refers to market abuse as one factor the FCA will take into account when considering a prohibition order against an approved person. Emphasising the interplay between deliberate abuse, fitness, probity and the FCA statutory objectives in justifying a prohibition, in the matter of *Andrew Kerr*,[94] the FSA considered that Kerr's deliberate engagement in market abuse and subsequent provision of false and misleading information to the Authority directly impugned his honesty, integrity and reputation, demonstrating that he was not a fit and proper person and presented a risk to the FCA's statutory objective of market confidence. Furthermore in *Massey v The Financial Services Authority*,[95] the Upper Tribunal linked a finding of market abuse with other misleading behaviour in the case and stated: 'On the evidence of this case he is in our view not a fit and proper person, and a prohibition order is justified',[96] although in the case the Tribunal did not consider the case was so serious that it justified a 'lifetime ban'.

APPLICATIONS TO THE COURT

12.56   In broader terms and in addition to the disciplinary measures explored above, the FCA has a number of enforcement measures available which may be viewed as protectionist rather than disciplinary in nature. Such additional measures may be taken where the FCA considers it is necessary to take enforcement action to ensure the protection of the market or individual investors. The FCA's Enforcement Guide is used to describe the FCA's approach to injunctions (see EG 10) and restitution (see EG 11). In both sections the FCA explains that injunction and restitution decisions are usually made by the RDC Chairman, or in urgent cases where the Chairman is not available, by the RDC Deputy Chairman. Further applicable provisions of EG are set out below.

Injunctions of the Court

12.57   Section 381 of the FSMA makes specific provision allowing the FCA to apply to the court for a range of orders to address market abuse. Section 381(1) addresses situations where a person has engaged in or may engage in market abuse allowing the court to 'restrain' the activity. In *Financial Conduct Authority v Da Vinci Invest Limited*[97], the FCA obtained a permanent injunction under section 381 restraining market abuse. FSMA, section 381 provides:

'If, on the application of the FCA, the court is satisfied–

(a)   that there is a reasonable likelihood that any person will engage in market abuse, or

(b)   that any person is or has engaged in market abuse and that there is a reasonable likelihood that the market abuse will continue or be repeated,

---

94   FSA Final Notice *Andrew Kerr* (1 June 2010), http://www.fsa.gov.uk/pubs/final/andrew_kerr.pdf.
95   *David Massey v the Financial Services Authority* [2011] UKUT 49 (TCC) Ref Fin/2009/0024.
96   *Massey* (note 95).
97   [2015] EWHC 2401.

the court may make an order restraining (or in Scotland an interdict prohibiting) the market abuse.'

Section 381(2) further makes provision allowing the court by order to require a person to take steps to remedy a market abuse. It provides:

'If on the application of the FCA the court is satisfied–

(a)   that any person is or has engaged in market abuse, and
(b)   that there are steps which could be taken for remedying the market abuse,

the court may make an order requiring him to take such steps as the court may direct to remedy it.'

12.58   Section 381(3) and (4) combine to make provision for an order to restrain a person from dealing with or disposing of assets. Section 381(3) provides:

'Subsection (4) applies if, on the application of the FCA, the court is satisfied that any person–

(a)   may be engaged in market abuse; or
(b)   may have been engaged in market abuse.'

Section 381(4) provides:

'The court may make an order restraining (or in Scotland an interdict prohibiting) the person concerned from disposing of, or otherwise dealing with, any assets of his which it is satisfied that he is reasonably likely to dispose of, or otherwise deal with.'

Factors the FCA may consider in determining whether to seek injunctions

12.59   The FCA sets out at EG 10.3 factors it will take into account when considering whether to apply for an order under section 381, although it states at EG10.3 that it will apply a 'broad test' of 'whether the application would be the most effective way to deal with the FSA's concerns'. The wider factors include consideration of the following:

'The nature and seriousness of a contravention or expected contravention ... [10.3(1)]

[Including for market abuse] the impact or potential impact on the financial system of the conduct in question [10.3(2)(a)] ... the extent and nature of any losses or other costs imposed ... [10.3.(2)(b)]

Whether the conduct in question has stopped or is likely to stop ... [10.3(3)]

Whether there are steps a person could take to remedy a contravention of a relevant requirement or market abuse ... [10.3(4)]

Whether there are steps a person could take to remedy a contravention have a relevant requirement or market abuse ... [10.3(4)]

Whether there is a danger of assets being dissipated ... [10.3(5)]

The costs the FCA would incur in applying for and enforcing an injunction and the benefits that would result [10.3(6)]

The disciplinary record and general compliance history of the person who is the subject of the possible application ... [10.3(7)]

Whether there is information to suggest that the person who is the subject of the possible application is involved in financial crime ... [10.3(10)]'

Restitution

12.60   Section 383 of the FSMA sets out provisions allowing the FCA to apply to the court for an order for a payment that will be passed on by the FCA to another person, who very generically might be referred to as the victim of the market abuse. Subject to where under section 383(3) the court is satisfied that a person 'believed on reasonable grounds, that his behaviour did not' amount to market abuse or 'he took all reasonable precautions and exercised due diligence to avoid' the market abuse behaviour, (being a defence analogous to the statutory market abuse defence in FSMA, section 123(2)), the court may where a person's market abuse behaviour has given rise to a profit (section 383(2)(a)), or other persons have suffered a loss or affected by the abuse (section 383(2)(b)) may pursuant to section 383(4) order the person to make a payment to the FCA. Further under section 383(5) the money received by the FCA under the restitution order must be 'paid' or 'distributed' to the person to whom under section 383(10) the abusers profits are 'attributable' or 'who has suffered the loss or adverse effect'.

12.61   In the FSA's market abuse enforcement case against *Barnett Michael Alexander*[98] due to Mr Alexander's on-going market abuse, the FSA applied an order under section 381 restraining him from committing market abuse and also under section 383 for restitution. The orders were agreed by consent between the parties including a restitution payment of £322,818, and a financial penalty of £700,000 agreed with the FSA under its settlement arrangements but ordered under FSMA, section 129.

12.62   At EG 11.3 the FCA sets out criteria that it will generally apply in deciding whether to utilise its powers to obtain or require restitution whether under section 383 or 384 (the power for the relevant regulator to require restitution). The basic premise at EG 11.3 is that the FCA 'will consider all the circumstances of the case', but specific factors considered include: 'Are the profits quantifiable?' (11.3(1)); 'Are the losses identifiable?' (11.3.(2)); 'The number of persons affected' (11.3(3)); 'The FCA's costs' (11.3 (4)); 'Is redress available elsewhere?' (11.3(5)); 'Can persons bring their own proceedings?' (11.3(7); 'What other powers are available to the FCA?' (11.3(9)).

The FCA's own requirements for restitution

12.63   Section 384(2) makes provision allowing the FCA, without the need for a court application, to require a person to make a payment in restitution if 'it is satisfied that a person (a) has engaged in market abuse, or (b) ... has required or encouraged another person to engage in behaviour which, if engaged in by the person concerned, would amount to market abuse. And under section 384(3),

---

98   FSA Final Notice *Barnett Michael Alexander* (14 June 2011) and *The Financial Services Authority v Barnett Alexander & ors* (2011) (unreported) HC 10C01696. A copy of the consent order in the case is appended to the FSA's final notice.

'profits have accrued to the person as a result of the market abuse; or ... one or more persons have suffered a loss or been adversely affected as a result of the abuse'. Similarly to section 383(3) the FCA, pursuant to section 384(4) may not require restitution where there are circumstances analogous to the section 123 statutory defence. Section 384(5) in essence stipulates that any amount that the FCA considers appropriate is to be paid or distributed to the persons (identified under section 384(6)) 'to whom the profits ... are attributable; or who has suffered the loss or adverse effect ...', thus distinguishing a restitution requirement under section 384 from a disgorgement of profits secured as part of a financial penalty.

12.64 Perhaps, however, the most significant question is whether the FCA should rely on its own powers under section 384 or make an application to court for restitution under section 383. In this respect the FCA states at EG 11.4 that it '... will first consider using its own administrative powers under section 384 [FSMA] before considering taking court action ...' but that it will go on to consider wider issues such as where there may be other court action against the person (11.5(1)); and perhaps most importantly where there is either 'a danger that assets ... may be dissipated ...' (11.5(3)) or where it considers that the sanction of breaching an order of the court is necessary because it has concerns that its own requirement under section 384 may not be complied with (11.5(4)).

Chapter 13

Compliance procedures and systems

INTRODUCTION

13.1   This chapter examines issues relating to the obligations imposed on
authorised persons to establish and maintain systems and controls to ensure
compliance with their obligations under the regulatory system.[1] In so doing
the chapter will consider compliance from the standpoints of both internal
firms governance arrangements and its 'compliance function' and how that
function serves to support the compliance arrangements established by a
firm. The Markets in Financial Instruments Directive (MiFID)[2] and Directive
2006/73,[3] one of MiFID's implementing measures, set out detailed provision
for minimum regulatory standards regarding the internal organisation of
investment firms. To a large extent these measures have shaped the Financial
Conduct Authority's (FCA) rules in its Senior Management Systems and
Controls sourcebook (SYSC). Additionally, enhanced regulation following
the global financial crisis has introduced prudential regulation for Banks and
certain investment firms that impacts how those firms are governed. Some of
these rules have been addressed within SYSC and the FCA's Prudential rules
for Investment Firms (IFPRU), and others have direct application through the
Capital Requirements Directive (CRD)[4] and Capital Requirements Regulations
(CRR).[5] In order to assess the impact these provisions have, the chapter will

---

1   See generally S Bazley, *Market Abuse Enforcement Practice and Procedure* (Bloomsbury
     Professional 2013) and Chapter 6 by S Bazley of *Special Report, The Regulation of
     Investment Services in Europe under MiFID: Implementation and Practice* (General Editor
     Emilios Avgouleas) (Tottel Publishing 2008).
2   Council Directive 2004/39/EC OJL145/1 on markets in financial instruments. In this
     chapter I refer to this directive as 'The Directive' and 'MiFID'. The Directive was amended
     by Council Directive 2006/31/EC OJL114/60 as regards certain deadlines.
3   Council Directive 2006/73/EC OJL241/26, implementing Directive 2004/39/EC as regards
     organisational requirements and operating conditions for investment firms and defined terms
     for the purpose of that Directive.
4   Directive 2013/36/EU bof the European Parliament on access to the activity of credit
     institutions and the prudential supervision of credit institutions and investment firms
     (Directive 2013/36/EU) and amending Directive 2002/87/EC and repealing Directives
     2006/48/EC and 2006/49/EC.
5   Regulation of the European Parliament and the Council on prudential requirements for credit
     institutions and investment firms (Regulation (EU) No 575/2013) and amending Regulation
     (EU) No 648/2012.

consider the provisions of MiFID, CRD and CRR as well as the rules and associated guidance of SYSC along with a number of relevant FSA and FCA Final Notices. It should be recognised that not all authorised firms are subject to the provisions of MiFID, such as insurers, although they may participate in market trading. Alternative provisions with the FCA's sourcebook SYSC set out governance and compliance obligations relating to other classes of authorised persons. A second Markets Instruments Directive (MiFID II) and supporting regulations (MiFIR) is due to come into force from January 2017, which will impact some of the governance arrangements applying to management bodies referred to in this chapter by bringing the obligations in line with the CRD.

13.2   When considering issues of compliance in respect of market abuse, a number of more discrete obligations concerning the prevention and detection of abuse should be considered. In so doing, this chapter will consider regulatory obligations to control record keeping and personal account trading, as well as the interaction between the compliance function and conflicts management (more detailed analysis of conflicts management is provided in Chapter 8). What should be evident, however, is that compliance is the responsibility of the authorised firm and its governing body and not merely something that can be delegated to a firm's compliance officer. Furthermore it is important to recognise the role of organisational culture in ensuring that a firm's business activities meet its regulatory obligations, as neither detailed provisions of the rulebook nor the appointment of a compliance function will by themselves ensure compliance with regulatory obligations. Furthermore the effectiveness of a firm's compliance function is influenced by the firm's senior management and its organisational culture; that is the right 'tone' for the business must be created by its governing body and senior management will determine how effectively a compliance function will operate. Clive Adamson, former FCA director of supervision, commenting on organisational culture stated: 'Setting the tone is all about creating a culture where everyone has ownership and responsibility for doing the right thing, because it is the right thing to do.'[6]

AUTHORISATION, GOVERNANCE, SENIOR MANAGEMENT AND COMPLIANCE

13.3   Before beginning an analysis of the detailed regulatory provisions relating to the firm's internal processes and compliance arrangements, it is important to consider a number of the basic provisions within the Financial Services and Markets Act 2000 (FSMA) that determine whether or not a firm meets the conditions for authorisation. Section 53 and Sch 6 of the FSMA, together with the Financial Services and Markets Act (Threshold Conditions) Regulations 2013,[7] impose a series of threshold conditions that firms must meet and demonstrate they are capable of continuing to meet in order to be considered fit and proper and be granted authorisation. The threshold conditions relating to 'suitability' and 'resources', it is submitted, have the most impact on the internal arrangements which firms must establish to secure compliance

---

6   Clive Adamson, FCA Director of supervision. Speech at the CFA Society 'The importance of culture in driving behaviours of firms and how the FCA will assess this' (19 April 2013) http://www.fca.org.uk/news/regulation-professionalism.
7   SI 2013/555.

with regulatory obligations.[8] Following amendments made by the Financial Services Act 2012, which created a twin peaks system of regulation, and the establishment of the Prudential Regulation Authority (PRA) and variation to the jurisdiction of the FCA, the threshold conditions are now divided between those applicable to firms authorised and regulated by the FCA, conditions relevant to the FCA but in relation to firms authorised by the PRA, conditions relevant to PRA authorisation of insurers, and conditions applicable to all other PRA authorised firms. In the following sections of this chapter consideration will be given to the threshold conditions applying to firms authorised and regulated by the FCA. The FCA provides guidance on its application of the threshold conditions in the conditions sourcebook (COND) of the FCA Handbook.

13.4 The suitability threshold condition at FSMA, Sch 6, para 2E requires the FCA to consider issues relating to the applicant firm's fitness and properness, in addition to a consideration of the antecedents of the firm and its controllers (see further Chapter 15). Consideration is also given to the applicant's suitability in the context of matters such as the nature and complexity of the regulated activities that it will carry on; along with how its business will be managed and controlled; that its business will be conducted appropriately and; 'the need to minimise the extent in which it is possible for the business carried on by [the firm] ... to be used for a purpose connected with financial crime'. The FCA guidance at COND 2.5.6G provides examples of matters the FCA will consider when assessing suitability, which in relation to the adequacy of internal controls and compliance arrangements includes consideration of whether:

'(1A) the firm has made arrangements to put in place an adequate system of internal control to comply with the requirements and standards for which the FCA is responsible under the regulatory system; ...

(7) the firm has put in place procedures which are reasonably designed to:(a) ensure that it has made its employees aware of, and compliant with, those requirements and standards under the regulatory system that apply to the firm for which the FCA is responsible and the regulated activities for which it has, or will have permission ...

(16) the firm has taken reasonable care to ensure that robust information and reporting systems have been developed, tested and properly installed;

(17) the firm has in place appropriate systems and controls against financial crime, including, for example, money laundering; ...'

13.5 In many respects the suitability condition overlaps with the resources threshold condition at FSMA, Sch 6 para 2D. This condition in part addresses the capital requirement imposed on an authorised firm, dependent on the category of business it undertakes. Although an assessment of regulatory capital is outside the scope of this book, for the purpose of analysis of systems and controls, it is important to highlight that a firm's capital position will be impacted by the risks of its business activities. The obligations in certain FCA prudential rules such as IFPRU at IFPRU 2.2.7R and 2.2.14R require firms to undertake a Pillar 2 assessment will which draws in analysis of the level

8 For further analysis of compliance systems relating to financial crime see B Rider (ed) Chapter 24 'Compliance', in *Research Handbook on Financial Crime* (Edward Elgar 2015).

321

of a firm's risks and address the capital provision it needs to make in order to manage those risks.[9] Additionally, however, the non-financial resources of a firm which under FSMA, Sch 6, para 1A(2) will include matters such as management experience, policies and internal systems, will be assessed (see Sch 6, para2D(4)). The FCA guidance at COND 2.4.4G concerning non-financial resources, including in the context of how it is prepared for the risks of its business, states: '... (d) whether the firm has taken reasonable steps to identify and measure any risks of regulatory concern that it may encounter in conducting its business (see COND 2.4.6 G) and has installed appropriate systems and controls and appointed appropriate human resources to measure them prudently at all times ...'.

13.6 In the context of the suitability condition, the MiFID regime provides a series of measures governing the appropriateness of a firm's senior management and their responsibilities within the firm. Article 9(1) of MiFID incorporated SYSC at 4.2.1R provides that Member States shall require the persons who effectively direct the business of an investment firm to be of sufficiently good repute and sufficiently experienced as to ensure the sound and prudent management of the investment firm. Pursuant to Article 9(3), 'the competent authority shall refuse authorisation if it is not satisfied that the persons who will effectively direct the business of the investment firm are of sufficiently good repute or sufficiently experienced, or if there are objective and demonstrable grounds for believing that proposed changes to the management of the firm pose a threat to its sound and prudent management'. (Further analysis relating to the suitability of senior personnel including compliance officers as well as those in control is provided in Chapters 14 and 15.)

13.7 MiFID stresses the role that a firm's senior management have in the operation of a firm's business, including their overall role in ensuring that the firm operates in compliance with its requirements. Regulators, such as the FCA, have sought to ensure that by having a compliance function within the firm, senior management benefit from dedicated oversight and advice on the standards of compliance within their business and are thus able to meet their personal responsibility for the management of the business. Article 9(1) of MiFID level 2 Directive 2006/73/EC provides that Member States should require investment firms 'to ensure that senior management, and, where appropriate, the supervisory function,[10] are responsible for ensuring that the firm complies with its obligations under the Directive [MiFID]. Article 9(1), as implemented by SYSC 4.3.1R, shapes the requirement for applicable authorised firms to undertake on-going monitoring of and remedy weaknesses in their internal control arrangements. It will be seen later in this chapter that monitoring and oversight is also a core component of the MiFID requirement for a Compliance Function. SYSC 4.3.1R provides: 'In particular, senior personnel and, where appropriate, the supervisory function must assess and periodically review the effectiveness of the policies, arrangements and procedures put in place to comply with the firm's obligations under the regulatory system and take appropriate measures to address any deficiencies.'

9   Certain firms are required to establish and maintain an internal Capital Adequacy Assessment Framework (ICAAP) with associated risk management arrangements in order for the firm's governing body to set the firm's risk appetite and set out how it will utilise capital to manage identified and emerging risks.

10   For the purpose of Article 9, supervisory function is defined as '... the function within an investment firm responsible for the supervision of its senior management.'.

GOVERNANCE AND THE NEED FOR POLICY, PROCESS, AND PROCEDURE

13.8 Effective governance is often viewed as essential to the effective and successful operation of an undertaking. An overarching obligation in relation to organisational control is provided by way of FCA High Level principle for business 3, stating: 'A firm must take reasonable care to organise and control its affairs responsibly and effectively, with adequate risk management systems.' By way of example of the FCA's reliance on Principle 3 to enforce control failings, in 2015 it imposed a financial penalty of £226,800,000 on Deutsche Bank AG, in part as a result of it failing to have in place specific financial benchmark systems and controls and having 'seriously defective systems and controls in place to support audit and investigation of trader misconduct ...'.[11]

13.9 FCA rules at SYSC 4.1.1R implementing Article 13(5) of the MiFID refer specifically to the need to have in place 'robust governance arrangements' which are defined as including 'effective processes to identify, manage, monitor and report the risks it is or might be exposed to and internal control mechanisms ...'. Additional and more prescriptive governance obligations are provided at SYSC 4.3A.1 in respect of firms subject to the EU Capital requirements regulations, including that such firm's management body 'defines, oversees and is accountable for the implementation of governance arrangements that ensure effective and prudent management of the firm ...'. The nature of the arrangements required under SYSC 4.1.1R, clarified further by provisions at SYSC 4.1.2, allows for the design of internal arrangements appropriate for a business in the context of individual risks, stating 'The arrangements, processes and mechanisms referred to in SYSC 4.1.1 R must be comprehensive and proportionate to the nature, scale and complexity of the risks inherent in the business model and of the ... firm's activities ...'. SYSC 4.1.4R(1)–(4) (implementing Article 5 of the MiFID implementing Directive) addresses more specific requirements concerning a firm's internal control arrangements which once again may be formulated to take account of the 'nature, scale and complexity' of the firm's business and includes the need to establish:

'... decision-making procedures and an organisational structure ...

... adequate internal control mechanisms designed to secure compliance with decisions and procedures at all levels of the firm;

... effective internal reporting and communication of information at all relevant levels of the firm; ...'

Systems for compliance and financial crime

13.10 Although the governance and general internal control obligations at SYSC 4 make discrete reference to compliance, more focused reference addressing both arrangements for securing compliance as well as the operation of a compliance function are provided for by SYSC. Article 13(2) of MIFID together with Article 6 of the implementing Directive, applied by the FCA at

---

11   FCA Final Notice *Deutsche Bank AG* (23 April 2015) http://www.fca.org.uk/your-fca/documents/final-notices/2015/deutsche-bank-ag.

13.10   *Compliance procedures and systems*

SYSC 6.1.1R requires that: 'A firm must establish, implement and maintain adequate policies and procedures sufficient to ensure compliance of the firm including its managers, employees and appointed representatives (or where applicable, tied agents) with its obligations under the regulatory system and for countering the risk that the firm might be used to further financial crime.' Indeed the compliance arrangements established by a firm (including those relating to conflicts management, wall crossing and personal account trading which are considered below at 13.33–13.42, may be sufficient to provide the 'reasonable grounds' defence to an allegation of market abuse at section 123(2) of the FSMA (see further Chapter 4). Financial crime is defined by section 1H of the FSMA as including any offences involving the following:

(a)   fraud or dishonesty;
(b)   misconduct in or misuse of information relating to a financial market; or
(c)   handling the proceeds of crime;
(d)   the financing of terrorism.

Section 1H(4) further defines 'offence' to include an act or omission, which would be an offence if it had taken place in the United Kingdom.

13.11   SYSC 6.1.1R draws out from its general compliance systems obligation a requirement that firms pay specific attention to the risk that they may be used to further financial crime. Moreover, the specific reference in the financial crime definition to misconduct in or misuse of information relating to the financial market will naturally include market abuse behaviours under section 118 of the FSMA but it is submitted that the offences of insider dealing under Part V of the Criminal Justice Act 1993 and market manipulation under Part 7 of the Financial Services Act 2012 are also included. In highlighting financial crime, both Article 13(2) of MIFID and the FCA provide an expectation that firms should put in place special financial crime compliance procedures and policies that supplement their general compliance systems.

13.12   Some key points emerge from Article 6 that should inevitably shape a firm's efforts to organise their compliance function under MiFID. It is clear that an obligation is established requiring the design as well as operation of policies and procedures. The use of the terms 'adequate' and 'designed to detect any risk of failure' in the context of firms' obligations under the Directive, help make it clear that firms' policies and procedures must be designed to meet their individual business model and the risks presented by that model. In the same mode, after initial authorisation, policies and procedures should be kept under review and adjustments to them made whenever the firm's regulatory risks alter. There is recognition at SYSC 6.1.2 that the scale and nature of the complexity of a firm's business should allow for it to determine appropriate policies and procedures to deal with its risk of non-compliance financial crime risk in much the same way at the more general provisions within SYSC 4. Equally, the compliance specific rules at SYSC 6.1.2R impose upon investment firms an obligation to carry out regular assessments of the adequacy of their compliance and financial crime risk procedures for the purpose of ensuring that such procedures continue to comply with the systems and controls obligations in SYSC 6.1.1R. The Authority does not provide any minimum expectation of the frequency of regular assessment, and in the same way that it provides scope for firms to determine the appropriateness of overall systems and controls, leaves the question of how regular assessment of financial crime risk management and systems and controls should be, to be determined by reference to the nature of the risk and complexity of the firm's business.

Investment firms might, therefore, consider that to comply with the regular assessment obligation, that alongside ad hoc reviews, they should review the extent to which their business is impacted by the risk of market abuse each and every time a change to business activities or service is planned.

THE COMPLIANCE FUNCTION AND REGULATORY CHARACTERISTICS

13.13 Many investment firms have traditionally established a compliance function as an integral part of their arrangements for the oversight of their compliance procedures, sales function and to provide regulatory advice to the firm's senior management and governing body. The need to operate a compliance function has become an inherent part of a firm's arrangements under Article 13 (organisational requirements) of MiFID and Article 6(2) of the MiFID implementing Directive. These provisions were brought into force in the UK by SYSC 6.1.3R.[12] These obligations in effect set out five key characteristics for a firm's compliance function, namely those of:

- permanence;
- effectiveness;
- operational independence;
- monitoring and assessment;
- providing advice and assistance.

SYSC 6.1.3R provides as follows

'A common platform firm ...must maintain a permanent and effective compliance function which operates independently and which has the following responsibilities:

(1)   to monitor and, on a regular basis, to assess the adequacy and effectiveness of the measures and procedures put in place in accordance with SYSC 6.1.2 R, and the actions taken to address any deficiencies in the firm's compliance with its obligations; and

(2)   to advise and assist the relevant persons responsible for carrying out regulated activities to comply with the firm's obligations under the regulatory system.'

Permanence

13.14 The requirement for permanence in SYSC 6.1.3R operates as a base line requirement for a firm's compliance function. It is submitted that the premise of permanency is based on a notion of the function being 'fixed' and 'routine', thus allowing them to operate continually, The European Securities and Markets Authority (ESMA) provides guidance[13] on the compliance

---

12   Whist most authorised firms are required to appoint a senior manager with responsibility for compliance oversight not all are. The provisions at SYSC 6.1.3, however, refer to the establishment of a Compliance Function.

13   The European Securities and Markets Authority Final report: Guidelines on certain aspects of the MiFID compliance function requirements (6 July 2012).

function and in relation to the issue of permanence includes at general guideline 6 reference to the following:

> 'Investment firms should … establish adequate arrangements for ensuring the responsibilities of the compliance officer are fulfilled when the compliance officer is absent, and adequate arrangements to ensure that the responsibilities of the compliance function are performed on an ongoing basis. These arrangements should be in writing.' (at [53])

And:

> 'The compliance function should perform its activities on a permanent basis and not only in specific circumstances. This requires regular monitoring on the basis of a monitoring schedule.' (at [56])

It may be argued that there is an overlap between the full time component of the permanency obligation and that of operational independence, given that (as will be examined below), the rules do provide some flexibility for operational independence in the context of the size and scale of the firm. In such circumstances it may be acceptable for the compliance function to maintain permanence whilst discharging other responsibilities.

Effectiveness

13.15   Effectiveness of the compliance function is partly established by the nature and extent of the arrangements that are put in place to meet the monitoring, review and advisory responsibilities under Article 6(2)(a) and (b) of Directive 2006/73/EC. Arguably, there is a very clear linkage between the arrangements under these provisions and the general organisational arrangements that a firm must have in place to meet its regulatory obligations. The latter may be designed in the context of the nature and complexity of the firm's business. Thus to allow Article 6(2), the compliance arrangements must also be capable of being designed in the context of the complexity and scale of the firm's business.

13.16   Effectiveness will also be determined by the compliance function's ability to operate and brings into consideration issues such as the compliance function's level of authority within the firm, its resources and whether these are sufficient, its expertise, both in terms of the firm's business as well as the regulatory environment relevant to the business and the access provided to relevant information within the firm.[14] Article 6(3), implemented at SYSC 6.14R, sets out conditions that must be met in order to demonstrate that the compliance function is able to properly meet its responsibilities, some of which touch upon the effectiveness component. SYSC 6.1.4R addresses effectiveness in terms of what might be described as organisational capability, stating that '(1) the compliance function must have the necessary authority, resources, expertise and access to all relevant information …'. Indeed FCA rules at SYSC 5.1.1R set out more general obligations relating to staff competence applying to compliance as well as all staff stating: 'A *firm* must employ personnel with the skills, knowledge and expertise necessary for the discharge of the responsibilities allocated to them.' The ESMA Compliance Function guidance[15]

---

14   Article 6(3)(a), Directive 2006/73/EC.
15   ESMA Compliance guidelines (note 13).

again addresses issues relating to capability including reference to resources as: 'Where an investment firm's business unit activities are significantly extended, the investment firm should ensure that the compliance function is similarly extended as necessary in view of changes to the firm's compliance risk. Senior management should monitor regularly whether the number of staff is still adequate for the fulfilment of the duties of the compliance function' (at [45]).

13.17 The appointment of a compliance officer is also an integral requirement of the effectiveness component of SYSC 6.1.3 R. Article 6(3)(b), implemented at SYSC 6.1.4(3)R requires that 'A compliance officer must be appointed and must be responsible for the compliance function and for any reporting as to compliance required by SYSC 4.3.2 R.' Chapter 14 will consider the liability that may arise for compliance officers along with the regulatory standards they are required to meet if approved to perform the FMSA controlled function of compliance oversight persons. At this juncture it is merely useful to highlight two approved person regulatory principles that operate to set standards of behaviour as well as positively impact the effectiveness of the compliance function, namely at Principle 6 of the Approved Person code: 'An approved person performing an accountable significant-influence function must exercise due skill, care and diligence in managing the business of the firm for which he is responsible in his accountable function'; and at Principle 7: 'An approved person performing an accountable significant-influence function must take reasonable steps to ensure that the business of the firm for which he is responsible in his accountable function complies with the relevant requirements and standards of the regulatory system.'

13.18 The ESMA Compliance Function guidance considers a number of factors relevant to the effectiveness of the appointed Compliance Officer, which in the main address that person's capability and experience both generally and in regard to the business undertaken by their firm, including:

'The compliance officer should have sufficiently broad knowledge and experience and a sufficiently high level of expertise so as to be able to assume responsibility for the compliance function as a whole and ensure that it is effective.' (at [44])

'The compliance officer should demonstrate sufficient professional experience as is necessary to be able to assess the compliance risks and conflicts of interest inherent in the investment firm's business activities. The required professional experience may have, amongst others, been acquired in operational positions, in other control functions or in regulatory functions.' (at [51])

'The compliance officer should have specific knowledge of the different business activities provided by the investment firm.' (at [52])

Operational independence

13.19 The requirement at SYSC 6.1.3R for firms to establish and maintain a permanent and effective compliance function which operates independently can raise a number of operational sensitivities for investment firms. Although larger investment firms will have the luxury of significant resource that allows them to identify compliance resources separate from their operational functions, the criteria for compliance independence can undoubtedly present challenges for many firms. SYSC 6.1.4(3)R (Article 6(3) of the Implementing Directive) provides that to ensure a compliance function discharges its responsibilities properly and independently, ' the relevant persons involved in the compliance function must not be involved in the performance of services or activities they monitor'.[16] ESMA guidance addressing this aspect of independence stresses the importance of the separation of compliance activity from the activity of other business units[17] (but see 13.21–13.22 below), including that:

'The tasks performed by the compliance function should be carried out independently from senior management and other units of the investment firm. In particular, the investment firm's organisation should ensure that other business units may not issue instructions or otherwise influence compliance staff and their activities.' (at [58])

13.20   The concept of independence also takes into account remuneration with SYSC 6.1.4(4)R providing, 'the method of determining the remuneration of the relevant persons involved in the compliance function must not compromise their objectivity and must not be likely to do so.'[18] This latter requirement suggests that a firm may have difficulties where its compliance staff remuneration, such as performance related pay, is linked to the financial performance of a business unit or division they monitor or advise.

13.21   However, some flexibility for the independence component may be available, particularly for smaller firms. SYSC 6.1.5 (Article 6(3) of the Implementing Directive) allows firms what may be described as an exit or 'opt out' from SYSC 6.1.4(3) or SYSC 6.1.4(4) if they can show that: 'In view of the nature, scale and complexity of its business, and the nature and range of financial services and activities, the requirements under those rules are not proportionate and that its compliance function continues to be effective.' If available and appropriate this limited exit, however, only partly assists firms, which still have to meet the base requirements for independence, and thus firms should always consider whether compliance staff with dual roles have sufficient independence and the ability to operate effectively. ESMA's guidelines[19] provide some assistance into how firms can formulate whether they can take advantage of the SYSC 6.1.5R proportionality opt out, with many aimed at smaller firms, such as:

'An investment firm may fall, for example, under the proportionality exemption if the performance of the necessary compliance tasks does not require a full-time position due to the nature, scale and complexity of the firm's business, and the nature and range of the investment services, activities and ancillary services offered.' (at [63]).

'While a compliance officer must always be appointed, it may be disproportionate for a smaller investment firm with a very narrow field of activities to appoint a separate compliance officer (i.e. one that does not perform any other function) ...'. (at [64])

13.22   The ESMA guidance proceeds to offer views on the extent to which a compliance function may be combined with other 'internal control functions',

---

16   Article 6(3)(c), Directive 2006/73/EC.
17   ESMA Compliance guidelines (note 13).
18   Article 6(3)(d), Directive 2006/73/EC.
19   ESMA Compliance guidelines (note 13).

although the ESMA view is that as a general rule it should not be combined with Internal Audit,[20] stating, '... this is likely to undermine the independence of the compliance function because the internal audit function is charged with the oversight of the compliance function ...' (at [69]). In general terms however ESMA does not rule out combing functions provided that the reason for doing so are documented so that a regulatory agency may assess the appropriates (at [67]). ESMA general guideline 9 states:

> 'The combination of the compliance function with other control functions may be acceptable if this does not compromise the effectiveness and independence of the compliance function ...' (at [67])

13.23 Additional complexity arises from the question as to whether the compliance function should have either representation on or a direct reporting line to the firm's governing body. The general organisational requirement, set out in Article 5 of the MiFID Implementing Directive as set out at SYSC 4.1.4R, in many ways shapes the basic structural obligations that underpin a firm's compliance arrangements, and how the compliance function will interact and communicate with the firm's senior management and other parts of the organisation. Although Article 5 is addressed towards the general organisation of a firm, many of its requirements also impact on how the compliance function should operate effectively; these areas include requirements broken down into areas covering procedures, responsibilities, internal control mechanisms, competence, effective internal reporting and communication and record keeping. Furthermore, Article 5 as set out at SYSC 4.1.4(1)R requires that a firm '... establish, implement and maintain decision-making procedures'[21] and an organisational structure which clearly and in a documented manner specifies reporting lines and allocates functions and responsibilities.[22] This still leaves open the question of the most appropriate reporting line for compliance. Article 6(3), as set out at SYSC 6.1.4(1)R, does refer to the necessity of the compliance functions 'authority' and indeed the FCA rules at SUP 10A.7.8(1)R state that the compliance oversight controlled function 'is the function of acting in the capacity of a director or senior manager who is allocated the function set out in ... SYSC 6.1.4R(2) ...' where the FCA defines 'senior manager' as including someone '... who, if the individual is employed by the firm, reports directly to: (i) the governing body; or (ii) a member of the governing body; or (iii) the chief executive; or (iv) the head of a significant business unit ...'. The solution is best left to be determined by following the proportionality provisions within SYSC 4.1.4R, that is, by 'taking into account the nature, scale and complexity of the business of the firm, and the nature and range of the financial services and activities undertaken in the course of that business ...'.

Monitoring

13.24 The monitoring component of the compliance functions responsibilities within SYSC 6.1.3R(1) is required to be performed on a 'regular basis' and for the purpose of assessing '... the adequacy and effectiveness of the [firms]' SYSC 6.1.2R compliance arrangements'

---

20   ESMA Compliance guidelines (note 13) at [67].
21   Article 5(1)(a), Directive 2006/73/EC.
22   Article 5(1)(a), Directive 2006/73/EC.

(see 13.11 above), 'and the actions taken to address any deficiencies in the firms compliance with its obligations ..'. This chapter earlier examined in the context of more general governance and systems and controls the obligation placed on firms to keep their internal control arrangements under review (see 13.7 above) and thus sensibly the SYSC 6.1.3R compliance monitoring component may be viewed as one part of an overall duty for a firm to keep its controls under review, albeit with the added benefit of independence. The ESMA compliance guidance relating to monitoring refers to the need for the compliance function to establish a monitoring programme (at [18]) and within the aim of that programme being '... to evaluate whether the investment firm's business is conducted in compliance with its obligations under MiFID and whether its internal guidelines, organisation and control measures remain effective and appropriate' (at [19]).

13.25 Before moving on from the examination of the compliance function monitoring component, some consideration can be given to the types of special market abuse relevant monitoring activity that are often conducted by a compliance function. At Chapter 10 some analysis was provided of the suspicious transaction reporting requirement under SUP 15.10R. The obligation at SUP 15.10.3 for firms to 'decide on a case-by-case basis whether there are reasonable grounds for suspicion' necessitates firms covered by SUP 15.10 (ie those that 'arrange or execute transactions with or for a client ...') from establishing formal methods for detecting reasonable suspicions. In its thematic review into asset management firms and market abuse (although not all such firms are regulated as MiFID firms), the FCA considered amongst others things the post trade surveillance arrangements stating in its report of the review:

> 'Post-trade surveillance has a key role to play in both detecting and deterring market abuse. We expect senior management to have processes to satisfy themselves that controls to identify and manage the risk of market abuse are working effectively.'[23]

Advice and assistance

13.26 The provision of advice and assistance to the firm's directors, managers and employees (see FCA Glossary definition of 'relevant person') 'to comply with the firm's obligations under the regulatory system' forms another key component of the compliance function responsibilities provided for under SYSC 6.1.3R(2). ESMA guidance[24] covers advice and assistance from the perspective of staff training and routine assistance to staff as well as 'participating in the establishment of new policies and procedures within the investment firm' (at [33]). The guidance emphasises the importance of the compliance functions involvement in the development of new business, arguably, it is submitted, because potential regulatory breaches can be avoided when the compliance function can advise the business on its regulatory obligations at the earliest opportunity. The guidance provides:

> 'In this context, the compliance function should be given the right to participate in the approval process for financial instruments to be taken up

---

23   FCA Asset management firms and the risk of market abuse TR15/1 (18 February 2015) at [10].
24   ESMA Compliance guidance (note 13).

in the distribution process. Senior management should therefore encourage business units to consult with the compliance function regarding their operations.' (at [41])

13.27 It is important that there is proper and efficient engagement between a firm's senior management and the compliance function. Proper communication of the efficiency of the firm's regulatory procedures in meeting the risk presented by the business as well as the efficacy of steps taken to deal with any identified risks helps to ensure senior management remains appropriately engaged with the firm's regulatory responsibility. This is particularly important given that the Directive makes clear that senior management are responsible for ensuring compliance. Article 9(2) provides that Member States shall require investment firms to ensure that their senior management receive on a frequent basis, and at least annually, written reports on the matters covered by Articles 6, 7 and 8, indicating in particular whether the appropriate remedial measures have been taken in the event of any deficiencies.

AUTHORISED FIRMS' OBLIGATION TO MAINTAIN RECORDS

13.28 All authorised firms are required by virute of their FCA regulatory responsibilities to maintain records relating to a wide variety of their business activity and conduct. In addition to the generic obligation presented by FCA Principle for Business 3 to 'organise and control its affairs responsibly and effectively' which no doubt creates record keeping expectations. General record keeping obligations are imposed in the FCA's Senior Management Systems and Controls sourcebook for investment firms at SYSC 9. The thrust of the SYSC record keeping obligations is that an authorised person must keep accessible records of its business operation and activities that are subject to regulatory requirements under FSMA. The obligations at SYSC 9 provide more specific detail of the FCA's record keeping obligations, implementing in particular Articles 13(6) and 51(1) and (2) of the MiFID Implementing Directive, and amongst other things make clear that a firm must maintain records of transactions as well as its business operation which are relevant to the FCA's ability to effectively supervise and monitor an authorised person's regulatory compliance, providing at SYSC 9.1.1R, 'A firm must arrange for orderly records to be kept of its business and internal organisation, including all services and transactions undertaken by it, which must be sufficient to enable the FCA ... to monitor the firm's compliance with the requirements under the regulatory system ...'. Moreover, SYSC 9 imposes more precise requirements relating to the record retention period, requiring at SYSC 9.1.2R that all records relating to '... MiFID business for a period of at least five years', and the accessibility of some records, which is relevant to the use that any such records may have for enquiries into abusive transactions. For example SYSC 9.1.3(1)R provides, 'the FCA ... must be able to access them readily and to reconstitute each key stage of the processing of each transaction'.

13.29 Record keeping obligations related to discrete regulatory obligations tend to be set out in each FCA sourcebook and often add to the generic obligations in SYSC 9 by making provision for the content of the record, the date when the record is to be made and the period of retention. As was evident from the analysis of the market abuse behaviours in Chapter 4, the exploitation of information is also a core component to market abuse and misconduct. As is explored in Chapters 10, 11 and 12, the FCA's information gathering, investigation and enforcement activity is reliant on timely access to accurate information regarding market conduct, necessitating authorised persons to keep timely, accurate and accessible records of the trading activities undertaken in their businesses. Moreover, given how sensitive information can be subject to exploitation, appropriate information controls are a necessary ingredient for the prevention of market abuse.

TRANSACTION RECORDS AND ELECTRONIC COMMUNICATIONS

13.30 The record-keeping provisions within COBS 11.5 address the recording of core information relating to client orders and transactions at the time of receipt (COBS 11.5.1), following execution of the transaction (COBS 11.5.2) and where the order has been transmitted to another person for execution (COBS 11.5.3). (The additional provisions relating to record keeping of employee personal dealing are addressed in 13.38–13.43 below.) The core information required to be recorded is set out in each of the provisions of COBS 11.5, which includes details of the client name, trading date and time, the nature of the order (such as buy or sell), the investment price or quantity ordered or obtained, the name of the counterparty and details of the execution venue (such as the exchange or where it was 'over the counter'). This not only provides information that in time can support the demonstration of compliance with the client order control requirements set out in COBS 11, but also provides integral information to allow firms so required to meet the FCA's transaction reporting requirements, which are examined in Chapter 10 on Information gathering.

13.31 The FCA also requires certain authorised persons (subject to a number of exemptions) to record telephone conversations or keep a record of electronic communications such as email or text messages relating to activities regarding the receipt, transmission and execution of both client and the authorised persons orders (see COBS 11.8.1R for the precise list of activities) and as provided by COBS 11.8.5R, extends to communications 'made with, sent or received on equipment (1) provided by the firm to an employee or contractor; or (2) the use of which by an employee or contractor has been sanctioned or permitted by the firm; to enable that employee or contractor to carry out the activities referred to in COBS 11.8.1R'. The obligation to make such records applies only to 'relevant conversations or communications' which, although fully defined in COBS 11.8.8R, may be summarised as including communications which conclude the receipt, transmission or execution of an order with clients or third parties on behalf of clients (such as a with a broker); and communications with professional clients or eligible counterparties or on their behalf with third parties with a view to concluding the receipt, transmission or execution of an order. Rather than attempting to prohibit authorised firms from allowing employees and contractors from using privately owned electronic equipment being used for 'relevant conversations or communications'. Needless to say the proliferation of privately owned electronic equipment such as mobile telephones and smart phones presents something of a challenge to record-keeping avoidance by employees and indeed there are instances of market abuse, such as in the matter of *Winterflood Securities v Financial Services*

Authority,[25] where the FSA had concluded that communciations between Winterflood and its client 'were undertaken on mobile telephones in order to avoid those conversations being taped'.[26]

13.32   Although the FCA's rules, which are not binding on employees (save where they may be FCA Approved Persons), through COBS 11.8.5A requires that authorised persons (firms) to address the risk of its non-recording by requiring them to "take reasonable steps to prevent employees or contractors from making, sending or receiving relevant telephone conversations and electronic communications on privately-owned equipment which the firm is unable to record of copy." Where the electronic communication record-keeping obligation arises, the FCA imposes under COBS 11.8.10R (1) a record retention period of 6 months, and specifies record accessibility standards under COBS 11.8.10R (2) which in particular allow the FCA to be able to follow through from an electronic communication record any transaction "corrections or other amendments" and any communications related to such corrections.

COMPLIANCE AND CONFLICTS MANAGEMENT, INFORMATION BARRIERS AND DEALING CONTROLS

13.33   Chapter 8 examined the law relating to conflicts of interest and considered some of the regulatory provisions regarding conflicts management and Chinese Walls. In this section further consideration is given to the use of Chinese Walls as part of a firm's overall compliance arrangements. Information about client orders or corporate transactions which have not been disclosed to the market can give rise to obligations to secure the information in order to ensure it is not improperly disclosed together with measures to manage or indeed eradicate conflicts of interest in the information between clients and the authorised person, clients and employees, employees and the authorised person and between clients. The FCA's regulatory standards addressing information control are presented in a cascade framework being derived from section 137P of the FSMA which provides at section 137P(2) the circumstances in which control of information rules may be used in the following terms:

'Control of information rules may–

(a)   require the withholding of information which A would otherwise have to disclose to a person ("B") for or with whom A does business in the course of carrying on any regulated or other activity;

(b)   specify circumstances in which A may withhold information which he would otherwise have to disclose to B;

(c)   require A not to use for the benefit of B information–
   (i)   which is held by A, and
   (ii)   which A would otherwise be required to use for the benefit of B;

(d)   specify circumstances in which A may decide not to use for the benefit of B information A holds which A would otherwise have to use in that way.'

---

25   *Winterfloods Securities Ltd, Stephen Sotiriou and Jason Robins v Financial Services Authority* [2010] EWCA Civ 423 ((2009) FIN 2008/0012, FIN 2008/0013, FIN 2008/0014).
26   FSA Final Notice *Winterflood Securities Ltd* (22 April 2010) at [81].

13.34 The FCA uses its Principles for Business and Senior Management Systems and Controls sourcebook to set out fundamental and generic information control obligations, with more conduct specific obligations set out in discrete sourcebooks of rules such as COBS. The FCA High Principles for Business address information control and conflict management in a number of ways including at Principle for Business 2, 'A firm must conduct its business with due skill, care and diligence' and Principle for Business 5, 'A firm must observe proper standards of market conduct' require authorised persons to address how they control and manage information. Additionally, Principle for Business 8 specifically targets the need for conflicts management providing that authorised persons 'must manage conflicts of interest fairly, both between itself and its customers and between a customer and another client'.

13.35 Rules in SYSC 10 relevant to authorised persons conducting MiFID business set out provision that recognise formal information barriers (referred to as 'Chinese Walls') as well as providing a market abuse safeguard for behaviour that complies with the FCA's Chinese wall provisions. The FCA's rules glossary defines a 'Chinese Wall' as 'an arrangement that requires information held by a person in the course of carrying on one part of its business to be withheld from, or not to be used for, persons with or for whom it acts in the course of carrying on another part of its business'. The FCA's core information barrier provision is set out in SYSC 10.2.2R(1) which recognises that information held behind the so called 'Chinese Wall' is excluded from having to be otherwise disclosed (which ordinarily might be the case where a conflict situation arises). The behavioural effect of the operation of the information barrier in the context of market abuse is described by the FCA in SYSC 10.2.5G and may be such that knowledge about the information held behind the barrier will not be attributed to persons 'on the other side of the wall' unless they have been wall crossed, that is the person has been given the information. It is essential for firms to consider their Chinese Wall obligations and wall crossing arrangements in the context of their internal systems of control. In this regard taking into account the provision at SYSC 6.1.1R the arrangements, which allow for the method of operation as well as the written processes should be 'sufficient to ensure compliance of the firm including its managers, employees and appointed representatives (or where applicable, tied agents) with its obligations under the regulatory system and for countering the risk that the firm might be used to further financial crime'.

13.36 In the FSA Final Notice to *Andrew Osborne*,[27] the FSA states: 'Wall crossing is a process whereby a company can legitimately provide inside information to a third party. A company may wall cross a variety of third parties ranging from large institutional shareholders to small shareholders or completely unrelated parties.' Compliance with the arrangements is particularly significant for concerns about market abuse behaviour as 'conformity with control of information rules' is a defence to the offences of misleading statement (Financial Services Act 2012, s 89(3)(b)) or misleading impressions (Financial Services Act 2012, s 91(9)(b)(ii)) and misleading statements in relation to benchmarks (Financial Services Act 2012, s 91(3)). Furthermore SYSC 10.2.2R(4) addresses market abuse and provides: 'For the purpose of section 118(5) (a) of … [FSMA], behaviour conforming with paragraph (1) [the establishment and maintenance of a Chinese Wall] does not amount to market abuse'. The FCA's enforcement actions against

---

27   FSA Final Notice *Andrew Jon Osborne* 15 February 2012 at [3.4].

David Einhorn,[28] *Greenlight Capital*[29] and *Andrew Osborne*[30] illustrate the regulatory significance of failing to have regard to Chinese Wall or information barrier arrangements. All three of the cases were concerned with discussions regarding a new share issue by Punch Taverns plc in June 2009. Mr Osborne worked at Merrill Lynch International, leading its broking team acting for Punch Taverns plc. Greenlight Inc, a US fund manager, was an existing Punch Tavern shareholder. Mr Einhorn was Greenlight's President and owner. It is common for existing investors to be approached about new share offerings and subject to confidentiality undertakings and restriction over trading any existing holdings, be given price sensitive information for the purpose of gauging their appetite for investing. In such circumstances the investors are 'wall crossed' and any trading in the investment prior to the information being formally released to the market will be abusive, that is it will not benefit from the protection set out in SYSC 10.2.2R(4). The FSA found that Mr Osborne disclosed inside information regarding the Punch Taverns new share issue to Greenlight and Mr Einhorn despite a refusal to be wall crossed, who having been given inside information (which they disputed) traded in Punch Tavern shares. In respect of Mr Osborne's control of the wall crossing, the FSA Final Notice states, 'bearing in mind the fact that Greenlight had refused to be wall crossed and that, as a result, significant legal and regulatory risk arose from a conversation proceeding between Punch management and Greenlight, Mr Osborne should have taken great care regarding the information he disclosed, and taken adequate steps to ensure that he complied with regulatory requirements'.[31]

13.37 For the 'wall crossing' process to work, the third party will need to consent to be given inside information and as a result will be prevented from trading until the inside information is announced to the market. In the FSA's Final Notice to David Einhorn, the FSA stated, 'Once a third party agrees to be wall crossed, it can be provided with inside information and it is then restricted from trading. The party is only able to trade in the company's shares again once the information it has been given is made public ...'.[32] The FCA recognises the legitimacy of 'wall crossing' at MAR 1.4.5E through a series of alternative evidential tests each of which includes '... the imposition of confidentiality requirements upon the person to whom the disclosure is made ...'.

PERSONAL ACCOUNT DEALING RULES

13.38 One consequence of information being held behind an information barrier is that it may present opportunities for an authorised person's employees to exploit it by trading on it for their personal account. Furthermore information about pending client orders in investments significant enough to cause a share price movement, can be exploited by staff placing personal orders in that same security ahead of the client orders being executed: a practice known as 'trading ahead' or 'pre-positioning.' The FCA uses rules in COBS 11 relating to the management of client dealing to address information control from the context of staff dealing, much of which addresses provisions of the MiFID implementing measures.

---

28 FSA Final Notice *David Einhorn* 15 February 2012.
29 FSA Final Notice *Greenlight Capital Inc* 15 February 2012.
30 FSA Final Notice *Andrew Jon Osborne* 15 February 2012.
31 FSA Final Notice *Andrew Jon Osborne* 15 February 2012 at [2.7(iii)].
32 FSA Final Notice *David Einhorn* 15 February 2012 at [3.11].

13.39   Addressing specifically the risk of trading ahead, the FCA implements Article 47(3) of the MiFID implementing measures at COBS 11.3.5R which provides that: 'A firm must not misuse information relating to pending client orders, and shall take all reasonable steps to prevent the misuse of such information by any of its relevant persons.' Indeed the provision at COBS 11.3.5R is not confined to trading ahead that might constitute s 118 market abuse behaviour. The FCA states its view at COBS 11.3.6G that even where misuse of client information does constitute market abuse that 'any use by a firm of information relating to a pending client order to deal on own account … should be considered a misuse of the information'. Additionally, provisions at COBS 12.2.5R implement Article 25(2) of the MiFID implementing measures and operate to prevent research analysts from trading ahead of the publication of their research. In certain circumstances, analyst reports upon publication have the capability of affecting the price of a company's securities, presenting the opportunity for analysts to exploit knowledge of the information with an unpublished report. COBS 12.2.5R recognises that the trading ahead limitation should only apply where the information in an analyst's report cannot be ascertained from information that is publicly available, but nonetheless COBS 12.2.5R (save in exceptional circumstances, which COBS 12.2.7G(2) indicates may arise in cases of personal financial hardship) prohibits analysts, other employees and connected persons such as spouses and dependent children, from carrying out personal transactions contrary to the analyst's recommendations.

13.40   The FCA's core personal account dealing rules are provided at COBS 11.7 (which implement Article 12 of the MiFID implementing measures) and set out a control framework of prevention, notification, record keeping and awareness and apply to a 'relevant person' defined by the FCA as including a director, partner, employee (including a contractor) and relates to 'personal transaction', which is defined by the FCA in its glossary (implementing Articles 2(7) and 11 of the MiFID implementing measures) as including 'trades carried out for … (a) the relevant person; (b) the spouse or partner of the relevant person …; (c) a dependent child or stepchild; (d) any other relative of the relevant person who has shared the same household as that person for at least one year on the date of the personal transaction concerned; (e) any person with whom he has close links' (close links are defined by the FCA as including a 20% or more interest in the voting rights of a company); and '(f) a person whose relationship with the relevant person is such that the relevant person has a direct or indirect material interest in the outcome of the trade, other than a fee or commission for the execution of the trade'.

13.41   It is essential for firms to consider their staff personal account dealing obligations in the context of their internal systems of control. The obligation to establish a framework of control for personal account dealing is provided at COBS 11.7.1R, which sets out a generally drafted obligation to 'establish, implement and maintain adequate arrangements' that, subject to COBS 11.7.4R, provides authorised firms with the flexibility to develop arrangements relevant to the personal account dealing and information control risks. It is submitted that the essence of the personal account dealing control framework as set out in COBS 11.7.1R is to prevent personal motivated transactions that exploit circumstances where 'relevant persons' have a conflict of interest, access to inside information or where they have 'other confidential information relating to clients transactions'. This basic proposition however is clarified by COBS 11.7.1(1), (2) and (3) which prohibits personal transactions, activity where the relevant person advises or procures another person to enter into a transaction, and the disclosure of information. In this sense it appears that the rules in COBS 11.7 supplement the information control rules in SYSC. More specifically the COBS 11.7 arrangements must be 'aimed at preventing' the following activity set out at COBS 11.7.1R:

'(1) entering into a personal transaction which meets at least one of the following criteria:

(a)   that person is prohibited from entering into it under the Market Abuse Directive,

(b)   it involves the misuse or improper disclosure of that confidential information,

it conflicts or is likely to conflict with an obligation of the firm to a customer under the regulatory system or any other obligation of the firm under MiFID or the UCITS Directive;

(2) advising or procuring, other than in the proper course of his employment or contract for services, any other person to enter into a transaction in designated investments which, if a personal transaction of the relevant person, would be covered by (1) or a relevant provision;

(3) disclosing, other than in the normal course of his employment or contract for services, any information or opinion to any other person if the relevant person knows, or reasonably ought to know, that as a result of that disclosure that other person will or would be likely to take either of the following steps:

(a)   to enter into a transaction in designated investments which, if a personal transaction of the relevant person, would be covered by (1) or a relevant provision;

(b)   to advise or procure another person to enter into such a transaction.'

13.42   An indication is given COBS 11.7.4R of the arrangements that are expected to be in place to meet COBS 11.7.1R including measures to ensure that relevant persons are aware of the arrangements including the trading restrictions, prompt notification of any 'personal transactions' and a requirement for the authorised person to keep a record of personal transactions. When considered as part of a firm's compliance arrangements, the personal account dealing rules will importantly operate as part of a firm's conflicts and Chinese Wall arrangements allowing a firm to safeguard any staff trading in shares that are currently restricted from trading due to the firm being in possession of inside information. Such a safeguard is required at COBS 11.7.4R(2), which provides that the firm '(a) is informed promptly of any personal transaction entered into by a relevant person, either by notification of that transaction or by other procedures enabling the firm to identify such transactions ...'.

13.43   In conclusion the rules we have considered relating to the compliance function and internal compliance arrangements form just a part of the strict governance and systems and controls rules applicable to investment firms. Nonetheless a number of the enforcement cases considered in this chapter and elsewhere in this book serve to illustrate how the outcome of a breakdown in a firm's internal arrangements can lead to non-compliance with discrete regulatory obligations including exposing firms and employees to market abuse and misconduct.

Chapter 14

Personal liability of senior managers and compliance officers

PERSONAL RESPONSIBILITY

14.1   The enormous financial penalties that have been imposed particularly in the USA and UK on financial institutions in recent years, primarily for compliance related failures, has been welcomed by many. In the main, however, these have been directly or indirectly the result of negotiated settlements with regulatory authorities and have not involved the courts. Having said this, because of the perception in the USA that bodies such as the Securities and Exchange Commission had become too soft, even to some degree captured by those whose conduct they oversee, there has been more emphasis on the criminal law. The problem with swingeing financial penalties against institutions, regardless of how they are imposed, is that they do not directly focus responsibility on those primarily responsible for the misconduct. Indeed, it is arguable that the penalties weaken the institution thereby harming investors, creditors, employees and many other stakeholders. This will no doubt have implications for those in senior management, certainly in terms of reputation and possibly financially through the loss of incentives and even employment. However, in practice these penalties are a blunt weapon and do not generally bring justice to those at fault. It is the case that regulators are not primarily enforcement agencies and they rightly have a responsibility to measure their actions alongside the other and often competing concerns that they have.[1] Furthermore, there is a genuine responsibility to ensure that the institution addresses the problems that have been exposed and in practice monitoring arrangements and the like have possibly a more constructive role to play.

14.2   Nonetheless, it is arguable that if integrity is to be promoted and better assured then there has to be a good possibility of those who engage in blameworthy conduct being effectively and efficiently brought to book. Public concern has traditionally, as we have seen,[2] justified the intervention of the criminal law. On the other hand for a variety of reasons that we need not elaborate upon here, for responsibility in the criminal law we generally require proof of culpability.

---

1   See for example, s 3B and in particular s 3B(b) of the Financial Services and Markets Act 2000 (FSMA) as amended by the Financial Services Act 2012.
2   See 1.5 *et seq*, 2.1 and 3.2 above.

We have seen that almost all fraud-related offences and those relating to the abuse of inside information require in effect proof that the individual concerned was dishonest. Given the high standard of proof that is required in the criminal law it is often, given the circumstances in which the suspected offence has taken place, too difficult to establish this level of culpability. While the recent financial crisis was caused by many factors, there is a widespread concern that with very few exceptions, the criminal law was unable to identify and bring anyone of significance to account. In part, it is argued, that this is because the requirement to show personal dishonesty in regard to often complicated and possibly structured and, thus, fragmented activity simply defeated the investigators – assuming that there was in fact the will to use the criminal law. We have already referred to the enactment of section 36 of the Financial Services (Banking Reform) Act 2013 which imposes criminal liability on senior officers or banks and building societies for participation in decisions that cause their institution to collapse. To be liable it must be shown that their conduct, or failure to act, fell far below the standard that could reasonably be expected of persons in their position. It is widely accepted that this standard is essentially one of recklessness. However, as we have pointed out[3] the same words are used in other places in the criminal law to impose liability for gross negligence, assuming that there is a difference – which is still a matter of debate. While there has been considerable concern expressed by many in the financial sector and their advisers, as to the criminalisation of recklessness given the fact that the consequences need to be catastrophic there is little likelihood of many cases arising.

THE ROLE OF THE LAW

14.3   In this chapter we will examine the circumstances where individuals may find themselves personally responsible under the criminal law, various regulatory systems and in the civil law. Of course, we have already considered many of the substantive offences that are relevant to a greater or lesser degree in controlling misconduct in the financial markets and we will not rehearse them again here.[4] Instead, we will focus rather more on the situation of an individual who becomes involved in a criminal investigation and or prosecution. We will also consider sentencing policy in regard to insider dealing and related offences and refer back to our discussion of confiscation. It is also pertinent to remember that in certain circumstances the criminal courts may order the payment of compensation.[5] Criminal proceedings may well impact on action in other areas of the law. For example, a criminal conviction may in limited circumstances be used as evidence of certain facts in a subsequent civil action.[6] A conviction will certainly have implications from the perspective of the regulators in the UK and overseas.

14.4   While not all financial services business will be incorporated the vast majority will be. Consequently, it is important to remember that the directors of such companies have a number of responsibilities to their companies. We have already examined the more significant duties that directors owe

---

3   See 6.74 above.
4   See Chapters 5, 6 and 7.
5   Sections 130 to 134 of the Powers of Criminal Courts Act 2000.
6   See Civil Evidence Act 1968, s 11.

to their companies in the context of conflicts of interest and insider abuse.[7] We emphasised, however, that these duties are owed to the company and not shareholders collectively, let alone individually.[8] It is only in exceptional circumstances that directors as directors will owe duties, whether fiduciary or of care, to shareholders and possibly other stakeholders.[9] We have also seen that generally speaking directors of one company owe no duties to other companies whether they are holding, subsidiary or sister companies. Having said this, it is probable that directors would be accountable to their company for profiting by the use of inside information that comes to them by virtue of their position.[10] It is also possible that directors may in exceptional circumstances also be liable for assisting others to profit through the use of inside information.[11] It is also increasingly recognised that directors have a duty to maintain the reputation of the company and protect it almost as an asset of the company.[12] The problem is that directors are not keen to sue themselves and in many cases they are well placed to frustrate inquiries and influence voting in general meetings. The law relating to the circumstances when a minority of shareholders can in effect sue on behalf of the company – deriving a right of action from the company, is complex and fairly beyond the scope of this work.[13] Suffice it to say, that in cases of insider abuse, where there is manifestly self-dealing and certainly where there is dishonesty, it is likely that a minority could maintain a derivative action.[14] Of course, as the action is effectively that of the company, recovery would go back to the company. We have also explored the extent to which others such as officers, employees and controllers might also step into a fiduciary relationship with the company and be similarly accountable.[15] In the case of partnerships the position is rather different as each partner owes his

7   See Chapters 2 and 9.
8   See 2.13 *et seq* above.
9   As we have seen the most likely category of stakeholders is the creditors. Section 127(3) of the Companies Act 2006 reflects the common law obligation on directors to consider the interests of creditors as the company approaches insolvency: see *Facia Footwear v Hinchcliffe* [1998] 1 BCLC 218. The directors need only know the facts giving rise to the actual or potential insolvency, they do not have to subjectively appreciate that an insolvency is imminent, see *Re HLC Environmental Products Ltd (in liquidation)* [2013] EWHC 2876 (Ch).
10 See Chapters 2 and 9. This is the position in the US, see *Brophy v Cities Services Co* 31 Del Ch 241 (1949), *In re Oracle Derivative Litigation*, 867 A 2d 904 (Del. Ch 2004), *Karz Corp. v T.H. Canty & Co Inc* 168 Conn 201 (1975) and the leading case of *Diamond v Oreamuno* 24 NY 2d 494 (1969). In *Ferris v Polycast Technology Corp*, 180 Conn 199 (1980), the Supreme Court of Connecticut stated: 'inside trading by a corporate fiduciary may be a violation of the common law duty which he owes to his corporation. That principle is not at issue.'
11 See 2.29 *et seq* above and see also 7.45 *et seq* above.
12 In the *Diamond* case (above) the New York Court of Appeal in part justified its decision on the basis that the insiders had damaged the reputation of their company by abusing the inside information. This would reflect adversely on the company's operations and its ability to secure additional financing. There remains debate in the US as to whether harm needs to be shown, or whether the abuse of loyalty is enough, as it appears to be in English law. See also *Malik & Another v Bank of Commerce and Credit International* [1997] IRLR 462 in regard to the reputation of a company vis à vis its employees.
13 See generally AJ Boyle *et al*, *Boyle and Birds' Company Law* (9th edn) (Jordan Publishing 2014), Ch 18 and AJ Boyle, *Minority Shareholders' Remedies* (Cambridge University Press 2002) (Cambridge Studies in Corporate Law) and see 2.10 above.
14 See B Rider and TM Ashe (eds), *The Fiduciary, the Insider and the Conflict* (Sweet and Maxwell 1995), Ch 12 and B Rider, 'Amiable Lunatics and the Rule in *Foss v. Harbottle*' (1978) *CLJ* 270.
15 See 2.10 above.

colleagues a duty of good faith.[16] Where the partners fail in a duty to customer or other third party other members of the partnership would be vicariously liable.[17]

THE DUTY OF FIDELITY

14.5   First, however, we will look at the civil law. We have already discussed in some detail the liability that arises where there has been a breach of a fiduciary duty.[18] The prerequisite for fiduciary liability is that there is a fiduciary relationship and we have seen that this may arise in a number of ways.[19] Indeed, it may arise as a result in part, of the conduct that is in issue. While the courts have been loath to hold that the categories of relationship that give rise to at least some fiduciary duties are closed, it would be exceptional for a court today to find an entirely new situation. Having said this, we have seen that in rather special circumstances at least some judges have been prepared to find a fiduciary relationship between directors and shareholders.[20] There is debate as to whether the duty of fidelity that employees owe to their employers has a fiduciary quality to it.[21] As we have seen employees are not in a fiduciary relationship with their employer *per se*.[22] However, a fiduciary relationship may arise by virtue of contractual provisions which require the employee to act generally or in certain respects solely in the employer's interest.[23] It would seem that in the case of most employees, unless there are highly unusual provisions in their contracts of engagement, they will be expected to eschew conflicts of interest and account for 'secret profits' and certainly bribes.[24] An employee who takes advantage of inside information obtained in the course of his employment or for that matter in breach of it, would probably be so accountable.[25] It is likely that an English Court would

16   See generally B Rider, 'Partnership Law and its impact on Domestic Companies' (1979) *CLJ* 148.
17   See Partnership Act 1890, s 10 and *Dubai Aluminium Ltd v Salaam & Others* [2003] 2 AC 366. See *Eaton v Caulfield* [2011] EWHC 173 in regard to the relationship of partners in limited liability partnerships incorporated under the Limited Liability Partnership Act 2000.
18   See Chapter 9.
19   See generally Chapters 2 and 8.
20   See 2.18 *et seq* above. Some judges have been prepared to stretch legal principles so as to deprive someone who has manifestly acted improperly of their gains, see for example, Lord Templeman in *Attorney General of Hong Kong v Reid* [1990] 1 AC 324 and Denning J in *Reading v The King* [1948] 2 KB 268 and our discussion at 2.31 *et seq* above. However, it is always important to distinguish the issue of liability, in other words whether there is a viable cause of action from the nature of the remedy. We have already noted that there has in certain areas of the law been a temptation for the judges to express the form of liability in a manner best suited to the award of an efficacious remedy.
21   See generally A Stratford and A Ritchie, *Fiduciary Duties, Directors and Employees* (2nd edn) (Jordan Publishing 2015).
22   See *University of Nottingham v Fishel* [2000] ICR 1462 and *Helmet Integrated Systems Ltd v Tunnard* [2007] IRLR 126. Note, however, that the more senior the employee's position the more likely the courts will be prepared to find a relationship. Furthermore, it may be possible that on the exceptional facts of the case the employee acts as a de facto or shadow director; see 2.39 *et seq* above.
23   See generally *Item Software (UK) Ltd v Fassihi* [2004] EWCA Civ 1244.
24   *Reading v The King* [1951] AC 507, *Boston Deep Sea Fishing and Ice Co v Ansell* (1888) 39 Ch D 339 and *Industrial Development Consultants Ltd v Cooley* [1972] 1 WLR 443.
25   The courts have found a fiduciary relationship in cases of fraud, *AGIP (Africa) Ltd v Jackson* [1990] Ch 260, per Millett J at 290 and *Tesco Stores Ltd v Pook* [2004] IRLR 618; and in the case of bribes, see *Attorney General for Hong Kong v Reid* (above).

consider that he is in the same position as a director of a company.[26] It is also the case that the betrayal of trust could amount to gross misconduct and justify dismissal as would, of course, the commission of a crime.[27] In many situations where the risk of abuse is better appreciated by employers then there are likely to be specific provisions in the contract of employment requiring compliance with relevant procedures. It is also the case that conduct that would attract the adverse attention of the regulators might well also justify dismissal. The extent to which an employer is able to bring an action for damages against an employee for misconduct amounting to breach of contract will depend upon the circumstances. Even where there are not relevant express terms in a contract, there will often be implied terms of fidelity and good conduct. It is also perhaps worth pointing out that employers also have significant and ever expanding duties to employees, including not to damage the employment prospects of their staff by allowing the company to be run fraudulently.[28]

14.6   One issue that has arisen, is the extent to which an employee is under a duty to bring to the attention of his employer facts which would justify dismissal or other disciplinary action. The law is not entirely clear. However, it would seem the better view, that employees are under no obligation in English law to disclose mere breach in the provisions of their contracts.[29] However, there is strong authority supporting the view that those who stand in a fiduciary relationship to their employer are obliged to disclose breaches of duty.[30] Of course, as we have seen the very breach of certain duties can effectively place the person responsible into a fiduciary relationship.

CONTRACT AND TORT

14.7   In the English civil law unlike in the criminal law there is no general concept, outside the law of restitution, analogous to accessory liability.[31] Given that in the civil law we are primarily concerned with compensation for harm that has been caused and is causally attributable to the acts or omissions of a specific individual, there is conceptually little scope for developing accessory liability. Of course, were there is participation in the infliction of recoverable

---

26   But see Lewison LJ in *Customer Services plc v Ranson* [2012] EWCA Civ 841 contrasting the position of directors and employees, and see *Crowson Fabrics Ltd v Rider* [2007] EWHC 2942 (Ch).

27   In *Neary v Dean of Westminster* [1999] IRLR 288 it was held that the 'conduct amounting to gross misconduct justifying dismissal must so undermine the trust and confidence which is inherent in the particular contract of employment that the master should no longer be required to retain the servant in employment'. In the majority of cases involving misconduct by employees that have come before the authorities involving allegations of insider dealing, the relevant employee has been dismissed or resigned.

28   See *Malik v Bank of Credit and Commerce International* [1997] IRLR 462.

29   *Bell v Lever Brothers Ltd* [1932] AC 161 and *Tesco Stores Ltd v Pook* [2003] EWHC 823 (Ch). Of course, where there is a contractual provision requiring disclosure the position will be different.

30   *Item Software (UK) Ltd v Fassihi* [2004] EWCA Civ 1244, *Governor of the Bank of Ireland v Jaffery* [2012] EWHC 1377 (Ch), *Crown Dilmun and Another v Sutton* [2004] EWHC 52 (Ch) and *Hanco ATM Systems Ltd v Cashbox ATM Systems Ltd* [2007] EWHC 1599 (Ch) in which it was held that the duty extended to the misconduct of employees.

31   See 2.29 *et seq* above and at 14.12 *et seq* below.

loss on another, by more than one party there may be joint and several liability.[32] For contractual liability in most cases it must be established that the parties are privy to the contract.[33] It may be possible to find a collateral contract, express or implied, but this is not something that the courts are over-willing to do, unless it represents the clear intention of those involved.[34]

14.8 In the law of tort, the defendant is either a tortfeasor or he is not. Of course, the relevant tort may be sufficiently encompassing in the imposition of its duty to impose liability on those who foresaw the consequences of an action, or exceptionally a failure to act, and who participated in the wrongdoing.[35] However, in such cases liability is as a participant not as an accessory in the tort. We have already considered the tort of conspiracy in the context of market manipulation[36] and deceit.[37] It is wide enough, however, to extend to a defendant who induces another person to divert a corporate opportunity in breach of his contract of employment and fiduciary relationship.[38]

14.9 Perhaps the closest the English law comes to in providing for liability as an accessory is in the tort of inducing or procuring a breach of contract by another person.[39] There must actually be a breach of contract and, contrary to early opinion,[40] mere interference with performance not amounting to a breach is insufficient for liability. On the other hand it is sufficient that he intends to cause a breach and not necessarily loss to the other contracting party. It is uncertain whether this tort extends to inducing or procuring breaches of other legal duties, not involving a contract. It probably does extend to breaching a

---

32 See for example, *Lumley v Gye* (1853) 2 Bl & Bl 216 and *Bowen v Hall* (1881) 6 QBD 333. However, note that in regard to the tort of inducing or procuring a breach of contract, the commentators and some judges do speak in terms of accessory liability as the procurer attracts an independent liability in tort for the breach of the contract.

33 Subject, of course, to the Contracts (Rights of Third Parties) Act 1999 which provides that a person who is not a party to a contract may enforce a contractual term if the contract expressly provides that he may. If the contract purports to confer a benefit on such a person he may enforce it provided on a proper construction of the contract it appears that the parties did not intend the benefit to be unenforceable. Note also the application of the general rule that there should also be 'privity' of consideration. There are, of course, other exceptions such as agency and trusts.

34 See for example, the discussion in *Evans (J) & Sons (Portsmouth) Ltd v Andrea Merzario Ltd* [1976] 2 All ER 930 between Lord Denning MR and Roskill and Geoffrey Lane LJJ.

35 See generally *Customs and Excise Commissioners v Barclays Bank Plc* [2007] AC 181 and in particular *Caparo Industries Plc v Dickman* [1990] 2 AC 605. In regard to failures to act, see *Stovin v Wise* [1996] AC 923 and Lord Hoffmann at 943.

36 See 6.17 *et seq* above. The tort of conspiracy 'involves an arrangement between two or more parties, whereby they … agree that at least one of them will use unlawful means against the claimant, and, although damage to the claimant need not be the predominant intention of any of the parties, the claimant must have suffered loss or damage as a result': *Revenue and Customs Commissioners v Total Network SL* [2008] UKHL 19 per Lord Neuberger and see also *Lonrho Plc v Fayed* [1992] 1 AC 448. The unlawful means utilised by the conspirators or one of them need not be independently actionable. Therefore it could be a crime such as insider dealing, which itself does not give rise to a cause of action. This is not, however, the position in regard to the tort of intentionally causing loss by unlawful means, see *OBG Ltd v Allan* [2008] 1 AC 1.

37 See 6.101 *et seq* above and see, in particular, *Concept Oil Services Ltd v En-Gen Group LLP* [2013] EWHC 1897 (Comm). While the Court of Appeal considered insider dealing 'a species of fraud' in *R v McQuoid* [2009] EWCA Crim 1301. it is debatable how far the mere abuse of inside information can be regarded as fraud in the conventional sense of the word.

38 See *Aerostar Maintenance International v Wilson* [2010] EWHC 2032. In this case Morgan J expressed concern that the principles applicable in the law of tort were different to and did not necessarily sit well with accessory liability in the law of restitution.

39 See *OBG Ltd v Allan* [2008] 1 AC 1.

40 *Torquay Hotel Co Ltd v Cousins* [1969] 2 Ch 106.

statutory duty where a statutory tort action has been recognised.[41] It has been argued that it might well extend to inducing or procuring a breach of a fiduciary duty, not involving a breach of trust. The basis, for this distinction was that in cases of a breach of trust those procuring or inducing such might well become trustees themselves. Whether such a distinction is now meaningful after recent decisions remains to be seen?[42]

14.10   There have been cases brought in the UK and particularly the US where it has been alleged that loss has been caused by virtue of the negligence of a compliance officer or official. As a general proposition banks and financial institutions do owe a duty of care both in contract and tort to their customers and it has been argued that this extends to forming an opinion as to whether, for example, a transaction is sufficiently suspicious to report to the authorities or not. It has also been argued that banks are under a duty of care to the customer once a report has been made to seek, in appropriate circumstances, a clearance from the authorities to enable a transaction to be completed.[43] Indeed, it has also been suggested that where the decision or conduct is itself wrongful this could expose the individuals and the institution to liability in regard to third parties who are harmed by the blocking of funds. There are important issues of public policy and although the courts have been prepared to require defendants to establish that they actually had the relevant suspicions, there appears to be a reluctance to go further.[44] The courts have also been reluctant to grant claimants disclosure as to the individuals who formed an opinion upon which a suspicion based report was filed.[45] It is also worth pointing out that there have also been allegations made against financial institutions and their officers and employees of defamation and infringement of privacy in regard to the making of statutory reports. In the absence of bad faith it is most unlikely such a claim would succeed.[46]

14.11   Compliance personnel will inevitably be in some kind of contractual relationship and this itself will impose express or implied obligations of care, but only between the parties to the contract.[47] Whether there is a broader

41   *Meade v Haringey LBC* [1979] 1 WLR 637.
42   *FHR European Ventures LLP v Cedar Capital Partners LLC* [2014] UKSC 58 discussed at 2.31 *et seq* above. In *OBG Ltd v Allan* [2008] 1 AC 1, Lord Nicholls, at 189 left open the question of how far the *Lumley v Gye* principle applies equally to breach of other actionable obligations such as statutory duties or equitable or fiduciary obligations.
43   See for example *Shah v HSBC Private Bank (UK) Ltd* [2012] EWHC 1283 (QB) and see 7.59 above.
44   In *Shah v HSBC Private Bank (UK) Ltd* above, Supperstone J was particularly impressed by the professionalism and honestly of the Money Laundering Reporting Officer who had formed a genuine suspicion.
45   See *Shah v HSBC Private Bank (UK) Ltd* [2011] EWCA Civ 1154. The bank was prepared to disclose the identity of the MLRO but not the employees who first reported their suspicions to the MLRO. The Court of Appeal did not consider, on the facts, that disclosure would assist the claimant and that he was essentially on a 'fishing expedition'. Consequently, it was not necessary to consider whether the bank would have been entitled to assert public interest immunity. The Court of Appeal dismissed as fanciful the allegation that one of the bank's employees had initiated the process which led to the MLRO making the report out of malice. At first instance Coulson J indicated that of there had been bad faith this may have undermined the bank's assertion that it had a genuine suspicion.
46   See above at note 44. Malice vitiates the defence of qualified privilege in the law of defamation. Indeed, it might expose that person to the tort of malicious falsehood. In regard to misuse of private information see *Campbell v MGN Ltd* [2004] UKHL 22. In addition to the law of tort equity protects confidential information and there may be specific statutory protection in certain cases.
47   It would be unlikely for an employer in the financial services sector to expressly provide in a contract of employment that an enforceable expectation would be accorded to customers. Where a contract purports to confer a benefit, as we have seen, on a third party under the

and potentially actionable obligation to others, such as the firm's clients is questionable. It may be the case that special circumstances arise where the competent fulfilment of the obligations of a compliance officer can be foreseen to have implications for another party and therefore, possibly give rise to a duty of care in the law of tort.[48] However, even in such cases it is more likely that the failure will be rather more that of the system than the individual and consequently attributable to the employer. If an individual deliberately causes harm, such as through deceit, then the position may be very different. Where an employee acting *bona fide* within the scope of his employment causes or, indeed, procures a breach of contract between his employer and another, then it is established that he cannot be sued for interference with the contractual obligations.[49] Again where he steps outside his employment the position will be different as he is not his employer's alter ego.[50] Finally, it should be emphasised that in many cases of tort the liability of the employer and the employee will be joint and several. In other words a claimant can choose to sue either or both. Given the costs of litigation it would normally be the employer that would be the primary target. However, proceeding against individual may well have tactical advantages in securing their cooperation against the employer. Indeed, there have been cases where allegations of defamation have been made against those directly responsible for reporting suspicious transactions to their employer and then to the authorities.

ACCESSORY LIABILITY IN EQUITY

14.12 We have seen that perhaps the most significant area of the law where the courts have been eager to develop a form of accessory liability is in the fast developing law relating to restitution.[51] Where a person receives into their control assets that have been transferred in breach of a trust the law has long regarded them as stepping into the position of a trustee. Debate has taken place as to the degree of knowledge that needs to be shown before it is appropriate to apply the onerous obligations of trusteeship. There has also been debate as to the nature of the assets and whether these principles apply to information and maturing business opportunities. Today, however, we recognise that really what is at stake is whether it is unconscionable to allow the recipient of trust property to retain it against the interests of other claimants. Thus, innocent receipt and the provision of consideration or a relevant change in position

Contracts (Rights of Third Parties) Act 1999, the burden is on the employer (as promisor) to rebut the presumption that the contracting parties intended this, *Nisshin Shipping Co Ltd v Cleaves & Co Ltd* [2003] EWHC 2602.
48   In *Caparo Industries Plc v Dickman* [1990] 2 AC 605 Lord Roskill stated at 628: 'There is no simple formula or touchstone to which recourse can be had in order to provide in every case a ready answer to the question whether, given certain facts, the law will or will not impose liability for negligence or, in cases where such liability can be shown to exist, determine the extent of that liability. Phrases such as "foreseeability", "proximity", "neighbourhood", "just and reasonable", "fairness" will be found used from time to time in different cases. But … such phases are not precise definitions. At best they are but labels or phrases descriptive of the very different factual situations which can exist in particular cases and which must be carefully examined in each case before it can be pragmatically determined whether a duty of care exists and, if so, what is the scope and extent of that duty.' The finding of a duty of care is essentially pragmatic, see *Rowling v Takaro Properties Ltd* [1988] AC 473.
49   *Said v Butt* [1920] 3 KB 497.
50   *DC Thomson & Co Ltd v Deakin* [1952] Ch 646 per Lord Evershed MR at 681.
51   See 2.32 and 2.52 above.

will generally absolve the recipient from liability.[52] As we have seen, in *FHR European Ventures LLP v Cedar Capital Partners LLC*,[53] the Supreme Court was prepared to allow tracing of property in cases where the breach of fiduciary duty did not involve property but a claim to an account. In other words, the distinction between proprietary claims and personal claims, which was thought to govern the availability of tracing and the constructive trust,[54] was in many respects redundant.

14.13 The courts have also been prepared to fashion a form of liability for those who no longer possess the relevant property or who have never come into possession or control.[55] This is a form of accessory liability and is essentially based on the dishonest assistance that the person concerned has provided those who innocently or otherwise have transferred property in breach of a trust, or arguably merely violated the principle of loyalty.[56] Given that this form of liability is also based on unconscionable conduct, including omissions, by the accessory, the issue of notice is crucial. The law has been perhaps unduly complicated by the fact that many of the cases that have arisen involve transactions relating to land, where it was reasonable and practical to expect purchasers to make certain inquiries as to the integrity of the transaction.[57] In the wider world of business to base liability on essentially a failure to know what an honest and reasonable person in the position of the recipient would know or deduce, has been thought a too exacting standard. Thus in the case of a proprietary claim against a bank, that has received suspect funds, it will be liable unless it can prove that it was a *bona fide* recipient without actual, constructive or imputed notice of the customer's fraud or other wrongdoing. In the case of a personal claim the issue will be whether the bank's conscience is sufficiently affected for it to be placed under an obligation to account to the person who has the relevant claim to the money. On the other hand it is important to remember that the test, in the civil law, is essentially objective and the test of honesty is that of normally accepted standards in the particular circumstances. For liability it needs to be shown that the bank either actually had knowledge which renders its receipt unconscionable or assistance dishonest or that the circumstances were such that turning a blind eye to 'commercially unacceptable conduct in a particular context' or 'acting in reckless disregard of other's possible proprietary rights' amounts to the same.[58] The extent to which

---

52 See generally A Burrows, *The Law of Restitution* (3rd edn) (Oxford University Press 2011) and in particular A Stafford and S Ritchie, *Fiduciary Duties, Directors and Employees* (Jordan Publishing 2015), Ch 9.
53 [2014] UKSC 45.
54 *Sinclair Investment Holdings SA v Versailles Trading Finance Ltd & Others* [2011] EWCA Civ 347 affirming *Lister & Co v Stubbs* (1890) 45 Ch D 1.
55 See for example *AGIP (Africa) Ltd v Jackson* [1990] Ch 265 aff'd [1991] Ch 547.
56 See for an illustration of the reach of these principles *Finers v Miro* [1991] 1 WLR 35.
57 For example, *Re Montagu's Settlement Trust* [1987] Ch 264 per Megarry VC at 272.
58 *Credit Agricole Corporation and Investment Bank v Papadimitriou* [2015] UKPC 13. In this case the Privy Council thought that 'the web of companies and the cost would have alerted a reasonable banker to the improper motive, namely to launder the money'. Lord Sumption observed that 'there must be something which the defendant actually knows (or would actually know if he has a reasonable appreciation of the meaning of the information in his hands) which calls for inquiry. The rule is that the defendant in this position cannot say that there might well have been an honest explanation if he has not made the inquiries suggested by the facts at his disposal with a view to ascertaining whether there really is … If there are features of the transaction such that if left unexplained they are indicative of wrongdoing, then an explanation must be sought before it can be assumed that there is none.' Reference should also be made to *Armstrong DLW GmbH v Winnington Networks Ltd* [2012] 3 All ER 425. See also at 7.48 *et seq* above.

financial institutions and their officers and employees could find themselves exposed to proprietary and more likely personal claims is real and reinforces many of the obligations that would normally be encountered in compliance systems.

14.14   Moving away from the common law, there are a number of statutory provisions which impose directly or indirectly the prospect of personal liability on persons performing particular functions. Perhaps the most significant in the context of our present discussion are those relating to reporting suspicions of money laundering under the Proceeds of Crime Act and the relevant anti-terrorist legislation.[59] While these provisions are addressed in Chapter 7 given their relevance to the civil law it is appropriate to set out the relevant issues here.

14.15   Having regard to the risks both legal and otherwise, that can arise for those involved, innocently or not, in the laundering of the proceeds of crime or the transfer of terrorist funds, ensuring proper and effective compliance with the statutory and other obligations is an important task of management. Oversight in terms of the establishment and support of such systems is an important issue in governance. In certain situations the failure of management and those responsible for governance might well result in legal and regulatory liability. It is also important to note that the complex web of law and regulation thrown up by anti-money laundering laws often has the effect of imposing obligations with the risk of legal consequences, internationally. For example, generally speaking under most laws, the offences relating to money laundering apply to conduct within jurisdiction, even if the criminal activity generating the property in question took place entirely out of jurisdiction. It is also the case that some provisions operate on wider notions of jurisdiction than would traditionally be encountered in most criminal justice systems. The significance that governments and, in particular inter-governmental organisations, now attach to combating serious crime, corruption and the funding of terror, through inhibiting the transfer and concealment of funds associated or representing such activity, means that regulators and indeed, even the courts, have been robust in the administration and application of relevant laws and procedures. A powerful illustration of the importance now attached to depriving criminals of their illicit wealth is provided in the new United Nations Convention against Corruption.[60] Article 51 states that pursing the proceeds of corruption is a fundamental principle of the Convention. It should be noted that many of the Conventions provisions might well have impact on the business world.[61] Furthermore, it must also be borne in mind that as it has proved in practice difficult to interdict property associated with crime and terror, law enforcement and regulatory authorities have adopted strategies designed rather more to disrupt criminal and subversive enterprises than interdict specific property. The problem with this approach is that the perimeters of what is acceptable, let alone lawful, disruptive conduct are not clear. It is also the case that often those being used knowingly or otherwise in the processes of disruption will be individuals and companies engaged in business or the financial sector. The

---

59   See B Rider and TM Ashe (eds), *Money Laundering Control* (Sweet & Maxwell 1996), Ch 1 and generally B Rider (ed), *International Financial Crime* (Edward Elgar 2015).

60   See generally B Rider, 'Recovering the Proceeds of Corruption', (2007) 10 *Journal of Money Laundering Control* 5.

61   See, for example, Article 12 in regard to anti-corruption initiatives in the private sector; Article 20 on unjust enrichment and Articles 21 and 22 in regard to bribery and embezzlement in the private sector.

legal risks in placing such persons in the 'front line' have not been sufficiently determined, or for that matter considered.

14.16   We have already emphasised particularly in our discussion of the law relating to criminal property and the offences of money laundering that rules of law no matter how well-crafted do not operate in a vacuum. While there is a reasonable degree of interface between the criminal law and the various obligations that have been developed within the regulatory system this is not always the case in regard to the civil law. Conceptually why this should be the case is not easy to explain, however, in practical terms it may well be due to the fact that very rarely are civil lawyers involved in crafting the various obligations that for perfectly understandable reasons have been imposed on those doing business in the financial sector. The complexity that arises by virtue of the very nature of transactions together with uncertainties and, indeed, in recent years the dynamic nature of the civil law and in particular the law relating to restitution, is sadly not always appreciated let alone understood by those engaged in the criminal and regulatory aspects of relevant conduct. In our discussion of the anti-money laundering provisions in Chapter 7 we have already discussed the offence of 'tipping off' and given the significance of this we return to it again in the context of our analysis of personal liability below. There are situations, however, where persons in receipt or control of property, that has been transferred in breach of trust or who may be at risk of being considered to be affording assistance to another who is in breach of a fiduciary obligation, are under a duty to take reasonable steps to search out and inform those who have a proper claim to the property in question.[62] There are other situations in which there is at least arguably a duty in the civil law to take steps to protect the relevant property or the proper interests of others, which might well have the effect of 'tipping off' those under suspicion.[63] Notwithstanding a reluctance in both the Treasury – until recently – and regulators to acknowledge such issues, the Courts have been required to consider the position of, in particular, banks that find themselves on the 'horns of a dilemma', and have rarely if ever been able to provide those at risk with particularly clear let alone determinative guidance.[64] Given the likelihood that in many financial transactions other

---

62   See for example *Finers v Miro* [1991] 1 WLR 35 and 2.55 above. In practice this has proved to be a 'minefield' for financial intermediaries, albeit few cases have come before the courts; see generally, *Banking on Corruption, The Legal Responsibilities of those who Handle the Proceeds of Corruption* (Sir Richard Scott and Lord Steel of Aikwood, 2000), Society of Advanced Legal Studies and B. Rider (ed), *Research Handbook on International Financial Crime* (Edward Elgar 2016) at Ch 60.

63   See, for example, *Bank of Scotland v A Ltd* [2001] EWCA Civ 52 and *Shah v HSBC Private Bank (UK) Limited* [2010] 3 All ER 477 (CA) discussed at 7.59 above. See also in this context *C v S* [1999] 2 All ER 343, *Amalgamated Metal trading Ltd v City of London Police Financial Investigation Unit* [2003] EWHC 703 (ComM) and *Hosni Tayeb v HSBBC and Al Farsan International* [2004] EWHC 1529 (Comm) and 7.45 below. As to the efficacy of the regime see *UK National Risk Assessment of Money Laundering and Terrorist Finance*, (October 2015) HM Treasury and the Home Office.

64   Section 37 of the Serious Crime Act 2015 adds subs 4A to s 388 (see 7.32 below) of the Proceeds of Crime Act and provides 'where an authorised disclosure is made in good faith no civil liability arises in respect of the disclosure on the part of the person by or on whose behalf it is made'. This is intended to address liability arising in common law 'in respect of the disclosure'. It does not address the issues that arise when the person making the disclosure by virtue of holding or controlling suspected property has obligations to third parties. Nor does it address the situation where the disclosure was not made in good faith such as was alleged, but not established, in *Shah v HSBC Private Bank (UK) Ltd* [2012] EWHC 1283 (see 7.59 below). It is unclear whether this new provision impacts on the duty of care. It has no application, of course, to proceedings overseas or to duties to report suspicions other than under POCA, such as to the FCA.

jurisdictions with their own laws and practices will be involved, legal and especially regulatory risk arising by virtue of a lack of proper interface is very real. Indeed, as we have already seen in our analysis as to the efficacy in law, as opposed to regulatory practice, of 'Chinese Walls,' in Chapter 8, it is not always appreciated that 'good practice' and adherence to regulatory guidance and even rules, will protect an intermediary from the legal implications of being in a conflict of interest or duty. Similarly, there is at least at the international level uncertainty as to how far an intermediary and or individual would be protected by domestic legislation or common law rules from allegations of, for example, defamation in making a report to the authorities on the basis of a suspicion. Traditionally those concerned with constructing compliance systems and advising on such have tended to focus disproportionately on the issues that arise under the FSMA 2000 and related legislation, together with specific areas of the criminal law, such as insider dealing and money laundering. Consequently, there are very real areas of potential risk which are not always adequately addressed in compliance procedures. It is not always the case that it is sufficiently appreciated that directors and officers of companies are under the degree of control and, thus risk pursuant to ordinary company law that they are. Indeed, as we attempt in this work to emphasise even just the control of insider abuse is a rather more complex issue, as a matter of law, than is often appreciated within essentially two dimensional compliance structures.

14.17   Of particular significance is section 330 of the Proceeds of Crime Act 2002 (POCA) which imposes an obligation on those in the regulated sector to report to the authorities their suspicions of laundering activity. Where a person fails to make the required disclosure as soon as is practicable, when he knows or suspects, or has reason for knowing or suspecting, another person is engaging in money laundering, and this information came to him in the course of his trade, profession, business or employment within the regulated sector, he commits a crime. Thus, a suspicion that property represents the benefit of criminal conduct committed overseas, including from inchoate offences such as conspiracy, would be caught under this provision. There is some protection, although not much, in that a person who does not in fact know or suspect that laundering is taking place, and has not had the benefit of the training that is required to be given the Regulations, will not be guilty of an offence. There are other limited defences. Where there is a reasonable excuse for non-disclosure then no offence is committed. Furthermore, a professional legal adviser will not be guilty for failing to disclose information that comes to him in privileged circumstances, provided such information is not in furtherance of criminal activity. Of course, under the general law, privilege is restricted in that it cannot serve to hide and facilitate crime. However, in this context it should also be noted that in *Bowman v Fels*,[65] the Court of Appeal confirmed that the obligation to report, in that case as a defence under section 328, did not override the common law legal professional privilege.

14.18   Section 331 of the Act imposes responsibility on nominated officers commonly referred to as Money Laundering Reporting Officers (MLROs) to pass on information that they receive. They are under an obligation to forward this information, in the prescribed manner, to the authorities as soon as practicable. However, in considering whether an offence has been committed, courts are required to consider whether the officer in question followed guidance issued, with the approval of the Treasury, by appropriate designated

---

65   [2005] EWCA Civ 226 and see *Shah v HSBC Private Bank (UK) Ltd* [2012] EWHC 1283 (QB).

bodies under Schedule 9 to the Act. Thus, compliance with, for example, the Guidance Notes of the Joint Money Laundering Steering Group of the British Bankers Association, the Law Society or the Financial Conduct Authority (FCA) would be relevant in the determination of guilt. In the case of the non-regulated sector, section 332 imposes similar obligations on nominated officers to report, as soon as practicable, knowledge or suspicion based on information that they have received. However, as we have seen here the test for liability is subjective rather than objective. Furthermore, they are not guilty if they have a reasonable excuse for non-compliance.

14.19 Reference has already been made to the offence of 'tipping off' contained in section 333 of the Act. This crime involves making a disclosure that is likely to prejudice a money laundering investigation. If a person knows or suspects that a protected or authorised disclosure has been made to the authorities or an employer and he makes a disclosure which is likely to prejudice any investigation that may be undertaken as a result of the protected or authorised disclosure, he commits an offence. This provision applies to everyone, including professional advisers. However, in the case of a professional legal adviser no offence will be committed in regard to the disclosure of information to a client or the client's representative, in regard to the provision of legal advice, or to any person in contemplation of, or in connection with, legal proceedings for the purpose of those proceedings, unless, of course, the disclosure was made with a view to furthering a criminal purpose. If the accused did not know or suspect that the disclosure was likely to prejudice an investigation, no offence is committed. Furthermore, as in the case of all the offences, there is no crime if what is done is pursuant to statutory authority or in the enforcement of the law.

14.20 Under section 342 of the Act any person who, knowing or suspecting that someone is acting or proposing to act in connection with a confiscation or money laundering investigation makes a disclosure that is likely to prejudice the investigation or interferes with evidence, is guilty of an offence. There are defences rather similar to those relating to an offence under section 333. Of course, where there is a deliberate interference with the administration of justice or destruction, concealment or falsification of evidence then there would be the prospect of prosecution for offences under the general criminal law.

14.21 Mention has been made of the possibility of liability resulting from the disclosure of information, pursuant to the statutory obligations in the Act, under the general law. In the case of disclosure by persons within the regulated sector, section 337 provides that they are protected from any legal or other obligation that might otherwise prevent them from revealing confidential information, provided the information upon which they acted came to them in the course of their trade, profession, business or profession. Such disclosures are referred to as 'protected disclosures'. Section 338(4) extends a similar protection to all authorised disclosures made under the provisions of the Act, whether by persons in the regulated sector or not. It is important to note that these provisions protect against liability, based on a breach of any restriction on the disclosure of information, however imposed. Thus, there would be no liability for breach of confidentiality arising, for example, by contract or a fiduciary relationship. However, this protection does not extend to, for instance, liability in the law of defamation. While it would be possible in most cases to assert a defence of qualified privilege, the threat of suit is a significant inhibition. Furthermore, it must not be forgotten that these statutory defences under the Act can only apply to proceedings within jurisdiction.

14.22   As far as penalties are concerned, section 334 provides that, anyone convicted on indictment of an offence under sections 327 to 329, is liable to a prison term of up to 14 years and an unlimited fine. In the case of sections 330 to 333, on conviction on indictment, the maximum penalty is five years imprisonment and an unlimited fine. Of course, in the case of summary convictions the maximum term of imprisonment is six months. Offences under these provisions might well be suitable for triggering proceedings for confiscation or asset recovery.

PERSONAL CRIMINAL LIABILITY

14.23   We have already considered when a person might be liable for market abuse and insider dealing offences and we do not intend to rehearse these offences again. What is clear is that individuals may commit the following offences, amongst others:

(a)   section 52 of the Criminal Justice Act 1993 (insider dealing);
(b)   sections 89–91 of the Financial Services Act 2012 (making misleading statements or impressions).

14.24   In addition, section 400 of the FSMA ensures that an officer of a company may also be guilty of an offence where the company is guilty of an offence under the 2000 Act if the offence was committed with the consent[66] or connivance[67] of that officer, or where the offence was attributable to any neglect on his part. This will include failure to comply when required to do so under Part XI of the 2000 Act on Information Gathering and Investigations.

14.25   Other legislation not directly concerned with insider dealing and market abuse also creates personal criminal liability, as we have seen in Chapter 6, including but not limited to:

(a)   section 19 of the Theft Act 1968, which creates the offence of making false statements by company directors (or officers of an unincorporated association) with intent to deceive members or creditors about the organisation's affairs;
(b)   the Fraud Act 2006, including the offences of fraud by false representation, by failing to disclose information or by abuse of position;
(c)   section 993 of the Companies Act 2006, which creates the offence of fraudulent trading, whereby every person who is knowingly a party to the carrying on of the business in the fraudulent manner commits an offence;
(d)   the Bribery Act 2010, including the offences of offering or receiving a bribe, or bribing a foreign public official. Where an offence is committed by a company, the senior officer or person purporting to act in that capacity may also be convicted if the offence was committed by the company with their consent or connivance;

---

66   In the Banking Act 1987 case of *Attorney General's Reference (No 1 of 1995)* [1996] 1 WLR 970 (CA), for consent: 'A defendant has to be proved to know the material facts which constitute the offence by the body corporate and to have agreed to its conduct of its business on the basis of those facts.'
67   The word 'connivance' was examined in *Huckerby v Elliott* [1970] 1 All ER 189 (QBD), in relation to failing to obtain a gaming licence and a person was said to connive where 'he is equally well aware of what is going on but his agreement is tacit, not actively encouraging what happens but letting it continue and saying nothing about it'.

(e)   the Proceeds of Crime Act 2002, the Terrorism Act 2000 and the Money Laundering Regulations 2007 offences as set out in Chapter 8, arising out of the obligations on compliance officers, professional advisers, directors and others.

CRIMINAL PROCEEDINGS

14.26   Criminal proceedings for market abuse and insider dealing are not generally dissimilar from criminal proceedings for any other offences, with some limited points of note.

14.27   First, the starting point is that criminal proceedings for the offence of insider dealing under Part V of the Criminal Justice Act 1993 cannot be instituted except by or with the consent of the Secretary of State or the Director of Public Prosecutions (see section 61 of the 1993 Act); however, despite this section, the FCA does not need such consent.[68] Other prosecution authorities may be bound by the requirement under section 61 where they also have the power to prosecute this offence. This will include the Crown Prosecution Service.

14.28   Second, there are evidential issues that must be taken into account. The FCA has the power under section 171 of the FSMA to compel persons to answer questions; a power that the Serious Fraud Office also has. The ability to compel a response is obviously subject to ECHR, Article 6 protection against self-incrimination and any compelled evidence cannot be used against a defendant in criminal proceedings. Section 174(2) of the FSMA states that, in criminal proceedings, no evidence relating to the statement may be adduced, and no question relating to it may be asked by or on behalf of the prosecution, unless evidence relating to it is adduced, or a question relating to it is asked, in the proceedings by or on behalf of that person. Section 174(3) creates exceptions for perjury, the offence of knowingly or recklessly providing false information pursuant to section 177(4) and the offence of knowingly or recklessly giving the FCA information which is false or misleading in a material particular.

14.29   Third, it is of note that civil and criminal proceedings are not exclusive. As the FCA notes in the enforcement section on its website: 'In some cases it will be appropriate for us to take both civil and criminal action. For example, we could take civil proceedings to secure assets, to obtain compensation for victims, and to prevent any further misconduct. We could then follow these by criminal proceedings to enable the Courts to deal with an offender for the misconduct which has already taken place.'[69]

14.30   Having noted the above, the main procedural point of note between charge and trial/conviction for the defendant will be whether or not the case is to be dealt with in the magistrates' court or the Crown Court. Where the charge is conspiracy, this is not an issue as conspiracy is triable only on indictment in the Crown Court.[70] The initial procedure for substantive cases

---

68   See *R (on the application of Uberoi) v Westminster Magistrates' Court* [2009] 1 WLR 1905 (CA), which dealt with the FCA's predecessor the Financial Services Authority, in which May LJ stated that 'it must have been the Parliamentary intention that the FSA would be able to institute proceedings under Part V of the 1993 Act without consent from outside'.
69   http://www.fca.org.uk/firms/being-regulated/enforcement/how-we-enforce-the-law/courts.
70   See s 1(1) of the Criminal Law Act 1977 and *Archbold: Criminal Pleading, Evidence and Practice* (Sweet and Maxwell, 2015) at 33-2. In regard, however, to the importance of reinforcing integrity in the markets, see *R v Hayes*, Court of Appeal, 21 December 2015, referred to at 6.13 note 21 above and in particular, 3.7 note 17 above.

that are triable either way is set out at section 17A of the Magistrates' Courts Act 1980; the defendant is asked whether or not he intends to plead guilty or not guilty.

14.31   If he pleads guilty, then the magistrates' court will treat the plea as a conviction in the magistrates' court and if it considers its sentencing powers to be insufficient,[71] the magistrates' court may commit the defendant to be sentenced in the Crown Court.

14.32   If he pleads not guilty, then the magistrates' court applies the process set out under sections 19–23 of the Magistrates' Courts 1980 and it shall decide whether the offence appears to it more suitable for summary trial or for trial on indictment. As well as taking into account the nature and circumstances of the offence, any previous convictions and any representations, the magistrates' court must consider whether the sentence which it could impose for the offence would be adequate and it must also have regard to any allocation guidelines issued as definitive guidelines under section 122 of the Coroners and Justice Act 2009.

SENTENCING POLICY

14.33   There is not a large amount of authority on sentencing policy for market abuse and insider trading.[72] This is not a surprise given that the number of prosecutions is low; the FCA reports in its 2014–15 Annual Report that it commenced just four prosecutions during that financial year.[73] Despite this, the authorities provide a fair amount of guidance as to the considerations that the court should take into account when sentencing for insider dealing.

14.34   Before turning to these authorities, the maximum sentences should be noted. The maximum that the Crown Court can impose for insider dealing is imprisonment of up to seven years and an unlimited fine. The maximum sentence that the magistrates' court can impose is imprisonment of up to six months and a fine not exceeding the statutory maximum.[74]

14.35   First, although insider dealing cannot be directly equated with theft, a comparison with breach of trust cases 'is not wholly devoid of relevance'.[75] In such breach of trust cases, sentences of five to nine years were merited where thefts of £250,000 to £1 million had been made.[76] Taking this into account, a sentence of five years' imprisonment was reduced in *R v Butt* to four years' imprisonment, for a net share of the profit made by the appellant of £237,000.

---

71   See the maximum terms for the offence and note that the magistrates' court cannot impose more than 12 months' imprisonment consecutively or six months' imprisonment for any one offence.
72   Indeed for offences pursuant to ss 87–89 of the Financial Services Act 2012, there is no reported authority.
73   Financial Conduct Authority, 'Annual Report and Accounts 2014/15' (FCA 2015).
74   See Criminal Justice Act 1993, s 61 and note 72 above.
75   *R v Butt* [2006] EWCA Crim 137.
76   On this point, see *R v Butt*, above; *R v McQuoid* [2010] 1 Cr App R (S) 43. For the key breach of trust case see *R v Clark* [1998] 2 Cr App R (S) 95 (CA).

14.36   Second, the starting point for insider trading, for reasons of deterrence, is a custodial sentence even for those not professionally involved in the City.[77] Previous good character does not diminish the criminality.[78]

14.37   Third, the fact that insider trading can also be dealt with by regulatory or disciplinary means does not mean to say that substantial sentences of imprisonment cannot be imposed.[79] It also does not matter if previously prosecution policy would have meant that one would have been dealt with by non-criminal methods.[80]

14.38   Fourth, the general considerations that a sentencing court should take into account include the following:[81]

(1)   the nature of the defendant's employment or retainer, or involvement in the arrangements which enabled him to participate in the insider dealing of which he is guilty;

---

77   In *R v Spearman* [2003] EWCA Crim 2893, Hughes J stated that: 'the judge was right in this case to say that an immediate custodial sentence was necessary for these offences, and secondly, we are quite sure that he was right to conclude that there needed to be an element of deterrence in such sentences. There has been for some years now a good deal of publicity about the process of insider trading. It has been well known for many years that it is conduct which is a serious criminal offence. We have little doubt that if the defendants had been professional City traders they could have expected a sentence significantly greater than the sentences which were imposed here.' These observations were adopted by Lord Judge CJ in *R v McQuoid*, above, as were the observations in the footnote below.

78   See *R v McQuoid*, above, per Lord Judge CJ: 'The principles of confidentiality and trust, which are essential to the operations of the commercial world, are betrayed by insider dealing and public confidence in the integrity of the system which is essential to its proper function is undermined by market abuse. Takeover arrangements are normally kept secret. Very few people are permitted to have advance knowledge of them. Those who are entrusted with advance knowledge are entrusted with that knowledge precisely because it is believed that they can be trusted. When they seek to make a profit out of the knowledge and trust reposed in them, or indeed when they do so recklessly, their criminality is not reduced or diminished merely because they are individuals of good character.'

79   *R v Spearman*, above, per Hughes J: 'We have been referred to the fact that new legislation enables some insider trading to be dealt with by means of regulatory or disciplinary process. That does not mean that the activity ceases to be a criminal offence which is likely to be prosecuted and if prosecuted likely in appropriate cases to be met by substantial sentences of imprisonment. Overall insider trading is a serious matter. On a large scale it corrupts the whole of the market in capital.' See also *R v McQuoid*, above, per Lord Judge CJ: 'We therefore emphasise that this kind of conduct does not merely contravene regulatory mechanisms. If there ever was a feeling that insider dealing was a matter to be covered by regulation, that impression should be rapidly dissipated. The message must be clear: when it is done deliberately, insider dealing is a species of fraud; it is cheating. Prosecution in open and public court will often, and perhaps much more so now than in the past, be appropriate. Although those who perpetrate the offence may hope, if caught, to escape with regulatory proceedings, they can have no legitimate expectation of avoiding prosecution and sentence.'

80   See *R v McQuoid*, above, per Lord Judge CJ: 'We understand the submission, but the answer to it is simple. Those involved in the earlier investigations when a different policy was apparently adopted (and assuming that a different policy was adopted) may have been very fortunate. But their good fortune cannot enure to the benefit of anyone else. It is not suggested that the former policy of using the regulatory system misled the appellant into thinking that insider dealing, if proved, would be, or could be, other than criminal, or that he had some kind of reasonable expectation that it would or even that it might. In these circumstances the complaint that somehow the prosecution was unfair, or that the fact of prosecution was unfair, and that the sentence, if the prosecution were successful, should have reflected the kind of financial penalty that would have followed from a regulatory intervention is not sustainable.'

81   See *R v McQuoid*, above, per Lord Judge CJ, who also stated immediately thereafter that: 'Age and a guilty plea will always be relevant. So, too, will good character. However, it must be borne in mind that it will often be the case that it is the individual of good character who

(2)   the circumstances in which he came into possession of confidential information and the use he made of it;

(3)   whether he behaved recklessly or acted deliberately, and almost inevitably therefore, dishonestly;

(4)   the level of planning and sophistication involved in his activity, as well as the period of trading and the number of individual trades;[82]

(5)   whether he acted alone or with others and, if so, his relative culpability;

(6)   the amount of anticipated or intended financial benefit or (as sometimes happens) loss avoided, as well as the actual benefit (or loss avoided);

(7)   although the absence of any identified victim is not normally a matter giving rise to mitigation, the impact (if any), where proved, on any individual victim; and

(8)   the impact of the offence on overall public confidence in the integrity of the market; because of its impact on public confidence it is likely that an offence committed jointly by more than one person trusted with confidential information will be more damaging to public confidence than an offence committed in isolation by one person acting on his own.

14.39   Fifth, the laundering of criminal proceeds will justify a consecutive sentence if the offence adds to the culpability of the conduct involved in the primary offence.[83] In particular, deliberately attempting to dispose of the proceeds of insider dealing within days of being contacted by the FSA has justified a consecutive sentence.[84]

14.40   As well as considering the issue of the appropriate length of imprisonment, whether suspended or not, a sentencing court may also in an appropriate case disqualify the convicted defendant from acting as the director of a company.[85] Under section 2 of the Company Directors Disqualification Act 1986, the defendant does not need to have been a director of the company and the court does not need to find that the individual is unfit to act as a company director. In criminal courts, there is no statutory minimum period

has been trusted with information just because he or she is an individual of good character. By misusing the information, the trust reposed as a result of the good character has been breached.' In addition, on the facts of this case, Lord Judge CJ found that full weight must be given to 'the impact on the appellant and his family, as well as the destruction of his professional reputation. This will be significant for the future. There is now no financial benefit. All his profit has been confiscated, and, no doubt because he elected to deny his guilt so that it had to be proved, he has been required to pay £30,000 towards the costs of the prosecution.' In this case, a sentence of 12 months' imprisonment was upheld for a single act of insider dealing resulting in profit of £48,919, for an appellant who was a solicitor and former General Counsel for a public limited company, who had become party to inside information regarding a takeover by another public limited company.

82   By way of example, see *R v Rollins* [2012] 1 Cr App R (S) 64 (CA), in which for a similar sum of money to that in *R v McQuoid*, above, a sentence of 15 months was justifiable rather than 12 months. Lord Judge CJ held that: 'Whilst the sums involved in each case are comparable, the appellant undertook five separate transactions over a period of weeks, as opposed to the single transaction in *McQuoid*.'

83   See *R v Linegar* [2009] EWCA Crim 648; *R v Greaves and Others* [2011] 1 Cr App R (S) 8 (CA).

84   See *R v Rollins* [2012] 1 Cr App R (S) 64 (CA), in which three months' imprisonment consecutive was imposed, reduced from six months given personal mitigation and the stress occasioned by the delay in bringing the matter to trial.

85   See *R v Goodman* (1993) 97 Cr App R 210 (CA), in which the defendant, a company director, arranged to sell 692,000 shares a few days before his company announced an unexpected loss. The Court of Appeal upheld the defendant's disqualification as a director pursuant to section 2 of the Company Directors Disqualification Act 1986. The offence was found to be in connection with the management of a company.

of disqualification. The maximum period of disqualification is 15 years in the Crown Court and five years in the magistrates' court.[86]

14.41   As noted above, the court may also, upon conviction, impose a confiscation order upon the defendant. The law relating to confiscation orders and discussion thereof can be found in Chapter 8 and we do not intend to repeat here what has already set out. It may be that the court may also fine a defendant, in addition to making a confiscation order.[87] The purpose of the fine is punitive. The purpose of the confiscation order is to deprive the defendant of the value of his criminal conduct.

14.42   Fining a defendant in excess of the profit made from insider dealing can be seen in the civil courts. In *Massey v The Financial Services Authority*,[88] the Upper Tribunal reduced a fine to the profit made (£100,000) plus 50% (£150,000 in total), where the applicant had persuaded himself on inadequate grounds that he could trade. Had the applicant deliberately traded knowing full well that he was committing market abuse, the Upper Tribunal would have upheld the original fine of £281,474, which would be equivalent to the profit plus over 180%.

14.43   In criminal courts, a fine may be combined with a sentence of imprisonment, in particular when there has been a substantial profit from the offence;[89] however the extent of any fine that might be imposed has not yet been tested in the relevant case law. There is also a lack of relevant authority as to the appropriateness and extent of any fines that can be made in market abuse and insider dealing cases after the making of a confiscation order.[90]

14.44   The other financial order that the court will consider is whether or not to make a compensation order pursuant to section 130 of the Powers of Criminal Courts (Sentencing) Act 2000. By virtue of section 130(3), a court is required, on passing sentence, to give reasons if it does not make a confiscation order under section 130(1) requiring the defendant to pay for any personal injury, loss or damage resulting from that offence or any other offences taken into consideration by the sentencing court. Two key principles may be of importance in cases involving compensation requests in market abuse and insider dealing cases. First, there must be a causal link for compensation to be ordered.[91] Second, when detailed and complex issues fall to be decided,[92] then compensation should be left to the civil courts.[93] In this context, and in the context of any regulatory proceedings that might follow, it is of note that a convicted defendant cannot use the civil courts as a means to initiate a

---

86   Guidance on the appropriate length of a disqualification was given in the civil law case of *Re Sevenoaks Stationers (Retail) Ltd* [1991] Ch 164 (CA). Periods over ten years should be reserved for particularly serious cases. These may include cases where a director who has already had one period of disqualification imposed on him falls to be disqualified yet again. Six to ten years' disqualification should apply for serious cases which do not merit the top bracket. Two to five years' disqualification should be applied where the case is, relatively, not very serious.
87   See POCA, s 15(3).
88   [2011] UKUT 49 (TCC).
89   See *Current Sentencing Practice* (Sweet and Maxwell 2015), at J1-3A.
90   See Proceeds of Crime Act 2002, s 15(4) for the general power to make a fine within 56 days of the making of a confiscation order, though such a fine will not be a consideration in those cases where the defendant has insufficient means to even repay his benefit from his crime.
91   See *R v Deary* (1993) 14 Cr App R (S) 648 (CA); *R v Derby* (1990–91) 12 Cr App R (S) 502 (CA).
92   Other than those already determined at trial or sentence.
93   See *R v Kneeshaw* (1974) 58 Cr App R 439 (CA); *R v Bewick* [2008] 2 Cr App R (S) 31(CA).

collateral attack on his conviction. This would constitute an abuse of process,[94] and the principle might be departed from only where there was fresh evidence which entirely changed the aspect of the case.[95]

REGULATORY LIABILITY AND APPROVED PERSONS

14.45   In this part of the chapter consideration is given to the personal liability that can arise under the regulatory system for approved persons such as compliance officers, money laundering reporting officers, senior managers and other persons that engage in market abuse, or otherwise fail to meet the standards required of them in relation to conduct in the market.

14.46   Part V of the FSMA sets out a framework of regulation applying to persons that perform controlled functions and in essence gives rise to a system of individual accountability. Such persons are required by section 59 of the FSMA to be approved by the relevant regulatory authority (the Prudential Regulation Authority (PRA) or the FCA as the case may be) in order for them to perform such a function. Once approved the approved person is required under section 64 of the FSMA to comply with provisions of the FS Handbook statements of principle and Code of Practice for Approved Persons (APER) and becomes subject to regulatory discipline and enforcement under section 66 in the event that they fail to comply with the provisions of APER. Liability that may arise from regulatory discipline and enforcement is considered further below and in Chapter 12.

14.47   The framework of regulation and personal accountability as it relates to senior managers and other certified persons working within the banking sector is subject to significant rule change coming into force on 31 Mach 2016. This part of the chapter addresses the regulatory framework currently in force and as it applies to non-PRA activity.

14.48   A series of controlled functions are prescribed in the supervision sourcebook (SUP) of the FS Handbook. The Table at SUP 10A 4.4R divides control functions between those classified as significant influence functions and the customer dealing function. The distinction between significant influence and the customer functions becomes important when one is considering the applicable provisions of APER and the regulatory standards that are expected of an individual approved person. It is indeed the case that the compliance oversight function coded in APER as CF 10 is for certain authorised persons a required function as well as classified as being 'significant'.[96]

14.49   In order to be approved the person must, in accordance with section 61(1) of the FSMA, satisfy the relevant regulatory authority that they are fit and proper and thus suitable to be so approved. Guidance provided in the FS Handbook at the sourcebook for 'The fit and proper test for persons' (FIT) indicates a series of issues relevant to an applicant's suitability.[97] This includes matters

---

94   See *Hunter v Chief Constable of the West Midlands Police & Others* [1982] AC 529 (HL).
95   See Earl Cairns LC in *Phosphate Sewage Co Ltd v Molleson* (1879) 4 App Cas 801.
96   Not all authorised persons are required to appoint a person with responsibility for compliance oversight. See SUP 10A.1 for details of the application of the controlled functions to different classes of authorised person.
97   See FS Handbook 'The Fit and Proper test for Approved Persons (FIT) at FIT 2 'Main assessment criteria.

such as: (a) the applicant's honesty, integrity and reputation; (b) their antecedents, including whether they have been convicted of any criminal offences, been the subject of adverse civil proceedings, been the subject of an investigation or proceedings of a disciplinary or criminal nature, contravened previously the requirements for the regulatory system, been a director, partner of or involved in the management of a business which has got into 'insolvency, liquidation or administration' during the period the applicant's connection with the business or within one year of being connected, and whether the applicant has been 'candid and truthful in all his dealings with' the relevant regulatory authority; (c) financial soundness, including outstanding judgment debts and arrangement with creditors or bankruptcy; and (d) competence and capability including whether the person's training and experience demonstrates suitability to perform the control function applied for whether they have 'adequate time to perform the controlled function meet the responsibilities associated with that function'. (Certain specified control functions such as those that are customer facing are subject to prescribed examination requirements, although these requirements do not apply to compliance functions specifically considered in this chapter.)

14.50   The statement of principles and approved persons code (APER) issued pursuant section 64 of the Financial Services and Markets Act makes provision for seven statements principles pursuant to along with guidance on the steps that may be taken to comply with the principles and evidential factors that the relevant regulatory authority may take into account to determine compliance by the approved person with the statements of principle. The Statements of principle, as set out in APER 2.1A.3 are as follows:

'Statement of Principle 1

An approved person must act with integrity in carrying out his accountable functions.

Statement of Principle 2

An approved person must act with due skill, care and diligence in carrying out his accountable functions.

Statement of Principle 3

An approved person must observe proper standards of market conduct in carrying out his accountable functions.

Statement of Principle 4

An approved person must deal with the FCA, the PRA and other regulators in an open and cooperative way and must disclose appropriately any information of which the FCA or the PRA would reasonably expect notice.

Statement of Principle 5

An approved person performing an accountable significant-influence function must take reasonable steps to ensure that the business of the firm for which he is responsible in his accountable function is organised so that it can be controlled effectively.

Statement of Principle 6

An approved person performing an accountable significant-influence function must exercise due skill, care and diligence in managing the business of the firm for which he is responsible in his accountable function

Statement of Principle 7

An approved person performing an accountable significant-influence
function must take reasonable steps to ensure that the business of the firm
for which he is responsible in his accountable function complies with the
relevant requirements and standards of the regulatory system.'

14.51   As set out by APER 3.1.7A, statements of principle 1–4 are of general
application, applying to all approved persons and setting the standards required
of them in carrying out their controlled function. Statements of principle 5–7
are applicable to those persons performing what are described as 'significant
influence functions'. Upon analysis, it is evident from the language of
principles 5–7 that they relate to standards required of the approved person in
managing and organising the affairs of the business they are responsible for,
including (as covered by the statement to principle 7) the extent to which the
approved person take steps to ensure the area of the business for which they are
responsible complies with the relevant regulatory standards.

14.52   The extent to which an approved person will be considered in breach
of the high-level principles is addressed to some extent in the introductory
sections of APER. Moreover at APER 3.1.3G the FS Handbook positions
compliance in the context of personal culpability and talks in terms of whether
the approved person's conduct in giving rise to the breach was deliberate or
falls 'below that which would be reasonable in all the circumstances'. This
is further confirmed at paragraph 6.2.7G of the FCA's Decisions Policies and
Procedures sourcebook (DEPP) which, in setting out the Authority's policy
towards the discipline of individuals, provides: '… disciplinary action will
not be taken against an approved person performing a significant influence
function simply because a regulatory failure has occurred in an area of business
for which he is responsible. The FCA will consider that an approved person
performing a significant influence function may have breached Statements of
Principle 5 to 7 only if his conduct was below the standard which would be
reasonable in all the circumstances at the time of the conduct concerned …'.
APER 3.1.5G makes clear the importance of the evidential provisions within
APER, providing that the Authority will consider whether the person has
'acted in a way that is stated to be in breach of a statement of principle'. In
addition APER 3.1.6R makes clear the importance of the code of practice that
supports the statements of principle in terms of the extent to which examples
provided in the code assist a person to identify whether or not their conduct
will be compliant. By way of example, and it is submitted of relevance to
a company's compliance officer, in the context of the management of a
compliance function, guidance at APER 4.5.8 addresses the suitability of
individuals working under the control of the significant person and considers
that it is a breach of Principle 5 for that approved person to '[fail] to take
reasonable steps to ensure that suitable individuals are responsible for those
aspects of the business under the control of the individual performing a
significant influence function'.

14.53   With regard to the Principle 6 obligation to exercise due skill care and
diligence, APER 4.6 addresses skill, care and diligence in relation to personal
decision-making as well as skill and care of the control of the business. Of
relevance to compliance officers and money laundering reporting officers,
APER 4.6.4 E sets out behaviour that the FCA considers gives rise to failure
to 'take reasonable steps to adequately inform himself of the affairs of the

business for which he is responsible ...'[98] and includes reference to 'permitting transactions without a sufficient understanding of the risks involved'; 'inadequately monitoring highly profitable transactions or business practices or unusual transactions or business practices'; and 'accepting implausible or unsatisfactory explanations from subordinates without testing the veracity of those explanations' The Financial Services Authority Final Notice to Alexander Edward Ten-Holter[99] illustrates the application of Principle 6 to a Compliance Officer in the context of market abusive transactions. Mr Ten-Holter was employed by Greenlight Capital (UK) LLP as its Compliance Offer (Controlled Function 10), Money Laundering Reporting Officer (Controlled Function 11), as well as a partner of the firm (Controlled Function 4) and to execute trades based on instructions from Greenlight Capital Inc (Customer Controlled Function 30). The FSA found that Greenlight Capital Inc had engaged in market abuse in that it had sold securities and executed contracts for differences in shares it owned in Punch Taverns plc, following a conversation with management at Punch Taverns during which price sensitive information was disclosed.[100] The order to execute the sell transaction was given to and executed by Mr Ten-Holter. The FSA identified that Mr Ten-Holter. 'was aware that: Greenlight had made the decision to sell all of its shares in Punch having just spoken to Punch management' and that at the time that he was given the sell order he had been told by the Greenlight analyst:

'a) Punch management would have told them "secret bad things" had Greenlight been prepared to sign a non-disclosure agreement ("NDA");

b) other shareholders had signed the NDA and in Greenlight's opinion would want to sell; and

c) Greenlight potentially had a window of a week to sell before the stock "plummets", although that "might be a lie".'

14.54 The FSA further identified that subsequent to the execution of the sell order, Mr Ten-Holter became aware of an unscheduled announcement by Punch Taverns concerning its intention to raise further finance, which caused a decline in the price of Punch Tavern Shares. The FSA considered that Mr Ten-Holter failed to 'question and to make reasonable enquiries prior to effecting the sell order' and that Mr Ten-Holter should have been alerted to the risk of market abuse by Punch Tavern's subsequent announcement. In this regard the FSA stated in its Final Notice that:

'Mr Ten-Holter did not recognise the risk and took no action. His behaviour whilst performing the Compliance oversight function at Greenlight UK was in breach of Statement of Principle 6 of APER. His behaviour also demonstrates a lack of competence and capability, such that he is not fit and proper to perform the Compliance oversight (CF10) and Money laundering reporting (CF11) significant influence functions.'

14.55 Importantly moreover, in respect of more specific standards required for a Compliance Officer, the FSA Final Notice commented on the failure in the context of 'detecting and preventing' market abuse being a 'key part' or

---

98   FS Handbook APER 4.6.3E.
99   FSA Final Notice *Alexander Edward Ten-Holter* 26 January 2012.
100   See further, FSA Final Notice *Greenlight Capital Inc* 12 January 2012.

Mr Ten-Holter's compliance role and of the need to consider risk of market abuse based on available information rather than in reliance on a personal view of the firms overall standards, stating: 'He relied on his view of Greenlight's high standards of compliance in making any assessment of risk. This was inappropriate; the possibility of risk should be considered on the basis of the information available.'

14.56 APER 4.6.12 considers the extent and depth to which a significant influence function approved person must understand the business which they are responsible for, in order to comply with Principle 6, recognising that such an approved person is 'unlikely to be an expert in all aspects of a complex financial services business'. In so doing, it sets an expectation that the approved person should have sufficient knowledge and understanding of risks relating to the firm's business activities and as further guidance at APER 4.6.12 G indicates, where he considers he is not an expert 'in a business area' and is unable to obtain 'an adequate explanation of issues within that business area' the approved person should obtain 'an independent opinion' possibly from outside of the business.

14.57 Principle 7 and its supporting guidance addresses specifically a significant influence approved person's responsibility to take reasonable steps to ensure that the areas of the business for which they are responsible comply with standards under the regulatory system. It is submitted that the guidance and evidential provisions in APER 4.7 set out a series of failures and behaviours relating to organisational systems and controls. Two such provisions are aimed firmly at the person with responsibility for compliance oversight and the money laundering reporting officer in the context of steps they should take to discharge their responsibilities. The provisions at APER 4.7.9E consider that the money laundering reporting officer will be in breach of principle 7 where the person fails to 'discharge the responsibilities imposed on him by the firm' pursuant to the provisions of SYSC. For instance, at SYSC 6.3.9R an authorised firm is required to 'appoint an individual as money-laundering reporting officer with responsibility for oversight of its compliance with the FCA's rules on systems and controls against money-laundering'. Similarly, in relation to compliance oversight, the provisions at APER 4.7.10E indicate that the applicable approved person will be in breach of principle 7 where they have failed 'to take reasonable steps to ensure that appropriate compliance systems and procedures are in place'.

Personal liability for compliance officers and failure to report reasonable suspicions

14.58 Article 6(9) of the EU Market Abuse Directive[101] implemented in the UK by rules in section 15.10 of the Supervision sourcebook of the FS Handbook, imposes an obligation on authorised persons to report to the FCA reasonable suspicions of market abuse. SUP 15.10.2R provides that 'A firm which arranges or executes a transaction with or for a client and which has reasonable grounds to suspect that the transaction might constitute market abuse must notify the FCA without delay.'

---

101 EU Directive on Insider dealing and market manipulation (market abuse) No 2003/6/EC.

14.59 In practice, it is often the case that the initial identification of suspicious arises either with persons reasonable for the receiving or orders to trade or execution of transactions or those involved with transaction surveillance. Once suspicious activity is first identified many authorised firms have established arrangements requiring the suspicious transaction to be assessed, and where necessary reported to the Financial Conduct Authority by the firm's compliance function. Indeed as examined in Chapter 13, rules in the senior management systems and controls sourcebook at SYSC 6.1.1R require: 'A firm must establish, implement and maintain adequate policies and procedures sufficient to ensure compliance of the ... with its obligations under the regulatory system and for countering the risk that the firm might be used to further financial crime.'

14.60 The FCA stresses the imperative of effective suspicious market abuse reporting and indeed a number of individual enforcement cases serve to highlight the individual liability that can arise for approved persons, including those holding the compliance oversight controlled function, when a suspicion of market abuse should be reasonably held but it is not reported. In *Carrimjee v Financial Conduct Authority* the Upper Tribunal considered an application relating to an FCA decision concerning whether Mr Carrimjee knew or suspected that one of his clients intended to engage in market abuse. In relation to the regulatory obligation to report suspicious transactions Judge Herrington stated:[102]

'As we have indicated ... the Authority relies on authorised firms and the approved persons who work for them to be vigilant as to suspicions of market abuse because of their position at the "coal face" in the market. If approved persons fail to meet the requirements market confidence can be damaged, financial crime can be facilitated and in this particular case, on the assumption that the trades concerned resulted or would have resulted in market abuse being committed, the impact on market participants could have been significant.'

14.61 Disciplinary liability for suspicious reporting failures, as they related to persons holding the Compliance Oversight Controlled Function was addressed in the FSA case against Mr Ten-Holter (the facts as described at **14.53** above) where the Authority stated in its Final Notice: 'The UK regulatory system requires individuals approved to hold the Compliance oversight (CF10) significant influence function to act with due skill, care and diligence and, in doing so, to recognise the signs of possible market abuse and to take action accordingly. Compliance failures of this nature can have a dramatic effect on the orderliness of the markets.'[103] In the case, the FSA considered that Mr Ten-Holter's failure to identify and react to 'warning signs' of market abuse amounted to a breach of Principle 6 in that he did not act with due skill care and diligence and as a consequence he was not competent and capable to hold the compliance controlled function. In reaching such decision the FSA stated:

'Individuals approved to hold the Compliance oversight (CF10) significant influence function are a fundamental part of the regulatory system and provide front line protection against market abuse for the firms for which

---

102 *Carrimjee v Financial Conduct Authority* [2015] UKUT 79 (TCC), FS/2013/0003, at [323].
103 FSA Final Notice *Alexander Edward Ten-Holter* 26 January 2012, at [5.5].

they work and the wider market. Mr Ten-Holter's conduct shows that he is unable to recognise signs of possible market abuse and has a flawed approach to compliance. As such, he does not have the requisite levels of competence and capability required to be fit and proper to hold the Compliance oversight (CF10) significant influence function. For the same reason he lacks sufficient competence and capability to hold the Money laundering reporting (CF11) significant influence function, which requires a similar level of alertness to warning signs.'[104]

---

104   Note 103, at [4.9].

Chapter 15

Control liability

RESPONSIBILITY AND CONTROL

15.1   In Chapter 14 we have examined the law and regulatory provisions which in certain circumstances might impose direct personal liability on individuals and in particular those involved with compliance, for misconduct related to insider abuse. In this chapter we will address the imposition of liability on those in managerial and supervisory positions for the misconduct of those for whom they have a responsibility. We will first examine the relevant English law and regulatory practice and then consider the position in the USA where control liability plays a much more significant part in promoting and maintaining integrity in the financial markets. The notion of imposing the risk of liability on those in authoritative relationships with those who commit or might commit wrongdoing is relatively foreign to the modern English law, where the emphasis is on personal responsibility for one's own culpable acts.[1] The position is, however, changing. We recognise that in many areas of activity where individuals are particularly vulnerable it may be justified to impose responsibilities on others to act in their or another's protection.[2] Their omission to protect or take steps to protect, in such circumstances, justifies the intervention of the criminal and civil law. Of course, these essentially paternalistic considerations are not particularly relevant in the financial markets albeit the ethos and, indeed, orientation of the law has become more like that relating to the protection of consumers.[3]

15.2   In addition to what might be described as the protection argument, we also recognise that in certain circumstances the temptation to abuse one's position will be influenced by the hurdles and risks that one is likely to encounter in achieving the illicit advantage or benefit. We have already discussed this in the context of insider dealing.[4] The imposition of potential liability on those who are in a supervisory position for a failure of, for example, a compliance system will, at least in theory, reinforce that system's efficacy. It will certainly encourage those in authority to better fund and support compliance and ensure that it is fit for purpose. We have already seen a manifestation of this approach

1   See for example the discussion in *G* [2004] 1 AC 1034.
2   See, for example, s 5(1) of the Domestic Violence, Crime and Victims Act 2004 in regard to allowing the death of a child or vulnerable adult.
3   We have already referred to the amendments introduced by the Financial Services Act 2012. The imposition of a fiduciary relationship or something approaching such can also import obligations to advance and protect the other parties' interests and property.
4   See generally Chapter 1 and in regard to the 'risk-benefit' approach, Edwin Sutherland, *White Collar Crime, The Uncut Version*, (Yale University 1983).

in regard to section 7 of the Bribery Act 2010.[5] There were many who wished to see the creation of an offence applicable to managers for failure to prevent, by adequate supervision and compliance, acts of bribery. In the result, however, the initial proposals were diluted into the form of a corporate offence.[6] We have already discussed whether imposing liability on individuals is likely to be more efficacious than on corporate employers.[7] While section 7 is of considerable interest because it imposes strict criminal liability on companies that cannot show that they did have in place adequate arrangements to address the risk that someone acting for them would commit the offence of bribery and in fact did so, it is unique in the context of integrity related law. It remains to be seen whether it could be used as a model for other areas of activity. As we have seen there are real practical issues in subjecting companies to the criminal justice system. However, there is evidence that the threat of a criminal prosecution particularly with the attendant adverse publicity has brought home to many in senior management positions the importance of funding adequate compliance procedures and training. Recent initiatives by the Serious Fraud Office involving corporate self-reporting of violations and deferred prosecution agreements have also played a role in underlining the importance of managerial responsibility.

15.3   The offence in section 7 is an entirely separate offence predicated on different criteria than the offence of the agent or other person who actually commits the crime of bribery. The wrong is the failure of the company to take proper steps to address and control the risk, rather like the approach of the Financial Conduct Authority (FCA) to failures of compliance by authorised persons. Outside the area of social regulatory offences and perhaps to some degree fiscal offences and those relating to national security, it is hard to find other examples in the English criminal law. As we have seen, there is an increasing tendency to place obligations that may result in criminal and regulatory liability on individuals and institutions to report their suspicions that certain crimes have or are taking place. This is, however, a personal responsibility and is not predicated on control or supervision.

VICARIOUS LIABILITY IN THE CRIMINAL LAW

15.4   We have already discussed the circumstances where a person may become involved in a criminal enterprise as a primary or secondary offender.[8] While in some cases this may resemble control liability, the responsibility of the individual under the criminal law is both direct and personal as an accessory or conspirator. Given the emphasis that the law places on the culpability of the defendant, strictly speaking there is no doctrine of vicarious liability in English criminal law.[9] Unlike in the law of tort where the object of the law is to provide compensation for wrongs and therefore find a deep pocket is appealing, the criminal law is primarily about punishing those who have committed crimes. Having said this there are circumstances in the criminal law where the acts and or state of mind of one person may be attributed to another, so as to resemble vicarious responsibility.[10] Of rather more significance is the willingness of the

5   See 6.82 above.
6   See 6.87 *et seq* above.
7   See 14.1 *et seq* above.
8   See 3.10 and Chapter 14 above.
9   *R v Huggins* (1730) 2 Str 883. The crime of public nuisance is an exception to the general rule, *R v Stephens* (1866) LR 1 QB 702, where an employer can be vicariously liable.
10   This may be under statute or according to the doctrine of delegation. However, neither is of particular relevance in our present discussion.

courts to simply treat the acts of an employee or agent as that of the employer.[11] We have already seen that this is not so much attribution of knowledge and responsibility, but merger of the culpability of the relevant actor with the personality of the person to be held accountable.[12] The courts have adopted this approach in cases involving complex financial and commercial dealings. While prosecutors have been reluctant to use this approach, it is not without interest that the Labour Party's Policy Review, Tackling Serious Fraud and White Collar Crime, quoting the second edition of this work, commended it as a sensible approach.[13] An important aspect of this approach is that provided what is done by the employee is in the course of employment it matters not that he is in breach of his employer's instructions. Indeed, the House of Lords has held that if what is forbidden does in fact take place, then by definition there has been a failure of compliance and management and these aspects are simply issues for mitigation.[14]

15.5 The infliction of criminal liability on companies is another aspect of control liability. As we have seen there is debate as to the practical value in imposing criminal as opposed to civil liability of companies given the fictitious nature of their personality and the impracticality of most forms of punishments. We have seen that in English law companies cannot be guilty of insider dealing under Part V of the Criminal Justice Act 1993. Notwithstanding the reluctance of many legal systems to bother attributing criminal responsibility to corporations, the English law for a number of pragmatic and policy reasons is prepared to threaten companies as if they are capable of committing many types of criminal activity in the same manner as a natural person. Crimes involving strict liability present few issues, although where it is necessary to identify *mens rea* – mental culpability – the matter is far more problematic. The law has fashioned and developed a number of theories which allow judges to transfer, impute and aggregate the knowledge and intentions, including recklessness, of one or more individual with that of the company.[15]

VICARIOUS LIABILITY IN THE LAW OF TORT

15.6 The civil law given its concern to assure adequate compensation for those who have suffered harm has always been rather more flexible and imaginative than the criminal law. On the other hand, as we have seen there, accessory liability with the exception of dishonest assistance in the breach of a

11 See for example, *Coppen v Moore (No 2)* [1898] 2 QB 306.
12 See 2.35 *et seq* above.
13 Labour Party (2013) 3.
14 *Re Supply of Ready Mixed Concrete (No 2)* [1995] 1 All ER 135 at 142 per Lord Templeman.
15 The two principal theories used in the criminal law are the so called alter ego and or directing mind theory, *Lennard's Carrying Co Ltd v Asiatic Petroleum Ltd* [1915] AC 705 and the identification theory, *DPP v ICR Haulage Ltd* [1944] KB 551 and *Moore v Bressler* [1944] 2 All ER 515 restricted in *Tesco Supermarkets Ltd v Nattrass* [1972] AC 153 to only very senior officials, whereby the approach becomes almost one of vicarious liability and see *Seaboard Offshore Ltd v Secretary of State for Transport* [1994] 1 WLR 541, but for a more flexible approach see the House of Lords in *Director General of Fair Trading v Pioneer Concrete plc* [1995] 1 AC 456. In *Meridian Global Funds Management Asia Ltd v Securities Commission* [1995] 2 AC 500, Lord Hoffmann in the Privy Council considered that there was no general rule relating to attribution, but it depended upon first determining whether the offence can be committed by a company and then determining whether the person with the requisite mental state is sufficiently high in the corporate structure. But note also the move to organisational liability in the Corporate Manslaughter and Corporate Homicide Act 2007.

fiduciary duty is very limited. Liability in the law of contract, in the context of our present discussion, is limited to the relevant parties. It is conceivable that in exceptional circumstances agency or a collateral contract might be invoked to place an obligation on someone who stands behind a wrongdoing party, but this would be highly exceptional. We have, however, already seen that the law of tort may in limited circumstances be relevant, such as in the case of inducing another breach of contract.[16] The two areas of civil law that are rather more pertinent are those of vicarious liability in the law of tort and in equity.

15.7 Vicarious liability in transmitting liability to another person does not relieve the person actually committing the wrong from liability.[17] However, as we have already noted in regard to the position of compliance officers, it will usually be far more attractive for a claimant to pursue the employer or principal as they are rather more likely to have access to funds. The basis of liability is that the person committing the wrong is in a particular relationship to the defendant and the wrong is referable to that relationship. We have already noted that employment will often give rise to the prospect of vicarious liability for the employer.[18] It is important to appreciate that the liability of the employer or principal in such cases does not depend on any fault as such on his or its part. Thus, this is an exception to the general reluctance of the civil law to contemplate strict liability other than under statute. It is also important to distinguish vicarious liability form an independent duty that an employer or principal may have, by virtue of some other relationship or situation to the claimant. Deciding which relationship can justify the imposition of vicarious responsibility on an employer has vexed the courts. The old approach based on control over the relevant employee is no longer thought to be suitable,[19] at least for all situations.[20] Today it is rather more common for the courts to adopt a test which looks at whether the relevant act was integral to the employer's business or was merely ancillary.[21] It is, however, necessary that all elements of the actionable wrong did in fact occur within the relationship. In other words the employee must himself be liable for a tort.[22]

15.8 The second important element is whether the wrong – the tort, is sufficiently connected to the relevant relationship so as to justify the imposition of vicarious liability on the employer or principal. In the case of those in an employment relationship or one that is taken to resemble such, the test is whether the wrong was committed in the course of that employment or perhaps in more recent decisions, whether it was in the scope of the duties attaching to the relationship. Of course, what is meant here is not whether the

---

16 See for example *Proform Sports Management Ltd v Proactive Sports Management Ltd* [2006] EWHC 22903 (Ch) and *Meretz Investments NV v ACP Ltd* [2008] Ch 244 and at 14.9 *et seq* above.

17 *Standard Chartered Bank v Pakistan National Shipping Corporation* [2002] UKHL 43.

18 The principle is not confined to employment contracts per se: see *Catholic Child Welfare Society v Institute of the Brothers of the Christian Schools* [2012] UKSC 56.

19 See above at note 16.

20 Where it can be applied then the test may survive, see *Jennings v Forestry Commission* [2008] EWCA Civ 581. While an employer is not liable for the torts of a truly independent contractor, sometimes it will be unclear as to whether an individual is an employee or contractor. The courts are inclined to see whether what is being done is of benefit to the 'employer' and is integral to his business. Employment law is not always the determinant of the relationship in this area of the law of tort.

21 See *Lee v Cheung* [1990] 2 AC 374. The court have also emphasised that there should be mutual obligations in the relationship.

22 *Credit Lyonnais Bank Nederland NV v ECGD* [2001] 1 AC 486.

commission of a wrong, by act or omission, was required by the employer, but whether the circumstances in which the wrong occurred was within the course or scope or the engagement. Thus, there will be liability if this is authorised, expressly or impliedly by the employer or is necessarily incidental thereto. It is the authorised performance or an authorised function or responsibility. So much, however, will depend upon the facts of the case. Indeed, the House of Lords in *Lister v Hesley Hall Ltd*[23] said that the test was really nothing more than whether what took place was closely connected with the employment or business and whether it was just to impose liability on the employer.

15.9   An issue which we have already touched upon in the context of accessory liability[24] is whether it makes any difference if the employee in committing his wrong was acting against the express instructions of his employer. It would seem on the authorities that it does not, provided what took place was still within the scope of employment.[25] It is also the case that it matters not whether the employee was not acting with the intention to benefit his employer, but rather in his own self-interest.[26] Indeed, where the employer has allowed the wrongdoer to appear to have authority and this has resulted in a fraud against a third party, then the employer may well be liable.[27] It is important, however, that the employer or principal has done something to contribute to the appearance of authority. However, it is no defence that the employer or principal may himself have also been wronged by the employee or agent. Indeed, in many cases involving vicarious liability the employer will have a claim in contract and or tort against the wrongdoer.

VICARIOUS RESPONSIBILITY IN RESTITUTION

15.10   Similar issues as in the criminal law and the law of tort have also manifested themselves in the law of restitution. In this context there are really three issues. First, there is the possibility of vicarious liability for the acts of others and in particular agents. Secondly, there is the attribution of knowledge and, of course, acts of an individual to a body corporate and, thirdly the attribution of knowledge and or a state of mind one person to another.[28] We have already considered on the context of the common law vicarious liability which traditionally has been invoked to provide a deeper pocket than that of the actual wrongdoer.[29] We have also noted that it is an exception to the general dislike of the civil law of strict liability. The employer or principal of the agent concerned will be liable regardless of any moral blame on his or its

---

23   [2002] 1 AC 215. Depending upon the nature of the tort, it may be where the employer can show that the employee was 'off on a frolic of his own' then it would be inappropriate to hold him vicariously liable, see *Joel v Morison* (1834) 6 C & P 501 per Parke B at 503.
24   See for example, 14.12 above.
25   See *In Re Supply of Ready Mixed Concrete (No 2)* [1995] 1 AC 456 and *Limpus v London General Omnibus Co* (1862) 1 H & C 526. But see at 2.38 *et seq* above.
26   *Lloyd v Grace, Smith & Co* [1912] AC 716 and *Uxbridge Permanent Benefit Society v Pickard* [1939] 2 KB 248 and in regard to theft by an employee of a third party's property see *Morris v CW Martin & Sons Ltd* [1966] 1 QB 716 and *Mendelssohn v Normand Ltd* [1970] 1 QB 177 and in regard to forgery *Dollars & Sense Finance Ltd v Nathan* [2008] NZSC 20.
27   See *Lloyd v Grace, Smith & Co*, above at note 26 and *Armagas Ltd v Mundogas SAQ* [1986] 1 AC 717.
28   See Moore-Bick LJ in *Man Nutzfahrzeuge AG v Freightliner Ltd* [2005] EWHC 2347 and *Moulin Global Eyecare Trading v Commissioner of Inland Revenue* [2014] HKFCA 22.
29   See *Dubai Aluminium Co Ltd v Salaam* [2003] 2 AC 366.

part. We have discussed the circumstances where the courts are prepared to hold individuals personally responsible as if they were constructive trustees for providing assistance dishonestly to another where there has been a breach of trust or fiduciary obligation.[30] As we have seen the House of Lords has accepted in the case of a partnership, that notwithstanding the innocence of all the partners save one, who had dishonestly facilitated a breach of trust, the firm – in this case of solicitors – was vicariously liable for the wrongdoing.[31] Indeed, the view was expressed that equity should and did follow the common law and was ready and willing to impose liability where the wrongdoing is one which can 'fairly be said to be reasonably incidental to the employer's business'.[32] A firm has been held vicariously liable for one of its employees bribing an employee of another company to provide him with confidential information. The claimant successfully alleged that the partner concerned had wrongfully induced their employee to breach his contract of employment.[33]

15.11   We have already referred to the attribution of knowledge and *mens rea* from an individual to a corporation in the context of the criminal law.[34] In the civil law the courts have adopted much the same approach as in the criminal law, but arguably with more flexibility. In the case of what used to be described as knowing receipt of property transferred in breach of trust and which today is probably better described as unconscionable possession or retention, we have seen that it must be established that the bank or other person holding the property, or what it has become, must have sufficiently knowledge for the court to consider their position unconscionable. The same is true in regard to where they no longer hold traceable property or have merely given assistance in circumstances that render their conduct, or conceivably their omissions, unconscionable.[35] Consequently, the ability to the attribute knowledge of the pertinent facts in the part of the individuals involved in the objectionable conduct to the company or partnership is of great importance.[36] The courts in such cases have tended to adopt an approach which asks whether the individual is performing his function for the company and therefore is effectively the company in regard to those acts. If so then it may be appropriate to attribute his state of mind to that of the company. While the formal position that an individual has in the corporate hierarchy might well be relevant, so are other issues.[37] Indeed, even a non-executive director if allowed by the board to

30   See Chapter 2.
31   See also *Dubai Aluminium Co Ltd v Salaam* [2003] 2 AC 366 and in particular Lord Millett who emphasised the jurisdiction that equity had always asserted to impose vicarious liability for dishonest breaches of fiduciary duty in the case of partnerships and trusts; see for example, *Brydges v Branfill* (1842) 12 Sim 369.
32   See Lord Millett supra at note 31 and see also Laddie J in *Balfron Trustees Ltd v Peterson* [2001] IRLR 758.
33   *Hamlyn v John Houston & Co* [1903] 1 KB 81 and see *UBS AG (London Branch) v Kommunale Wasserwerke Leipzig GmbH* [2014] EWHC 3615.
34   See 15.5 at note 15 above and also the excellent discussion of this topic in Cheong-Ann Png, *Corporate Liability, A Study in the Principles of Attribution* (Kluwer 2001) and A. Stafford and S. Ritchie, *Fiduciary Duties, Directors and Employees* (Jordan Publishing 2014) at Chapter 8.
35   See in particular *Credit Agricole Corporation and Investment Bank v Papadimitriou* [2015] UKPC 13.
36   See *El Ajou v Dollar Land Holdings Ltd* [1994] 2 All ER 685.
37   See for example, *Meridian Global Funds Management Asia Ltd v Securities Commission* [1995] 2 AC 500 and *Man Nutzfahrzeuge AG v Freightliner Ltd* [2005] EWHC 2347. This approach is based on the directing mind theory propounded by Viscount Haldane in *Lennard's Carrying Co Ltd v Asiatic Petroleum Ltd* [1915] AC 705 as developed into what is sometimes referred to as the organic theory, which seeks to identify the relevant organ of the company.

represent the company in discussions may effectively be the company.[38] The courts have also been prepared to use agency as a test for imputation.[39] This involves a determination that, for example, the bank or company, expressly or impliedly, authorised an individual, or for that matter another corporation, to receive communications on its behalf. In such circumstances the bank or other institution will not be able to deny that it had the relevant knowledge if it is proved that its agent in fact had it.

15.12   The Courts have accepted that in line with the general law of agency, a company as principal will be estopped from denying knowledge that it gave its agent actual, apparent or ostensible authority to receive from others. Where it was known or indeed, intended that the information would not be passed on or would be distorted the position would be different.[40] It is debatable the extent to which it is possible to aggregate the knowledge of two or more individuals and fix the company with this composite state of mind.[41] While some judges have come close to doing this in circumstances where it is clear that the company did act in fact improperly, the better view is that it is desirable to identify one individual who has a sufficient state of mind to justify the imposition of liability for receipt or assistance. As we have already seen in regard to the law of tort, knowledge will not generally be imputed where the agent or other fiduciary, such as a director, is defrauding the principal.[42] As Lord Philips observed on *Stone & Rolls Ltd v. Moore Stephens* '… it is contrary to common sense and justice to attribute to a principal knowledge of something that his agent would be anxious to conceal from him'.[43]

DIRECTORS' KNOWLEDGE

15.13   The question as to the comprehensiveness and depth of knowledge that a company has or can be taken to have as a result of one or more of its directors having the relevant information is of course, a wider issue than

---

38   See *El Ajou v Dollar Land Holdings Ltd* [1994] 2 All ER 685 but see *Man Nutzfahrzeuge AG v Freightliner Ltd* [2005] EWHC 2347. See also in regard to the position of those who influence the boards of companies at 2.39 *et seq* above.

39   See *El Ajou v Dollar Land Holdings Ltd* [1994] 2 All ER 685 and *Jafari-Fini v Skillglass* [2007] EWCA Civ 261.

40   The courts may be prepared, however, to be rather more robust where there is evidence that individuals have deliberately structured their activity to obscure what is afoot, *El Ajou v Dollar Land Holdings Ltd* [1994] 2 All ER 685 and see *Adams v R* [1995] 1 WLR 52.

41   See for example *London County Freehold & Leasehold Properties Ltd v Berkeley Property & Investment Co* [1941] 2 All ER 379.

42   See *Bilta (UK) Ltd v Nazir (No 2)* [2014] Ch 52. The principle is applicable to other types of liability than fraud see *Safeway Stores Ltd v Twigger* [2011] 2 All ER 841 and see the leading case of *Re Hampshire Land* [1896] 2 Ch 743. The exception does not, of course, apply in regard to the company's liability for the fraudulent acts of its directors or employees to third parties and seemingly cannot be relied upon in regard to allegations against its auditors, see *Stone & Rolls Ltd v Moore Stephens* [2009] AC 1 1391, restrictively interpreted by the Court of Appeal in *Bilta (UK) Ltd v Nazir (No 2)* [2014] Ch 52. Where the company is essentially a one person company and is essentially being used as a 'engine of fraud' the exception will not apply, see *Berg, Sons & Co Ltd v Mervyn Hampton Adams* [2002] Ll Rep PN 41 cited with approval in *Stone & Rolls Ltd*, by Lord Phillips.

43   See above at note 42 and see also *Group Josi Re v Walbrook Insurance Co Ltd* [1996] 1 WLR 1152 at 1170 and *Belmont Finance Corporation Ltd v Williams Furniture Ltd* [1979] Ch 250 in which the Court of Appeal rejected the argument that the company could be considered a conspirator with two directors in regard to conduct which was illegal and detrimental to the company.

justifying liability for restitution to third parties. As we have seen, if in all cases a director's knowledge were attributed to the company, the company would not be in apposition to challenge the director for a failure in his duties to the company. The company would itself be tainted. Consequently, it is necessary to consider these issues from the standpoint of who the complainant is and what the relevance of knowledge is to that particular claim. The courts have accepted that not all knowledge that a director has can reasonably be attributed. Indeed, directors might reasonably forget information[44] or be under a duty not to disclose it, albeit this may result in a conflict of interest.[45] While directors and agents are under a duty to communicate relevant information to their company or principal, the courts have adopted a realistic approach and have been prepared to accept that this might not always be a duty that is properly discharged.[46]

15.14   Many of the issues that we have canvassed are complicated by the very nature of the separate personality of corporations. This is something we have already noted. Generally speaking the courts are reluctant to look behind incorporation and fix liability on those who stand behind a company, including other companies.[47] Having said this where incorporation is used to evade a duty of disclosure or facilitate a fraud including the drawing down of the proceeds of such[48] the courts are very prepared to look through to the reality.[49]

---

44   This will, however, be exceptional, see Arden LJ in *Real Estate Opportunities Ltd v Aberdeen Managers Ltd* [2008] 2 BCLC 116 and *El Ajou v Dollar Land Holdings Ltd* [1994] 2 All ER 685. There is also a question of timing. What if a director, with knowledge has ceased to be a director at the material time? Is it reasonable to impute knowledge over a period of time? In practice the court will examine the facts. Similar issues have arisen in the so called corporate opportunity cases, see Chapters 2 and 8 above where a director has left a company taking with him a maturing business opportunity.
45   See generally Chapter 8 above.
46   See *El Ajou v Dollar Land Holdings Ltd* [1994] 2 All ER 685. Where the agent is required to investigate and report on a matter then it will be presumed, vis à vis a third party that this has occurred justifying imputation. Of course, if a third party is aware that the information has not or will not be effectively communicated to the company or principle the position will be different, *Blackley v National Mutual Life Insurance* [1914] 3 KB 722. Where the duty to investigate is imposed directly on the company or principal, which might well be the case in the so called knowing receipt and assistance cases and an agent is instructed to discharge this duty then the knowledge of the agent will be imputed.
47   See the classic justifications in *Saloman v Saloman & Co* [1897] AC 422.
48   The courts while traditionally conservative have no problem in disregarding the corporate form where it has been invoked as part of a fraud or other crime. The use of an existing company, which has incurred obligations to others, is more problematic. The willingness of judges to look behind incorporation – lift the veil of incorporation, or effectively disregard it – pierce the veil, is not confined to fraud and crime, but extends to a much wider spectrum of obligations, see for example, Burton J in *Antonio Gramsci Shipping Corp v Stepanovs* [2011] EWHC 33 who held that there was 'no good reason of principle or jurisprudence why the victim cannot enforce the agreement against both the puppet company and the puppeteer who, all the time, was pulling the strings' and see also *Alliance Bank JSC v Aquanta Corporation* [2011] EWHC 3281 and the approach of Lord Denning in *Wallersteiner v Moir (No 2)* [1975] QB 373.
49   See *Prest v Petrodel Resources Ltd* [2013] UKSC 34 and *VTB Capital plc v Nuteitek International Corporation* [2013] UKSC 5. In *Prest* at paragraph 35, Lord Sumption stated: 'There is a limited principle in English law which applies when a person is under an existing legal obligation or liability or subject to an existing legal restriction which he deliberately evades or whose enforcement he deliberately frustrates by interposing a company under his control. The court may then pierce the corporate veil for the purpose, and only for the purpose, of depriving the company or its controller of the advantage that they would otherwise have obtained by the company's separate legal personality.'

FINANCIAL SERVICES REGULATION AND CONTROL LIABILITY

15.15 This part of the chapter will examine issues concerned with accountability and liability under the regulatory system for those persons involved in the control and management of firms authorised to carry on regulated investment business in the United Kingdom. As a matter of policy, the regulatory system seeks to hold to account those persons in senior management positions that effectively direct the affairs of an authorised business. A series of business failures in the 1990s heightened the desire to ensure that the regulatory system did not allow for senior management to avoid personal responsibility for organisational failure and at the same time allow for them to merely move to another regulated financial services business following the failure and possible collapse of their former employer. Following the collapse of Barings Bank in 1995 the Securities and Futures Authority experienced press criticism for its dealings with senior management at the Bank.[50] Although many of the agencies regulating financial services business prior to the coming into force of the Financial Services and Markets Act 2000 (FSMA) introduced rules and arrangements to ensure that senior personnel within firms they regulated could be subject to personal discipline, the FSMA introduced into law a statutory system of regulatory approval and as a consequence liability for persons holding 'controlled functions'. Subsequently and following the banking crisis, the significance of accountability along with the complexities associated with liability for those persons holding control in relation to banking was emphasised by the Parliamentary Commission on Banking Standards as follows:

> 'The complex structure and diverse activities of many large banks obscured senior executives' understanding of what was really going on in the businesses they were supposedly running. When conduct and risk failures came to light, this ignorance allowed many leaders to profess their shock at what had been happening, duck personal accountability and instead blame systems failures or rogue individuals. Many banks had a structure of cross-cutting functions and committees which meant that key decisions and risks were not owned by single executives but were shared, undermining a sense of individual responsibility.'[51]

15.16 Regulatory discipline against those that control the affairs of an authorised person (such as its senior executives) is not always straightforward and regulatory misconduct within an authorised firm may not necessarily give rise to liability for those in control, unless it can be shown in accordance with evidential standards, that the persons in control are in breach of the regulatory obligation they are obliged to meet (such as those set out with the FS Handbook's Approved Persons Code (APER)). The Financial Services Authority (FSA) attempt to discipline John Pottage, the Chief Executive Officer of the wealth management businesses of UBS AG and UBA Wealth Management (UK) Limited (collectively referred to as UBS), for failing to take reasonable steps to ensure UBS complied with regulatory requirements failed. In a decision of

---

50 Anthony Hilton, 'SFA backing off over the Barings accused' *The Evening Standard* (London: 10 December 1996) City Comment 33.
51 Parliamentary Commission on Banking Standards *Changing Banking for Good* Fifth report Volume II, Chapters 1-11 [94].

the Upper Tribunal following a reference by Mr Pottage, Sir Stephen Oliver judge of the Upper Tribunal stated:[52]

> 'Our views of the evidence as a whole and of those points in particular have led us to the conclusion that the FSA has not established its case that Mr Pottage had committed misconduct. There were, as we have found in Part II of this Decision, and as UBS AG have in some respects admitted, failings in the Firm's compliance with relevant standards of the regulatory system (see APER 4.7.3E). The FSA has not satisfied us however from the evidence as a whole that Mr Pottage's standard of conduct was "below that which would be reasonable in all the circumstances" (see APER 3.1.4G). In particular we are not satisfied that his failure to institute a Systematic Overhaul at an earlier date (than when the LORR was initiated) was beyond the bounds of reasonableness. Put positively, we think that the actions that Mr Pottage in fact took prior to July 2007 to deal with the operational and compliance issues as they arose were reasonable steps.'

15.17   Not all issues relating to senior management responsibility necessarily results in formal regulatory proceedings and indeed what may be described as extended regulatory influence can and has resulted in criticism of senior management. Illustrating the extent to which external accountability can operate, following the FSA's first enforcement case relating to the manipulation of LIDOR,[53] the UK Treasury Select Committee heard in evidence from the then Chairman of the FSA, Lord Turner and the then Governor of the Bank of England, Sir Mervyn King, of the existence of concerns about the senior management at Barclays.[54] Shortly after there followed a series of resignations from Barclays senior management, including its Chief Executive Officer, Mr Bob Diamond.

15.18   It would be erroneous to assume, that control of a financial services business is exercised only by the directors and senior management within the firm. An organisation's business activity can be influenced significantly by those that own or control the business capital, such as a limited company's shareholders. Indeed it is the case that when considering issues relating to regulatory control liability and accountability that one has to consider the statutory system for authorisation within FSMA and the consideration it requires for both the owners in influencers of would be authorised persons as well as those persons that work as its directors and senior managers.

Control liability and misleading the FCA and PRA

15.19   FSMA, as we have seen in Chapter 6, makes provision for a small number of what might be classified as regulatory disclosure offences, which if committed by a corporate body or partnership may in defined circumstances expose the directors, officers or partners of the company or partnership to prosecution. It is an offence under section 398 of the FSMA[55] for a person when complying with a requirement under FSMA to knowingly or recklessly give the Prudential Regulation Authority (PRA) or FCA false or misleading information. Section 398 does however limit the offence to where the false

---

52   *John Pottage v The Financial Services Authority* [2012] Upper Tribunal (Tax and Chancery Chamber) Financial Services. FS/2010/33.
53   FSA Final Notice, *Barclays Bank plc* 27 June 2012.
54   'Barclays sailed close to the wind, Bank governor says', BBC News, 17 July 2012, http://www.bbc.co.uk/news/business-18870461.
55   Section 398 was amended by s 36 of the Financial Services Act 2012.

or misleading information is material. Section 400 of the FSMA[56] expressly extends liability for an offence under section 398 to directors, officers or partners where the offence was committed with the 'consent' or' connivance' of the officer or partner or 'attributable to any neglect on his part'. Liability for the section 398 disclosure offence may conceivably arise in any case where a firm is required under FSMA to inform or disclosure information to the FCA or PRA, such as in applications for authorisation or variations to business permissions, applications for approval to perform a controlled function, and disclosures or notification of information, such as where an authorised firm is required to disclose information pursuant to an obligation under Principle 11. Of particular interest is whether the section 398 offence can committed in connection with information that is omitted from a disclosure.

15.20   In *R v Vijay Sharma*[57] the defendant pleaded guilty to charges under sections 178(1) and 191 of the FSMA for failing to give the FSA prior notice of his taking a controlling interest in an authorised firm as well as a charge under section 398 of the FSMA of making false and misleading statements to the FSA by virtue of him failing to disclose information that the FSA considered material to 'an assessment of whether he was fit and proper to acquire control'.[58] In a press release following the case, the FSA's then Director of Enforcement, Margaret Cole, drew attention to the nature of the misleading disclosure, saying:

'… This was made worse by the false and misleading statements he made in his applications to the FSA about the control change and his former employment in the financial services industry …'[59]

CONTROL LIABILITY AND AUTHORISATION

15.21   Schedule 6 to the FSMA sets out the threshold conditions that must be satisfied by applicant authorised firms in order to be granted authorisation by the PRA or FCA and, once authorised, they must continue to meet. In respect of conduct-related matters, three of the conditions are of direct relevance to the question of the capability of those that control the authorised firm. Guidance on the matters that will be considered for the assessment of the Threshold Conditions are provided in the FS handbook at 'COND' including matters such as: the 'effective supervision' which deals with, amongst other things, the extent to which the applicant for authorisation may be influenced by other members of its Group of companies and persons with whom it has 'close links'. Both of these may be considered in terms of persons that control the authorised firm; suitability of the applicant firm and thirdly its resources, which covers both financial and non-financial resources. Paragraph 1A(2) of Schedule 6 to the FSMA defines non-financial resource as including matters such as systems and controls and human resource. A number of these threshold conditions take into account the nature and extent of persons that have 'control' of or are

---

56 Section 400 was amended by s 37 of the Financial Services Act 2012.

57 *R v Vijay Sharma* [2009] (Unreported) City of Westminster Magistrates Court.

58 Note 57, Witness Statement in the case of *R v Sharma*, Graeme Ashley-Fenn, FSA Director of Permissions, Reporting and Decisions [para 2] http://www.fsa.gov.uk/pages/Library/Communication/PR/2009/120.shtml.

59 FSA press release, 'Mortgage Broker fined by Court in FSA's first criminal prosecution for change of control failures' FSA/PN/120/2009. 10 September 2009 http://www.fsa.gov.uk/pages/Library/Communication/PR/2009/120.shtml.

connected with the applicant, and thus allow the FCA or PRA to consider whether such control of connection impacts on a decision to authorise the firm. For example, in relation to the suitability condition at paragraph 2E of Schedule 6 to the FSMA, the decision to authorise an applicant will have regard to matters such as the applicant's 'connection with any person' and 'whether those who manage [the applicants] affairs have adequate skill and experience and act with probity'. The FCA provides specific guidance on the type of matters it will take into account when considering the persons connected with it such as (COND 2.5.6G) the connected person's antecedents including whether the connected person has ever been in contravention of financial services regulation.

15.22   In regard to an authorised person's non-financial resources, the threshold conditions seek to consider whether these are 'sufficient'. Paragraph 2D(4) of Schedule 6 to the FSMA, (for firms which do not carry on PRA regulated activity) provides:

'The matters which are relevant in determining whether A has appropriate non-financial resources include –

(a)   the skills and experience of those who manage A's affairs;

(b)   whether A's non-financial resources are sufficient to enable A to comply with –

   (i)   requirements imposed or likely to be imposed on A by the FCA in the course of the exercise of its functions;

   (ii)   any other requirement in relation to whose contravention the FCA would be the appropriate regulator for the purposes of any provision of Part 14 of this Act.'

Controllers

15.23   The Effective Supervision Threshold Condition set out at paragraph 2C of Schedule 6 (for non PRA activity) and paragraph 3B of Sch 6 (for PRA activity) requires the FCA to consider the extent to which persons that 'control' or have close links with the authorised firm. Both paragraphs 2C and 3B define 'close link' in consistent terms The definition taken from paragraph 2B is:

'A [the authorised firm] *has close links with CL* [The close link] *if –*

(a)   CL is a parent undertaking of A;

(b)   CL is a subsidiary undertaking of A;

(c)   CL is a parent undertaking of a subsidiary undertaking of A;

(d)   CL is a subsidiary undertaking of a parent undertaking of A;

(e)   CL owns or controls 20% or more of the voting rights or capital of A; or

(f)   A owns or controls 20% or more of the voting rights or capital of CL.'

APPROVED PERSONS

15.24   The 'approved person' regime is a necessary tool to ensure accountability, impose liability and responsibility and in extreme cases restrict access to the regulated financial services markets only those persons that are considered fit and proper. However, large elements of the regime are concerned with articulating the standards of behaviour expected of approved persons and thus arguably are directed at preventing regulatory problems from occurring.

15.25 Part V of the FSMA sets out a statutory regime for the approval of persons performing 'controlled functions' including provisions for their approval, the setting of a statement of conduct and disciplinary powers in the event of misconduct (amendments made by the Financial Services (Banking and Reform) Act 2013, make a number of modifications to Part V of the FSMA, which will be touched upon further below. At this juncture, it is important to highlight that provisions in section 56 of the FSMA extend to all persons performing regulatory activity and not merely approved persons, thus allowing for the FCA to prohibit any person from performing regulated activity where it considers the person is not fit and proper.

15.26 Section 66 of the FSMA sets out the FCA's disciplinary powers in regards to persons covered by Pt V of the FSMA, providing in section 66(1) that it may take action where the person is '… guilty of misconduct' and '… it is appropriate in all the circumstances to take action against him'. Section 66(2) goes on to describe when a person is guilty of misconduct and identifies two instances while the person is an approved person, namely (a) a failure 'to comply with a statement of principle issued under section 64' (which will be examined further in this chapter), or (b) being, 'knowingly concerned in a contravention by the relevant authorised person of a requirement imposed on that authorised person by or under this Act …'.

15.27 An example of section 66(2) being used to address issues of being knowingly concerned (albeit not in connection with a case of market abuse) is found in the Final Notice on March 2013 to Mr Tidjane Thiam, the then Chief Executive Officer of the Prudential. Mr Thiam was censured by the FCA for being knowingly concerned with the Prudential's failing to meet its obligation under High Level Principle for Business 11 to be open and cooperative with the FCA, arising from the Prudential's failure to inform the FCA of a proposed takeover.[60] In its press release following the notice, it was stated by Tracy McDermot, the FCA's then Director of Enforcement and Financial Crime, 'This case should send a clear message to all board members of their collective and individual responsibility for the decisions they make on behalf of their companies.'

15.28 Pursuant to section 66(3) where there has been misconduct the FCA may take the following types of action:

* impose a financial penalty;
* suspend approval from any control function;
* impose a limitation or restriction; or
* publish a statement concerning the misconduct.[61]

Fitness and properness

15.29 Guidance on the matters considered when assessing whether a person is fit and proper is set out in the FS handbook at 'FIT', and covers issue relating to the approved persons applicant's antecedents as well as their competence.

---

60 FCA Final Notice, *Mr Cheick Tidjane Thiam* 27 March 2013. See also FCA Final Notice *The Prudential Assurance Company Limited* 27 March 2013 and FCA Final Notice *Prudential plc* 27 March 2013.
61 Analysis of the FCA approach to enforcement is provided in Chapter 12.

15.30   The FCA rules at the Supervision provisions of the FS Handbook (referred to as 'SUP') provides at SUP 10A.4 an exhaustive list of the controlled functions referred to in section 60 of the FSMA. The applicability of individual controlled functions to different types of authorised firms is provided at SUP 10A.1R and it is important to note that not all of the functions are applicable to every class of authorised firm. The range of controlled functions is divided into 'significant influence functions' and 'customer-dealing functions'. The significant influence functions, which as is further examined below, carrying increased responsibility under the approved persons code and are divided into 'governing functions' (such as executive and non-executive directors, chief executive), 'required functions' (such as the compliance oversight function and money laundering reporting function, 'systems and controls function' and 'significant management function' all four of which are collectively referred to as 'significant influence functions').

The Approved Person Code and its impact

15.31   The FCA's approved person code (referred to as 'APER') and its accompanying guidance sets out seven high-level Statements of Principle designed to address the obligations of those approved to undertake controlled functions. Principles 5, 6 and 7 of the code apply to 'significant influence' approved persons. Analysis of these significance influence principles reveal that they are aimed at embedding individual responsibility for the organisation and management of the firm's business, unlike Principles 1–4 which arguably will apply to more generic behaviour not limited to what a person does as a significant influence function holder. By way of illustration, Statement of Principle 1 provides that 'An Approved Person must act with integrity in carrying out his accountable function'. In guidance to APER at APER 4.1. the FCA indicates (and of relevance to issues concerning market abuse) that it considers that behavioural activity includes matters such as 'falsifying documents', 'mismarking the value of investments or trading positions', 'failing to disclose dealings where disclosure is required by the firm's personal account dealing rules', and 'deliberately misusing the assets or confidential information of a client or of his firm'. Whereas Principle 7 addresses responsibility for the firms regulatory obligations and provides: 'An approved person performing an accountable significant influence function must take reasonable steps to ensure that the business of the firm for which he is responsible in his accountable function complies with the relevant requirements and standards of the regulatory system.' In the APER guidance to Principle 7 at APER 4.7 the FCA indicates (and once again of relevance to market abuse issues) that a person will not comply with Principle 7 where there is a: 'Failing to take reasonable steps to implement (either personally or through a compliance department or other departments) adequate and appropriate systems of control to comply with the relevant requirements and standards of the regulatory system in respect of the regulated activities of the firm in question.' Indeed guidance at APER addresses the expected behavioural standards of both the Compliance Officer (see APER 4.7.10E) and Money Laundering Reporting officer (see APER 4.7.9E) by reference to how the FCA expects those persons to how they meet the systems and controls obligations referred to in SYSC. Thus for example APER 4.7.10E provides, 'In the case of an approved person performing a significant influence function responsible for compliance under SYSC 3.2.8 R, SYSC 6.1.4 R or SYSC 6.1.4A R, failing to take reasonable steps to ensure that appropriate compliance systems and procedures are in place falls within APER 4.7.2A E… [APER 4.7.2A being the FCA's opinion on the type of behaviour that is non-compliant with APER Principle 7].' There is no doubt that FCA does instate enforcement proceedings by reference to APER 7, including instances of senior personnel of firms engaged in manipulation. In its Final Notice of 22 January 2014 to David Caplin[62] the Chief Executive of Martins Brokers UK Limited, Mr Caplin agreed an administrative settlement resulting in a financial penalty of £210,000 and an FCA order prohibiting him from performing any significant influence function. The enforcement action against Mr Caplin was in connection with Martins having engaged in the manipulation of LIBOR[63] and was settled by reference to APER Principle 7. In particular the FCA referred in the Final Notice to Mr Caplin failing to 'ensure the timely and adequate implementation of recommendations made … to carry out a risk review', and 'to identify and remedy Martins' lack of controls to prevent Brokers making or receiving corrupt inducements'.

LIABILITY WHEN ACTING WITHOUT APPROVAL

15.32 Although so far we have examined the liability that attaches to persons that are approved to perform a controlled function, provisions addressing persons that perform such 'functions without approval should not be overlooked. Section 63A of the FSMA provides the FCA and PRA with power to impose a financial penalty on such persons regardless of whether or not there has been any underlying misconduct, where they 'knew or could have reasonably been expected to have known that [they] were performing a controlled function without approval'. Indeed such 'unapproved performance may in extreme cases be such that the FCA may consider exercising its powers under section 56 to prohibit that person from performing'.

SIGNIFICANT MANAGEMENT REGIME AND CERTIFIED PERSONS

15.33 Hitherto in this chapter we have given consideration to the regimes for approved persons as well as others that have control authorised persons. Following recommendations made by the Parliamentary Commission on Banking Standards in relation to conduct in the banking sector,[64] significant change to the approved persons regime set out in Part 4 of the Financial Services (Banking Reform) Act 2013 will come into force on 7 March 2016,[65] including amendments to the FSMA, section 66A definition of misconduct, introducing a presumption of responsibility through what has been referred to as a reverse burden of proof.[66] The regime is applicable to persons working

---

62 FCA Final Notice *David Caplin* 22 January 2015. See also FCA Final Notice *Jeremy Kraft* 22 January 2015. Mr Kraft had been Martins Brokers UK Ltd Compliance Oversight Approved Person (CF10).

63 FCA Final Notice *Martins Brokers UK Limited*.

64 Parliamentary Commission on Banking Standards, *Changing Banking for Good* (HL 27, HC 175) 19 June 2013.

65 *Strengthening Individual Accountability in Banking and Insurance* – response to CP14/14 and CP 26/14. The Prudential Regulation Authority. March 2015 http://www.bankofengland. co.uk/pra/Documents/publications/ps/2015/ps315.pdf.

66 Financial Services (Banking Reform Act) 2013, s 32 which amends s 66A of the FSMA.

in firms authorised by the PRA, classified as senior managers and those that subject to firm based certification that are classified as performing 'significant harm' functions. Under the new regime, senior managers will be subject to regulatory approval; however, PRA firms will be required to ensure that these persons have assigned to them the major responsibilities for the management of the firm and that their fitness to perform the activity of senior managers is reviewed regularly. The regime for certified persons whilst not subjecting those persons to regulatory approval requires that firm assess the fitness and competence of those persons. Despite the imminent implementation of this new regime, the Government introduced into Parliament the Bank of England and Financial Services Bill on 14 October 2015 and HM Treasury on 15 October announced that the senior managers and certified persons regime would be extended to all regulated financial services sectors and that, at the same time, it intended to reform the regime that was in the process of implementation, including replacing the reverse burden of proof provisions with a statutory duty or responsibility for all senior managers. In response to HM Treasury's announcement, Tracy McDermot, Acting Chief Executive of the FCA said:[67]

> 'Extending the Senior Managers' and Certification Regime is an important step in embedding a culture of personal responsibility throughout the financial services industry ...

> While the presumption of responsibility could have been helpful, it was never a panacea. There has been significant industry focus on this one, small element of the reforms, which risked distracting senior management within firms from implementing both the letter and spirit of the regime ...'

As a result, the Treasury has amended the FSMA, s 66A definition of misconduct to ensure that the PRA or FCA would have the burden of proving that a senior manager did not take reasonable steps to stop a breach.

15.34   Under the Federal Deposit Insurance Corporation Act of 1991 ('the FDIC Act 1991'), US bank regulators and prosecutors can bring cases against individuals – senior and mid-level – for failure to meet their duties. For example, the FDIC Act 1991 authorises regulators to bring civil lawsuits against former directors and officers of a failed bank for a demonstrated failure to satisfy the duties of loyalty and care. The degree of protection afforded to directors of failed banks by the FDIC under the business judgment rule has often been the subject of litigation. Similarly, Title II of the Dodd-Frank Act 2010 provides that in the event of a receivership of a large financial institution, the Orderly Liquidation Authority can impose personal liability on directors and officers in a civil action brought by the FDIC for gross negligence or conduct that demonstrates a greater disregard of a duty of care than gross negligence, including intentional tortious conduct. Furthermore, under clawback provisions, the FDIC is authorised to recover incentive payment and other compensation from directors and senior executives for the two years prior to the company's failure if they are found to be substantially responsible for the failure. Moreover, the Securities and Exchange Commission recently proposed a rule to implement s 954 of the Dodd-Frank Act that would, among other provisions, require listed issuers, including but not limited to banks, to

---

67   Financial Conduct Authority Press Release, Statement from the Financial Conduct Authority following the announcement by HM Treasury of changes to the Senior Managers' Regime. 15 October 2015 http://www.fca.org.uk/news/hm-treasury-changes-to-the-senior-managers-regime.

develop, implement, and disclose policies requiring clawback of 'erroneously awarded compensation' in the event of an accounting restatement.[68]

15.35   US banking regulators can dismiss employees as part of enforcement actions against regulated institutions and can take enforcement actions against directors and officers (and other so-called 'institution-affiliated parties') for violations of laws, breach of fiduciary duties, and unsafe and unsound practices. For example, the Federal Reserve bank regulation division can remove any officer, director, or employee of a foreign banking organisation involved in its US branch or other operations upon a finding of improper conduct or as a result of being convicted of certain criminal offences.

15.36   Despite strong US regulatory and enforcement powers, the US business judgment rule presumption generally affords directors and officers protection from personal liability for prudent, informed business decisions made in good faith. As in the UK and other European jurisdictions, directors and officers generally obtain protection from personal liability through indemnification agreements and directors and officers liability insurance in the absence of bad faith or malfeasance, but such protections are limited in certain circumstances by law and regulation.

---

68   See discussion in Shearman & Sterling LLP, 'SEC Proposes Highly Anticipated Clawback Rules' (9 July 2015) (on file with author). Specifically, issuers would be required to recover incentive-based compensation received by any executive officer in the three years prior to a material restatement of the issuer's financial statements that is in excess of the compensation that would have been received if the compensation had been determined based on the restated financial statements. The clawback would be required regardless of the reason for the restatement, ie not limited to restatements required because of misconduct, and including restatements that are required because of no-fault computational errors.

Chapter 16

The impact of other laws: domestic and overseas

INTRODUCTION

16.1   The globalisation of financial markets has resulted in increased interaction among securities firms and investors in different jurisdictions. The securities and derivatives markets underpin economic growth and development and the overall strength of market economies by, for example, supporting corporate initiatives, providing finance for new ideas and facilitating the management of financial risk. Sound and effective regulation can, in turn, enhance market confidence and the integrity and development of securities markets. Increasingly, globalised and integrated securities markets pose significant challenges for regulators. Share transactions are increasingly international in character. In global and integrated securities markets, national regulators must be able to monitor and assess cross-border conduct if they are to ensure the integrity, efficiency, and transparency of their domestic markets.

16.2   Globalised securities and derivatives markets have led to increasing interdependence amongst national regulators. Accordingly, there must be strong cooperation and coordination between regulators and capability to give effect to those links. Cross-border trading in securities has caused a great deal of overlap in the regulatory responsibilities of national regulators and, in some instances, where economically powerful countries (eg the United States) impose their regulations extra-territorially, it can result in a diminution in sovereignty of affected nation states. Indeed, the world's largest and most liquid securities and derivatives market is the United States and many non-US companies are subject to extra-territorial jurisdiction under US securities and banking laws because of their contacts with US commerce and financial markets. This chapter discusses some of the issues of institutional coordination in the EU/EEA in applying the Market Abuse Directive and examines the extraterritorial aspects of US anti-fraud law for insider dealing and market manipulation under the US securities laws. This chapter also analyses emerging international standards and principles to control insider dealing and market abuse in an international context. These international standards, principles and rules that relate to market abuse and insider dealing have been promulgated by the world's leading international body of securities regulators, the International Organisation of Securities Commissions (IOSCO). IOSCO

383

has adopted international standards and principles to protect investors against market abuse and has set out standards for national regulators to use while investigating and prosecuting those who attempt to use unlawful means to manipulate securities markets.[1]

16.3   The barriers to a global securities market are diminishing: financial information has become inexpensive to obtain and advances in technology allow more complicated cross-border share transactions. Ultimately, the forces of liberalisation and technology will link most financial markets with the result that regulators should develop improved regulatory links to improve the effectiveness and efficiency of their financial markets. More efficient cross-border enforcement necessitates bilateral and multilateral agreements between national regulatory authorities that allocate jurisdictional authority amongst regulators so that they can have the capacity to investigate and enforce market abuse that occurs on a cross-border basis.

IMPACT OF EU LAW ON MARKET ABUSE AND COOPERATION IN INVESTIGATIONS AND ENFORCEMENT

16.4   The European Union has adopted the policy objective of financial integration for EU financial markets. To this end, the EU Council and Parliament approved in June 2001 the Financial Services Action Plan (FSAP) that contained 42 legislative measures which have been adopted and implemented by all EEA/EU states.[2] The Market Abuse Directive 2003 was one of these legislative measures that required all EEA states to adopt a civil offence for insider dealing and market manipulation.[3] The Market Abuse Directive required EEA states to create a single regulatory authority for investigations and enforcement which must serve as a point of contact with other EEA regulators for coordinating cross-border surveillance, investigations and enforcement in cases involving cross-border elements between EEA states. Moreover, the Market Abuse Directive required all home state authorities to keep records of all transactions, ie the number of instruments bought and sold and the dates, times and transaction prices. The home state is obliged to exchange this information upon request with host state regulators during investigations of financial service firms based in other EEA states who are operating in the host jurisdiction. Host state authorities continue to be responsible for supervising

---

1   IOSCO Mutilateral Memorandum of Understanding (May 2002), Article 4(a) (describing the MOU's application to national laws and regulations dealing with insider dealing, market abuse and securities fraud). The IOSCO standards are important for understanding how the FSA may interpret the UK market abuse regime and how EEA states may implement these principles in their regulatory practices.

2   The FSAP sets out a policy agenda to achieve a common European market in financial services. See European Commission, 'Financial Services: Implementing the Framework for Financial Markets: Action Plan' (1999) COM 232 (11 May 1999), p 23.

3   See the Directive on Insider Dealing and Market Manipulation ('Market Abuse Directive') (2003/6/EC). The Criminal Justice Act 1993, Pt V, implemented the requirement of Council Directive 89/552 that all Member States of the EU adopt laws creating a criminal offence of insider dealing for natural persons. See 89/552/EEC (13 November 1989) (OJ L 334, 18.11, 1989, p 30). The Market Abuse Directive replaced the Insider Trading Directive 1989. The Market Abuse Regulation 2014 (EU MAR) replaces the Market Abuse Directive as the applicable EU legislation governing the civil offence of market abuse.

and regulating all firms and persons operating within host state territory for conduct of business-related issues.[4]

16.5   As discussed in 4.47–4.50 above, the Market Abuse Regulation (EU MAR) and the Market Abuse Directive 2 (MAD 2) were adopted by the European Parliament and Council in July 2014. EU MAR and MAD 2 replace MAD 1 and require Member States to adopt implementing legislation to comply with it by July 2016.[5] EU MAR extends the scope of the civil offence of market abuse to all OTC derivatives instruments traded on EU multilateral trading facilities and organised trading facilities, even if the referenced assets are not traded on regulated markets. MAD 2 imposes an obligation on all Member States to create criminal sanctions for market abuse[6] and requires the harmonisation of administrative and civil sanctions across Member States. As with MAD 1,[7] MAD 2 requires EEA competent authorities – both home and host state – to facilitate transnational investigations and enforcement of market abuse laws and regulations in the following way. If a financial firm with a passport from another EEA state is suspected or found to have violated market abuse laws, the host state regulator must take the following steps in order to address the breach: (a) approach the firm's home state regulator to seek assistance in conducting an investigation, and then (b) to co-operate with the home state regulator regarding any enforcement action. Generally, the host state must take all appropriate measures at its disposal to end the violation and to adopt measured procedures in seeking cooperation and information before undertaking direct enforcement. Officials of the home and host state competent authorities are bound by professional secrecy in respect of proprietary information they obtain from individuals or regulated entities during the course of their duties. These restrictions on disclosure of proprietary and other confidential information, however, are qualified to allow home and host state authorities to provide mutual assistance in conducting oversight, investigations and enforcement. Under MAR, these principles and obligations between home and host states are maintained and enhanced.

16.6   The EU MAR and MAD 2 incorporate the provisions of MAD 1 that allow Member States to enter into mutual assistance agreements with third countries (eg countries outside the EEA) so long as the information exchanged is covered by guarantees of secrecy equivalent to those provided in Article 25 of MAD 1. The UK has entered into many mutual assistance agreements and memoranda of understanding (MOU) with countries outside the EEA that provide for the exchange of information and evidence to support investigations and enforcement actions by national authorities. For instance, the UK–US 1986 MOU[8] is a non-binding statement of principles and procedures for making requests for information in regard to investigations and enforcement actions in

---

4   The Market Abuse Directive provides that the 'competent regulatory authority' may periodically require all investment firms with branches or agency offices in their jurisdictions to report on their activities and to provide all information necessary for monitoring their compliance with the Market Abuse Directive.

5   Directive 2003/6/EC (MAD 1).

6   Council Directive 2014/57/EU of 16 April 2014 on criminal sanctions for market abuse (Market Abuse Directive) [2014] OJ L 173/179 (**MAD 2**).

7   European Communities Directive on Insider Dealing and Market Manipulation (Market Abuse), Articles 6–10 (encouraging cooperation in enforcement matters by allowing national regulators to obtain necessary information).

8   The relevant agencies today would be the US Securities and Exchange Commission and the Commodities and Futures Trading Commission and the UK Financial Conduct Authority and the Serious Fraud Office.

regard to alleged breaches of securities laws. Each national authority retains discretion whether to cooperate in the disclosure of requested information.[9] The UK–US MOU covers insider dealing, misrepresentations in the course of dealing and market manipulation and it applies to securities or futures traded within the territorial jurisdiction of each regulatory authority.[10] The impact of EU law and mutual assistance agreements has been substantial in requiring UK authorities to take account of international developments in financial regulation and to adopt practices that are similar to those taken by other regulatory authorities. Conflicts occur, however, when the laws of some jurisdictions are imposed unilaterally and in an extra-territorial manner without the consent of UK authorities. This has become a major issue in regard to the extra-territorial application of US insider trading and market manipulation laws as discussed below.

16.7   The Market Abuse Directive established a viable institutional and legal framework to enhance investor confidence and market integrity that has gone beyond enhancing 'co-operation between supervisors' by establishing a more common approach to detection and investigation as well as to enforcement'.[11] Nevertheless, many EU national regulators agree that there should be more harmonisation regarding the standards of market practice enforced across Member States and in the criteria used to decide whether to investigate and enforce, and in the type and level of sanctions applied, market abuse laws.[12] The European Securities and Markets Authority (ESMA) have been tasked by the European Commission with adopting regulatory implementing standards and technical implementing standards to give effect to the EU MAR and Market Abuse Directive 2. ESMA will play a crucial role in devising more harmonised approaches for EEA competent authorities to implement the MAR and MAD 2.

EXTRA-TERRITORIAL APPLICATION OF US SECURITIES LAWS, FOREIGN ISSUERS AND ANTI-FRAUD PROVISIONS

16.8   This section addresses the extra-territoriality of US securities laws in the context of how the anti-fraud provisions apply to foreign issuers and to transactions involving activities that take place, in part, in non-US territories. The extraterritorial dimension of US anti-fraud law merits discussion because of the close links between US and UK securities markets. US securities laws can expose UK persons and other non-US persons to civil and criminal

---

9   For example, the UK Secretary of State may deny requests for cooperation on the grounds of public interest.

10   Paragraph 11 of the MOU provides for spontaneous provision of information by one agency to another.

11   For instance, the Market Abuse Directive sets 'common disciplines for trading floors to enhance investor confidence in an embryonic single securities market'. See also FESCO, 'Market Abuse: FESCO's Response to the Call for Views from the Securities Regulators Under the EU's Action Plan for Financial Services' (1999) COM 232 (29 June 2000).

12   The Committee of European Securities Regulators (CESR) recognised the importance of promoting more harmonised regulation and supervisory practices in a report that called for the establishment of an EU securities regulatory framework. See the initial report of the 'Committee of Wise Men' on the regulation of the European securities markets (9 November 2000), pp 26, 35 and Annex 1. CESR was created based on recommendations of the Lamfalussy Committee in 2000, which were adopted by the EU Council and Parliament.

liability for insider dealing and market manipulation. Most US case law addressing the extra-territorial application of US securities laws focuses on the anti-fraud provisions of the Securities and Exchange Act 1934.[13] The courts have developed two tests for determining subject matter jurisdiction in civil securities fraud cases. One test relies on the 'effects test' that assesses the effects in the United States of conduct that occurs in foreign countries, while the other focuses on the 'conduct' of foreign persons within the United States. Under the Dodd Frank Act, the Exchange Act now provides that the courts have jurisdiction over actions by the Securities and Exchange Commission (SEC) or Department of Justice (DOJ) involving '(1) conduct within the United States that constitutes significant steps in furtherance of the violation, even if the securities transaction occurs outside the United States and involves only foreign investors; or (2) conduct occurring outside the United States that has a foreseeable substantial effect within the United States.'[14] Regarding the 'conduct' test, the Dodd-Frank Act extends extraterritorial jurisdiction beyond that applied by the US Supreme Court in *Morrison v National Australia Bank*.[15]

Anti-fraud provisions of the US Securities and Exchange Act 1934, section 10(b)

16.9 Section 10(b) of the Securities and Exchange Act 1934 makes it unlawful, *inter alia*, to use or employ any manipulative or deceptive device or contrivance 'in connection with the purchase or sale of any security'. Moreover, section 27 of the Act vests the district courts with jurisdiction of all actions 'to enforce any liability or duty created by this title or the rules and regulations thereunder'. The federal courts, therefore, have jurisdiction to enforce the provisions of section 10(b), while the SEC has authority under Rule 10b-5 to enforce section 10(b) as a regulatory offence. The federal circuit courts have interpreted the anti-fraud provisions to have extra-territorial effect in a number of circumstances. Generally, the courts apply alternative tests: the 'conduct' test or the 'effects' test.[16] Under the conduct test, the court has subject matter jurisdiction 'where conduct material to the completion of the fraud occurred in the United States'.[17] Mere preparatory activities and conduct far removed from the conduct of the fraud will not suffice;[18] rather, '[o]nly where conduct "within the United States directly caused" the loss will a district court have jurisdiction ...'. Essentially, jurisdiction exists when 'substantial acts in furtherance of the fraud were committed in the United States'.[19] The test is met whenever the defendant's activities in the US are more than 'merely preparatory' to a securities fraud committed abroad, and the 'activities or culpable failures to act within the United States "directly caused" the claimed losses'.[20]

16.10 Under the 'effects' test, the court has jurisdiction 'whenever a predominantly foreign transaction has substantial effects within the

13 15 USCA, s 78a et seq.
14 15 U.S.C. § 78aa(b).
15 561 U.S. 247, 130 S. Ct. 2869 (2010).
16 *Butte Mining plc v Smith* 76 F 3d 287 (9th Cir, 1996).
17 *United States v Vilar*, 729 F.3d 62 (2d Cir. 2013), *Morrison v National Australia Bank Ltd.* 561 U.S. 247, 130 S. Ct. 2869 (2010), *SEC v Berger* 322 F. 3d 187, 193 (2nd Cir, 2003); *Psimenos v E F Hutton & Co* 722 F 2d 1041, 1046 (2nd Cir, 1983).
18 *Psimenos v EF Hutton*, 722 F 2d at 1045.
19 *IIT v Vencap Ltd* 519 F.2d 1001, 1018 (2nd Cir 1975).
20 *Itoba Ltd v Lep Group PLC* 54 F.3d 118, 121–122 (2nd Cir 1995).

United States'.[21] Thus, remote or indirect effects in the United States do not confer subject matter jurisdiction.

The Second Circuit Court of Appeals held in *Schoenbaum v Firstbrook*[22] that extra-territorial jurisdiction could be imposed on a transaction involving securities issued by a foreign corporation that were listed on a US stock exchange and held by US citizens on the grounds that such a transaction affected US securities markets. The court found that extra-territorial subject matter jurisdiction was justified under the federal securities laws on the basis that the challenged foreign transaction had an 'effect' on domestic US securities markets. Similarly, the Ninth Circuit also found extra-territorial jurisdiction based on the 'effects' test[23] in a case involving a takeover of a Canadian corporation by a US corporation that involved the improper use of the US corporation's securities, which were registered and listed on a US national exchange and had adversely affected both the foreign plaintiffs and the US securities markets. Further, extra-territorial jurisdiction can be imposed on foreign actors who make misrepresentations to US investors in the sale of foreign securities that were only traded in foreign markets.[24] In this case, the Second Circuit premised jurisdiction upon domestic conduct and the direct effect on US investors. Therefore, the US courts will consider two factors in determining whether extraterritorial subject matter jurisdiction will be applied: (1) whether the wrongful conduct substantially occurred in the US; or (2) whether the wrongful conduct had a substantial effect in the US or upon US citizens, wherever they are located.[25] However, extra-territorial jurisdiction will not be conferred on a transaction or occurrence if its only connection to US territory are activities in the United States that are 'merely preparatory' to the actual fraud.[26]

16.11   The extra-territorial scope of the anti-fraud provisions also extends to the acts of a defendant based in the United States who perpetrates fraud upon non-US persons in a foreign country. The Second Circuit observed that the jurisdictional basis was sufficient in this case because Congress could not have intended 'to allow the United States to be used as a base for manufacturing fraudulent security devices for export, even when … peddled only to foreigners'.[27] Moreover, foreign nationals who are resident in the United States are protected to the same extent as US nationals so long as their claims arise at the time they are resident in the United States. This rule applies even though the fraudulent scheme is devised and set into motion abroad,[28] but a foreign corporation whose sole shareholder and chief executive officer was a foreigner

---

21   *Consolidated Gold Fields plc v Minorco SA* 871 F 2d 252, 261–262 (2nd Cir, 1989).
22   405 F 2d 200 (2nd Cir, 1968); cert denied 395 US 906 (1969).
23   *Des Brisay v Goldfield Corpn* 549 F 2d 133 (9th Cir, 1977).
24   *Leasco Data Processing Equipment v Maxwell* 468 F 2d 1326 (2nd Cir, 1972).
25   *Europe and Overseas Commodity Traders, SA v Banque Paribas London* 147 F.3d 118, 125 (2nd Cir 1998). But the effects test will not create extraterritorial subject matter jurisdiction over the federal securities claims of foreign investors against foreign persons if the wrongful conduct in question was predominantly foreign. See *In re Alstom SA*, 406 F. Supp. 2d 346 (2005).
26   *SEC v Berger* 322 F 3d at 193; *Zoelsch v Arthur Andersen & Co* 824 F 2d 27 (DC Cir, 1987); *Bersch v Drexel Firestone Inc* 519 F 2d 974 (2nd Cir, 1975).
27   *Consolidated Gold Fields plc v Minorco SA* 871 F 2d 252 (2nd Cir, 1989); see also *IIT v Vencap Ltd* 519 F 2d 1001, 1017 (2nd Cir, 1975); on remand 411 F Supp 1094 (SDNY, 1975).
28   *O'Driscoll v Merrill Lynch, Pierce, Fenner & Smith Inc* Fed Sec L Rep 99, 486 (SDNY, 1983).

residing in the United States was required to prove that losses incurred on account of the fraudulent scheme were directly caused by acts within the United States.[29] However, deception of a foreigner who is a sole shareholder within the United States, while necessary to demonstrate a fraudulent scheme, has thus been held insufficient proof of direct causation of loss.[30]

16.12 The Eighth Circuit imposed extra-territorial subject matter jurisdiction on foreign conduct that involved the use of the US telephone system and US mail to further a fraudulent scheme, even though the only victim of the fraud was a foreign corporation purchasing stock in another foreign company.[31] In this case, the foreign defendant sellers relied, in part, on the US telephone system and US mail fraudulently to induce foreign investors to purchase securities of a foreign company not listed on a US exchange. The court imposed extra-territorial jurisdiction, despite the fact that no transaction occurred in the United States nor involved US securities, by finding that the defendants' conduct (use of the US telephone and mail system) was significant – not 'merely preparatory' – and constituted a fraud devised and completed in the United States.[32]

16.13 The Second and Third Circuits have also upheld extra-territorial subject matter jurisdiction based on conduct in the United States that directly caused a foreign plaintiff's losses, even though the fraud had no direct effect on US securities markets or upon investors in the United States.[33] Therefore, foreigners purchasing securities in the United States are protected by US federal securities laws.[34] Jurisdiction, however, will not extend to conduct that is, at most, 'ancillary' or peripheral and therefore not the direct cause of the plaintiff's losses. The Second Circuit took this position in *Fidenas AG v Compagnie Internationale Pour L' informatique CII Honeywell Bull SA*,[35] when it denied extra-territorial jurisdiction to the claims of foreign investors against a foreign subsidiary that was wholly-owned by a US parent on the grounds that knowledge by the US parent of fraudulent conduct committed by its foreign subsidiary was insufficient US conduct. In a subsequent suit filed against the US parent for the same fraud, the court denied jurisdiction on the basis that mere knowledge of the fraud was insufficient to confer extra-territorial subject matter jurisdiction upon US courts. The court then relied on the Second Circuit's view that the transactions were 'predominantly foreign' and thereby dismissed the suit for failing to satisfy either the 'conduct' or 'effects' test for subject matter jurisdiction.

16.14 Similarly, the US District Court for the Southern District of New York applied the transaction test to deny extra-territorial subject matter jurisdiction in a case where the primary fraud and every fact essential to the plaintiff's claim of fraudulent misconduct was committed or occurred in Costa Rica.[36] The transaction was considered not to have had significant enough effects on US securities markets and the fraudulent conduct in question was ancillary to

---

29 *O'Driscoll v Merrill Lynch, Pierce, Fenner & Smith Inc* WL 1360, 1361 (1983).
30 Ibid.
31 *Continental Grain (Australia) Pty Ltd v Pacific Oilseeds Inc* 592 F 2d 409 (8th Cir, 1979).
32 *Continental Grain (Australia) Pty Ltd v Pacific Oilseeds Inc* at 420.
33 *SEC v Kasser* 548 F 2d 109 (3rd Cir, 1977); cert denied 431 US 938 (1977).
34 *IIT v Cornfeld* 619 F 2d 909, 918 (2nd Cir, 1980). See also *Arthur Lipper Corpn v SEC* 547F 2d 171 (2nd Cir, 1976); cert denied 434 US 1009 (1978).
35 606 F 2d 5 (2nd Cir, 1979).
36 *Mormels v Girofinance SA* 544 F Supp 815 (SDNY, 1982).

the US and was 'predominantly foreign'.[37] In addition, extra- territorial subject matter jurisdiction will not be conferred where US investors used circuitous means (by setting up an overseas shell corporation) in order to conceal their US nationality so that they could participate in a foreign public offering in which they purchased the non-US securities of a foreign corporation. The court held that the plaintiffs were estopped from bringing a claim under the US securities laws because they had gone to great efforts to avoid and evade the Act's requirements.[38]

Extraterritorial criminal liability for insider trading

16.15   In *United States v Vilar*, the Second Circuit extended the 'conduct test' to determine extraterritorial criminal liability for insider trading.[39] In *Vilar*, the Second Circuit applied the 'presumption against extraterritoriality' for civil liability cases to claims of criminal liability under Section 10(b) of the Securities Exchange Act. In doing so, the Second Circuit expressly extended the Supreme Court's 2010 decision in *Morrison v National Australia Bank Ltd.* – a civil case in which the Court barred federal fraud suits by foreign investors over foreign-traded securities – to criminal actions brought by the Department of Justice. Rejecting the government's argument that *Morrison* only applies to civil actions, the Second Circuit concluded that criminal and civil defendants alike can only be found liable under Section 10(b) if the fraud occurred in connection with 'a security listed on a U.S. exchange' or with 'a security purchased or sold in the United States'.

16.16   Because none of the securities at issue in *Vilar* were listed on an American exchange, the Second Circuit followed *Morrison* and questioned whether the securities transactions constituted a domestic purchase or sale of securities. The Second Circuit held that a securities transaction is considered domestic 'when the parties incur irrevocable liability to carry out the transaction within the United States or when title is passed in the United States'. The Second Circuit concluded that, because certain alleged victims entered into and renewed agreements in Puerto Rico and New York, a jury would have found that the defendants engaged in fraud in connection with a domestic purchase or sale of securities and upheld the defendants' convictions. By focusing on the nature of the securities transaction, the Second Circuit's analysis in *Vilar* materially limits the conduct that is susceptible to extraterritorial criminal liability, thereby limiting the applicability of the 'conduct test'.

Extraterritorial Jurisdiction and the Dodd Frank Act 2010

16.17   The Dodd-Frank Wall Street Reform and Consumer Protection Act 2010 contains certain provisions that amend the Exchange Act (and other securities laws) to acknowledge expressly the federal courts' extraterritorial reach when enforcing the federal securities laws. Under the Dodd Frank Act, the Exchange Act now provides that the courts have jurisdiction over actions by the SEC or DOJ involving: '(1) conduct within the United States that constitutes significant steps in furtherance of the violation, even if the

37   *Mormels v Girofinance SA.*
38   *MCG Inc v Great Western SA* 544 F Supp 815 (SDNY, 1982).
39   *United States v Vilar*, 729 F.3d 62 (2d Cir. 2013).

securities transaction occurs outside the United States and involves only foreign investors; or (2) conduct occurring outside the United States that has a foreseeable substantial effect within the United States.'[40] The Dodd Frank Act has arguably extended the extraterritorial reach of the 'conduct' test and thus supersedes *Vilar*'s more limited jurisdictional test, while reaffirming a robust application of the 'effects' test.

16.18   Based on the above cases and legislation, the following propositions can be made about the extra-territorial application of the anti-fraud provisions of the US securities laws:

• that jurisdiction will be conferred on acts of material importance that occur in a foreign country if such acts cause losses in the sale of securities to US resident investors in the United States;

• that jurisdiction will be conferred on acts of material importance that occur in the United States if they cause losses in the sale of securities to US residents abroad;

• that extraterritorial jurisdiction can apply to foreign persons so long as the wrongful conduct substantially occurred within the US; and

• that jurisdiction will *not* be conferred on transactions that result in losses in the sale of securities to foreigners outside US territory *unless* acts within the United States directly caused such losses.[41]

Reporting and disclosure requirements

16.19   The collapse of Enron and WorldCom in 2002 demonstrated the importance of accurate and non-misleading reporting by companies whose securities are listed on US exchanges and/or make public offerings to US investors. The jurisdictional scope of the US securities laws' disclosure and reporting requirements, however, are more narrowly defined. A foreign issuer's filing of misleading reports to the SEC will not of itself provide a sufficient jurisdictional basis to support a private right of action by foreign investors. This means that there will be no US jurisdiction over claims by foreign investors residing abroad against a foreign corporation for filing misleading reports with the SEC, even though the misrepresentations were contained in documents filed with the SEC and also were circulated in the US press.[42] In contrast, there will be US jurisdiction where a non-US national residing abroad brings an action against a foreign corporation for fraud in connection with the sale of US securities since some of the acts that were a part of the fraud occurred in the United States.[43] Jurisdiction will also extend to misrepresentations in a prospectus delivered outside US territory by a foreign corporation to foreign investors residing abroad if negotiations relating to the prospectus took place in US territory.[44] The Sarbanes-Oxley Act 2002 creates extraterritorial subject matter jurisdiction over a foreign issuer and its chief executive and chief financial officer for signing annual or quarterly reports that are materially incorrect which can lead to civil and criminal liability. Generally, however, the extra-territorial application of US securities law's reporting and disclosure requirements will not

---

40   15 U.S.C. § 78aa(b).
41   See *Bersch v Drexel Firestone Inc* 519 F 2d 974 at 993 (2nd Cir, 1975); cert denied 423 US 1018 (1975).
42   *Kaufman v Campeau Corpn* 744 F Supp 808 (SD Ohio, 1990) at 810–812.
43   *Kaufman v Campeau Corpn.*
44   *Alfadda v Fenn* 935 F 2d 475 (2nd Cir, 1991).

permit a foreign shareholder of a US-listed non-US company to bring a private right of action against the foreign company arising out of misrepresentations in a prospectus or other similar documents if the plaintiff cannot provide adequate proof of causation from acts that took place in the United States.

Foreign manipulation of US markets

16.20   The US government imposes criminal liability on non-US persons or business entities that are engaged in off-shore manipulations affecting US markets or US issuers.[45] The basis for such jurisdiction is the Securities and Exchange Act 1934, section 9(a) that prohibits 'any person' from using 'any means or instrumentality of interstate commerce' (including e-mails, faxes and telephones) or of the mail, 'or of any facility of a national securities exchange [for a] manipulative or deceptive device or contrivance' in contravention of the SEC rules.[46] Moreover, the SEC, the Department of Justice and the Commodities Futures Trading Commission (CFTC) are targeting foreign traders that utilise algorithmic trading and other types of high frequency trading methods to manipulate markets and unfairly benefit from privileged inside information.[47] The US Department of Justice (DOL) in February 2015 indicted a British trader for contributing to the 2010 US 'Flash Crash' through wire fraud, commodities fraud and market manipulation.[48] The DOL is seeking extradition following his arrest by the British authorities in relation to the 'Flash Crash'. This raises important policy issues about how insider dealing and market manipulation regulation should be applied to technologically sophisticated trading activity, including high frequency trading.

16.21   US courts have generally held that, given the principal purpose of US securities laws to protect US investors exposed to fraudulent or manipulative activities that implicate the jurisdictional means of interstate commerce, foreign activities by foreign nationals producing such a result in the United States or affecting US investors will be subject to US jurisdiction, which will displace the foreign law and will, as a matter of conflict of laws, allow US courts to apply US laws to foreign nationals.

Extra-territorial jurisdiction over commodities trading and civil RICO

16.22   Where a cause of action arose from trading on US commodities exchanges, US courts will uphold extra-territorial subject matter jurisdiction, even though the parties to the suit were non-resident US aliens and the fraudulent transactions and conduct occurred in a foreign country.[49] In *Tamari*, the court relied on the 'effects' test to find that 'where the ... transactions involve trading on domestic exchanges, harm can be presumed, because the

---

45   *General Foods Corpn v Brannon* 170 F 2d 220, 234 (7th Cir, 1998).
46   *Cargill Inc v Hardin* 452 F 2d 1154 at 1163 (8th Cir, 1971).
47   See Report on the US 'Flash Crash'. Report of the Staffs of the CFTC and SEC To The Joint Advisory Committee on Emerging Regulatory Issues, 'Findings Regarding the Events of May 6, 2010' (30 September 2010).
48   See US DOL Criminal Complaint AO 91 (Rev. 11/11), www.justice.gov/sites/default/files/opa/press-releases/attachments/2015/04/21/sarao_criminal_complaint.pdf.
49   *Tamari v Bache & Co (Lebanon) SAL* 547 F Supp 309 (ND Ill, 1982); order affd 730 F 2d 1103 (7th Cir, 1984); cert denied 469 US 871 (1984).

fraud … implicates the integrity of the American market'.[50] The court also noted that extra-territorial jurisdiction could attach to a foreign defendant's transmission of orders on behalf of the foreign plaintiffs when such transmissions went from Lebanon to the commodities exchange in Chicago. Such transmissions constituted 'conduct within the United States that was of substantial importance to the success of the fraudulent scheme'.[51]

16.23   The Racketeer Influenced Corrupt Organisations Act ('RICO') contains no express provision regarding its extra-territorial application.[52] RICO applies to civil and criminal actions and provides an express private right of action for those who were defrauded by individuals who used their controlling influence over a business enterprise to commit a fraud. To determine extra-territorial jurisdiction, the courts seek guidance from precedents 'concerning subject matter jurisdiction for international securities transactions and anti-trust matters'.[53] Therefore, the courts will look to the cases discussed above to determine issues of extra- territoriality under RICO.

13.24   In addition, jurisdiction may be imposed on the activities of non-US persons residing abroad when their activities affect the US marketplace. The Ninth Circuit in *Bourassa v Desrochers*[54] held that the jurisdictional link was satisfied by a Canadian broker's telephone call from Canada to an investor in the United States and later the US investor was able to serve the writ on the Canadian defendant while the defendant was on holiday in Florida. Jurisdiction was not satisfied, however, in a case where defrauded US investors brought an action for aiding and abetting liability against a foreign auditor for producing a report that was used by a foreign company without the consent of the auditor.[55] A US court also dismissed a claim based on lack of jurisdiction when it involved US investors who owned American Depository Receipts (ADRs) and had received a press release announcing a UK company's tender offer for shares in a UK target company whose securities were trading in the United States through the use of ADRs.[56] The determination of whether to impose extra-territorial subject matter jurisdiction will be a highly factual inquiry which must be made on a case-by-case basis.[57]

IOSCO AND UK EFFORTS AT INTERNATIONAL COOPERATION

16.25   IOSCO is the leading international body concerned with the regulation of securities markets.[58] Its membership comprises regulatory bodies from over 100 countries who have responsibility for day-to-day oversight and administration of securities laws. The preamble of IOSCO's byelaws states:

'Securities authorities resolve to co-operate together to ensure a better regulation of the markets, on the domestic as well as on the international level, in order to maintain just, efficient and sound markets.'

50   *Tamari v Bache & Co (Lebanon) SAL* at 313.
51   *Tamari v Bache & Co (Lebanon) SAL* at 315.
52   See *John Doe v UNOCAL Corpn* 110 F Supp 2d 1294, 1310 (CD Cal, 2000).
53   *North South Finance Corpn v Al-Turki* 100 F 3d 1046, 1051 (2nd Cir, 1996).
54   938 F 2d 1056 (9th Cir 1991).
55   *Reingold v Deloitte Haskins & Sells* 599 F Supp 1241 (SDNY, 1984).
56   *Plessey Co v General Electric Co* 628 F Supp 477 (D Del, 1986).
57   *Dept of Economic Development v Arthur Andersen & Co* 683 F Supp 1463 (SDNY, 1988).
58   See IOSCO's website: www.iosco.org.

To accomplish this, IOSCO encourages its member regulatory bodies to co-ordinate the establishment of standards and mutual assistance with other regulators as follows: (a) to exchange information on their respective experiences in order to promote the development of domestic securities markets, (b) to unite national efforts to establish standards and an effective surveillance of international securities transactions, and (c) to provide mutual assistance to ensure the integrity of the markets by a vigorous application of the standards and effective enforcement against offences.

16.26 IOSCO seeks to develop international standards to provide advice for national regulators which serves as a yardstick against which national regulatory efforts can be measured. IOSCO also recognises that providing minimum international standards and effective international cooperation in establishing, maintaining and investigating standards will not only result in investor protection, but also reduce systemic risk. IOSCO recognises that the increasing integration and liberalisation of global financial markets poses significant challenges for the regulation of securities markets. Moreover, markets, especially emerging markets, have experienced remarkable growth in recent years, but have also been exposed to the volatility of short-term capital flows which have resulted in some countries experiencing financial instability and the increased risk of contagion. This has been exacerbated by the lack of transparency and disclosure of material information for investors to assess risks in emerging markets. National regulators must now take account of transactions and activities that occur in other countries and IOSCO seeks to establish standards to assess the nature of cross-border conduct with a view to ensuring the fair, efficient and transparent operation of securities markets.

IOSCO and market abuse

16.27 IOSCO recognises that investors should be protected from misleading, manipulative or fraudulent practices. IOSCO adopts a broad definition of 'manipulative or fraudulent' conduct to include insider trading, front running or trading ahead of customers and the misuse of client assets. IOSCO has designated the principle of full disclosure of material information to be the primary principle for ensuring investor protection. Full disclosure reduces information asymmetries in the marketplace and thereby improves the investor's position to assess the potential risks and rewards of their investments.

16.28 IOSCO asserts that a key component of full disclosure requirements is adequate accounting and auditing standards, which should be of a high and sufficiently robust standard to inspire international confidence. Moreover, only duly licensed or authorised persons should be allowed to hold themselves out to the public as providing investment services. This should also apply in the case of market intermediaries and the operators of exchanges. IOSCO also encourages national authorities to require initial and ongoing capital requirements for those licence holders and authorised persons. These standards should be designed to achieve an environment in which a securities firm can meet the current demands of its counterparties and, if necessary, wind down its business without losses to its customers.

16.29 IOSCO also encourages national authorities to adopt strict standards of supervision for market intermediaries for the purpose of achieving investor protection by setting minimum standards for market participants. Investors should be treated in a just and equitable manner by market intermediaries based on standards that should be established in rules of business conduct. An effective system of surveillance is needed which would entail inspection, oversight and internal compliance programmes for investment firms and intermediaries.

16.30 Investors are particularly vulnerable in securities markets to misconduct by intermediaries and others, but the capacity of individual investors to take action may be limited. Further, the complex character of securities transactions and of fraudulent schemes requires strong enforcement of securities laws. In the event a violation occurs, investors should be protected through effective enforcement of the law.

16.31 IOSCO also sets out the principle that investors should have access to neutral fora, such as courts or administrative tribunals, to seek redress for damages and other injuries arising from market abuse and other misconduct. Remedies should include adequate compensation and/or restitution. The network of mutual assistance agreements that IOSCO has encouraged national regulators to adopt should lead to more effective enforcement. Effective cross-border supervision and enforcement will depend on close cooperation and coordination by national regulators. The Financial Services and Markets Act 2000 (FSMA) contains provisions that implement many of these principles and standards adopted by IOSCO.

16.32 The FSMA authorises the Financial Conduct Authority (FCA) to co-ordinate their investigations and to subpoena documents and witnesses from foreign jurisdictions and to prosecute parties allegedly committing acts in foreign jurisdictions that breach the market abuse provisions of the FSMA.[59] Part X provides for more effective information gathering to be collected as part of investigations in foreign jurisdictions and thereby provides mechanisms for cooperation with foreign authorities.

16.33 More specifically, the FSMA 2000, section 139 refers to 'assistance to overseas regulators' and lists a number of matters that the FCA must take into account before deciding whether to exercise its investigative powers or not. Sections 140 and 141 of the FSMA authorise broad powers for the FCA to gather information and documents from an authorised firm, its employees and even a member firm within the authorised firm's corporate or entity group.

16.34 The FSMA, section 139(6) makes it mandatory for the FCA to respond to requests for cooperation and information from other EU Member State authorities. Further, the FSMA develops safeguards to provisions authorising disclosure to foreign regulators by more narrowly defining and reducing the categories that can be relied on by UK authorities to reject requests for information and to coordinate investigations and enforcement actions. For example, the FSMA, section 305(1) tightly restricts the disclosure of all confidential information that arises from fiduciary and privileged relationships. Such information can only be provided with the consent of the person from whom it was sought. The FSMA, section 306(1) provides exceptions to this restriction on disclosure that are more specifically defined by secondary legislation. This list of prescribed recipients will be entitled to take, obtain and utilise information that would otherwise be non-disclosable.

---

59   Part I of the consultation document issued with the Financial Services and Markets Bill emphasised the need for 'extensive co-operation with regulatory bodies in other countries'.

16.35   The principle of reciprocity will determine the willingness of the FCA to intervene on behalf of foreign authorities in investigations and enforcement actions.[60] The FCA will act if there is a corresponding legal obligation in the requesting jurisdiction that would allow them to provide comparable assistance to the FCA, if asked. The principle of reciprocity is a key component of the UK MOU and mutual legal assistance treaties that authorise UK authorities to coordinate information collection, investigations and enforcement with foreign jurisdictions if those jurisdictions allow UK authorities to have reciprocal rights in UK investigations and enforcement actions. The FSMA, Pts IV and XII both provide detailed procedures that authorise the FCA, acting on a request from an EU Member State or other jurisdiction with which it has an agreement guaranteeing reciprocal rights, to support an enforcement action of a foreign regulator by allowing the FCA to vary, cancel and intervene in a regulated firm's ability to conduct permitted financial services activities whilst operating in the UK. Part IV addresses disclosure of information from foreign firms which seek to carry on regulated financial activities in the UK. Part XII authorises the FCA to intervene in order to protect the integrity and good governance of UK financial markets by imposing jurisdiction extra-territorially on persons or transactions outside the UK that may affect UK markets.

16.36   The FSMA, sections 42 and 164 allow the FCA ultimately to exercise discretion as to whether it should exercise its broad powers. It should be noted that such discretion may appear to be an obstacle to enhanced transnational cooperation, yet this discretion is expressly denied if the foreign authority requesting assistance is an EU Member State.[61] Outside the EU, this discretion can only be restrained by bilateral or multilateral agreement.

CONCLUSION

16.37   The barriers to a global securities market are diminishing; financial information is becoming available and inexpensive to obtain and it has been become easier to effect share transactions abroad.[62] Ultimately, the forces of liberalisation and technology will link most financial markets with the result that regulators should develop improved regulatory links to improve the effectiveness and efficiency of their financial markets. National regulatory authorities will come under pressure to enter agreements that allocate jurisdictional authority amongst regulators in different jurisdictions in order to forge a more coordinated attack on those who engage in complex and cross-border market manipulation, insider dealing and fraud. The EU Market Abuse Regulation and the Market Abuse Directive 2 will result in a more harmonised approach to investigations, enforcement and sanctions. This should result in a more consolidated and efficient European regulatory regime that can address some of the main challenges in cross-border market misconduct.

16.38   The impact of foreign laws, especially extraterritorial US anti-fraud securities laws, will pose a major challenge for regulatory compliance by UK companies and other market participants. US courts apply alternative tests:

---

60   See discussion in FSA Consultation Paper 17 (2001) discussing the FSA's powers to intervene on behalf of foreign authorities.
61   FSMA, s 139.
62   See Merritt B Fox, 'Securities Disclosure in a Globalising Market: Who Should Regulate Whom' (1997) 95 *Mich L Rev* 2498.

the 'conduct' test or the 'effects' test. Under the 'conduct' test, the court has subject matter jurisdiction where conduct material to the completion of the fraud occurred in the United States. Under the 'effects' test, the court has jurisdiction whenever a predominantly foreign transaction has substantial effects within the United States. The close links between US and UK securities markets require an analysis of how US securities laws can expose UK persons and other non-US persons to civil and criminal liability for insider dealing and market manipulation. Finally, the efforts of IOSCO have been instrumental in developing international standards in the areas of market abuse and insider dealing that have been generally adopted by most IOSCO countries. The IOSCO standards are important for understanding how the FCA will interpret and enforce the market abuse regime and for how the UK Upper Tribunal and courts will interpret the regime in legal proceedings.

16.39 Overall, the implementation of the Market Abuse Directive into the UK market abuse regime has created more effective cross-border cooperation and coordination between EEA/EU regulators by requiring states to establish a single regulatory agency to coordinate cross-border investigations and enforcement. This has led to more effective regulatory action within Europe for addressing some of the complexities of cross-border market misconduct. The Market Abuse Directive amended the FSMA to give the FSA express authority to engage in investigations and enforcement actions in market abuse cases that occur partly or solely in the UK so long as it relates to qualifying investments on a prescribed or regulated market in a EEA state. The FSA, and its successor the FCA, however, have mainly limited their enforcement to cases with a significant link to the UK financial market. HM Treasury's authority to prescribe markets on recognised investment exchanges that could be based outside the UK constitutes a potentially significant extension of the UK Treasury's and the FCA's regulatory authority. UK financial policy might be guided by a principle that allows it to regulate extraterritorial market misconduct – acts or omissions – that take place in foreign jurisdictions, but have a significant or direct effect on UK markets, so long as substantial wrongful conduct occurs in the UK or conduct outside the UK relates to qualifying investments traded on a UK regulated market. Indeed, these legal and regulatory issues will continue to pose complex challenges for regulators, firms and practitioners who will find it increasingly difficult to reconcile different market practices and attitudes to market misconduct across jurisdictions, while effectively managing risk in today's turbulent financial markets.

Index

Index